P9-CQQ-511

Biology
for the IB DIPLOMA

Biology
for the IB DIPLOMA

C.J.Clegg

HODDER
EDUCATION
PART OF HACHETTE LIVRE UK

The cover image shows a green anole (*Anolis carolinensis*), a tree-dwelling reptile found in parts of North and South America that may grow to a length of 20 cm. Here it is perched momentarily upon a pitcher plant. These active, agile carnivores have pads on their feet that enable them to cling, climb and run on virtually any surface, as they hunt for crickets, cockroaches, spiders and moths. Prey is caught in the wide jaws, with the aid of a long, forked tongue. Their skin is characteristically scaly, and the anole, typically green coloured, can change its colour, as the related chameleon lizards do.

Pitcher plants are examples of 'carnivorous' plants; they grow and compete well on soils typically deficient in essential ions, such as nitrates. These photosynthetic organisms trap insects and other tiny animals in their tall-sided pitchers, lined internally with smooth, down-pointing scales. When the 'prey' dies it decays by bacterial action, aided by enzymes secreted in the pitcher. The ions released are actively absorbed into the plant's cells, enabling essential metabolic processes such as protein synthesis.

Although every effort has been made to ensure that website addresses are correct at time of going to press, Hodder Education cannot be held responsible for the content of any website mentioned in this book. It is sometimes possible to find a relocated web page by typing in the address of the home page for a website in the URL window of your browser.

Hachette's policy is to use papers that are natural, renewable and recyclable products and made from wood grown in sustainable forests. The logging and manufacturing processes are expected to conform to the environmental regulations of the country of origin.

This material has been developed independently by the publisher and the content is in no way connected with, nor endorsed by, the International Baccalaureate Organization.

Orders: please contact Bookpoint Ltd, 130 Milton Park, Abingdon, Oxon OX14 4SB. Telephone: (44) 01235 827720. Fax: (44) 01235 400454. Lines are open 9.00–5.00, Monday to Saturday, with a 24-hour message answering service. Visit our website at www.hoddereducation.co.uk.

© C.J.Clegg 2007
First published in 2007 by
Hodder Murray, an imprint of Hodder Education,
part of Hachette Livre UK,
338 Euston Road
London NW1 3BH

Impression number   5 4 3
Year   2010 2009 2008

All rights reserved. Apart from any use permitted under UK copyright law, no part of this publication may be reproduced or transmitted in any form or by any means, electronic or mechanical, including photocopying and recording, or held within any information storage and retrieval system, without permission in writing from the publisher or under licence from the Copyright Licensing Agency Limited. Further details of such licences (for reprographic reproduction) may be obtained from the Copyright Licensing Agency Limited, Saffron House, 6–10 Kirby Street, London EC1N 8TS.

Cover photo © David Aubrey/Science Photo Library
Illustrations by Oxford Designers & Illustrators, Barking Dog Art
Typeset in 10/12pt Goudy and Frutiger families by Eric Drewery
Printed in Italy

A catalogue record for this title is available from the British Library

ISBN: 978 0340 92652 9

Contents

Section 2: Additional higher level

Section 3: Options

available on the CD-ROM accompanying this book

Introduction

The International Baccalaureate Diploma programme, a pre-university course for 16–19-year-olds, is designed to develop not only a breadth of knowledge, skills and understanding, but well-rounded individuals and engaged world citizens. One of the Diploma's key requirements is concurrent study in six academic areas, at least one of which is an experimental science. Of these, biology, whether taken at standard or higher level, is the choice of many students. **This book is designed to serve them.**

Within the IB Diploma programme, the theory content for biology is organised into compulsory core topics and options. The organisation of this book follows that syllabus sequence:

- **Section 1** is the **common core material for standard and higher-level students**: Chapters 1–7;
- **Section 2** is the **additional higher level material for higher-level students**: Chapters 8–12;
- **Section 3** consists of the **options,** of which three are available to standard students only (Chapters 13–15), four are for standard and higher-level students (Chapters 16–19), and one is available to higher-level students only (Chapter 20).

The syllabus is presented as topics and options, and most are the subject of a single chapter in *Biology for the IB Diploma* (see pages xi and xii). The exceptions are Topics 3 and 4, which are split between two chapters in each case, in order to facilitate design and delivery of individual teaching programmes. The topic on statistical analysis is presented in Chapter 21.

Special features of the chapters of *Biology for the IB Diploma*:

- each begins with 'Starting points' that summarise the essential concepts on which the chapter is based; where the issues to be addressed have their genesis in earlier chapters, these are identified
- the text is written in straightforward language, uncluttered by phrases or idioms that might confuse **students for whom English is a second language**; the depth of treatment of topics carefully reflects the objectives and action verbs in which the syllabus assessment statements are phrased
- photographs, electron micrographs and full-colour **illustrations are linked to support the relevant text**, with annotations included to elaborate the context, function or applications
- the main sections within chapters specify the **IB syllabus subtopics paragraph numbers** being addressed, so links between text and syllabus are self-evident
- explanations of structure are linked to function and behaviour in living things, and the habitat and environment of organisms are identified where appropriate; application of biology in industry, and the economic, environmental and ethical consequences of developments are highlighted, where appropriate
- **processes of science** (science methods) and something of the history of developments are introduced selectively to aid appreciation of the possibilities and limitations of science
- self-assessment questions (**SAQs**) are phrased so as to assist comprehension and recall, but also help familiarise students with the assessment implications of the action verbs; at the end of chapters, typical examination questions are given
- links to the interdisciplinary **Theory of Knowledge** (TOK link) element of the IB course are made at appropriate points in most chapters.

Using this book

The sequence of chapters in *Biology for the IB Diploma* follows the sequence of the syllabus contents. However, the IB Diploma biology syllabus is not designed as a teaching syllabus, and the order in which the syllabus content is presented is not necessarily the order in which it should be taught. Different schools and colleges need to design a course delivery model based on individual circumstances. How this may be tackled is discussed in **Chapter 22**.

In addition to the study of theory issues on which this book focuses, IB science students are also involved in practical investigations and project work. Investigations are ultimately presented for the **internal assessment**, based on given assessment criteria. How all these components are integrated is also the subject of Chapter 22. This has been written by **guest author Gary Seston**, an experienced and enthusiastic teacher of IB Diploma biology, who, importantly, also has examiner experience. Prior to his present post at Sotogrande International School, Cadiz, Gary taught at the United World College of South East Asia in Singapore. This chapter is an excellent guide of interest to both teachers and students, though possibly at different stages of their experience of the course.

Author's acknowledgements

I am indebted to IB teachers who have welcomed me into their Departments, and updated me on the delivery of the Diploma programme, including:

- Chris Hall, Head of Science, Malvern College, Worcester, UK
- Carolyn Halliday, Head of Biology, and Keith Allen, St Clare's, Oxford, UK
- John Cherverton, Head of Biology, Oakham School, Rutland, UK.

These colleagues also read early drafts of chapters of the manuscript, and their advice guided me to the best approach, following helpful discussion with Katie Mackenzie Stuart, Science Publisher, of Hodder Murray.

To Gary Seston, of Sotogrande International School, Cadiz, I owe a special debt. His perceptive comments on the appropriateness of the presentation to students for whom English is a second language, together with his advice on organisms familiar to students across other continents, and especially his observations on content and approach to syllabus issues of all chapters, were invaluable.

On particular aspects of the IB Diploma biology syllabus, I had the advantage of insights from experts:

- Dr Robin Cook, The Marine Laboratory, Aberdeen, Scotland, concerning the conservation of marine fish stocks
- Professor Robert Turner, Wellcome Department of Imaging Neuroscience, Institute of Neurology, University College, London, concerning fMRI scanning of the brain
- Dr Richard Johnson, Aberdeen University, Scotland, concerning electron microscopy
- Dr Kevin McKenzie, School of Medical Science, Aberdeen University, concerning electron microscopy
- Dr Neil Millar, Head of Biology, Hecknondwike Grammar School, Kirklees, West Yorkshire, UK, for permission to introduce Merlin, his unique statistical package for biology students, which is made freely available for educational and non-profit use.

Finally, I am indebted to the Science publishing team of Phillipa Allum and Helen Townson at Hodder Murray, and freelances Penelope Lyons and Gina Walker, all of whose skill and patience brought together text and illustration as I have wished, and I am most grateful to them.

Dr Chris Clegg
Salisbury
Wiltshire
UK
May 2007

Matching chapters with the IB Diploma biology syllabus

Colour key for syllabus levels

Standard and higher levels
Higher level only
Standard level only

Chapter	IB Diploma biology syllabus topic	
Chapter 1: Cells – the building blocks	Topic 2: Cells	■ ■
	2.1 Cell theory	■ ■
	2.2 Prokaryotic cells	■ ■
	2.3 Eukaryotic cells	■ ■
	2.4 Membranes	■ ■
	2.5 Cell division	■ ■
Chapter 2: The chemistry of life	Topic 3: The chemistry of life (part a)	■ ■
	3.1 Chemical elements and water	■ ■
	3.2 Carbohydrates, lipids and proteins	■ ■
	3.3 DNA structure	■ ■
	3.4 DNA replication	■ ■
	3.5 Transcription and translation	■ ■
	3.6 Enzymes	■ ■
Chapter 3: Energy transfer in cells	Topic 3: The chemistry of life (part b)	■ ■
	3.7 Cell respiration	■ ■
	3.8 Photosynthesis	■ ■
Chapter 4: Genetics	Topic 4: Genetics (part a)	■ ■
	4.1 Chromosomes, genes, alleles and mutations	■ ■
	4.2 Meiosis	■ ■
	4.3 Theoretic genetics	■ ■
Chapter 5: Genetic engineering and biotechnology	Topic 4: Genetics (part b)	■ ■
	4.4 Genetic engineering and biotechnology	■ ■
Chapter 6: Ecology, evolution and biodiversity	Topic 5: Ecology and evolution	■ ■
	5.1 Communities and ecosystems	■ ■
	5.2 The greenhouse effect	■ ■
	5.3 Populations	■ ■
	5.4 Evolution	■ ■
	5.5 Classification	■ ■
Chapter 7: Human physiology, health and reproduction	Topic 6: Human health and physiology	■ ■
	6.1 Digestion	■ ■
	6.2 The transport system	■ ■
	6.3 Defence against infectious disease	■ ■
	6.4 Gas exchange	■ ■
	6.5 Nerves, hormones and homeostasis	■ ■
	6.6 Reproduction	■ ■
Chapter 8: Nucleic acids and proteins	Topic 7: Nucleic acids and proteins	■
	7.1 DNA structure	■
	7.2 DNA replication	■
	7.3 Transcription	■
	7.4 Translation	■
	7.5 Proteins	■
	7.6 Enzymes	■
Chapter 9: Energy transfer in cells II	Topic 8: Cell respiration and photosynthesis	■
	8.1 Cell respiration	■
	8.2 Photosynthesis	■
Chapter 10: Plant science	Topic 9: Plant science	■
	9.1 Plant structure and growth	■
	9.2 Transport in angiospermophytes	■
	9.3 Reproduction in angiospermophytes	■

Cells – the building blocks

STARTING POINTS
- The **cell** is the basic unit of life; living things are made of cells.
- Cells are small, too small to be seen with the naked eye. They must be viewed using a **microscope**.
- Plant and animal cells have common features, including the **nucleus**, **cytoplasm** and cell membrane (**plasma membrane**).
- Many living things consist of a single cell (**unicellular organisms**), others are built of many cells (**multicellular organisms**).
- In most multicellular organisms, the cells perform specialised functions.

The cell is the basic unit of living matter – the smallest part of an organism which we can say is alive. It is cells that carry out the essential processes of life. We think of them as self-contained units of structure and function.

Introducing cells

2.1.1–2.1.10, 2.2.1–2.2.4, 2.3.1–2.3.6

Figure 1.1 Introducing unicellular organisation

Some organisms are made of a single cell, and are known as unicellular. Examples of **unicellular** organisms are introduced in Figure 1.1. In fact, there are vast numbers of different unicellular organisms in the living world, many with a very long evolutionary history.

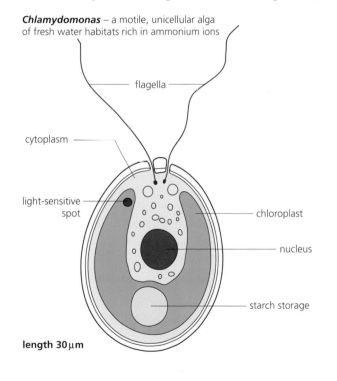

Chlamydomonas – a motile, unicellular alga of fresh water habitats rich in ammonium ions

- flagella
- cytoplasm
- light-sensitive spot
- chloroplast
- nucleus
- starch storage

length 30 μm

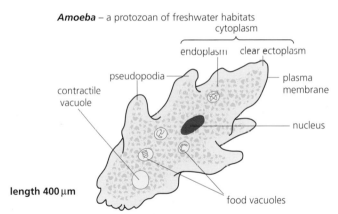

Amoeba – a protozoan of freshwater habitats

- cytoplasm
- endoplasm
- clear ectoplasm
- pseudopodia
- plasma membrane
- contractile vacuole
- nucleus
- food vacuoles

length 400 μm

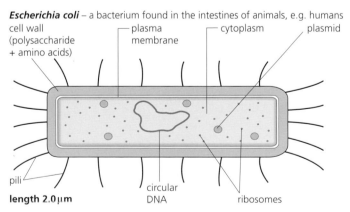

Escherichia coli – a bacterium found in the intestines of animals, e.g. humans

- cell wall (polysaccharide + amino acids)
- plasma membrane
- cytoplasm
- plasmid
- pili
- circular DNA
- ribosomes

length 2.0 μm

1 State the essential processes characteristic of living things.

Other organisms are made of many cells, and are known as **multicellular** organisms. Examples of multicellular organisms are the mammals and flowering plants. Much of the biology in this book is about multicellular organisms, including humans, and the processes that go on in these organisms. But remember, single-celled organisms carry out all the essential functions of life too, occurring within the confines of a single cell.

Cell size

Cells are extremely small – most are only visible as distinct structures when we use a **microscope** (although a few types of cell are just large enough to be seen by the naked eye).

Observations of cells were first reported over 300 years ago, following the early development of microscopes (Figure 1.2). Today we use a compound light microscope to investigate cell structure – perhaps you are already familiar with the light microscope as a piece of laboratory equipment. You may have used one to view living cells, such as the single-celled animal, *Amoeba*, shown in Figure 1.1.

Since cells are so small, we need appropriate units to measure them. The **metre** (symbol **m**) is the standard unit of length used in science (it is an internationally agreed unit, or **SI unit**). Look at Table 1.1 below, showing the subdivisions of the metre used to measure cells and their contents. These units are listed in descending order of size. You will see that each subdivision is one thousandth of the unit above it. The smallest units are probably quite new to you; they may take some getting used to.

1 metre (m)	= 1000 millimetres (mm)
1 mm	= 1000 micrometres (μm) (or microns)
1 μm	= 1000 nanometres (nm)

Table 1.1 Units of length used in microscopy

2 Calculate:
a how many cells of 100 μm diameter will fit side by side along a millimetre
b the magnification of the image of *Escherichia coli* in Figure 1.1.

So, the dimensions of cells are expressed in the unit called a **micrometre** or micron (μm). Notice this unit is one thousandth (10^{-3}) of a millimetre. This gives us a clear idea about how small cells are when compared to the millimetre, which you can see on a standard ruler.

Bacteria are really small, typically 0.5–10 μm in size, whereas the cells of plants and animals are often in the range 50–150 μm or larger. In fact, the lengths of the unicells shown in Figure 1.1 are approximately:

- *Chlamydomonas* 30 μm
- *Escherichia coli*   2 μm
- *Amoeba*   400 μm (but its shape, and therefore length, varies greatly).

The features of cells

A cell consists of a **nucleus** surrounded by cytoplasm, contained within the cell membrane. The nucleus is the structure that controls and directs the activities of the cell. The **cytoplasm** is the site of the chemical reactions of life, which we call 'metabolism'. The cell membrane, known as the **plasma membrane**, is the barrier controlling entry to and exit from the cytoplasm.

Newly formed cells grow and enlarge. A growing cell can normally divide into two cells. Cell division is very often restricted to unspecialised cells, before they become modified for a particular task.

Cells may develop and specialise in their structure and in the functions they carry out. A common outcome of this is that many fully specialised cells are no longer able to divide, for example. But as a consequence of specialisation, **cells show great variety in shape and structure**. This variety in structure reflects the evolutionary adaptations of cells to different environments, and to different specialised functions – for example, within multicellular organisms.

Cell theory – a summary statement

The **cell theory** – the statement that cells are the unit of structure and function in living things – contains three very basic ideas:

- cells are the building blocks of structure in living things;
- cells are the smallest unit of life;
- cells are derived from other cells (pre-existing cells) by division.

Today we can confidently add two concepts:

- cells contain a blueprint (information) for their growth, development and behaviour;
- cells are the site of all the chemical reactions of life (metabolism).

The origins of cell theory

Figure 1.2 Early steps in the development of the cell theory

Many biologists contributed to the development of the cell theory. This concept evolved gradually in western Europe during the nineteenth century as a result of a steadily accelerating pace of developments in **microscopy** and **biochemistry**. You can see a summary of the earliest steps in Figure 1.2.

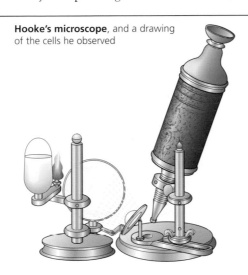

Hooke's microscope, and a drawing of the cells he observed

Robert Hooke (1662), an expert mechanic and one of the founders of the Royal Society in London, was fascinated by microscopy. He devised a compound microscope, and used it to observe the structure of cork. He described and drew cork cells, and also measured them. He was the first to use the term 'cells'.

Anthony van Leeuwenhoek (1680) was born in Delft. Despite no formal training in science, he developed a hobby of making lenses, which he mounted in metal plates to form simple microscopes. Magnifications of ×240 were achieved, and he observed blood cells, sperms, protozoa with cilia, and even bacteria (among many other types of cells). His results were reported to the Royal Society, and he was elected a fellow.

Robert Brown (1831), a Scottish botanist, observed and named the cell nucleus. He also observed the random movements of tiny particles (pollen grains, in his case) when suspended in water (Brownian movement).

Matthias Schleiden (1838) and Theodor Schwann (1839), German biologists, established cells as the natural unit of form and function in living things: 'Cells are organisms, and entire animals and plants are aggregates of these organisms arranged to definite laws.'

Rudolf Virchow (1856), a German pathologist, established the idea that cells arise only by division of existing cells.

Louis Pasteur (1862), a brilliant French microbiologist, established that life does not spontaneously generate. The bacteria that 'appear' in broth are microbes freely circulating in the air, which contaminate exposed matter.

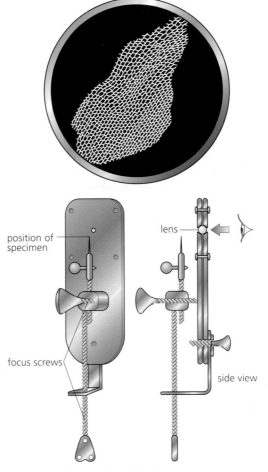

position of specimen

lens

focus screws

side view

Leeuwenhoek's microscope

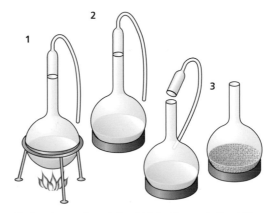

Pasteur's experiment, in which broth was sterilised (**1**), and then either exposed to air (**3**) or protected from air-borne spores in a swan-necked flask (**2**). Only the broth in **3** became contaminated with bacteria.

What evidence do we have in total, to support the cell theory?

Although cells were observed as long ago as the seventeenth century, it was not until the nineteenth century that biologists were confident enough to state what we now call the 'cell theory', categorically (Figure 1.2). Subsequent developments in many aspects of biological investigation have supported this concept. Cell theory has not been challenged, although it took some time for the true cause of apparent 'spontaneous generation of life' – the sudden appearance of living things in water that had previously seemed devoid of life, for example – to be understood.

Today, the study of the structure of cells, called **cytology**, is integrated within a larger, major branch of biology called **cell biology**. We know that cells contain the hereditary material **deoxyribonucleic acid (DNA)** in their nucleus (page 63). The structure and role of the DNA double helix in the control of metabolism and of growth via protein synthesis are understood. Now, developments in cell biology are closely linked to developments in genetics, biochemistry, biophysics, electron microscopy, biotechnology, enzymology, genetic engineering, and medicine – including oncology (the study of cancer), as we shall see. Table 1.2 is a summary of the evidence for the cell theory, and identifies where it is discussed further.

Concept	Evidence
living things are made of cells	**observations by microscopists** (light microscopy and electron microscopy) on the structure of unicellular and multicellular organisms, especially on the structure of tissues and organs (histology, page 7)
cells are the smallest units of life	**discovery of viruses** as particles that are 'crystalline' (non-cellular) when outside a host cell, and that can only reproduce themselves at the expense of their host cell's metabolic machinery (page 19)
	biochemical investigations of organelles (tiny substructures in cells, e.g. chloroplasts) showing their ability to function outside of a cell, under laboratory-controlled conditions, for a limited time (page 281)
cells come from pre-existing cells	**Pasteur's observations** on the origins of microbes in fermenter vessels (Figure 1.2), and related discoveries that cases of apparent 'spontaneous generations' of microorganisms in pond or puddle waters were due to the presence of (unnoticed) pre-existing cells
	discovery that the life cycles of many microorganisms include a resistant spore phase, and the linked discovery that spores of many microorganisms and unicellular protoctista are ubiquitous, but that they become active only in favourable growing conditions
	observations on the behaviour of cells at division (mitosis, page 31 and meiosis, page 94) and during reproduction (cytology)
cells contain a blueprint for growth, development and behaviour	**observations on the behaviour of chromosomes** and the establishment of the nature and role of genes / DNA in the day-to-day control of cells (page 66), and in the process of heredity (page 91)
	experimental evidence of the effects on cells of the deliberate transfer of genes between organisms (genetic engineering, page 117)
cells are the site of the chemical reactions of life	**discovery of enzymes** and the enzyme machinery of cellular processes such as cell aerobic respiration and fermentation (page 80)
	discovery of biochemical events in cells, such as the formation of proteins from amino acids (page 69)
	discovery of cell ultrastructure, of the presence of discrete organelles and of the biochemical events located in particular organelles (electron microscopy and biochemistry, page 14)

Table 1.2 The evidence for the cell theory – a review

Maintaining cell growth

The materials required for growth and maintenance of a cell enter through the outermost layer of the cytoplasm, a membrane called the **plasma membrane**. Similarly, waste products must leave the cell through the plasma membrane.

The rates at which materials can enter and leave a cell depend on the surface area of that cell, but the rates at which materials are used and waste products are produced depend upon the amount of cytoplasm present within the cell. Similarly, heat transfer between the cytoplasm and environment of the cell is determined by surface area.

Cell surface:volume ratios and cell size

As the cell grows and increases in size, an important difference develops between the surface area available for exchange and the volume of the cytoplasm in which the chemical reactions of life occur. The volume increases faster than the surface area; the **surface area:volume ratio** falls (Figure 1.3). So, with increasing size of a cell, less and less of the cytoplasm has access to the cell surface for exchange of gases, supply of nutrients, and loss of waste products.

Figure 1.3 The effect of increasing size on the surface area:volume ratio

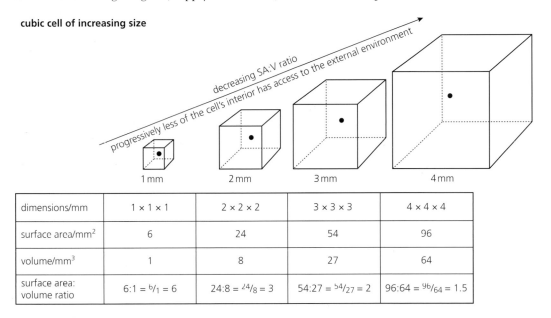

cubic cell of increasing size

decreasing SA:V ratio

progressively less of the cell's interior has access to the external environment

| | 1 mm | 2 mm | 3 mm | 4 mm |

dimensions/mm	$1 \times 1 \times 1$	$2 \times 2 \times 2$	$3 \times 3 \times 3$	$4 \times 4 \times 4$
surface area/mm^2	6	24	54	96
volume/mm^3	1	8	27	64
surface area: volume ratio	$6:1 = {}^6/_1 = 6$	$24:8 = {}^{24}/_8 = 3$	$54:27 = {}^{54}/_{27} = 2$	$96:64 = {}^{96}/_{64} = 1.5$

3 For imaginary cubic 'cells' with sides 1, 2, 4 and 6 mm:

  a **calculate** the volume, surface area and ratio of surface area to volume for each
  b **state** the effect on the SA:V ratio of a cell as it increases in size
  c **explain** the effect of increasing cell size on the efficiency of diffusion in the removal of waste products from cell cytoplasm.

Put another way, we can say that the smaller the cell is, the more quickly and easily can materials be exchanged between its cytoplasm and environment. One consequence of this is that cells cannot continue growing larger, indefinitely. When a maximum size is reached, cell growth stops. The cell may then divide. The process of cell division is discussed later (page 30).

Metabolism and cell size

The extent of chemical reactions that make up metabolism in a cell (the subject of later chapters) is not directly related to the surface area of the cell, but it does relate to the amount of cytoplasm, expressed as the cell mass. In summary, we can say that the rate of metabolism of a cell is a function of its mass, whereas the rate of exchange of materials and heat energy that metabolism generates is a function of the cell's surface area.

Introducing animal and plant cells

No 'typical' cell exists – there is a very great deal of variety among cells. However, we shall see that most cells have features in common. Viewed using a compound microscope, the initial appearance of a cell is of a simple sac of fluid material, bound by a membrane, and containing a nucleus. Look at the cells in Figure 1.4.

Figure 1.4 Animal and plant cells from multicellular organisms

Canadian pondweed (*Elodea*) grows submerged in fresh water

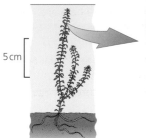

5 cm

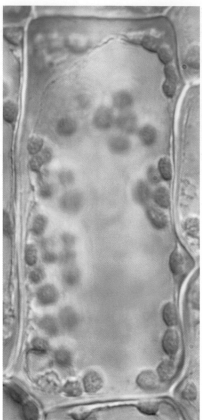

human

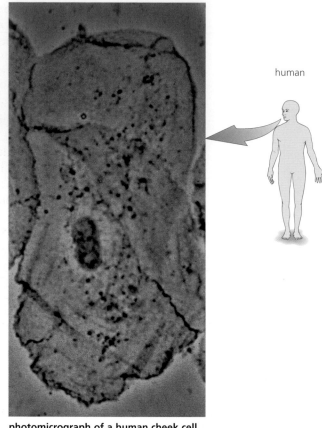

1 m

photomicrograph of a leaf cell of *Elodea* (×400)

photomicrograph of a human cheek cell (×800)

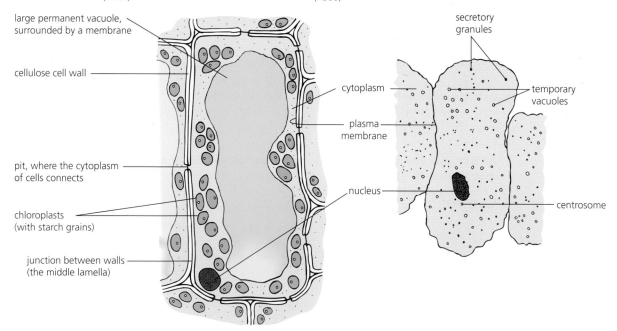

large permanent vacuole, surrounded by a membrane

cellulose cell wall

pit, where the cytoplasm of cells connects

chloroplasts (with starch grains)

junction between walls (the middle lamella)

secretory granules

cytoplasm

temporary vacuoles

plasma membrane

nucleus

centrosome

Animal and plant cells have at least three structures in common. These are their **cytoplasm** with its **nucleus**, surrounded by a **plasma membrane**. In addition, there are many tiny structures in the cytoplasm, called **organelles**, most of them common to both animal and plant cells. An organelle is a discrete structure within a cell, having a specific function. Organelles are all too small to be seen at this magnification. We have learned about the structure of organelles using the electron microscope (page 14).

There are some important basic differences between plant and animal cells (Table 1.3). For example, there is a tough, slightly elastic **cell wall**, made largely of cellulose, present around plant cells (page 16). Cell walls are absent from animal cells.

A **vacuole** is a fluid-filled space within the cytoplasm, surrounded by a single membrane. Plant cells frequently have a large, permanent vacuole present. By contrast, animal cells may have small vacuoles, but these are mostly temporary.

Green plant cells also contain organelles called **chloroplasts** in their cytoplasm. These are not found in animal cells. The chloroplasts are the sites where green plant cells manufacture elaborated food molecules by a process known as photosynthesis.

The **centrosome**, an organelle that lies close to the nucleus in animal cells (Figure 1.4), is not present in plants. This tiny organelle is involved in nuclear division in animal cells.

Finally, the **storage carbohydrate** (energy store) differs, too. Animal cells may store glycogen (page 47); plant cells normally store starch.

Plant cells	Feature	Animal cells
cellulose cell wall present	**cell wall**	no cellulose cell walls
many cells contain chloroplasts; site of photosynthesis	**chloroplasts**	no chloroplasts; animal cells cannot photosynthesise
large, fluid-filled vacuole typically present	**permanent vacuole**	no large permanent vacuoles
no centrosome	**centrosome**	a centrosome present outside the nucleus
starch	**carbohydrate storage product**	glycogen

Table 1.3 Differences between plant and animal cells

Multicellular organisms – specialisation and division of labour

Unicellular organisms are structurally simple in that they perform all the functions and activities of life within a single cell. The cell feeds, respires, excretes, is sensitive to internal and external conditions (and may respond to them), may move, and eventually divides or reproduces. You have seen examples of unicellular organisation in Figure 1.1.

By contrast, the majority of multicellular organisms are like the mammals (and flowering plants) in that they are made of cells, most of which are highly **specialised** to perform particular functions. Specialised cells occur organised into **tissues** and **organs**. A tissue is a group of similar cells specialised to perform a particular function, such as heart muscle tissue of a mammal. An organ is a collection of different tissues which performs a specialised function, such as the heart of a mammal. So the tissues and organs of multicellular organisms consist of specialised cells.

Control of cell specialisation

We have noted that the nucleus of each cell is the structure that controls and directs the activities of the cell, and that the information required for this exists in the form of a nucleic acid, DNA. The nucleus of a cell contains the DNA in thread-like **chromosomes**, which are linear sequences of **genes** (page 92). Genes control the development of each cell within the mature organism. We can define a gene in different ways, including:

- a specific region of a chromosome which is capable of determining the development of a specific characteristic of an organism;
- a specific length of the DNA double helix (hundreds or thousands of base pairs long) which codes for a protein.

So, when a cell is becoming specialised – we say the cell is **differentiating** – some of its genes are being activated and expressed. These genes determine how the cell develops. What happens during gene expression, and the mechanism by which a cell's chemical reactions are controlled, are explored in the next chapter.

For the moment we can just note that the nucleus of each cell contains all the information required to make each type of cell present within the whole organism, only a selected part of which is needed in any one cell and tissue. The potential of each cell to specialise in any number of different ways is called **totipotency**. Which genes are activated and how a cell specialises are controlled by the immediate environment of the differentiating cell, and its position in the developing organism.

The cost of specialisation

Specialised cells are efficient at carrying out their particular function, such as transport, or support, or protection. We say the resulting differences between cells are due to **division of labour**. By specialisation, increased efficiency is achieved, but at a price. The specialised cells are now totally dependent on the activities of other cells. For example, in animals, nerve cells are adapted for the transport of nerve impulses, but dependent on blood cells for oxygen, and on heart muscle cells to pump the blood. This modification of cell structure to support differing functions is another reason why no 'typical cell' really exists.

■ Extension: Non-cellular organisation – an exceptional condition

In addition to the familiar unicellular and multicellular organisation of living things, there are a few examples of multinucleate organs and organisms, without divisions into separate cells. This type of organisation is called acellular. An example of an **acellular organism** is the pin mould *Rhizopus*, where the 'plant' body consists of fine, thread-like structures called hyphae. An example of an **acellular organ** is the striped muscle fibres that make up the skeletal muscles of mammals (Figure 1.5).

Figure 1.5 Acellular organisation in *Rhizopus* and in skeletal muscle fibres

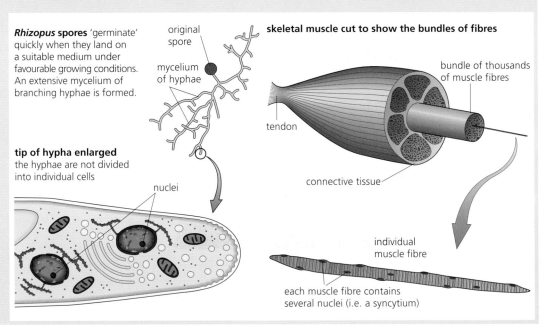

Rhizopus **spores** 'germinate' quickly when they land on a suitable medium under favourable growing conditions. An extensive mycelium of branching hyphae is formed.

original spore

mycelium of hyphae

tip of hypha enlarged
the hyphae are not divided into individual cells

nuclei

skeletal muscle cut to show the bundles of fibres

bundle of thousands of muscle fibres

tendon

connective tissue

individual muscle fibre

each muscle fibre contains several nuclei (i.e. a syncytium)

Emergent properties of the multicellular organism

It has been said that a multicellular organism has properties that in total are greater than the sum of the individual parts – that is, of all the cells, tissues and organs of which it is made up. Such properties are described as **emergent**.

4 **Suggest** emergent properties of a human, as an example of a multicellular organism.

Examining cells, and recording structure and size

We use microscopes to magnify the cells of biological specimens in order to view them. Figure 1.6 shows two types of light microscope.

In the simple microscope (**hand lens**), a single biconvex lens is held in a supporting frame so that the instrument can be held very close to the eye. Today, a hand lens is mostly used to observe external structure, although some of the earliest detailed observations of living cells were made with single-lens instruments.

In the **compound microscope**, light rays are focused by the **condenser** on to a specimen on a microscope slide on the stage of the microscope. Light transmitted through the specimen is then focused by two sets of lenses (hence the name compound microscope). The **objective lens** forms an image (in the microscope tube) which is then further magnified by the **eyepiece lens**, producing a greatly enlarged image.

Biological material to be examined by compound microscopy must be sufficiently transparent for light rays to pass through. When bulky tissues and parts of organs are to be examined, thin sections are cut. Thin sections are largely colourless.

TOK Link

Researching the development of the microscope and the early history of The Royal Society may support your study of the methods of science. If so, the following websites provide useful links:

■ The Royal Society
www.royalsoc.ac.uk

■ Royal Microscopical Society
www.rms.org.uk

Figure 1.6 Light microscopy

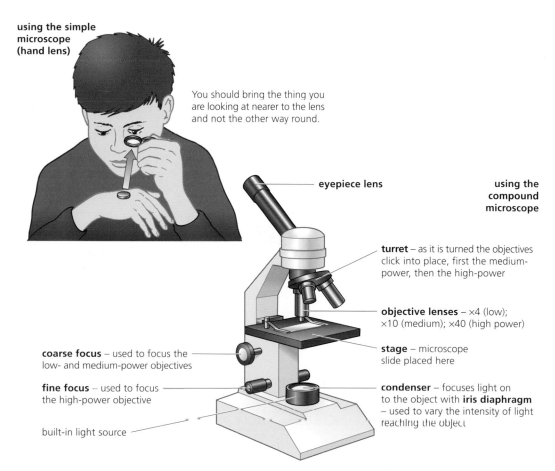

using the simple microscope (hand lens)

You should bring the thing you are looking at nearer to the lens and not the other way round.

using the compound microscope

eyepiece lens

turret – as it is turned the objectives click into place, first the medium-power, then the high-power

objective lenses – ×4 (low); ×10 (medium); ×40 (high power)

stage – microscope slide placed here

condenser – focuses light on to the object with **iris diaphragm** – used to vary the intensity of light reaching the object

coarse focus – used to focus the low- and medium-power objectives

fine focus – used to focus the high-power objective

built-in light source

Recording observations

Images of cells and tissues viewed may be further magnified, displayed or projected and saved for printing out by the technique of **digital microscopy** (Figure 1.7). A digital microscope is used, or alternatively an appropriate video camera is connected by microscope coupler or eyepiece adaptor that replaces the standard microscope eyepiece. Images are displayed via video recorder, TV monitor, or computer, and may be printed out by the latter.

Alternatively, a record of what you see via the compound microscope may be recorded by drawings of various types (Figure 1.8). For a clear, simple drawing:

- use a sharp HB pencil and a clean eraser;
- use unlined paper and a separate sheet for each specimen you record;
- draw clear, sharp outlines, avoiding shading or colouring (density of structures may be represented by degrees of stippling);
- label each sheet or drawing with the species, conditions (living or stained; if stained, which stains), TS or LS, and so forth;
- label your drawing fully, with labels well clear of the structures shown, remembering that label lines should not cross;
- annotate (add notes about function, role, development) if appropriate;
- include a statement of the magnification under which the specimen has been observed.

Figure 1.7 Digital microscopy in action.

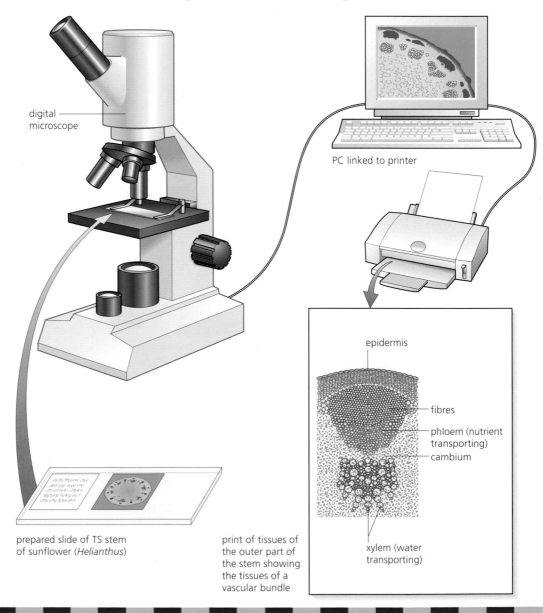

digital microscope

PC linked to printer

prepared slide of TS stem of sunflower (*Helianthus*)

print of tissues of the outer part of the stem showing the tissues of a vascular bundle

epidermis

fibres

phloem (nutrient transporting)

cambium

xylem (water transporting)

Figure 1.8 Recording cell
structure by drawing

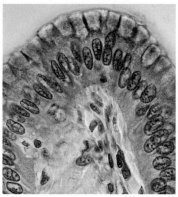

**view (phase contrast) of the layer of
cells (epithelium) lining the stomach wall**

The lining of the stomach consists of columnar
epithelium. All cells secrete mucus copiously.

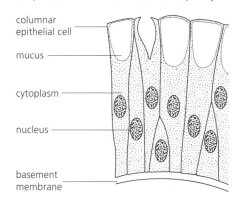

columnar
epithelial cell

mucus

cytoplasm

nucleus

basement
membrane

Figure 1.9 Measuring
the size of cells

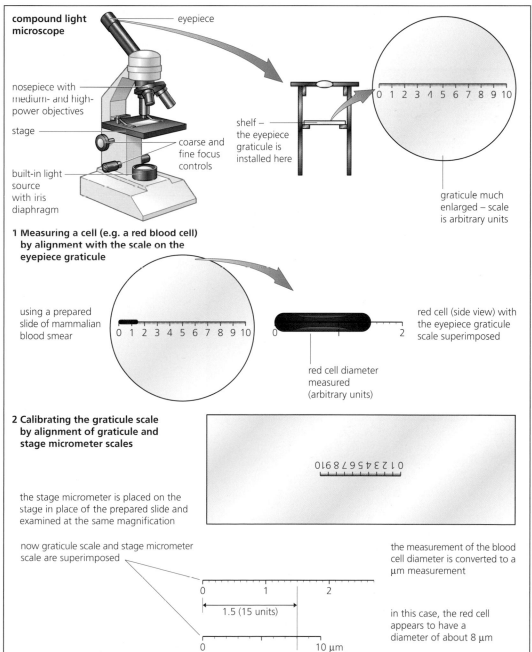

**compound light
microscope**

eyepiece

nosepiece with
medium- and high-
power objectives

stage

built-in light
source
with iris
diaphragm

coarse and
fine focus
controls

shelf –
the eyepiece
graticule is
installed here

0 1 2 3 4 5 6 7 8 9 10

graticule much
enlarged – scale
is arbitrary units

**1 Measuring a cell (e.g. a red blood cell)
by alignment with the scale on the
eyepiece graticule**

using a prepared
slide of mammalian
blood smear

0 1 2 3 4 5 6 7 8 9 10

0   2

red cell (side view) with
the eyepiece graticule
scale superimposed

red cell diameter
measured
(arbitrary units)

**2 Calibrating the graticule scale
by alignment of graticule and
stage micrometer scales**

0 1 2 3 4 5 6 7 8 9 10

the stage micrometer is placed on the
stage in place of the prepared slide and
examined at the same magnification

now graticule scale and stage micrometer
scale are superimposed

0   1   2

1.5 (15 units)

0   10 μm

the measurement of the blood
cell diameter is converted to a
μm measurement

in this case, the red cell
appears to have a
diameter of about 8 μm

Measuring microscopic objects

The size of a cell can be measured under the microscope. A transparent scale called a **graticule** is mounted in the eyepiece at the focal plane (there is a ledge for it to rest on). In this position, when the object under observation is in focus, so too is the scale. The size (e.g. length, diameter) of the object may then be recorded in arbitrary units. Next, the graticule scale is calibrated using a **stage micrometer** – in effect, a tiny, transparent ruler, which is placed on the microscope stage in place of the slide and then observed. With the eyepiece and stage micrometer scales superimposed, the true dimensions of the object can be estimated in microns. Figure 1.9 shows how this is done.

Once the size of a cell has been measured, a scale bar line may be added to a micrograph or drawing to record the actual size of the structure, as illustrated in the photomicrograph in Figure 1.10.

Figure 1.10 Recording size by means of scale bars

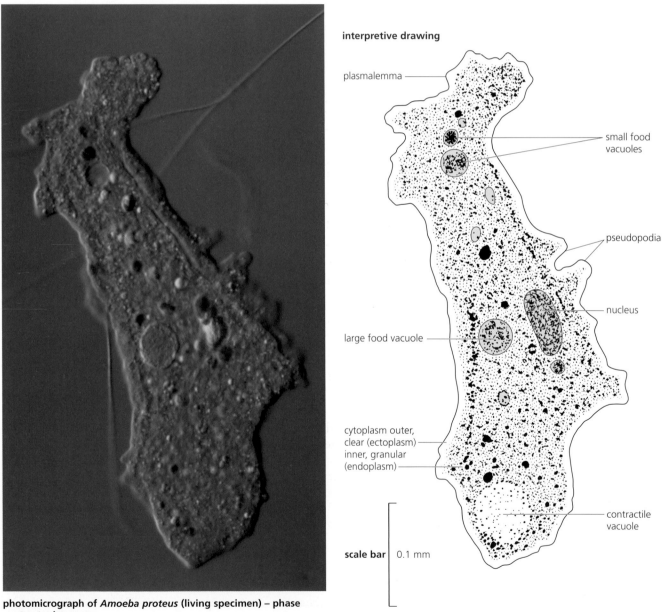

interpretive drawing

plasmalemma

small food vacuoles

pseudopodia

nucleus

large food vacuole

cytoplasm outer, clear (ectoplasm) inner, granular (endoplasm)

contractile vacuole

scale bar | 0.1 mm

photomicrograph of *Amoeba proteus* (living specimen) – phase contrast microscopy

5 Using the scale bar given in Figure 1.10, **calculate** the maximum observed length of the *Amoeba* cell.

Magnification and resolution of an image

Magnification is the number of times larger an image is than the specimen. The magnification obtained with a compound microscope depends on which of the lenses you use. For example, using a ×10 eyepiece and a ×10 objective lens (medium power), the image is magnified ×100 (10 × 10). When you switch to the ×40 objective (high power) with the same eyepiece lens, then the magnification becomes ×400 (10 × 40). These are the most likely orders of magnification used in your laboratory work.

Actually, there is **no limit to magnification**. For example, if a magnified image is photographed, then further enlargement can be made photographically. This is what may happen with photomicrographs shown in books and articles. Magnification is given by the formula:

$$\text{magnification} = \frac{\text{size of image}}{\text{size of specimen}}$$

So, for a particular plant cell of 150 µm diameter, photographed with the microscope and with the image enlarged photographically, the magnification in a print showing the cell at 15 cm diameter (150 000 µm) is:

$$\frac{150\,000}{150} = 1000$$

If a further enlargement is made, to show the same cell at 30 cm diameter (300 000 µm), then the magnification is:

$$\frac{300\,000}{150} = 2000$$

In this case, the image size has been doubled, but **the detail will be no greater**. You will not be able to see, for example, details of cell membrane structure, however much the image is enlarged. This is because the layers making up a cell's membrane are too thin to be seen as separate structures using the light microscope (Figure 1.11).

6 Calculate what magnification occurs with a ×6 eyepiece and a ×10 objective.

Figure 1.11 Magnification without resolution

chloroplast enlarged (×6000)

a) from a transmission electron micrograph

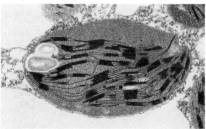

b) from a photomicrograph obtained by light microscopy

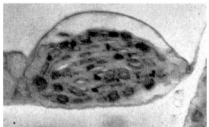

The **resolution** (resolving power) of the microscope is its ability to separate small objects which are very close together. If two separate objects cannot be resolved they will be seen as one object. Merely enlarging them will not separate them. Resolution is a property of lenses quite different from their magnification – and is more important.

Resolution is determined by the wavelength of light. Light is composed of relatively long wavelengths, whereas shorter wavelengths give the better resolution. For the light microscope, the limit of resolution is about 0.2 µm. This means two objects less than 0.2 µm apart may be seen as one object.

Electron microscopy

In the **electron microscope**, an electron beam is used to make a magnified image. Because an electron beam has a much shorter wavelength than light, resolution is much greater in the electron microscope than it is in the light microscope. For the electron microscope used with biological materials, the limit of resolution is about 5 nm (the size of nanometres is given in Table 1.1, page 2).

In **transmission electron microscopy** (**TEM**), the electron beam is passed through an extremely thin section of material. Membranes and other structures present are stained with heavy metal ions, making them electron-opaque so they stand out as dark areas in the image. We cannot see electrons, so the electron beam is focused onto a fluorescent screen for viewing, or onto a photographic plate for permanent recording (Figure 1.12).

In **scanning electron microscopy** (**SEM**) a narrow electron beam is scanned back and forth across the surface of the specimen. Electrons that are reflected or emitted from this surface are detected and converted into a three-dimensional image (Figures 10.17, 12.1).

Figure 1.12 A transmission electron microscope in use

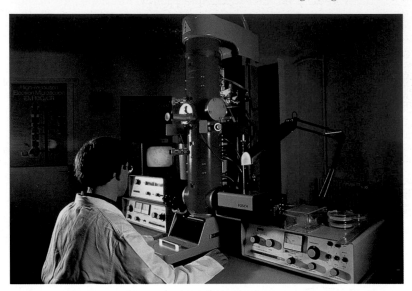

The impact of electron microscopy on cell biology

The nucleus is the largest substructure (organelle) of a cell, and may be observed with the light microscope. Most organelles cannot be viewed by light microscopy, and none is large enough for internal details to be seen. It is the electron microscope that we use to learn about the fine details of cell structure (Figure 1.13).

7 **Distinguish** between resolution and magnification.

Prokaryotic and eukaryotic organisation

Living things have traditionally been divided into two major groupings: animals and plants. However, the range of biological organisation is more diverse than this. The use of the electron microscope in biology has led to the discovery of two types of cellular organisation, based on the presence or absence of a nucleus.

Cells of plants, animals, fungi and protoctista have cells with a large, obvious nucleus. The surrounding cytoplasm contains many different membranous organelles. These types of cells are called **eukaryotic cells** (meaning a 'good nucleus').

On the other hand, bacteria contain no true nucleus and their cytoplasm does not have the organelles of eukaryotes. These are called **prokaryotic cells** (meaning 'before the nucleus').

This distinction between prokaryotic and eukaryotic cells is a fundamental division and is more significant than the differences between plants and animals. We will shortly return to examine the detailed structure of the prokaryotic cell, choosing a bacterium as our example (page 16). First, we need to look into the main organelles in eukaryotic cells.

The ultrastructure of the eukaryotic cell

Our knowledge of the fine structure (known as **ultrastructure**) of cells has been built up by the examination of numerous TEMs. In effect, the eukaryotic cell is a bag of organelles suspended in a fluid matrix, contained within a special membrane, the plasma membrane.

The ultrastructure of a mammalian liver cell is shown in Figure 1.13. The functions of each of the six types of organelle shown (**nucleus, mitochondria, ribosomes, rough endoplasmic reticulum (rER), lysosomes**, and **Golgi apparatus**) are included on their labels.

Figure 1.13
Ultrastructure of a
eukaryotic animal cell

TEM of liver cells

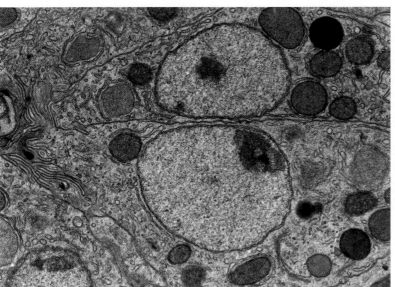

interpretive drawing

mitochondria – site of pathway of aerobic
respiration and ATP formation

ribosomes – site of synthesis of proteins
that remain in the cell

**rough endoplamic
reticulum (rER)** – site of synthesis of proteins that
will be exported from cells

lysosomes – membrane-bound vesicles
containing enzymes

Golgi apparatus – site of synthesis of chemicals
required by the cell, which are
packaged into vesicles before
these 'bud off' from the margins

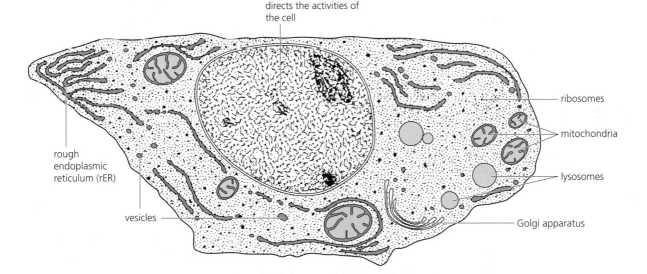

nucleus – controls and
directs the activities of
the cell

ribosomes

mitochondria

lysosomes

Golgi apparatus

rough
endoplasmic
reticulum (rER)

vesicles

Cells may have extracellular components

We have noted that the contents of cells are contained within the plasma membrane. However, cells may secrete material outside the plasma membrane; for example, plant cells have an external wall, and many animal cells secrete glycoproteins.

The plant cell and its wall

The plant cell differs from an animal cell in that it is surrounded by a wall. This wall is completely external to the cell. The plant cell wall is not an organelle. Plant cell walls are primarily constructed of cellulose – a polysaccharide and an extremely strong material. Cellulose molecules are very long, and are arranged in bundles called microfibrils (Figure 1.14).

Cell walls make the boundaries of plant cells easy to see when plant tissues are examined by microscopy. The presence of this strong structure allows the plant cell to develop high internal pressure due to water uptake, without danger of the cell bursting. This is a major difference between the cell water relations of plants and animals.

8 Outline how the electron microscope has increased our knowledge of cell structure.

Figure 1.14 The cellulose of a plant cell wall

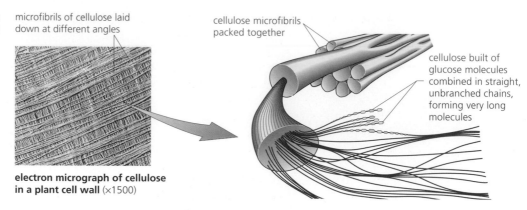

microfibrils of cellulose laid down at different angles

cellulose microfibrils packed together

cellulose built of glucose molecules combined in straight, unbranched chains, forming very long molecules

electron micrograph of cellulose in a plant cell wall (×1500)

The effect of hydrated cell contents pressing against a cell wall (which is distinctly non-elastic) creates an internal pressure which supports the herbaceous (non-woody) plant, its stem, leaves and roots. For example, try cutting a 1 cm × 1 cm × 10 cm potato 'chip' from a potato tuber, and standing it in tap water for an hour or two. Then remove and gently bend it. The now turgid tissue may audibly snap, so stretched are the potato cells!

Extracellular glycoproteins around animal cells

Many animal cells have the ability to adhere to each other. We see the importance of this property in the ways in which cells may form compact tissues and organs. Other animal cells occur in simple sheets or layers, attached to a basement membrane below them. These cases of adhesion are brought about by glycoproteins that the cells have secreted. Glycoproteins are large molecules of protein to which quite large sugar molecules (called oligosaccharides) are attached. Glycoproteins play a part in the support and movement of cells.

The structure of the prokaryotic cell

Figure 1.15 The structure of *Escherichia coli*

Figure 1.15 shows the structure of a prokaryotic cell called *Escherichia coli*. The bacteria and cyanobacteria are prokaryotes.

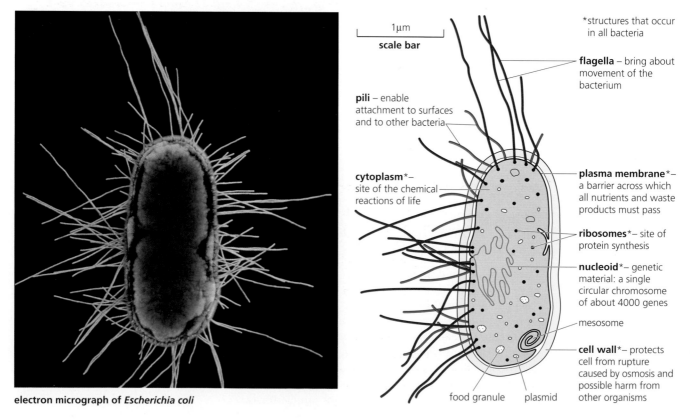

1 µm
scale bar

*structures that occur in all bacteria

flagella – bring about movement of the bacterium

pili – enable attachment to surfaces and to other bacteria

cytoplasm* – site of the chemical reactions of life

plasma membrane* – a barrier across which all nutrients and waste products must pass

ribosomes* – site of protein synthesis

nucleoid* – genetic material: a single circular chromosome of about 4000 genes

mesosome

cell wall* – protects cell from rupture caused by osmosis and possible harm from other organisms

food granule   plasmid

electron micrograph of *Escherichia coli*

E. coli is a common bacterium of the human gut – it occurs in huge numbers in the lower intestine of humans and other endothermic (once known as 'warm-blooded') vertebrates, such as the mammals, and it is a major component of the faeces of these animals. This tiny organism was named by a bacteriologist, Professor T. Escherich, in 1885. Notice the scale bar in Figure 1.15. This bacterium is typically about $1 \times 3\ \mu m$ in length – about the size of a mitochondrion in a eukaryotic cell. The cytoplasm lacks the range of organelles found in eukaryotic cells and there is no large nucleus surrounded by a double membrane.

In Figure 1.15, the ultrastructure of E. coli is shown. The functions of each of the structures (cell wall, plasma membrane, cytoplasm, **pili**, **flagella**, **ribosomes** and **nucleoid**) are included on their labels.

Finally, we can note that all prokaryote cells are capable of extremely rapid growth when conditions are favourable for them. In such environments, prokaryote cells frequently divide into two cells (known as 'binary fission'). New cells formed then grow to full size and divide again.

9 Calculate the approximate magnification of the image of E. coli in Figure 1.15.

Prokaryotic and eukaryotic cells compared

By contrasting Figures 1.13 and 1.15 we can see that there are fundamental differences, both in cell size and cell complexity. In Table 1.4, prokaryotic and eukaryotic cells are compared.

Prokaryotes (e.g. bacteria, cyanobacteria)	Feature	Eukaryotes (e.g. animals, plants, fungi)
cells are extremely small, typically 5–10 µm	**size**	cells are larger, typically 50–150 µm
nucleus absent; circular strand of DNA helix in the cytoplasm, not supported by histone protein, and called a 'nucleoid'	**genetic material**	nucleus has distinct nuclear membrane (with pores), and chromosomes of linear DNA helix supported by histone protein
cell wall present (not of cellulose)	**cell wall**	cell wall present in plants and fungi
few organelles; membranous organelles absent or very simple	**organelles**	many organelles bounded by double membrane (e.g. mitochondria, nucleus) or single membrane (e.g. Golgi apparatus, lysosome, vacuole, rough endoplasmic reticulum)
proteins synthesised in small ribosomes (70S)	**protein synthesis**	proteins synthesised in large ribosomes (80S)
some cells have simple flagella, 20 nm in diameter	**motile organelles**	some cells have cilia or flagella with internal structures, 200 nm in diameter

Table 1.4 Prokaryotic and eukaryotic cells compared

■ Extension: A possible origin for mitochondria and chloroplasts

Present-day prokaryotes are similar to fossil prokaryotes, some of which are 3500 million years old. By comparison, the earliest eukaryote cells date back only 1000 million years. Thus eukaryotes must have evolved surrounded by prokaryotes that were long-established organisms. It is possible that, in the evolution of the eukaryotic cell, prokaryotic cells that were taken up into food vacuoles came to survive as organelles inside the 'host' cell, rather than being digested as food items. If so, they have become integrated into the biochemistry of their 'host' cell, with time.

If this hypothesis is correct, it would explain why mitochondria (and chloroplasts) contain a ring of DNA double helix, just like a bacterial cell. They also contain small ribosomes like those of prokaryotes. These features have caused some evolutionary biologists to suggest that these organelles may be descendants of free-living prokaryotic organisms that came to inhabit larger cells. It may seem a fanciful idea, but not impossible.

The life history of the cell and the nature of stem cells

Figure 1.16 The life history of a cell and the role of stem cells

Multicellular organisms begin life as a single cell, which grows and divides, forming very many cells, and these eventually form the adult organism. So cells arise by division of existing cells. The time between one cell division and the next is known as the **cell cycle** (Figure 1.16).

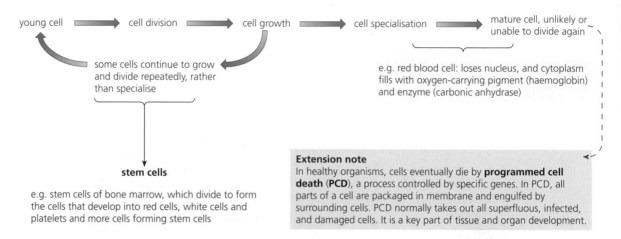

young cell ⟹ cell division ⟹ cell growth ⟹ cell specialisation ⟹ mature cell, unlikely or unable to divide again

some cells continue to grow and divide repeatedly, rather than specialise

e.g. red blood cell: loses nucleus, and cytoplasm fills with oxygen-carrying pigment (haemoglobin) and enzyme (carbonic anhydrase)

stem cells

e.g. stem cells of bone marrow, which divide to form the cells that develop into red cells, white cells and platelets and more cells forming stem cells

Extension note
In healthy organisms, cells eventually die by **programmed cell death** (**PCD**), a process controlled by specific genes. In PCD, all parts of a cell are packaged in membrane and engulfed by surrounding cells. PCD normally takes out all superfluous, infected, and damaged cells. It is a key part of tissue and organ development.

We have noted that most of the cells of a multicellular organism like ourselves have become highly specialised for a particular function. Many specialised cells are then unable to divide again, or can only do so if a special need arises such as when they are damaged (e.g. mammalian liver cells). However, a few cells are able to continue to divide and do so frequently throughout the life of the organism. These are the body's **stem cells**. Adult stem cells can divide an unlimited number of times, producing a new stem cell and a new body tissue cell each time. For example, blood stem cells, present in our bone marrow, produce the full range of different types of blood cell. In other positions in the body, stem cells are capable of producing other body tissue cells. In fact, stem cells may be able to grow into any of the 300 different kinds of cell in the human body.

Human stem cell research seeks to use human embryonic stem (ES) cells, obtained from embryos a few days old. ES cells are more flexible in that they may be coaxed to grow into any type of mature cell. ES cells may be extracted from human embryos that have been discarded during fertility treatments (page 230). Alternatively, therapeutic cloning is the creation of human embryos for the sole purpose of producing of ES cells (rather than cloning with the aim of producing a new human).

The hope is the ES cells, grown up in the laboratory, may eventually be successfully implanted in patients to treat diseases like Alzheimer's, Parkinson's or Type I diabetes. Perhaps genetically engineered stem cells could eventually be available to treat the genetic fault underlying sickle cell disease (page 101). Similarly, people with cystic fibrosis (page 576) might be treated with their own stem cells, removed and genetically engineered with the cystic fibrosis gene. Such cells would then be planted back in the patient in a way that might lead to the formation of healthy cells lining the airways of their lungs. This would eliminate the problem of tissue rejection that occurs in traditional transplant surgery.

Because these techniques are controversial and experimental, international scientists have agreed a consensus of principles guiding their work. New developments and challenges arise all the time around this therapy for human diseases. You can keep in touch with developments in this (and other) aspects of modern biology by reference to journals such as *New Scientist* (www.newscientist.com), and *Scientific American* (www.sciam.com). Other organisations and sources, including the BioNews website (www.bionews.org.uk), may be accessed using an internet search engine.

Introducing the viruses

Viruses are disease-causing agents, rather than organisms. They are not made of cells. A virus consists of a **core of nucleic acid**, either of DNA or RNA. This is surrounded by a **protein coat** called a capsid (Figure 1.17). In some viruses there is an additional external envelope of membrane made of lipids and proteins (e.g. human immunodeficiency virus – HIV).

All viruses are all extremely small, most are in the size range 20–400 nm (0.02–0.4 μm). Consequently, they are visible only by means of electron microscopy.

Viruses reproduce inside specific living cells only. Here they function as parasites in their host organism. However, they have to be transported in some way between hosts. Viruses are mostly highly specific to particular host species, some to plant species, some to animal species and some to bacteria. An example of a plant virus is shown in Figure 1.17.

Figure 1.17 Tobacco mosaic virus (TMV) – an example of a virus

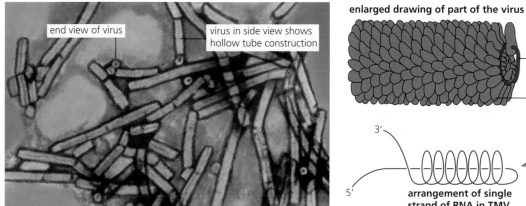

end view of virus

virus in side view shows hollow tube construction

transmission electron micrograph of TMV (×40 000) negatively stained

enlarged drawing of part of the virus

position of RNA

protein coat (capsid) of polypeptide building blocks arranged in a spiral around the canal containing RNA

3′

5′

arrangement of single strand of RNA in TMV

10 **State** which characteristics of living things are not shown by viruses.

Relative sizes of molecules, macromolecules, viruses and organisms

There are great disparities of size among organisms, viruses, and the molecules they are built from. We measure size using the SI unit of length, the metre, and the accepted subdivisions (Table 1.1, page 2). In Figure 1.18, size relationships of biological and chemical levels of organisation are compared. The scale is logarithmic to accommodate the diversities in size in the space available, so each division is ten times larger than the division immediately below it. In science, 'powers to ten' are used to avoid writing long strings of zeros.

Remember, although sizes are expressed by a single length or diameter, all cells and organisms are three-dimensional structures, with length, breadth and depth.

11 **Distinguish** between the following pairs of terms:

a cell wall and plasma membrane
b nucleus and nucleoid
c flagella and pili.

Figure 1.18 Size relationships on a logarithmic scale

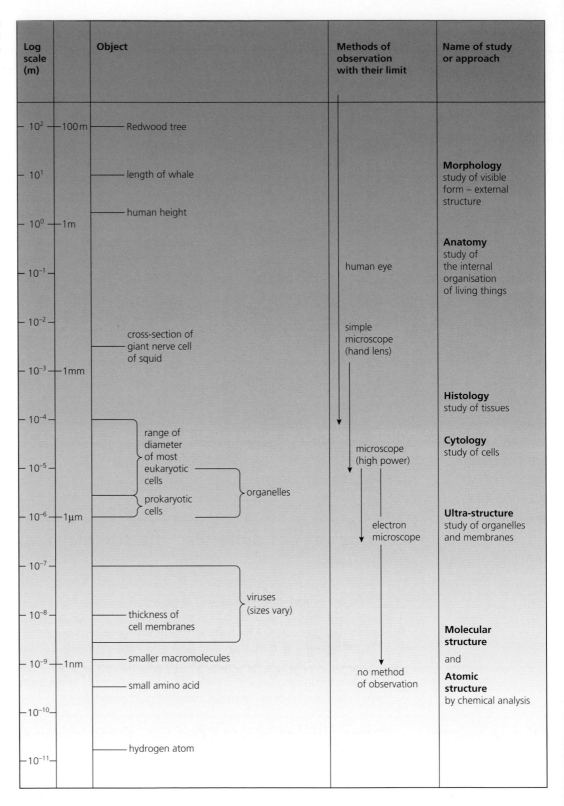

Membranes

We have seen that a plasma membrane is a structure common to eukaryotic and prokaryotic cells. The plasma membrane maintains the integrity of the cell (it holds the cells contents together). Also, it is a barrier across which all substances entering and leaving the cell pass.

The structure of the plasma membrane

The plasma membrane is made almost entirely of protein and lipid, together with a small and variable amount of carbohydrate. How are these components assembled into the plasma membrane? Figure 1.19 shows the molecular structure of the plasma membrane, which is known as the **fluid mosaic model**. The plasma membrane is described as *fluid* because the components (lipids and proteins) are on the move, and *mosaic* because the proteins are scattered about in this pattern.

Figure 1.19 The fluid mosaic model of the plasma membrane

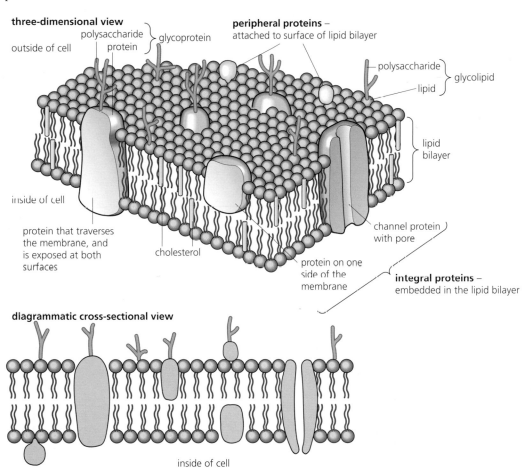

12 Draw a copy of the diagrammatic cross-section of the fluid mosaic membrane (part of Figure 1.19). **Label** it correctly, using the terms: phospholipid bilayer, cholesterol, glycoprotein, integral protein, peripheral protein.

The lipid of membranes is **phospholipid**. The chemical structure of phospholipid is shown in Figure 2.13, page 50.

Take a look at its structure, now.

You see that phospholipid has a 'head' composed of a glycerol group to which is attached one ionised phosphate group. This latter part of the molecule has **hydrophilic properties** (water-loving). For example, hydrogen bonds readily form between the phosphate head and water molecules.

The remainder of the phospholipid consists of two long, fatty acid residues consisting of hydrocarbon chains. These 'tails' have **hydrophobic properties** (water-hating).

So phospholipid is unusual in being partly hydrophilic and partly hydrophobic.

Figure 1.20 Phospholipid molecules and water – the formation of monolayers and bilayers

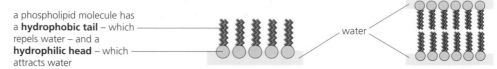

Phospholipid molecules **in contact with water** form a **monolayer**, with heads dissolved in the water and the tails sticking outwards.

When **mixed with water**, phospholipid molecules arrange themselves into a **bilayer**, in which the hydrophobic tails are attracted to each other.

a phospholipid molecule has a **hydrophobic tail** – which repels water – and a **hydrophilic head** – which attracts water

water

What are the consequences of this dual nature of phospholipid?

A small quantity of phospholipid in contact with water will float with the hydrocarbon tails exposed above the water, forming a monolayer of phospholipid molecules (Figure 1.20). When more phospholipid is available, the molecules arrange themselves as a bilayer, with the hydrocarbon tails facing together. This is the situation in the plasma membrane (Figure 1.21).

In the lipid bilayer, attractions between the hydrophobic hydrocarbon tails on the inside, and between the hydrophilic glycerol/phosphate heads and the surrounding water on the outside make a stable, strong barrier.

Figure 1.21 Plasma membrane structure; evidence from the electron microscope

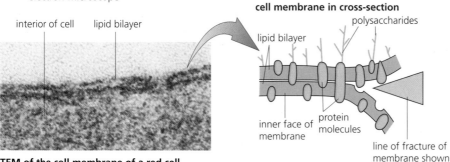

interior of cell   lipid bilayer

TEM of the cell membrane of a red cell (×700 000)

cell membrane in cross-section

lipid bilayer

polysaccharides

inner face of membrane

protein molecules

line of fracture of membrane shown to the right

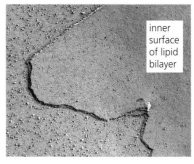

inner surface of lipid bilayer

electron micrograph of the cell membrane (freeze-etched)

The proteins of plasma membranes are **globular proteins** (page 257). Some of these proteins occur partially or fully buried in the lipid bilayer, and are described as integral proteins. Others are superficially attached on either surface of the lipid bilayer and are known as peripheral proteins. The functions of the membrane proteins are various; some are channels for transport of metabolites, some are enzymes or carriers, and some receptors or antigens (Figure 1.22).

The **carbohydrate** molecules of the membrane are relatively short-chain polysaccharides, some attached to the proteins (**glycoproteins**) and some to the lipids (**glycolipids**). This glycocalyx, as it is known, occurs only on the outer surface of the plasma membrane. Its various functions involve, for example, cell–cell recognition, acting as receptor sites for chemical signals, and the binding of cells into tissues.

13 State the difference between a lipid bilayer and the double membrane of many organelles.

Movement across the plasma membrane

Movement of molecules across the plasma membrane of living cells is continuous and heavy. Into and out of cells pass **water**, **respiratory gases** (oxygen and carbon dioxide), **nutrients** such as glucose, **essential ions**, and **excretory products**.

Cells may secrete substances such as **hormones** and **enzymes**, and they may receive **growth substances** and certain hormones. Plants secrete the chemicals that make up their walls through their cell membranes, and assemble and maintain the wall outside the membrane. Certain mammalian cells secrete **structural proteins** such as collagen, in a form that can be assembled outside the cells.

In addition, the plasma membrane is where the cell is identified by surrounding cells and organisms. For example, **protein receptor sites** are recognised by hormones, by neurotransmitter substances from nerve cells, and by other chemicals sent from other cells. Figure 1.23 is a summary of this movement, and Figure 1.24 summarises the mechanisms of transport across membranes, into which we need to look further.

Figure 1.22 The functions of membrane proteins

1 channels for transport of metabolites or water

channel protein for passage through membrane – each channel allows one specific substance to pass

pump protein for active transport across membrane – energy from ATP is used selectively to move one (or two) specific substances across

ADP + P$_i$

ATP

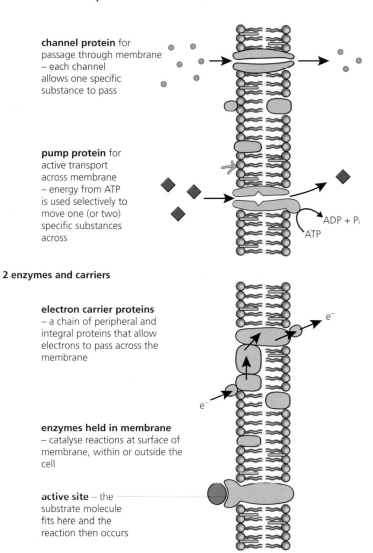

2 enzymes and carriers

electron carrier proteins – a chain of peripheral and integral proteins that allow electrons to pass across the membrane

e$^-$

e$^-$

enzymes held in membrane – catalyse reactions at surface of membrane, within or outside the cell

active site – the substrate molecule fits here and the reaction then occurs

3 receptors, antigens, cell–cell recognition and cell binding sites

binding protein for attachment of a specific hormone – a signal is then generated that is transmitted inside the cell

cell–cell recognition site – attachment may result in cells binding together

binding sites for antigen–antibody reaction (page 196)

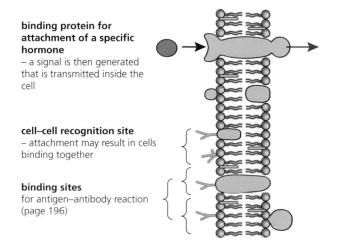

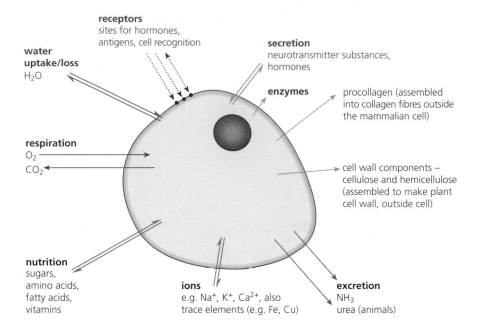

Figure 1.23 Movements across the plasma membrane

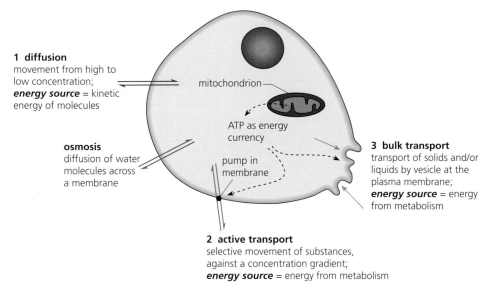

Figure 1.24 Mechanisms of movement across membranes

Movement by diffusion

The atoms, molecules and ions of liquids and gases undergo continuous random movements. These movements result in the even distribution of the components of a gas mixture and of the atoms, molecules and ions in a solution. So, for example, from a solution we are able to take a tiny random sample and analyse it to find the concentration of dissolved substances in the whole solution – because any sample has the same composition as the whole. Similarly, every breath we take has the same amount of oxygen, nitrogen and carbon dioxide as the atmosphere as a whole.

Continuous random movements of all molecules ensures complete mixing and even distribution, given time, in solutions and gases.

Diffusion is the free passage of molecules (and atoms and ions) from a region of their high concentration to a region of low concentration.

Where a difference in concentration has arisen in a gas or liquid, random movements carry molecules from a region of high concentration to a region of low concentration. As a result, the particles become evenly dispersed. The energy for diffusion comes from the **kinetic energy** of molecules. *Kinetic* means that a particle has this energy because it is in continuous motion.

Diffusion in a liquid can be illustrated by adding a crystal of a coloured mineral to distilled water. Even without stirring, the ions become evenly distributed throughout the water (Figure 1.25). The process takes time, especially as the solid has first to dissolve.

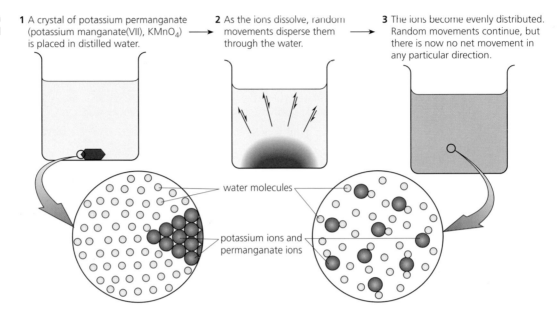

Figure 1.25 Diffusion in a liquid

1 A crystal of potassium permanganate (potassium manganate(VII), KMnO₄) is placed in distilled water.

2 As the ions dissolve, random movements disperse them through the water.

3 The ions become evenly distributed. Random movements continue, but there is now no net movement in any particular direction.

water molecules

potassium ions and permanganate ions

Diffusion in cells

Diffusion across the cell membrane occurs where:

- The plasma membrane is fully permeable to the solute. The lipid bilayer of the plasma membrane is permeable to non-polar substances, including steroids and glycerol, and also oxygen and carbon dioxide in solution, all of which diffuse quickly via this route.
- The pores in the membrane are large enough for a solute to pass through (Figure 1.26). Water diffusing across the plasma membrane passes via the protein-lined pores of the membrane, and via tiny spaces between the phospholipid molecules. This latter occurs easily where the fluid mosaic membrane contains phospholipids with unsaturated hydrocarbon tails, for here these hydrocarbon tails are spaced more widely. The membrane is consequently especially 'leaky' to water, for example.

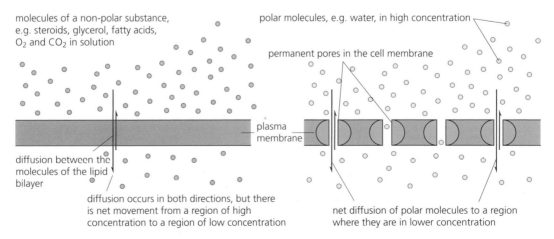

Figure 1.26 Diffusion across the plasma membrane

molecules of a non-polar substance, e.g. steroids, glycerol, fatty acids, O_2 and CO_2 in solution

polar molecules, e.g. water, in high concentration

permanent pores in the cell membrane

plasma membrane

diffusion between the molecules of the lipid bilayer

diffusion occurs in both directions, but there is net movement from a region of high concentration to a region of low concentration

net diffusion of polar molecules to a region where they are in lower concentration

14 Students were provided with cubes of slightly alkaline gelatine of different dimensions, containing an acid–alkali indicator that is red in alkali but yellow in acid. The cubes were placed in dilute acid solution, and the time taken for the colour in the gelatine to change from red to yellow was measured.

Dimensions/mm	Surface area/mm²	Volume/mm³	Time/minutes
10 × 10 × 10	600.0	1000.0	12.0
5 × 5 × 5	150.0	125.0	4.5
4 × 4 × 4	96.0	64.0	4.2
2.5 × 2.5 × 2.5	37.5	15.6	4.0

a For each block, **calculate** the ratio of surface area to volume (SA:V).

b Plot a graph of the time taken for the colour change (vertical or *y* axis) against the SA:V ratio (horizontal or *x* axis).

c **Explain** why the colour changes more quickly in some blocks than others.

Facilitated diffusion

In facilitated diffusion, a substance that otherwise is unable to diffuse across the plasma membrane does so as a result of its effect on particular molecules present in the membrane. In the presence of the substance, these membrane molecules, made of globular protein, form into pores large enough to allow diffusion; they close up again when the substance is no longer present (Figure 1.27). In facilitated diffusion, the energy comes from the kinetic energy of the molecules involved, as is the case in all forms of diffusion. Energy from metabolism is not required. Important examples of facilitated diffusion are the movement of ADP into mitochondria and the exit of ATP from mitochondria (page 80).

Figure 1.27 Facilitated diffusion

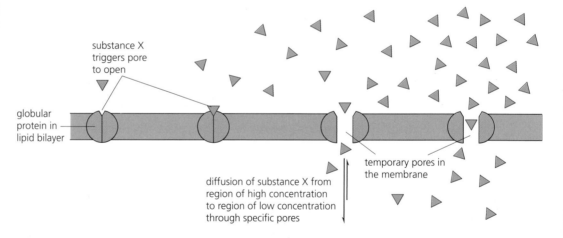

substance X triggers pore to open

globular protein in lipid bilayer

diffusion of substance X from region of high concentration to region of low concentration through specific pores

temporary pores in the membrane

15 **Distinguish** between diffusion and facilitated diffusion.

Osmosis – a special case of diffusion

Osmosis is a special case of diffusion. It is the diffusion of water molecules across a membrane which is permeable to water (**partially permeable**). Since water makes up 70–90% of living cells and cell membranes are partially permeable membranes, osmosis is very important in biology.

Why does osmosis happen?

Dissolved substances attract a group of polar water molecules (page 38) around them. The forces holding the water molecules in this way are weak chemical bonds, including **hydrogen bonds**. Consequently, the tendency for random movement by the dissolved substances and their surrounding water molecules is restricted. Organic substances like sugars, amino acids, polypeptides and proteins, and inorganic ions like Na^+, K^+, Cl^- and NO_3^-, have this effect on the water molecules around them.

The stronger the solution (i.e. the more solute dissolved per volume of water) the greater the number of water molecules that are slowed up and held almost stationary. So, in a very concentrated solution, very many more of the water molecules have restricted movement than in a dilute solution. In pure water, all of the water molecules are free to move about randomly, and do so.

When a solution is separated from water (or a more dilute solution) by a membrane permeable to water molecules (such as the plasma membrane), water molecules free to move tend to diffuse, while dissolved molecules and their group of water molecules move very much less, if at all. So there is a net flow of water, from a more dilute solution into a more concentrated solution, across the membrane. The membrane is described as partially permeable.

Osmosis is the net movement of water molecules (solvent), from a region of high concentration of water molecules to a region of lower concentration of water molecules, across a selectively permeable membrane (Figure 1.28). Alternatively, we can state the following.

> **Osmosis is the passive movement of water molecules, across a partially permeable membrane, from a region of lower solute concentration to a region of higher solute concentration.**

Figure 1.28 Osmosis

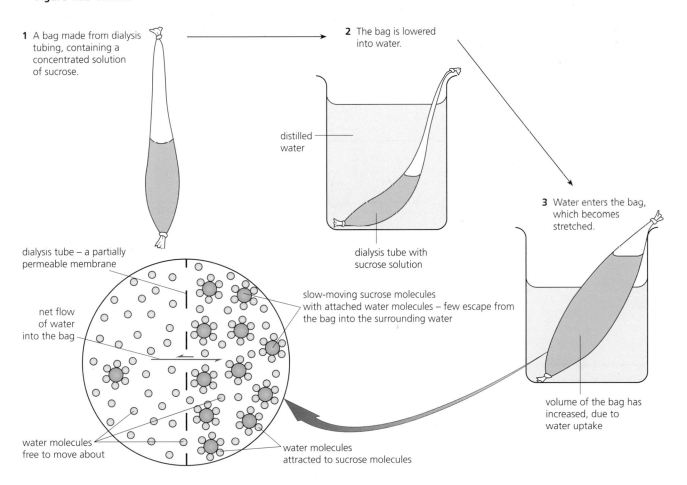

1 A bag made from dialysis tubing, containing a concentrated solution of sucrose.

2 The bag is lowered into water.

distilled water

3 Water enters the bag, which becomes stretched.

dialysis tube – a partially permeable membrane

net flow of water into the bag

dialysis tube with sucrose solution

slow-moving sucrose molecules with attached water molecules – few escape from the bag into the surrounding water

volume of the bag has increased, due to water uptake

water molecules free to move about

water molecules attracted to sucrose molecules

16 When a concentrated solution of glucose is separated from a dilute solution of glucose by a partially permeable membrane, **determine** which solution will show a net gain of water molecules.

Movement by active transport

We have seen that diffusion is due to random movements of molecules, and occurs spontaneously, from a high to a low concentration. However, many of the substances required by cells have to be absorbed from a weak external concentration and taken up into cells that contain a higher concentration. Uptake against a concentration gradient cannot occur by diffusion. Instead, it requires a source of energy to drive it. This type of uptake is known as **active transport**.

In active transport, metabolic energy produced by the cell, held as ATP, is used to drive the transport of molecules and ions across cell membranes. Active transport has characteristic features distinctly different from those of movement by diffusion.

1 **Active transport occurs against a concentration gradient**

It occurs from a region of low concentration to a region of higher concentration. The cytoplasm of a cell normally holds some reserves of molecules and ions valuable in metabolism, like nitrate ions in plant cells, or calcium ions in muscle fibres. The reserves of useful molecules and ions do not escape; the cell membrane retains them inside the cell. Yet when more of these or other useful molecules or ions become available for uptake, they too are actively absorbed into the cells. This happens even though the concentration outside the cell is lower than that inside.

2 **Active uptake is highly selective**

For example, in a situation where potassium chloride (K^+ and Cl^- ions) is available to an animal cell, K^+ ions are more likely to be absorbed, since they are needed by the cell. Where sodium nitrate (Na^+ and NO_3^- ions) is available to a plant cell, it is likely that more of the NO_3^- ions are absorbed than the Na^+, since this reflects the needs of plant cells.

Figure 1.29 Active transport of a single substance

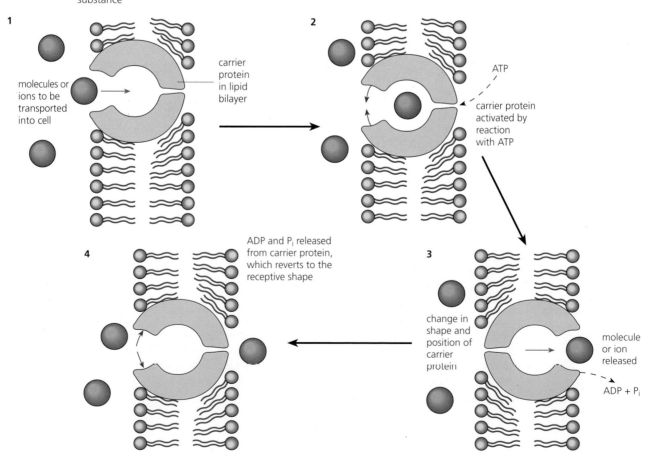

1

molecules or ions to be transported into cell

carrier protein in lipid bilayer

2

ATP

carrier protein activated by reaction with ATP

ADP and P_i released from carrier protein, which reverts to the receptive shape

4

3

change in shape and position of carrier protein

molecule or ion released

ADP + P_i

3 Active transport involves special molecules of the membrane, called pump molecules

The pump molecules pick up particular molecules or ions and transport them to the other side of the membrane, where they are then released. The pump molecules are globular proteins, sometimes also called carrier proteins, that span the lipid bilayers (Figure 1.29). Movements by the pump molecules require reaction with ATP; this reaction supplies metabolic energy to the process. Most membrane pumps are specific to particular molecules or ions and this is the way selective transport is brought about. If the pump molecule for a particular substance is not present, the substance will not be transported.

Active transport is a feature of most living cells. We meet examples of active transport in the gut where absorption occurs (Chapter 7), in the active uptake of ions by plant roots (Chapter 20), in the kidney tubules where urine is formed, and in nerve fibres where an impulse is propagated (Chapter 13).

The protein pumps of plasma membranes are of different types. Some transport a particular molecule or ion in one direction (Figure 1.29), while others transport two substances (like Na^+ and K^+) in opposite directions (Figure 1.30). Occasionally, two substances are transported in the same direction; for example, Na^+ and glucose (Figure 20.13, page 654).

17 Samples of five plant tissue discs were incubated in dilute sodium chloride solution at different temperatures. After 24 hours, it was found that the uptake of ions from the solutions was as follows (arbitrary units).

	Sodium ions	Chloride ions
Tissue at 5 °C	80	40
Tissue at 25 °C	160	80

Comment on how absorption of sodium chloride occurs, giving your reasons.

Figure 1.30 The sodium/potassium ion pump

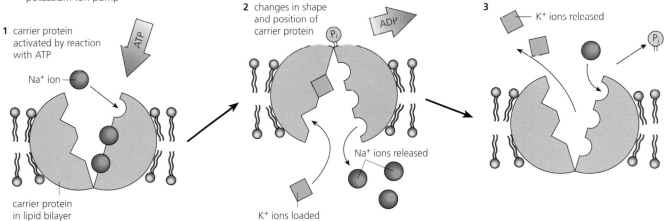

1 carrier protein activated by reaction with ATP

Na^+ ion

carrier protein in lipid bilayer

2 changes in shape and position of carrier protein

P_i

ADP

Na^+ ions released

K^+ ions loaded

3

K^+ ions released

P_i

Movement by bulk transport

Another mechanism of transport across the plasma membrane is known as **bulk transport**. It occurs by movements of **vesicles** of matter (solids or liquids) across the membrane by processes known generally as **cytosis**. Uptake is called **endocytosis** and export is **exocytosis**.

The strength and flexibility of the fluid mosaic membrane makes this activity possible. Energy from metabolism (ATP) is also required to bring it about. For example, when solid matter is being taken in (**phagocytosis**), part of the plasma membrane at the point where the vesicle forms is pulled inwards and the surrounding plasma membrane and cytoplasm bulge out. The matter thus becomes enclosed in a small vesicle.

Vesicles are used to transport materials within cells, for example, between the rough endoplasmic reticulum (rER) and the Golgi apparatus, and on to the plasma membrane (Figure 1.13, page 15).

In the human body, there is a huge number of phagocytic cells (phagocytosis means 'cell eating'). These are called the **macrophages**. The macrophages engulf the debris of damaged or dying cells and dispose of it. For example, we break down about 2×10^{11} red cells each day. This number are ingested and disposed of by macrophages, every 24 hours.

Bulk transport of fluids is referred to as pinocytosis (Figure 1.31).

Figure 1.31 Transport by cytosis

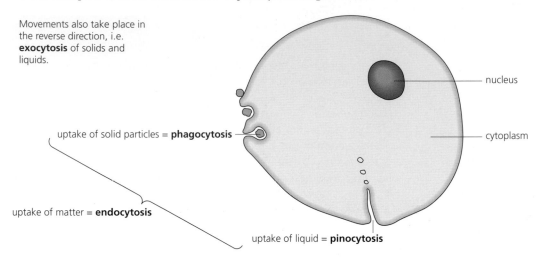

Movements also take place in the reverse direction, i.e. **exocytosis** of solids and liquids.

uptake of solid particles = **phagocytosis**

uptake of matter = **endocytosis**

uptake of liquid = **pinocytosis**

nucleus

cytoplasm

18 **Distinguish** between the following pairs:

a proteins and lipids in cell membranes

b active transport and bulk transport

c endocytosis and exocytosis.

Cell division

2.5.1–2.5.6

New cells arise by division of existing cells. Unicellular organisms grow quickly under favourable conditions, then divide into two cells. The growth and division cycle is repeated while conditions are suitable. Multicellular organisms begin life as a single cell which grows and divides, forming many cells which eventually make up the adult organism. In these situations, it is important that division of a nucleus produces two new cells (daughter cells) containing identical sets of chromosomes; this is achieved by **mitosis**.

The cell division cycle

The cycle of growth and division of a cell is called the cell division cycle. The **cell division cycle** has three main stages:

- **interphase**;
- division of the nucleus by **mitosis**;
- **cytokinesis** (cell division).

In each stage of the cell cycle particular events occur. These events are summarised in Figure 1.32, and they are discussed below.

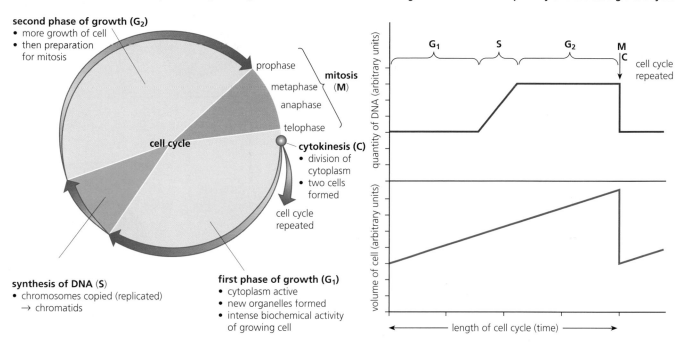

the cell cycle consists of interphase and mitosis

interphase = G$_1$ + S + G$_2$

change in cell volume and quantity of DNA during a cell cycle

second phase of growth (G$_2$)
- more growth of cell
- then preparation for mitosis

prophase
metaphase } **mitosis (M)**
anaphase
telophase

cell cycle

cytokinesis (C)
- division of cytoplasm
- two cells formed

cell cycle repeated

synthesis of DNA (S)
- chromosomes copied (replicated) → chromatids

first phase of growth (G$_1$)
- cytoplasm active
- new organelles formed
- intense biochemical activity of growing cell

quantity of DNA (arbitrary units)

G$_1$ S   G$_2$ M
C
cell cycle repeated

volume of cell (arbitrary units)

← length of cell cycle (time) →

Figure 1.32 The stages of the cell cycle

Interphase

Interphase is always the longest part of the cell cycle, but it is of extremely variable length. When growth is fast, as in a developing human embryo, and the growing point of a young stem, interphase may last about 24 hours or less. On the other hand, in mature cells that infrequently divide it lasts a very long period – possibly indefinitely. For example, some cells, once they have differentiated, rarely or never divide again. Here the nucleus remains at interphase permanently.

What happens to the nucleus in interphase?

At first glance the nucleus appears to be resting, but this is not the case. The chromosomes cease to be visible as thread-like structures at interphase, becoming dispersed as chromatin. Now they are actively involved in protein synthesis. From the chromosomes, copies of the information in particular genes or groups of genes are taken for use in the cytoplasm (page 69). In organelles of the cytoplasm called ribosomes, proteins are assembled by combining amino acids in sequences dictated by the information from the gene.

During interphase, the synthesis of new organelles takes place in the cytoplasm. There is intense biochemical activity in the cytoplasm and the organelles, and there is an accumulation of stored energy before nuclear division occurs again.

Also in this period, between nuclear divisions, each chromosome **replicates** (makes a copy of itself). The two identical structures formed are called **chromatids**. The chromatids remain attached until they divide during mitosis.

Mitosis

When cell division occurs, the nucleus divides first. In mitosis, the chromosomes, present as the chromatids formed during interphase, are separated, and accurately and precisely distributed to two daughter nuclei (Figure 1.33). In the following description, mitosis is presented and explained as a process in four phases, but remember this is for convenience of description only. Mitosis is a continuous process with no breaks between the phases.

In **prophase**, the chromosomes become visible as long thin threads. They increasingly shorten and thicken by a process of supercoiling. Only at the end of prophase is it possible to see that they consist of two chromatids held together at the **centromere**. At the same time, the nucleolus gradually disappears and the nuclear membrane breaks down.

Figure 1.33 Mitosis in an animal cell

For simplicity, the drawings show mitosis in a cell with a single pair of homologous chromosomes.

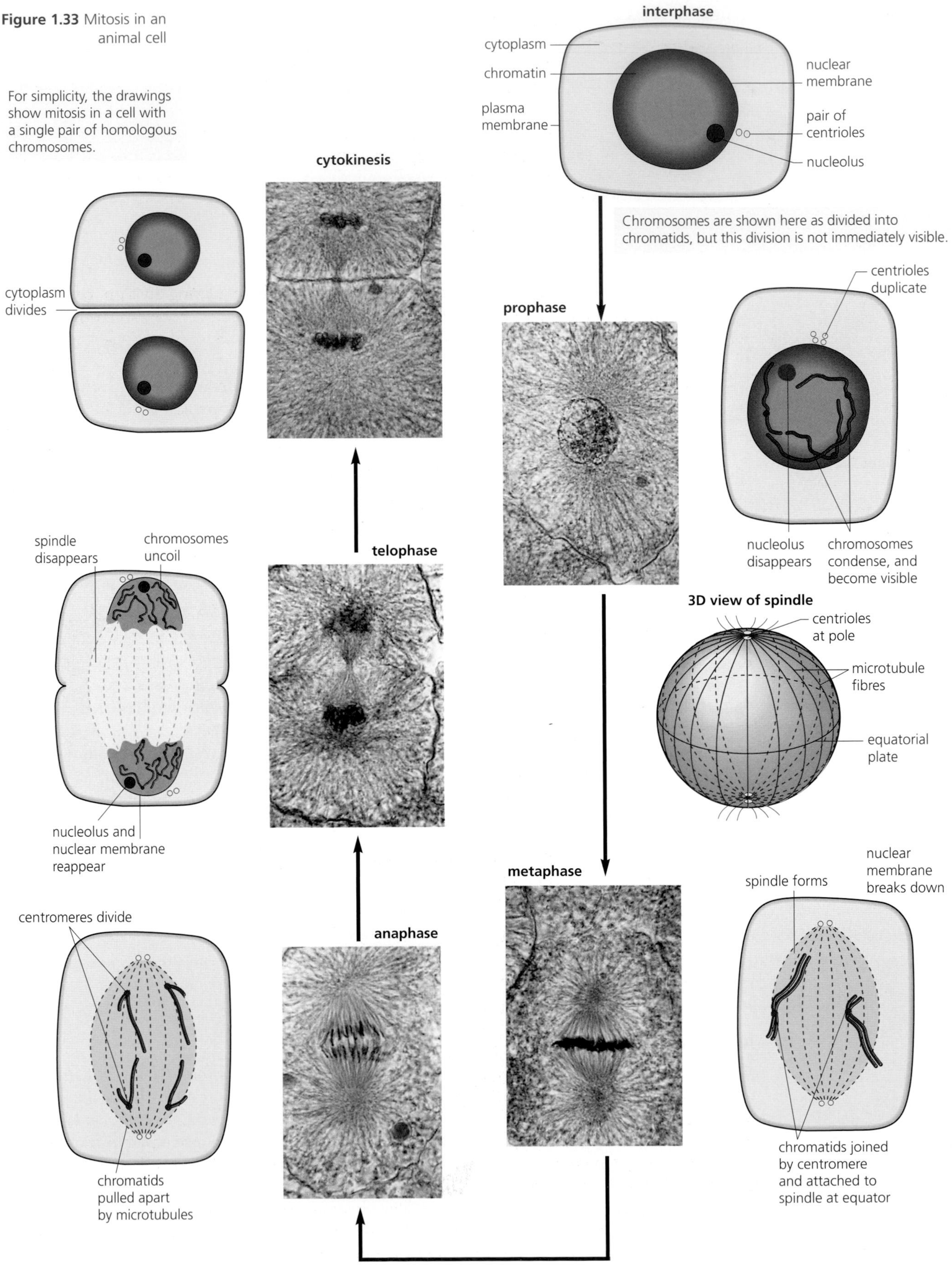

interphase

cytoplasm

chromatin

plasma membrane

nuclear membrane

pair of centrioles

nucleolus

Chromosomes are shown here as divided into chromatids, but this division is not immediately visible.

cytokinesis

cytoplasm divides

prophase

centrioles duplicate

nucleolus disappears

chromosomes condense, and become visible

spindle disappears

chromosomes uncoil

telophase

nucleolus and nuclear membrane reappear

3D view of spindle

centrioles at pole

microtubule fibres

equatorial plate

centromeres divide

anaphase

metaphase

nuclear membrane breaks down

spindle forms

chromatids pulled apart by microtubules

chromatids joined by centromere and attached to spindle at equator

In **metaphase**, the centrioles move to opposite ends of the cell. Microtubules in the cytoplasm start to form into a spindle, radiating out from the centrioles (Figure 1.33, page 32). Microtubules attach to the centromeres of each pair of chromatids, and these are arranged at the equator of the spindle. (Note: in plant cells, a spindle of exactly the same structure is formed, but without the presence of the centrioles.)

In **anaphase**, the centromeres divide, the spindle fibres shorten, and the chromatids are pulled by their centromeres to opposite poles. Once separated, the chromatids are referred to as chromosomes.

In **telophase**, a nuclear membrane reforms around both groups of chromosomes at opposite ends of the cell. The chromosomes decondense by uncoiling, becoming chromatin again. The nucleolus reforms in each nucleus. Interphase follows division of the cytoplasm.

Cytokinesis

Division of the cytoplasm, known as **cytokinesis**, follows telophase. During division, cell organelles such as mitochondria and chloroplasts become distributed evenly between the cells. In animal cells, division is by in-tucking of the plasma membrane at the equator of the spindle, 'pinching' the cytoplasm in half (Figure 1.33).

In plant cells, the Golgi apparatus forms vesicles of new cell wall materials which collect along the line of the equator of the spindle, known as the cell plate. Here the vesicles coalesce forming the new plasma membranes and cell walls between the two cells (Figure 1.34).

Figure 1.34 Cytokinesis in a plant cell

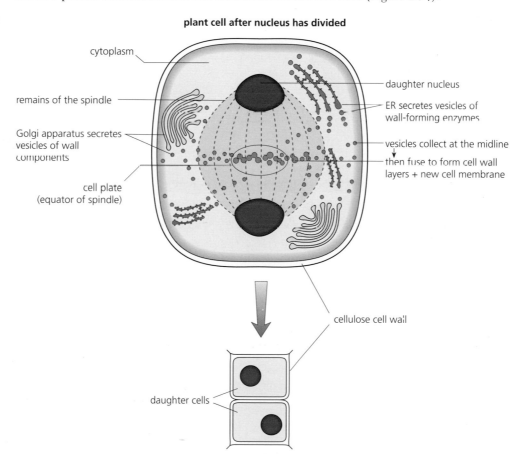

plant cell after nucleus has divided

cytoplasm

remains of the spindle

Golgi apparatus secretes vesicles of wall components

cell plate (equator of spindle)

daughter nucleus

ER secretes vesicles of wall-forming enzymes

vesicles collect at the midline then fuse to form cell wall layers + new cell membrane

cellulose cell wall

daughter cells

Observing chromosomes during mitosis

Actively dividing cells, such as those at the growing points of the root tips of plants, include many cells undergoing mitosis. This tissue can be isolated, stained with an orcein ethanoic (acetic orcein) stain, squashed, and then examined under the high-power lens of a microscope. Nuclei at interphase appear red–purple with almost colourless cytoplasm, but the chromosomes in cells undergoing mitosis will be visible, rather as they appear in the photomicrographs in Figure 1.33. The procedure is summarised in the flow diagram in Figure 1.35.

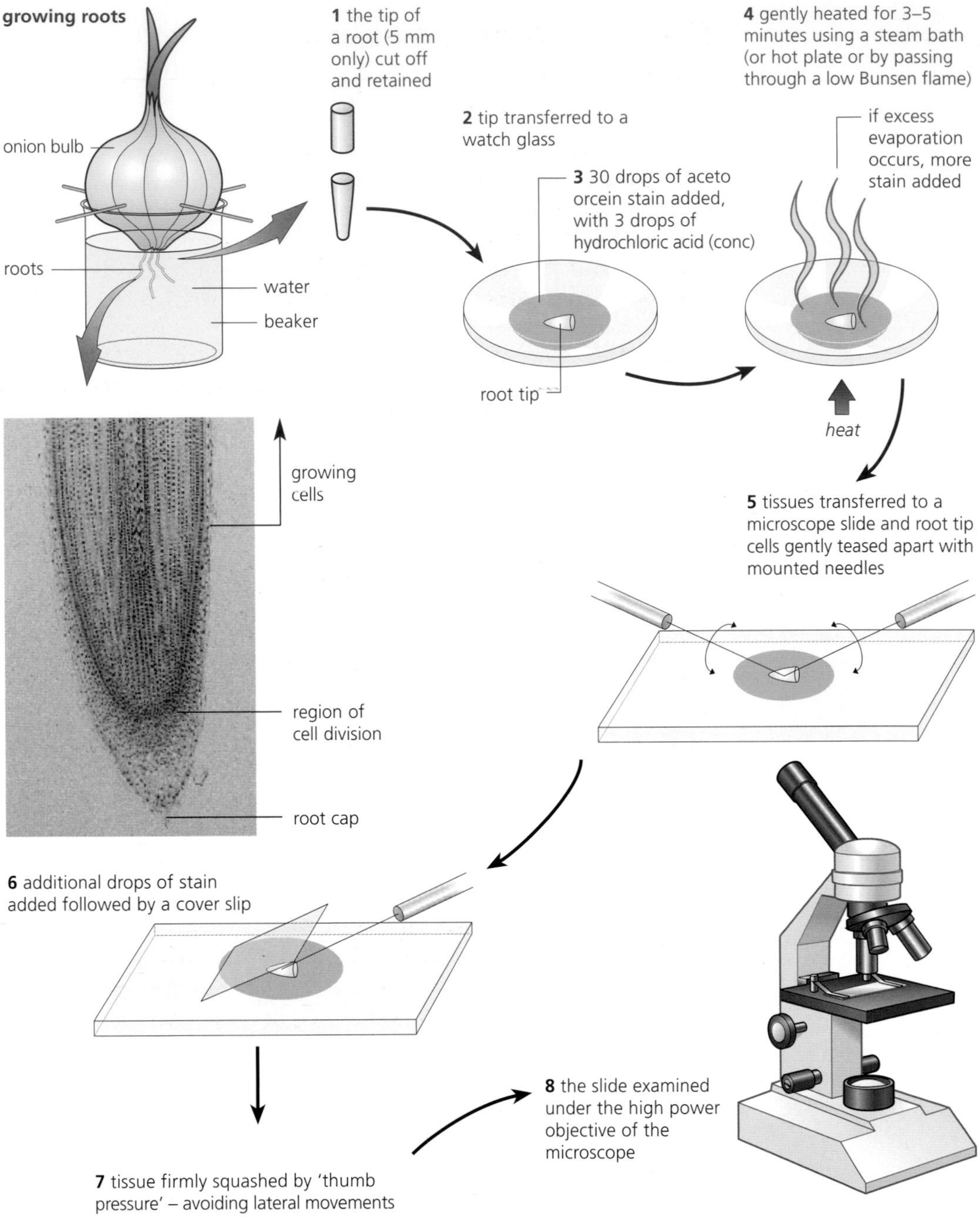

Figure 1.35 The orcein ethanoic stain of an onion root tip squash

growing roots

1 the tip of a root (5 mm only) cut off and retained

2 tip transferred to a watch glass

3 30 drops of aceto orcein stain added, with 3 drops of hydrochloric acid (conc)

4 gently heated for 3–5 minutes using a steam bath (or hot plate or by passing through a low Bunsen flame)

if excess evaporation occurs, more stain added

onion bulb

roots

water

beaker

root tip

heat

5 tissues transferred to a microscope slide and root tip cells gently teased apart with mounted needles

growing cells

region of cell division

root cap

root tip in LS (HP)

6 additional drops of stain added followed by a cover slip

8 the slide examined under the high power objective of the microscope

7 tissue firmly squashed by 'thumb pressure' – avoiding lateral movements

19 Using slides they had prepared to observe chromosomes during mitosis in a plant root tip (Figure 1.35), five students observed and recorded the number of nuclei at each stage in mitosis in 100 cells as shown in the table below.

	Number of nuclei counted by				
Stage of mitosis	student 1	student 2	student 3	student 4	student 5
prophase	64	70	75	68	73
metaphase	13	10	7	11	9
anaphase	5	5	2	8	5
telophase	18	15	16	13	13

a **Calculate** the mean % of dividing cells at each stage of mitosis and present your results as a pie chart.
b Assuming that mitosis takes about 60 minutes to complete in this species of plant, **deduce** what these results imply about the lengths of the four steps.

The significance of mitosis

Daughter cells produced by mitosis have a set of chromosomes identical to each other and to the parent cell from which they were formed. This occurs because:

- an **exact copy** of each chromosome is made by accurate replication (page 66) during interphase, when two chromatids are formed;
- **chromatids remain attached** by their centromeres during metaphase of mitosis, when each becomes attached to a spindle fibre at the equator of the spindle;
- centromeres then divide during anaphase and the chromatids of each pair are pulled apart to **opposite poles** of the spindle; thus, one copy of each chromosome moves to each pole of the spindle;
- the chromosomes at the poles **form the new nuclei** – two to a cell at this point;
- two cells are then formed by division of the cytoplasm at the midpoint of the cell, **each with an exact copy of the original nucleus.**

In **growth and development of an embryo**, it is important that all cells carry the same genetic information as the existing cells from which they are formed, and which they share with surrounding cells or tissues. Similarly, when **repair of damaged or worn out cells** occurs, they are exact copies of what they replace. In fact, this is essential for growth, development and repair, because otherwise different parts of our body might start working to conflicting blueprints. The results would be chaos.

Mitotic cell division is also the basis of all forms of **asexual reproduction** (page 133), in which the offspring produced are identical to the parent.

Cancer – disease caused by uncontrolled cell division

There are very many different forms of cancer, affecting different tissues of the body. Cancer is not thought of as a single disease. However, in cancer, cells divide by mitosis repeatedly, without control or regulation, forming an irregular mass of cells, called a tumour. Sometimes tumour cells break away and are carried to other parts of the body, where they form a secondary tumour. Unchecked, cancerous cells ultimately take over the body at the expense of the surrounding, healthy cells, leading to malfunction and death.

Cancer is caused by damage to DNA of chromosomes. 'Mistakes' of different types build up in the DNA of the body cells. The accumulation of mistakes with time explains why the majority of cancers arise in older people. Different types of mistake can occur, and this explains why cancer is not one single disease. Another cause of cancer is damage to the gene that codes for a protein known as p53 which stops the copying of damaged DNA. This p53 protein and the gene that codes for it are called 'the guardians of the genome'.

Damage to DNA has many potential causes, including the effects of ionising radiation (X-rays, gamma rays and others), certain chemicals (such as components of the tar in tobacco smoke) and some virus infections. Another set of factors is inherited, so that the members of some families are more likely to suffer from certain cancers than others.

20 **Describe** how the behaviour of cancerous cells differs from that of normal cells.

■ *Examination questions – a selection*

Questions 1–5 are taken from past IB Diploma biology papers.

Q1 The diagram represents an animal cell. Which processes occur in the locations labelled?

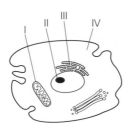

	Transcription	Translation	Glycolysis
A	II	III	I
B	III	II	I
C	II	III	IV
D	III	II	IV

Standard Level Paper 1, May 06, Q3

Q2 Which of the following is a characteristic of organelles?
A They are only found in eukaryotic cells.
B They are only found in prokaryotic cells.
C They are sub-cellular structures.
D They are all membrane-bound.
Standard Level Paper 1, May 04, Q2

Q3 **a** List **two** functions of membrane proteins. (1)
b Oxygen (O_2) moves across the membrane by diffusion. Define the term diffusion. (1)
c Potassium can move across the membrane by passive or active transport. Distinguish between active and facilitated diffusion of ions. (2)
d The hormone insulin leaves the cell by exocytosis. Describe the process of exocytosis. (2)

Standard Level Paper 2, May 06, Q3

Q4 The width of a human hair is 0.1 mm. What is the width in μm?
A 10 μm   **B** 100 μm   **C** 1000 μm   **D** 10 000 μm
Higher Level Paper 1, May 06, Q2

Q5 **a** State **two** processes which involve mitosis. (2)
b Explain the importance of the surface area to volume ratio as a factor limiting cell size. (3)
c State **one** difference between the proteins produced by free ribosomes and those produced by ribosomes attached to the endoplasmic reticulum. (1)
Higher Level Paper 2, May 05, Q2

Questions 6–10 cover other syllabus issues in this chapter.

Q6 List the features animal and plant cells have in common. Construct a table of the differences in structure between typical plant and animal cells. (6)

Q7 The stages of the cell cycle are interphase, mitosis and cytokinesis. Four distinct phases make up the process of mitosis itself.
a Outline the events of interphase which establish that this is not a 'resting' stage in the cell cycle. (4)
b List the major changes that occur to the chromosomes of a nucleus undergoing mitosis during:
i prophase (the first phase)
ii anaphase (the third phase). (6)
c Explain how mitosis produces two genetically identical nuclei. (4)
d Distinguish between stem cells and cancer cells. (2)

Q8 The structure of a plasma membrane is represented by the fluid mosaic model. It is a barrier that has to be crossed by material entering or leaving a cell.
a Draw and label a diagram to illustrate the structure of the plasma membrane as seen in cross-section. (6)
b Explain how the properties of phospholipids help maintain the structure of the plasma membrane. (3)
c List the essential conditions necessary for diffusion. (4)
d Explain the process by which water moves across the plasma membrane. (4)

Q9 **a** Draw and label a diagram of a generalised prokaryotic cell. Annotate your diagram with the functions of each named structure. (6)
b Explain how the size of a prokaryotic cell relates to the size of some organelles typically found in animal cells. (2)
c Define binary fission. (2)

Q10 a List three ideas contained within the cell theory. (3)
b Outline the differences between the processes typically observed in a eukaryotic unicellular organism and a **named** highly differentiated animal cell. (4)

2 Chemistry of life

STARTING POINTS
■ **Elements** are the basic units of pure substances. An **atom** is the smallest part of an element that can take part in a chemical change. At the centre of an atom is a nucleus of **protons** (positively charged particles), and usually also **neutrons** (uncharged particles). Around the nucleus are tiny particles called **electrons** (negatively charged). A **molecule** is a group of like or different atoms held together by chemical forces. A **compound** contains two or more elements chemically combined together.
■ The element **carbon** has a branch of chemistry to itself, known as **organic chemistry**. Compounds built from carbon are called **organic compounds**.
■ A vast number of organic compounds make up living things, but most of them fall into one of **four groups** of compounds, each with distinctive structures and properties. They are: **carbohydrates**, **lipids** (e.g. fats and oils), **proteins**, and **nucleic acids**.
■ Most cells are at least **80% water** by mass. The properties of water are vital to life.

Chemical **elements** are the units of pure substance that make up our world. The Earth is composed of about 92 stable elements in all, in varying quantities, and living things are built from some of them. In Table 2.1 there is a comparison of the most common elements in the Earth's crust and in us. You can see that the bulk of the Earth is composed of the elements oxygen, silicon, aluminium and iron. Of these, only oxygen is a major component of cells.

	Earth's crust		Human body	
1	oxygen	47%	hydrogen	63%
2	silicon	28%	oxygen	25.5%
3	aluminium	7.9%	carbon	9.5%
4	iron	4.5%	nitrogen	1.4%
5	calcium	3.5%	calcium	0.31%
6	sodium	2.5%	phosphorus	0.22%

Table 2.1 Most common elements

Chemical elements and water   3.1.1–3.1.6

About 16 elements are required by cells, and are therefore essential for life. Consequently, the full list of essential elements is a relatively short one. Furthermore, about 99% of living matter consists of just four elements: **carbon, hydrogen, oxygen** and **nitrogen**.

Why do these four elements predominate in living things?

The elements carbon, hydrogen and oxygen predominate because living things contain large quantities of **water**, and also because most other molecules present in cells and organisms are compounds of carbon combined with hydrogen and oxygen, including the **carbohydrates** and **lipids**. The element nitrogen is combined with carbon, hydrogen and oxygen in compounds called amino acids from which **proteins** are constructed.

The roles of a selection of the other **essential elements** are listed in Table 2.2. Note that several of these elements are required in tiny, 'trace' amounts only; in fact, more of some would actually be very harmful to the body.

Element	In plants	In animals	In prokaryotes
sulphur	■ in some amino acids and proteins ■ in some vitamins	■ in some amino acids and proteins ■ in some vitamins	■ in some amino acids and proteins ■ in some vitamins
calcium	■ cell wall formation between dividing plant cells ■ co-factor for certain enzymes	■ constituent of bones ■ reacts in muscle fibre contraction, blood clotting and synapses ■ co-factor for certain enzymes	■ co-factor for certain enzymes ■ contributes to heat resistance of bacterial endospores
phosphorus	■ synthesis of nucleotides ■ ATP	■ synthesis of nucleotides ■ ATP ■ constituent of bones	■ synthesis of nucleotides ■ ATP
iron	■ constituent of electron transport molecules (e.g. cytochromes) ■ chlorophyll synthesis	■ constituent of electron transport molecules (e.g. cytochromes and haem – part of haemoglobin)	■ constituent of electron transport molecules ■ chlorophyll synthesis in photosynthetic prokaryotes
sodium	■ involved with **potassium** in membrane function	■ involved with **potassium** in membrane function and nerve impulse transport	■ involved with **potassium** in membrane function

Other essential elements include:
■ **magnesium** (in chlorophyll – in green plants and certain prokaryotes);
■ **manganese**, **copper**, **cobalt**, **zinc**, **molybdenum** (all in trace amounts, in certain enzymes).

Table 2.2 Roles of certain other elements in living organisms

The difference between atoms, molecules and ions

The fundamental unit of chemical structure is the atom.

> **An atom is the smallest part of an element that can take part in a chemical change.**

Atoms group together to form molecules, and molecules are the smallest part of certain elements and compounds that can exist alone under normal conditions. For example, both oxygen and nitrogen naturally combine with another atom of the same type to form a molecule (O_2 and N_2).

Alternatively, if an atom gains or loses an electron an ion is formed.

1 Distinguish between the terms 'atom' and 'ion'.

> **Ions are formed when atoms gain or lose electrons to form positively or negatively charged ions.**

Water

Living things are typically solid, substantial objects, yet water forms the bulk of their structures – between 65% and 95% by mass of most multicellular plants and animals (about 80% of a human cell consists of water). Despite this, and the fact that water has some unusual properties, water is a substance that is often taken for granted.

Water is composed of atoms of the elements hydrogen and oxygen. One atom of oxygen and two atoms of hydrogen combine by sharing electrons (**covalent bonding**). However, the water molecule is triangular rather than linear, and the nucleus of the oxygen atom draws electrons (negatively charged) away from the hydrogen nuclei (positively charged) – with an interesting consequence. Although overall the water molecule is electrically neutral, there is a net negative charge on the oxygen atom and a net positive charge on the hydrogen atoms. In other words, the water molecule carries an unequal distribution of electrical charge within it. This arrangement is known as a **polar molecule** (Figure 2.1).

2 Distinguish between ionic and covalent bonding.

Hydrogen bonds

With water molecules, the positively charged hydrogen atoms of one molecule are attracted to negatively charged oxygen atoms of nearby water molecules by forces called **hydrogen bonds**. These are weak bonds compared to covalent bonds, yet they are strong enough to hold water molecules together and attract water molecules to charged particles or a charged surface. In fact, hydrogen bonds largely account for the unique properties of water. We examine these properties next.

Figure 2.1 The water molecule and the hydrogen bonds it forms

one oxygen atom combines with two hydrogen atoms by sharing electrons (covalent bond)

↓

in the water molecule the oxygen nucleus draws electrons (negatively charged) away from the hydrogen nucleus (positively charged)

↓

the water molecule carries an **unequal distribution of electrical charge**, even though overall it is electrically neutral

↓

polar water molecule

↓

there is electrostatic attraction between the positively charged region of one water molecule and the negatively charged region of a neighbouring one, giving rise to weak bonds called **hydrogen bonds**

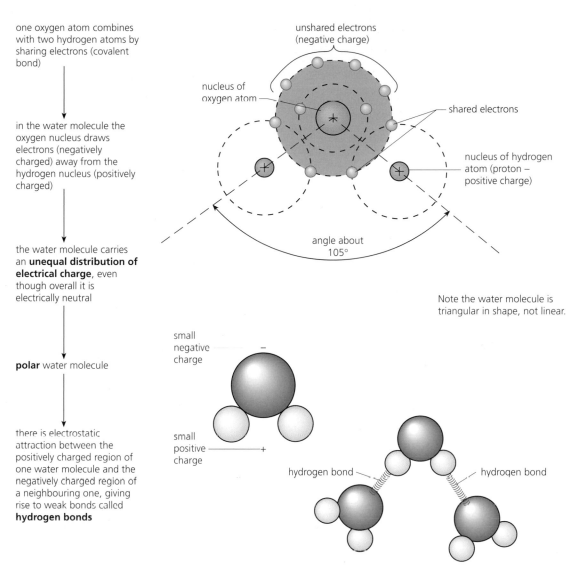

unshared electrons (negative charge)

nucleus of oxygen atom

shared electrons

nucleus of hydrogen atom (proton – positive charge)

angle about 105°

Note the water molecule is triangular in shape, not linear.

small negative charge

small positive charge

hydrogen bond

hydrogen bond

Thermal properties of water

Heat energy and the temperature of water

A lot of heat energy is required to raise the temperature of water. This is because much energy is needed to break the hydrogen bonds that restrict the movements of water molecules. This property of water is its **specific heat capacity**. The specific heat capacity of water is the highest of any known substance. Consequently, aquatic environments like streams and rivers, ponds, lakes and seas are very slow to change temperature when the surrounding air temperature changes. Aquatic environments have much more stable temperatures than terrestrial (land) environments do.

Another consequence is that cells and the bodies of organism do not change temperature readily. Bulky organisms, particularly, tend to have a stable temperature in the face of a fluctuating surrounding temperature, whether in extremes of heat or cold.

Evaporation and heat loss

The hydrogen bonds between water molecules make it difficult for them to be separated and vaporised (evaporated). This means that much energy is needed to turn liquid water into water vapour (gas). This amount of energy is the **latent heat of vaporisation**, and for water it is very high. Consequently, the evaporation of water in sweat on the skin, or in transpiration from green leaves, causes marked cooling. The escaping molecules take a lot of energy with them. You experience this when you stand in a draught after a shower. And since a great deal of heat is lost with the evaporation of a small amount of water, cooling by evaporation of water is economical on water, too.

Heat energy and freezing

The amount of heat energy that must be removed from water to turn it to ice is very great, as is that needed to melt ice. This amount of energy is the **latent heat of fusion**, and is very high for water. As a result, both the contents of cells and the water in the environment are always slow to freeze in extreme cold.

The density of ice

Most liquids contract on cooling, reaching maximum density at their freezing point. Water is unusual in reaching its maximum density at 4 °C. So as water freezes, the ice formed is less dense than the cold water around it. As a consequence, ice floats on top of very cold water (Figure 2.2). The floating layer of ice insulates the water below. The consequence is that lakes rarely freeze solid; aquatic life can generally survive a freeze-up.

Figure 2.2 Ice forms on the surface of water

Because ice freezes from below, it is difficult to judge its depth. It can therefore be very dangerous to walk on!

The angle between the covalent bonds in the water molecule is very close to the angles of a perfect tetrahedron. In ice the molecules form a regular tetrahedral arrangement, and are spaced more widely apart than they are in liquid water.

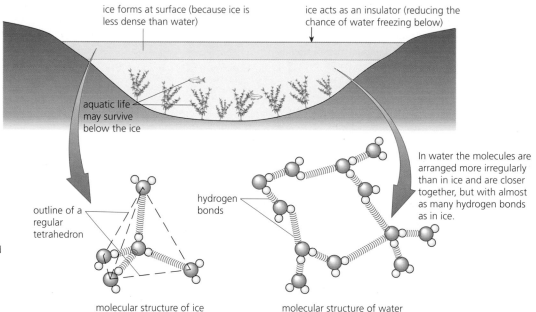

ice forms at surface (because ice is less dense than water)

ice acts as an insulator (reducing the chance of water freezing below)

aquatic life may survive below the ice

outline of a regular tetrahedron

hydrogen bonds

In water the molecules are arranged more irregularly than in ice and are closer together, but with almost as many hydrogen bonds as in ice.

molecular structure of ice

molecular structure of water

Cohesive properties of water

Cohesion is the force by which individual molecules stick together. Water molecules stick together as a result of hydrogen bonding. These bonds continually break and reform with other, surrounding water molecules, but at any one moment, a large number are held together by their hydrogen bonds. **Adhesion** is the force by which individual molecules cling to surrounding material and surfaces. Materials with an affinity for water are described as **hydrophilic** (see 'Solvent properties of water' on page 42). Water adheres strongly to most surfaces and can be drawn up long columns, through narrow tubes like the xylem vessels of plant stems, without danger of the water column breaking (Figure 2.3). Compared with other liquids, water has extremely strong adhesive and cohesive properties that prevent it breaking under tension.

Related to the property of cohesion is the property of **surface tension**. The outermost molecules of water form hydrogen bonds with water molecules below them. This gives a very high surface tension to water – higher than any other liquid except mercury. The surface tension of water is exploited by insects that 'surface skate' (Figure 2.4). The insect's waxy cuticle prevents wetting of its body, and the mass of the insect is not great enough to break the surface tension.

Below the surface, water molecules slide past each other very easily. This property is described as low **viscosity**. Consequently, water flows readily through narrow capillaries and tiny gaps and pores.

Figure 2.3 Water is drawn up a tree trunk

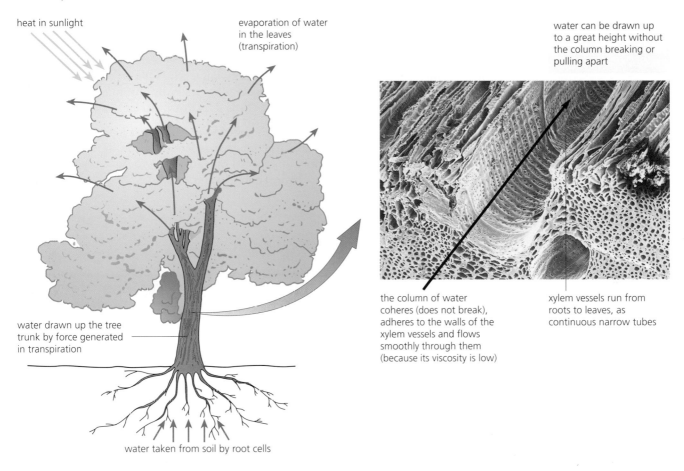

heat in sunlight

evaporation of water in the leaves (transpiration)

water can be drawn up to a great height without the column breaking or pulling apart

water drawn up the tree trunk by force generated in transpiration

the column of water coheres (does not break), adheres to the walls of the xylem vessels and flows smoothly through them (because its viscosity is low)

xylem vessels run from roots to leaves, as continuous narrow tubes

water taken from soil by root cells

Figure 2.4 A pond skater moving over the water surface

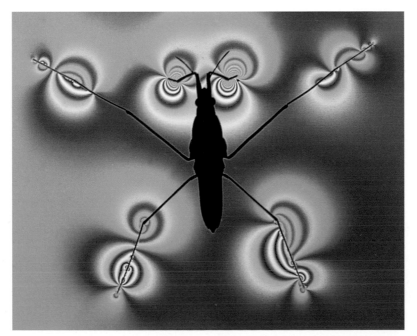

the photograph shows the interference patterns created by the water's surface tension

Solvent properties of water

Water is a powerful solvent for polar substances. These include the following:

- Ionic substances like sodium chloride (Na^+ and Cl^-, page 695). All cations (positively charged ions) and anions (negatively charged ions) become surrounded by a shell of orientated water molecules (Figure 2.5).
- Carbon-containing (organic) molecules with ionised groups (such as the carboxyl group $-COO^-$, and amino group $-NH_3^+$). Soluble organic molecules like sugars dissolve in water due to the formation of hydrogen bonds with their slightly charged hydroxyl groups ($-OH$).

Once they have dissolved, molecules (the **solute**) are free to move around in water (the **solvent**), and as a result, are more chemically reactive than when in the undissolved solid.

On the other hand, non-polar substances are repelled by water, as in the case of oil on the surface of water. Non-polar substances are **hydrophobic** (water-hating).

Figure 2.5 Water as universal solvent

Ionic compounds like NaCl dissolve in water,

$$NaCl \rightleftharpoons Na^+ + Cl^-$$

with a group of orientated water molecules around each ion:

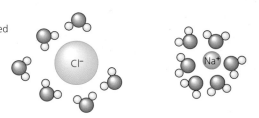

Sugars and alcohols dissolve due to hydrogen bonding between polar groups in their molecules (e.g. —OH) and the polar water molecules:

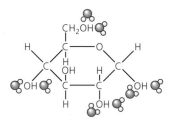

3 In an aqueous solution of glucose, **state** which component is the solvent and which the solute.

■ **Extension:** ## Solvent properties arise because water is not a gas

Water has a relative molecular mass of only 18, yet it is a liquid at room temperature. This is surprising; it contrasts with other small molecules, which are **gases**. For example, methane (CH_4) = 16; ammonia (NH_3) = 17; and carbon dioxide (CO_2) = 44. But **none of these latter molecules contains hydrogen bonds**.

In gases, molecules are widely spaced and free to move about independently. In liquids, molecules are closer together. In the case of water, hydrogen bonds pull the molecules very close to each other, which is why water is a liquid at the temperatures and pressure that exist over much of the Earth's surface. As a result, we have a liquid medium which life exploits (Table 2.3).

Water is transparent

Because light penetrates water, aquatic photosynthetic plants can live at some depth (Figure 2.6). These plants support aquatic food chains, and therefore animal life. Light aids sight in aquatic animals.

Figure 2.6 Seaweed can survive at depth

In warm, shallow seas, the plant life includes attached seaweeds and an abundance of tiny, unicellular, floating phytoplankton. These support animal life, including shoals of fish, and many non-vertebrates such as sessile corals like the large Toadstool Leather Coral seen here, in the Banda Sea, Indonesia.

Property	Benefit to life
1 a liquid at room temperature, water dissolves more substances than any other common liquid	liquid medium for living things and for the chemistry of life
2 much heat energy needed to raise the temperature of water	aquatic environment slow to change temperature bulky organisms have stable temperatures
3 evaporation requires a great deal of heat	evaporation causes marked cooling (much heat is lost by evaporation of a small quantity of water)
4 much heat has to be removed before freezing occurs	cell contents and water in aquatic environments are slow to freeze in cold weather
5 ice is at maximum density at 4 °C	ice forms on the surface of water, insulating the water below and allowing much aquatic life to survive freezing
6 surface water molecules orientate with hydrogen bonds formed inwards	water forms droplets and rolls off surfaces certain animals exploit surface tension to move over water surface
7 water molecules slide past each other easily (low viscosity)	water flows easily through narrow capillaries, and through tiny spaces (e.g. in soils, spaces in cell walls)
8 water molecules adhere to surfaces	water adheres to walls of xylem vessels as it is drawn up the stem to the leaves, from the roots
9 water column does not break or pull apart under tension	water can be lifted by forces applied at the top, and so can be drawn up xylem vessels of tree trunks by forces generated in the leaves
10 water is transparent	aquatic plants can photosynthesise at some depth in water

Table 2.3 Water and life – summary

4 Explain the significance to organisms (plants and animals) of water as a coolant and transport medium, in terms of it properties.

Carbohydrates, lipids and proteins

Carbohydrates, lipids and proteins are examples of compounds of carbon. Carbon is a relatively uncommon element of the Earth's crust, but in cells and organisms it is the second most abundant element by mass, after oxygen.

Compounds containing carbon that are found in living organisms are called organic compounds. The exceptions are the gas carbon dioxide (CO_2), hydrogen carbonates (the product of CO_2 when dissolved in water), and mineral calcium carbonate ($CaCO_3$), which are classified as non-organic carbon.

Carbon has remarkable properties. It is a relatively small atom, and is able to form four strong, stable, covalent bonds. Also, carbon atoms are able to react with each other to form extended chains. These carbon 'skeletons' may be straight chains, branched chains, or rings. Carbon also bonds covalently with other atoms, such as oxygen, hydrogen, nitrogen and sulphur, forming different groups of organic molecules with distinctive properties. So, there are vast numbers of organic compounds – more than the total of known compounds made from other elements, in fact. Biologists think the diversity of organic compounds has made possible the diversity of life.

5 Suggest where non-organic forms of carbon exist in the biosphere.

Fortunately, very many of the organic chemicals of living things fall into one of four discrete groups or 'families' of chemicals with many common properties. These families are the carbohydrates, lipids, proteins, and nucleic acids.

Carbohydrates

Carbohydrates are the largest group of organic compounds found in living things. They include sugars, starch, glycogen and cellulose. Carbohydrates contain only three elements: carbon, hydrogen and oxygen, with hydrogen and oxygen always present in the ratio 2:1 (as they are in water – H_2O), so they can be represented by the general formula $C_x(H_2O)_y$. Table 2.4 is a summary of the three types of carbohydrates commonly found in living things.

Carbohydrates – general formula $C_x(H_2O)_y$

Monosaccharides	Disaccharides	Polysaccharides
■ simple sugars (e.g. glucose and fructose – 6 carbon atoms; ribose – 5 carbon atoms)	■ two simple sugars condensed together (e.g. sucrose, lactose, maltose)	■ very many simple sugars condensed together (e.g. starch, glycogen, cellulose)

Table 2.4 Carbohydrates of cells and organisms

Monosaccharides – the simple sugars

Monosaccharides are carbohydrates with relatively small molecules. They taste sweet and are soluble in water. In biology, **glucose** is an especially important monosaccharide because:

- all green leaves manufacture glucose using light energy;
- our bodies transport glucose in the blood;
- all cells use glucose in respiration – we call it one of the respiratory substrates;
- in cells and organisms, glucose is the building block for very many larger molecules.

The structure of glucose

Glucose has the chemical or **molecular formula** $C_6H_{12}O_6$. This type of formula tells us what the component atoms are, and the numbers of each in the molecule. For example, glucose is a 6-carbon sugar, or **hexose**. But the molecular formula does not tell us the structure of the molecule.

Glucose can be written on paper as a linear molecule but it cannot exist in this form (because each carbon arranges its four bonds into a tetrahedron, so the molecule cannot be 'flat'). Rather, glucose is folded, taking a ring or cyclic form. Figure 2.7 shows the structural formula of glucose.

6 Suggest why simple sugars like glucose are not commonly found as a storage form of carbohydrate in cells or tissues.

The carbon atoms of an organic molecule may be numbered. This allows us to identify which atoms are affected when the molecule reacts and changes shape. For example, as the glucose ring forms, the oxygen on carbon-5 attaches itself to carbon-1. Note that the glucose ring contains five carbon atoms and an oxygen atom (Figure 2.7).

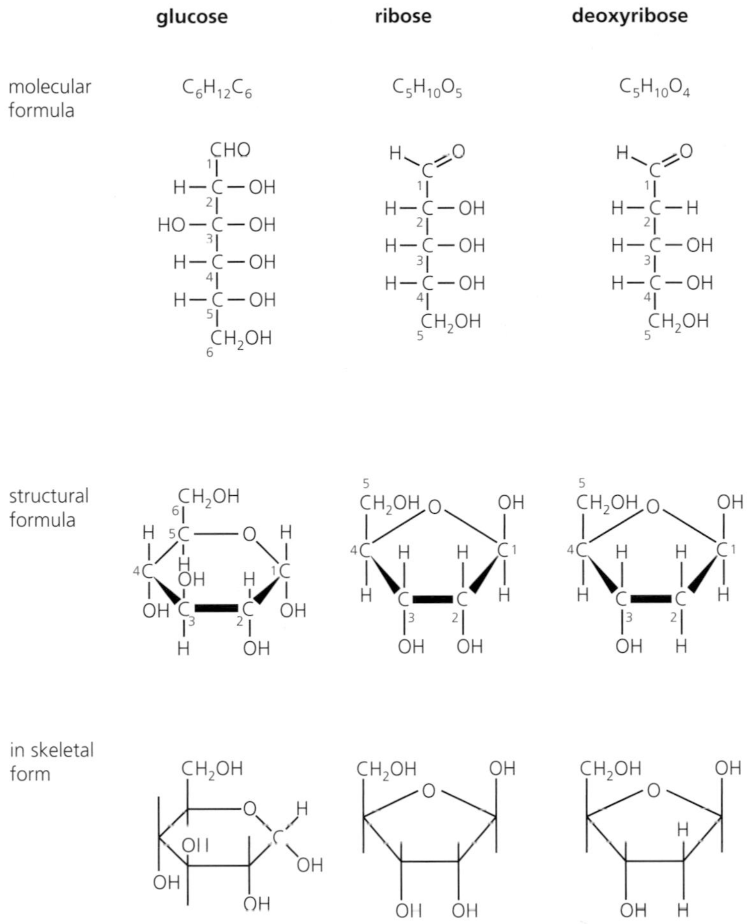

Figure 2.7 Structural formulae of some monosaccharides

	glucose	ribose	deoxyribose
molecular formula	$C_6H_{12}C_6$	$C_5H_{10}O_5$	$C_5H_{10}O_4$

Other monosaccharides of importance in living cells

Glucose, fructose and galactose are examples of hexose sugars commonly occurring in cells and organisms.

Other monosaccharide sugars produced by cells and used in metabolism include:

- 3-carbon sugars (**trioses**), early products in photosynthesis (page 284);
- 5-carbon sugars (**pentoses**), namely ribose and deoxyribose.

The pentoses ribose and deoxyribose are components of the nucleic acids (page 63). The structures of both these pentoses are also shown in Figure 2.7.

Disaccharides

Disaccharides are carbohydrates made of two monosaccharides combined together. For example, sucrose is formed from a molecule of glucose and a molecule of fructose chemically combined together.

Condensation and hydrolysis reactions

When two monosaccharide molecules are combined to form a disaccharide, a molecule of water is also formed as a product, and so this type of reaction is known as a **condensation reaction**. The linkage between monosaccharide residues, after the removal of H—O—H between them, is called a **glycosidic linkage** (Figure 2.8). This comprises strong, covalent bonds. The condensation reaction is brought about by an enzyme.

In the reverse process, disaccharides are 'digested' to their component monosaccharides in a hydrolysis reaction. This reaction involves adding a molecule of water (hydro-) as splitting (-lysis) of the glycosidic linkage occurs. It is catalysed by an enzyme, too, but it is a different enzyme from the one that brings about the condensation reaction.

Figure 2.8 Disaccharides, and the monosaccharides that form them

sucrose   +   water $\underset{\text{condensation}}{\overset{\text{hydrolysis}}{\rightleftharpoons}}$ glucose   +   fructose

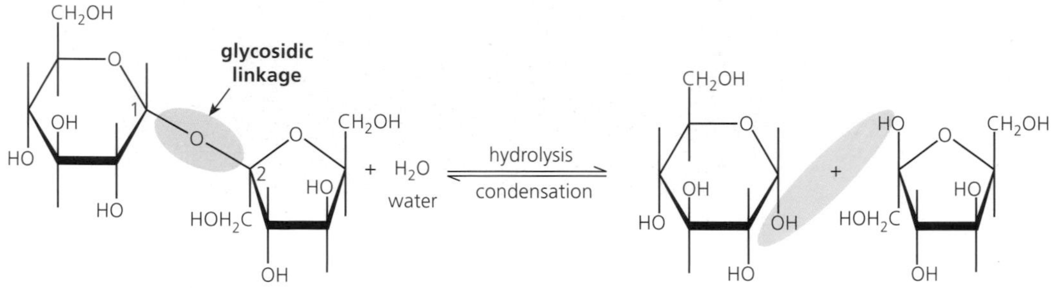

This structural formula shows us how the glycosidic linkage forms/breaks, but the structural formulae of disaccharides should not be memorised.

maltose   +   water $\underset{\text{condensation}}{\overset{\text{hydrolysis}}{\rightleftharpoons}}$ glucose   +   glucose

lactose   +   water $\underset{\text{condensation}}{\overset{\text{hydrolysis}}{\rightleftharpoons}}$ galactose   +   glucose

Apart from sucrose, other disaccharide sugars produced by cells and used in metabolism include:

- **maltose**, formed by condensation reaction of two molecules of glucose;
- **lactose**, formed by condensation reaction of galactose and glucose.

Polysaccharides

Polysaccharides are built from very many monosaccharide residues condensed together, all linked by glycosidic linkages. Poly- means 'many', and in fact thousands of monosaccharide residues make up a polysaccharide. They are examples of molecules known as polymers – that is, huge molecules normally made of only one type of repeated monomer residue.

Examples of polysaccharides produced by cells and used in metabolism include:

- **starch**, which is a polymer of glucose, and is in fact a mixture of two polysaccharides: amylose (an unbranched chain of glucose residues) and amylopectin (which has branches at points along its chain) – each chain in starch takes the form of a helix, and the whole molecule is stabilised by countless hydrogen bonds;
- **glycogen**, which is a polymer of glucose chemically similar to amylopectin, although larger and more highly branched (Figure 2.9);
- **cellulose**, which is a giant polymer also made of repeating glucose units, arranged in straight, unbranched, parallel chains held together in fibres by numerous hydrogen bonds (Figure 1.14, page 16).

Examples of some important carbohydrates are given in Table 2.5.

7 Define the terms 'monomer' and 'polymer', giving examples from the carbohydrates.

Figure 2.9 Glycogen granules in a liver cell

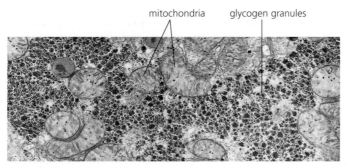

mitochondria   glycogen granules

TEM of a liver cell (×7000)

Animals		Plants	
Monosaccharides		**Monosaccharides**	
glucose	■ transported to cells in the blood plasma ■ used as a respiratory substrate for cellular respiration or converted to glycogen (storage carbohydrate, see below)	glucose	■ a first product of photosynthesis
galactose	■ used in the production of lactose (milk sugar)	fructose	■ produced in cellular respiration as an intermediate of glucose breakdown ■ used in the production of sucrose
Disaccharides		**Disaccharides**	
lactose	■ produced in mammary glands and secreted into the milk as an important component in the diet of very young mammals	sucrose	■ produced in green leaves from glucose and fructose ■ transported in plant in solution, in the vascular bundles
		maltose	■ breakdown product in the hydrolysis of starch
Polysaccharides		**Polysaccharides**	
glycogen	■ storage carbohydrate formed from glucose in the liver and other cells (but not in brain cells) when glucose is not immediately required for cellular respiration (Figure 2.9)	cellulose	■ manufactured in cells and laid down externally, in bundles of fibres, as the main component of the cell walls
		starch	■ storage carbohydrate

Table 2.5 Examples of carbohydrates important in animals and plants

Lipids

Lipids occur in living things as animal **fats** and plant **oils**, and also as the **phospholipids** of cell membranes, for example. Fats and oils seem rather different substances, but their only difference is that at about 20 °C (room temperature) oils are liquid and fats are solid.

Lipids contain the elements carbon, hydrogen and oxygen, as do carbohydrates, but in lipids the proportion of oxygen is much less.

Lipids are insoluble in water. In fact they generally behave as 'water-hating' molecules, a property described as **hydrophobic**. However, lipids can be dissolved in organic solvents such as alcohol (e.g. ethanol) and propanone (acetone).

Fats and oils

Fats and oils are compounds called **triglycerides**. They are formed by reactions in which water is removed (another case of a condensation reaction) between fatty acids and an alcohol called glycerol. Here the bond formed is known as an **ester linkage**. The structure of a fatty acid commonly found in cells, and of glycerol, is shown in Figure 2.10, and the steps of triglyceride formation in Figure 2.11. In cells, enzymes catalyse the formation of triglycerides, and also the breakdown of glycerides by hydrolysis.

Figure 2.10 Fatty acids and glycerol, the building blocks

Fatty acid

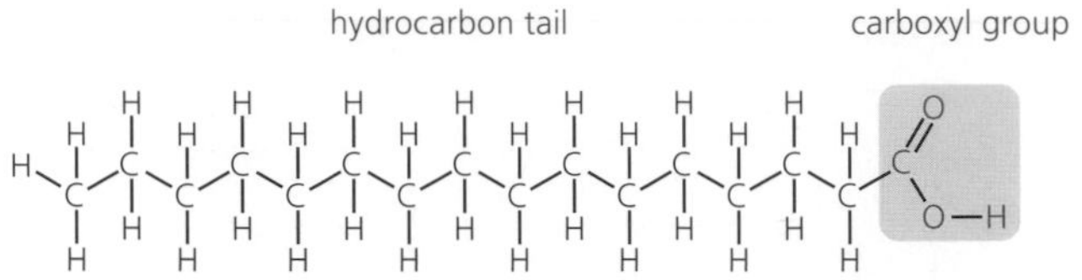

hydrocarbon tail   carboxyl group

this is palmitic acid with 16 carbon atoms

the carboxyl group ionises to form hydrogen ions, i.e. it is a weak acid

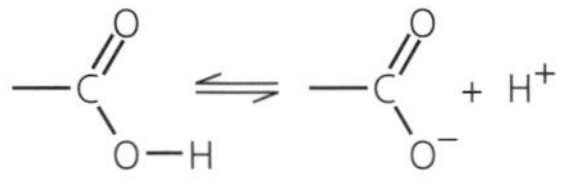

molecular formula of palmitic acid

$CH_3(CH_2)_{14}COOH$

Glycerol

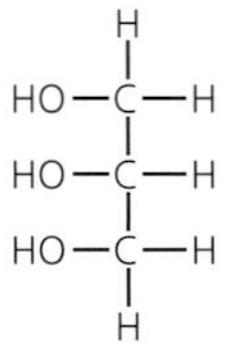

molecular formula of glycerol

$C_3H_5(OH)_3$

The fatty acids combined in fats and oils have long hydrocarbon 'tails', typically of about 16–18 carbon atoms, but may be anything between 14 and 22. The hydrophobic properties of triglycerides are due to these hydrocarbon tails. A molecule of triglyceride is quite large, but relatively small when compared to polymer macromolecules such as starch and cellulose. It is because of their hydrophobic properties that triglyceride molecules clump together (aggregate) into huge globules, making them appear to be macromolecules.

8 Distinguish between condensation and hydrolysis reactions. Give an example of each.

The roles of fats and oils in living things

1 Energy store and metabolic water source
When triglycerides are oxidised in respiration a lot of energy is transferred (and used to make, for example, ATP – page 77). Mass for mass, fats and oils transfer more than twice as much energy as carbohydrates do, when they are respired (Table 2.6). This is because fats are comparatively low in oxygen atoms (the carbon of lipids is more reduced than that of carbohydrates), so more of the oxygen in the respiration of fats comes from the atmosphere. In the oxidation of carbohydrate, more oxygen is present in the carbohydrate molecule itself. Fat and oils, therefore, form a concentrated energy store.

They are insoluble, too, so the presence of fat or oil in cells does not cause osmotic water uptake there. A fat store is especially typical of animals that endure long unfavourable seasons in which they survive on reserves of food stored in the body. Oils are often a major energy store in plants, their seeds and fruits, and it is common for fruits and seeds – including maize, olives and sunflower seeds – to be used commercially as a source of edible oils for humans.

Figure 2.11 Formation of triglyceride

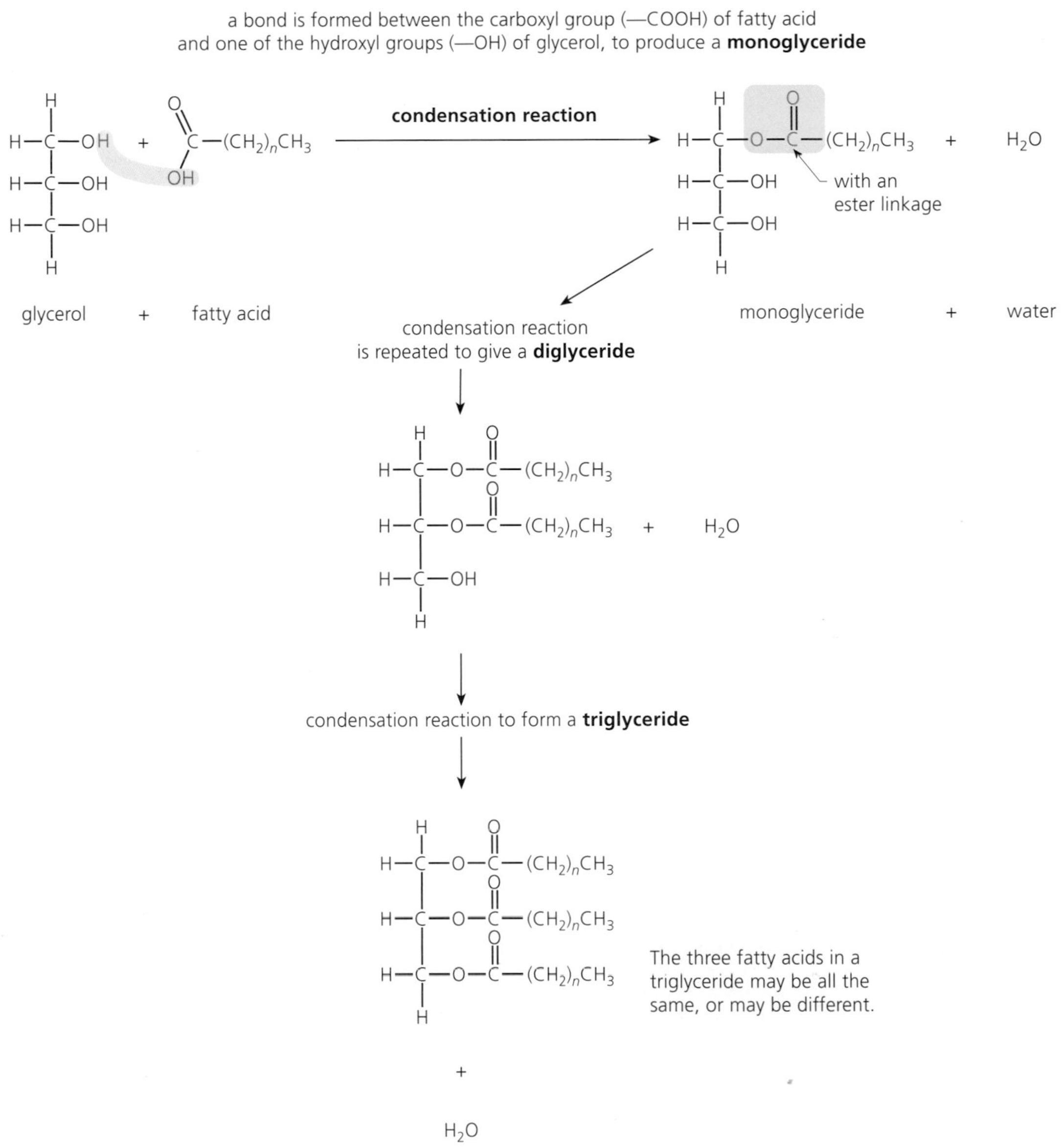
a bond is formed between the carboxyl group (—COOH) of fatty acid
and one of the hydroxyl groups (—OH) of glycerol, to produce a **monoglyceride**
condensation reaction
with an
ester linkage
glycerol + fatty acid
monoglyceride + water
condensation reaction
is repeated to give a diglyceride
condensation reaction to form a triglyceride
The three fatty acids in a
triglyceride may be all the
same, or may be different.

Complete oxidation of fats and oils produces a large amount of water, far more than when the same mass of carbohydrate is respired. Desert animals like the camel and the desert rat retain much of this metabolic water within the body, helping them survive when there is no liquid water for drinking. The development of the embryos of birds and reptiles, while in their shells, also benefits from metabolic water formed by the oxidation of the stored fat in their egg's yolk.

Lipids	Role	Carbohydrates
more energy per gram than from carbohydrates	**energy store**	less energy per gram than from lipids
much metabolic water is produced on oxidation	**metabolic water source**	less metabolic water is produced on oxidation
insoluble, so osmotic water uptake is not caused	**solubility**	sugars are highly soluble in water, causing osmotic water uptake
not quickly 'digested'	**ease of breakdown**	more easily hydrolysed – energy transferred quickly

Table 2.6 Lipids and carbohydrates as energy stores – a comparison

2 Subcutaneous fat as a buoyancy aid (and thermal insulation)

Fat is stored in animals as adipose tissue, typically under the skin, where it is known as subcutaneous fat (Figure 2.12). In aquatic diving mammals, which have a great deal of subcutaneous fat, it is identified as blubber. Blubber undoubtedly gives buoyancy to the body since fat is not as dense as muscle or bone.

If fat reserves like these have a restricted blood supply (as is normally the case), then the heat of the body is not especially distributed to the fat under the skin. In these circumstances the subcutaneous fat also functions as a heat insulation layer.

Figure 2.12 Adipose tissue

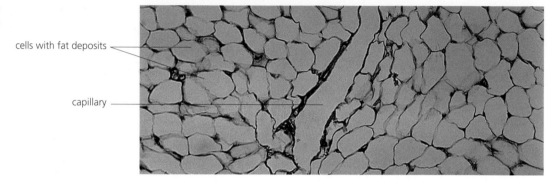

cells with fat deposits

capillary

3 Water-proofing of hair and feathers

Oily secretions of the sebaceous glands, found in the skin of mammals, act as a water repellent, preventing fur and hair from becoming waterlogged when wet. Birds have a preen gland that fulfils the same function for feathers.

4 Electrical insulation

Myelin lipid in the membranes of Schwann cells, forming the sheaths around the long fibres of nerve cells (page 211), electrically isolates the cell plasma membrane and facilitates the conduction of the nerve impulse there.

Phospholipid

A phospholipid has a similar chemical structure to triglyceride; here, one of the fatty acid groups is replaced by phosphate (Figure 2.13). This phosphate is ionised and therefore water soluble. So phospholipids combine the hydrophobic properties of the hydrocarbon tails with hydrophilic properties of the phosphate.

Phospholipid molecules form monolayers and bilayers in water (Figure 1.20, page 22). A phospholipid bilayer is a major component of the plasma membrane of cells.

9 Describe the property given to a lipid when it combines with a phosphate group.

Figure 2.13 Phospholipid

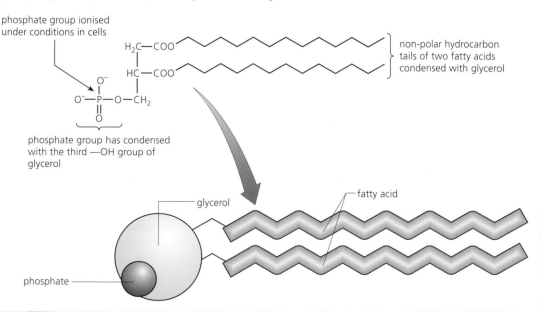

phosphate group ionised under conditions in cells

H_2C-COO }
$HC-COO$ } non-polar hydrocarbon tails of two fatty acids condensed with glycerol

$O^--P-O-CH_2$

phosphate group has condensed with the third —OH group of glycerol

glycerol

fatty acid

phosphate

Amino acids, peptides and proteins

Proteins make up about two-thirds of the total dry mass of a cell. They differ from carbohydrates and lipids in that they contain the element nitrogen, and usually the element sulphur, as well as carbon, hydrogen and oxygen.

Amino acids are the molecules from which peptides and proteins are built – typically several hundred or even thousands of amino acid molecules are combined together to form a protein. The terms 'polypeptide' and 'protein' can be used interchangeably, but when a polypeptide is about 50 amino acid residues long it is generally agreed to have become a protein.

Once the chain is constructed, a protein takes up a specific shape. Shape matters with proteins – their shape is closely related to their function. This is especially the case in proteins that are enzymes, as we shall shortly see.

Amino acids – the building blocks of peptides

Figure 2.14 shows the structure of an amino acid. As their name implies, amino acids carry two groups:

- an **amino group** (—NH$_2$);
- an **organic acid group** (carboxyl group —COOH).

These groups are attached to the same carbon atom in the amino acids which get built up into proteins. Also attached here is a side-chain part of the molecule, called an **R group**.

Proteins of living things are built from just **20 different amino acids**, in differing proportions. All we need to note is that the R groups of these amino acids are all very different and consequently amino acids (and proteins containing them) have different chemical characteristics.

Figure 2.14 The structure of amino acids

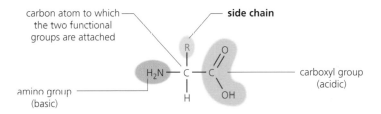

The 20 different amino acids that make up proteins in cells and organisms differ in their side chains. Below are three illustrations but *details of R groups are not required*.

glycine   alanine   leucine

Some amino acids have an additional —COOH group in their side chain (= acidic amino acids).
Some amino acids have an additional —NH$_2$ group in their side chain (= basic amino acids).

Peptide linkages

Two amino acids combine together with the loss of water to form a **dipeptide**. This is one more example of a condensation reaction. The amino group of one amino acid reacts with the carboxyl group of the other, forming a **peptide linkage** (Figure 2.15).

A further condensation reaction between the dipeptide and another amino acid results in a tripeptide. In this way, long strings of **amino acid residues**, joined by peptide linkages, are formed. Thus, peptides or protein chains are assembled, one amino acid at a time, in the presence of a specific enzyme (page 72).

Figure 2.15 Peptide linkage formation

amino acids combine together, the amino group of one with the carboxyl group of the other

amino acid 1   amino acid 2   dipeptide   water

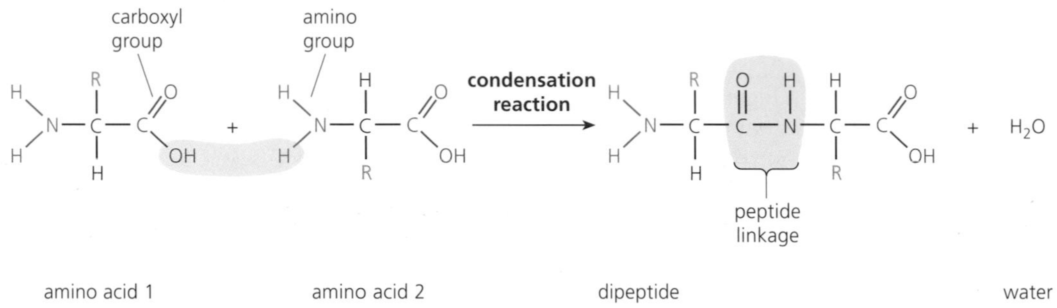

When a further amino acid residue is attached by condensation reaction, a tripeptide is formed. In this way, long strings of amino acid residues are assembled to form polypeptides and proteins.

10 The possible number of different polypeptides, P, that can be assembled is given by $P = A^n$
    where A = the number of different types of amino acids available,
    and n = the number of amino acid residues in the polypeptide molecule.

    Given the naturally occurring pool of 20 different amino acids, **calculate** how many different polypeptides are possible if constructed from 5, 25 and 50 amino acid residues, respectively.

■ Enzymes – biological catalysts   3.6.1–3.6.5

Most chemical reactions do not occur spontaneously. In a laboratory or in an industrial process, chemical reactions may be made to occur by applying high temperatures, high pressures, extremes of pH, and by maintaining high concentrations of the reacting molecules. If these drastic conditions were not applied, very little of the chemical product would be formed. On the other hand, in cells and organisms, many chemical reactions occur simultaneously, at extremely low concentrations, at normal temperatures, and under the very mild, almost neutral, aqueous conditions we find in cells.

How is this brought about?

It is the presence of enzymes in cells and organisms that enables these reactions to occur at incredible speeds, in an orderly manner, yielding products that the organism requires, when they are needed. Sometimes, reactions happen even though the reacting molecules are present in very low concentrations. Enzymes are truly remarkable molecules.

Enzymes are biological catalysts made of protein.

By 'catalyst' we mean a substance that **speeds up the rate of a chemical reaction**. In general, catalysts:

■ are **effective in small amounts**;
■ remain **unchanged at the end of the reaction**.

Another important property of enzymes and catalysts is that they speed up the rate at which an equilibrium position is reached. In a reversible reaction:

$$A + B \rightleftharpoons C + D$$

A and B react to form C and D. This is a reversible reaction as shown by the sign $\rightleftharpoons$. As soon as C and D start to accumulate, some will react to re-form A and B. The reversible reaction reaches an equilibrium point when the rate of the forward reaction equals the rate of the reverse reaction. Most enzyme-catalysed reactions are reversible; the presence of the enzyme for these reactions means the equilibrium position is reached quickly.

The enzyme active site

In a reaction catalysed by an enzyme, the starting substance is called the **substrate**, and what it is converted to is the **product**. An enzyme works by binding to the substrate molecule at a specially formed pocket in the enzyme. This binding point is called the **active site**.

An active site is a region of an enzyme molecule where the substrate molecule binds.

As the enzyme and substrate form a complex, the substrate is raised to a transition state and instantly breaks down to products which are released, together with unchanged enzyme (Figure 2.16). The enzyme is available for use again.

Figure 2.16 The enzyme–substrate complex and active site

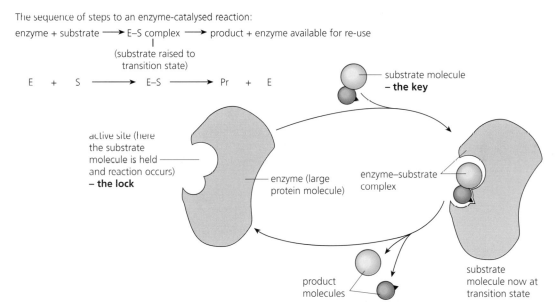

The sequence of steps to an enzyme-catalysed reaction:

enzyme + substrate ⟶ E–S complex ⟶ product + enzyme available for re-use
                                    |
                          (substrate raised to
                            transition state)

E + S ⟶ E–S ⟶ Pr + E

substrate molecule
– **the key**

active site (here the substrate molecule is held and reaction occurs) – **the lock**

enzyme (large protein molecule)

enzyme–substrate complex

product molecules

substrate molecule now at transition state

Enzymes are typically large globular protein molecules. Most substrate molecules are quite small molecules by comparison. Even when the substrate molecules are very large, such as certain macromolecules like the polysaccharides, only one bond in the substrate is in contact with the enzyme active site. The active site takes up a relatively small part of the total volume of the enzyme.

The active site and enzyme specificity

Enzymes are highly specific in their action – they catalyse only one type of reaction or only a very small group of highly similar reactions. This means that enzymes 'recognise' a very small group of substrate molecules or even only a single type of molecule. This is because the active site where the substrate molecule binds has a **precise shape** and **distinctive chemical properties** (meaning the presence of particular chemical groups and bonds). Only particular substrate molecules are attracted to a particular active site and can fit there. All other substrate molecules are unable to fit and so cannot bind.

To emphasise this, the binding of enzyme and substrate is referred to as the **lock and key hypothesis** of enzyme action. The enzyme is the 'lock', the substrate is a 'key' that fits it, and the point of link-up is the active site on the enzyme, as shown in Figure 2.16.

Enzymes control metabolism

There is a huge array of chemical reactions that go on in cells and organisms – collectively the chemical reactions of life are called **metabolism**.

Since the reactions of metabolism can only occur in the presence of a specific enzyme, we know that if an enzyme is not present then the reaction it catalyses cannot occur. Many enzymes are always present in cells and organisms, but some enzymes are produced only under particular conditions or at certain stages. By making some enzymes and not others, cells can control what chemical reactions happen in the cytoplasm. Sometimes it is the presence of the substrate molecule that triggers the synthesis machinery by which the enzyme is produced. Very many of the proteins made by cells are enzymes.

Later in this chapter we shall see how protein synthesis (and therefore enzyme production) is controlled by the cell nucleus.

Where do enzymes operate?

Some enzymes are exported from cells, such as the digestive enzymes (page 180). Enzymes like these, that are parcelled up and secreted and work externally, are called **extracellular enzymes**. However, very many enzymes remain within cells and work there. These are the **intracellular enzymes**. They are found inside organelles, and in the membranes of organelles, in the fluid medium around the organelles, known as the cytosol, and in the plasma membrane.

11 **Explain** why the shape of globular proteins that are enzymes is important in enzyme action.

Factors affecting the rate of enzyme-catalysed reactions

Reactions catalysed by enzymes are typically extremely fast. However, the rate of an enzyme-catalysed reaction is sensitive to environmental conditions. Many factors within cells affect enzymes and therefore alter the rate of the reaction being catalysed. In extreme cases, proteins become **denatured**.

Denaturation of protein

Many of the properties of proteins depend on the three-dimensional shape of the molecule. This is true of enzymes, which are large, globular proteins where a small part of the surface is an active site. Here the precise chemical structure and physical configuration is critical. Provided the active site is unchanged, substrate molecules can attach and reactions can be catalysed.

> **Denaturation is a structural change in a protein that alters its three-dimensional shape and causes the loss of its biological properties.**

Denaturation occurs when the bonds within the globular protein, formed between different amino acid residues, break. Possibly different bonds are formed. Temperature rises and changes in pH of the medium may cause denaturation of the protein of enzymes.

How may denaturation be brought about?

Exposure to heat causes atoms to vibrate violently and this disrupts bonds within globular proteins. Protein molecules change chemical characteristics. We see this most dramatically when a hen's egg is cooked. The translucent egg 'white' is a globular protein called albumen, which becomes irreversibly opaque and insoluble. Heat has triggered irreversible denaturation of this globular protein.

Small changes in pH of the medium similarly alter the shape of globular proteins. The structure of an enzyme may spontaneously re-form when the optimum pH is restored, but exposure to strong acids or alkalis is usually found to irreversibly denature enzymes.

It was investigation of the effect of change in factors such as temperature, pH and concentration of substrate that particularly helped our understanding of how enzymes work.

Temperature

Examine the investigation of the effects of temperature on the hydrolysis of starch by the enzyme amylase, shown in Figure 2.17. When starch is hydrolysed by the enzyme amylase, the product is maltose, a disaccharide (page 46). Starch gives a blue–black colour when mixed with iodine solution (iodine in potassium iodide solution), but maltose gives a red colour. The first step in this experiment is to bring samples of the enzyme and the substrate (the starch solution) to the temperature of the water bath before being mixed – a step called pre-incubation.

Figure 2.17 The effects of temperature on hydrolysis of starch by amylase

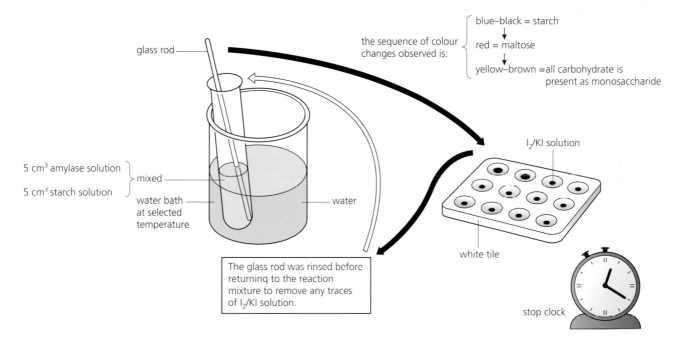

The experiment is **repeated at a range of temperatures,** such as at 10, 20, 30, 40, 50 and 60 °C.

A **control tube** of 5 cm³ of starch solution + 5 cm³ of distilled water (in place of the enzyme) should be included and tested for the presence/absence of starch, at each temperature used.

The progress of the hydrolysis reaction is then followed by taking samples of a drop of the mixture on the end of the glass rod, at half-minute intervals. These are tested with iodine solution on a white tile. Initially, a strong blue–black colour is seen confirming the presence of starch. Later, as maltose accumulates, a red colour predominates. The endpoint of the reaction is when all the starch colour has disappeared from the test spot. Using fresh reaction mixture each time, the investigation is repeated at a series of different temperatures, say at 10, 20, 30, 40, 50 and 60 °C. The times taken for complete hydrolysis at each temperature are recorded and the rate of hydrolysis in unit time is plotted on a graph (Figure 2.18).

A characteristic curve is the result – although the optimum temperature varies from reaction to reaction and with different enzymes.

How is the graph interpreted?

As temperature is increased, molecules have increased active energy, and reactions between them go faster. The molecules are moving more rapidly and are more likely to collide and react. In chemical reactions, for every 10 °C rise in temperature the rate of the reaction approximately doubles. This property is known as the **temperature coefficient** (Q_{10}) of a chemical reaction.

Figure 2.18
Temperature and the rate
of an enzyme-catalysed
reaction

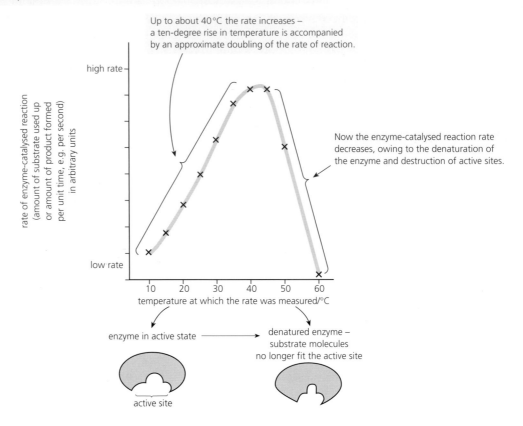

Other variables – such as the concentrations of the enzyme and substrate solutions –
were kept constant.

However, in enzyme-catalysed reactions the effect of temperature is more complex, for
proteins are denatured by heat. The rate of denaturation increases at higher temperatures, too.
So as the temperature rises the amount of active enzyme progressively decreases, and the rate is
slowed. As a result of these two effects of heat on enzyme-catalysed reactions, there is an
apparent optimum temperature for an enzyme.

Not all enzymes have the same optimum temperature. For example, the bacteria in hot
thermal springs have enzymes with optima between 80 °C and 100 °C or higher, whereas
seaweeds of northern seas and the plants of the tundra have optima closer to 0 °C. Humans have
enzymes with optima at or about normal body temperature. This feature of enzymes is often
exploited in the commercial and industrial uses of enzymes (page 61).

12 In studies of the effect of temperature on enzyme-catalysed reactions, **suggest** why the enzyme and
substrate solutions are pre-incubated to a particular temperature before they are mixed.

pH

Change in pH can have a dramatic effect on the rate of an enzyme-catalysed reaction. Each
enzyme has a range of pH in which it functions efficiently. This is often at or close to neutrality
point (pH 7.0). This effect of pH is because the structure of a protein (and therefore the shape of
the active site) is maintained by various bonds within the three-dimensional structure of the
protein. A change in pH from the optimum values alters the bonding patterns, progressively
changing the shape of the molecule. The active site may quickly be rendered inactive. However,
unlike temperature changes, the effects of pH on the active site are normally reversible –
provided, that is, the change in surrounding acidity or alkalinity is not too extreme. As the pH
reverts to the optimum for the enzyme, the active site may reappear.

Figure 2.19 pH effect on enzyme shape and activity

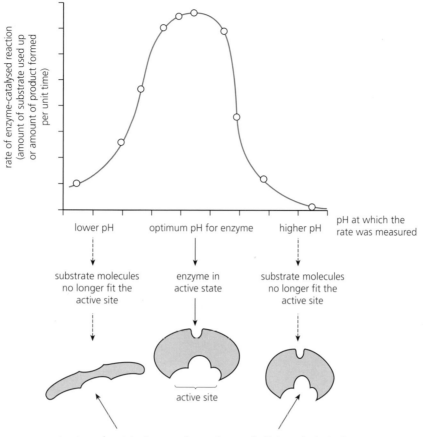

structure of protein changes when a change of pH alters the ionic charge on
—COO⁻ (acidic) and —NH₃⁺ (basic) groups in the peptide chain, so the shape of the active site is lost

the optimum pH of different human enzymes

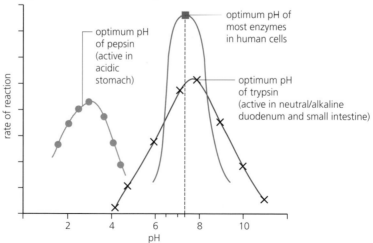

13 **Explain** what a buffer solution is and why such solutions are often used in enzyme experiments.

Some of the digestive enzymes of the gut have different optimum pH values from the majority of other enzymes. For example, those adapted to operate in the stomach, where there is a high concentration of acid during digestion, have an optimum pH which is close to pH 2.0 (Figure 2.19).

Substrate concentration

The effect of different concentrations of substrate on the rate of an enzyme-catalysed reaction can be shown using an enzyme called catalase. This enzyme catalyses the breakdown of hydrogen peroxide:

$$2H_2O_2 \xrightarrow{\text{catalase}} 2H_2O + O_2$$

Catalase occurs very widely in living things; it functions as a protective mechanism for the delicate biochemical machinery of cells. This is because hydrogen peroxide is a common by-product of reactions of metabolism, but it is also a very toxic substance (a very powerful oxidising agent, page 270). Catalase inactivates hydrogen peroxide as it forms, before damage can occur.

You can demonstrate the presence of catalase in fresh liver tissue by dropping a small piece into dilute hydrogen peroxide solution (Figure 2.20). Compare the result obtained with that from a similar piece of liver that has been boiled in water (we have seen that high temperature denatures enzymes). If you do not wish to use animal tissues, then you can use potato or soaked and crushed dried peas, instead.

Figure 2.20 Liver tissue in dilute hydrogen peroxide solution, a demonstration

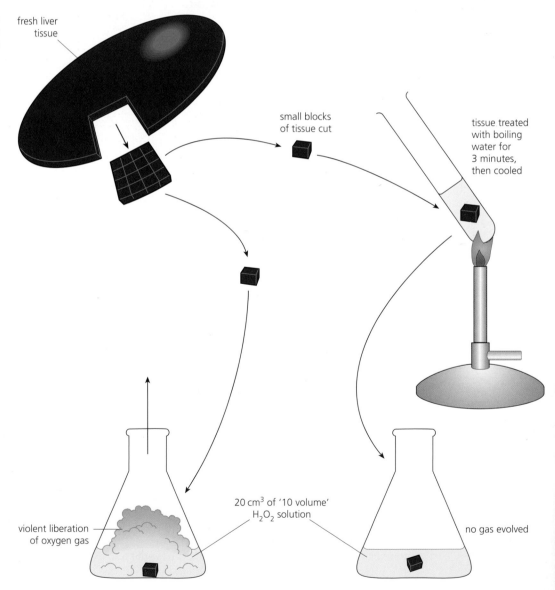

fresh liver tissue

small blocks of tissue cut

tissue treated with boiling water for 3 minutes, then cooled

violent liberation of oxygen gas

20 cm³ of '10 volume' H_2O_2 solution

no gas evolved

When measuring the rate of enzyme-catalysed reactions, we measure the amount of substrate that has disappeared from a reaction mixture, or the amount of product that has accumulated, in a unit of time. For example, in Figure 2.17 it is the rate at which the substrate starch disappears from a reaction mixture that is measured.

Working with catalase, it is convenient to measure the rate at which the product (oxygen) accumulates – the volume of oxygen that has accumulated at 30-second intervals is recorded (Figure 2.21).

Over a period of time, the initial rate of reaction is not maintained, but falls off quite sharply. This is typical of enzyme actions studied outside their location in the cell. The fall-off can be due to a number of reasons, but most commonly it is because the concentration of the substrate in the reaction mixture has fallen. Consequently, it is the initial rate of reaction that is measured. This is the slope of the tangent to the curve in the initial stage of reaction.

14 Calculate the initial rate of reaction shown in the graph in Figure 2.21.

Figure 2.21 Measuring the rate of reaction using catalase

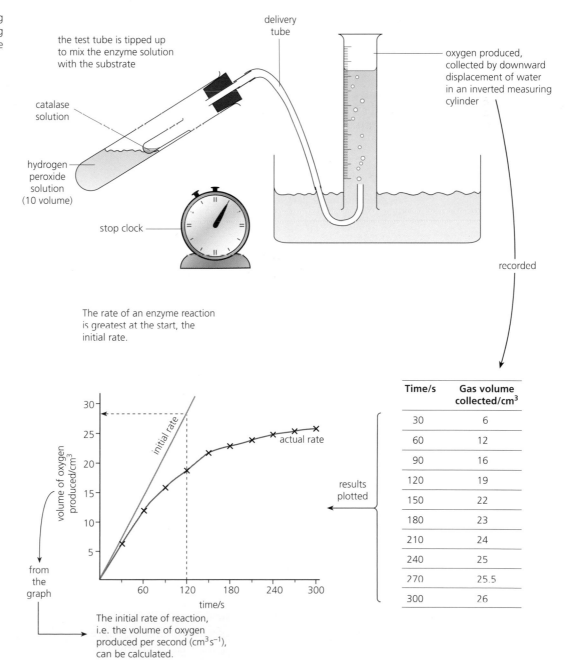

Time/s	Gas volume collected/cm^3
30	6
60	12
90	16
120	19
150	22
180	23
210	24
240	25
270	25.5
300	26

To investigate the effects of substrate concentration on the rate of an enzyme-catalysed reaction, the experiment shown in Figure 2.21 is repeated at different concentrations of substrate, and the initial rate of reaction plotted in each case. Other variables such as temperature and enzyme concentration are kept constant.

When the initial rates of reaction are plotted against the substrate concentration, the curve shows two phases. At lower concentrations, the rate increases in direct proportion to the substrate concentration – but at higher substrate concentrations, the rate of reaction becomes constant, and shows no increase.

Now we can see that the enzyme catalase works by forming a short-lived enzyme–substrate complex. At low concentration of substrate, all molecules can find an active site without delay. Effectively, there is an excess of enzyme present. Here the rate of reaction is set by how much substrate is present – as more substrate is made available the rate of reaction increases.

However, at higher substrate concentrations, there comes a point when there is more substrate than enzyme. Now, in effect, substrate molecules have to 'queue up' for access to an active site. Adding more substrate merely increases the number of molecules awaiting contact with an enzyme molecule, so there is now no increase in the rate of reaction (Figure 2.22).

Figure 2.22 The effect of substrate concentration

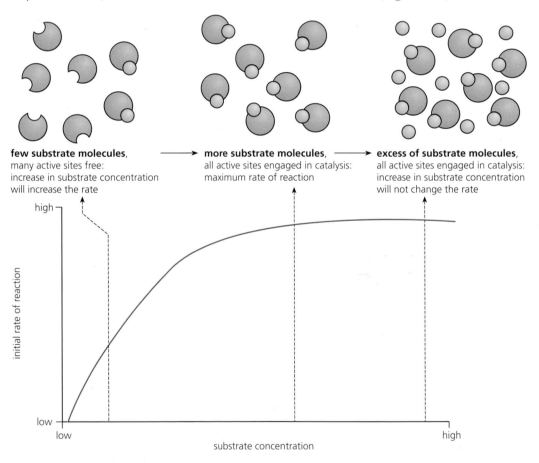

15 When there is an excess of substrate present in an enzyme-catalysed reaction, **explain** the effects on the rate of reaction of increasing the concentration of:

   a the substrate
   b the enzyme.

Enzymes and a link with homeostasis

The requirements of enzymes for specific conditions – for example, of temperature and pH – have led to the need to control the internal environment of the body, a phenomenon known as **homeostasis** (page 217).

Industrial uses of enzymes

There is a tradition of using enzymes as biological catalysts in some long-established industries, all over the world. Here are some examples.

- In **leather tanning**, hides have been softened and hair removed using proteases naturally present in the faeces of carnivorous animals.
- In **brewing**, enzymes in barley grains at germination are used to convert the starch stored in the grain to sugars. These sugars are converted to ethanol by the fermentation enzymes of yeast.
- In **cheese manufacture**, the proteins in milk are coagulated (made insoluble), using the enzyme rennet (rennin, page 181), originally from young mammals.

Today, there are many new uses for enzymes as industrial catalysts, a part of the current development of **biotechnology**. Biotechnology is the industrial and commercial applications of biology, particularly of microorganisms, enzymology and genetic engineering (page 117). The use of enzymes in industrial processes is known as enzyme technology.

Advantages of enzymes as industrial catalysts

Enzymes are produced by living cells but often they may be separated from cells and continue to function outside the cell. They can be used in test tubes or industrial reactor vessels (known as *in vitro* conditions). Enzymes have advantages over inorganic catalysts in industrial processes because they are:

16 Define what we mean by *'in vitro'* and *'in vivo'*.

- **specific**, typically catalysing one particular compound or one type of bond only;
- **efficient**, requiring only a tiny quantity to catalyse the production of a huge quantity of product;
- able to **work at normal temperatures and pressures**, and so require much less input of energy than a chemical catalyst normally requires.

Sources of industrial enzymes

Useful enzymes are obtained from plant and animal sources; for example, enzymes for use in medicine in the treatment of thromboses are extracted from pineapple juice. However, the majority of enzymes for enzyme technology are from microorganisms, mainly from bacteria and fungi. Features of microorganisms making them valuable as a source of enzymes include the following.

- Microorganisms may be cultured economically and at high growth rates, in bulk fermenters, often using relatively low-grade nutrients.
- Some microorganisms occur naturally under extreme environmental conditions, and consequently may contain enzymes adapted to function efficiently under extremes of temperature and pH – for example, enzymes from hot springs' bacteria are used in biological washing powders.

Lactose-free milk – an example of industrial use of enzymes

People unable to produce lactase in their pancreatic juice or on the surface of the villi of the small intestine (page 183) fail to digest milk sugar. Lactose passes on to their large intestine without being hydrolysed to its constituent monosaccharides (page 44). As a result, bacteria in the large intestine feed on the lactose, producing fatty acids and methane, causing diarrhoea and flatulence. Such people are said to be lactose intolerant.

The enzyme lactase is produced in the gut of all human babies while they are dependent on milk. However, it is only found in adults from Northern Europe (and their descendents, wherever they now live) and from a few African tribes. On the other hand, people from the Orient, Arabia and India, most African people and those from the Mediterranean typically produce little or no lactase as adults.

Such people may be prescribed **lactose-free milk**; this product can be supplied by the application of enzyme technology, using lactase obtained from bacteria.

How can bacterial lactase be used safely in this context?

Initially, enzymes were used in industrial processes as **whole-cell preparations**. This meant applying a culture of particular microorganisms, usually some species of bacteria. This is not efficient, and may be highly inappropriate for a food product such as liquid milk. **Cell-free preparations of enzymes** have tended to replace the use of whole cells, especially where the enzymes are secreted by the microorganism into the culture medium, and so are relatively easily isolated for use. However, isolated enzymes, once applied, cannot be used over and over again, and removal of the enzyme may be expensive.

The favoured, alternative arrangement is the use of **immobilised enzymes**. Figure 2.23 illustrates the ways in which enzymes may be effectively immobilised. The advantages of using an immobilised enzyme in industrial productions are:

- it permits re-use of the enzyme preparation;
- the product is obtained enzyme free;
- the enzyme may be much more stable and long lasting, due to protection by the inert matrix.

Today, lactose-free milk is produced by passing milk through a column containing immobilised lactase. The enzyme is obtained from bacteria, purified, and enclosed in capsules (Figure 2.24).

Figure 2.23 Methods of immobilising enzymes

1 **entrapment** of enzyme molecules between fibres: the enzyme is not chemically attached

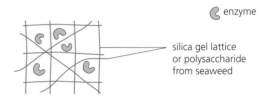

silica gel lattice or polysaccharide from seaweed

2 **covalent bonding** of enzyme to matrix, which prevents enzyme molecules from being leached away

matrix of a polymer such as cellulose or collagen

3 **entrapment** of enzyme molecules in permeable microcapsules; the enzyme is held securely

capsule wall

4 **direct crosslinking** of enzyme molecules by covalent bonding with bridging molecules

glutaraldehyde molecules forming the crosslinks

5 **adsorption** of enzyme on to a surface, where it is bonded with bridging molecules

ion-exchange resin or clay

Figure 2.24 Production of lactose-free milk

17 **Define** the term 'catalyst'. **List** two differences between inorganic catalysts and enzymes.

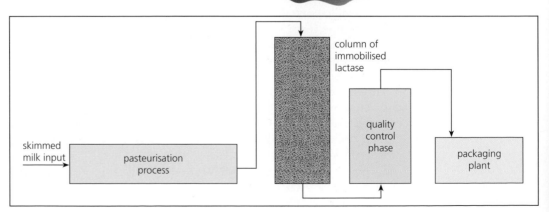

skimmed milk input — pasteurisation process — column of immobilised lactase — quality control phase — packaging plant

Nucleic acids

Nucleic acids are the **information molecules** of cells found throughout the living world. This is because the code containing the information in nucleic acids, known as the **genetic code**, is a universal one. That means that it makes sense in all organisms. It is not specific to a few organisms or to just one group, such as bacteria.

There are two types of nucleic acid found in living cells: **deoxyribonucleic acid (DNA)**, and **ribonucleic acid (RNA)**. DNA is the genetic material and occurs in the chromosomes of the nucleus. But while some RNA also occurs in the nucleus, most is found in the cytoplasm – particularly in the ribosomes. Both DNA and RNA have roles in the day-to-day control of cells and organisms, as we shall shortly see. First, we will look into the structure of nucleotides and the way they are built up to form the unique **DNA double helix**.

Nucleotides

A nucleotide consists of three substances combined together. These are:

- a **nitrogenous base** – the four bases of DNA are cytosine (C), guanine (G), adenine (A), and thymine (T);
- a **pentose sugar** – deoxyribose occurs in DNA and ribose in RNA;
- **phosphoric acid**.

These components are combined by condensation reaction to form a nucleotide with the formation of two molecules of water. Since any one of the four bases can be selected, four different types of nucleotide are formed to make DNA. How these components are combined together is shown in Figure 2.25, together with the diagrammatic way the components are represented to illustrate their spatial arrangement. Simple shapes are used rather than complex structural formulae, and these shapes are all that are required here.

Figure 2.25 The components of nucleotides

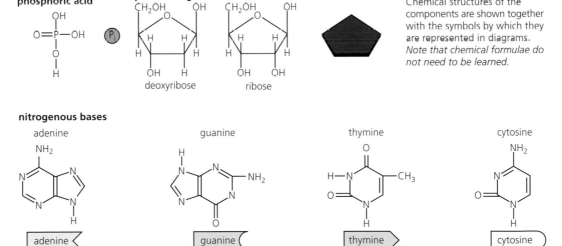

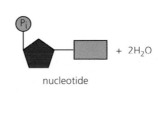

Nucleotides become nucleic acid

Nucleotides themselves then condense together, one nucleotide at a time, to form huge molecules called nucleic acids or **polynucleotides** (Figure 2.26). So, nucleic acids are very long, thread-like macromolecules with alternating sugar and phosphate molecules forming the 'backbone'. This part of the nucleic acid molecule is uniform and unvarying. However, also attached to each of the sugar molecules along the strand is one of the bases, and these project sideways. Since the bases vary, they represent a unique sequence that carries the coded information held by the nucleic acid.

Figure 2.26 How nucleotides make up nucleic acid

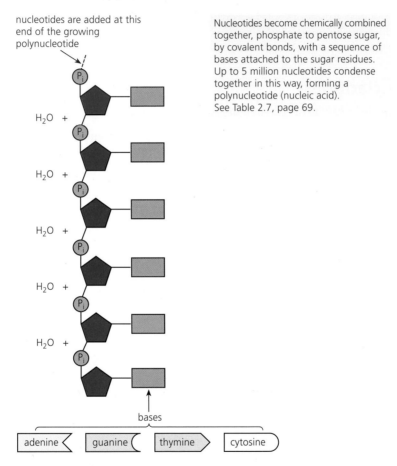

nucleotides are added at this end of the growing polynucleotide

Nucleotides become chemically combined together, phosphate to pentose sugar, by covalent bonds, with a sequence of bases attached to the sugar residues. Up to 5 million nucleotides condense together in this way, forming a polynucleotide (nucleic acid). See Table 2.7, page 69.

bases

adenine   guanine   thymine   cytosine

18 Distinguish between a nitrogenous base and a base found in inorganic chemistry.

The DNA double helix

The DNA molecule consists of two polynucleotide strands, paired together, and held by hydrogen bonds. The two strands take the shape of a double helix (Figure 2.27). The pairing of bases is between **adenine (A)** and **thymine (T)**, and between **cytosine (C)** and **guanine (G)**, simply because these are the only combinations that fit together along the helix. This pairing, known as **complementary base pairing**, also makes possible the very precise way that DNA is copied in a process called **replication**. The existence of the DNA double helix was discovered, and the way DNA holds information was suggested, by Francis Crick and James Watson in 1953 – they received a Nobel Prize for this work (Figure 2.28).

Figure 2.27 The DNA double helix

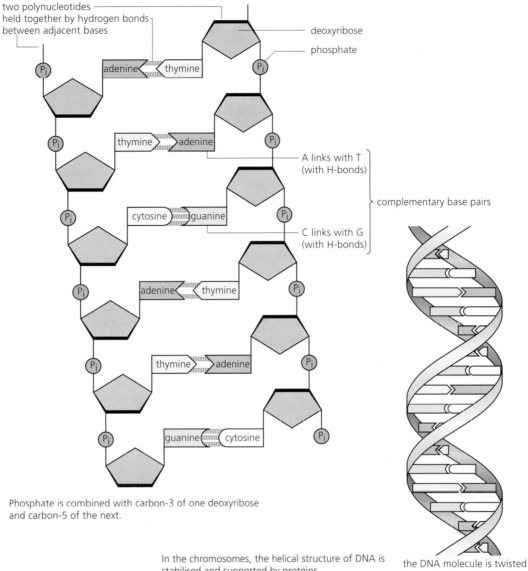

two polynucleotides held together by hydrogen bonds between adjacent bases

deoxyribose

phosphate

A links with T (with H-bonds)

C links with G (with H-bonds)

} complementary base pairs

Phosphate is combined with carbon-3 of one deoxyribose and carbon-5 of the next.

In the chromosomes, the helical structure of DNA is stabilised and supported by proteins.

the DNA molecule is twisted into a double helix

TOK Link

Crick and Watson had a distinctive method of working, including re-interpreting already published data and developing studies they had access to. Research this for your study of the **methods of science**. Try these resources.

1 Crick and Watson's original, short 'letter' to *Nature*, published 25 April 1953, if your school or college can make a copy available for you. For a one-off fee, the paper can be obtained from: www.nature.com/nature/archive

2 Their own accounts in:
James D. Watson (1965), *The Double Helix*, Weidenfeld & Nicolson
Francis Crick (1988), *What Mad Pursuits*, Penguin

3 Find out about the contribution of Rosalind Franklin:
Brenda Maddox (2003), *The Dark Lady of DNA*, Harper Collins

Francis Crick (1916–2004) and **James Watson** (1928–) laid the foundations of a new branch of biology – **cell biology** – and achieved this while still young men. Within two years of their meeting in the Cavendish Laboratory, Cambridge (1951), Crick and Watson had achieved their understanding of the nature of the gene in chemical terms.

Crick and Watson brought together the experimental results of many other workers, and from this evidence they deduced the likely structure of the DNA molecule.

- **Edwin Chergaff** measured the exact amount of the four organic bases in samples of DNA, and found the ratio of A:T and of C:G was always close to 1.

Chergaff's results suggest consistent base pairing in DNA from different organisms.

Organism	Ratio of bases in DNA samples	
	Adenine : Thymine	Guanine : Cytosine
Cow	1.04	1.00
Human	1.00	1.00
Salmon	1.02	1.02
Escherichia coli	1.09	0.99

- **Rosalind Franklin** and **Maurice Wilkins** produced X-ray diffraction patterns by bombarding crystalline DNA with X-rays.

Watson and Crick with their demonstration model of DNA

Rosalind Franklin produced the key X-ray diffraction pattern of DNA at Kings College, London

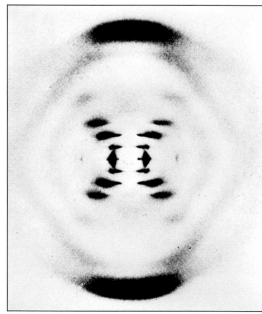

X-ray diffraction pattern of DNA

Watson and Crick concluded that DNA is a double helix consisting of:

- two polynucleotide strands with nitrogenous bases stacked on the inside of the helix (like rungs on a twisted ladder)
- parallel strands are held together by hydrogen bonds between the paired bases (A–T, C–G)
- ten base pairs occur per turn of the helix
- the two strands of the double helix are antiparallel.

Figure 2.28 The discovery of the role of DNA

They built a model. See Figure 2.27 (page 65) for a simplified model of the DNA double helix.

Replication – how DNA copies itself

In order that a copy of each chromosome can pass into the daughter cells at cell division, the DNA of the chromosomes must first be copied (replicated). As the DNA carries the genetic message, replication must be extremely accurate. Remember, it is a process that takes place in the interphase nucleus, well before the events of nuclear division (page 31).

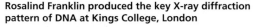

In replication, the DNA double helix must unwind, and the hydrogen bonds holding the strands together be broken. This allows the two strands of the helix to separate. An enzyme, **helicase**, is involved in these steps and holds the strands apart while replication occurs.

Both strands of DNA act as templates in replication. New nucleotides with the appropriate complementary bases line up opposite the bases of the exposed strands. Adenine pairs with thymine, cytosine with guanine. Because of this process of base pairing, the sequence of bases in one strand exactly determines the sequence of bases in the other strand. The two strands are said to be complementary. The bases of the two strands fit together only if the sugar molecules they are attached to point in opposite directions. The strands are said to be antiparallel.

Hydrogen bonds then form between the complementary bases, holding them in place. Finally, the sugar and phosphate groups of adjacent nucleotides of the new strand condense together. This reaction is catalysed by an enzyme called **DNA polymerase**. DNA replication is summarised in Figure 2.29.

Figure 2.29 DNA replication

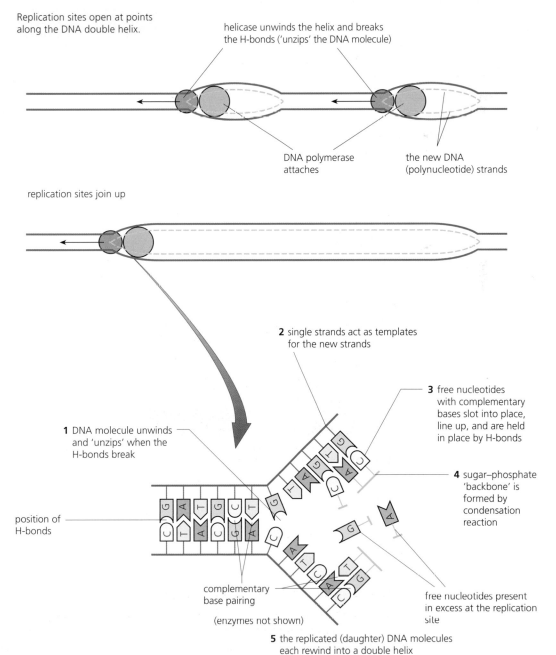

Replication sites open at points along the DNA double helix.

helicase unwinds the helix and breaks the H-bonds ('unzips' the DNA molecule)

DNA polymerase attaches

the new DNA (polynucleotide) strands

replication sites join up

2 single strands act as templates for the new strands

3 free nucleotides with complementary bases slot into place, line up, and are held in place by H-bonds

1 DNA molecule unwinds and 'unzips' when the H-bonds break

4 sugar–phosphate 'backbone' is formed by condensation reaction

position of H-bonds

complementary base pairing

(enzymes not shown)

free nucleotides present in excess at the replication site

5 the replicated (daughter) DNA molecules each rewind into a double helix

Each new pair of double strands winds up into a double helix. One strand of each new double helix came from the original chromosome and one is a newly synthesised strand. This arrangement is known as **semi-conservative replication** because half the original molecule is kept the same (Figure 2.30).

DNA polymerase also has a role in 'proof-reading' the new strands. Any mistakes that start to happen (such as the wrong bases attempting to pair up) are corrected. Each new DNA double helix is an exact copy of the original.

Figure 2.30 Semi-conservative versus conservative replication

Crick and Watson suggested replication of DNA would be 'semi-conservative', and this has since been shown experimentally, using DNA of bacteria 'labelled' with a 'heavy' nitrogen isotope.

In **semi-conservative replication** one strand of each new double helix comes from the parent chromosome and one is a newly synthesised strand (i.e. half the original molecule is conserved)

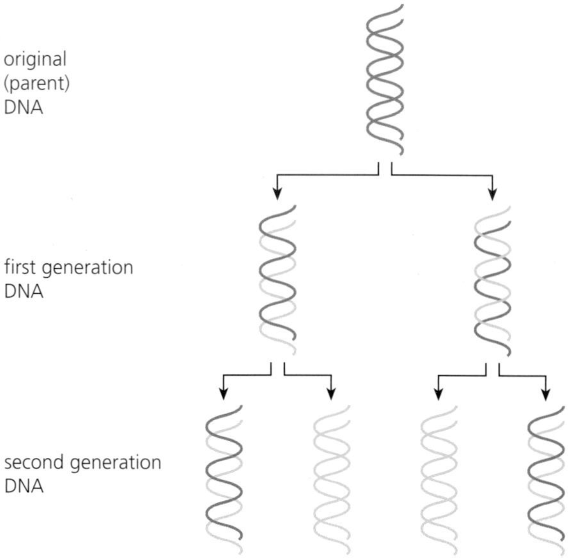

original (parent) DNA

first generation DNA

second generation DNA

If an entirely new double helix were formed alongside the original, then one DNA double helix molecule would be conserved without unzipping, in the next generation (i.e. **conservative replication**).

parent DNA

first generation DNA

second generation DNA

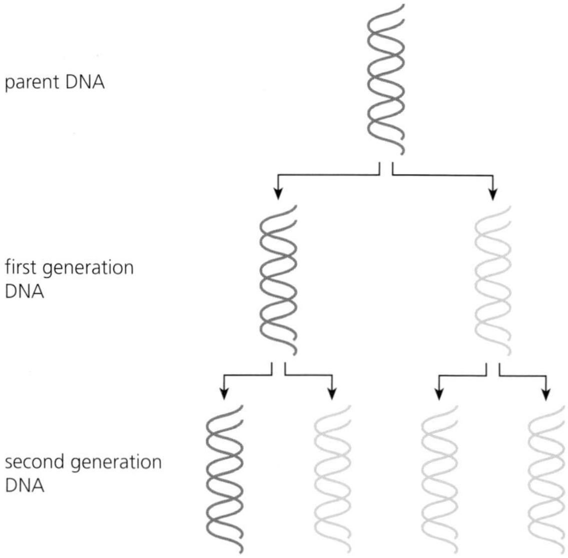

Protein synthesis

Proteins are linear series of amino acids condensed together – most proteins contain several hundred amino acid residues. There are only 20 different amino acids used in protein synthesis; all cell proteins are built from these. The unique properties of a protein lie in:

- **which amino acids** are involved in its construction;
- **the sequence** in which these amino acids are condensed together.

The sequence of bases in DNA dictates the order in which specific amino acids are assembled and combined together. The huge length of the DNA molecule in a single chromosome codes for a very large number of proteins. Within this extremely long molecule, the relatively short length of DNA that codes for a single protein is called a **gene**. Proteins are very variable in size and, therefore, so are genes. A very few genes are as short as 75–100 nucleotides. Most are at least 1000 nucleotides long, and some are more.

Proteins are formed at ribosomes in the cytoplasm, so a copy of the gene's information is first required, and transported to the site of protein synthesis. That copy is made of RNA, and is called messenger RNA. So both DNA and RNA are involved in protein synthesis.

Introducing RNA

RNA molecules are relatively short in length when compared with DNA. In fact, RNAs tend to be from a hundred to thousands of nucleotides long, depending on the particular role they have. The RNA molecule is a single strand of polynucleotide in which the sugar is ribose. The bases found in RNA are cytosine, guanine, adenine, and **uracil** (which replaces thymine of DNA). There are three functional types of RNA, known as **messenger RNA (mRNA)**, **transfer RNA (tRNA)**, and **ribosomal RNA** (Table 2.7). While mRNA is formed in the nucleus and passes out to ribosomes in the cytoplasm, tRNA and ribosomal RNA occur only in the cytoplasm.

DNA	Feature	RNA
very long strands, several million nucleotides	**length**	relatively short strands, 100 to several thousand nucleotides
contains deoxyribose	**sugar**	contains ribose
contains bases C, G, A and T (not U)	**bases**	contains C, G, A and U (not T)
consists of two polynucleotide strands of complementary base pairs (C with G and A with T) held by H-bonds in the form of a double helix	**forms**	consists of single strands, and in three functional forms: messenger RNA (mRNA) transfer RNA (tRNA) ribosomal RNA

Table 2.7 The differences between DNA and RNA

Transcription – the first step in protein synthesis

Stage 1 of protein synthesis occurs in the nucleus where a complementary copy of the code is made by the building of a molecule of mRNA. This process is called **transcription** (Figure 2.31), and the enzyme is **RNA polymerase**. The DNA double helix unwinds and the hydrogen bonds are broken at the site of the gene being transcribed. At this site there is a pool of free nucleotides. Then, one strand of the DNA, the coding strand, is used as the template for transcription by complementary base pairing. Of course, in RNA synthesis it is uracil which pairs with adenine. Once the mRNA strand is formed, it leaves the nucleus through pores in the nuclear membrane and passes to ribosomes in the cytoplasm, where the information can be 'read' and used in the synthesis of a protein.

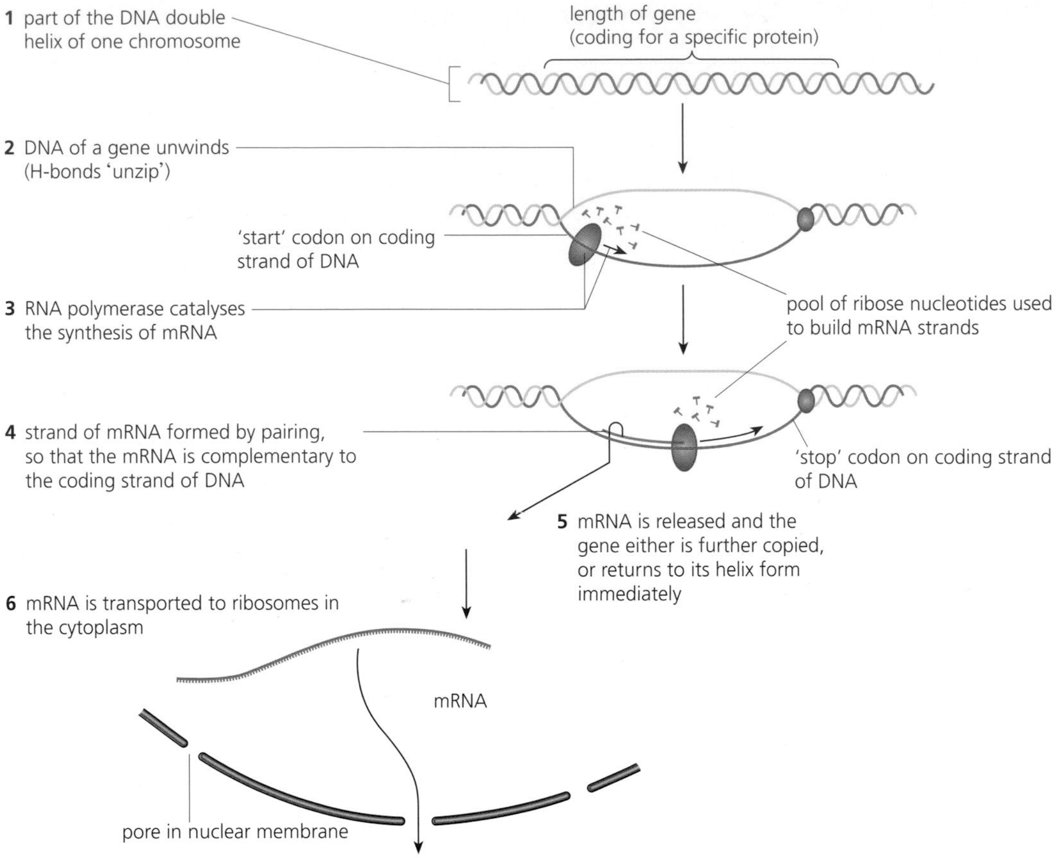

Figure 2.31
Transcription

1 part of the DNA double helix of one chromosome

length of gene (coding for a specific protein)

2 DNA of a gene unwinds (H-bonds 'unzip')

'start' codon on coding strand of DNA

3 RNA polymerase catalyses the synthesis of mRNA

pool of ribose nucleotides used to build mRNA strands

4 strand of mRNA formed by pairing, so that the mRNA is complementary to the coding strand of DNA

'stop' codon on coding strand of DNA

5 mRNA is released and the gene either is further copied, or returns to its helix form immediately

6 mRNA is transported to ribosomes in the cytoplasm

mRNA

pore in nuclear membrane

The genetic code

The sequence of bases in nucleic acid dictates the order in which specific amino acids are to be assembled and combined to make proteins. The code is a three-letter or **triplet code**, meaning that each sequence of three bases stands for one of the 20 amino acids, and is called a **codon**.

In fact, with the four-letter alphabet of DNA (C, G, A, T) there are 64 possible different triplet combinations ($4 \times 4 \times 4$). In other words, the genetic code has many more codons than there are amino acids – since only 20 amino acids require coding. This type of code is described as **degenerate** since most amino acids have two or three similar codons that code for them. A degenerate code has more than one base triplet (codon) to code for one amino acid.

Of course, some of the codons represent the 'punctuations' of the code, meaning there are 'start' and 'stop' triplets. Thus the enzyme machinery involved in protein synthesis is instructed where to begin and to end a particular protein sequence.

Amino acid activation – the second step in protein synthesis

In Stage 2 of protein synthesis, the amino acids of the pool available for incorporation into protein are activated by combining with short lengths of a different sort of RNA, tRNA. This activation occurs in the cytoplasm. The special significance of tRNA is that translates a three-base sequence into an amino acid sequence.

How does this occur?

All the tRNAs have a cloverleaf shape, but there is a different tRNA for each of the 20 amino acids involved in protein synthesis. At one end of each tRNA molecule is a site where one particular amino acid of the 20 involved can be joined. At the other end, there is a sequence of three bases called an **anticodon**. This anticodon is complementary to the codon of mRNA that codes for the specific amino acid (Figure 2.32).

Figure 2.32 Amino acid activation

Each amino acid is linked to a specific transfer RNA (tRNA) before it can be used in protein synthesis. This is the process of amino acid activation. It takes place in the cytoplasm.

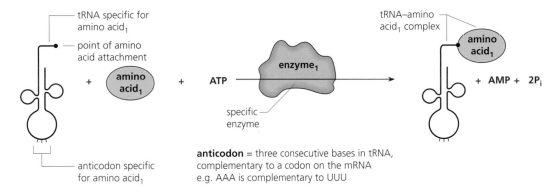

anticodon = three consecutive bases in tRNA, complementary to a codon on the mRNA e.g. AAA is complementary to UUU

The amino acid becomes attached to its tRNA by an enzyme in a reaction that also requires ATP. These enzymes are specific to the particular amino acids (and types of tRNA) to be used in protein synthesis. The specificity of the enzymes is a way of ensuring the correct amino acids are used in the right sequence.

Translation – the last step in protein synthesis

In Stage 3, the final stage, a protein chain is assembled, one amino acid residue at a time, in tiny organelles called ribosomes. These move along the messenger RNA 'reading' the codons from the 'start' codon. In the ribosome, for each mRNA codon, the complementary anticodon of the tRNA–amino acid complex slots into place and is temporarily held in position by hydrogen bonds. While held there, the amino acids of neighbour tRNA–amino acid complexes are joined by a peptide linkage. This frees the first tRNA which moves back into the cytoplasm for re-use. Once this is done, the ribosome moves on to the next mRNA codon. The process continues until a ribosome meets a 'stop' codon (Figure 2.33).

19 Outline the different forms of RNA involved in transcription and translation, and state the roles of each.

One gene – one enzyme?

So far we have assumed that each gene works by coding for the synthesis of one particular protein, such as an enzyme.

Do we know this is the case? If so, how?

The answer is that evidence came from two American scientists, G. W. Beadle and E. L. Tatum, who worked together in America in 1940. Their work is summarised below, and in Figure 2.34.

TOK Link

While the details of Beadle and Tatum's experiments are not required, comparison of their **experimental approach** with that of Watson and Crick may support your discussion of the methods of science.

Beadle and Tatum worked with a fungus called *Neurospora* that was a pest organism in bakeries, causing bread to turn mouldy. This simple organism was easily cultured on laboratory agar plates containing a **minimal medium** of sugar, mineral ions, the vitamin biotin, and a source of nitrogen such as nitrate or ammonium ions. The fungus naturally manufactures all other organic compounds required, including all the amino acids, from this medium – hence the term 'minimal'.

They exposed some of their cultures of *Neurospora* to X-rays that caused the formation of mutants. A **mutant** organism has altered genetic material. Interestingly, some of the mutant forms produced by chance were unable to grow on the minimal medium, but could still grow normally on media enriched with amino acids used in protein synthesis.

Further investigations with these mutants showed that most needed only one particular amino acid added to minimal medium in order to be able to grow and reproduce. These mutants had lost the ability to synthesise one particular enzyme.

In a whole series of experiments, many different mutants were produced and cultured – each unable to synthesise a different enzyme. They also conducted breeding experiments between mutants and unaltered *Neurospora* cultures, and found that the new characteristics of mutant *Neurospora* were inherited just as other, naturally occurring characteristics were (Figure 2.34).

Figure 2.33 Translation

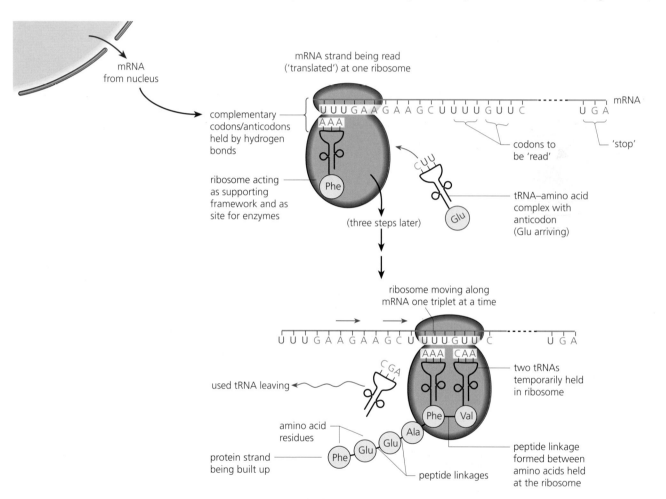

Several ribosomes may move along the mRNA at one time. This structure (mRNA, ribosomes plus growing protein chains) is called a **polysome**.

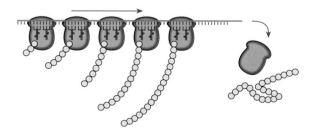

Figure 2.34 The 'one gene – one enzyme' experiments with *Neurospora* – a summary

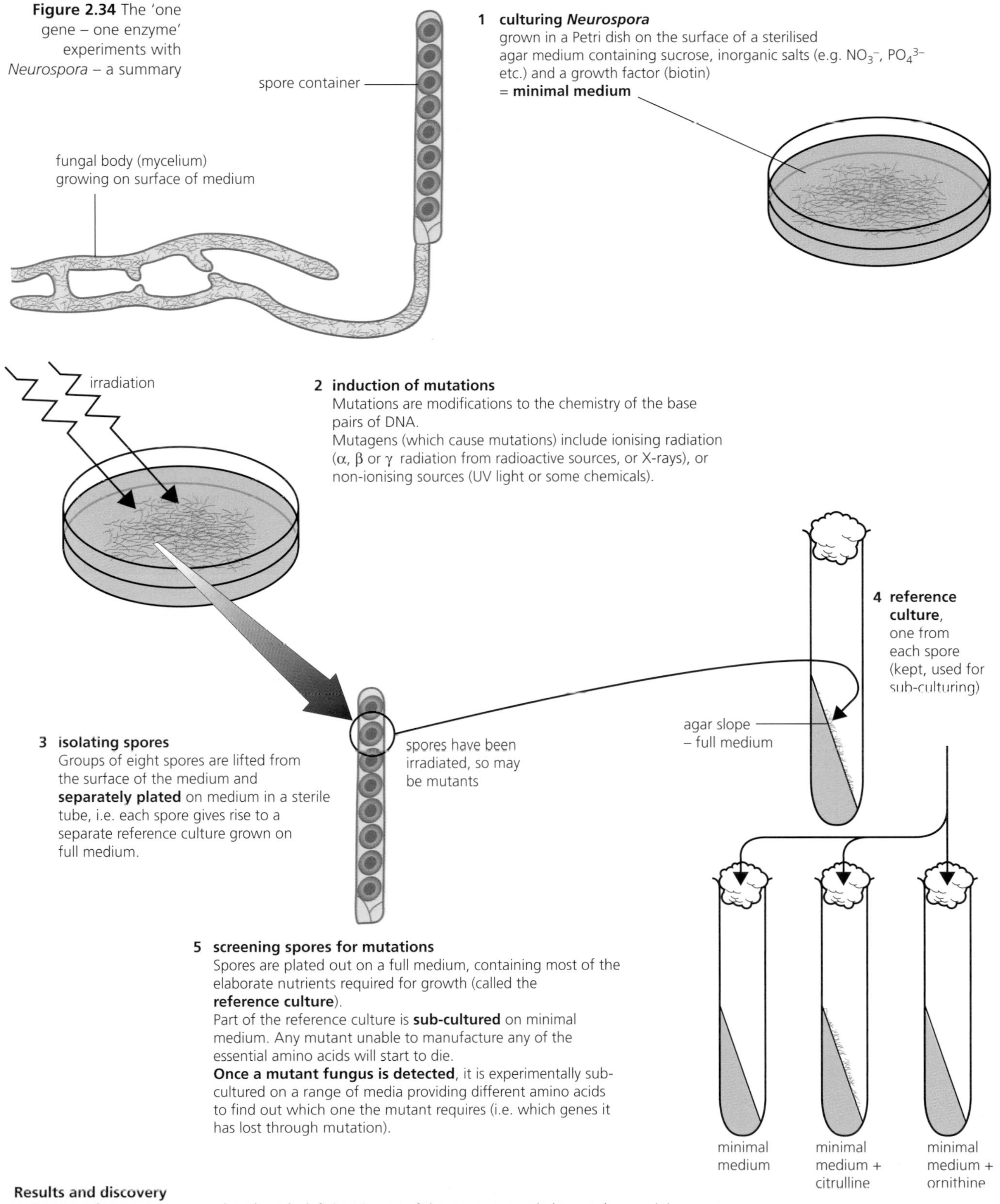

spore container

fungal body (mycelium) growing on surface of medium

1 culturing *Neurospora*
grown in a Petri dish on the surface of a sterilised agar medium containing sucrose, inorganic salts (e.g. NO_3^-, PO_4^{3-} etc.) and a growth factor (biotin)
= **minimal medium**

irradiation

2 induction of mutations
Mutations are modifications to the chemistry of the base pairs of DNA.
Mutagens (which cause mutations) include ionising radiation (α, β or γ radiation from radioactive sources, or X-rays), or non-ionising sources (UV light or some chemicals).

4 reference culture, one from each spore (kept, used for sub-culturing)

agar slope – full medium

3 isolating spores
Groups of eight spores are lifted from the surface of the medium and **separately plated** on medium in a sterile tube, i.e. each spore gives rise to a separate reference culture grown on full medium.

spores have been irradiated, so may be mutants

5 screening spores for mutations
Spores are plated out on a full medium, containing most of the elaborate nutrients required for growth (called the **reference culture**).
Part of the reference culture is **sub-cultured** on minimal medium. Any mutant unable to manufacture any of the essential amino acids will start to die.
Once a mutant fungus is detected, it is experimentally sub-cultured on a range of media providing different amino acids to find out which one the mutant requires (i.e. which genes it has lost through mutation).

minimal medium

minimal medium + citrulline

minimal medium + ornithine

Results and discovery
- A range of mutants were produced, each deficient in one of the enzymes needed to produce arginine.
- Arginine production in *Neurospora* starts with glutamic acid, and involves two intermediates and three enzymes:

glutamic acid $\xrightarrow{\text{enzyme 1}}$ ornithine $\xrightarrow{\text{enzyme 2}}$ citrulline $\xrightarrow{\text{enzyme 3}}$ arginine

- In different mutants, enzymes 1, or 2, or 3 were no longer produced, e.g. one mutant lacked enzyme 2, and could not produce citrulline (only if citrulline was added to the minimal medium would growth occur).

Beadle and Tatum concluded that in an organism **each gene coded for a particular enzyme**. This was known as the **one gene – one enzyme hypothesis**.

This work was carried out in the middle of the last century, well before Crick and Watson's work on the chemical nature of the gene. Beadle and Tatum's contribution earned them a Nobel Prize. Interestingly, the same conclusions about the role of a gene had been proposed by a doctor studying inherited human diseases of metabolism several years earlier, but his work was ignored, and so was unknown to the American scientists at the time of their study.

Subsequently, as protein chemistry became better understood, several proteins were found to consist of two (or more) polypeptide chains. Also, of course, not all proteins are enzymes, so the hypothesis was modified to **one gene – one polypeptide**.

Another development has been the appreciation that in different parts of an organism (or at different times), selected genes are switched on or switched off. The existence of **regulator genes** which activate or suppress the action of neighbouring genes has been demonstrated in, for example, prokaryotes (page 244).

Human haemoglobin consists of two sorts of polypeptide chain, α (**alpha**) **chains** and β (**beta**) **chains**. In the fetus, the β chains are replaced by γ (**gamma**) **chains**, the effect of which gives fetal haemoglobin a higher affinity for oxygen (page 667). Control of haemoglobin production may involve:

- a gene that codes for α chains – always switched on;
- a gene that codes for γ chains – switched on in the fetal stage only;
- a gene that codes for β chains – switched off at the fetal stage but switched on at birth;
- other genes that switch on and off the β gene and the γ gene.

20 Not all proteins formed in cells are enzymes. **State** the other important roles proteins may have.

Consequently, the picture has emerged of genes with a range of roles, sometimes activated, but possibly inactivated at other times. The combined effect of gene action, however, is the realisation of the characteristics of an organism by the interactions of gene products, not all of which are enzymes.

■ *Examination questions – a selection*

Questions 1–4 are taken from past IB Diploma biology papers.

Q1 Which property of water is most important to plants living below the surface of water?
 A cohesion
 B oxygen solubility
 C surface tension
 D transparency
 Higher Level Paper 1, May 06, Q8

Q2 **a** Define the term *active site* of an enzyme. (1)
 b Outline how enzymes catalyse biochemical reactions. (2)
 c Explain the effect of pH on enzyme activity. (3)
 d State three functions of lipids. (2)
 Higher Level Paper 1, May 03, Q3

Q3 Where do transcription and translation occur in eukaryotic cells?

	Transcription	Translation
A	cytoplasm	cytoplasm
B	cytoplasm	mitochondria
C	nucleus	cytoplasm
D	nucleus	nucleus

 Standard Level Paper 2, May 05, Q8

Q4 Which of the following elements is most common in living organisms?
 A sodium
 B oxygen
 C iron
 D nitrogen
 Standard Level Paper 1, May 04, Q6

Questions 5–8 cover other syllabus issues in this chapter.

Q5 Carbohydrates, lipids and proteins make up the bulk of the organic compounds found in organisms.
 a Identify a monosaccharide commonly found in both animal and plant cells. (1)
 b State the polysaccharide with a role as energy store found in skeletal muscle, and what monomer it is constructed from. (2)
 c Draw a generalised structural formula for:
  i an amino acid
  ii a fatty acid. (4)
 d Define the type of chemical reaction involved in the formation of a peptide linkage between two amino acids, and state the other product, in addition to a dipeptide. (2)
 e List three advantageous features of lipids as energy stores for terrestrial animals. (3)

Q6 **a** State at which period in a cell cycle the replication process takes place. (1)
 b For the process of DNA replication, draw a diagrammatic representation of the structure of a 'replication fork' in which two important enzymes essential to replication are shown *in situ*. Annotate your diagram to make clear the roles of these enzymes. (6)
 c Explain the part played by complementary base pairing in replication. (2)
 d Explain why the replication process is described as semi-conservative. (2)

Q7 **a** Outline the key features of biological macromolecules. (1)
 b Glycogen and protein are both polymers. Explain why there is only one type of glycogen but many different types of protein. (2)

Q8 **a** Nucleic acids are the information molecules of cells, and structurally consist of nucleotides combined together. State what three substances combine together to form a nucleotide. (3)
 b List the structural differences between RNA and DNA. (2)
 c Describe the types of RNA that occur in cells, what roles each type has, and where each type is commonly found in growing cells. (3)
 d Outline the difference in roles of DNA polymerase and RNA polymerase. (2)

Energy transfer in cells

- **Organisms require energy** to maintain cells and carry out their activities and functions.
- **Cellular respiration** occurs in every living cell, making energy available.
- Green plants manufacture glucose by **photosynthesis**, using energy from sunlight.
- **Chloroplasts** contain chlorophyll and are the site of photosynthesis.

Living things require **energy** to build and repair body structures, and to maintain all the activities of life, such as movement, reproduction, nutrition, excretion and sensitivity. The need for energy for protein synthesis, and for the active transport of molecules and ions across membranes by membrane pumps, has already been discussed (Chapter 1).

Energy is transferred in cells by the breakdown of nutrients, principally of carbohydrates like glucose. The process by which energy is made available from nutrients in cells is called **cellular respiration**; this process is investigated first in this chapter.

Organisms require a supply of nutrients to sustain respiration, but they obtain their nutrients in very different ways. Green plants synthesise sugars from simpler substances by **photosynthesis**. Photosynthesis is discussed later in this chapter. On the other hand, animals and other heterotrophic organisms take nutrients into the body tissues following the digestion of food (Chapter 7, page 178).

■ Cellular respiration – the controlled release of energy

3.7.1–3.7.4

We can measure the total amount of energy that can be released from the nutrient glucose by means of a simple **calorimeter** (Figure 3.1). Here, a known amount of glucose is placed in the crucible in a closed environment, and burnt in oxygen. The energy, released as heat, is transferred to the surrounding jacket of water, and the rise in temperature of the water is measured. Then the energy value of the glucose sample may be calculated, based on the fact that it takes 4.2 joules (J) of heat energy to raise 1 g of water by 1 °C. One well known outcome of this technique is the energy value labelling of manufactured foods that we can read on the packaging – and the publicity that 'low-calorie' items may receive in slimming diets.

Figure 3.1 A calorimeter for measuring energy value

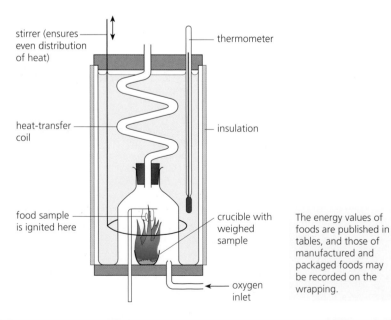

Samples are completely oxidised in air.

stirrer (ensures even distribution of heat)

thermometer

heat-transfer coil

insulation

food sample is ignited here

crucible with weighed sample

The energy values of foods are published in tables, and those of manufactured and packaged foods may be recorded on the wrapping.

oxygen inlet

People sometimes talk about 'burning up food' in respiration. In fact, likening respiration to combustion is unhelpful. In combustion, energy in fuel is released in a one-step reaction, as heat (Figure 3.2). Such a violent change would be disastrous for body tissues. In cellular respiration, a large number of small steps occur, each catalysed by a specific enzyme. Because energy in respiration is transferred in small quantities, much of the energy is made available to the cells, and may be trapped in the energy currency molecule **adenosine triphosphate (ATP)**. However, some energy is still lost as heat in each step – we notice how warm we become with strenuous physical activity!

Cellular respiration is the controlled release of energy, in the form of ATP, from organic compounds in cells.

Figure 3.2 Combustion and respiration compared

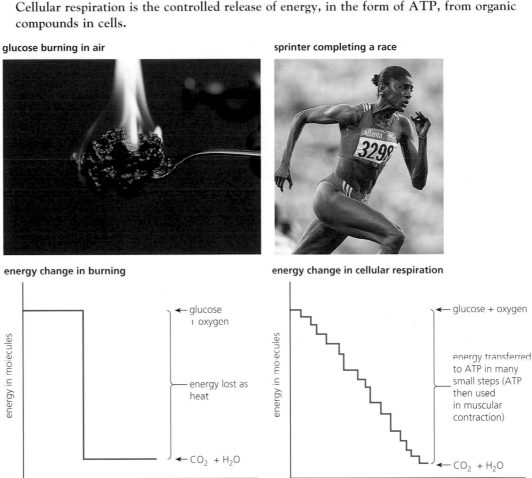

glucose burning in air

sprinter completing a race

energy change in burning

← glucose + oxygen

energy lost as heat

← CO_2 + H_2O

time

energy change in cellular respiration

← glucose + oxygen

energy transferred to ATP in many small steps (ATP then used in muscular contraction)

← CO_2 + H_2O

time

ATP – the universal energy currency

Energy made available within the cytoplasm is transferred to a molecule called adenosine triphosphate (ATP). ATP is referred to as **energy currency** because, like money, it can be used in different contexts, and it is constantly recycled.

ATP is a **nucleotide** (page 63) with an unusual feature. It carries three phosphate groups linked together in a linear sequence (Figure 3.3). ATP may lose both of the outer phosphate groups, but usually only one at a time is lost. ATP is a relatively small, soluble organic molecule. It occurs in cells at a concentration of $0.5–2.5$ mg cm^{-3}.

Like many organic molecules of its size, ATP contains a good deal of chemical energy locked up in its structure. What makes ATP special as a reservoir of stored chemical energy, is its role as a common intermediate between energy-yielding reactions and energy-requiring reactions and processes. Energy-yielding reactions include many of the individual steps in respiration. Energy-requiring reactions include the synthesis of cellulose from glucose, the synthesis of proteins from amino acids, and the contraction of muscle fibres.

Figure 3.3 ATP, ADP and AMP

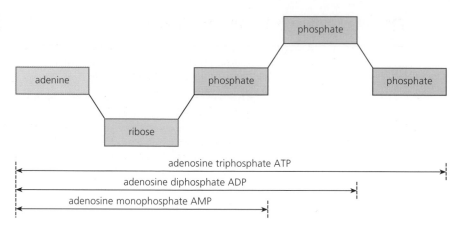

In summary, ATP is a molecule universal to all living things; it is the source of energy for chemical change in cells, tissues and organisms. The important features of ATP are that it is:

- a substance that moves easily within cells and organisms – by facilitated diffusion;
- able to take part in many steps of cellular respiration and in very many reactions of metabolism;
- able to deliver energy in relatively small amounts, sufficient to drive individual reactions.

The ATP–ADP cycle and metabolism

In cells, ATP is formed from **adenosine diphosphate (ADP)** and **phosphate ion (P_i)** using energy from respiration (Figure 3.4). Then, in the presence of enzymes, ATP participates in energy-requiring reactions. The free energy available in ATP is approximately 30–34 kJ mol^{-1}. Some of this energy is lost as heat in a reaction, but much free energy is made available to do useful work, more than sufficient to drive a typical energy-requiring reaction of metabolism (Figure 3.4).

Sometimes ATP reacts with water (a hydrolysis reaction) and is converted to ADP and P_i. For example, direct hydrolysis of the terminal phosphate groups happens in muscle contraction.

Mostly, ATP reacts with other metabolites and forms phosphorylated intermediates, making them more reactive in the process. The phosphate groups are released later, so both ADP and P_i become available for re-use as metabolism continues.

1 Outline why ATP is an efficient energy currency molecule.

Figure 3.4 The ATP–ADP + P_i cycle

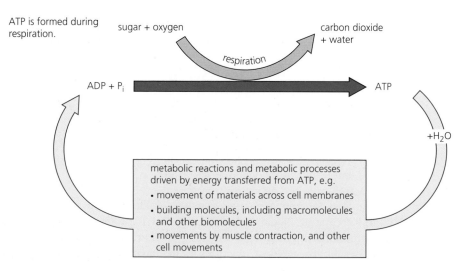

The steps of cellular respiration

In the first steps of cellular respiration, the glucose molecule (a 6-carbon sugar) is split into two 3-carbon molecules. Then the products are converted to an organic acid called pyruvic acid (also a 3-carbon compound). Under conditions in the cytoplasm, organic acids are weakly ionised, and therefore pyruvic acid exists as the **pyruvate** ion.

Obviously, two molecules of pyruvate are formed from each molecule of glucose. In addition, there is a small amount of ATP formed, using a little of the energy that had been locked up in the glucose molecule. No molecular oxygen is required for these first steps of cellular respiration.

Because glucose has been split into smaller molecules, these steps are known as **glycolysis** (glyco + lysis). The enzymes that catalyse these reactions are found in the cell cytoplasm generally, but not inside an organelle. Throughout cellular respiration, a series of oxidation–reduction reactions occur. (What oxidation and reduction consist of is explained on page 270.)

In summary:

$$\text{glucose} \xrightarrow{\text{enzymes in the cytoplasm}} \text{pyruvate + small amount of ATP}$$

Aerobic and anaerobic cellular respiration

While no oxygen is required for the formation of pyruvate by cells in the early steps of cellular respiration, most animals and plants and very many microorganisms do require oxygen for cell respiration, in total. We say that they respire aerobically.

In **aerobic cellular respiration**, sugar is completely oxidised to carbon dioxide and water and much energy is made available. The steps of aerobic respiration can be summarised by a single equation:

$$\text{glucose} + \text{oxygen} \longrightarrow \text{carbon dioxide} + \text{water} + \text{ENERGY}$$
$$C_6H_{12}O_6 + 6O_2 \longrightarrow 6CO_2 + 6H_2O + \text{ENERGY}$$

This equation is a balance sheet of the inputs (raw materials) and the outputs (products). It tells us nothing about the separate steps, each catalysed by a specific enzyme, by which cellular respiration occurs. It does not mention pyruvate, for example.

What happens to pyruvate in aerobic respiration?

If oxygen is available to cells and tissues, the pyruvate is completely oxidised to carbon dioxide, water and a large quantity of ATPs. Before these reactions take place, the pyruvate first passes into mitochondria by facilitated diffusion. This is because it is only in mitochondria that the required enzymes are found (Figure 3.5).

In summary:

$$\text{pyruvate} \xrightarrow{\text{enzymes in the mitochondria}} \text{carbon dioxide} + \text{water} + \text{large amount of ATP}$$

In this phase of cellular respiration, the pyruvate is oxidised by:

- removal of hydrogen atoms by hydrogen acceptors (oxidising agents);
- addition of oxygen to the carbon atoms to form carbon dioxide.

These reactions occur one at a time, each catalysed by a different enzyme.

Also, it is in the mitochondria that the reduced hydrogen acceptor molecules (these carry H) react with oxygen to form water. The reduced hydrogen acceptor is re-oxidised (loses its H), and is available for re-use in the production of more pyruvate. The majority of ATP molecules (the key product of respiration for the cell) are generated in this step, also.

The sites of cellular respiration

The enzymes of cellular respiration occur partly in the cytoplasm (the enzymes of glycolysis) and partly in the mitochondria (the enzymes of pyruvate oxidation and most ATP formation). After formation, ATP passes to all parts of the cell. Both ADP and ATP pass through the mitochondrial membranes by facilitated diffusion. The locations of the different stages of aerobic respiration are shown in Figure 3.5.

Figure 3.5 The sites of cellular respiration in cells

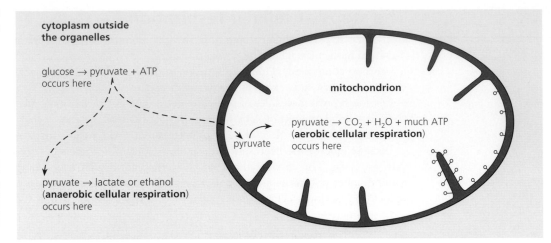

2 State which steps in cellular respiration occur whether or not oxygen is available to cells.

Anaerobic respiration – fermentation

In the absence of oxygen, many organisms (and sometimes tissues in organisms, when these have become deprived of oxygen) will continue to respire pyruvate by different pathways, known as fermentation or **anaerobic respiration**, at least for a short time.

Many species of yeast (*Saccharomyces*) respire anaerobically, even in the presence of oxygen. The products are ethanol and carbon dioxide. You will already be aware that **alcoholic fermentation** of yeast has been exploited by humans in wine and beer production for many thousands of years:

glucose ⟶ ethanol + carbon dioxide + ENERGY

Vertebrate muscle tissue can respire anaerobically, too, but in this case it involves the formation of lactic acid rather than ethanol. Once again, under conditions in the cytoplasm, lactic acid is weakly ionised, and therefore exists as the **lactate** ion.

Lactic acid fermentation occurs in muscle fibres, but only when the demand for energy for contractions is very great, and cannot be fully met by aerobic respiration. In lactic acid fermentation the sole waste product is lactate.

glucose ⟶ lactate + ENERGY

■ **Extension:** Out of general interest we can also note that just a few organisms respire only in the absence of oxygen. One such is the tetanus bacillus *Clostridium tetani* which causes tetanus, also called lock-jaw. This bacterium is active in oxygen-free environments rich in nutrients, such as occur in deep body wounds. Otherwise the bacteria merely survive as resistant spores in the soil or among the faeces of the lower gut of many animals. *Clostridium tetani* (during growth, but not as a dormant spore) produces toxins which, when released inside wounds, are carried around the body in the blood circulation, and cause agonising muscular spasms. Today, tetanus may be prevented by vaccination, supported by periodic booster injections.

What happens to pyruvate in anaerobic respiration?

In human skeletal muscle tissue, when oxygen is not available, the pyruvate remains in the cytoplasm and is converted to lactate. In yeast, whether or not oxygen is available, the pyruvate is converted to the alcohol called ethanol.

How is the supply of pyruvate maintained in cells in the absence of oxygen?

This is the key issue in the breakdown of pyruvate in the absence of oxygen. Remember, in pyruvate formation, hydrogen acceptor molecules are reduced (take up hydrogen atoms). Without using oxygen, these must be re-oxidised (lose their H) if production of pyruvate is to continue.

The answer is that in anaerobic cellular respiration the reduced hydrogen acceptor molecules donate their hydrogen to form lactate or ethanol from pyruvate. This is how they are re-oxidised. In this way the acceptor molecules are available for further pyruvate synthesis. Pyruvate formation is able to continue.

3 Identify two products of anaerobic respiration in muscle.

We can summarise this as:

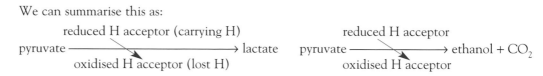

$$\text{pyruvate} \xrightarrow[\text{oxidised H acceptor (lost H)}]{\text{reduced H acceptor (carrying H)}} \text{lactate} \qquad \text{pyruvate} \xrightarrow[\text{oxidised H acceptor}]{\text{reduced H acceptor}} \text{ethanol} + CO_2$$

Anaerobic respiration is 'wasteful'

Anaerobic respiration is 'wasteful' of respiratory substrate. This is the case because the total energy yield per molecule of glucose respired, in terms of ATP generated, in both alcoholic and lactic acid fermentation is limited to the net two molecules of ATP produced in pyruvate formation. No additional energy is transferred in the latter steps and made available in cells.

So we can think of both lactate and ethanol as energy-rich molecules. (That is correct; ethanol is sometimes used as a fuel in cars, for example.) The energy locked up in these molecules may be used later, however. For example, in humans, lactate is transported to the liver and later metabolised aerobically. Energy yields of cellular respiration are compared in Table 3.1.

Table 3.1 Energy yield of aerobic and anaerobic cellular respiration compared

Yield from each molecule of glucose respired		
Aerobic respiration		Anaerobic respiration
2 ATPs	**glycolysis**	2 ATPs
up to 36 ATPs	**fates of pyruvate**	nil
38 ATPs	**Totals**	2 ATPs

Investigating respiration

The rate of respiration of an organism is an indication of its demand for energy. Respiration rate, the uptake of oxygen per unit time, may be measured by means of a **respirometer**. This apparatus, a form of manometer, detects change in pressure or volume of a gas. Respiration by tiny organisms (germinating seeds or fly maggots are ideal) trapped in the chamber of the respirometer alters the composition of the gas there, once the screw clip has been closed (Figure 3.6).

Figure 3.6 ∧ respirometer to measure respiration rate

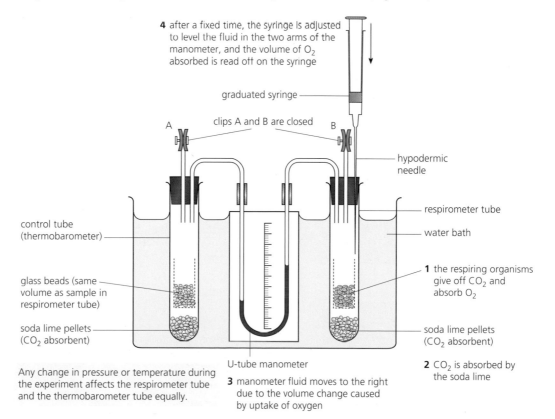

4 after a fixed time, the syringe is adjusted to level the fluid in the two arms of the manometer, and the volume of O_2 absorbed is read off on the syringe

graduated syringe

clips A and B are closed

A   B

hypodermic needle

respirometer tube

control tube (thermobarometer)

water bath

glass beads (same volume as sample in respirometer tube)

1 the respiring organisms give off CO_2 and absorb O_2

soda lime pellets (CO_2 absorbent)

soda lime pellets (CO_2 absorbent)

Any change in pressure or temperature during the experiment affects the respirometer tube and the thermobarometer tube equally.

U-tube manometer

3 manometer fluid moves to the right due to the volume change caused by uptake of oxygen

2 CO_2 is absorbed by the soda lime

Soda lime removes carbon dioxide gas as it is released by the respiring organism. Consequently, only oxygen uptake causes a change in volume. The bubble of coloured liquid in the attached capillary tube will move in response. The change in the volume of air in the respirometer tube, due to oxygen uptake, can be estimated from measurements of the movement of the manometric fluid during the experiment. In this apparatus, the volume of gas absorbed per unit time is given by readings on the syringe – the volume of air from the syringe that must be added to the respirometer tube to make the manometric fluid level in the two arms is equal to the volume of oxygen taken up by the respiring organisms.

> **4** In the respirometer (Figure 3.6), **explain** how changes in temperature or pressure in the external environment are prevented from interfering with measurement of oxygen uptake by respiring organisms in the apparatus.

■ Photosynthesis

3.8.1–3.8.8

Green plants use the energy of sunlight to produce **sugars** from the inorganic raw materials **carbon dioxide** and **water**, by a process called **photosynthesis**. The waste product is oxygen. Photosynthesis occurs in plant cells that contain the organelles called **chloroplasts** (page 6) – such as many of the cells of the leaves of green plants. Here energy of light is trapped by the green pigment **chlorophyll**, and becomes the chemical energy in molecules such as **glucose** and in **ATP**. Note that we now say that **light energy is transferred to organic compounds** in photosynthesis, rather than talking of the 'conversion of energy' – a term that was once widely used.

Sugar formed in photosynthesis may temporarily be stored as starch, but sooner or later most is used in metabolism. For example, plants manufacture other carbohydrates, together with the lipids, proteins, growth factors, and all other metabolites they require. For this they additionally need certain mineral ions, which are absorbed from the soil solution. Figure 3.7 is a summary of photosynthesis and its place in plant metabolism.

Figure 3.7
Photosynthesis and its place in plant nutrition

photosynthesis: a summary

The process in the chloroplast can be summarised by the equation:

carbon dioxide	+	water	+	LIGHT ENERGY	$\xrightarrow[\text{in chloroplast}]{\text{chlorophyll}}$	organic compounds, e.g. sugars	+	oxygen
raw materials				*energy source*		*products*		*waste product*
$6CO_2$	+	$6H_2O$	+	light	$\xrightarrow[\text{in chloroplast}]{\text{chlorophyll}}$	$C_6H_{12}O_6$	+	$6O_2$

plant nutrition: a summary

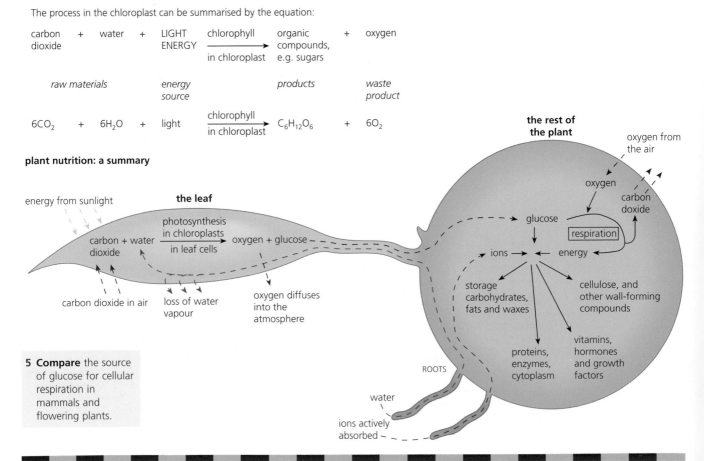

> **5 Compare** the source of glucose for cellular respiration in mammals and flowering plants.

What is light?

Light is a form of the electromagnetic radiation produced by the Sun. Visible light forms only a part of the total magnetic radiation reaching the Earth. When this visible 'white' light is projected through a prism, we see a continuous spectrum of light – a rainbow of colours, from red to violet. Different colours have different wavelengths. The wavelengths of electromagnetic radiation and of the components of light are shown in Figure 3.8.

The significance of the spectrum of light in photosynthesis is that not all the colours of the spectrum present in white light are absorbed equally by chlorophyll. Some are even transmitted (or reflected), rather than being absorbed.

Which of these individual colours does chlorophyll absorb and then exploit as the energy source for photosynthesis?

Figure 3.8
Electromagnetic radiation and the spectrum of visible light

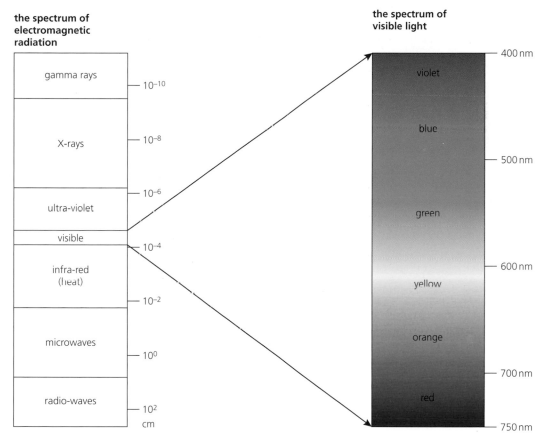

Investigating chlorophyll

Some plant pigments are soluble in water, but chlorophyll is not. While we cannot extract chlorophyll from leaves with water, it can be extracted by dissolving in an organic solvent like propanone (acetone). With this solvent, extraction of chlorophyll is straightforward. Figure 3.9 shows how it may be done.

With chlorophyll in solution, the colours of light it absorbs can be investigated. We have seen that white light consists of a roughly equal mixture of violet, blue, green, yellow, orange and red light (Figure 3.8). When these different colours are projected through the chlorophyll solution in turn, we see that the greatest absorption occurs in the blue and red parts of the spectrum, whereas green light is transmitted or reflected (Figure 3.10).

The chemical structure of the chlorophyll molecule allows absorption of the energy of blue and red light. When extracted from the chloroplasts and dissolved in organic solvent, chlorophyll still absorbs light, but it cannot now use the energy gained to cause photosynthesis to take place. This is because, in the extraction process, the chlorophyll has been separated from the membrane systems and enzyme systems that surround it in chloroplasts, and which are essential for carrying out the biochemical steps of photosynthesis.

Figure 3.9 Steps in the extraction of chlorophyll

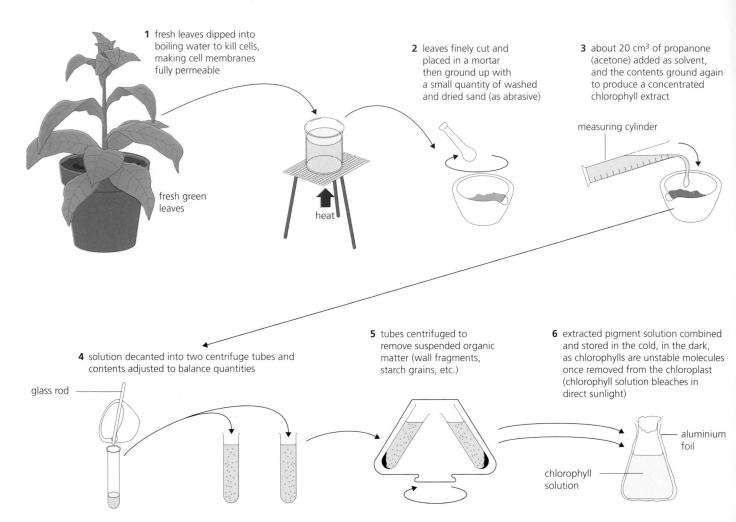

1 fresh leaves dipped into boiling water to kill cells, making cell membranes fully permeable

fresh green leaves

heat

2 leaves finely cut and placed in a mortar then ground up with a small quantity of washed and dried sand (as abrasive)

3 about 20 cm³ of propanone (acetone) added as solvent, and the contents ground again to produce a concentrated chlorophyll extract

measuring cylinder

4 solution decanted into two centrifuge tubes and contents adjusted to balance quantities

glass rod

5 tubes centrifuged to remove suspended organic matter (wall fragments, starch grains, etc.)

6 extracted pigment solution combined and stored in the cold, in the dark, as chlorophylls are unstable molecules once removed from the chloroplast (chlorophyll solution bleaches in direct sunlight)

aluminium foil

chlorophyll solution

Green plants suitable to use for chlorophyll extraction
• spinach
• bougainvillea
• hibiscus
• green grass
• in Asia, the leaf vegetables kai lan or kang kong

6 Evaluate the essential safety precautions required when chlorophyll is extracted as shown in Figure 3.9.

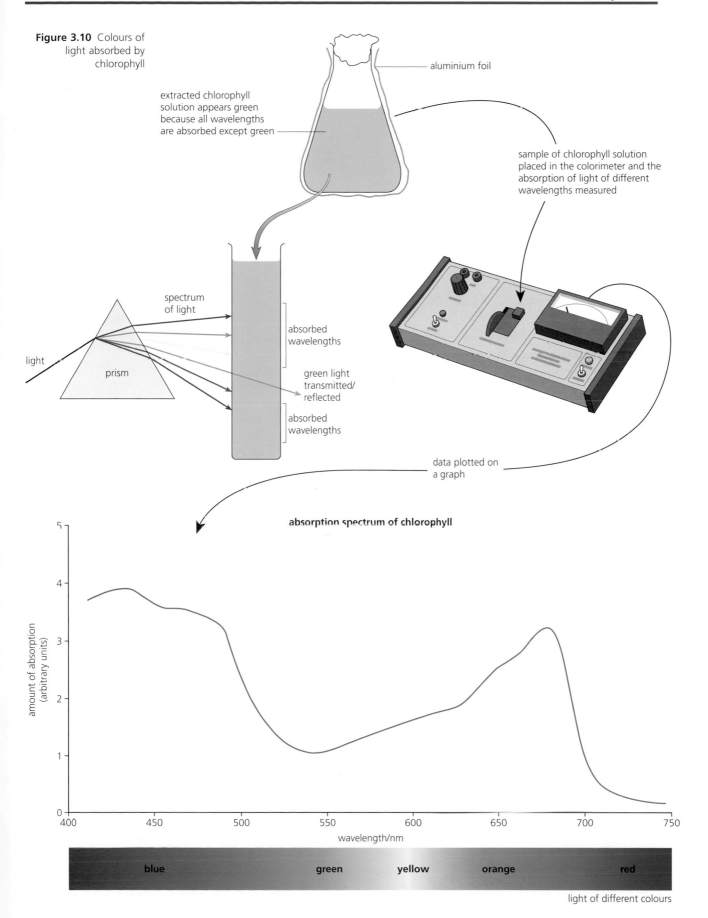

Figure 3.10 Colours of light absorbed by chlorophyll

aluminium foil

extracted chlorophyll solution appears green because all wavelengths are absorbed except green

sample of chlorophyll solution placed in the colorimeter and the absorption of light of different wavelengths measured

spectrum of light

absorbed wavelengths

green light transmitted/ reflected

absorbed wavelengths

light

prism

data plotted on a graph

absorption spectrum of chlorophyll

amount of absorption (arbitrary units)

wavelength/nm

blue   green   yellow   orange   red

light of different colours

■ Extension: Which wavelengths are used in photosynthesis?

Figure 3.11 Engelmann's investigation of light and photosynthesis

We can see that chlorophyll absorbs light energy most strongly in the blue and red ranges of the spectrum. How can we tell that this light energy, once absorbed, is being used to drive photosynthesis in chloroplasts?

cell structure of *Spirogyra* (a filamentous alga)

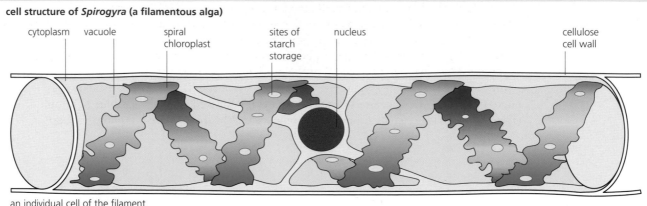

cytoplasm vacuole spiral chloroplast sites of starch storage nucleus cellulose cell wall

an individual cell of the filament

Engelmann's investigation

Spirogyra with *Pseudomonas* in the dark

Spirogyra with *Pseudomonas* with parts of the algal filament illuminated selectively

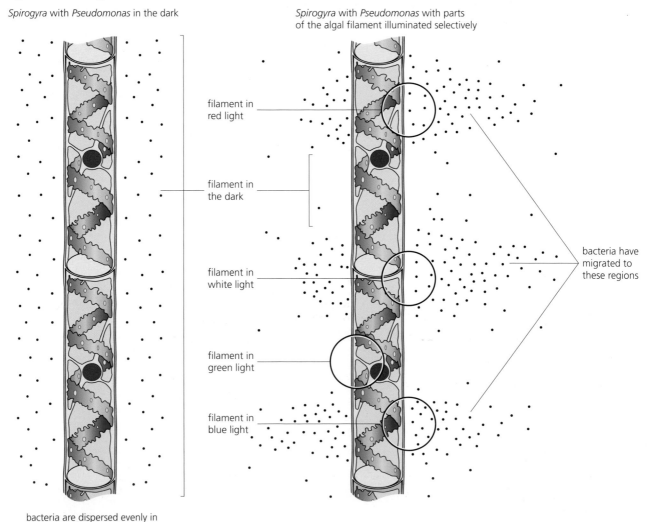

filament in red light

filament in the dark

filament in white light

filament in green light

filament in blue light

bacteria have migrated to these regions

bacteria are dispersed evenly in the medium around the filament

This question was first resolved by a German biologist, T. W. Engelmann, in 1882. Using filamentous algae such as *Spirogyra* (an aquatic, photosynthetic organism), he shone fine beams of white light and of light of different wavelengths onto different parts of a filament of the alga – so different parts were exposed to blue, green or red light, or to full (white) light. The other parts of the filament were in darkness.

Present in the water around the filament was a population of a motile bacterium (*Pseudomonas* sp.). This is a strongly aerobic species – the bacterium requires a supply of oxygen to survive, and migrates away from regions where oxygen is scarce.

Where algal cells are carrying out photosynthesis, oxygen diffuses out and is dissolved in the water immediately around the cell. Engelmann found that the bacteria migrated to only certain of the illuminated regions, and were visible there when the filaments were examined microscopically. They occurred around the parts illuminated with red and blue light only (Figure 3.11). He concluded that it is these wavelengths that are used in photosynthesis.

What happens in photosynthesis?

Photosynthesis is a set of many reactions occurring in chloroplasts in the light. However, these can be conveniently divided into two main steps:

1 **Light energy is used to split water (photolysis)**
   This releases the waste product of photosynthesis, oxygen, and allows the hydrogen atoms released to be retained on hydrogen acceptor molecules. The hydrogen is one requirement of step 2. At the same time, ATP is generated from ADP and phosphate, also using energy from light.

2 **Sugars are built up from carbon dioxide**
   We say that carbon dioxide is fixed to make organic molecules. To do this, both energy of ATP and hydrogen atoms from the reduced hydrogen acceptor molecules are required.

Figure 3.12 Two steps of photosynthesis

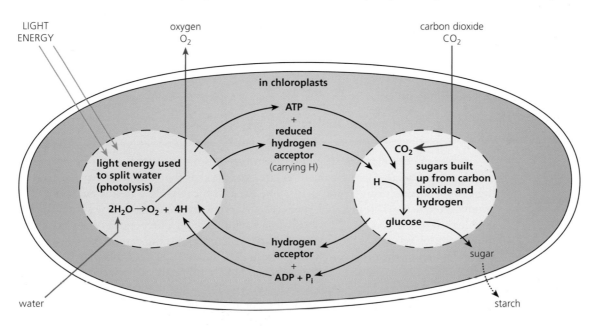

7 State from where a green plant obtains **a** carbon and **b** hydrogen used to build up glucose molecules.

Measuring the rate of photosynthesis

Measuring the rate of photosynthesis is a straightforward task in the laboratory. The rate can be estimated indirectly, by measuring the **increase in biomass** in samples of illuminated leaves, since most of the sugar produced in the light is immediately stored as starch in the cells. This technique is illustrated in Figure 3.13. It is best to destarch the leaves of the plant beforehand by keeping the intact plant in the dark for 48 hours first. The result is a more accurate estimate of gain in mass due to photosynthesis.

Figure 3.13 Rate of photosynthesis estimated by dry mass increase in leaf discs

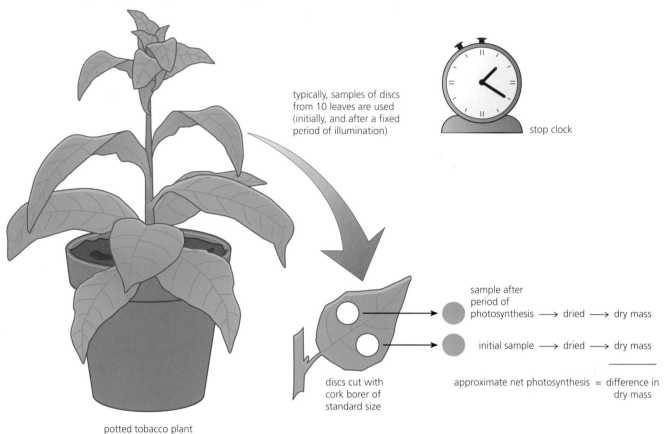

typically, samples of discs from 10 leaves are used (initially, and after a fixed period of illumination)

stop clock

sample after period of photosynthesis ⟶ dried ⟶ dry mass

initial sample ⟶ dried ⟶ dry mass

approximate net photosynthesis = difference in dry mass

discs cut with cork borer of standard size

potted tobacco plant

8 Suggest the likely fate of starch stored in a green leaf, during the destarching process.

The rate of photosynthesis can also be estimated using an oxygen sensor probe connected to a data-logging device or, using a microburette, measured as the **volume of oxygen given out in the light** by an aquatic plant (Figure 3.14). The experiment requires a freshly cut shoot of a pondweed which, when inverted, produces a vigorous stream of gas bubbles from the base. The bubbles tell us the pondweed is actively photosynthesising. The pondweed is placed in a very dilute solution of sodium hydrogencarbonate, which supplies the carbon dioxide (as $—HCO_3$ ions) required by the plant for photosynthesis. The quantity of gas evolved in a given time, say in 30 minutes, is measured by drawing the gas bubble that collects into the capillary tube, and measuring its length. This length is then converted to a volume.

Alternatively, the **uptake of carbon dioxide in the light** can be measured. Using an aquatic plant, the dissolved carbon dioxide absorbed from the water will cause the pH to rise and this may be monitored with a pH meter connected to a data-logging monitor.

Using this apparatus the effects of external conditions such as light intensity, carbon dioxide concentration and temperature on the rate of photosynthesis have been investigated.

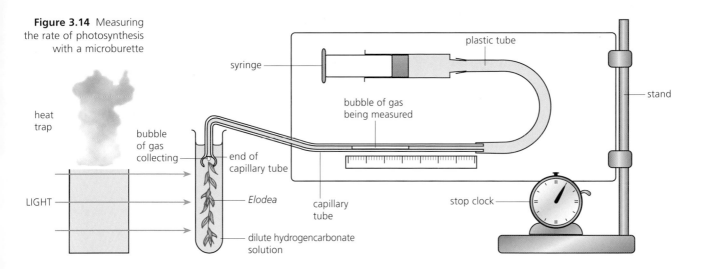

Figure 3.14 Measuring the rate of photosynthesis with a microburette

9 A thermometer is not shown in the apparatus in Figure 3.14. **Predict** why one is required, and **state** where.

External factors and the rate of photosynthesis

The effect of the **concentration of carbon dioxide** on the rate of photosynthesis is shown in Figure 3.15. Look at this figure now – note the shape of the curve.

In this experiment, when the concentration of carbon dioxide is at zero there is no photosynthesis, of course. As the concentration is steadily increased, the rate of photosynthesis rises, and the rate of that rise is positively correlated with the increasing carbon dioxide concentration. However, at much higher concentrations of carbon dioxide, the rate of photosynthesis reaches a plateau – now there is no increase in rate with rising carbon dioxide concentration.

The effect of **light intensity** on the rate is shown in Figure 3.16. Look at this graph now – the shape of the curve is familiar.

In this experiment, when light intensity is low, the rate of photosynthesis is directly proportional to light intensity. However, at much higher light intensities, there is no increase in rate with rising light intensity – this rate had reached a plateau, too.

Figure 3.15 The effect of carbon dioxide concentration on photosynthesis

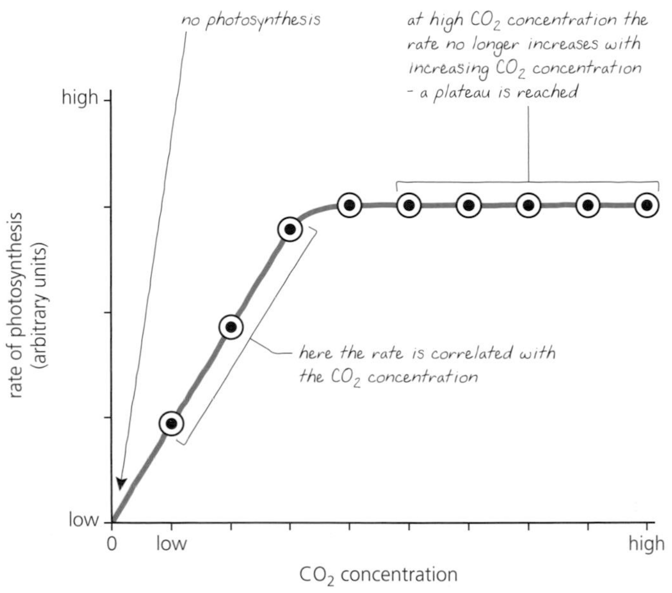

Figure 3.16 The effect of light intensity on photosynthesis

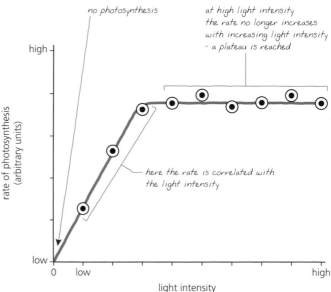

Figure 3.17 The effect of temperature on photosynthesis

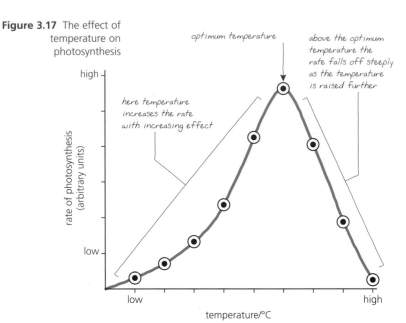

optimum temperature

above the optimum temperature the rate falls off steeply as the temperature is raised further

here temperature increases the rate with increasing effect

high

rate of photosynthesis (arbitrary units)

low

low   high

temperature/°C

The effect of **temperature** on the rate of photosynthesis is shown in Figure 3.17. Here the curve of the graph is an entirely different shape. At relatively low temperatures, as the temperature increases, the rate of photosynthesis increases more and more steeply. However, at higher temperatures, the rate of photosynthesis abruptly stops rising and actually falls steeply. The result is a clear optimum temperature for photosynthesis.

10 Suggest why we should expect that high external temperatures cause the rate of photosynthesis to fall off very rapidly.

■ *Examination questions – a selection*

Questions 1–3 are taken from past IB Diploma biology papers.

Q1 In which process of photosynthesis is light directly involved?
- **A** conversion of ATP to ADP
- **B** the fixing of carbon
- **C** the splitting of water
- **D** the conversion of pyruvate to ethanol
    Standard Level Paper 1, May 06, Q11

Q2 In the following generalised diagram of anaerobic respiration, which molecules are represented by I, II and III?

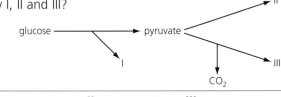

glucose ⟶ pyruvate

II

I

III

CO₂

	I	II	III
A	ATP	ethanol	lactate
B	ethanol	ATP	lactate
C	lactate	ethanol	ATP
D	ATP	lactate	ethanol

Higher Level Paper 1, May 05, Q5

Q3
- **a** State the main photosynthesis pigment in plants. (1)
- **b** State the **two** materials used to convert carbon dioxide to organic molecules in plants. (2)
- **c** Explain **two** ways in which the rate of photosynthesis can be measured. (4)
    Standard Level Paper 2, May 04, Q4

Questions 4–8 cover other syllabus issues in this chapter.

Q4 Define cell respiration. Include the essential raw materials, *and* the products. (2)
State where respiration occurs in a living organism. (2)

Q5 Explain the composition of ATP and the role of this molecule in cell metabolism. (2)

Q6 Construct a flow diagram to show the steps in aerobic cellular respiration. Demonstrate which steps are restricted to the cytoplasm, and which to a mitochondrion, and the connection between these steps. (6)

Q7 Photosynthesis involves the transfer of light energy to chemical energy of glucose and other organic molecules.
- **a** State why photosynthesis is restricted to green plants in the light. (1)
- **b** State the waste product of photosynthesis. (1)
- **c** Define the term 'photolysis'. (1)
- **d** Photosynthesis leads to an increase in biomass of a green plant. Suggest the metabolic process mostly responsible for reducing the amount of biomass present in the plant. (1)

Q8 Design an experiment to test whether temperature has an effect on photosynthesis. Predict what outcome you would expect. (6)

4 Genetics

- The **nucleus** is the largest organelle in a cell. It contains the **chromosomes** on which **genes**, the blueprints (coded instructions) for the cell, occur.
- When cells divide, the **nucleus divides first**, and each new (daughter) cell receives a nucleus.
- The nucleus **controls and directs the activities** of the cell throughout life; it **contains the hereditary material** which is passed from generation to generation during reproduction.

Genetics is the study of inheritance and of variation in the inherited characteristics that **chromosomes** control. The nucleus contains the chromosomes, as we have already seen. The chromosomes hold the blueprint (coded instructions) for the organisation and activities of cells and for the whole organism, in the form of **genes**. Genes are involved both in the continuous control of cell activity and in reproduction, carrying instructions from one generation to the next.

Chromosomes, genes, mutations and meiosis
4.1.1–4.1.4, 4.2.1–4.2.7

Chromosomes can be seen in cells by staining them with certain dyes (Figure 1.33, page 34). At the time a nucleus divides, the chromosomes become compact, much-coiled structures, and are clearly visible. At all other times, the chromosomes are very long thin, uncoiled threads. In this condition, they give the stained nucleus a granular appearance. The granules are called chromatin.

Each chromosome consists of **DNA**, a huge molecule consisting of **two paired strands in the form of a double helix** (Figure 2.27, page 64). The DNA molecule runs the full length of the chromosome, and is supported by protein. About 50% of a chromosome is built of protein. While some of these proteins are enzymes that are involved in copying and repair reactions of DNA, the bulk of chromosome protein has a support and packaging role for DNA.

There are five features of the chromosomes of organisms which it is helpful to note now.

1 **The number of chromosomes per species is fixed**
   The number of chromosomes in the cells of different species varies, but in any one species the number of chromosomes per cell is normally constant. For example, the mouse has 40 chromosomes per cell, the onion has 16, humans have 46, and the sunflower has 34. Each species has a characteristic chromosome number. Note, these are all even numbers.

2 **The shape of a chromosome is characteristic**
   Chromosomes are long thin structures of a particular, fixed length. Somewhere along the length of the chromosome is a narrow region called the **centromere**. Centromeres may occur anywhere along the chromosome, but they are always in the same position on any given chromosome. The position of the centromere, as well as the length of a chromosome, is how they are identified in photomicrographs (photographs taken down a light microscope, see page 10).

3 **The chromosomes of a cell occur in pairs called homologous pairs**
   The word 'homologous' just means 'similar in structure'. One of each pair came originally from one parent, and the other from the other parent. So, for example, the human has 46 chromosomes, 23 coming originally from each parent in the process of sexual reproduction. This is why chromosomes occur in homologous pairs.

Homologous chromosomes resemble each other in structure. They occur in a diploid cell, contain the same sequence of genes, but have come from different parents.

You can see this from the photomicrographs in Figure 4.1. Here, chromosomes of a human male are shown at a stage of the nuclear division called **mitosis** (page 31). They are cut out of a photomicrograph and arranged in numbered descending order of size. This type of enlarged photographic image of the mitotic chromosomes of a cell, arranged in pairs in order of size, is called a **karyotype**.

The procedure of karyotyping is used by genetic counsellors, in conjunction with other techniques, to detect the presence of (rare) abnormalities, such as Down's syndrome (page 98), in a patient's chromosome set. This is discussed later in this chapter.

Figure 4.1
Chromosomes as homologous pairs, as seen during nuclear division

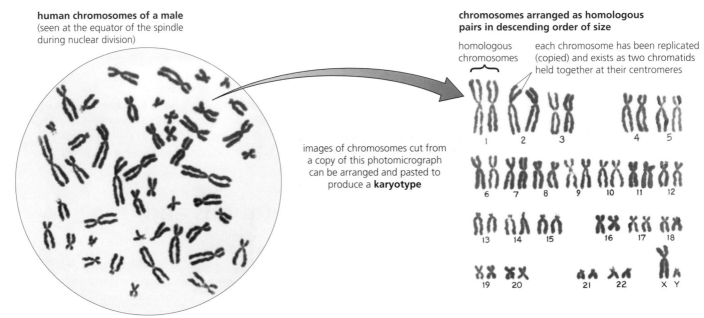

human chromosomes of a male
(seen at the equator of the spindle during nuclear division)

chromosomes arranged as homologous pairs in descending order of size

homologous chromosomes

each chromosome has been replicated (copied) and exists as two chromatids held together at their centromeres

images of chromosomes cut from a copy of this photomicrograph can be arranged and pasted to produce a **karyotype**

4 Chromosomes hold the hereditary factors – genes

The chromosomes are effectively a linear series of genes (Figure 4.2). We can define 'gene' in different ways. For example, a gene is a:

a specific region of a chromosome which is capable of determining the development of a specific characteristic of an organism;

b specific length of the DNA double helix, hundreds or (more typically) thousands of base pairs long, which codes for a protein;

c unit of inheritance.

A particular gene always occurs on the same chromosome in the same position.

The position of a gene is called a **locus** (plural, **loci**).

Each gene has two or more forms, called **alleles**. The word 'allele' just means 'alternative form'.

The total of all the genetic information – all the genes present on an organism's chromosomes – is called the **genome** of the organism.

5 Chromosomes copy themselves

Between nuclear divisions, while the chromosomes are uncoiled and cannot be seen, each chromosome makes a copy of itself. It is said to **replicate**.

Replication occurs in the cell cycle, during interphase (page 31). The two identical structures formed are called **chromatids** (Figure 4.3). The chromatids remain attached by their centromeres until they are divided during nuclear division. After division of the centromeres, the chromatids are recognised as chromosomes again.

Of course, when chromosomes copy themselves, the critical event is the copying of the DNA double helix that runs the length of the chromosome. Replication occurs in a very precise way, brought about by specific enzymes, as we have already discussed (page 66).

1 Explain why chromosomes occur in homologous pairs in cells.

Figure 4.2 Genes and alleles of a homologous pair of chromosomes

The **loci** are the positions along the chromosomes where genes occur, so alleles of the same gene occupy the same locus.

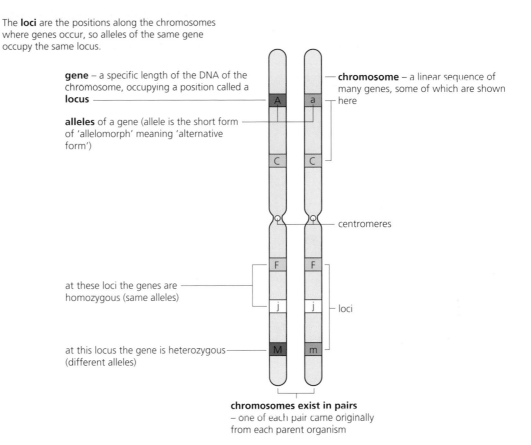

gene – a specific length of the DNA of the chromosome, occupying a position called a **locus**

alleles of a gene (allele is the short form of 'allelomorph' meaning 'alternative form')

chromosome – a linear sequence of many genes, some of which are shown here

centromeres

at these loci the genes are homozygous (same alleles)

loci

at this locus the gene is heterozygous (different alleles)

chromosomes exist in pairs
– one of each pair came originally from each parent organism

Figure 4.3 One chromosome as two chromatids

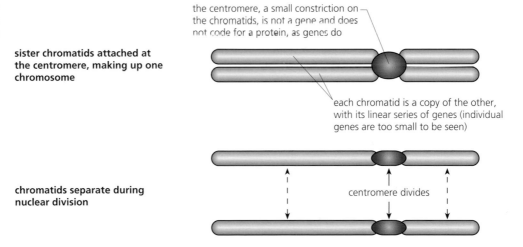

the centromere, a small constriction on the chromatids, is not a gene and does not code for a protein, as genes do

sister chromatids attached at the centromere, making up one chromosome

each chromatid is a copy of the other, with its linear series of genes (individual genes are too small to be seen)

chromatids separate during nuclear division

centromere divides

Nuclear divisions and the fate of chromosomes

Divisions of the nucleus are very precise processes, ensuring the correct distribution of chromosomes between the new cells (daughter cells). There are two types of nuclear division, known as mitosis and meiosis.

In **mitosis**, the daughter cells produced have the same number of chromosomes as the parent cell, typically two of each type, known as the **diploid (2n)** state. Mitosis is the nuclear division that occurs when cells grow, old cells are replaced, and when an organism reproduces asexually. The way mitosis works is explained in Chapter 1, page 32.

In **meiosis**, the daughter cells contain half the number of chromosomes of the parent cell. That is, one chromosome of each type is present in the nuclei formed; this is known as the **haploid (n)** state. Meiosis is the nuclear division that occurs when sexual reproduction occurs, normally during the formation of the gametes.

The differences between mitosis and meiosis are summarised in Figure 4.4.

Figure 4.4 Mitosis and meiosis, the significant differences

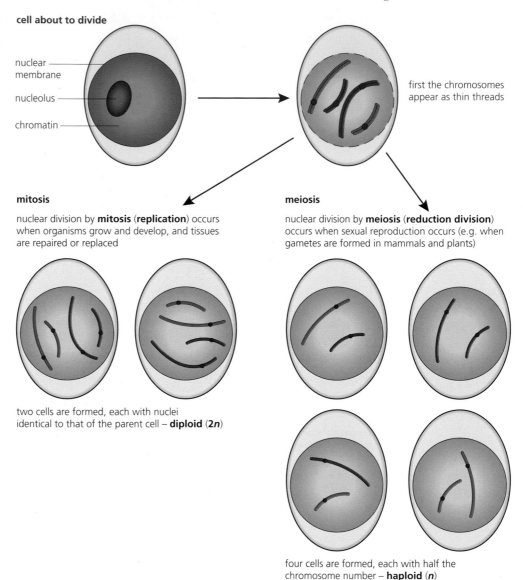

cell about to divide

nuclear membrane

nucleolus

chromatin

first the chromosomes appear as thin threads

mitosis

nuclear division by **mitosis (replication)** occurs when organisms grow and develop, and tissues are repaired or replaced

meiosis

nuclear division by **meiosis (reduction division)** occurs when sexual reproduction occurs (e.g. when gametes are formed in mammals and plants)

two cells are formed, each with nuclei identical to that of the parent cell – **diploid (2n)**

four cells are formed, each with half the chromosome number – **haploid (n)**

2 **Suggest** why it is essential that nuclear division is a precise process.

Meiosis, the reduction division

Meiosis is part of the life-cycle of every organism that reproduces sexually. In meiosis, four daughter cells are produced – each with half the number of chromosomes of the parent cell. Halving of the chromosome number of gametes is essential because at fertilisation the number is doubled.

How does meiosis work?

Meiosis involves **two divisions** of the nucleus, known as **meiosis I** and **meiosis II**, both of which superficially resemble mitosis. As in mitosis, chromosomes replicate to form chromatids during interphase, before meiosis occurs. Then, early in meiosis I, **homologous chromosomes pair up**. By the end of meiosis I, homologous chromosomes have separated again, but the chromatids they consist of do not separate until meiosis II. Thus, meiosis consists of two nuclear divisions but only **one replication of the chromosomes**.

Figure 4.5 What happens to chromosomes in meiosis

The process of meiosis

The key events of meiosis are summarised in Figure 4.5.

during interphase

during meiosis I

during meiosis II

chromosomes separate and enter daughter cells

cytokinesis

division of cytoplasm

product of meiosis is four haploid cells

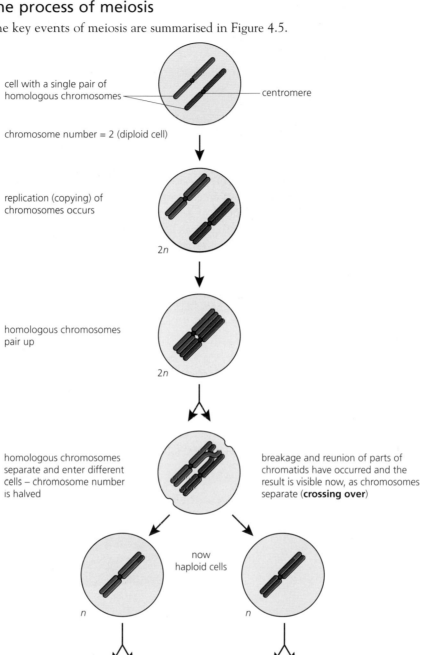

cell with a single pair of homologous chromosomes

centromere

chromosome number = 2 (diploid cell)

replication (copying) of chromosomes occurs

2*n*

homologous chromosomes pair up

2*n*

homologous chromosomes separate and enter different cells – chromosome number is halved

breakage and reunion of parts of chromatids have occurred and the result is visible now, as chromosomes separate (**crossing over**)

now haploid cells

n

n

n

n

n

n

In the interphase that precedes meiosis, the chromosomes are replicated as chromatids, but between meiosis I and II there is no further interphase, so no replication of the chromosomes occurs during meiosis.

As meiosis begins, the chromosomes become visible. At the same time, homologous chromosomes pair up. (Remember, in a diploid cell each chromosome has a partner that is the same length and shape and with the same linear sequence of genes. It is these partner chromosomes that pair.)

When the homologous chromosomes have paired up closely, each pair is called a **bivalent**. Members of the bivalent continue to shorten.

During the coiling and shortening process within the bivalent, the **chromatids frequently break**. Broken ends rejoin more or less immediately. When non-sister chromatids from homologous chromosomes break and rejoin they do so at exactly corresponding sites, so that a cross-shaped structure called a chiasma is formed at one or more places along a bivalent. The event is known as a **crossing over** because lengths of genes have been exchanged between chromatids.

Then, when members of the bivalents start to repel each other and separate, the bivalents are (initially) held together by one or more chiasmata. This temporarily gives an unusual shape to the bivalent. So, crossing over is an important mechanical event (as well as a genetic event).

Next, the spindle forms. Members of the bivalents become attached by their centromeres to the fibres of the spindle at the equatorial plate of the cell. Spindle fibres pull the homologous chromosomes apart, to opposite poles, but the **individual chromatids remain attached** by their centromeres.

Meiosis I ends with two cells each containing a single set of chromosomes each made of two chromatids. These cells do not go into interphase, but rather continue smoothly into meiosis II. This takes place at right angles to meiosis I, but is exactly like mitosis. Centromeres of the chromosomes divide and **individual chromatids now move to opposite poles**. Following division of the cytoplasm, there are four cells – each with half the chromosome number of the original parent cell (haploid).

Figure 4.6 Genetic variation due to crossing over between non-sister chromatids

The effects of genetic variation are shown in one pair of homologous chromosomes.
Typically, two, three or more chiasmata form between the chromatids of each bivalent at prophase I.

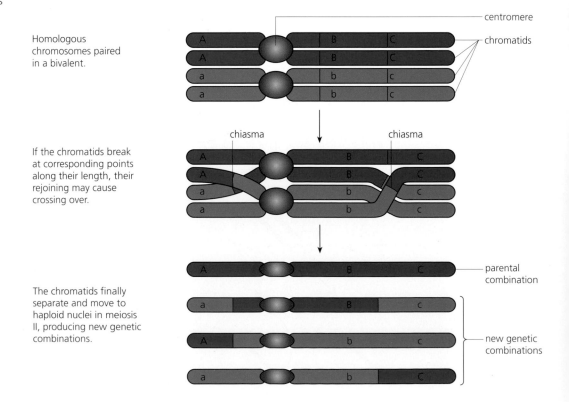

Meiosis and genetic variation

The four haploid cells produced by meiosis differ genetically from each other for two reasons.

- There is **independent assortment** of maternal and paternal homologous chromosomes. This happens because the way the bivalents line up at the equator of the spindle in meiosis I is entirely random. Which chromosome of a given pair goes to which pole is unaffected by (independent of) the behaviour of the chromosomes in other pairs.
- There is **crossing over** of segments of individual maternal and paternal homologous chromosomes. These events result in new combinations of genes on the chromosomes of the haploid cells produced (Figure 4.6).

Independent assortment is illustrated in Figure 4.7, in a parent cell with a diploid number of 4 chromosomes. In human cells, the number of pairs of chromosomes is 23; the number of possible combinations of chromosomes that can be formed by random orientation during meiosis is 2^{23}, which is over 8 million. We see that independent assortment alone, generates a huge amount of variation in the coded information carried by different gametes into the fertilisation stage.

Figure 4.7 Genetic variation due to independent assortment

Independent assortment is illustrated in a parent cell with two pairs of homologous chromosomes (four bivalents). The more bivalents there are, the more variation is possible. In humans, for example, there are 23 pairs of chromosomes giving over 8 million combinations.

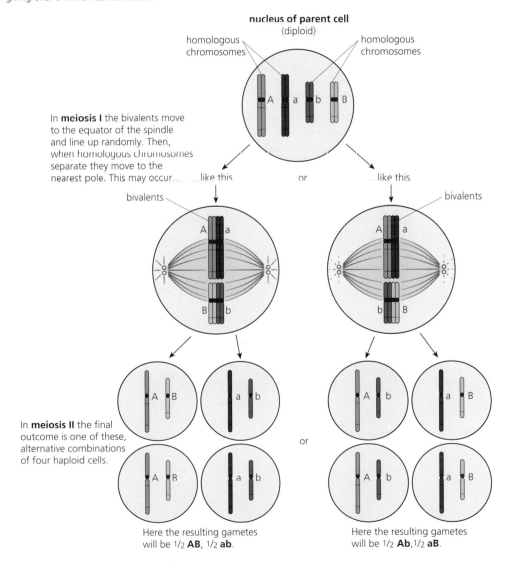

Abrupt change in hereditary information – mutations

An abrupt change in the structure, arrangement or amount of DNA of chromosomes may result in a change in the characteristics of an organism or an individual cell in which they occur. This is because the change, called a **mutation**, results in the alteration or non-production of a cell protein (and of the **mRNA** which codes for it, page 69). Mutations can occur spontaneously as a result of errors in normal cell processes such as DNA replication, although this is rare. Alternatively, they can be induced by certain chemicals or types of radiations that cells are sometimes exposed to.

Mutations occurring in body cells of multicellular organisms are called **somatic mutations**. They are only passed on to the immediate descendents of that cell. However, we have already noted that somatic mutations can also be the cause of a cancer (page 35). Somatic mutations do occur with increasing frequency as an organism ages; cancers are more common in elderly people than in the young.

On the other hand, mutations occurring in the cells of the gonads (called **germ line mutations**) that give rise to gametes with an altered genome can be inherited by the offspring and so be the cause of genetic changes in future generations.

> **A mutation is a change in the amount or chemical structure of DNA which may result in a change in the characteristics of an organism.**

Chromosome mutations

In chromosome mutations, there is a change in the number or the sequence of genes, brought about in a number of different ways. Additional sets of chromosomes may occur; for example, the cultivated potato has double the number of chromosomes of the smaller, wild potato (polyploidy, page 467).

Alternatively, there may be an alteration to part of the chromosome set. Sometimes, chromosomes that should separate and move to opposite poles during the nuclear division of gamete formation do not separate but instead move to the same pole.

> **Non-disjunction is the term for the failure of a pair of chromatids to separate and go to opposite poles during division of the nucleus. In meiosis, this results in gametes with more than and less than the haploid number of chromosomes.**

For example, people with Down's syndrome have an extra chromosome 21, giving them a total of 47 chromosomes. How this case of non-disjunction arises is illustrated in Figure 4.8. The symptoms of Down's syndrome are variable, but when severe they include congenital heart defects, defects in the eyes, subsequent learning difficulties and immune system deficiencies.

How are chromosome mutations detected?

A chromosome mutation is exposed by karyotyping the chromosome set of a fetus, after fetal cells have been obtained by amniocentesis or chorionic villus sampling (Figure 4.9).

Gene mutations

Gene mutations are changes in the sequence of bases in the DNA of a gene. They may occur spontaneously as a result of errors in DNA replication although this is extremely rare since DNA polymerase has a built-in checking mechanism as it operates (page 67).

Alternatively, gene mutations can be caused by environmental agents we call **mutagens**. These can include ionising radiation in the form of X-rays, cosmic rays, and radiation from radioactive isotopes (α, β and γ rays). Any of these can cause the break-up of the DNA molecule. Non-ionising mutagens include UV light and various chemicals, including carcinogens in tobacco smoke (tar compounds). These act by modifying the chemistry of the base pairs of DNA.

Base substitution mutation and sickle cell condition

The smallest form of gene mutation change occurs when one base is replaced by another – this is called base substitution. An example of this type of gene mutation is the cause of the human condition known as sickle cell anaemia.

Figure 4.8 Down's syndrome, an example of a chromosome mutation

An extra chromosome causes Down's syndrome. The extra one comes from a meiosis error. The two chromatids of chromosome 21 fail to separate, and both go into the daughter cell that forms the secondary oocyte.

karyotype of a person with Down's syndrome

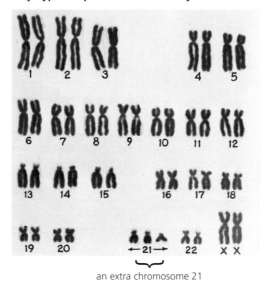

an extra chromosome 21

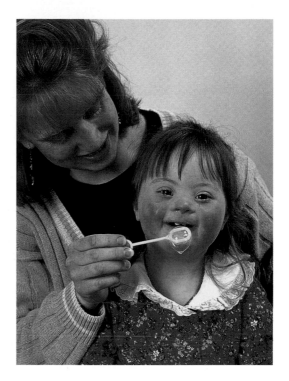

Steps of non-disjunction in meiosis
(illustrated in nucleus with only two pairs of homologous chromosomes – for clarity)

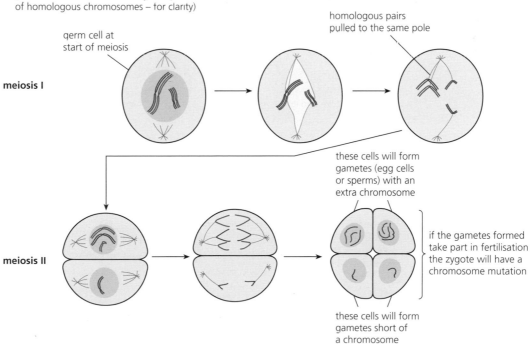

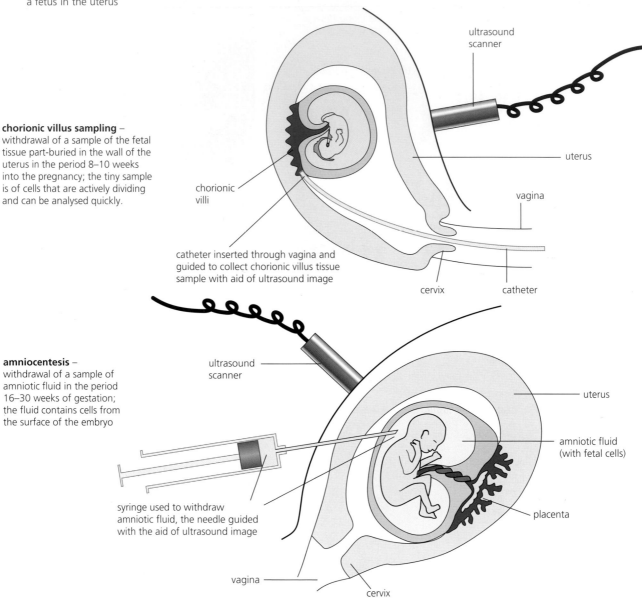

Figure 4.9 Screening of a fetus in the uterus

ultrasound scanner

chorionic villus sampling – withdrawal of a sample of the fetal tissue part-buried in the wall of the uterus in the period 8–10 weeks into the pregnancy; the tiny sample is of cells that are actively dividing and can be analysed quickly.

uterus

chorionic villi

vagina

catheter inserted through vagina and guided to collect chorionic villus tissue sample with aid of ultrasound image

cervix

catheter

ultrasound scanner

amniocentesis – withdrawal of a sample of amniotic fluid in the period 16–30 weeks of gestation; the fluid contains cells from the surface of the embryo

uterus

amniotic fluid (with fetal cells)

placenta

syringe used to withdraw amniotic fluid, the needle guided with the aid of ultrasound image

vagina

cervix

Figure 4.10 Human karyotype used in a genetic screening for counselling

3 **Analyse** the human karyotype in Figure 4.10 to determine the gender of the patient and whether non-disjunction has occurred.

Figure 4.11 Sickle cell anaemia; an example of a gene mutation

Anaemia is a disease typically due to a deficiency in healthy red cells in the blood.

Haemoglobin occurs in red cells – each contains about 280 million molecules of haemoglobin. A molecule consists of two α-haemoglobin and two β-haemoglobin subunits, interlocked to form a compact molecule.

The **mutation** that produces sickle cell haemoglobin (**Hg^S**) is in the gene for β-haemoglobin. It results from the substitution of a single base in the sequence of bases that make up all the codons for β-haemoglobin.

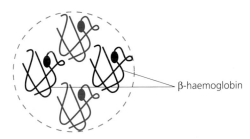

β-haemoglobin

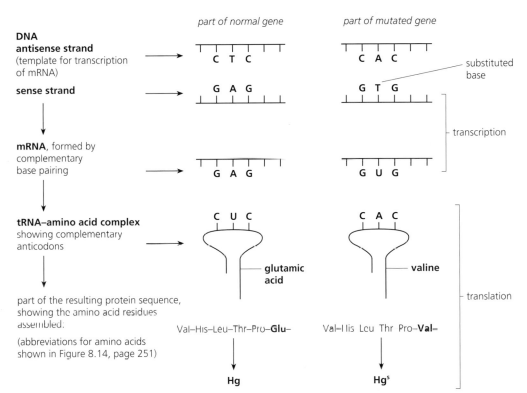

part of normal gene   *part of mutated gene*

**DNA
antisense strand**
(template for transcription of mRNA)

→   C T C   C A C

substituted base

sense strand

→   G A G   G T G

transcription

mRNA, formed by complementary base pairing

→   G A G   G U G

tRNA–amino acid complex
showing complementary anticodons

→   C U C   C A C

glutamic acid   valine

part of the resulting protein sequence, showing the amino acid residues assembled:

(abbreviations for amino acids shown in Figure 8.14, page 251)

Val–His–Leu–Thr–Pro–**Glu**–   Val–His–Leu–Thr–Pro–**Val**–

Hg   **Hg^s**

translation

drawing based on a photomicrograph of a blood smear, showing blood of a patient with sickle cells present among healthy red cells

phenotypic appearance of **HgHg** red cells and sickle cells (**Hg^{s}Hg**)

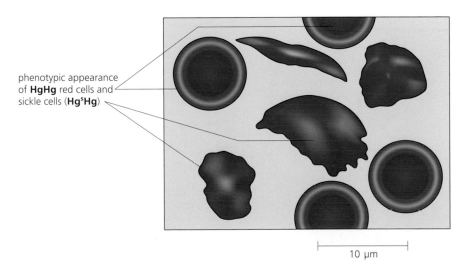

10 μm

Haemoglobin, the oxygen-transporting pigment of red cells, is made of four protein molecules that interlock to form a compact molecule. Two of the haemoglobin molecules are known as α haemoglobin and two are β haemoglobin. The gene that codes for the amino acid sequence of β haemoglobin occurs on chromosome 11, and is prone to a substitution of the base A to T in a codon for the amino acid glutamic acid. As a consequence, the amino acid valine appears at that point, instead, as illustrated in Figure 4.11. Note the consequence of this substitution at the transcription and translation stages.

The effects on the properties of the haemoglobin molecule of this simple change of one amino acid residue for another within the whole β haemoglobin molecule are dramatic. The molecules with this unusual haemoglobin, known as **haemoglobin S (Hbˢ)**, tend to clump together and form long fibres that distort the red cells into sickle shapes. In this condition, they transport little oxygen and the sickle cells may even block smaller vessels.

People who are heterozygous for haemoglobin S (**Hb Hbˢ**) have less than 50% haemoglobin S. Such a person is said to have **sickle cell trait**, and they are only mildly anaemic. However, people who are homozygous for haemoglobin S (**Hbˢ Hbˢ**) have a serious problem, and are described as having **sickle cell anaemia**. Heart and kidney failure problems are common in people affected with sickle cell anaemia.

An advantage in having sickle cell trait?

Malaria is the most important of all insect-borne diseases. It is in Africa south of the Sahara that about 80% of the world's malaria cases are found, and here that most fatalities due to the disease occur. It is estimated that some 400 million people are infected, of whom 1.5 million (mostly children under 5 years) die each year.

Malaria is caused by *Plasmodium*, a protozoan, which is transmitted from an infected person to another person by blood-sucking mosquitoes of the genus *Anopheles*. Only the female mosquito is the vector (the male mosquito feeds on plant juices).

Plasmodium completes its life cycle in red cells, but it cannot do so in red cells containing haemoglobin S. People with sickle cell trait are protected to a significant extent. Where malaria is endemic in Africa, possession of one mutant gene (having sickle cell trait, not full anaemia) is advantageous. This means that 'survival of the fittest' ensures this allele is selected for. Fewer of the alleles for normal haemoglobin are carried into the next generation (Figure 4.12).

Figure 4.12 How sickle cell trait may confer an advantage

distribution of haemoglobin S is virtually the same as that of malaria

distribution of malaria caused by *Plasmodium falciparum* or *P. vivax* (the forms of malaria that are most frequently fatal, especially in childhood)

distribution of sickle cell gene in the population

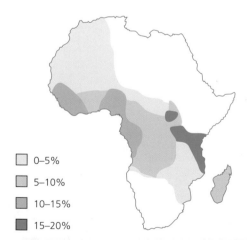

- ☐ 0–5%
- ☐ 5–10%
- ☐ 10–15%
- ☐ 15–20%

Sickle cell anaemia is a genetically transmitted disease of the blood caused by an abnormal form of haemoglobin. Red cells with 'sickle' haemoglobin do not carry oxygen and can cause blockage of arterioles. Normally, sickle cell anaemia confers a disadvantage, but the malarial parasite (page 595) is unable to complete its life cycle in red cells with haemoglobin S, so the gene for sickle cell is selected for in regions of the world where malaria occurs.

4 Explain how knowledge of the cause of sickle cell trait and sickle cell anaemia supports the concept of a gene as a linear sequence of bases.

Chromosomes and the mechanism of inheritance

4.3.1–4.3.12

The mechanism of inheritance was successfully investigated before chromosomes had been observed or genes were known about. It was **Gregor Mendel** who made the first discovery of the fundamental laws of heredity (Figure 4.13).

Figure 4.13 Gregor Mendel – founder of modern genetics

Gregor Mendel was born in Moravia in 1822, the son of a peasant farmer. As a young boy, he worked to support himself through schooling, but at the age of 21 he was offered a place in the monastery at Bruno (now in the Czech Republic). The monastery was a centre of research in natural sciences and agriculture, as well as in the humanities. Mendel was successful there. Later, he became Abbot.

Mendel discovered the principles of heredity by studying **the inheritance of seven contrasting characteristics of the garden pea plant**. These did not 'blend' on crossing, but retained their identities, and were inherited in fixed mathematical ratios.

He concluded that hereditary factors (we now call them genes) determine these characteristics, that these factors occur in duplicate in parents, and that the two copies of the factors segregate from each other in the formation of gametes.

Today, we often refer to Mendel's laws of heredity, but Mendel's results were **not presented as laws** – which may help to explain the difficulty others had in seeing the significance of his work at the time.

Mendel was successful because:

- his experiments were carefully planned, and used large samples
- he carefully recorded the numbers of plants of each type but expressed his results as ratios
- in the pea, contrasting characteristics are easily recognised
- by chance, each of these characteristics was controlled by a single factor (gene)* rather than by many genes, as most human characteristics are
- pairs of contrasting characters that he worked on were controlled by factors (genes) on separate chromosomes*
- in interpreting results, Mendel made use of the mathematics he had learnt.

* Genes and chromosomes were not known then.

Features of the garden pea

round v. wrinkled seeds

green v. yellow cotyledons (seed leaves)

dwarf v. tall plants

TOK Link

At the time of Mendel, it was thought that the characteristics of parents 'blended' in their offspring. What features of Mendel's methods enabled him to avoid this error?

Mendel's investigation of the inheritance of a single contrasting characteristic is known as a **monohybrid cross**. Mendel had noticed that the garden pea plant was either tall or dwarf. How was this contrasting characteristic controlled?

Figure 4.14 summarises the steps of his investigation of the inheritance of height in the pea plants. Note that his experiment began with plants that always 'bred true'; that is, the tall plants produced progeny that were all tall and the dwarf plants produced progeny that were all dwarf, when each was allowed to self-fertilise. Self-fertilisation is the normal condition in the garden pea plant.

In Mendel's interpretation of the monohybrid cross he argued that because the dwarf characteristic had apparently disappeared in the F_1 generation and reappeared in the F_2 generation, there must be a factor controlling dwarfness that remained intact from one generation to another. However, this factor did not express itself in the presence of a similar factor for tallness. In other words, as characteristics, tallness is dominant and dwarfness is recessive. Logically there must be two independent factors for height, one from one parent and the other factor from the other parent in the cells of an organism. A sex cell (gamete) must contain only one of these factors.

Mendel saw that a 3:1 ratio could be the product of randomly combining two pairs of unlike factors (**T** and **t**, for example). This can be shown using a grid, now known as a Punnett grid, after the mathematician who first used it (Figure 4.15).

Mendel's conclusions from the monohybrid cross were that:

- within an organism there are breeding factors controlling characteristics such as 'tall' and 'dwarf';
- there are two factors in each cell;
- one factor comes from each parent;
- the factors separate in reproduction, and either can be passed on to an offspring;
- the factor for 'tall' is an alternative form of the factor for 'dwarf';
- the factor for 'tall' is dominant over the factor for 'dwarf'.

Figure 4.14 The steps of Mendel's monohybrid cross

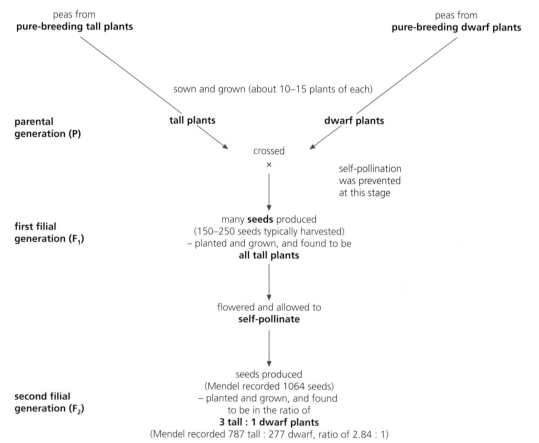

Figure 4.15 Genetic diagram showing the behaviour of alleles in Mendel's monohybrid cross.

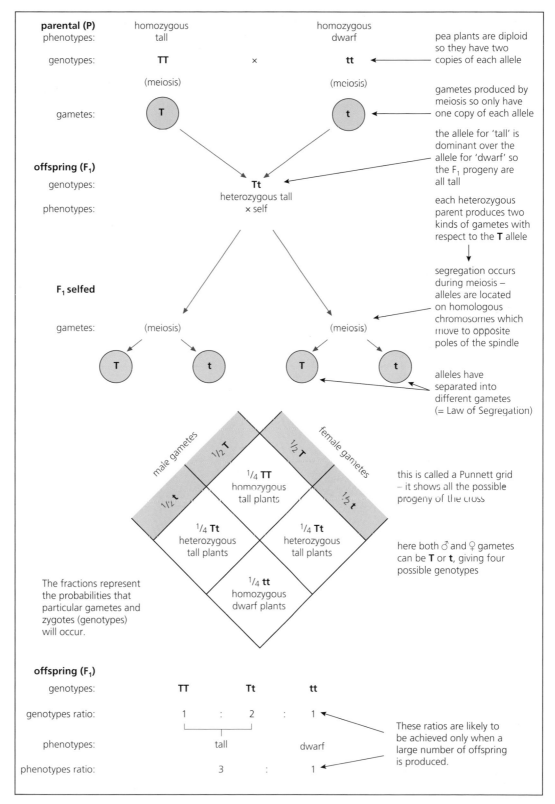

5 From the Punnett grid (Figure 4.15), a ratio of 3 tall to 1 dwarf pea plants was predicted. In fact, a ratio of 2.84:1 occurred (Figure 4.14). **Suggest** what chance events may influence the actual ratios of offspring obtained in breeding experiments like these.

Mendel never stated his discoveries as laws, but it might have helped others understand his work had he done so. For example, he might have said, 'Each characteristic of an organism is determined by a pair of factors of which only one can be present in each gamete'. Today we call a similar statement Mendel's First Law, the **Law of Segregation: 'The characteristics of an organism are controlled by pairs of alleles which separate in equal numbers into different gametes as a result of meiosis.'**

Genotype, phenotype and the test cross

The alleles that an organism carries (present in every cell) make up the genotype of that organism. A genotype in which the two alleles of a gene are the same is said to 'breed true' or, more scientifically, to be **homozygous** for that gene. In Figure 4.15, the parent pea plants (P generation) were either homozygous tall or homozygous dwarf.

If the alleles are different, the organism is **heterozygous** for that gene. In Figure 4.15, the progeny (F_1 generation) were heterozygous tall.

So the **genotype** is the genetic constitution of an organism. Alleles interact in various ways and with environmental factors. The outcome is the phenotype. The **phenotype** is the way in which the genotype of the organism is expressed – including the appearance of the organism. Here the heights of the plants were their phenotypes.

If an organism shows a recessive characteristic in its phenotype (like the dwarf pea) it must have a homozygous genotype (**tt**). But if it shows the dominant characteristic (like the tall pea) then it may be either homozygous for a dominant allele (**TT**) or heterozygous for the dominant allele (**Tt**). **In other words, TT and Tt look alike**. They have the same phenotype but different genotypes.

You could tell plants like these apart only by the offspring they produced in a particular cross. When the tall heterozygous plants (**Tt**) are crossed with the homozygous recessive plants (**tt**), the cross yields 50% tall and 50% dwarf plants (Figure 4.16). This type of cross has become known as a **test cross**. If the offspring produced had all been tall then we would have known that the tall plants under test were homozygous plants (**TT**). Of course, sufficient plants have to be used to obtain these distinctive ratios.

Figure 4.16 Genetic diagram of Mendel's test cross

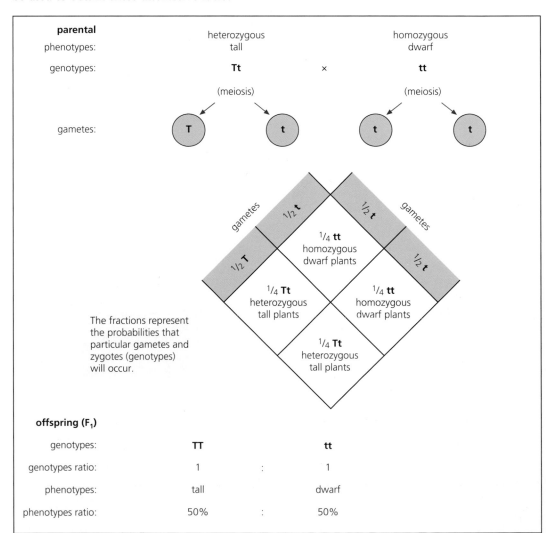

6 **Construct** a table to explain the relationship between Mendel's Law of Segregation and meiosis.

Modification of the 3:1 monohybrid ratio

In certain types of monohybrid cross the 3:1 ratio is not obtained. Two of these situations are illustrated next.

Codominance – when both alleles are expressed

In the case of some genes, both alleles may be expressed simultaneously, rather than one being dominant and the other recessive in the phenotype, as has been illustrated up to now. For example, in the common garden flower *Antirrhinum*, when red-flowered plants are crossed with white-flowered plants, the F_1 plants have pink flowers. When pink-flowered *Antirrhinum* plants are crossed, the F_2 offspring are found to be red, pink and white in the ratio 1:2:1 respectively.

Pink coloration of the petals occurs because both alleles have been expressed in the heterozygote and two pigment systems are present, rather than that of a dominant allele only. Red and white are **codominant alleles**. In genetic diagrams, codominant alleles are represented by a capital letter for the gene, and different superscript capital letters for the two alleles, in recognition of their equal influence (Figure 4.17).

Figure 4.17
Codominance in the garden flower, *Antirrhinum*

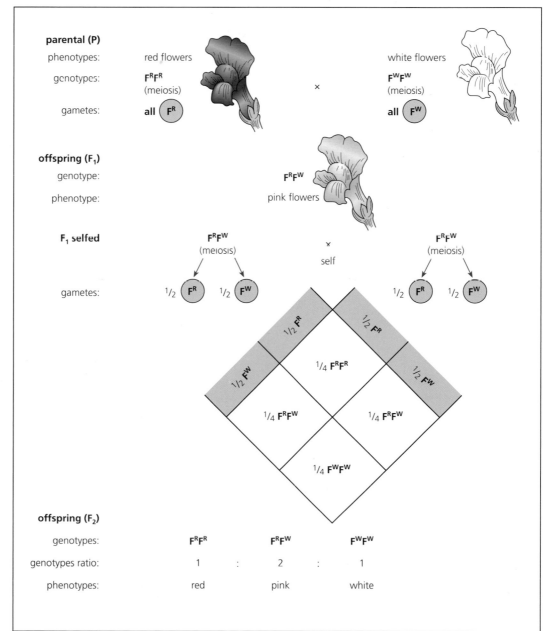

7 **Construct** for yourself (pencil and paper) a monohybrid cross between cattle of a variety that has a gene for coat colour with codominant alleles, for red and white coats. Homozygous parents produce roan offspring (red and white hairs together). **Predict** what offspring you would expect and in what proportions, when a sibling cross (equivalent to selfing in plants) occurs between roan offspring.

More than two alleles exist for a particular locus

The genes introduced so far exist in two forms (two alleles), like the height gene of the garden pea, existing as tall or dwarf alleles. That means that in genetic diagrams we can represent alleles by a single letter (here, **T** or **t**) according to whether they are dominant or recessive.

For simplicity we began by considering inheritance of a gene for which there are just two alleles. However, we now know that not all genes are like this. In fact, most genes have more than two alleles, and these are cases of **multiple alleles**.

With multiple alleles, we choose a single capital letter to represent the locus at which the alleles may occur, and the individual alleles are then represented by an additional single letter (usually capital) in a superscript position (Table 4.1) – as with codominant alleles. An excellent example of multiple alleles is found in those controlling the ABO blood group system of humans. Human blood belongs to one of four groups: A, B, AB or O. Table 4.1 lists the possible phenotypes and the genotypes that may be responsible for each.

Table 4.1 The ABO blood groups – phenotypes and genotypes

Phenotype	Genotypes
A	$I^A I^A$ or $I^A i$
B	$I^B I^B$ or $I^B i$
AB	$I^A I^B$
O	$i^i i^i$

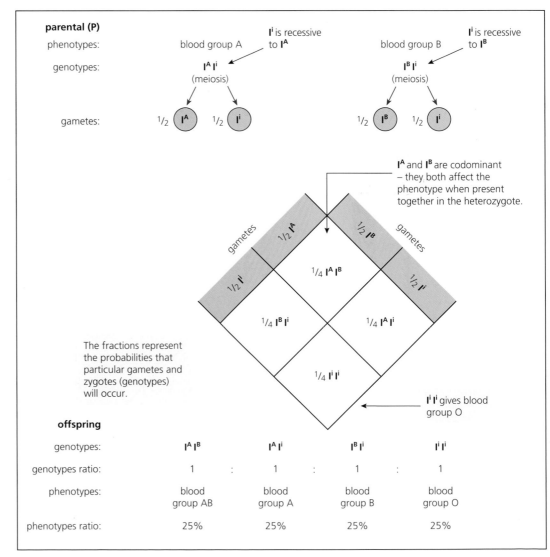

Figure 4.18 Inheritance of blood groupings A, B, AB, and O

So, the ABO blood group system is determined by combinations of alternative alleles. In each individual, only two of the three alleles exist, but they are inherited as if they were alternative alleles of a pair. However, I^A and I^B are codominant alleles and both I^A and I^B are dominant to the recessive I^i. In Figure 4.18 the way the alternative blood groups may be inherited is shown.

8 One busy night in an understaffed maternity unit, four children were born about the same time. Then the babies were muddled up by mistake; it was not certain which child belonged to which family. Fortunately the children had different blood groups: A, B, AB and O.

The parents' blood groups were also known:

Mr and Mrs Jones	A × B	Mr and Mrs Lee	B × O
Mr and Mrs Gerber	O × O	Mr and Mrs Santiago	AB × O

The nurses were able to decide which child belonged to which family. **Deduce** how this was done.

Reviewing the genetic terms learned so far

Table 4.2 lists these essential genetic terms and defines each, succinctly.

Cover the right-hand column with a piece of paper, temporarily, and see if you can define each correctly, in your own words.

Gene	the basic unit of inheritance by which inherited characteristics are transferred from parents to offspring, consisting of a length of DNA on a chromosome
Allele	one alternative form of a gene, occupying a specific position (locus) on a chromosome
Loci	the positions along the chromosomes where genes occur, so alleles of the same gene occupy the same locus (singular)
Genotype	the genetic constitution of an organism
Phenotype	the characteristics displayed by the organism – the way in which the genotype is expressed (appearance of an organism)
Dominant allele	an allele that affects the phenotype of the organism, whether present in the heterozygous or homozygous condition
Recessive allele	an allele that affects the phenotype of the organism only when the dominant allele is absent (in homozygous recessive individuals)
Homozygous	a diploid organism that has inherited the same allele (for any particular gene) from both parents
Heterozygous	a diploid organism that has inherited different alleles from each parent
Test cross	testing a suspected heterozygote by crossing it with a known homozygous recessive
Codominant alleles	pairs of alleles that both affect the phenotype when present in a heterozygote
Carrier	an individual with a recessive allele of a gene that does not affect their phenotype – especially one responsible for a genetic disorder such as colour blindness or haemophilia (page 114)

Table 4.2 Essential genetic terms

Human inheritance investigated by pedigree chart

Studying human inheritance by experimental crosses (with selected parents, sibling crosses, and the production of large numbers of progeny) is out of the question. Instead, we may investigate the pattern of inheritance of a particular characteristic by researching a family pedigree, where appropriate records of the ancestors exist. A human pedigree chart uses a set of rules. These are identified in Figure 4.19.

9 In the human pedigree chart in Figure 4.19 (page 110) **state**:

a who are the female grandchildren of Richard and Judith
b who are Alan's (i) grandparents; (ii) uncles
c how many people in the chart have parents unknown to us
d the names of two offspring who are cousins.

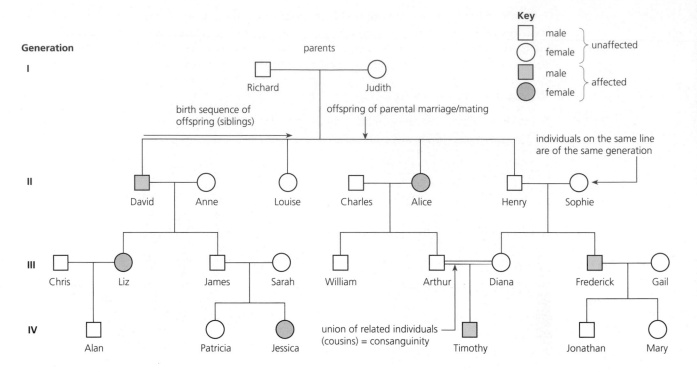

Figure 4.19 An example of a human pedigree chart

We can use a pedigree chart to detect conditions likely to be due to dominant and recessive alleles. In the case of a characteristic due to a dominant allele, the characteristic tends to occur in one or more members of the family in every generation (Figure 4.19). On the other hand, a recessive characteristic is seen infrequently, often skipping many generations.

For example, albinism is a rare inherited condition of humans (and other mammals) in which the individual has a block in the biochemical pathway by which the pigment melanin is formed. Albinos have white hair, very light-coloured skin and pink eyes. Albinism shows a pattern of recessive monohybrid inheritance in humans (Figure 4.20). In the chart shown of a family with albino members, albinism occurs infrequently, skipping two generations altogether.

Figure 4.20 Pedigree chart of a family with albino members

Albino people must be homozygous for the recessive albino allele (**pp**). People with normal skin pigmentation may be homozygous normal (**PP**) or carriers (**Pp**).

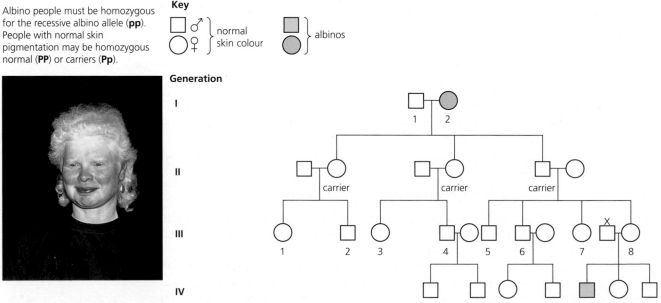

This is a typical family tree for inheritance of a characteristic controlled by a recessive allele.

Brachydactyly is a rare condition of humans in which the fingers are very short. Brachydactyly is due to a mutation in the gene for finger length. Unusually, the mutant allele is dominant, so brachydactyly shows a pattern of dominant monohybrid inheritance among members of a family in which it occurs; that is, it tends to occur in every generation (Figure 4.21). Indeed, the frequencies of brachydactylous and normal handed people are similar to those obtained in a test cross (page 106).

Figure 4.21
Brachydactyly, and pedigree chart of a family with brachydactylous genes

X-ray of bones of hand of normal length

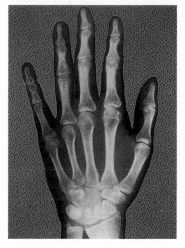

Drawing of brachydactylous hand

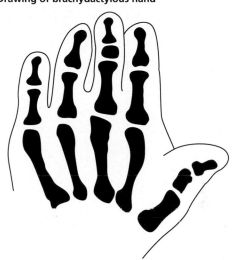

Pedigree chart of family with brachydactylous alleles

10 If a homozygous normal-handed parent (**nn**) were crossed with a heterozygous brachydactylous parent (**Nn**) **calculate** the probability of an offspring with brachydactylous hands, using a Punnett grid. **Construct** a genetic diagram to show your workings.

In **generation I** the parents are assumed to be normal male (**nn**) and brachydactylous female (heterozygous **Nn**), as the ratio of offspring is similar to that of a test cross.

In **each subsequent generation** about half the offspring are brachydactylous (i.e. **Nn** or **NN**) and half are normal (**nn**).

Sex chromosomes and gender

In humans, gender is determined by specific chromosomes known as the **sex chromosomes**. Each of us has one pair of sex chromosomes (either XX or XY chromosomes) along with the 22 other pairs (known as **autosomal chromosomes**).

Egg cells produced by meiosis all carry an X chromosome, but 50% of sperms carry an X chromosome and 50% carry a Y chromosome. At fertilisation, an egg cell may fuse with a sperm carrying an X chromosome leading to a female offspring. Alternatively, the egg cell may fuse with a sperm carrying a Y chromosome, leading to a male offspring. So, the gender of offspring in humans (and all mammals) is determined by the male partner. Also, we would expect equal numbers of male and female offspring to be produced by a breeding population, over time (Figure 4.22).

Figure 4.22 X and Y chromosomes and the determination of sex

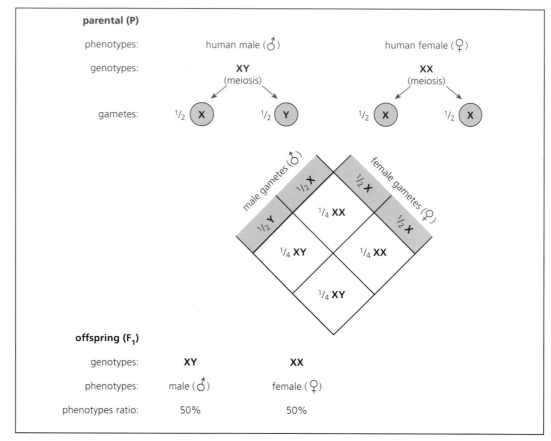

Human X and Y chromosomes and the control of gender

Initially, male and female embryos develop identically in the uterus. At the seventh week of pregnancy, however, a cascade of developmental events is triggered, leading to the growth of male genitalia if a Y chromosome is present in the embryonic cells.

On the Y chromosome is the **prime male-determining gene**. This gene codes for a protein – the **testis-determining factor (TDF)**. TDF functions as a molecular switch; on reaching the embryonic gonad tissues, TDF initiates the production of a relatively low level of testosterone. The effect of this hormone at this stage is to inhibit the development of female genitalia, and to cause the embryonic genital tissues to form testes, scrotum and penis.

In the absence of a Y chromosome, the embryonic gonad tissue forms an ovary. Then, partly under the influence of hormone from the ovary, the female reproductive structures develop.

■ Extension: Non-disjunction and the sex chromosomes

We have noted already that non-disjunction in meiosis results in gametes with more and less than the haploid number of chromosomes (page 98). Table 4.3 identifies cases that occur in the determination of gender, and how frequently they arise.

Table 4.3 Non-disjunction of X and Y chromosomes

Genotype	Condition	Incidence at birth
XO ♀	**Turner's syndrome:** common at conception, but normally fatal (99% naturally aborted); infertile adult	1 in 2500
XXY ♂	**Klinefelter's syndrome:** male with feminine features; often infertile; typically mildly mentally disabled	1 in 1000
XXX ♀	normal individual	1 in 1000
XYY ♂	almost normal individual	1 in 1000

Pairing of X and Y chromosomes in meiosis

We know that homologous chromosomes pair up early in meiosis (Figure 4.5, page 95). Pairing is an essential step in the mechanism of meiosis. However, only a very small part of the X and Y chromosomes of humans have complementary alleles and can pair up during meiosis. The bulk of the X and Y chromosomes contain genes that have no corresponding alleles on the other (Figure 4.23).

> The short Y chromosome carries genes specific for male sex determination and sperm production, including the gene that codes for TDF, which switches development of embryonic gonad tissue to testes early in embryonic development.

> The X chromosome carries an assortment of genes, very few of which are concerned with sex determination.

We shall examine the effects of some of the alleles of these genes next.

Figure 4.23 The pairing of X and Y chromosomes in meiosis

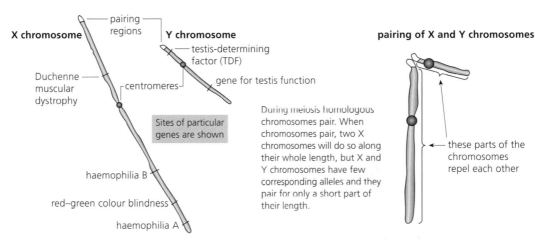

Sex linkage

Genes present on the sex chromosomes are inherited with the sex of the individual. They are said to be sex-linked characteristics.

> Sex linkage is a special case of linkage occurring when a gene is located on a sex chromosome (usually the X chromosome).

The inheritance of these sex-linked genes is different from the inheritance of genes on the autosomal chromosomes. This is because the X chromosome is much longer than the Y chromosome (because many of the genes on the X chromosome are absent from the Y chromosome). In a male (XY), an allele present on the X chromosome is most likely to be on its own and will be apparent in the phenotype *even if it is recessive*.

Meanwhile, in a female, a single recessive gene is often masked by a dominant allele on the other X chromosome, and in these cases the recessive allele is not expressed. A human female can be homozygous or heterozygous with respect to sex-linked characteristics whereas males will have only one allele.

An individual with a recessive allele of a gene that does not have an effect on their phenotype (i.e. is heterozygous for that allele) is known as a **carrier**. They carry the allele but it is not expressed. So, female carriers are heterozygous for sex-linked recessive characteristics. Of course, the unpaired alleles of the Y chromosome are all expressed in the male. However, the alleles on the (short) Y chromosome are mostly concerned with male structures and male functions.

Examples of recessive conditions controlled by genes on the X chromosome are: Duchenne muscular dystrophy, red–green colour blindness, and haemophilia. In the case of these **genetically controlled diseases**, if a single recessive allele is present in a male human, the disease-triggering allele will be expressed. However, a female must be homozygous recessive for a sex-linked characteristic for the allele to be expressed.

Red–green colour blindness

A red–green colour blind person sees green, yellow, orange and red as all the same colour. The condition afflicts about 8% of males, but only 0.4% of females in the human population. This is because a female with normal colour vision may by homozygous for the normal colour vision allele ($X^B X^B$) or she may be heterozygous for normal colour vision ($X^B X^b$). For a female to be red–green colour blind, she must be homozygous recessive for this allele ($X^b X^b$), and this occurs extremely rarely. On the other hand a male with a single recessive allele for red–green colour vision ($X^b Y$) will be affected.

The inheritance of red–green colour blindness is illustrated in Figure 4.24. It is helpful for those who are red–green colour blind to recognise their inherited condition. Red–green colour blindness is detected by the use of multicoloured test cards.

Figure 4.24 Detection and inheritance of red–green colour blindness

Colour blindness is detected by multicoloured test cards. A mosaic of dots is arranged on the cards so that those with normal vision see a pattern that is not visible to those with colour blindness.

11 State how the genetic constitution of a female who is red–green colour blind is represented. **Explain** why it is impossible to have a 'carrier' male.

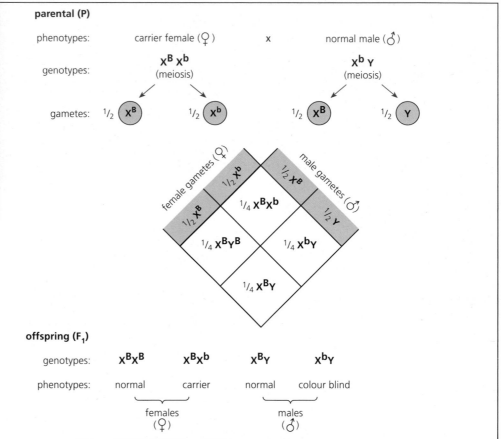

Haemophilia

If a break occurs in the circulatory system of a mammal, there is a risk of uncontrolled bleeding. This is normally overcome by the blood clotting mechanism that causes any gap to be plugged (page 349). Haemophilia is a rare, genetically determined, condition in which the blood will not clot normally. The result is frequent, excessive bleeding.

There are two forms of haemophilia, known as haemophilia A and haemophilia B. They are due to a failure to produce adequate amounts of particular blood proteins essential to the complex blood clotting mechanism. Today, haemophilia is effectively treated by the administration of the clotting factor the patient lacks.

Haemophilia is a sex-linked condition because the genes controlling production of the blood proteins concerned are located on the X chromosome. Haemophilia is caused by a recessive allele. As a result, haemophilia is largely a disease of the male since a single X chromosome carrying the defective allele ($X^h Y$) will result in disease. For a female to have the disease, she must be homozygous for the recessive gene ($X^h X^h$), but this condition is usually fatal in the uterus, typically resulting in a natural abortion.

A female with only one X chromosome with the recessive allele ($X^H X^h$) is described as a carrier. She has normal blood clotting. When a carrier is partnered by a normal male, there is a 50% chance of the daughters being carriers and a 50% chance of the sons having haemophilia (Figure 4.25).

Figure 4.25 The inheritance of haemophilia

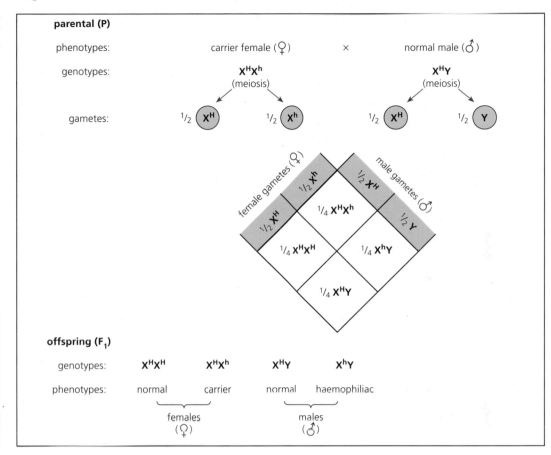

12 Haemophilia results from a sex-linked gene. The disease is most common in males, but the haemophilia allele is on the X chromosome. **Explain** this apparent anomaly.

■ *Examination questions – a selection*

Questions 1–4 are taken from past IB Diploma biology papers.

Q1 Which response summarises meiosis?

	Pairing of chromosomes	Number of divisions	Result
A	no	one	two diploid cells
B	no	two	four diploid cells
C	yes	one	two haploid cells
D	yes	two	four haploid cells

Higher Level Paper 1, May 02, Q8

Q2 The diagram below shows the pedigree of a family with red–green colour blindness, a sex-linked condition.

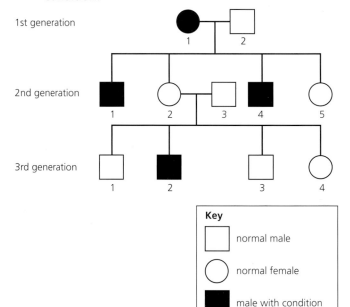

1st generation

2nd generation

3rd generation

Key

☐ normal male

○ normal female

■ male with condition

● female with condition

a Define the term *sex linkage*. (1)
b Deduce, with a reason, whether the allele producing the condition is dominant or recessive. (2)
c i Determine all the possible genotypes of the individual (2nd generation-1) using appropriate symbols. (1)
  ii Determine all the possible genotypes of the individual (3rd generation-4) using appropriate symbols. (1)

Standard Level Paper 2, May 03, Q2

Q3 What is the genetic cross called between an individual of unknown genotype and an individual who is homozygous recessive for a particular trait?
A test cross
B hybrid cross
C dihybrid cross
D F_1 cross

Higher Level Paper 1, May 06, Q11

Q4 When red shorthorn cattle are crossed with white shorthorn cattle, the offspring are roan, a colour that has both red and white hairs. What does this cross illustrate?
A codominance
B multiple alleles
C sex linkage
D mutation

Standard Level Paper 1, May 03, Q15

Questions 5 and 6 cover other syllabus issues in this chapter.

Q5 Mendel carried out a breeding experiment with garden pea plants in which pure-breeding pea plants grown from seeds with a smooth coat were crossed with plants grown from seeds with a wrinkled coat. All the seeds produced (called the F_1 generation) were found to have a smooth coat. When plants were grown from these seeds and allowed to self-pollinate, the second generation of seeds (the F_2 generation) included both smooth and wrinkled seeds in the ratio of 3:1.
a In Mendel's explanation of his results he used the term 'hereditary factor'. Identify our term for 'factors' and state where in the cell they occur. (2)
b The parent plants have diploid cells, while the gametes (sex cells) are haploid. Define what we mean by *haploid* and *diploid*. (4)
c By reference to the above experiment, define the following terms and give an example of each:
  i *homozygous* and *heterozygous* (4)
  ii *dominant* and *recessive* (4)
  iii *genotype* and *phenotype*. (4)
d Using appropriate symbols for the alleles for smooth and wrinkled coat, construct a genetic diagram (including a Punnett grid) to show the behaviour of the alleles in this experiment. (6)

Q6 a Define the term *mutation*. (2)
b By means of specific examples, explain the difference between chromosome mutation and gene mutation. (4)

Genetic engineering and biotechnology

STARTING POINTS

- Chromosomes are a linear sequence of **genes**. They consist of **a length of DNA double helix**, hundreds or thousands of base pairs long.
- The sequence of bases in nucleic acid forms the **genetic code**. The code dictates the order in which specific amino acids are assembled and combined to make **proteins**.
- The **code is universal** to prokaryotes and eukaryotes.
- Many of the proteins coded for by genes and produced in cells function as **enzymes**. Reactions of metabolism are catalysed by specific enzymes.
- **Bacteria are prokaryotes** and have a distinctive cell structure. They lack chromosomes enclosed in a nucleus, but have a **nucleoid** – a single, circular chromosome of DNA in the cytoplasm, attached to the plasma membrane.

The practical skill of animal and plant breeding made possible the first great revolution in human history. This is known as the **Neolithic Revolution**. It commenced after the last Ice Age, about 10 000 years ago. At this time, groups of *Homo sapiens* stopped their nomadic existence and became farmers in settled communities.

The greatest achievement of these Neolithic (new stone age) peoples was the breeding of **domesticated animals** and the cultivation of many **crop plants**, all from the wild stock around them. This technology, now called **artificial selection**, was developed without theoretical knowledge of heredity. Many of the plant and animal species of modern farming were first bred at this time.

Today a new type of genetic modification is also in use. Genes from one organism are transferred to the set of genes (the genome) of another, unrelated organism. The process is called recombinant DNA technology or **genetic engineering**. The outcomes are new varieties of organisms, mostly but not exclusively of microorganisms such as bacteria. Genetic material can be transferred because the **genetic code is universal** (page 251). This means that any particular triplet code represents the same amino acid whether it is being read in a bacterium, cyanobacterium, green plant, fungus or animal. Thus the amino acid sequence of the protein coded for by the gene is the same wherever that gene occurs or is placed.

Gene technology has important applications in, for example, the pharmaceuticals industry, medicine, agriculture, horticulture and forensic science. It is a branch of **biotechnology** – the industrial and commercial application of biology. Another aspect of biotechnology is the industrial exploitation of enzymes (page 61).

1 Define the terms 'genome' and 'gene'.

Genetic engineering and its applications 4.4.1–4.4.13

The steps of genetic engineering

The five steps of genetic engineering are discussed, each in turn, below.

Isolating the gene from the source genome

The long double strand of DNA of a chromosome is functionally divided into genes, the units of inheritance. A chromosome holds a linear sequence of very many genes. For example, there is an average of 2200 genes on each human chromosome. Genes are variable in their length, but usually consist of hundreds or thousands of bases. Each gene codes for a particular protein. For genetic engineering to take place, individual genes may have to be isolated (and eventually identified).

How can one gene be found and isolated among so many?

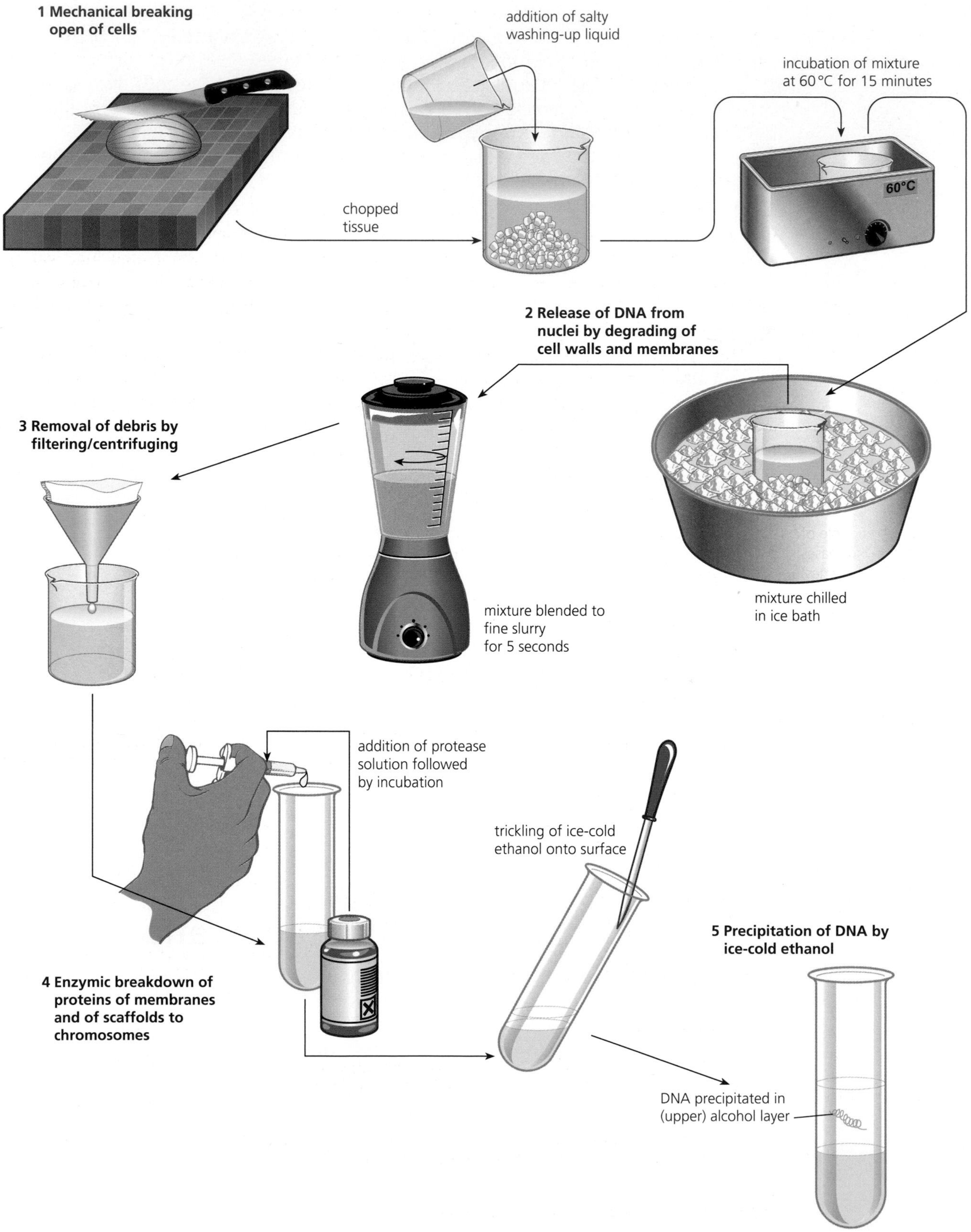

Figure 5.1 The extraction of DNA – the procedure or protocol

1 Mechanical breaking open of cells

addition of salty washing-up liquid

chopped tissue

incubation of mixture at 60 °C for 15 minutes

60°C

2 Release of DNA from nuclei by degrading of cell walls and membranes

3 Removal of debris by filtering/centrifuging

mixture blended to fine slurry for 5 seconds

mixture chilled in ice bath

addition of protease solution followed by incubation

trickling of ice-cold ethanol onto surface

4 Enzymic breakdown of proteins of membranes and of scaffolds to chromosomes

5 Precipitation of DNA by ice-cold ethanol

DNA precipitated in (upper) alcohol layer

DNA may be extracted from tissue samples by mechanically breaking up the cells, filtering off the debris, and breaking down cell membranes by treatment with detergents. After this, the protein framework of the chromosomes, often called a scaffold, is removed by incubation with a protein-digesting enzyme (protease). As a result the DNA is now present as long naked threads and can be isolated from the mixture of chemicals by precipitation with ethanol; it is thus 'cleaned' (Figure 5.1). The DNA strands are then re-suspended in aqueous, pH-buffered medium and are ready for 'slicing' into fragments.

> 2 **State** the products of digestion of proteins by protease enzymes.

Cutting up of DNA

Genetic engineering really began with the discovery of restriction endonucleases (**restriction enzymes**). These enzymes occur naturally in bacteria. Here they protect against the activity of viruses by cutting up viral DNA that enters the bacterium, and thereby completely inactivating it. Viral DNA might otherwise take over the host cell. The viruses that specifically parasitise bacteria have a special name. They are called bacteriophage or phage. Restriction enzymes were so named because they *restrict* the multiplication of phage viruses.

Many different restriction enzymes have been discovered and purified, and today they are used widely in genetic engineering experiments. Restriction enzymes cut at particular base sequences, and are of two types, forming either **blunt ends** or **sticky ends** to the cut fragments. Sticky ends are single-stranded extensions formed in the double-stranded DNA after 'digestion' with a restriction enzyme that cuts in a staggered fashion (Figure 5.2).

In experiments, a selected restriction enzyme is used to cut the DNA extracted from cells of an organism known to carry a required gene.

Figure 5.2 The role of restriction endonucleases (restriction enzymes)

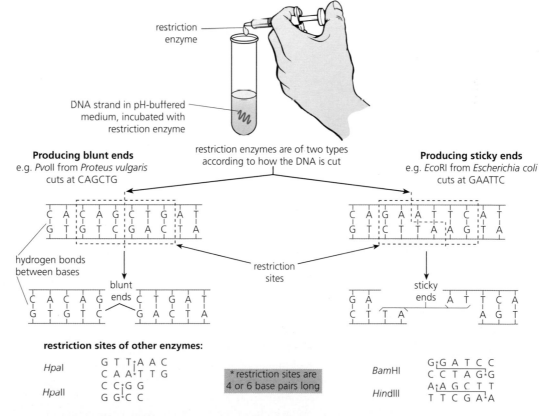

Restriction enzymes are named after the microorganisms they are found in. Roman numbers are added to distinguish different enzymes from the same microorganism.

> 3 **Outline** why we describe DNA as double stranded.

Isolating DNA fragments – electrophoresis

Electrophoresis is a process used to separate particles, including biologically important molecules such as DNA, RNA, proteins and amino acids. Electrophoresis is typically carried out on an agarose gel (a very pure form of agar) or on polyacrylamide gel (PAG). Both these substances contain tiny pores which allow them to act like a **molecular sieve**. Small particles can move quite quickly through these gels whereas larger molecules move much more slowly.

Biological molecules separated by electrophoresis also carry an **electrical charge**. In the case of DNA, it is the phosphate groups in DNA fragments that give them a net negative charge. Consequently, when these molecules are placed in an electric field they migrate towards the positive pole.

So, in electrophoresis, separation occurs according to the size of the molecule and the charge carried. This is the double principle of electrophoretic separations. Separation of DNA fragments produced by the actions of restriction enzyme is shown in Figure 5.3.

Figure 5.3
Electrophoretic separation
of DNA fragments

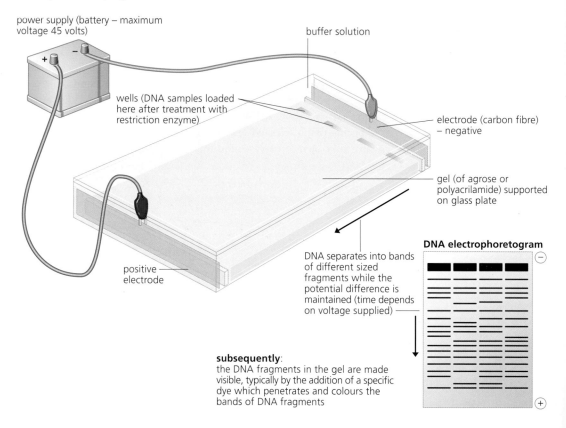

electrophoresis in progress

power supply (battery – maximum voltage 45 volts)

buffer solution

wells (DNA samples loaded here after treatment with restriction enzyme)

electrode (carbon fibre) – negative

gel (of agrose or polyacrilamide) supported on glass plate

positive electrode

DNA separates into bands of different sized fragments while the potential difference is maintained (time depends on voltage supplied)

DNA electrophoretogram

subsequently:
the DNA fragments in the gel are made visible, typically by the addition of a specific dye which penetrates and colours the bands of DNA fragments

Vectors for cloning

Electrophoresis is used to sort the DNA fragments by size. The required gene will occur in fragments of a particular size (Figure 5.4). The gene fragment required can be identified eventually, after it has been copied (a process known as **cloning**). For these steps to be carried out, the gene has to be added to a **vector** by which it is transferred to a receiving organism. These steps and techniques of genetic engineering are outlined next.

In biology, a vector is an agent that transports between one organism and another. In genetic engineering, a vector is 'carrier DNA' into which a DNA fragment containing a particular gene can be inserted, and which is then used to introduce the gene into a new organism. One such vector is commonly found in bacteria.

A bacterium such as *E. coli* (page 16) contains two types of genetic material. One is the long, double strand of DNA in the form of a ring, which we can think of as a single, circular chromosome. This is called the **nucleoid**.

Figure 5.4 Locating the required gene

Restriction endonuclease enzyme cuts DNA strands into fragments of differing lengths at the restriction sites. One fragment will contain the **required gene.**

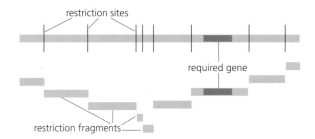

Figure 5.5 Plasmids as vectors

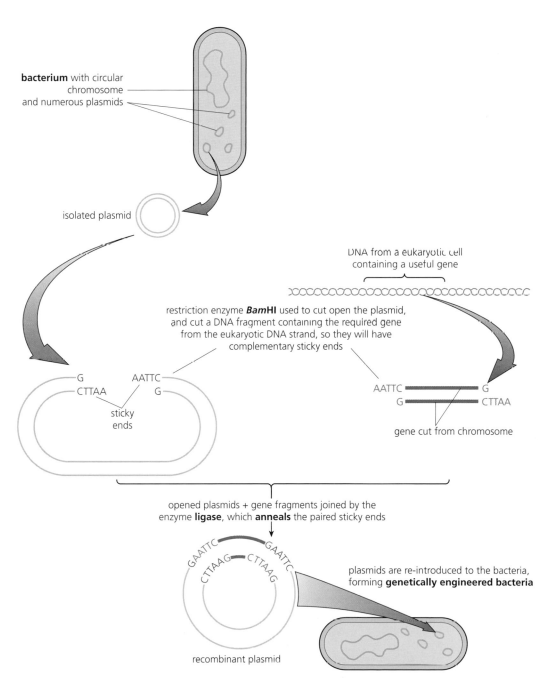

The other type of DNA in bacteria takes the form of numerous smaller rings, called **plasmids** (Figure 5.5). Plasmids are easily isolated from a bacterium and can be re-introduced to a bacterial cell, too. They are therefore extremely useful as vectors. In the bacterium, plasmids copy themselves (replicate) independently of the chromosome, so any gene added to a plasmid is also copied many times. This is how the isolated gene is cloned, once inside a bacterial cell.

Using plasmids as vectors

To prepare isolated plasmids as vectors, a restriction enzyme that forms sticky ends is used to cut open the plasmid. The *same* restriction enzyme is used to cut out the gene from longer strands of DNA, previously separated by electrophoresis. In this way, both will carry complementary sticky ends. Then the opened plasmids and the gene-containing fragments may be combined together by a second enzyme, **ligase**.

Ligase occurs naturally in the nuclei of organisms where it will repair DNA damaged in replication. Ligase catalyses the joining of sugar–phosphate backbones of adjacent DNA strands (a process called **annealing**), after their sticky ends have aligned by complementary base pairing (Figure 5.6).

Figure 5.6 The action of ligase

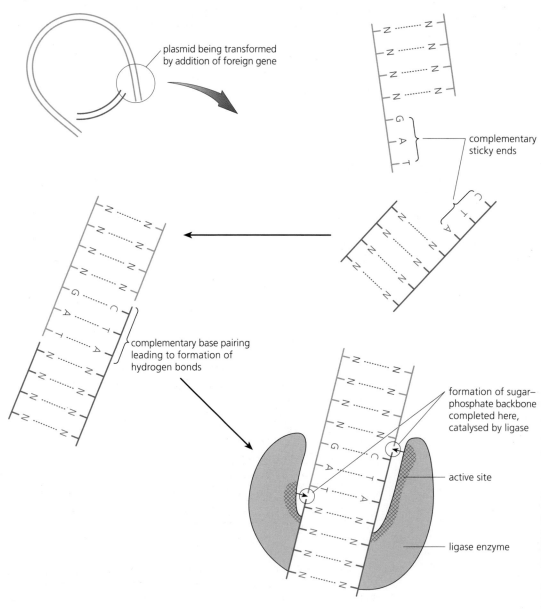

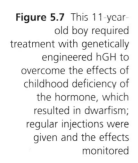

4 State the property of DNA that makes complementary sticky ends hold together.

Finally, genetically engineered plasmids are re-introduced to the bacterium. This may occur by mixing bacterial cells and engineered plasmids in the presence of a salt (calcium chloride) which makes the bacterial cell walls especially permeable to plasmids. Some of the recombinant plasmids enter the cytoplasm of the bacteria. Because the genetic code is universal, the bacterium can translate the code and produce the gene's protein product.

Current uses of genetically modified organisms

Genetically modified (GM) bacteria, animals and plants all have roles in the world we live in today.

The production of transformed bacteria

One of the earliest applications of the techniques of genetic engineering was in the production of GM bacteria containing human genes, or genes taken from other eukaryotes. The manufacture of human growth hormone by the pharmaceutical industry is a good example.

Human growth hormone (hGH), also known as somatostatin, is one of a group of hormones normally synthesised in the pituitary gland and circulated around the body in the blood stream. It stimulates growth of body cells, particularly those of the skeleton and skeletal muscles. It works by enhancing cell protein synthesis, and the uptake of amino acids by the plasma membrane, from the plasma and tissue fluid. Also, it enhances conversion of glycogen to glucose in the liver, so tending to cause blood sugar level to rise.

Failure to secrete sufficient hGH in children and young people in their growth years leads to a condition called **pituitary dwarfism**. This can be overcome by a series of injections of hGH (Figure 5.7). It proved extremely difficult to extract a significant quantity of the equivalent hormone from, for example, sheep – and such hormone was largely not effective in humans.

Figure 5.7 This 11-year-old boy required treatment with genetically engineered hGH to overcome the effects of childhood deficiency of the hormone, which resulted in dwarfism; regular injections were given and the effects monitored

Hence the importance of a supply of hGH from GM bacteria.

This hormone is produced from cultures of the bacterium *E. coli* that have been engineered to carry the gene for hGH. This is a mutant form of *E. coli* – one that requires special laboratory conditions to survive at all. This is an obvious **safety precaution**, since otherwise genetically engineered bacteria might escape and exchange genes with a gut population of *E. coli*, with possibly unpredictable consequences.

Interestingly, hGH is a short protein (a polypeptide, in this case), only 14 amino acid residues in length. Consequently, it was found easier to manufacture an artificial gene coding for the hormone, than to isolate the real gene from human chromosomes. The artificial gene was inserted into plasmids and introduced into host bacteria. Transformed bacteria with the hGH gene 'switched on' are cultured in large vats called fermenters, where they produce hGH polypeptide in significant quantities. This is extracted and purified from the culture medium.

5 Calculate the *minimum* number of nucleotides an artificial gene (a polynucleotide) coding for hGH would need in length, given that in addition to codons for 14 amino acids, 'stop' and 'start' codons are also required, and the plasmid vector has to be 'cut open' with *Eco*RI restriction enzyme (Figure 5.2) to create sticky ends.

In eukaryotes

Manipulating genes in eukaryotes is a more difficult process than in prokaryotes. There are several reasons for this, including the following.

- Plasmids, the most useful vehicle for moving genes, do not occur in eukaryotes (except in yeasts) and, if introduced, do not always survive there to be replicated.
- Eukaryotes are diploid organisms, so two forms (alleles) for every gene are required to be engineered into the nucleus. By comparison, prokaryotes have a single, circular 'chromosome', so only one copy of the gene has to be engineered into their chromosome.

Producing transgenic animals

Transgenic organisms have genetic material introduced artificially from another organism. Despite the difficulties of engineering eukaryotic cells, several varieties of transgenic animal have been produced. For example, transgenic sheep have been successfully engineered to produce in their milk rare and expensive human proteins that may be useful as medicines.

One example is the production of a special human blood protein, known as AAT. Production of **AAT protein** in our bodies enables us to **maintain lung elasticity** which is essential in breathing movements. Patients with a rare genetic disease are unable to manufacture AAT protein at all, and they develop emphysema (destruction of the walls of the air sacs, so that the lungs remain full of air during expiration).

The chemical industry is unable to manufacture AAT protein in the laboratory on a practical scale. However, the human gene for AAT protein production has been identified and isolated, and it has been cloned into sheep, together with a promoter gene (a sheep's milk protein promoter) attached to it. Consequently the sheep's mammary glands produce the human protein and secrete it in their milk, during lactations (Figure 5.8). Thus, human AAT protein is made available for use with patients.

Another product important to medicine is the human blood clotting factor known as factor IX, now obtained from the milk of GM sheep for use with patients whose bodies are unable to synthesise this protein.

Producing transgenic plants

Many commercially valuable plant species have been genetically engineered and field trials undertaken. The crops most involved are cotton, tobacco, oilseed rape, maize, potatoes, soya and tomatoes. The improvements achieved include:

- herbicide resistance in crop plants, so that application of weed killer will remove weeds without harm to the crop (Figure 5.10, page 128);
- rice varieties that contain β carotene (vitamin A precursor);
- tomato varieties able to ripen on the plant and develop full flavour, without rotting quickly when picked and marketed as red fruit (traditionally, tomatoes are picked green and induced to ripen but in this state they may lack flavour);
- resistance to insect pests – crop plant tissue contains a naturally occurring insecticide which is harmless to other animal species;
- oilseed rape varieties that make and store commercially useful oils;
- thale cress (*Arabidopsis thaliana*), engineered as a cheap, renewable source of the biodegradable plastic called polyhydrobutyrate (most plastics come from petrochemicals and are slow to degrade; reserves of petrochemicals are limited).

Transgenic flowering plants may be formed using tumour-forming *Agrobacterium*. This soil-inhabiting bacterium sometimes invades broad-leaved plants at the junction of stem and root, forming a huge growth called a tumour or crown gall. The gene for tumour formation occurs naturally in a plasmid in the bacterium, known as a Ti plasmid. Useful genes may be added to the Ti plasmid, using restriction enzyme and ligase, and the recombinant plasmid placed back into *Agrobacterium*. A host crop plant is then infected by the modified bacterium. The gall tissue that results may be cultured into independent plants, all of which also carry the useful gene. All the plants will make the particular useful gene product that has been introduced (Figure 5.9).

6 **Explain** why a gene that is inserted into the nucleus of a fertilised egg cell is also passed to the progeny of the animal that forms from the zygote.

7 **Explain** why plants formed from the gall tissue will contain the recombinant gene that has been added to the Ti plasmid.

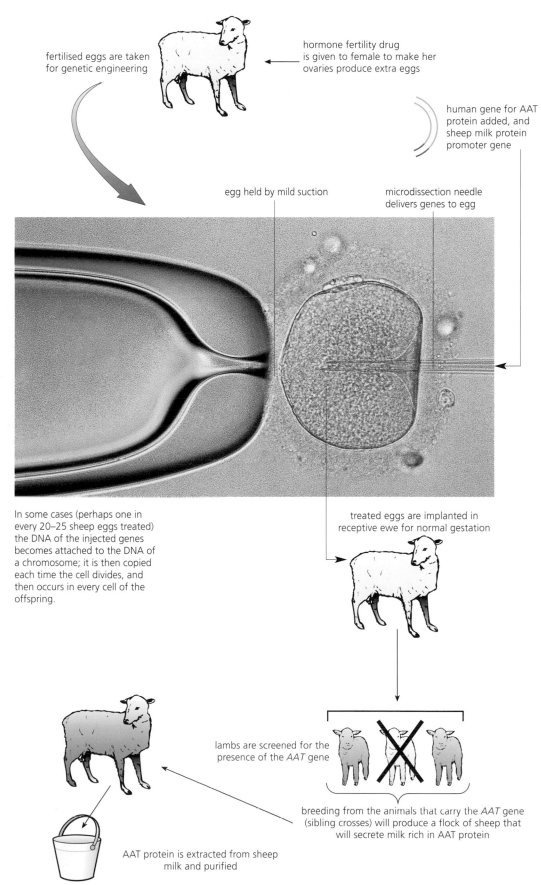

Figure 5.8 The cloning of transgenic sheep to secrete human AAT protein

hormone fertility drug is given to female to make her ovaries produce extra eggs

fertilised eggs are taken for genetic engineering

human gene for AAT protein added, and sheep milk protein promoter gene

egg held by mild suction

microdissection needle delivers genes to egg

In some cases (perhaps one in every 20–25 sheep eggs treated) the DNA of the injected genes becomes attached to the DNA of a chromosome; it is then copied each time the cell divides, and then occurs in every cell of the offspring.

treated eggs are implanted in receptive ewe for normal gestation

lambs are screened for the presence of the *AAT* gene

breeding from the animals that carry the *AAT* gene (sibling crosses) will produce a flock of sheep that will secrete milk rich in AAT protein

AAT protein is extracted from sheep milk and purified

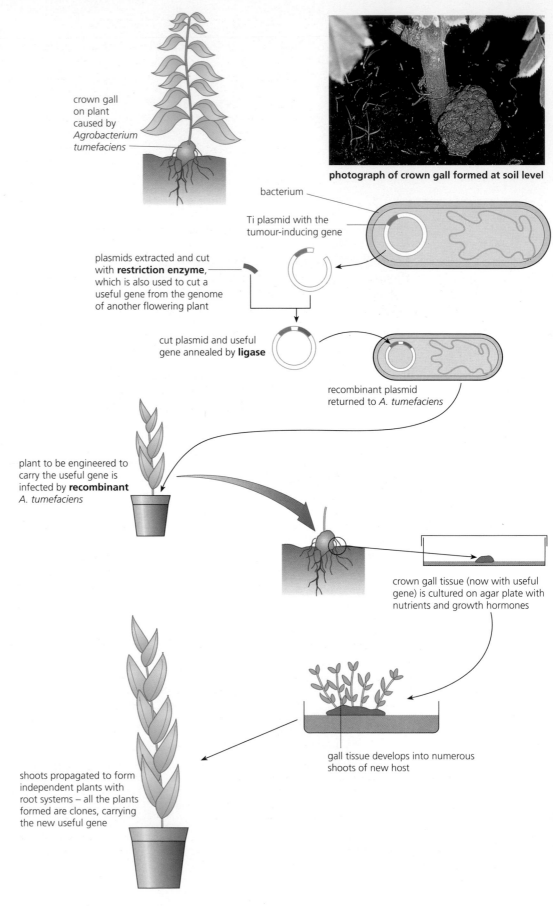

Figure 5.9 Transgenic plants via the Ti plasmid of *Agrobacterium*

crown gall on plant caused by *Agrobacterium tumefaciens*

photograph of crown gall formed at soil level

bacterium

Ti plasmid with the tumour-inducing gene

plasmids extracted and cut with **restriction enzyme**, which is also used to cut a useful gene from the genome of another flowering plant

cut plasmid and useful gene annealed by **ligase**

recombinant plasmid returned to *A. tumefaciens*

plant to be engineered to carry the useful gene is infected by **recombinant** *A. tumefaciens*

crown gall tissue (now with useful gene) is cultured on agar plate with nutrients and growth hormones

gall tissue develops into numerous shoots of new host

shoots propagated to form independent plants with root systems – all the plants formed are clones, carrying the new useful gene

Issues raised by genetic engineering

There are many examples of genetic modification of organisms that are beneficial. However, geneticists are really producing new organisms when genes are transferred. Consequently, this work is potentially a source of hazards and it certainly generates concerns. These include the following.

- Will a gene, added to a genome, function in an unforeseen manner – perhaps, for example, triggering some disease in the recipient?
- Might an introduced gene for resistance to adverse conditions get transferred from a crop plant or farm animal into a weed species or to some predator?
- Is it possible that a harmless organism such as the human gut bacterium *E. coli* might, with recombinant DNA technology, be transformed into a harmful pathogen that escapes the laboratory and infects the population?
- Is there an important overriding principle that humans should not 'change nature' in a deliberate way?
- Genetic engineering is a costly technology, mostly beneficial to the health and life expectancy of people of developed nations. If the funds were made available for more basic problems of housing, health and nutrition in less developed countries instead, vastly more humans would benefit immediately.

An evaluation of the potential benefits and possible harmful effects of genetic modification of plants is presented in the following case study (Table 5.1 and Figure 5.10).

Case study: Consider the production of herbicide-tolerant crops, such as sugar beet modified to be tolerant of glyphosate herbicide applications. This herbicide normally kills plants it comes in contact with, but is inactivated in a 'tolerant' plant (Figure 5.10).

Benefits	Dangers
Use of herbicide eradicates weeds around sugar beet crops, where loss of yield due to competition with weeds is very high.	Fewer weed species on farmland, and longer periods without weeds growing, breaks the wildlife food chain.
Glyphosate herbicide is transported all around the weed plant, killing even the largest weeds with extensive roots.	Selection of a glyphosate-resistant crop plant ties the grower to one particular herbicide product – choice is lost.
Glyphosate inhibits an enzyme for the production of essential amino acids in plants. This enzyme is absent from animals, so glyphosate has very low toxicity.	Will GM plant material, when consumed by humans, release novel toxins or otherwise adversely affect enzyme systems in the human digestive system?
An average of five sprays of herbicides are applied to sugar beet in conventional cultivation, whereas with GM sugar beet a maximum of three spays (and normally only one or two) are needed because of the greater activity of glyphosate.	Genetically engineered genes are vectored in plasmids containing an antibiotic-resistant gene – to facilitate GM processes in the lab. This latter gene might be accidentally transferred to human gut bacteria, via food eaten.
Cereals normally precede spring-sown sugar beet. Cereal stubble is an important source of food for bird life in autumn and winter. With glyphosate herbicide applied to GM beet being so effective, there is no need for weed control in stubble the preceding autumn – so wild birds' food sources are available for longer.	'Superweeds' may develop by cross-pollination between herbicide-tolerant crop plants and compatible weed species (fat-hen, sea beet and weed beet are naturally occurring near relatives of sugar beet). Superweeds would be difficult to eradicate from crops.
Glyphosate herbicide provides good weed control, allowing cultivation by discs or tines (conservation tillage) rather than by ploughing. These systems have less harmful effects on soil organisms, and increase moisture, improve soil structure, and reduce tillage costs	There is a possibility of cross-pollination between GM crops and conventional and organic crops. The maintenance of sufficient distance or the devising of effective barriers to prevent or reduce pollen transfers between crops may be difficult to achieve.
Glyphosate herbicide is applied as large droplets from coarse nozzles, rather than as a fine mist of tiny droplets that are prone to drift onto surrounding habitats.	If glyphosate herbicide droplets do reach hedgerow plants (or further), their size and chemical activity in plants means they are more likely to do damage.

Table 5.1 Benefits from and dangers of GM herbicide tolerance in a crop plant such as sugar beet

Figure 5.10 Herbicide-tolerant sugar beet and the action of glyphosate

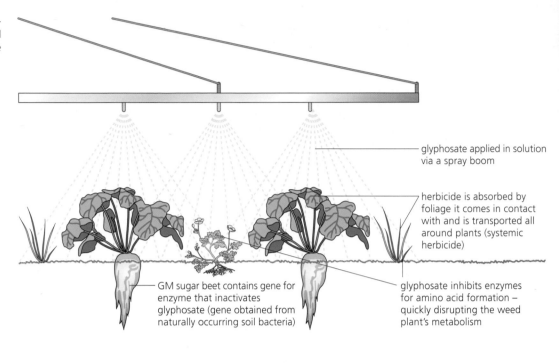

glyphosate applied in solution via a spray boom

herbicide is absorbed by foliage it comes in contact with and is transported all around plants (systemic herbicide)

GM sugar beet contains gene for enzyme that inactivates glyphosate (gene obtained from naturally occurring soil bacteria)

glyphosate inhibits enzymes for amino acid formation – quickly disrupting the weed plant's metabolism

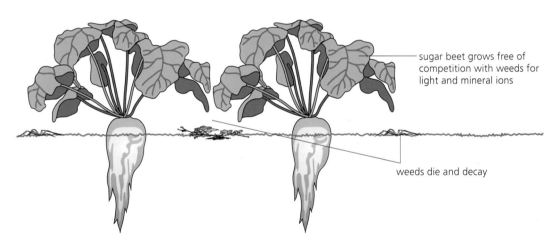

sugar beet grows free of competition with weeds for light and mineral ions

weeds die and decay

8 **Suggest** what advantage would result from the eventual transfer of genes for nitrogen fixation from nodules in leguminous plants to cereals such as wheat.

TOK Link

'Frankenstein foods!' Occasional articles in the press make strong criticisms of genetic modification of food organisms, sometimes with alarmist headlines. Select such an article and prepare the following to use in a discussion with your peers:

1 a concise summary of the criticisms made, avoiding extremist language or unnecessary exaggeration

2 a list of balancing arguments in favour of genetic modification of food organisms

3 a concise statement of your own view on this issue.

DNA profiling

DNA profiling exploits the techniques of genetic engineering to identify a person or organism from a sample of their DNA. The DNA of our chromosomes, which is unique, includes that of our genes.

Actually, the bulk of our DNA does not code for proteins. In these regions, short sequences of bases are repeated many times. While some of these sequences are scattered throughout the length of the DNA molecule, many are joined together in major clusters. It is these major lengths of the non-coding, 'nonsense' DNA, often known as **satellite DNA**, that are used in genetic profiling. Between 10% and 25% of our total DNA is made up of short sequences of 5–10 nucleotides (**microsatellites**) repeated thousands of times. We inherit a distinctive combination of these apparently non-functional repeat regions, half from our mother and half from our father. Consequently, each of us has a unique sequence of nucleotides in our DNA (except for identical twins, who share the same pattern).

To produce a genetic 'fingerprint' a sample of DNA is cut with a restriction enzyme which recognises specific sequences in the DNA. Electrophoresis (Figure 5.3, page 120) is used to separate pieces according to length and size, and the result is a pattern of bands similar to a bar code (Figure 5.11). The steps to produce a DNA fingerprint are as follows.

1 A sample of cells is obtained from blood, semen, hair root, or body tissues, and the DNA is extracted. Where a tiny quantity of DNA is all that can be recovered, this is precisely copied (polymerase chain reaction, below) to obtain sufficient DNA to analyse.
2 The DNA is cut into small, double-stranded fragments using a particular restriction enzyme chosen because it 'cuts' close to, but not within, the satellite DNA.
3 The resulting DNA fragments are of varying lengths, and are separated by gel electrophoresis into bands (invisible, at this stage).
4 The gel is treated to split DNA into single strands, and then a copy is transferred to a membrane.
5 Selected, radioactively labelled DNA probes are added to the membrane to bind to particular bands of DNA, and then the excess probes are washed away.
6 The membrane is now overlaid with X-ray film which becomes selectively fogged by emission from the retained labelled probes.
7 The X-ray film is developed, showing up the positions of the bands (fragments) to which probes have attached. The result is a profile with the appearance of a bar code.

DNA profiling has applications in forensic investigations

DNA profiles are produced from samples taken from serious crime scenes, both from victims and suspects, as well as from others who have certainly not been involved in the crime, as a control. The greatest care has to be taken to ensure the authenticity of the sample. There must be no possibility of contamination if the outcome of subsequent testing is to be meaningful. DNA profiling helps eliminate innocent suspects, and to identify a person or people who may be responsible or related. It cannot prove with absolute certainty anyone's guilt or connection. An example is shown in Figure 5.11.

Crimes such as suspected murder and burglaries may be solved in cases where biological specimens are left at the scene of the crime, such as a few hair roots or a tiny drop of blood. Also, specimens may be collected from people suspected of being present at the crime. DNA fingerprinting may also help forensic scientists identify corpses otherwise too decomposed for recognition, or where only parts of the body remain, as may occur after bomb blasts or other violent incidents, including natural disasters.

Note: There are various circumstances where the amount of DNA available or which can be recovered (such as at a crime scene) is very small indeed – apparently too little for analysis, in fact. It is now possible to submit such minute samples to a process known as the **polymerase chain reaction (PCR)** in which the DNA is replicated in an entirely automated process, *in vitro*, to produce a large amount of the sequence. A single molecule is sufficient as the starting material, should this be all that is available. The product is exact copies in quantities sufficient for analysis.

Figure 5.11 DNA profiles used to investigate relatedness

1 DNA profiles used to establish family relationships

Is the male (F) the parent of both children?

Examine the DNA profiles shown to the right.

Look at the children's bands (C).

Discount all those bands that correspond to bands in the mother's profile (M).

The remaining bands match those of the biological father.

DNA fingerprinting has been widely applied in biology. In ornithology, for example, DNA profiling of nestlings has established a degree of 'promiscuity' in breeding pairs, the male of which was assumed to be the father of the whole brood. In birds, the production of a clutch of eggs is extended over a period of days, with copulation and fertilisation preceding the laying of each egg. This provides the opportunity for different males to fertilise the female.

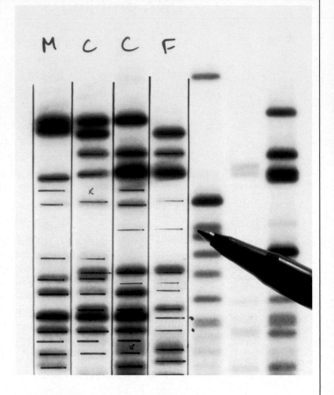

2 DNA profiling in forensic investigation

Identification of criminals

At the scene of a crime (such as a murder or burglary), hairs – with hair root cells attached – or blood may be recovered. If so, the resulting DNA profiles may be compared with those of DNA obtained from suspects.

Examine the DNA profiles shown to the right, and suggest which suspect should be interviewed further.

Identification in a rape crime involves the taking of vaginal swabs. Here, DNA will be present from the victim and also from the rapist. The result of DNA analysis is a complex profile that requires careful comparison with the DNA profiles of the victim and of any suspects. A rapist can be identified with a high degree of certainty, and the innocence of others established.

Identification of a corpse which is otherwise unidentifiable is achieved by taking DNA samples from body tissues and comparing their profile with those of close relatives or with DNA obtained from cells recovered from personal effects, where these are available.

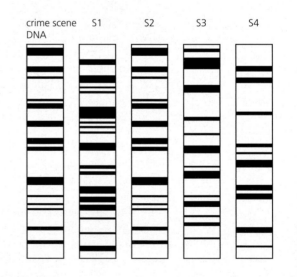

DNA profiling has applications in determining paternity

Another very important application of DNA profiling is in issues of parentage. A range of samples of DNA of the people who are possibly related are analysed side by side. The banding patterns are then compared (Figure 5.11). Because a child inherits half his DNA from his mother and half from his father, the bands in a child's DNA fingerprint that do not match his mother's must come from the child's father.

DNA profiling also has wide applications in studies of wild animals – for example, concerning breeding behaviour, and in the identification of unrelated animals as mates in captive breeding programmes of species in danger of extinction. Note the use of a DNA profile in Figure 5.13 (page 134), for example.

9 **Distinguish** between the following pairs:

a genotype and genome
b restriction endonuclease and ligase
c 'blunt ends' and 'sticky ends'
d bacterial chromosome and a plasmid.

Human Genome Project

The Human Genome Project (HGP), an initiative to map the entire human genome, is a publicly funded project that was launched in 1990.

The ultimate objectives of the HGP were to discover the location of each human gene and the base sequence within its DNA structure.

The work was shared among more than 200 laboratories around the world, avoiding duplication of effort. However, in 1998 the task became a race when a commercially funded company set out to achieve the same outcome in only three years, by different techniques. Because of a fear that a private company might succeed, patent the genome, and then sell access to it (rather than making the information freely available to all), the HGP teams accelerated their work.

In fact, both teams were successful well ahead of the project completion dates. On the 26th June 2000, a joint announcement made at the White House in Washington DC (USA) established that the sequencing of the human genome had been achieved. At the same time as the HGP had got under way, teams of scientists set about the sequencing of the DNA of other organisms, and more than 30 have been completed to date.

Outcomes of the HGP

Ultimately, most if not all aspects of biological investigation will be enhanced by the outcomes of this project. At this stage, we can illustrate the impact of the HGP with three examples.

How many individual genes do we have and how do they work?
The three billion bases that make up the human genome represent 30 000 to 45 000 genes – far fewer than the expected 100 000. This is only a few thousand more than the genes of a sea urchin. Even *Drosophila* (the fruit fly) has almost half our number. A rice plant has many more genes than a human – up to 55 000 genes.

How is the structural, physiological and behavioural complexity of humans delivered by so relatively few genes?

The secret of our complexity may lie not in the number of our genes but how we use them. Promoters and enhancers are associated with many genes and may determine which cells express genes, when they are expressed, and at what level.

Another issue is the effect of experience. The genetic code of DNA is not altered by the environment (except in cases of mutation) – information flows out of genes and not back into them. However, while our genes are immune to direct outside influence, can our experience regulate the expression of particular genes? Genes may be switched on and off by promoters, and this may occur in response to external factors. If so, our genes may be responding to our actions as well as causing them.

This field of investigation is in its infancy compared with its likely final impact.

Locating the cause of genetic disease

Another outcome of the HGP is the ability to locate genes responsible for human genetic diseases. Genetic diseases cause suffering in about 1–2% of the population.

More than half of all genetic diseases are due to a mutation of a single gene, and the mutant gene is commonly recessive. To prove a gene is associated with a disease it must be shown that patients have a mutation in that gene, but unaffected individuals do not. The outcome of the mutation in affected people is the loss of the ability to form the normal product of the gene. Common genetic diseases include cystic fibrosis (page 576), sickle cell disease (page 100), and haemophilia (page 114).

Development of gene therapy

The discovery of genes responsible for human genetic disease generates the possibility of a fundamental cure by gene therapy.

Gene therapy is the use of recombinant DNA technology to overcome genetic disease, where this is thought safe and ethically sound. Gene therapy is a very recent, and is a highly experimental science. One approach is to supply the body with the missing gene's product (and then periodically re-supply it). More difficult, but a permanent solution, would be to supply the missing gene to body cells in such a way that it remains permanently functional. This approach is illustrated here by reference to the genetic disease **familial hypercholesterolaemia (FH)**.

Lipids are transported around the body and across cell membranes as lipoproteins, such as low-density lipoproteins (LDLs). In the genetic disease FH, the membrane receptors for LDLs are defective, and LDLs accumulate in the blood, leading to atherosclerosis (page 664) and coronary heart disease.

Gene therapy for FH involves engineering a healthy human gene into a sample of liver cells so that genetically corrected cells may be re-established in the liver and restore correct functioning (Figure 5.12).

Figure 5.12 Familial hypercholesterolaemia (FH); correcting liver cell functions

Samples of liver tissue may be removed, the cells genetically modified, and then returned. The human body quickly regenerates missing liver tissue. If removed liver cells are returned to the body they may be rapidly incorporated into the liver.

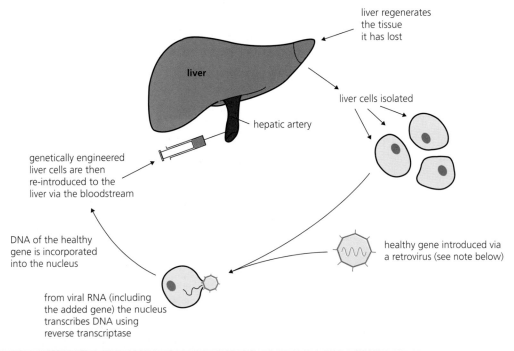

liver regenerates the tissue it has lost

liver

hepatic artery

liver cells isolated

genetically engineered liver cells are then re-introduced to the liver via the bloodstream

healthy gene introduced via a retrovirus (see note below)

DNA of the healthy gene is incorporated into the nucleus

from viral RNA (including the added gene) the nucleus transcribes DNA using reverse transcriptase

10 Suggest the factors that tend to maintain the levels of alleles for a genetic disease within a population, despite their unfavourable effects on quality and length of life of those affected.

Note: An *alternative vector* is used in this case because plasmids are not components of eukaryotic cells. **Retroviruses** are viruses that, on entry to the host cell, convert their RNA into DNA and add it to a host chromosome. They use a special enzyme for this, reverse transcriptase (page 573). Once the added genes are installed, they may be transcribed and translated in the usual way.

The new discipline of bioinformatics

Bioinformatics is the storage, manipulation and analysis of biological information via computer science. At the centre of this development is the creation and maintenance of databases concerning nucleic acid sequences and the proteins derived from them. Already, the genomes of several prokaryotes and eukaryotes have been sequenced, as well as that of humans. This represents a deluge of data that requires organisation, storage and indexing to facilitate subsequent effective analysis involving applied mathematics, informatics, statistics and computer science.

From these database resources, potentially highly rewarding discoveries may follow, including:

- the location of specific genes in the DNA sequences of various organisms, as well as the sequences that regulate genes (remember, within a genome not all the nucleotides are genes);
- development of methods of predicting the structure and suggesting the function of newly discovered proteins and RNA sequences that the genes code for;
- establishment of evolutionary relationships between species (by comparing genes of different species); new phylogenetic trees would follow, based on molecular genetics – it would become possible to trace the evolutionary relationship of a large number of organisms by measuring changes in their DNA, and to estimate the point in geological time when related organisms diverged (page 499).

Cloning

Clones are identical things.

Genetic engineers clone genes when a single gene is introduced into a plasmid. Bacteria are then induced to take up the recombinant plasmid (page 122). Once this has occurred, the plasmid is replicated many times in the cytoplasm. In this way, very many identical copies of the gene are produced. This is an important step in recombinant DNA technology. This is one important aspect of cloning with which we are already familiar.

A clone is also defined as a group of **genetically identical individuals** or cells produced by **asexual reproduction** from a single parent cell or individual. There are numerous cases of asexual reproduction in plants, animals and protoctista. Cloning has been used widely in commercial plant propagation for many years.

Human clones occur naturally, too, in the persons of identical twins. In sexual reproduction, the fertilised egg cell divides to form a tiny hollow ball of cells called a blastocyst, as it passes down the oviduct. In the uterus, the blastocyst becomes embedded in the wall, and forms a group of cells, the inner cell mass, that will go on to form the embryo (page 385). If this cell mass (unusually) divides into two separated masses before it embeds, then both cell masses go on to form embryos, and these become genetically identical twins.

In recent years, animal clones have been produced by **nuclear transfer techniques**. Dolly the sheep was the first mammal to be cloned from non-embryonic cells. This was achieved at the Roslin Institute, Edinburgh in 1996. Dolly was produced from a fully differentiated udder cell taken from a six-year-old ewe. The isolated cell was induced to become 'dormant' or genetically quiescent, and then converted to the embryonic state by fusion with an egg cell from which the nucleus had been removed, taken from a different ewe. The process is summarised in Figure 5.13.

Human cloning?

Preliminary experiments have shown that it may be possible to clone humans, too. However, the ethical issues of such a move have stimulated opposition and comment from many people and organisations, and human cloning is currently banned in many countries.

In 2004, the UK's Human Fertilisation and Embryology Authority (HFEA) gave a Newcastle biomedical team permission to create human embryos that are clones of patients. The team is licensed to use the embryos to make embryonic stem cells to investigate diabetes, though their work could be relevant to diseases such as Alzheimer's and Parkinson's, also.

steps in the production of Dolly the clone

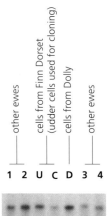

donor cells taken from udder of a Finn Dorset ewe

unfertilised egg cell taken from Scottish blackface ewe

cultured in medium low in nutrients, depriving the cells of essentials and causing active genes to be 'shut down'

nucleus removed by micropipette

egg cell without nucleus

cells fused together – stimulus for fusion is an electric pulse

fused cell

cell division triggered by electric pulse

early embryo formed

embryo implanted in uterus of surrogate mother ewe

gestation of 148 days

Dolly born – genetically identical with Finn Dorset ewe from which the nucleus was taken (see genetic profile)

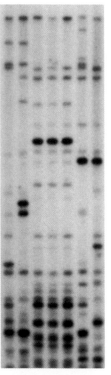

other ewes | cells from Finn Dorset (udder cells used for cloning) | cells from Dolly | other ewes

1 2 U C D 3 4

genetic profile of Finn Dorset ewe cells, Dolly's cells and other ewes

Like the team who cloned Dolly the sheep, this team use nuclear transfer techniques – in this case, replacing the DNA of a human embryo cell with the DNA from a human skin cell. The embryos created in these Newcastle experiments will never be implanted in a uterus because reproductive cloning is illegal in the UK.

Instead, the team work on embryonic **stem cells** derived from the embryos. Stem cells have the ability to produce a variety of cells (page 18). It is thought these cells may have great potential in treating disease by replacing damaged tissue. Unlike an organ transplant, stem cells are not expected to be rejected by the patient's body, as the process ensures the engineered cells have the same DNA as the patient.

This is the first licence for cloning experiments in humans that the HFEA has issued. The Chair of the HFEA said:

'After careful consideration of all the scientific, ethical, legal and medical aspects of the project, the HFEA Licence Committee agreed to grant an initial one-year research licence to the Newcastle Centre for Life. This is an important area of research and a responsible use of technology. The HFEA is there to make sure any research involving human embryos is scrutinised and properly regulated.'

Since human clones can form naturally, and because experiments in human cloning are being planned, permitted and funded in several countries around the world, this controversial issue needs our careful, informed consideration.

Opponents of research cloning served an application for a judicial review on the HFEA over its decision to issue the first research licence granting permission to create cloned human embryos. At the time, UK 'pro-life' groups condemned the move and have mounted a legal challenge. This remains a controversial issue.

Arguments for and against human cloning are listed in Table 5.2.

What views do you hold?

Points against human cloning	Points in favour of human cloning
Human beings might be planned and produced with the sole intention of supplying 'spare parts' for a related human being with some passing health problem.	Parents at high risk of producing offspring with genetic disease would have the opportunity of healthy children. Infertile couples could have children of their own.
Cloning could facilitate 'improving' humans by designing and delivering a race of 'superior' people (like attempts to 'improve' by some arbitrary standards proposed in earlier, discredited, eugenics movements).	Cloning technologies are being developed to deliver organs for transplants that are entirely compatible and are not rejected by the recipient's immune system. New treatments for genetic diseases are planned and may shortly be achieved.
Cloning techniques are experimental and unreliable, resulting in the death of many embryos and newborns, since there are still so many unknown factors operating.	Cloning techniques are as safe and reliable as other comparable medical procedures, given this early stage in development and our limited experiences.
The traditional concept of 'family' is of a group of people with individuality, and with a clear sense of personal worth.	Clones are not true duplicates because environmental factors and personal experiences influence development and who we are.
Clones might have diminished rights and a lessened sense of individuality.	Identical twins have a strong sense of individuality and personal worth.
Some aspects of human life should exist above the values and standards of the laboratory. Many believers consider that cloning is against the will of their god. Human inventiveness must not tamper with 'nature', regarding human life issues.	All new developments take time for acceptance. Most improvements in medical technologies have received trenchant opposition which has receded with familiarity, and as the advantages are perceived.

Table 5.2 The cases for and against human cloning

■ *Examination questions – a selection*

Questions 1–4 are taken from past IB Diploma biology papers.

Q1 What is a clone?

    A a group of organisms which could interbreed and produce fertile offspring

    B a group of cells descended from two parent cells

    C a group of organisms of the same species living together and interbreeding

    D a group of organisms with identical genotype

        Higher Level Paper 1, May 02, Q10

Q2 **a** Outline how the process of meiosis can lead to Down's syndrome. (4)

    b Discuss the advantages and disadvantages of genetic screening for chromosomal and genetic disorders. (8)

    c Describe the technique for the transfer of the insulin gene using *E. coli*. (6)

        Standard Level Paper 2, May 06, QB6

Q3 What is copied by the polymerase chain reaction (PCR)?

    A polypeptides

    B polysaccharides

    C polynucleotides

    D polyunsaturated fatty acids

        Standard Level Paper 1, May 04, Q16

Q4 Which of the following conditions has been treated by gene therapy?

    A emphysema

    B SCID

    C coronary heart disease

    D colon cancer

        Standard Level Paper 1, May 06, Q14

Questions 5–8 cover other syllabus issues in this chapter.

Q5 **a** By means of examples, explain what is meant by:

      i therapeutic cloning

      ii reproductive cloning. (6)

    b Suggest three reasons why many people may object in principle to the cloning of human embryos as being unethical. (3)

Q6 DNA profiling uses the techniques of genetic engineering to identify an individual (typically a human) from a sample of their DNA.

    a It is satellite DNA that is used. Explain what you understand by *satellite DNA*. (1)

    b Restriction endonuclease is the enzyme that cuts DNA into short lengths. Identify at what specific points along the DNA molecule the restriction enzyme selected for use in DNA profiling cuts nucleic acid. (2)

    c Outline the processes by which gel electrophoresis separates (sieves out) DNA fragments. (2)

    d During forensic investigation, application of the polymerase chain reaction (PCR) is sometimes required prior to DNA profiling. Explain what the PCR does and in what circumstances it is required. (2)

Q7 Many human communities appear highly critical of attempts at the genetic modification of farm crops or animals. Choosing a specific example with which you are familiar, list the points you would make if you attempted to change their outlook to being supportive. (6)

Q8 **a** Outline what you understand by the term *biotechnology*. Give examples that show its relevance to human communities over time. (2)

    b Suggest reasons why the application of enzymes is so highly significant in biotechnological processes. (4)

6 Ecology, evolution and biodiversity

STARTING POINTS
- **Ecology** is the study of living things in their environment.
- **Energy** reaching the green plants as light is transferred to the chemical energy of **nutrients** during **photosynthesis**.
- During **feeding**, energy is transferred from organism to organism, but is eventually returned to the environment as heat.
- **Cell respiration** is a process by which nutrients are broken down and much energy transferred to carry out the **activities and functions of cells and organisms**.
- **ATP** is the **energy currency** molecule of cells and organisms.

Ecology is the study of living things in their environment. It is an essential component of modern biology. Understanding the relationships between organisms and their environment is just as important as knowing about the structure and physiology of animals and plants.

Communities and ecosystems

5.1.1–5.1.14

One of the ideas that ecologists have introduced is that of the **ecosystem**. This is defined as a **community of organisms** and their surroundings, the **environment in which they live** and with which they interact. An ecosystem is a basic functional unit of ecology since the organisms that make up a community cannot realistically be considered apart from their physical environment.

Examples such as woodlands or a lake illustrate two important features of an ecosystem, namely that it is:

- a largely **self-contained** unit, since most organisms of the ecosystem spend their entire lives there and their essential nutrients will be endlessly recycled around and through them;
- an **interactive** system, in that the kinds of organism that live there are largely decided by the physical environment, and the physical environment is constantly altered by the organisms; the organisms (community) of an ecosystem are called the **biotic** component, and the physical environment is known as the **abiotic** component.

Ecology	The study of living things within their environment.
Ecosystem	A stable, settled unit of nature consisting of a community of organisms, interacting with each other and with their surrounding physical and chemical environment. Examples of ecosystems are ponds or lakes, woods or forests, sea shores or salt marshes, grassland, savannah or tundra.
	Ecosystems are necessarily very variable in size.
Habitat	The locality in which an organism occurs. It is where the organism is normally found.
	If the area is extremely small, we call it a microhabitat. The insects that inhabit the crevices in the bark of a tree are in their own microhabitat. Conditions in a microhabitat are likely to be very different from conditions in the surrounding habitat.
Population	All the living things of the same species in a habitat at any one time. The members of a population have the chance of interbreeding, assuming the species concerned reproduces sexually. The boundaries of populations are often hard to define, but those of aquatic organisms occurring in a small pond are clearly limited by the boundary of the pond.
Community	All the living things in a habitat or ecosystem, the total of all the populations. So, for example, the community of a well-stocked pond would include the populations of rooted, floating and submerged plants, the populations of bottom-living animals, the populations of fish and non-vertebrates of the open water, and the populations of surface-living organisms – typically a very large number of organisms.
Species	A group of individuals of common ancestry that closely resemble each other and that are normally capable of interbreeding to produce fertile offspring.

Table 6.1
An introduction to ecological terms

1 **Suggest** why the dominant plant species of a habitat may more or less determine the types of animal life present.

Environment is a term we commonly use to mean 'surroundings'. In biology, we talk about the environment of cells in an organism, or the environment of organisms in a habitat. It is also our term for the external conditions affecting the existence of organisms, so 'environment' is a rather general, unspecific term, but useful, nonetheless.

Alternatively, there are several other terms that ecologists have introduced and regularly use that have precise meaning. Table 6.1 gives definitions of these ecological terms; you can refer to it as the need arises.

Feeding relationships – producers, consumers and decomposers

Think of an ecosystem that you are very familiar with. Perhaps it is one near your home, school or college. It might be savannah, forest, a lake, woodland or meadow. Whatever you have in mind, it will certainly contain a community of plants, animals, and microorganisms, all engaged in their characteristic activities. Some of these organisms will be much easier to observe than others, possibly because of their size, or the times of day (or night) at which they feed, for example.

However, the essence of survival of organisms is their activity. To carry out these activities organisms need **energy**. We have already seen that the immediate source of energy in cells is the molecule **ATP** (page 77) produced by respiration. The energy ATP represents has been transferred from sugar and other organic molecules, the respiratory substrates. These organic molecules are obtained from nutrients as a result of the organism's mode of nutrition.

We know that green plants make their own organic nutrients from an external supply of inorganic molecules, using energy from sunlight in photosynthesis (page 82). The nutrition of the green plants is described as **autotrophic** (meaning 'self feeding') and in ecology, green plants are known as **producers**.

> **An autotroph is an organism that synthesises its organic molecules from simple inorganic substances.**

In contrast, animals and most other types of organism use only existing nutrients, which they obtain by digestion and then absorb into their cells and tissues for use. Consequently, animal nutrition is dependent on plant nutrition either directly or indirectly. Animal nutrition is described as **heterotrophic** (meaning 'other nutrition') and in ecology, animals are known as **consumers**.

> **A heterotroph is an organism that obtains organic molecules from other organisms.**
> **A consumer is an organism that ingests other organic matter that is living or recently killed.**

Some of the consumers, known as herbivores, feed directly and exclusively on plants. **Herbivores are primary consumers.** Animals that feed exclusively on other animals are carnivores. **Carnivores** feeding on primary consumers are known as **secondary consumers**. Carnivores that feed on secondary consumers are called **tertiary consumers**, and so on.

Eventually all producers and consumers die and decay. Organisms that feed on dead plants and animals, and on the waste matter of animals, are described as **saprotrophs** (meaning 'putrid feeding'), and in ecology these feeders are known as **detritivores** or **decomposers**.

> **A saprotroph is an organism that lives on or in dead organic matter, secreting digestive enzymes into it and absorbing the products of digestion.**
> **A detritivore or a decomposer is an organism that ingests dead organic matter.**

Feeding by saprotrophs releases inorganic nutrients from the dead organic matter, including carbon dioxide, water, ammonia, and ions such as nitrates and phosphates. Sooner or later, these inorganic nutrients are absorbed by green plants and re-used. We will look in more detail at the cycling of nutrients in the biosphere later in this chapter.

Drawing up a food chain

A feeding relationship in which a carnivore eats a herbivore which itself has eaten plant matter is called a **food chain** (Figure 6.1). Here, light is the initial energy source, as it is with most other food chains. Note that in a food chain the arrows point to the consumers, and so indicate the direction of energy flow. Food chains from contrasting ecosystems are shown in Figure 6.2.

Figure 6.1 A food chain

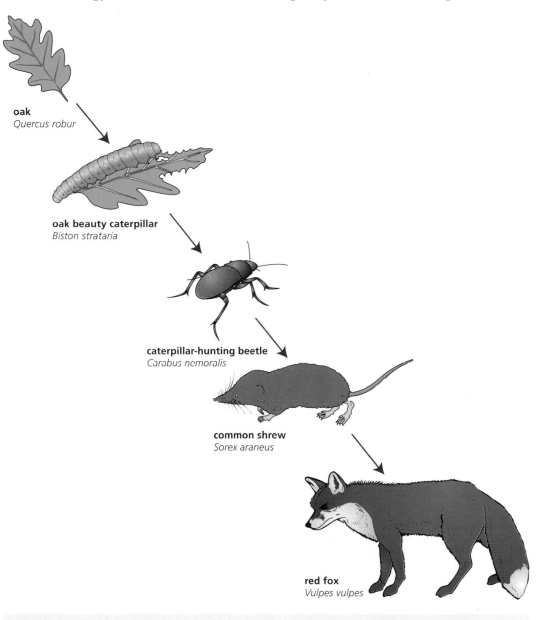

oak
Quercus robur

oak beauty caterpillar
Biston strataria

caterpillar-hunting beetle
Carabus nemoralis

common shrew
Sorex araneus

red fox
Vulpes vulpes

2 **Apply** one or more of the terms below to describe each of the listed features of a freshwater lake:

population   **ecosystem**   **habitat**   **abiotic factor**   **community**   **biomass**

a the whole lake

b all the frogs of the lake

c the flow of water through the lake

d all the plants and animals present

e the total mass of vegetation growing in the lake

f the mud of the lake

g the temperature variations in the lake

Figure 6.2 Food chains from contrasting ecosystems

A in a tropical rainforest

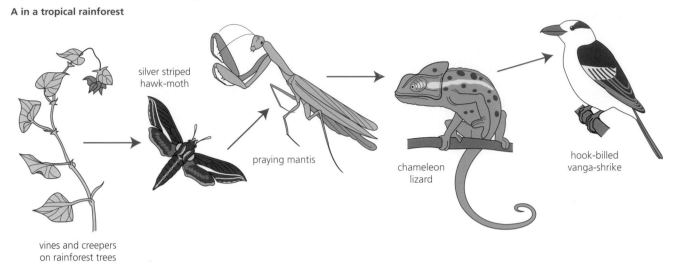

silver striped
hawk-moth

praying mantis

chameleon
lizard

hook-billed
vanga-shrike

vines and creepers
on rainforest trees

B on the savannah of the Serengeti, East Africa

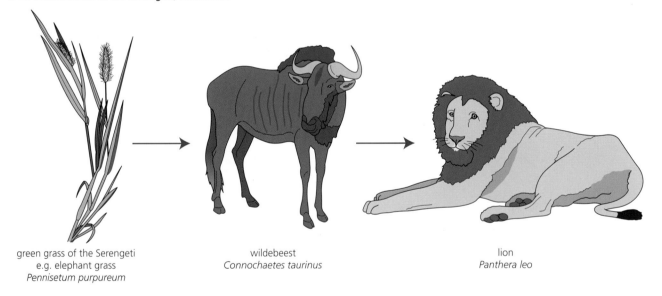

green grass of the Serengeti
e.g. elephant grass
Pennisetum purpureum

wildebeest
Connochaetes taurinus

lion
Panthera leo

3 Using the information in the food web in Figure 6.3 B, **construct** two individual food chains from the marine ecosystem, each with at least three linkages (four organisms).

Identify each organism with its common name, and **state** whether each is a producer, primary consumer, secondary consumer, etc.

Food webs

In an ecosystem the food chains are not isolated. Rather, they interconnect with other chains. This is because most prey species have more than one predator. Predators, as well as having preferences, need to exploit alternative food sources when any one source becomes scarce. They also take full advantage of gluts of food as particular prey populations become temporarily abundant.

Consequently, individual food chains may be temporary, and are interconnected so that they may form a **food web**. Two examples of food webs are shown in Figure 6.3, one from a woodland ecosystem and one from a marine ecosystem.

Examine these now.

Note that food chains tell us about the feeding relationships of organisms in an ecosystem, but they are entirely **qualitative** relationships (we know which organisms are present as prey and as predators) rather than providing **quantitative** data (we do not know the numbers of organisms at each level).

Figure 6.3 Examples of food webs

A a woodland food web

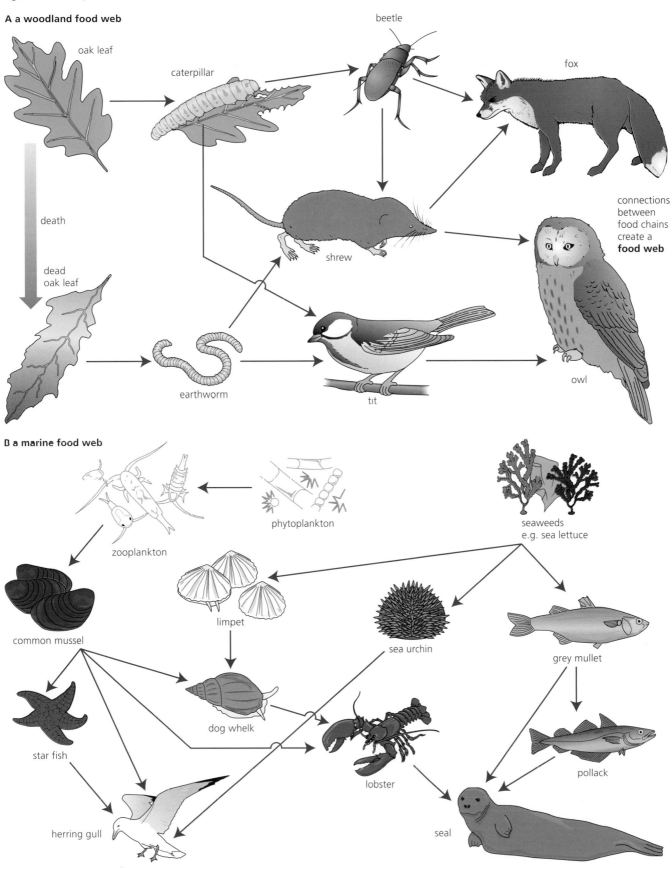

B a marine food web

Trophic levels

The level at which an organism feeds in a food chain is called its **trophic level** (feeding level). In this way of classifying feeding relationships, the **producers** are designated as **trophic level 1**, because energy has been transferred once, from Sun to plant. All the herbivores make up **trophic level 2**, because here energy has been transferred twice, and so on. The trophic levels of organisms in some of the above food chains and food webs are classified in Table 6.2.

Trophic level	Woodland	Rainforest	Savannah
Producer Level 1	oak	vines and creepers on rainforest trees	grass
Primary consumer Level 2	caterpillar	silver striped hawk-moth	wildebeest
Secondary consumer Level 3	beetle	praying mantis	lion
Tertiary consumer Level 4	shrew	chameleon lizard	
Quaternary consumer Level 5	fox	hook-billed vanga-shrike	

Table 6.2 An analysis of trophic levels

4 **Identify** the initial energy source for almost all communities.

Note that there is not a fixed number of trophic levels to a food chain, but typically they have three, four or five levels only. There is an important reason why stable food chains remain quite short. We will come back to this point, shortly.

Sometimes it can be difficult to decide at which trophic level to place an organism. For example, an **omnivore** feeds on both plant matter (level 2 – primary consumer) and on other consumers (level 3 – secondary consumer, or higher). In the woodland food chain of Figure 6.1, the fox more commonly feeds on beetles than shrews because there are many more beetles about, and they are easier to catch.

5 **Suggest** what trophic levels humans occupy. Give examples.

Energy flow

Between each trophic level there is an energy transfer. At the base of the food chain, green plants, the producers, transfer light energy into the chemical energy of sugars in photosynthesis. Much of the light energy is not retained in the green leaf. Some is reflected, some transmitted, and some lost as heat energy. Heat is also a waste product of the reactions of respiration and of the plant's metabolism, as sugar is converted into lipids and amino acids, for example. Some of these metabolites are used in the growth and development of the plant, and by these reactions, energy is locked up in the organic molecules of the plant body.

Inevitably, energy is transferred every time the tissues of a green plant are consumed by herbivores.

Finally, on the death of the plant, the remaining energy passes to detritivores and saprotrophs when dead plant matter is broken down and decayed. The diverse routes of energy flow through a primary producer are summarised in Figure 6.4.

Consumers eat producers or primary or secondary consumers, according to where they occur in a food chain. In this way, energy is transferred to the consumer. The consumer in turn, transfers energy in muscular movements by which it hunts and feeds, and as it seeks to escape from predators. Some of the food eaten remains undigested, passing through the consumer unchanged, and is lost in the faeces. Also, heat energy, a waste product of the reactions of respiration and of the animal's metabolism, is continuously lost as the consumer grows and develops and forms body tissues. If the consumer is itself caught and consumed by another, larger consumer, energy is again transferred. Finally, on the death of the consumer, the remaining energy passes to detritivores and saprotrophs when dead matter is broken down and decayed.

The flow of energy through a consumer is summarised in Figure 6.5.

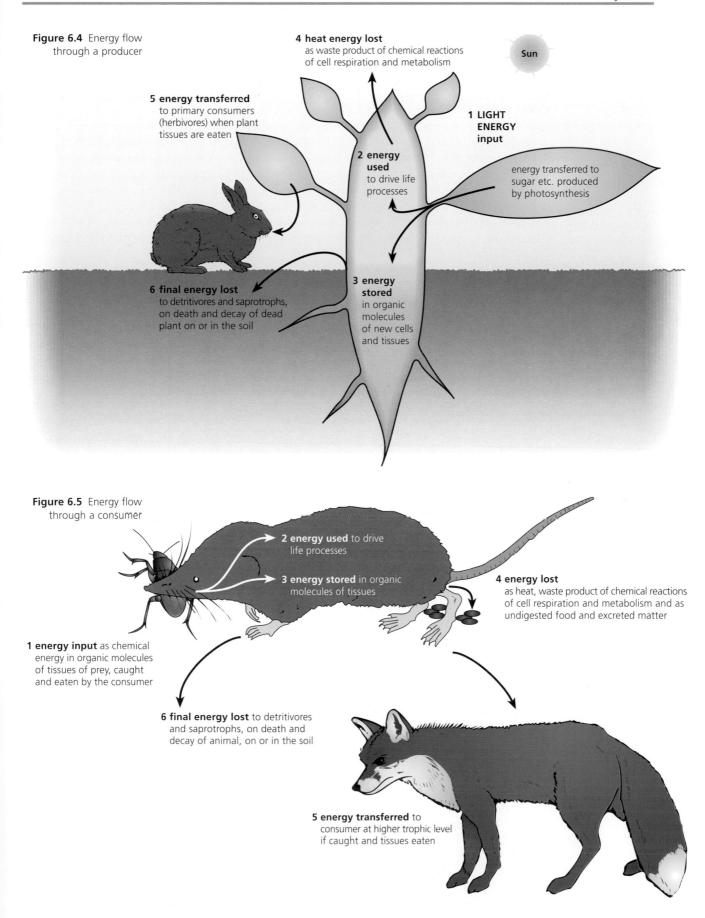

Figure 6.4 Energy flow through a producer

4 **heat energy lost** as waste product of chemical reactions of cell respiration and metabolism

Sun

5 **energy transferred** to primary consumers (herbivores) when plant tissues are eaten

1 **LIGHT ENERGY input**

2 **energy used** to drive life processes

energy transferred to sugar etc. produced by photosynthesis

6 **final energy lost** to detritivores and saprotrophs, on death and decay of dead plant on or in the soil

3 **energy stored** in organic molecules of new cells and tissues

Figure 6.5 Energy flow through a consumer

2 **energy used** to drive life processes

3 **energy stored** in organic molecules of tissues

4 **energy lost** as heat, waste product of chemical reactions of cell respiration and metabolism and as undigested food and excreted matter

1 **energy input** as chemical energy in organic molecules of tissues of prey, caught and eaten by the consumer

6 **final energy lost** to detritivores and saprotrophs, on death and decay of animal, on or in the soil

5 **energy transferred** to consumer at higher trophic level if caught and tissues eaten

So, energy is transferred from one organism to another in a food chain, but only some of the energy transferred becomes available to the next organism in the food chain. In fact, only about 10% of what is eaten by a consumer is built into that organism's body, and so is potentially available to be transferred on in predation or browsing. There are two consequences of this.

■ The energy loss at transfer between trophic levels is the reason why food chains are short. Few transfers can be sustained when so little of what is eaten by one consumer is potentially available to the next step in the food chain. Consequently, it is very uncommon for food chains to have more than four or five links between producer (green plant) and top carnivore, at most.
■ Feeding relationships of a food chain may be structured like a pyramid. At the start of the chain is a very large amount of living matter (biomass) of green plants. This supports a smaller biomass of primary consumers, which in turn supports an even smaller biomass of secondary consumers. A generalised ecosystem pyramid diagram, representing the structure of an ecosystem in terms of the biomass of the organisms at each trophic level, is shown in Figure 6.6.

6 **Explain** why, in a food chain, a large amount of plant material supports a smaller mass of herbivores and an even smaller mass of carnivores.

Figure 6.6 Energy flow through a food chain – the pyramid of biomass

A linear food chain – energy flow

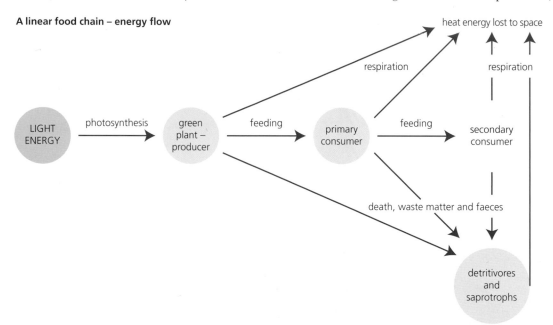

B food chain as pyramid of biomass showing energy flow
(Note: materials are recycled)

Energy enters the food chain from sunlight and leaves as heat energy lost to space.

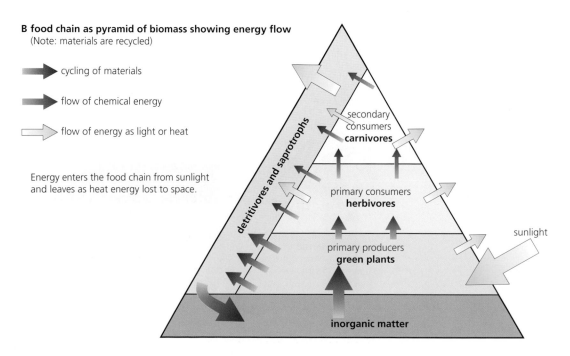

Pyramids of numbers, biomass and energy

Ecological pyramids are a practical means of analysing ecosystems. For example, they have been used to express seasonal changes in one ecosystem, or to compare different ecosystems at comparable times.

Initially, **pyramids of numbers** were produced. All the organisms at each trophic level within a given area were recognised and counted. The data were relatively easily obtained without destroying the organisms (given that the experimenter recognised all the organisms). The results were presented as rectangular blocks, stacked on top of each other, representing the numbers of organisms at each trophic level in a bar diagram.

In this approach, no allowance was made for differences in size of individual organisms; a giant oak tree and a single microscopic green alga counted the same. Consequently, the pyramids of numbers sometimes created strange shapes of limited meaning (Figure 6.7).

Figure 6.7 Examples of ecological pyramids of numbers

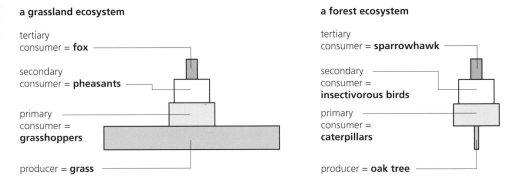

This problem of erratically shaped 'pyramids' was overcome by producing **pyramids of biomass**. To do this, the fieldwork involved estimating the numbers of organisms of each type at each trophic level, and then finding the biomass (dry weight) of a representative sample of each type of organism.

However, problems emerged with pyramids of biomass, too. A pyramid of biomass represents matter in different organisms at the moment the analysis was made, but the data do not indicate how fast matter is being added or consumed. Consequently, a pyramid based on the inflow of energy to each trophic level is preferred. This is called a **pyramid of energy**.

There are few examples of pyramids of energy because obtaining the data is difficult and time-consuming, and is a destructive activity. In practice, pyramids of biomass can be converted to pyramids of energy using published values of energy content, made in previous experiments in habitats that are comparable. The amounts of energy (kJ) measured are expressed per square metre of area occupied by the community per year ($kJ\,m^{-2}\,year^{-1}$).

Figure 6.8 A generalised pyramid of energy

Only energy taken in at one trophic level and then built in as chemical energy in the molecules making up the cells and tissues is available to the next trophic level. This is about 10% of the energy.

The reasons are:

• Much energy is used for cell respiration to provide energy for growth, movement, feeding, and all other essential life processes.

• Not all food eaten can be digested. Some passes out with the faeces. Indigestible matter includes bones, hair, feathers, and lignified fibres in plants.

• Not all organisms at each trophic level are eaten. Some escape predation.

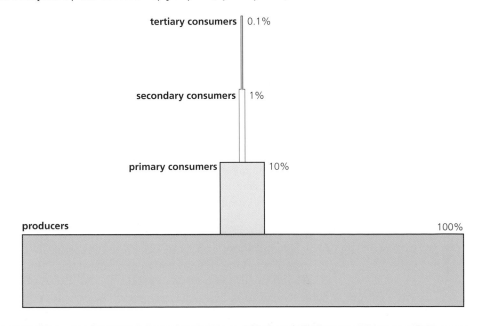

A generalised pyramid of energy is shown in Figure 6.8. It is annotated to summarise the reasons why the shape is always pyramidal. Figure 6.9 shows a researched example – a study made over 50 years ago by an American ecologist working on a river system in Florida, USA. It is interesting to note that it is a quite sweeping generalisation to say that only about 10% of energy is available for the next trophic level. For example, in the Florida river analysis it was found that 17% of energy of the producers (green aquatic plants) was transferred to primary consumers. The reason in this case was that the plants concerned were almost entirely of highly digestible matter. They lacked any woody tissues common to most terrestrial plant matter.

Figure 6.9 Pyramid of energy for a river ecosystem at Silver Springs, Florida

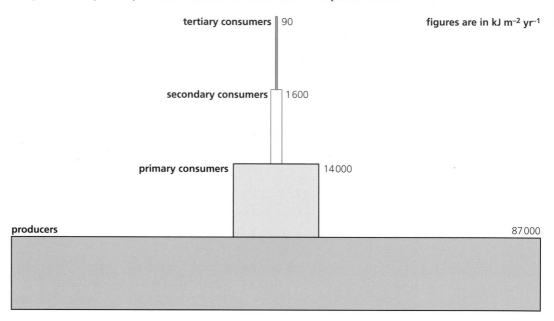

tertiary consumers ‖ 90   figures are in kJ m^{-2} yr^{-1}

secondary consumers ‖ 1600

primary consumers ‖ 14000

producers   87000

Cycling of nutrients

We have seen that energy enters ecosystems as light energy, is transferred to chemical energy in the nutrient molecules that sustain the growth of the tissues of producers and consumers, but ultimately is lost to space as heat. Energy continuously flows through ecosystems in this way. On the other hand, the **nutrients** of the ecosystem are not lost – they are **recycled and re-used**.

Nutrients provide the chemical elements that make up the biochemical molecules of cells and organisms. We have seen that all organisms are made of carbon, hydrogen and oxygen, together with mineral elements nitrogen, calcium, phosphorus, sulphur and potassium, and several others, in increasingly small amounts (Table 2.2, page 38). Plants obtain their essential nutrients as carbon dioxide and water, from which they manufacture sugar. With the addition of mineral elements absorbed as ions from the soil solution, they build up the complex organic molecules they require (Figure 3.7, page 82). Animals, on the other hand, obtain nutrients as complex organic molecules of food which they digest, absorb and assimilate into their own cells and tissues.

Recycling of nutrients is essential for the survival of living things, because the available resources of many elements are limited. When organisms die, their bodies are broken down and decomposed, mainly by **bacteria and fungi**, and the nutrients are released. Elements may become part of the soil solution, and some may react with chemicals of soil or rock particles, before becoming part of living things again by being reabsorbed by plants.

The cycling processes by which essential elements are released and re-used are called **biogeochemical cycles** because the cycle of changes involves both living things (the biota) and the non-living (abiotic) environment, consisting of atmosphere, hydrosphere (oceans, rivers and lakes) and the lithosphere (rocks and soil). All the essential elements take part in biogeochemical cycles – one example is the carbon cycle, which we will discuss shortly.

Roles of detritivores and saprotrophs in recycling

When organisms die, their bodies are broken down to simpler substances (for example, CO_2, H_2O, NH_3 and various ions) by a succession of organisms (mostly microorganisms), as illustrated in Figure 6.10. Scavenging actions of detritivores often begin the process, but saprotrophic bacteria and fungi always complete the breakdown processes.

Ultimately, both plants and animals depend on the activities of saprotrophic microorganisms to release matter from dead organisms for re-use. There is a limited supply of many of the chemical elements required as nutrients, so recycling is essential for life. Microorganisms are the main contributors in the vital recycling that goes on in the environment, largely unseen.

Figure 6.10 The sequence of organisms involved in decay

dead animal

1 break up
of animal body by scavengers and detritivores e.g. carrion crow, magpie, fox

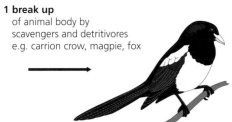

2 succession of microorganisms
– mainly bacteria, feeding:
• firstly on simple nutrients such as sugars, amino acids, fatty acids
• secondly on polysaccharides, proteins, lipids
• thirdly on resistant molecules of the body, such as keratin and collagen

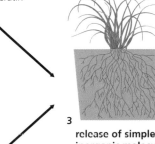

3
release of simple inorganic molecules
such as CO_2, H_2O, NH_3, ions such as Na^+, K^+, Ca^{2+}, NO_3^-, PO_4^-, all available to be reabsorbed by plant roots for re-use

2 succession of microorganisms
– mainly fungi, feeding:
• firstly on simple nutrients such as sugars, amino acids, fatty acids
• secondly on polysaccharides, proteins, lipids
• thirdly on resistant molecules such as cellulose and lignin

1 break up
of plant body by detritivores e.g. slugs and snails, earthworms, wood-boring insects

dead plant

7 **Explain** how it is that animal life is dependent on the actions of saprotrophs.

Greenhouse effect

5.2.1–5.2.6

Carbon dioxide is present in the atmosphere at about 0.038% by volume (which represents 0.057% by mass). This amount of atmospheric carbon dioxide is maintained by a balance between the fixation of this gas during photosynthesis and release of carbon dioxide into the atmosphere by respiration, combustion, and decay by microorganisms – an interrelationship illustrated in the carbon cycle (Figure 6.11).

Photosynthesis withdraws about as much carbon dioxide during the daylight each day as is released into the air by all the other processes, day and night – or nearly so.

In fact, the level of atmospheric carbon dioxide is now rising for reasons we will examine shortly. First, we need to look at the effect of low levels of atmospheric carbon dioxide because this natural component of the atmosphere maintains **a favourable environmental temperature on Earth** – a phenomenon known as the **greenhouse effect**.

Figure 6.11 The carbon cycle

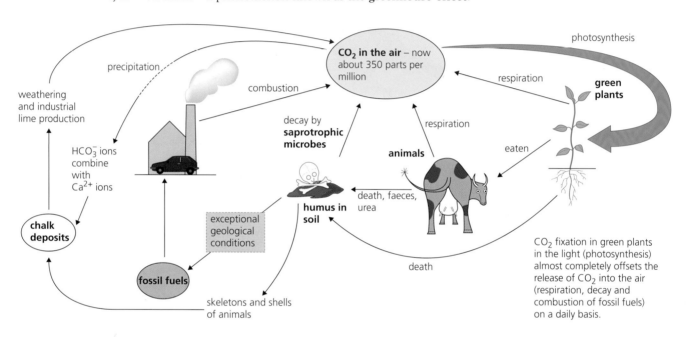

The mechanism of the greenhouse effect

The radiant energy reaching the Earth from the Sun includes visible light (short wave radiation), and infra-red radiation (longer wave radiation – heat), which warms up the sea and the land. As it is warmed, the Earth radiates infra-red radiation back towards space. However, much of this heat does not escape from our atmosphere. Some is reflected back by clouds and much is absorbed by gases in the atmosphere which are warmed. In this respect, the atmosphere is working like the glass in a greenhouse, which is why the effect is called the greenhouse effect (Figure 6.12). We must stress that the greenhouse effect is very important to life on the Earth: without it surface temperatures would be too cold for life.

Gases in the atmosphere that absorb infra-red radiation are referred to as **greenhouse gases**. **Carbon dioxide** is not the only component of our atmosphere with this effect – both **water vapour** and **methane** are naturally occurring greenhouse gases. In addition, atmospheric pollutants such as the oxides of nitrogen (particularly **nitrous oxide**) and the **chlorofluorocarbons (CFCs)** also have greenhouse properties. Oxides of nitrogen are waste products of the combustion of fossil fuels (natural gas, oil and coal), and a particularly abundant source is the exhaust fumes of internal combustion engines. CFCs, on the other hand, are unreactive molecules that were deliberately manufactured by the chemical industry to use as propellants in aerosol cans and as the coolant in refrigerators. With the passage of time these gases have escaped into the atmosphere, and have slowly been carried up to the stratosphere.

8 In the cycling of carbon in nature, **state** in what forms inorganic carbon can exist in:

a the atmosphere
b the hydrosphere
c the lithosphere.

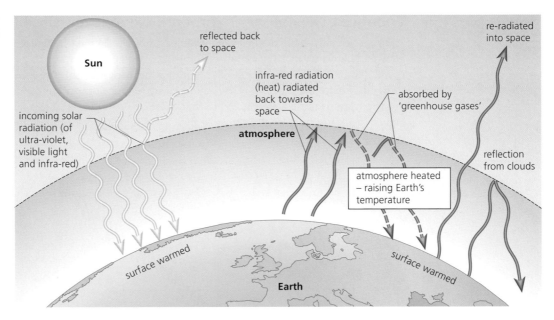

Figure 6.12 The greenhouse effect

An enhanced greenhouse effect leading to global warming?

The composition of the atmosphere has changed over time. That is beyond dispute.

How are current and historic levels of atmospheric carbon dioxide known?

The best **long-term records** of changing levels of greenhouse gases (and associated climate change) are based on evidence obtained from ice cores drilled in the Antarctic and Greenland ice sheets. For example, data from the Vostok ice core in East Antarctic and evidence from the composition of the bubbles of gas obtained from these cores, show us how methane and carbon dioxide levels have varied over no less than 400 000 years. Similarly, variations in the concentration of oxygen isotopes from the same source indicate how temperature has changed during the same period (Figure 6.13).

Clearly, the levels of greenhouse gas in the atmosphere can be closely correlated with global temperature. Environmental conditions on Earth have changed as a consequence, and we may anticipate further changes unless the current, rising levels of atmospheric carbon dioxide are reversed by internationally agreed action. We need to examine this issue next.

Figure 6.13 Three types of data recovered from the Vostok ice cores over 400 000 years of Earth history

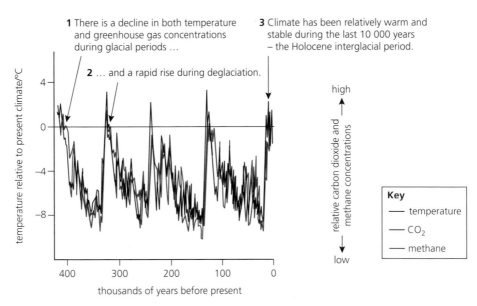

Changes in atmospheric carbon dioxide levels since 1957

Appropriate measuring devises were established at the Mauna Low monitoring station on Hawaii, beginning in 1957 as part of the International Geophysical Year initiative, to monitor the global environment. The most recent data furnished by this on-going investigation are shown in Figure 6.14. Seasonal variations cause fluctuations in atmospheric carbon dioxide, but the trend is unmistakeable. Note that there are differences in the scales of the graphs in Figures 6.13 and 6.14, so the slopes of the curves appear profoundly different.

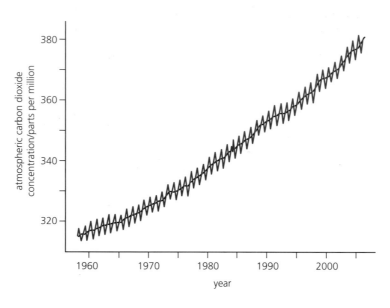

Figure 6.14 Atmospheric carbon dioxide levels recorded at Mauna Low, Hawaii, 1957–2005

9 From the data given in Figure 6.14:

   a **calculate** the % change in mean atmospheric carbon dioxide between 1960 and 2000
   b **explain** why it is that the atmospheric carbon dioxide varies between high and low values within each 12-month period of the graph.

The causes of raised levels of atmospheric carbon dioxide

From the graphs in Figures 6.13 and 6.14, we can see that while the levels of carbon dioxide have risen at times during the past 20 000 years, it is since the beginnings of the industrial revolutions in the developed countries of the world (the past 200 years or so) that levels have been consistently high and steadily rising.

We may assume that when the carbon dioxide levels were raised in earlier Earth history, processes like volcanic eruptions and the weathering of chalk and limestone rocks added additional carbon dioxide. Today, the release of carbon dioxide from volcanoes is estimated to contribute only about 1% of the amounts released by human activities.

The most recent sharp rise is attributed to the burning of fossil fuels (natural gas, coal and oil). Fossil fuels were mostly laid down in the Carboniferous Period, so we are now adding to our atmosphere carbon dioxide containing carbon that has been locked away for about 350 million years. This is an entirely new development in geological history. This enhanced global warming is beginning to generate problems that pose a major environmental threat to life as we know it.

Global warming and the Precautionary Principle

The Precautionary Principle is summed up by the expression 'Better safe than sorry'! Given that this idea is generally accepted once it is put to people in a particular context, it is surprising that the principle has not been clearly defined. However, no official definition has been shown to be other than vague, on careful consideration. The most common definition used is:

> **When an activity raises threats of harm, measures should be taken, even if a cause-and-effect relationship has not been established scientifically.**

To evaluate the relevance of this principle as a justification for strong action to combat the threats posed by enhanced global warming, we need to identify:

- the most likely consequences that may result from failure to slow down the rising level of atmospheric carbon dioxide and then reduce it to earlier values;
- the actions needed to deliver measures that enable us to achieve this.

In Table 6.3 these aspects are identified.

Table 6.3 Evaluating the threats posed by global warming and appropriate strong actions to rectify or avoid the resulting environmental degradation

Likely consequences of unchecked enhanced global warming	Effective strong actions that may combat these threats
■ complete melt-down of the polar ice caps and the glaciers of mountain regions, releasing vast amounts of water into the seas, so raising sea levels	■ conserve fossil fuel stocks, using them only sparingly, and only where there are no apparent alternatives (such as oils from biofuel sources)
■ warming of sea waters, causing them to expand in volume, so further raising sea levels	■ develop nuclear power sources to supply electricity for industrial, commercial and domestic needs
■ permanent flooding of much lowland territory where currently vast numbers of the human population live and where the most agriculturally productive land occurs	■ develop so-called renewable sources of power, exploiting environmental energy sources, such as wave energy and wind power
■ raising of the sea water temperature to levels where surface waters (where algae may flourish) is no longer ion-enriched by natural mixing with deep, colder water, causing failure of algal photosynthesis (a major CO_2-sump) so further raising atmospheric CO_2 levels	■ develop biofuel sources of energy that exploit organic waste matter that will naturally decay anyway, and biofuel crops that are renewable sources of energy using current photosynthesis products
■ destruction of forests by global temperatures that, in many parts of the world, are too high to support the survival and natural growth of trees	■ reduce use of fuels for heating of homes (where necessary) to minimum levels by designing well-insulated houses
■ interruption of ocean current systems that distribute warm waters from the tropical regions of the globe northwards, thereby disrupting agricultural production levels that sustain the human food chain for many peoples	■ reduce use of fuels for transport systems
	■ terminate the destruction of forests in general and, in particular, of rainforest all around the tropical regions of the Earth, since these are major CO_2-sumps

To be effective, strong actions taken in response to these challenges need to:

- be agreed internationally as acceptable to all nations and be acted on by everyone simultaneously;
- recognise that existing developed countries have previously experienced their industrial revolutions (which largely initiated these processes of environmental damage) and need to fully share the benefits with less-developed countries that would otherwise be required to forego some of the benefits of development.

Figure 6.15 summarises the problem.

In less-developed countries
natural resources such as rainforest may be the only product people can market to earn foreign currency to purchase goods and services, often at developed-world prices – and there is huge demand for their resources from developed and developing countries.

In developed countries
the destruction of natural resources like rainforest elsewhere in the world is seen as a threat to stable environmental conditions essential for an established, comfortable way of life. This way of life is often based on earlier exploitation of similar resources.

Figure 6.15 The environmental conundrum for today's world!

These contrasting needs cannot be met without huge sacrifices on both sides – yet it is easier for each country to recognise only what other countries need to do!

Is effective international agreement possible?

The need is for drastic cuts in global emissions of carbon dioxide and other greenhouse gases. An international agreement to limit release of greenhouse gases by all industrial countries and emerging industrial countries was first agreed at the **Earth Summit** in Rio de Janeiro in 1992. The initiative, known as **Agenda 21**, was launched. Subsequently, at the **Kyoto Conference** in Japan a first attempt was made to meet the pledges made at Rio. Carbon dioxide emission targets for the industrial nations were set for the period 2009–2012.

However, nations were allowed to offset emissions with devices such as carbon sinks – mechanisms by which atmospheric carbon dioxide is removed from the air either permanently, or on a long-term basis. For example, carbon dioxide may be absorbed by additional forest trees and become the carbon of wood that is not harvested and burnt. However, many of the arrangements are so complex as to be difficult to enforce. Real progress is extremely slow.

The Arctic and the consequences of global temperature rise – a case study

Arctic ecosystems consist of areas of permanent **ice desert** and huge areas of low-lying treeless land with an environment and vegetation regime described as **tundra** (Figure 6.16). The few plants present all through the year are sedges, lichens and sometimes dwarf willows – often described as low cushion plants. Trees do not grow because the growing season is too short for them, the winters too cold and dry, and what soil exists there is unable to provide support for the growth of significant root systems. Most of the year the temperatures are well below freezing point, so the moisture, soil and organic remains present are frozen hard as rock (permafrost). Dead organic matter accumulates, because the periods of the year when bacteria and fungi might decay this to humus in the usual way are far too short. Thus, the bulk of nutrients are locked away and few are released in growing periods. Nevertheless, during the brief growing season the surface of the substratum melts and plant growth is briefly spectacular, including flowering and seed dispersal, accompanied by a tremendous number of insects.

Figure 6.16 Arctic ecosystems

Some arctic ecosystems consist of **permanent ice desert**.

Other areas are of low-lying land with vegetation described as **tundra**.

The consequences of global warming for arctic ecosystems include:

- loss of the ice habitats, leading to extensive flooding of surrounding low-lands, at least temporarily;
- significant decay by microorganisms of the accumulated detritus, once released from its permafrost state, leading to huge releases into the atmosphere of methane and carbon dioxide, previously locked away in dead organic matter; this contributes to further global warming;
- an expansion in the range of habitats as significant quantities of soil rich in humus are formed;
- appearance and growth of conifers, forming boreal forests (also known as taiga); these areas absorb radiant heat energy from sunlight and contribute to further warming of the region, since they replace ice, snow and frozen tundra;
- appearance of insect-eating species, particularly of birds, able to take advantage of further increasing numbers of insects;
- a wider flora including annual plants typical of alpine meadows and grassland in summer seasons, where these appear;
- appearance of small mammals such as the alpine marmot, able to take advantage of the expanding range of plant biota and habitats (in winter periods such mammals need to be able to retreat into excavated dens for group hibernation);
- predators for the expanded vertebrate populations, mostly birds of prey (raptors) that can fly on when winter returns;
- increased presence of pathogens that parasitise the expanded range of animal and plant life the changing habitat supports.

■ **Extension:** **The enhanced greenhouse effect – important sources**

Evidence on the causes and effects of enhanced global warming continues to be sought and the data interpreted, not least so that steps and proposals for action to avoid an environmental disaster may be effective. However, all aspects of the issue are controversial to some extent. Our understanding is likely to continue to develop in what is a fast-changing situation. Consequently, there are very likely to be relevant developments within the time span of your International Baccalaureate programme, and you may need to consult other sources. In the table below are some references currently pertinent to this issue.

Environmental change due to global warming will be less extreme than predicted
www.newscientist.com/article/mg18524861.500.html 'Meet the global warming sceptics', 12 February 2005
W. Kininmonth (2004), *Climate change: A Natural Hazard,* Multi-Science Publishing Co. ISBN 09065 22269
Evidence of how global temperatures have regularly fluctuated in geological time
Search Google for 'Climate and the Carboniferous Period'. You may well find articles providing a graph of atmospheric CO_2 and average global temperature variation for the past 600 million years of Earth history.
Current and recent human activities as the cause of enhanced global warming, the disastrous consequences, and necessary action now
James Lovelock (2006) *The Revenge of Gaia: Why the Earth is Fighting Back – and How We Can Still Save Humanity,* Allen Lane (London) ISBN 07139 99144
Al Gore (2006) *An Inconvenient Truth: The Planetary Emergency of Global Warming and What We Can Do About It,* Bloomsbury Publishing ISBN 07475 89062

Table 6.4 Sources on the issues of enhanced global warming

■ # Populations

5.3.1–5.3.4

Another practical approach to analysing what goes on in an ecosystem is to find out how the separate populations which make up the ecosystem grow and maintain themselves. Remember, a population is defined as a group of individuals of the same species that have the potential to breed with each other. In an ecosystem such as a wood or lake, the numbers of some species remain remarkably stable, but other species have times of rapid growth, and sometimes populations 'crash'. So, populations can vary greatly.

What are the factors in an ecosystem that control population size?

Population growth

First, think of the situation where a small number of young rabbits enter a large, well-stocked meadow area from which other rabbits continue to be excluded. The rabbits initially familiarise themselves with the new territory, and establish burrows. Then, benefiting from the more or less unrestricted access to food supplies, breeding would commence.

The population of rabbits would increase very rapidly, but eventually, because of the very large numbers of rabbits produced, the vegetation would be used up faster than it grew. Further increases in population now stop, and the population enters a plateau or stationary phase. In this situation, the supply of food has become a limiting factor in the growth of the rabbit population.

If we had maintained a careful census of rabbit numbers throughout this experiment, a graph of number of individuals plotted against time would give us an S-shaped (sigmoid) curve (Figure 6.17).

Figure 6.17 The sigmoid curve of growth

The pattern of growth of a population of microorganisms after being inoculated into a fresh medium sample is shown. The distinct phases to growth are identified.

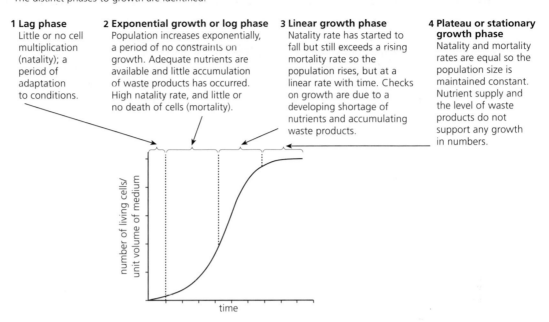

1 Lag phase
Little or no cell multiplication (natality); a period of adaptation to conditions.

2 Exponential growth or log phase
Population increases exponentially, a period of no constraints on growth. Adequate nutrients are available and little accumulation of waste products has occurred. High natality rate, and little or no death of cells (mortality).

3 Linear growth phase
Natality rate has started to fall but still exceeds a rising mortality rate so the population rises, but at a linear rate with time. Checks on growth are due to a developing shortage of nutrients and accumulating waste products.

4 Plateau or stationary growth phase
Natality and mortality rates are equal so the population size is maintained constant. Nutrient supply and the level of waste products do not support any growth in numbers.

number of living cells/ unit volume of medium

time

This situation of a population in the wild is similar to the change in population produced when a quantity of microbiological growth medium, called a broth, is inoculated by a few bacteria, under controlled laboratory conditions, and the growth of the bacterial population is measured. The bacteria reproduce by a process called binary fission in which fully grown bacteria each divide into two and these cells then grow to full size. The bacteria feed on the nutrients in the medium (such as glucose, amino acids, and growth factors), slowly using them up. Waste products start to accumulate.

The typical change in this population with time is shown by the graph in Figure 6.17. As in the case of the rabbit population described above, we see that the population numbers pass through distinct phases. Each phase is identified by a descriptive name:

- organisms become adapted to the medium (**lag phase**);
- growth proceeds at an exponential rate (exponential growth or **log phase**);
- growth proceeds at a more steady rate (**linear growth phase**);
- growth slows down and stops (stationary or **plateau phase**).

Exponential growth cannot be maintained

So, when a population has access to ideal conditions, there is an exponential period of growth, whether it is a population of mammals or microorganisms. In exponential growth, the population doubles in each generation: one individual becomes 2, then they become 4, 8, 16, 32, 64, 128, 256, and so on. This type of increase in a population is quick, but is not maintained because there are insufficient resources for it.

As a population increases, it begins to experience environmental resistance, because:

- space and resources are reduced;
- competition for space and resources increases.

The population tends to stabilise at a level which ecologists call the **carrying capacity** of the habitat.

If the numbers start to increase above carrying capacity, shortage of resources reduces the numbers of offspring produced, and the population regulates itself at the carrying capacity. If the population is reduced, say by heavy predation, the additional resources that then become available lead to an increase in reproductive rate, and the carrying capacity is again reached.

In other words, populations tend to be naturally self-regulating.

10 **Suggest** what factors might:

a lead to an increase in a population of a species of songbird in a wood or forest habitat near you
b eventually limit the growth of that population.

Why populations fluctuate in the wild

In practice, most populations in an ecosystem are already established, but do show significant fluctuations in numbers over a period of time. One example is seen in the study of the populations of phytoplankton (producers) and zooplankton (primary consumers) in a fresh water lake, studied for a 12-month period (Figure 6.18). We can see there is a significant spring 'bloom' in the phytoplankton population in the third and fourth months of the year, and that a corresponding surge in the zooplankton population occurred shortly afterwards. Note that the abiotic factors of essential nutrients, light and mean temperature were also measured and recorded.

Figure 6.18 Plankton of a fresh water lake in Northern Europe, with data on abiotic factors

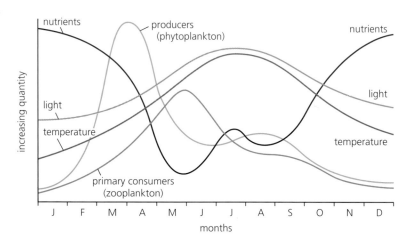

11 **Examine** the results of the ecological study shown in Figure 6.18, and then **suggest**:

  a two soluble nutrients in the lake water that would be taken up by phytoplankton and facilitate their rapid growth rate in March and April
  b why the numbers of phytoplankton decrease significantly by May and June, despite the favourable conditions of light and temperature
  c the most likely source of the increase in nutrients that begins in October.

So, in ecosystems the numbers in each population may fluctuate to varying degrees with time. In fact, population sizes vary for the following reasons:

- the birth rate (**natality**) varies;
- the death rate (**mortality**) varies;
- mobile members of the population may move away to new habitats, referred to as **emigration**;
- new members of species may arrive from other habitats, referred to as **immigration**.

In addition, it is possible that:

- A sudden, rapid change in one or more of the physical or chemical components of the environment may occur, reducing the size of the population or reducing the birth and death rates. This might be due to severe drought, or intense cold, for example. The effects of such change are unrelated to the density of the population. They are called **density-independent factors**.
- The effect of other members of the population and of members of other populations, in the form of competition for resources, predation and grazing, and parasitism, may all affect the population numbers adversely. The effects of these factors increase with increasing population numbers. They are known as **density-dependent factors**.

Evolution

By 'evolution' we mean 'the gradual development of life in geological time'. The word 'evolution' is used very widely, but in biology it specifically means 'the processes by which life has been changed from its earliest beginnings to the diversity of organisms we know about today, living and extinct'. It is the development of new types of living organisms from pre-existing types by the accumulation of genetic differences over long periods of time.

> **Evolution is the process of cumulative change in the heritable characteristics of a population.**

Evidence for evolution

Evidence for evolution comes from many sources, including from the study of fossils, from artificial selection in the production of domesticated breeds, and from studies of the comparative anatomy of groups of related organisms.

Fossils

We learn about the history of life from the evidence of the fossils that have been found. Fossilisation is an extremely rare, chance event. This is because predators, scavengers and bacterial action normally break down dead plant and animal structures before they can be fossilised. Of the relatively few fossils formed, most remain buried, or if they do become exposed, are overlooked or are accidentally destroyed before discovery.

Nevertheless, numerous fossils have been found – and more continue to be discovered all the time. The various types of fossil and the steps of fossil formation by petrification are illustrated in Figure 6.19. Where it is the case that the fossil or the rock that surrounds it can be accurately dated (as is often the case, using radiometric dating techniques that exploit natural radioactivity – as in ^{14}carbon or the ratio of ^{40}potassium to ^{40}argon), we have good evidence of the history of life.

Figure 6.19 Fossilisation

Fossil forms

petrification – organic matter of the dead organism is replaced by mineral ions
mould – the organic matter decays, but the space left becomes a mould, filled by mineral matter
trace – an impression of a form, such as a leaf or a footprint, made in layers that then harden
preservation – of the intact whole organism; for example, in amber (resin exuded from a conifer, which then solidified) or in anaerobic, acidic peat

Steps of fossil formation by petrification

1 dead remains of organisms may fall into a lake or sea and become buried in silt or sand, in anaerobic, low-temperature conditions
2 hard parts of skeleton or lignified plant tissues may persist and become impregnated by silica or carbonate ions, hardening them
3 remains hardened in this way become compressed in layers of sedimentary rock
4 after millions of years, upthrust may bring rocks to the surface and erosion of these rocks commences
5 land movements may expose some fossils and a few are discovered by chance but, of the relatively few organisms fossilised, very few will ever be found by humans

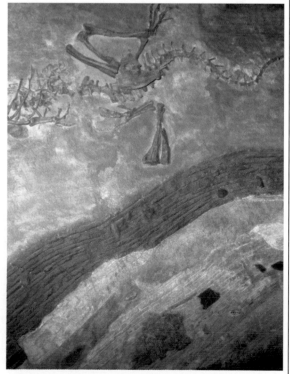

Sedimentary rock layers (with a fault line) and the remains of extinct fossil species

12 Many fossils are preserved in sedimentary rocks. **Explain** why is this so, and how sedimentary rocks formed.

Figure 6.20 Charles Darwin's observation of pigeon breeding

From his breeding of pigeons, Darwin noted that there were more than a dozen varieties that, had they been presented to an ornithologist as wild birds, would have been classified as separate species.

jacobin

pouter

rock dove (*Columbia livia*) from which all varieties of pigeon have been derived

fantail

Figure 6.21 Dog breeding

wolf (*Canis lupus*)
differences in size and other features of American, European and Asian wolves are reflected in the dog breeds that have been developed from them

The dog was domesticated from the wolf about 13 000 years ago. It was the first animal to be domesticated.

bloodhound
selectively bred for following air and ground scent in hunting

Irish setter
selectively bred for recreational hunting (with guns), along with pointers and retrievers

collie dog
selectively bred to herd and control flocks of domestic animals

Artificial selection

Artificial selection is the process by which all the plants and animals used by humans (in horticulture, agriculture, transport, companionship and leisure) have been derived from wild organisms. Artificial selection involves identifying the largest, the best or the most useful of the progeny for the intended purpose, and using them as the next generation of parents. The continuous culling out of progeny deficient in the desired features, generation by generation, leads to deliberate genetic change in the population; the genetic constitution of the population changes rapidly (Figures 6.20, 6.21).

13 Charles Darwin argued that the great wealth of varieties we have produced in domestication supports the concept of evolution. **Outline** how this is so.

14 Alsatians, Pekinese and Dachshunds are different in appearance yet are all classified as members of the same species. **Explain** how this is justified.

Comparative anatomy

Studies of the comparative anatomy of many groups of related organisms show that, although adapted to different habitats or life styles, often their underlying organisation is similar (that is, they have **homologous structures**). In such cases, a likely explanation is that they share a common ancestor, and show adaptive radiation from a basic plan (Figure 6.22). On the other hand, fundamentally different structures that have similar functions show only superficial resemblances. These are described as **analogous structures**.

Figure 6.22
Homologous and analogous structures

Homologous structures:

- are similar in fundamental structure
- are similar in position and development, but not necessarily in function
- are similar because of common ancestry

Examples of homologous structures are the **limbs of vertebrates**, all of which appear to be modifications on an ancestral five-fingered (pentadactyl) limb.

Analogous structures:

- resemble each other in function
- differ in their fundamental structure
- illustrate only superficial resemblances

Examples of analogous structures are the **wings of birds and insects**, which are similar only in their function as aerofoils.

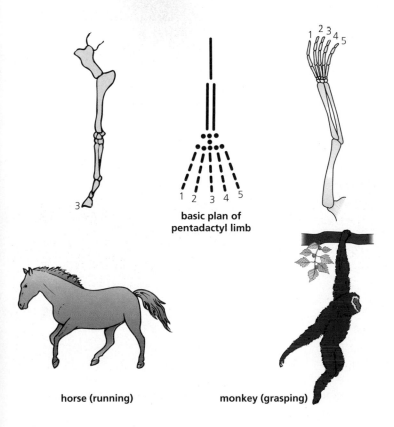

basic plan of pentadactyl limb

horse (running)

monkey (grasping)

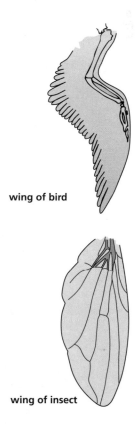

wing of bird

wing of insect

Evolution by natural selection – the ideas and arguments

Charles Darwin (1809–82) was a careful observer and naturalist who made many discoveries in biology. After attempting to become a doctor (at Edinburgh University) and then a clergyman (at Cambridge University), he became the unpaid naturalist on an Admiralty-commissioned expedition to the southern hemisphere, on a ship called HMS *Beagle*. On this five-year expedition around the world and in his later investigations and reading, he developed the idea of **organic evolution by natural selection**.

Darwin remained very anxious (always) about how the idea of evolution might be received, and he made no moves to publish it until the same idea was presented to him in a letter by another biologist and traveller, **Alfred Russel Wallace**. Only then (1859) was *On the Origin of Species by Natural Selection* completed and published. The arguments and ideas in the *Origin of Species* are summarised in Table 6.5.

		Statement / deduction
S1		Organisms produce a far greater number of progeny than ever give rise to mature individuals.
S2		The number of individuals in species remain more or less constant.
	D1	Therefore, there must be a high mortality rate.
S3		The individuals in a species are not all identical, but show variations in their characteristics.
	D2	Therefore, some variants will succeed better than others in the competition for survival. So the parents for the next generation will be selected from those members of the species better adapted to the conditions of the environment.
S4		Hereditary resemblance between parents and offspring is a fact.
	D3	Therefore, subsequent generations will maintain and improve in the degree of adaptation of their parents, by gradual change.

Table 6.5
Charles Darwin's ideas about the origin of species, summarised in four statements (S) and three deductions (D) from these statements

Neo-Darwinism

Charles Darwin (and nearly everyone else in the scientific community of his time) knew nothing of Mendel's work. Instead, biologists generally subscribed to the concept of 'blending inheritance' when mating occurred (which would reduce the genetic variation available for natural selection).

Neo-Darwinism is an essential restatement of the concepts of evolution by natural selection in terms of Mendelian and post-Mendelian genetics, as follows.

Organisms produce many more offspring than survive to be mature individuals

Darwin did not coin the phrase 'struggle for existence', but it does sum up the point that the over-production of offspring in the wild leads naturally to their competition for resources. Table 6.6 is a list of the normal rate of production of offspring in some common species.

Organism	No. of eggs / seeds / young per brood or season
rabbit	8–12
great tit	10
cod	2–20 million
honey bee (queen)	120 000
poppy	6 000

Table 6.6
Numbers of offspring produced

How many of these offspring survive to breed themselves?

In fact, in a stable population, a breeding pair may give rise to a single breeding pair of offspring, on average. All their other offspring are casualties of the 'struggle'; many organisms die before they can reproduce.

So, populations do not show rapidly increasing numbers in most habitats, or at least, not for long. Population size is naturally limited by restraints we call **environmental factors**. These include space, light, and the availability of food. The never-ending competition for resources results in the majority of organisms failing to survive and reproduce. In effect, the environment can only support a certain number of organisms, and the number of individuals in a species remains more or less constant over a period of time.

The individuals in a species are not all identical, but show variations in their characteristics

Today, modern genetics has shown us that there are several ways by which **genetic variations** arise in **gamete formation** during meiosis, and at **fertilisation**. We have seen that genetic variations arise via:

- **random assortment** of paternal and maternal chromosomes in meiosis (occurs in the process of gamete formation, page 224);
- **crossing over** of segments of individual maternal and paternal homologous chromosomes (results in new combinations of genes on the chromosomes of the haploid gametes produced by meiosis, page 96);
- the **random fusion** of male and female gametes in sexual reproduction (this source of variation was understood in Darwin's time).

Additionally, variation arises due to **mutations** – either chromosome mutations or gene mutations, page 98.

As a result of all these, the individual offspring of parents are not identical. Rather, they show variations in their characteristics.

Natural selection results in offspring with favourable characteristics

When genetic variation has arisen in organisms:

- the favourable characteristics are expressed in the phenotypes of some of the offspring;
- these offspring may be better able to survive and reproduce in a particular environment; others will be less able to compete successfully to survive and reproduce.

Thus, natural selection operates to determine the survivors and the genes that are perpetuated in future progeny. In time, this selection process may lead to new varieties and new species.

The operation of natural selection is sometimes summarised in the phrase **survival of the fittest**, although these were not words that Darwin used, at least not initially.

To avoid the criticism that 'survival of the fittest' is a circular phrase (how can fitness be judged except in terms of survival?), the term 'fittest' is understood in a particular context. For example, the fittest of the wildebeest of the African savannah (hunted herbivores) may be those with the acutest senses, quickest reflexes, and strongest leg muscles for efficient escape from predators. By natural selection for these characteristics, the health and survival of wildebeests is assured.

15 Deduce the importance of modern genetics to the theory of the origin of species by natural selection.

Environmental change and speciation

When environmental changes put selected individuals at a disadvantage, then natural selection is likely to operate on individuals and causes changes to gene pools. We have already noted that individuals possessing a particular allele, or combination of alleles, may be more likely to survive, breed, and pass on their alleles than other, less well-adapted individuals are. This process is also referred to as **differential mortality**; two examples follow.

1 Multiple antibiotic resistance in bacteria

This is an example of the situation in which, while the majority of an existing form of an organism may no longer be best suited to the environment, some unusual or abnormal forms of the population have a selective advantage.

Certain bacteria cause disease. Patients with bacterial infections are frequently treated with an antibiotic to help them overcome the infection. Antibiotics are very widely used. In a large population of a species of bacteria, some may carry a gene for resistance to the antibiotic in question. Sometimes, such a gene arises by spontaneous mutation; sometimes the gene is acquired in a form of sexual reproduction between bacteria of different populations.

The resistant bacteria in the population have no selective advantage *in the absence of the antibiotic*, and must compete for resources with non-resistant bacteria. But when the antibiotic is present, most bacteria of the population will be killed off. The resistant bacteria are very likely to survive and be the basis of the future population. In the new population, all now carry the gene for resistance to the antibiotic; the genome has been changed abruptly (Figure 6.23).

Figure 6.23 Multiple antibiotic resistance in bacteria

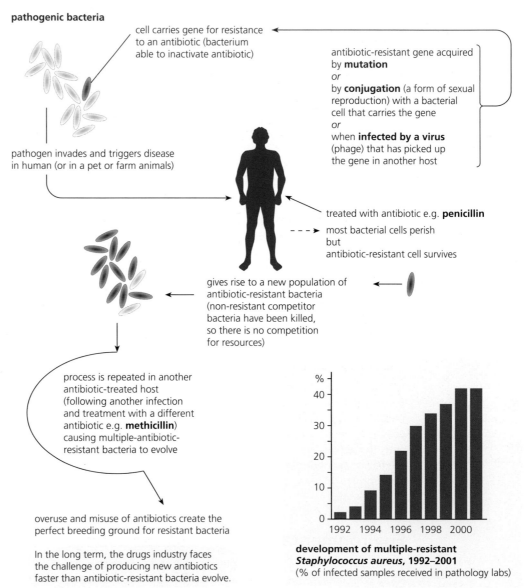

pathogenic bacteria

cell carries gene for resistance to an antibiotic (bacterium able to inactivate antibiotic)

antibiotic-resistant gene acquired by **mutation**
or
by **conjugation** (a form of sexual reproduction) with a bacterial cell that carries the gene
or
when **infected by a virus** (phage) that has picked up the gene in another host

pathogen invades and triggers disease in human (or in a pet or farm animals)

treated with antibiotic e.g. **penicillin**

most bacterial cells perish
but
antibiotic-resistant cell survives

gives rise to a new population of antibiotic-resistant bacteria (non-resistant competitor bacteria have been killed, so there is no competition for resources)

process is repeated in another antibiotic-treated host (following another infection and treatment with a different antibiotic e.g. **methicillin**) causing multiple-antibiotic-resistant bacteria to evolve

overuse and misuse of antibiotics create the perfect breeding ground for resistant bacteria

In the long term, the drugs industry faces the challenge of producing new antibiotics faster than antibiotic-resistant bacteria evolve.

development of multiple-resistant *Staphylococcus aureus*, 1992–2001 (% of infected samples received in pathology labs)

16 **Explain:**

a why doctors ask patients to ensure that they complete their course of antibiotics fully
b why the medical profession tries to combat resistance by regularly alternating the type of antibiotic used against an infection.

2 Heavy metal tolerance in plants

This is a phenomenon associated with those plants able to survive and even flourish on the otherwise bare waste tips and spoil heaps commonly found at mining sites. Here, heavy metals such as zinc, copper, lead, and nickel may be present as ions dissolved in soil moisture at concentrations that generate toxic conditions for plants normally present on the surrounding unpolluted soils. We have seen that several heavy metal ions are essential for normal plant growth when present in trace amounts (page 38). In mining spoils, these levels are frequently exceeded, and spoil heaps from eighteenth- and nineteenth-century mining activities in several countries around the world remain largely bare of plant cover, even when surrounding, unpolluted soils have dense vegetation cover. Seeds from these plants regularly fall on spoil heap soil, but plants fail to establish themselves.

However, careful observations of spoil heaps at many locations have disclosed the presence of local populations of plants that have evolved tolerance. One example is the grass *Agrostis tenuis* (Bent grass), populations of which are tolerant of otherwise toxic concentrations of copper (Figure 6.24).

A variety of biochemical and physiological mechanisms have evolved in tolerant species, including:

a the selective ability to avoid uptake of heavy metal ions;
b the accumulation of ions that enter in insoluble compounds in cell walls by formation of stable complexes with wall polysaccharides;
c transport of toxic ions into the vacuoles of cells, the membranes of which are unable to pump them out again, so avoiding interactions with cell enzymes.

The evolution of this form of tolerance has been demonstrated in several species of terrestrial plants, and also in species of seaweeds now tolerant of copper-based antifouling paints frequently applied to the hulls of ships.

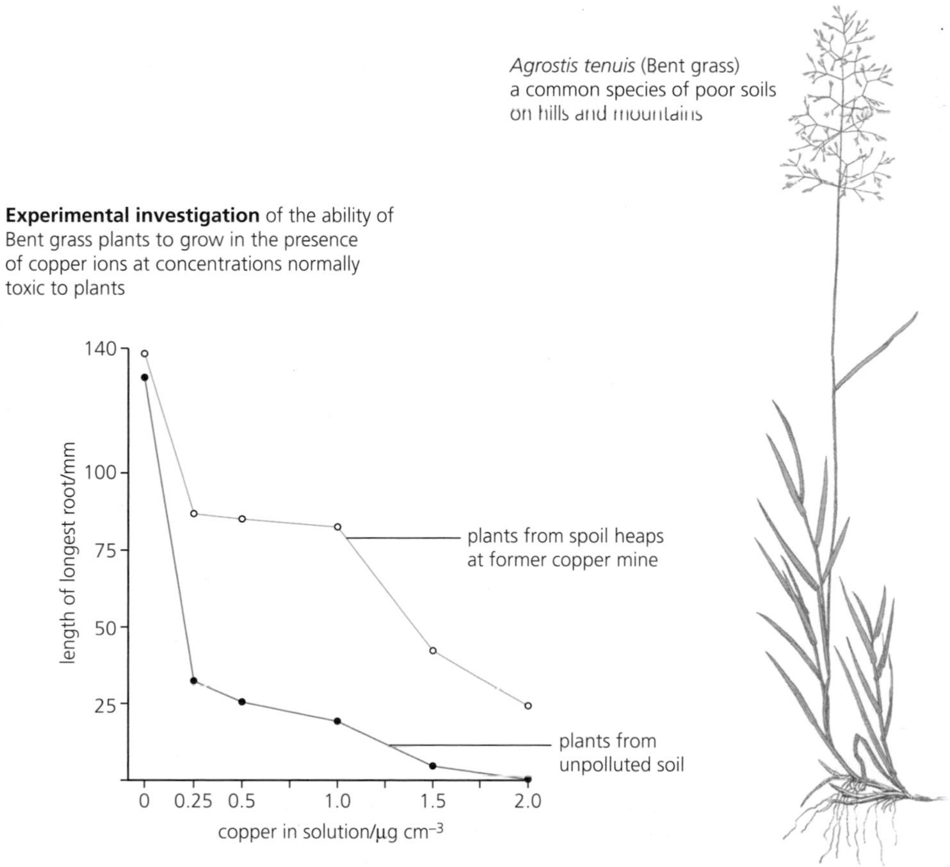

Figure 6.24 Copper ion tolerance in populations of Bent grass

Agrostis tenuis (Bent grass) a common species of poor soils on hills and mountains

Experimental investigation of the ability of Bent grass plants to grow in the presence of copper ions at concentrations normally toxic to plants

■ Extension: The development of the ideas of evolution

The idea of biological evolution is closely linked to the name of **Charles Darwin**, but in fact evolution was discussed by **Erasmus Darwin** (1731–1802), Charles's grandfather, and by other biologists and geologists long before the publication of Charles Darwin's controversial theory shocked Victorian Britain.

The earliest, significant contribution was the realisation that the **Earth was extremely old**. In Western culture, the biblical account of creation was generally accepted as authoritative until the eighteenth century, at least. Furthermore, the chronology detailed in the Bible suggested that life had appeared on Earth a mere few thousand years ago. This timescale, which meant that the Earth was only 5000–6000 years old, was widely accepted in Europe until well into the nineteenth century.

James Hutton (1726–97), a doctor, farmer and experimental scientist, realised that the sedimentary rocks of many existing mountain ranges had once been the beds of lakes and seas and, before that, had been the rocks of even older mountains. He made no estimate of the age of the Earth, but he realised that, in contrast to biblical estimates, the **Earth's timescale** virtually had **no beginning and no end**. Nowadays, geologists estimate the age of the Earth to be **4500 million years**, and **life to have originated 3500 million years ago**. With these timescales it became possible to imagine organic evolution by gradual change.

17 **Explain** the significance for evolution theory of the realisation by early geologists that the Earth was more than a few thousand years old.

18 **Suggest** what sort of events might, in the past, have caused violent and speedy habitat change over a substantial part of the surface of the Earth.

TOK Link

The word 'theory' comes from a Greek word meaning 'seeing'. Today, a scientific theory normally explains something, usually via some mental model. However, there is diversity of scientific theories. They are not always precise and mathematical, like those of Isaac Newton (1642–1727), which seized people's imaginations and enabled them to see science as extremely precise and exact. This remains a very commonly held view.

Dip into the *The Origin of Species* – say Chapter 7. Find the paragraph on the Greenland whale and the evolution of the baleen plates. How would you describe this reasoning? What sort of 'theory' is presented here?

■ Classification

5.5.1–5.5.5

Classification is essential to biology because there are far too many different living things to sort out and compare unless they are organised into manageable categories. With an effective classification system in use, it is easier to organise our ideas about organisms and make generalisations. The scheme of classification has to be flexible, allowing newly discovered living organisms to be added into the scheme where they fit best. It should also include fossils, since we believe living and extinct species are related.

The process of **classification** involves:

■ giving every organism an **agreed name**;
■ arrangement of organisms into **groupings of apparently related organisms**, as far as these relationships are understood, so imposing an overall scheme on the diversity of living things.

The binomial system of naming

Many organisms have local names, but these often differ from locality to locality around the world, so they do not allow observers to be confident they are talking about the same thing. For example, in America the name 'robin' refers to a bird of the size of the European blackbird and altogether different from the European robin (Figure 6.25). To avoid confusion, scientists use an international approach called the **binomial system** (meaning 'a two-part name'). By this system everyone, anywhere knows exactly which organism is being referred to.

Figure 6.25 Two robins of the northern hemisphere

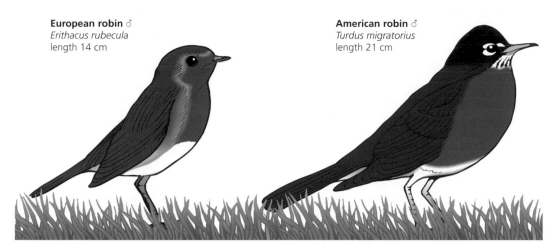

European robin ♂
Erithacus rubecula
length 14 cm

American robin ♂
Turdus migratorius
length 21 cm

In the binomial system, each organism is given a scientific name consisting of two Latin words. The first (a noun) designates the **genus**, the second (an adjective) names the **species**. The generic name begins with a capital letter, and is followed by the specific name, which begins with a lowercase letter. Conventionally, this name is written in *italics* when in print (or is underlined in handwriting). As shown in Figure 6.26, closely related organisms have the same generic name; only their species names differ. You will see that when organisms are frequently referred to in a piece of writing, the full name is given initially and thereafter the generic name is shortened to the first (capital) letter. Thus, in continuing references to humans in an article or scientific paper, *Homo sapiens* becomes *H. sapiens*.

Figure 6.26 Naming organisms by the binomial system

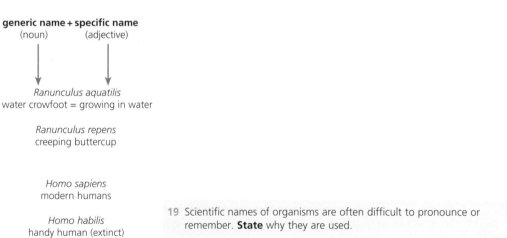

generic name + specific name
(noun)   (adjective)

Ranunculus aquatilis
water crowfoot = growing in water

Ranunculus repens
creeping buttercup

Homo sapiens
modern humans

Homo habilis
handy human (extinct)

19 Scientific names of organisms are often difficult to pronounce or remember. **State** why they are used.

The scheme of classification

The science of classification is called taxonomy. The word comes from taxa (singular, taxon), which is the general name for groups or categories within a classification system. The taxa used in taxonomy are given in Figure 6.27.

Biological classification schemes are the invention of biologists, based on the best available evidence at the time. In classification, the aim is to use as many characteristics as possible in placing similar organisms together and dissimilar ones apart. Just as similar **species** are grouped together into the same **genus** (plural, **genera**), so similar genera are grouped together into **families**. This approach is extended from families to **orders**, then **classes**, **phyla** and **kingdoms**. This is a hierarchical scheme of classification, each successive group containing more and more different kinds of organism.

Figure 6.27 Taxa used in taxonomy, applied to genera from two different kingdoms

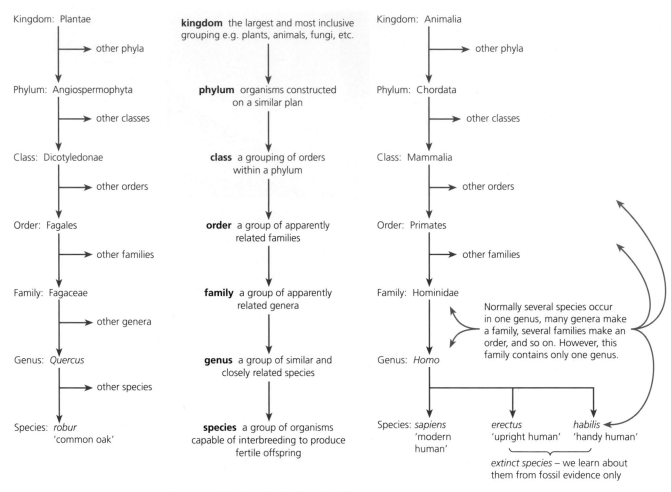

Kingdom: Plantae
→ other phyla
Phylum: Angiospermophyta
→ other classes
Class: Dicotyledonae
→ other orders
Order: Fagales
→ other families
Family: Fagaceae
→ other genera
Genus: *Quercus*
→ other species
Species: *robur* 'common oak'

kingdom the largest and most inclusive grouping e.g. plants, animals, fungi, etc.

phylum organisms constructed on a similar plan

class a grouping of orders within a phylum

order a group of apparently related families

family a group of apparently related genera

genus a group of similar and closely related species

species a group of organisms capable of interbreeding to produce fertile offspring

Kingdom: Animalia
→ other phyla
Phylum: Chordata
→ other classes
Class: Mammalia
→ other orders
Order: Primates
→ other families
Family: Hominidae
Genus: *Homo*

Normally several species occur in one genus, many genera make a family, several families make an order, and so on. However, this family contains only one genus.

Species: *sapiens* 'modern human'   *erectus* 'upright human'   *habilis* 'handy human'

extinct species – we learn about them from fossil evidence only

(a mnemonic to remember the hierarchy of taxa:
King **P**eter **C**alled **O**ut **F**or **G**enuine **S**cientists)

---

20 **Design** a method of classifying animals and plants commonly found in gardens that might be useful to an enthusiastic gardener.

Classification of the plant kingdom

The green plants are terrestrial organisms, adapted to life on land, although some do occur in aquatic habitats. They are eukaryotic organisms, with a wall containing cellulose around each cell. In their nutrition, green plants are autotrophic organisms, manufacturing sugar by photosynthesis in their chloroplasts. The sugar is then stored or used immediately to sustain the whole of their metabolism.

A distinctive feature of green plants is their rather **complex life cycle**: there are two stages or generations, a gametophyte generation that produces gametes, and a sporophyte generation that forms spores. *The details of this feature do not concern us here, but it does account for some otherwise puzzling aspects of green plant structures and life cycles.*

The phyla that make up the green plants

Green plants range from simple, tiny mosses to huge trees – incidentally, trees include some of the largest and oldest living things. The four main phyla of green plants are the mosses (Phylum Bryophyta); ferns (Phylum Filicinophyta); conifers (Phylum Coniferophyta) and flowering plants (Phylum Angiospermophyta). Figures 6.28–31 present the **simple recognition features of the four phyla**, in turn.

Figure 6.28 The mosses – Phylum Bryophyta

the moss *Funaria* is an early coloniser of land after a fire has killed larger plants in woods or heathland

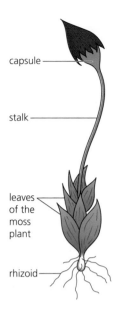

capsule

stalk

leaves of the moss plant

rhizoid

Introducing the Bryophyta

- All are land plants, yet poorly adapted to terrestrial conditions – typically restricted to damp environments.

- Plant constructed of a tiny stem and radially arranged leaves. Roots absent, but stem anchored by hair-like rhizoids.

- Leaves not protected from water loss by a waxy cuticle, and stem contains no water-conducting cells or supporting 'fibres'.

- Spore-containing capsule grows on the main (haploid) plant on a long stalk with its 'foot' in the moss stem.

- Spore capsule may have an elaborate spore-dispersing valve mechanism.

- Alternatively, some Bryophyta exist as flat leaf-like structures on the soil surface, and are known as liverworts.

Figure 6.29 The ferns – Phylum Filicinophyta

the fern *Dryopteris*

leaves

roots

rhizome

the fern Bracken

developing leaf rolled

rhizome

growing point

Introducing the Filicinophyta

- Ferns are green plants with stems, leaves and roots, and are well-adapted to terrestrial conditions. (Stems growing just below ground are called rhizomes.)

- Within stem, leaves and roots is vascular tissue for conducting water and nutrients around the plant.

- The leaves are elaborate structures that form tightly coiled up, and uncoil in early growth.

- Leaves are covered by a waxy cuticle that protects against water loss by evaporation.

- Spore-producing structures (sporangia) occur in clusters on the under-surface of the leaves, protected below a flap of tissue.

- Spores are released explosively, thrown some distance and then germinate to produce a tiny, independent leaf-like plant.

- This tiny gamete-forming plant (haploid) is where the zygote is formed that then grows into a new fern plant.

- Present day ferns are relatively small survivors of an ancient group, dominant within the Carboniferous period (about 355 million years ago). Huge forests grew across a swampy land, with tree-like ferns – now present as today's fossil fuels.

Figure 6.30 The conifers
– Phylum Coniferophyta

the conifer tree *Pinus*

**branch showing
position of
female cones**

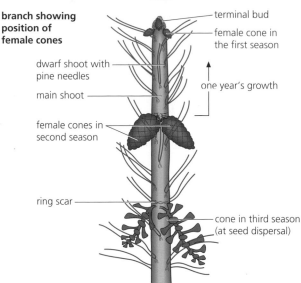

terminal bud

female cone in
the first season

dwarf shoot with
pine needles

one year's growth

main shoot

female cones in
second season

ring scar

cone in third season
(at seed dispersal)

Introducing the Coniferophyta

- Cone-bearing trees, usually large with strong stem (trunk). They grow well, even on poor soils, and are the dominant plants in northern (boreal) forests, for example.

- The main trunk continues to grow straight, and side branches are typically formed in whorls, below, giving the trees a simple cone-shaped outline, at least as young trees.

- Leaves are usually waxy and needle-shaped. They are mostly evergreen, the leaves able to resist damage in low temperatures and heavy snow fall, when water supplies are locked away as ice.

- Seed-bearing plants, the seeds formed in female cones. Male and female cones often occur on the same tree. Typically, the seed takes 2–3 years to form from arrival of pollen (from male cone) to release and dispersal of seeds.

- Survival on poor soils is aided by their mutually advantageous relationship with soil fungi in modified roots (mycorrhiza) in which fungal threads (hyphae) 'trade' ions from the soil for excess sugar that forms in the tree.

- Since confers mostly grow fast and straight, they form economically important crops of timbers known as 'soft woods'.

Figure 6.31 The
flowering plants – Phylum
Angiospermophyta

the monocotyledon grass *Poa*

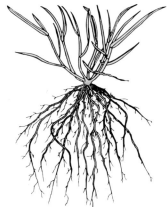

**the dicotyledon
*Ranunculus***

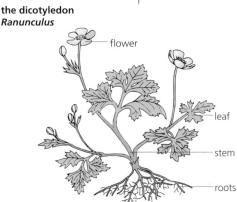

flower

leaf

stem

roots

Introducing the Angiospermophyta

- The Angiospermophyta are the dominant group of land plants. Many are herbaceous (non-woody) plants, others are trees (hard woods) or shrubs.

- The stem, leaves and roots contain vascular tissue (xylem and phloem) that delivers water and nutrients all around the plant.

- Leaves are elaborate structures with a waxy, waterproof covering and pores (stomata) in the surface.

- Flowers are unique to the Angiospermophyta, and from them seeds are formed. Seeds are enclosed in an ovary, and after fertilisation, the ovary develops into a fruit.

- With development of the flower have come complex mechanisms of pollen transfer and seed dispersal, often involving insects, birds, mammals or wind and water.

- The Angiospermophyta are divided into the monocotyledons and dicotyledons.

- The monocotyledons (e.g. the grasses) mostly have parallel veins in their leaves, and have a single seed-leaf in the embryo in the seed.

- The dicotyledons (the broad-leaved plants) have net veins in their leaves and two seed leaves in the embryo.

Classification of the animal kingdom

Animals are multicellular, eukaryotic organisms with heterotrophic nutrition. Typically, the body of an animal has cells highly specialised by their structure and physiology to perform particular functions, such as muscle cells for movement. Specialised tissues often occur together to form organs, which perform a particular function in the body as a whole. Most animals have some form of nervous system to coordinate their body actions and responses. These features of animal structure and function are mostly explored in relation to the human mammal, in Chapter 7.

A point of contrast with plants is the simplicity of the life cycle of animals (although some parasitic animals are an exception to this). Their life cycle is diploid, with the adult producing haploid gametes (sperms and ova) by meiosis. After fertilisation, the zygote divides to produce an embryo, which early in development becomes a characteristic hollow ball of cells, called a **blastula** (page 384).

An animal's life style may be reflected in its body plan – many animals are in more or less constant movement, often in search of food, for example. The symmetry of the body of a motile organism is typically **bilateral**, meaning that there is only one plane that cuts the body into two equal halves. Also, with motility comes a compact body, elongated in the direction of movement, so shaped to offer least resistance to the surrounding medium, air or water. Since the anterior (front) end experiences the changing environment first, sense organs become located there. The result is the evolution of a head distinct from the rest of the body, a developmental process called **cephalisation**.

However, the body of an animal with a non-motile or sessile life style may show radial symmetry. The body is approximately cylindrically organised, with body parts arranged around a central axis. There are many planes by which the body can be cut into equal halves. No head is formed.

Some non-vertebrate phyla of the animal kingdom

The phyla of animals introduced here are a selection of non-vertebrate groups only, namely the sponges (Phylum Porifera); jellyfishes and sea anemones (Phylum Cnidaria); flatworms (Phylum Platyhelminthes), roundworms (Phylum Nematoda), the molluscs (Phylum Mollusca), and the jointed-limbed animals (Phylum Arthropoda).

Figures 6.32–6.37 present the **simple recognition features of these six phyla**, in turn.

Figure 6.32 The sponges – Phylum Porifera

the sponge *Leucosolenia*

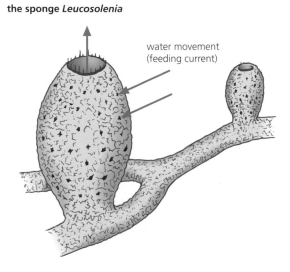

water movement (feeding current)

Leucosolenia (1–2 cm wide)

Introducing the Porifera

- The Porifera are the simplest multicellular animals, structurally little more than colonies of cells. They are aquatic and mostly marine animals (once thought to be plants).

- Sponges are formed into simple sac-like structures of cells in two layers, arranged around a central (gastric) cavity.

- Cells of the walls of the sponge specialise for feeding, structural support or reproduction. They form the only multicellular animals to entirely lack any nervous system.

- Feeding is on tiny suspended particles – plankton – which are drawn in through pores in the walls, and are taken up by individual cells and digested.

- Sponges may reproduce asexually by budding, and also sexually – forming a free-swimming larva which is the dispersal stage for this sedentary animal.

Figure 6.33 The jellyfishes and sea anemones – Phylum Cnidaria

Hydra
a fresh water hydroid cnidarian

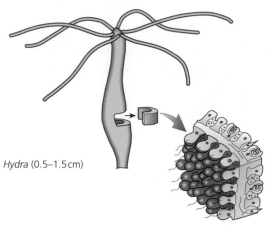

Hydra (0.5–1.5 cm)

Aurelia
a marine jellyfish
where the medusoid form
is the dominant stage

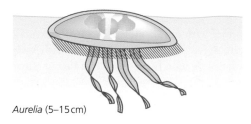

Aurelia (5–15 cm)

Introducing the Cnidaria

- The Cnidaria or coelenterates (meaning 'hollow gut') are aquatic animals, mostly marine, with radially symmetrical body plans.

- The body cavity is a gut with a single opening for ingestion of food and egestion of waste matter.

- The body wall is of two layers of cells – an outer **ectoderm** and an inner **endoderm** – separated by a layer of jelly, the **mesoglea**.

- The ectoderm includes **stinging cells** which may be triggered by passing prey. With these cells, prey is poisoned, paralysed and held until it is pushed into the gut for digestion.

- The stinging cells are found especially on the tentacles.

- Behaviour of the body is coordinated by a nerve net in the mesoglea, in contact with the bases of all wall cells.

- There are alternative body forms in the Cnidaria – either a sessile **hydroid** form (illustrated by *Hydra*) or a floating **medusa** form (illustrated by the jellyfish). These body forms typically alternate in the life cycle.

- The Cnidaria also include the sea anemones and corals.

Figure 6.34 The flatworms – Phylum Platyhelminthes

Planaria
a free-living flatworm

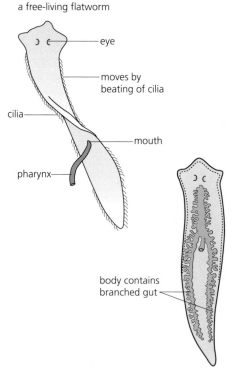

- eye
- moves by beating of cilia
- cilia
- mouth
- pharynx
- body contains branched gut

Introducing the Platyhelminthes

- The Platyhelminthes are flat, unsegmented animals with a body built from three cell layers (**triploblastic organisation**).

- There is no cavity in the middle layer. They have a mouth and a gut with numerous branches, but there is no anus. Feeding is by scavenging or predating on other small animals.

- There is no circulatory system in the platyhelminth body, but the generally small, thin, often flat body means that oxygen can diffuse easily to most cells.

- There are 'flame cells' present for excretion and regulation of water and ions in the body.

- Platyhelminthes often have both male and female reproductive organs in one individual (hermaphrodite organisation), but the chances of self-fertilisation are minimal.

- Some are free-living flatworms, but others are parasitic flukes or tapeworms. The phylum contains many important parasites.

Figure 6.35 The roundworms – Phylum Nematoda

Ascaris
a roundworm parasite of humans

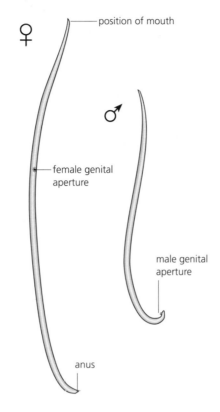

- position of mouth

♀

♂

female genital aperture

male genital aperture

anus

Introducing the Nematoda

- The nematode worms, also known as roundworms, have narrow bodies, round in cross-section and pointed at both ends. They are unsegmented.

- The body is covered by a thin, transparent, elastic protein cuticle. Within, the muscles are all longitudinal, and their contraction produces thrashing movements through liquid media.

- The body contains a long, unbranched gut with mouth and anus.

- Nematodes live in vast numbers in moist soil and in the mud at the bottom of lakes – playing a part in decomposition and nutrient cycling. Others are parasites of plants, and about 50 species are human parasites.

Figure 6.36 The molluscs – Phylum Mollusca

Helix
the snail

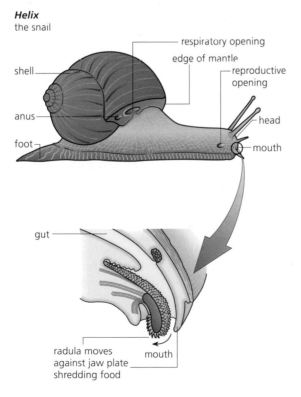

respiratory opening
edge of mantle
shell
reproductive opening
anus
head
foot
mouth

gut

radula moves against jaw plate shredding food
mouth

Introducing the Mollusca

- The molluscs are the slugs, snails, limpets, mussels and octopuses. They are a huge and diverse group of organisms, the second largest phylum in terms of numbers of species. Most are aquatic and found in fresh water or marine habitats, but a few are terrestrial.

- They are animals with generally soft, flexible bodies which show little or no evidence of segmentation. The body is divided into a head, a flattened muscular foot and a hump or visceral mass often covered by a shell, secreted by a layer of tissue called the mantle.

- The compact body shape of molluscs means that diffusion is not effective for the transport of nutrients, and molluscs have gills or occasionally lungs for gaseous exchange, as well as a well-developed blood circulation.

- Most molluscs have a rasping, tongue-like radula used for feeding.

Figure 6.37 The jointed-limbed animals – Phylum Arthropoda

the locust

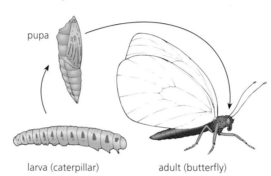

adult

grows through several moults

larval stage

the butterfly

pupa

larva (caterpillar)

adult (butterfly)

Introducing the Arthropoda

- The Arthropoda are the most numerically successful of all animals, and are divided into five distinct groups: the **crustaceans**, the **arachnids**, the **centipedes**, the **millipedes**, and the **insects**.

- These animals have segmented bodies, covered by a hard external skeleton made of chitin, with jointed limbs (after which they are named). Typically, there is one pair of legs per segment, but this pattern has been lost from some arthropods.

- The exoskeleton cannot grow with the animal, so it has to be shed periodically (moulting), and replaced with a larger one into which the enlarging animal grows.

- The blood circulation is open; the blood is in a haemocoel cavity surrounding all the organs of the body. A tubular heart pumps blood into the haemocoel.

- The functioning of the body is co-ordinated by a ventral nerve cord with nerves running to each segment. There is a concentration of nerves at the front of the body.

- The insects are by far the most numerous and have:
  – a body divided into head, thorax and abdomen
  – three pairs of legs and two pairs of wings attached to the thorax
  – a pair of compound eyes and a pair of antennae on the head
  – head with mouthparts that are modified paired limbs
  – air piped to the tissues by a system of tubes, called tracheae.

The construction of dichotomous keys

The process of naming unknown organisms we come across – for example, in ecological field work – is important but time-consuming. We often attempt this by comparisons, using identification books that are illustrated with drawings and photographs, and that provide information on habitat and habits to give us clues to the identity of organisms.

Alternatively, the use of **keys** may assist us in the identification of unknown organisms. The advantage of using keys is that it requires careful observation. We learn a great deal about the structural features of organisms and get some understanding of how different organisms may be related.

The steps in the construction of a dichotomous key are illustrated first.
Follow the steps, then put them into practice yourself.

Steps in key construction

The steps in key construction are illustrated using eight different tree leaves as shown in Figure 6.38. In selecting the leaves, care must be taken to ensure that each is entirely representative of the majority of leaves the tree has.

First, each leaf is carefully examined and the most significant features of structure are listed in a matrix where their presence (or absence) is recorded against each specimen, as shown in Figure 6.39.

Then, from the matrix, a characteristic shown by half (or thereabouts) of the leaves is selected. This divides the specimens into two groups. A dichotomous flow diagram is constructed, progressively dividing the specimens into smaller groups. Each division point is labelled with the critical diagnostic feature(s), as shown in Figure 6.40.

Finally, a dichotomous key is constructed, reducing the dichotomy points in the flow diagram to alternative statements to which the answer is either 'yes' or 'no'. To each alternative is given a number to which the reader must refer to carry on the identification, until all eight leaves have been identified (Figure 6.41).

Figure 6.38 Collection of leaves for the construction of a dichotomous key

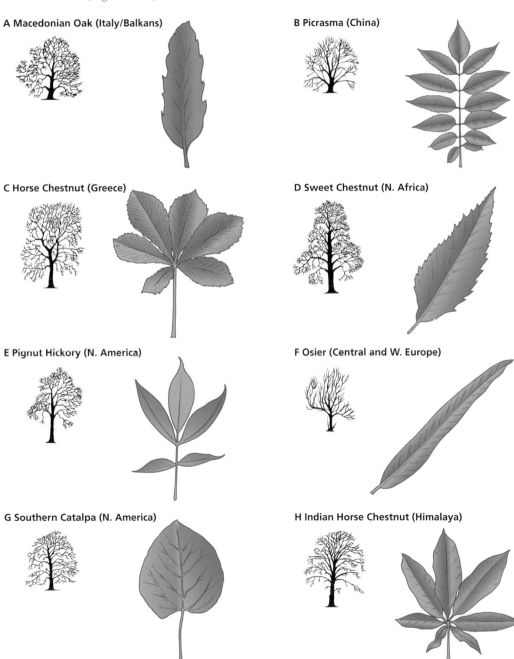

A Macedonian Oak (Italy/Balkans)

B Picrasma (China)

C Horse Chestnut (Greece)

D Sweet Chestnut (N. Africa)

E Pignut Hickory (N. America)

F Osier (Central and W. Europe)

G Southern Catalpa (N. America)

H Indian Horse Chestnut (Himalaya)

Figure 6.39 Matrix of characteristics shown by one or more of the sample

Feature of leaf: present (✓) or absent (−)	Tree leaves, identified by number							
	A Macedonian Oak	B Picrasma	C Horse Chestnut	D Sweet Chestnut	E Pignut Hickory	F Osier	G Southern Catalpa	H Indian Horse Chestnut
leaf not divided into leaflets (leaf entire)	✓	−	−	✓	−	✓	✓	−
leaf consists of leaflets	−	✓	✓	−	✓	−	−	✓
leaf blade narrow, with almost parallel sides	✓	−	−	−	−	✓	−	−
leaf blade broad	−	−	−	✓	−	−	✓	−
leaflets radiate from one point (palmate)	−	−	✓	−	−	−	−	✓
leaflets arranged in two rows along stalk	−	✓	−	−	✓	−	−	−
leaf / leaflet margin smooth	−	−	−	−	✓	✓	✓	✓
leaf / leaflet margin toothed, like a saw	✓	✓	✓	✓	−	−	−	−
leaf blade heart-shaped	−	−	−	−	−	−	✓	−
leaf blade boat-shaped (widest in middle)	−	−	−	✓	−	−	✓	−
leaflet paddle-shaped, widest near one end	−	−	✓	−	−	−	−	−
leaflets 5 in number or less	−	−	−	−	✓	−	−	−
leaflets between 6 and 10 in number	−	−	✓	−	−	−	−	✓
leaflets more than 10 in number	−	✓	−	−	−	−	−	−

Figure 6.40 Dichotomous flow diagram of leaf characteristics

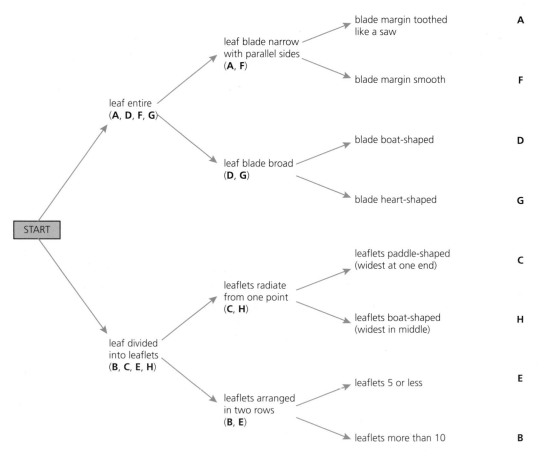

Figure 6.41
Dichotomous key to the
sample of eight tree
leaves

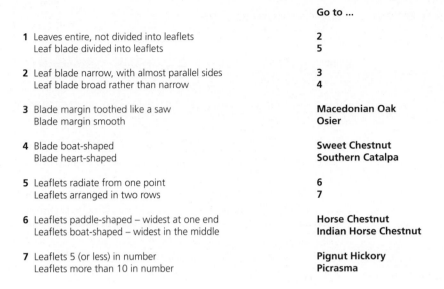

Go to ...

1 Leaves entire, not divided into leaflets — **2**
Leaf blade divided into leaflets — **5**

2 Leaf blade narrow, with almost parallel sides — **3**
Leaf blade broad rather than narrow — **4**

3 Blade margin toothed like a saw — **Macedonian Oak**
Blade margin smooth — **Osier**

4 Blade boat-shaped — **Sweet Chestnut**
Blade heart-shaped — **Southern Catalpa**

5 Leaflets radiate from one point — **6**
Leaflets arranged in two rows — **7**

6 Leaflets paddle-shaped – widest at one end — **Horse Chestnut**
Leaflets boat-shaped – widest in the middle — **Indian Horse Chestnut**

7 Leaflets 5 (or less) in number — **Pignut Hickory**
Leaflets more than 10 in number — **Picrasma**

Practising key construction

Joseph Camin, a biology teacher at Kansas University, designed a family of 'animals' in order to introduce the principles of classification in a practical way. Some of his 'caminacules' are shown in Figure 6.42. Use a copy of these to construct a key, following the steps detailed above. Alternatively, use a suitable selection of eight living biological specimens.

Figure 6.42 A selection of Camin's 'caminacules'

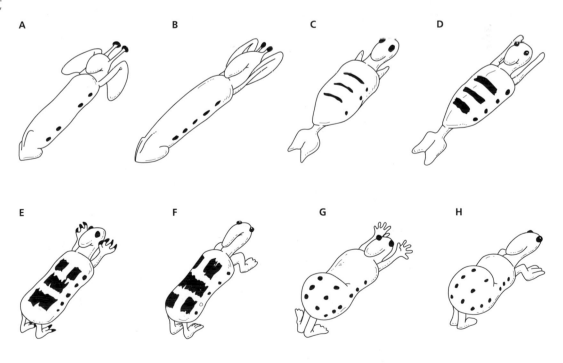

■ Extension: The five kingdoms

At one time the living world seemed to divide naturally into two kingdoms:

Plants	Animals
photosynthetic (autotrophic nutrition)	ingestion of complex food (heterotrophic nutrition)
mostly rooted (therefore, stationary) organisms	typically mobile organisms

These two kingdoms grew from the original disciplines of biology, namely **botany**, the study of plants, and **zoology**, the study of animals. Fungi and microorganisms were 'added' to botany.

Initially there was only one problem: fungi possessed the typically 'animal' heterotrophic nutrition but were 'plant-like' in structure. Later, with the use of the **electron microscope**, came the discovery of the two types of cell structure, namely **prokaryotic** and **eukaryotic** (page 14). As a result, the bacteria with their prokaryotic cells could no longer be 'plants' since plants have eukaryotic cells. The divisions of living things into kingdoms needed overhauling.

Figure 6.43 Possible evolutionary relationship of the five kingdoms

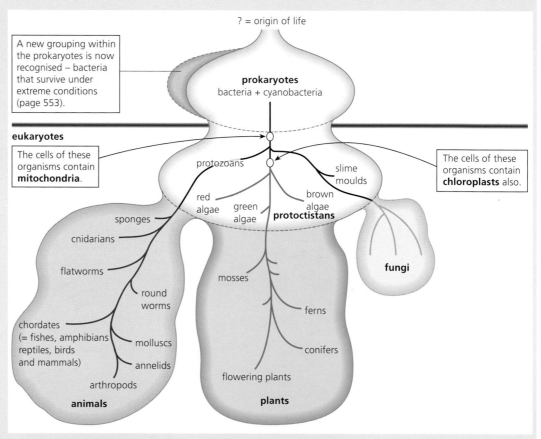

Today, the agreed division of living things is into five kingdoms (Figure 6.43):

- **Prokaryotae** – the prokaryote kingdom, the bacteria and cyanobacteria (photosynthetic bacteria), predominantly unicellular organisms;
- **Protoctista** – the protoctistan kingdom (eukaryotes), predominantly unicellular, and seen as resembling the ancestors of the fungi, plants and animals;
- **Fungi** – the fungal kingdom (eukaryotes), predominantly multicellular organisms, non-motile, and with heterotrophic nutrition;
- **Plantae** – the plant kingdom (eukaryotes), multicellular organisms, non-motile, with autotrophic nutrition;
- **Animalia** – the animal kingdom (eukaryotes), multicellular organisms, motile, with heterotrophic nutrition.

■ *Examination questions – a selection*

Questions 1–5 are taken from past IB Diploma Biology papers:

Q1 Which characteristics apply to all evolving populations?
I overproduction of offspring
II there are differing genotypes in the population
III different chances of survival

A I and II only   C II and III only
B I and III only   D I, II and III
Standard Level Paper 1, May 02, Q21

Q2 Which of the following represents a kingdom?
A eukaryotes   C protoctista
B viruses   D mammals
Higher Level Paper 1, May 06, Q18

Q3 Which of the following correctly identifies the role(s) of bacteria in an ecosystem?
A autotroph
B autotroph and detritivore
C detritivore and heterotroph
D autotroph, detritivore and heterotroph
Standard Level Paper 1, May 05, Q21

The following diagram refers to questions 4 and 5. It shows part of the food web of the community that inhabits Antarctica.

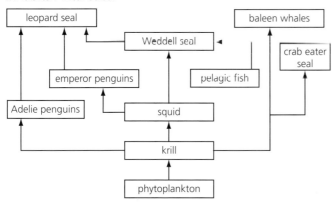

Q4 What trophic level do squid belong to?
A tertiary consumers
B secondary consumers
C primary consumers
D producers
Standard Level Paper 1, May 04, Q18

Q5 Which human activity would have the greatest impact on the food web?
A overfishing the krill
B killing the crab eater seals for their skins
C a continued ban on hunting whales
D building an airstrip through the emperor penguin nesting colony
Standard Level Paper 1, May 04, Q19

Questions 6–10 cover other syllabus issues in this chapter.

Q6 By means of concise definition and examples, distinguish between the following terms:
a *ecosystem* and *habitat*   (4)
b *population* and *community*   (4)
c *species* and *genus*.   (4)

Q7 a Carbon is present in all organic compounds and in carbon dioxide gas in the atmosphere. Suggest where else inorganic carbon is commonly found in the biosphere, and in what forms it occurs.   (4)
b Describe by what processes the carbon of organic compounds will be converted to carbon of carbon dioxide.   (2)
c State where conversion of carbon dioxide to organic compounds occurs and what source of energy is involved.   (2)
d Explain the fact that the average concentration of atmospheric carbon dioxide is almost stable on a daily basis.   (2)
e Identify the part played by the oceans, and organisms in them, in the carbon cycle.   (3)

Q8 The individuals in a species are not identical, but show variations in their characteristics. Explain how variations may arise, and what part variations may play in the evolution of species by natural selection.   (6)

Q9 a Draw a graph of the growth of an animal population after introduction to a new, highly favourable environment. Annotate the stages of the curve to establish the factors influencing change in population size at each stage.   (6)
b In a natural environment the numbers of a population in the community of organisms present normally fluctuate unpredictably. Identify the natural influences that change population numbers in these circumstances.   (6)

Q10 Use a table as shown to state one external feature characteristic of each group.   (7)

Group	Characteristic external feature
cnidarians	
chordates	
mosses	
arthropods	
ferns	
annelids	
flowering plants	

7 Human physiology, health and reproduction

STARTING POINTS

- The bulk of the **carbon compounds** that make up the cytoplasm of cells consist of **carbohydrates**, **lipids** and **proteins**.
- In cells, **energy** is transferred by the breakdown of **nutrients**, principally carbohydrates such as glucose, by the process of **cell respiration**.
- Animals obtain nutrients by **digestion** of food substances, followed by absorption of the products of digestion – described as **heterotrophic nutrition**.
- **Enzymes** are biological catalysts made of **protein**, produced by cells to bring about **chemical changes** inside cells, such as cell respiration, or outside cells, such as **digestion**.
- **Entry into cells** occurs by **diffusion** or **active transport**. Water enters by **osmosis**, a special case of diffusion.
- Microorganisms are a diverse group, some **prokaryotes**, some **eukaryotes**, and some **protoctista**. **Viruses** are not living organisms.
- Reproduction is a characteristic of living things. In sexual reproduction two sex cells (**gametes**) fuse (**fertilisation**) to form a **zygote**.
- As the chromosome number is doubled at fertilisation, the process of gamete formation involves **meiosis** (reductive nuclear division).

Physiology is about how and why the parts of the body function the way they do. Linked with physiology is **anatomy** – the study of structure. Structure gives vital clues to function, as when the structures of our arteries and veins are compared, for example.

Physiology is also an experimental science. For example, physiological experiments have established that cells of organisms function best in an internal environment that stays fairly constant, held and maintained within quite narrow limits. We talk about a **constant internal environment** – which is certainly the case in mammals such as the human, on which we focus here.

In this chapter, we first examine how the body **obtains nutrients**, breathes and **exchanges gases** with the air, and maintains an efficient **internal transport system**.

Pathogens, many of them microorganisms, may bring disease to healthy organisms. Accordingly, cells of our blood circulation also have roles in **defence against communicable diseases**. Finally, the roles of **nerves** and **hormones**, the processes of **homeostasis**, and aspects of **sexual reproduction** are discussed.

■ Nutrition

6.1.1–6.1.7

An animal takes in food, which is complex organic matter, and digests it in the **alimentary canal** or gut, producing molecules suitable for absorption into the body cells via the blood circulation system. This is known as **holozoic nutrition** (meaning 'feeding like an animal'). Holozoic nutrition is just one of the forms of **heterotrophic nutrition** (meaning 'feeding on complex, ready-made foods') to obtain the required nutrients. The important ecological point to remember about all heterotrophs is their dependence, directly or indirectly, on organisms that manufacture their own elaborated foods. These organisms are the photosynthetic green plants, known as autotrophs. This dependence is demonstrated in food chains (page 139).

1 State two forms of heterotrophic nutrition, other than holozoic.

Digestion, where and why

The food an animal requires has to be searched for or possibly hunted. Some mammals eat only plant material (**herbivores**), some eat only other animals (**carnivores**), and others eat both animal and plant material (**omnivores**). Whatever is eaten, a balance of the essential nutrients is required by the body. The sum total of the nutrients eaten is the diet.

The mammalian gut is a long, hollow muscular tube connecting mouth to anus. Along the gut are several glands, and the whole structure is specialised for the movement and digestion of food and for the absorption of the useful products of digestion. The regions of the human gut are shown in Figure 7.1, and the steps of nutrition in Table 7.1.

Figure 7.1 The layout of the human gut

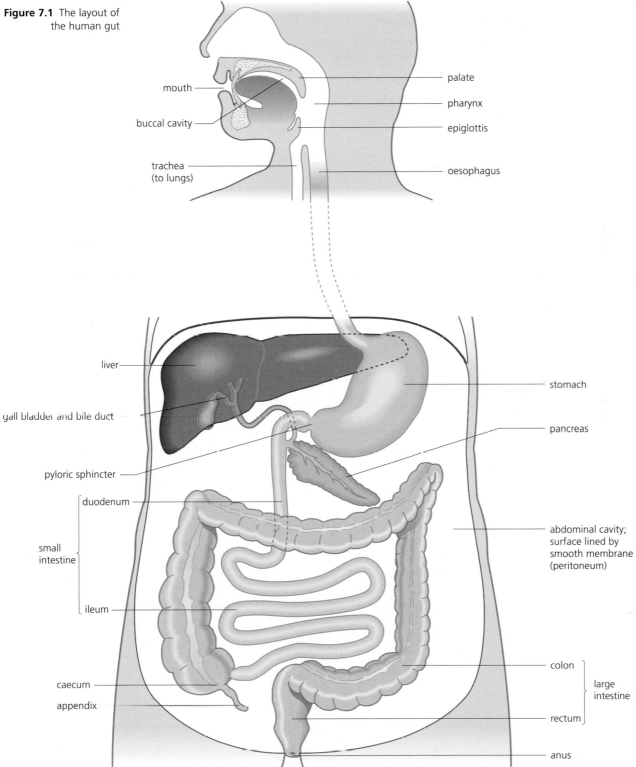

Step	Process
ingestion	food taken into mouth for processing in the gut
digestion	▪ mechanical digestion by the action of teeth and the muscular walls of the gut ▪ chemical digestion by enzymes, mainly in the stomach and intestine
absorption	soluble products of digestion absorbed into blood circulation system (into lymphatic system if fat droplets)
assimilation	products of digestion absorbed from blood into body cells (such as liver and muscle cells) and used or stored
egestion	undigested food and dead cells from the lining of the gut, together with bacteria from the gut flora, expelled from the body as faeces

Table 7.1 The five steps of holozoic nutrition

Figure 7.2 Chemical digestion – the steps

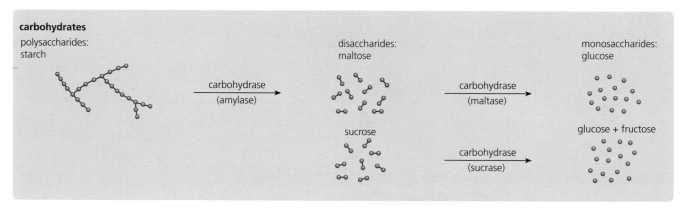

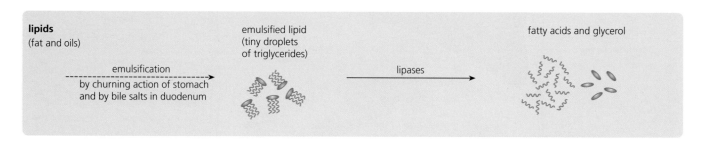

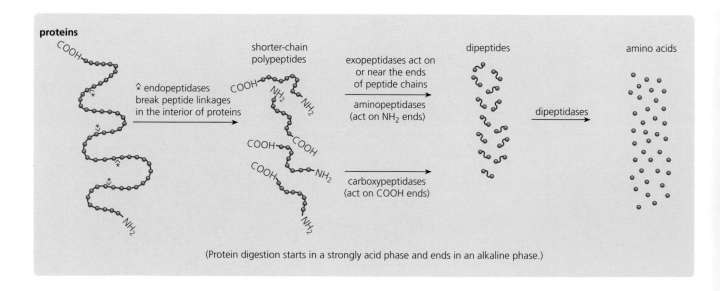

Digestion is an essential step because the bulk of the food taken in consists of insoluble molecules that are far too large to cross the gut wall and enter the blood stream. The bulk of our diet consists of carbohydrates, lipids and proteins. These must be hydrolysed to monosaccharides, fatty acids and glycerol, and free amino acids, before they can be absorbed and, later, built up into the carbohydrates, lipids and proteins required by our bodies. The chemical structure of carbohydrates, lipids and proteins is discussed in Chapter 2. The chemical changes that occur to large, insoluble carbohydrates, lipids and proteins during digestion are summarised in Figure 7.2. Food cannot be said to have truly entered the body until it has been digested and the products absorbed across the gut wall.

The first stage in the breakdown of large, insoluble food molecules, then, is **mechanical digestion**. This occurs by the action of the jaws and teeth in the mouth, and then later, through the churning action of the muscular walls as the food is moved along the gut, particularly in the stomach. Throughout the gut, waves of contraction and relaxation of the circular and longitudinal muscles of the wall propel food along. This process is known as **peristalsis**. (Gut muscles are described as involuntary muscles because they are not under conscious control.)

The **chemical digestion** that follows is brought about by enzymes. Digestive enzymes are protein catalysts produced in specialised cells in glands associated with the gut. Several different enzymes are secreted onto the food as it passes along the gut. The action of these enzymes very greatly speeds up the breakdown of insoluble food substances. They work efficiently at the relatively low temperature the body is maintained at. To complete the digestion processes, enzymes secreted onto the food work together with those held in the plasma membranes of cells of the gut lining. Examples of digestive enzymes are listed in Table 7.2

2 a Explain why digestion is an essential stage in nutrition.
b State two essential foods that do not require digestion.
c Identify a polysaccharide the human gut cannot digest.

Enzyme	Source	Substrate	Product	Optimum pH
amylase	salivary glands	starch	maltose	6.5–7.5
pepsin	gastric glands	protein	polypeptides	2.0
lipase	pancreas	triglyceride	fatty acids and glycerol	7.0

Table 7.2 Examples of digestive enzymes

Digestion in the stomach

Figure 7.3 Gastric glands, structure and function

The human stomach is a J-shaped muscular bag located high in the abdominal cavity, below the diaphragm and liver. The function of this organ is to retain a meal while enzymic digestion of protein begins.

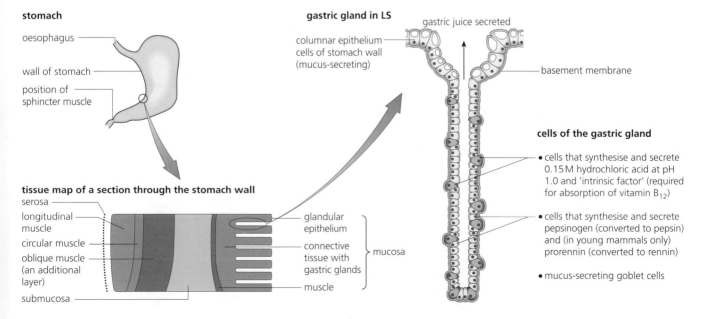

stomach
- oesophagus
- wall of stomach
- position of sphincter muscle

tissue map of a section through the stomach wall
- serosa
- longitudinal muscle
- circular muscle
- oblique muscle (an additional layer)
- submucosa
- glandular epithelium
- connective tissue with gastric glands
- muscle
- mucosa

gastric gland in LS
gastric juice secreted
- columnar epithelium cells of stomach wall (mucus-secreting)
- basement membrane

cells of the gastric gland
- cells that synthesise and secrete 0.15M hydrochloric acid at pH 1.0 and 'intrinsic factor' (required for absorption of vitamin B_{12})
- cells that synthesise and secrete pepsinogen (converted to pepsin) and (in young mammals only) prorennin (converted to rennin)
- mucus-secreting goblet cells

Present in the wall of the stomach are millions of tiny pits called **gastric glands** which secrete the components of **gastric juice** (Figure 7.3). This juice includes **hydrochloric acid** – sufficiently acidic to create an environment of pH 1.5–2.0, which is the optimum pH for protein digestion by the **protease enzymes** of the gastric juice. These proteases, of which **pepsin** is one (Table 7.2), are formed in cells of the gastric glands and secreted in an inactive state. The hydrochloric acid then activates them, and it also kills many bacteria present in the incoming food.

The whole stomach lining is supplied with **goblet cells** that secrete mucus. Mucus bathes the interior lining of the stomach, forming an effective barrier to both the hydrochloric acid and the proteases of the gastric juices, preventing **autolysis** (self-digestion) of the stomach wall.

As the food is mixed with gastric juice and churned by muscle action it becomes a semi-liquid called **chyme**. The churning action of the stomach is an important part of the mechanical digestion process. A typical meal may spend up to four hours in the stomach.

> **3 Predict** why it is essential that the protease enzymes of digestion are secreted in inactive forms.

The roles of the small intestine

It is in the small intestine that completion of digestion of carbohydrates, lipids and proteins occurs, and the useful products of digestion are absorbed. In humans, the small intestine is about five metres long. Throughout its length, the innermost layer of the wall is formed into vast numbers of finger-like or leaf-like projections called villi.

Digestion in the small intestine

Food enters the first part of the small intestine (known as the **duodenum**) a little at a time. Here the chyme meets bile from the bile duct, and the pancreatic juice from the **pancreas**. Bile is strongly alkaline and neutralises the acidity of the chyme. It also lowers the surface tension of large fat globules, causing them to break into tiny droplets, a process called **emulsification**. This speeds digestion by the enzyme lipase later on. Bile itself contains no enzymes.

Pancreatic juice contains several enzymes, including an **amylase** that catalyses the hydrolysis of starch to maltose, a **lipase** that catalyses the hydrolysis of fats to fatty acids and glycerol, and **proteases** that hydrolyse proteins to polypeptides, and shorter-length peptides to free amino acids (Table 7.3).

All these enzymes act as the chyme, bile and pancreatic juice are mixed together by a churning action (a form of peristalsis) called segmentation (Figure 7.4).

Figure 7.4 Chyme meets bile and pancreatic juice

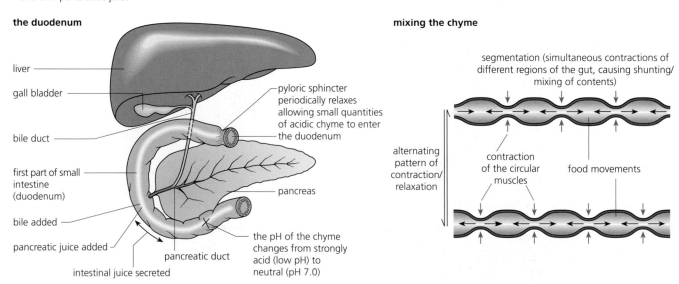

Enzyme	Substrate	Products
amylases	starch	maltose
lipases	lipids	fatty acids and glycerol
proteases	proteins + polypeptides	polypeptides + amino acids

Table 7.3 The groups of hydrolytic enzymes operating in the small intestine

Absorption in the small intestine

The products of digestion, mostly monosaccharide sugars, amino acids, fatty acids and glycerol, together with various vitamins and mineral ions, are absorbed as they make contact with the epithelial cells of the villi of the small intestine (Table 7.4). The process is efficient because the small intestine has a huge surface area, due to the vast number of **villi** (Figure 7.5). Epithelial cells expend energy in the **active transport** process by which most of the products of digestion are taken into the cells. Transport involves protein pump molecules in the plasma membrane, activated by reaction with ATP.

Figure 7.5 The small intestine – the absorption surface

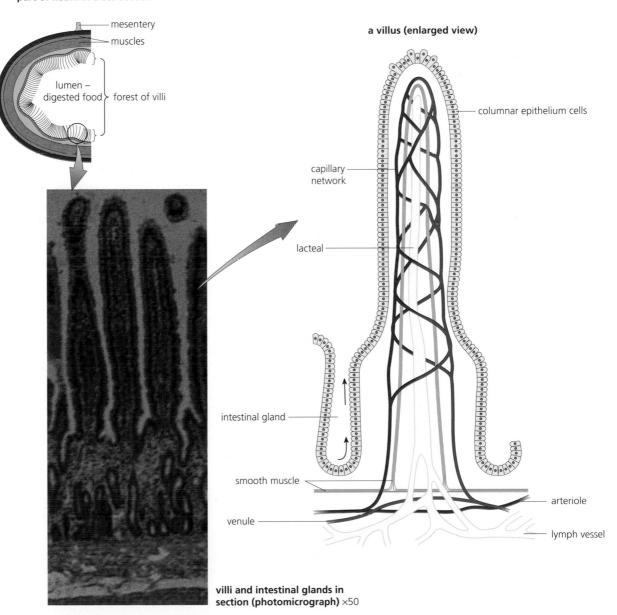

part of ileum in cross-section

mesentery
muscles
lumen – digested food — forest of villi

a villus (enlarged view)

columnar epithelium cells
capillary network
lacteal
intestinal gland
smooth muscle
venule
arteriole
lymph vessel

villi and intestinal glands in section (photomicrograph) ×50

Feature	Description/function
villi	provide a huge surface area for absorption
epithelium cells	single layer of small cells, packed with mitochondria – the source of ATP (metabolic energy) for active uptake across the plasma membrane
pump proteins in the plasma membrane of epithelial cells	actively transport nutrients across the plasma membrane into the villi
network of capillaries	large surface area for uptake of amino acids, monosaccharides, and fatty acids and glycerol into blood circulation
lacteal	branch of the lymphatic system into which triglycerides (combined with protein) pass for transport to body cells
mucus from goblet cells in epithelium	lubricates movement of digested food among the villi and protects plasma membrane of epithelial cells

Table 7.4 Functions of the absorption surface of the small intestine

Assimilation follows absorption

The fate of absorbed nutrients is termed **assimilation**. In the first stage of assimilation, absorbed nutrients are transported from the intestine. In the villi, **sugars** are passed into the capillary network, and from here they are transported to the liver. The liver maintains a constant level of blood sugar (page 222). The **amino acids** are also passed into the capillary network and transported to the liver. Here they contribute to the pool or reserves of amino acids from which new proteins are made in cells and tissues all over the body.

Finally, **lipids** are absorbed as fatty acids and glycerol and are largely absorbed into the lacteal vessels. From there they are carried by the lymphatic system to the blood circulation outside the heart.

4 Distinguish between absorption and assimilation.

Role of the large intestine

The large intestine wall has no villi, but the surface area for absorption is increased somewhat by numerous folds of the inner lining. At this point in the gut, most of the useful products of digestion have been absorbed. What remains is the undigested matter (such as plant fibre), mucus, dead intestinal cells, bacteria, some mineral ions and water. Water is an important component of our diet, and many litres of water are also secreted onto the chyme in the form of digestive juices.

In the colon, water and mineral salts (such as Na^+ and Cl^- ions) are absorbed. What remains of the meal is now referred to as faeces. Bacteria compose about 50% of the faeces, and some of these microorganisms produce gases and odoriferous substances. Bile pigments (excretory products formed from the routine breakdown of red cells), which were added in the duodenum, uniformly colour the faeces.

The rectum is a short muscular tube which terminates at the anus. Discharge of faeces from the body at the anus is controlled by sphincter muscles.

The transport system

6.2.1–6.2.7

Living cells require a supply of water and nutrients such as glucose and amino acids, and most need oxygen. The waste products of cellular metabolism have to be removed. In single-celled organisms and very small organisms, internal distances are small, so movements of nutrients can occur efficiently by **diffusion**, although some substances require to be transported across membranes by **active transport**. In larger organisms, these mechanisms alone are insufficient – an internal transport system is required to service the needs of the cells.

Internal transport systems at work are examples of **mass flow**. The more active an organism is, the more nutrients are likely to be required by cells, and so the greater is the need for an efficient system for internal transport. Larger animals have a **blood circulatory system** that links the parts of the body and makes resources available where they are required.

Transport in mammals

Mammals have a **closed circulation** in which blood is pumped by a powerful, muscular heart and circulated in a continuous system of tubes – the **arteries, veins** and **capillaries** – under pressure. The heart has four chambers, and is divided into right and left sides. Blood flows from the right side of the heart to the lungs, then back to the left side of the heart. From here it is pumped around the rest of the body and back to the right side of the heart. As the blood passes twice through the heart in every single circulation of the body, the system is called a **double circulation**.

The circulatory system of mammals is shown in Figure 7.6, alongside alternative systems. Looking at these other systems helps us to understand the features of the mammalian circulation. It becomes clear that the major advantages of the mammalian circulation are:

- simultaneous high-pressure delivery of oxygenated blood to all regions of the body;
- oxygenated blood reaches the respiring tissues, undiluted by deoxygenated blood.

Figure 7.6 Open and closed circulations

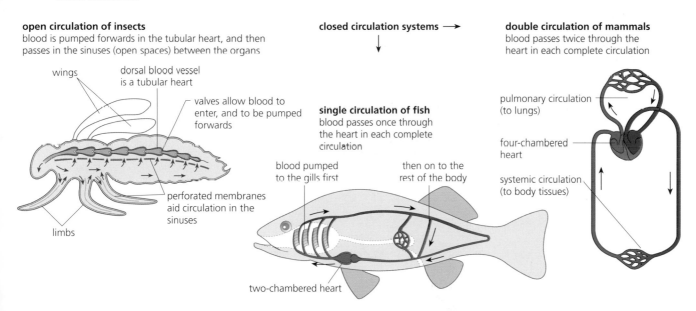

open circulation of insects
blood is pumped forwards in the tubular heart, and then passes in the sinuses (open spaces) between the organs

wings

dorsal blood vessel is a tubular heart

valves allow blood to enter, and to be pumped forwards

perforated membranes aid circulation in the sinuses

limbs

closed circulation systems →

single circulation of fish
blood passes once through the heart in each complete circulation

blood pumped to the gills first

then on to the rest of the body

two-chambered heart

double circulation of mammals
blood passes twice through the heart in each complete circulation

pulmonary circulation (to lungs)

four-chambered heart

systemic circulation (to body tissues)

5 In an open circulation there is 'little control over circulation'. **Suggest** what this means.

The transport medium – the blood

Blood is a special tissue consisting of a liquid medium called **plasma** in which are suspended red cells or **erythrocytes**, white cells or **leucocytes**, and the platelets (Figures 7.7 and 7.8). The plasma is the medium for exchange of substances between cells and tissues, the erythrocytes are involved in transport of respiratory gases, and the leucocytes are adapted to combat infection. The roles of the components of blood are summarised in Table 7.5.

Figure 7.7 The composition of the blood

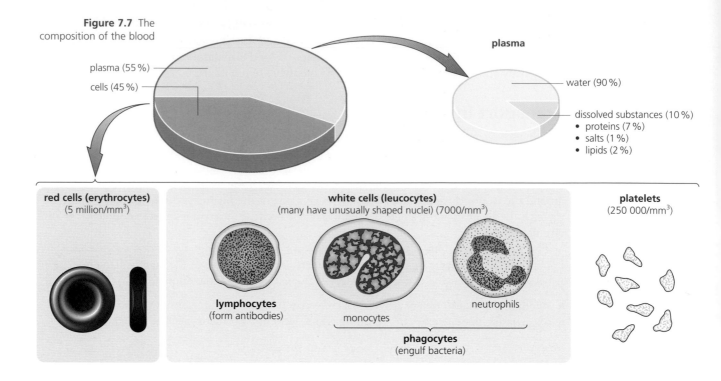

plasma (55%)

cells (45%)

plasma

water (90%)

dissolved substances (10%)
• proteins (7%)
• salts (1%)
• lipids (2%)

red cells (erythrocytes)
(5 million/mm³)

white cells (leucocytes)
(many have unusually shaped nuclei) (7000/mm³)

platelets
(250 000/mm³)

lymphocytes
(form antibodies)

monocytes

neutrophils

phagocytes
(engulf bacteria)

Figure 7.8 Examining a blood smear

preparing a blood smear for staining

Once the smear has dried, it is usually double-stained.

The first stain is selected to dye the cytoplasm of white cells. The second stain will dye the nuclei. When coloured in this way, the few white cells in a blood sample are easy to find.

This technique might be used in a hospital pathology laboratory to search for abnormalities in the blood cells.

1 drop of blood is spread by edge of glass slide

2

3 forming a thin layer that is then allowed to dry

The taking of blood samples and the handling of human blood in school and college laboratories are **forbidden** because of the remote danger of infection from hepatitis and AIDS viruses. The technique shown here is used in the manufacture of prepared slides by a laboratory supplier, and is carried out under proper sterile procedures.

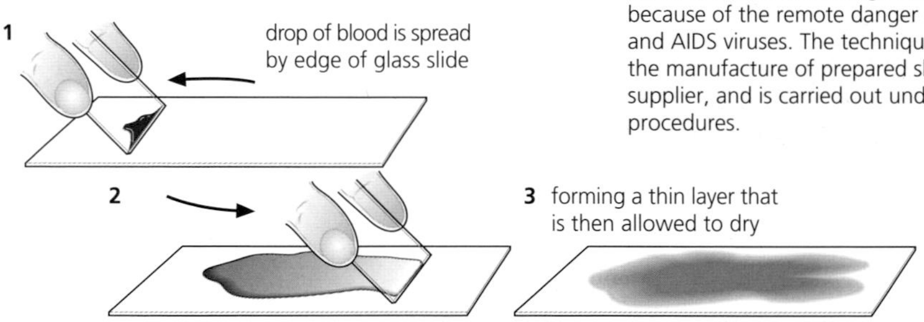

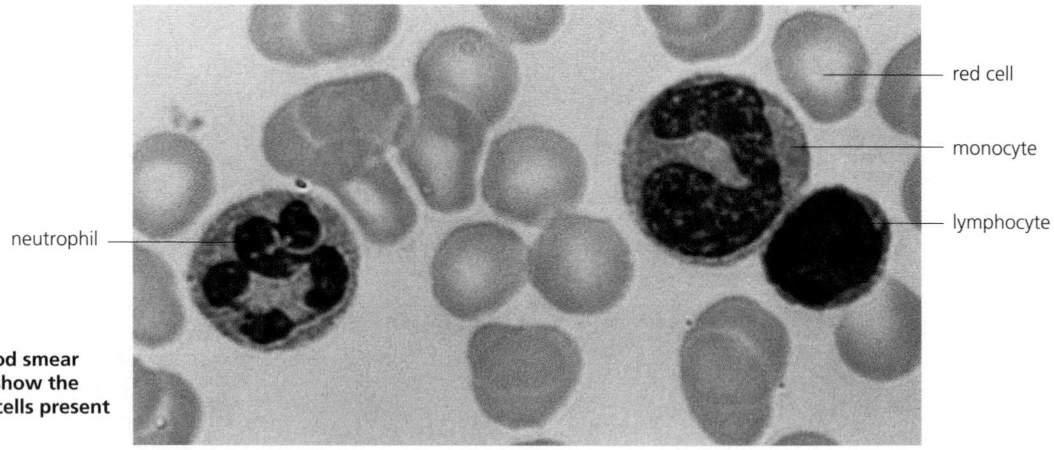

red cell

monocyte

lymphocyte

neutrophil

human blood smear stained to show the few white cells present
(×4500)

Component	Role
plasma	transport of: ■ **nutrients** from gut or liver to all the cells ■ excretory products such as **urea** from the liver to the kidneys ■ **hormones** from the endocrine glands to all tissues and organs ■ **dissolved proteins** which have roles including regulating the osmotic concentration (water potential) of the blood ■ dissolved proteins which are **antibodies** ■ **heat** distribution to all tissues
erythrocytes	transport of: ■ **oxygen** from lungs to respiring cells ■ **carbon dioxide** from respiring cells to lungs (also carried in plasma)
lymphocytes	important in the **immune system** because they form antibodies
phagocytes	**ingest bacteria** or cell fragments
platelets	play a part in the **blood clotting mechanism**

Table 7.5 The components of the blood and their roles

6 Outline where in the body phagocytic leucocytes function.

The plumbing of the circulation system – arteries, veins and capillaries

There are three types of vessel in the circulation system:

■ **arteries**, which carry blood away from the heart;
■ **veins**, which carry blood back to the heart;
■ **capillaries**, which are fine networks of tiny tubes linking arteries and veins.

Both arteries and veins have strong, elastic walls, but the walls of the arteries are very much thicker and stronger than those of the veins. The strength of the walls comes from the collagen fibres present, and the elasticity is due to the elastic and involuntary (smooth) muscle fibres. The walls of the capillaries, on the other hand, consist of endothelium only (endothelium is the innermost lining layer of arteries and veins). Capillaries branch profusely and bring the blood circulation close to cells – no cell is far from a capillary.

Blood leaving the heart is under high pressure, and travels in waves or **pulses**, following each heart beat. By the time the blood has reached the capillaries it is under very much lower pressure, without a pulse. This difference in blood pressure accounts for the differences in the walls of arteries and veins (Table 7.6). Figure 7.9 shows an artery, vein and capillary vessel in section, and details the wall structure of these three vessels. Because of the low pressure in veins there is a possibility of backflow here. Veins have **valves** at intervals that prevent this (Figure 7.10).

Figure 7.9 The structure of the walls of arteries, veins and capillaries

TS artery and vein, LP (×20)

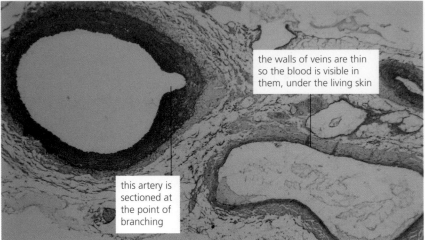

the walls of veins are thin so the blood is visible in them, under the living skin

In sectioned material (as here), veins are more likely to appear squashed, whereas arteries are circular in section.

this artery is sectioned at the point of branching

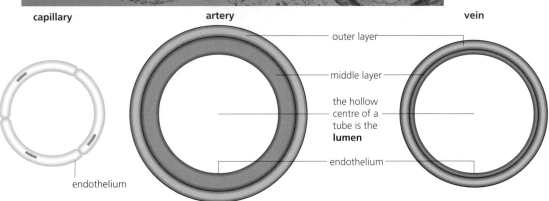

capillary

artery

vein

outer layer

middle layer

the hollow centre of a tube is the **lumen**

endothelium

endothelium

	Capillary – site of exchange between blood and body tissues	Artery – carries blood under high pressure away from the heart	Vein – carries blood under low pressure back to the heart
Outer layer (collagen fibres)	absent	present	present
Middle layer (elastic fibres and involuntary muscle fibres)	absent	thick layer	thin layer
Inner layer or endothelium (pavement epithelium)	present	present	present
Valves	absent	absent	present

Table 7.6 Structural differences between arteries, veins and capillaries

Valves are especially common in the veins of the limbs.

pressure from movements of the surrounding tissues, including contractions of the muscles, which compresses the vein

blood flow reversed

blood flow back to the heart

valve is closed by blood pressure from in front

valve is opened by blood pressure from behind

Figure 7.10 The valves in veins

The arrangement of arteries and veins

We have already noted that mammals have a double circulation. It is the role of the right side of the heart to pump deoxygenated blood to the lungs, and the arteries, veins and capillaries serving the lungs are known as the **pulmonary circulation**. The left side of the heart pumps oxygenated blood to the rest of the body, and the arteries, veins and capillaries serving the body are known as the **systemic circulation**.

In the systemic circulation, organs are supplied with blood by an artery branching from the main **aorta**. Within the organ, the artery branches into numerous arterioles (smaller arteries), and the smallest arterioles supply the capillary networks. Capillaries drain into venules (smaller veins), and venules join to form veins. The veins join the **vena cava** carrying blood back to the heart. The branching sequence in the circulation is, therefore:

aorta → artery → arteriole → capillary → venule → vein → vena cava

Arteries and veins are often named after the organs they serve (Figure 7.11). The blood supply to the liver is via the hepatic artery, but the liver also receives blood directly from the small intestine, via a vein called the **hepatic portal vein**. This brings much of the products of digestion, after they have been absorbed into the capillaries of the villi.

Figure 7.11 The layout of the human circulation

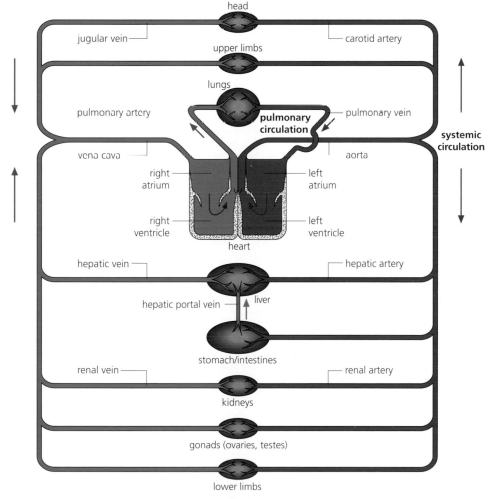

The circulatory system as shown here is simplified, e.g. limbs, lungs, kidneys and gonads are paired structures in the body.

■ The heart as a pump

The human heart is the size of a clenched fist. It is found in the thorax between the lungs and beneath the breast bone (sternum). The heart is a hollow organ with a muscular wall, and is contained in a tightly fitting membrane, the pericardium – a strong, non-elastic sac that anchors the heart within the thorax.

The cavity of the heart is divided into four chambers, with those on the right side of the heart completely separate from those on the left. The two upper chambers are thin-walled **atria** (singular, **atrium**). These receive blood into the heart. The two lower chambers are thick-walled

Figure 7.12 The structure of the heart

heart viewed from the front of the body with pericardium removed

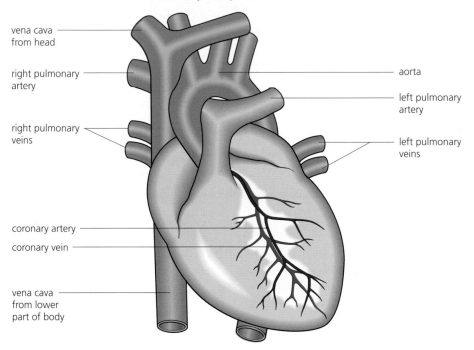

vena cava from head

right pulmonary artery

right pulmonary veins

coronary artery

coronary vein

vena cava from lower part of body

aorta

left pulmonary artery

left pulmonary veins

heart in LS

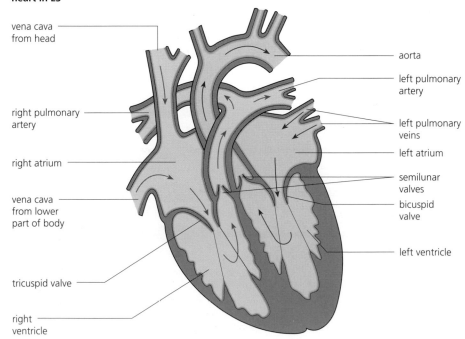

vena cava from head

right pulmonary artery

right atrium

vena cava from lower part of body

tricuspid valve

right ventricle

aorta

left pulmonary artery

left pulmonary veins

left atrium

semilunar valves

bicuspid valve

left ventricle

ventricles, with the muscular wall of the left ventricle much thicker than that of the right ventricle. However, the volumes of the right and left sides (the quantities of blood they contain) are identical. The ventricles pump blood out of the heart.

Note that the walls of the heart (the heart muscle) are supplied with oxygenated blood via **coronary arteries** (Figure 7.12). These arteries, and the capillaries they serve, deliver to the muscle fibres of the heart the oxygen and nutrients essential for the pumping action.

The **valves** of the heart prevent backflow of the blood, thereby maintaining the direction of flow through the heart. You can see these valves in action, in the lower drawing in Figure 7.12. The **atrio-ventricular valves** are large valves, positioned to prevent backflow from ventricles to atria. The edges of these valves are supported by tendons anchored to the muscle walls of the ventricles below, and which prevent the valves from folding back due to the (huge) pressure that develops here with each heart beat. Actually, these atrio-ventricular valves are individually named: on the right side is the **tricuspid valve**, on the left is the **bicuspid** or mitral valve.

A different type of valve separates the ventricles from pulmonary artery (right side) and aorta (left side). These are pocket-like structures called **semilunar valves**, rather similar to the valves seen in veins. These cut out backflow from aorta and pulmonary artery into the ventricles as the ventricles relax between heart beats.

The action of the heart

The heart normally beats about 75 times per minute – approximately 0.8 seconds per beat. In each beat, the heart muscle contracts strongly, followed by a period of relaxation. As the muscular walls of a chamber of the heart contract, the volume of that chamber decreases. This increases the pressure on the blood contained there, forcing the blood to a region where pressure is lower. Since the valves prevent blood flowing backwards, blood consistently flows on through the heart.

Look at the steps of contraction and relaxation in Figure 7.13, illustrated in the left side of the heart. (Both sides function together, in exactly the same way, of course.)

We start at the point where the **atrium contracts**. Blood is pushed into the ventricles (where the contents are under low pressure) by contraction of the walls of the atrium. This contraction also prevents backflow by blocking off the veins which brought the blood to the heart.

The **atrium now relaxes**.

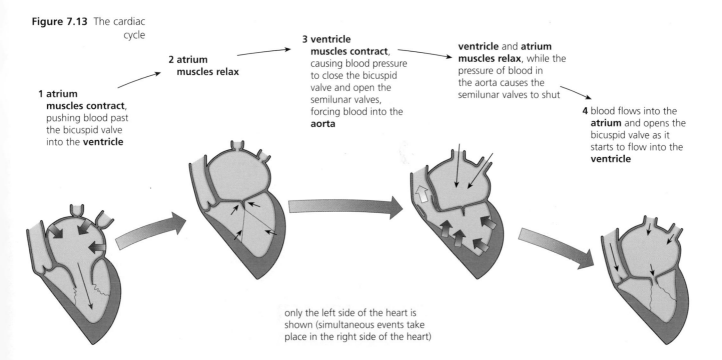

Figure 7.13 The cardiac cycle

1 atrium muscles contract, pushing blood past the bicuspid valve into the **ventricle**

2 atrium muscles relax

3 ventricle muscles contract, causing blood pressure to close the bicuspid valve and open the semilunar valves, forcing blood into the **aorta**

ventricle and **atrium muscles relax**, while the pressure of blood in the aorta causes the semilunar valves to shut

4 blood flows into the **atrium** and opens the bicuspid valve as it starts to flow into the **ventricle**

only the left side of the heart is shown (simultaneous events take place in the right side of the heart)

Next the **ventricle contracts**, and contraction of the ventricle is very forceful indeed. The high pressure this generates slams shut the atrio-ventricular valve and opens the semilunar valves, forcing blood into the aorta. A pulse, detectable in arteries all over the body, is generated.

This is followed by **relaxation of the ventricles**. Each contraction of cardiac muscle is followed by relaxation and elastic recoil.

7 The edges of the atrio-ventricular valves have non-elastic strands attached, which are anchored to the ventricle walls (Figure 7.12). **Suggest** the role of these strands.

Origin of the heart beat

The heart beats rhythmically throughout life, without rest, apart from the momentary relaxation between beats. Even more remarkably, the origin of each beat is within the heart itself – we say the heart beat is **myogenic** in origin.

Beats originate in a structure in the muscle of the wall of the right atrium, called the **pacemaker** (Figure 7.14). Special muscle fibres radiate out from the pacemaker, conducting the impulse to the muscles of both atria, triggering contraction there. Then a second structure picks up the excitation and passes it to the ventricles. Now ventricular contraction is triggered. Then, after every contraction, cardiac muscle has a period of insensitivity to stimulation (in effect, a period of enforced non-contraction), when the heart refills with blood. This period is a relatively long one in heart muscle, and is undoubtedly important in enabling the heart to beat throughout life.

The heart's natural rhythm, set by the pacemaker, is about 50 beats per minute, but we are well aware that conditions in our body override this basic rate and increase heart performance.

How is the pacemaker regulated?

Nervous control of the heart is by reflex action – it is an involuntary response, not under our conscious control. The heart receives impulses from a **control centre** in the hindbrain (medulla), via two nerves. One nerve, when stimulated, triggers speeding up of the heart rate, and the other nerve triggers a slowing down of the heart (Figure 7.14). Since these nerves have opposite effects we say they are **antagonistic**.

Figure 7.14 The pacemaker and control of heart rate

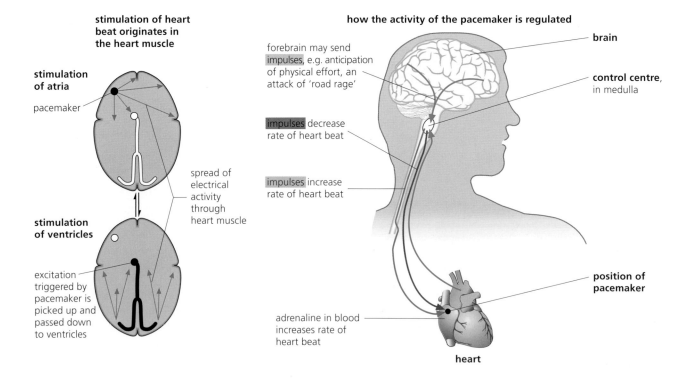

stimulation of heart beat originates in the heart muscle

how the activity of the pacemaker is regulated

stimulation of atria

pacemaker

stimulation of ventricles

excitation triggered by pacemaker is picked up and passed down to ventricles

spread of electrical activity through heart muscle

forebrain may send impulses, e.g. anticipation of physical effort, an attack of 'road rage'

impulses decrease rate of heart beat

impulses increase rate of heart beat

adrenaline in blood increases rate of heart beat

brain

control centre, in medulla

position of pacemaker

heart

Nerves supplying the control centre in the hindbrain bring impulses from strategically placed stretch receptors located in the walls of the aorta and various arteries, and indeed from the heart wall itself. As a result, when blood pressure is high in the arteries, the rate of heart beat is lowered by impulses from the control centre. When blood pressure is low, the rate of heart beat is increased. The rate of heart beat is also influenced by impulses from the higher centres of the brain – for example, emotion, stress and anticipation of events can all cause impulses that speed up heart rate.

8 Suggest likely conditions or situations in which the body is likely to secrete adrenaline.

In addition, the hormone **adrenaline**, which is secreted by the adrenal glands and carried in the blood, causes the pacemaker to increase the heart rate.

The roles of the blood circulation system

The blood circulation has roles in the body's defence against diseases (see below) as well as being the all-important transport system of the body (Table 7.7). Nutrients from digestion, oxygen and carbon dioxide, urea, hormones and antibodies are all transported. In the tissues of the body, exchange between the blood and cells of the tissues occurs from the capillaries, the walls of which are permeable and highly 'leaky'.

Function	Transport of
tissue respiration	O_2 from lungs to all tissues CO_2 back to the lungs
hydration	**water** to all the tissues
nutrition	**nutrients** (sugars, amino acids, lipids, vitamins) and inorganic ions to all cells
excretion	waste product **urea** to kidneys
development and co-ordination	**hormones** from endocrine glands to target organs
temperature regulation	distribution of **heat**
defence against disease	**antibodies** are circulated in the blood stream

Table 7.7 Transport roles of the blood circulation

Defence against infectious disease

6.3.1–6.3.8

Infectious disease is caused when another organism or virus invades the body and lives there parasitically. The invader is known as a **pathogen** and the infected organism – a human in this case – is the **host**.

> **A pathogen is an organism or virus that causes a disease. Most, but not all, are microorganisms.**

Pathogens may pass from diseased host to healthy organisms, so these diseases are known as infectious or **communicable diseases**. Disease in general is defined as an 'unhealthy condition of the body', and this rather broad definition includes some distinctly different forms of ill-health. For example, ill-health may be caused by unfavourable environmental conditions. Diseases of this type are non-infectious or **non-communicable** diseases, and they include conditions such as cardiovascular disease, malnutrition and cancer.

Good health is more than the absence of harmful effects of a disease. This point is emphasised by the **World Health Organization (WHO)** which identifies health as 'a state of complete physical, mental and social well-being, and not merely the absence of disease or infirmity'.

Pathogens and disease

The range of **disease-causing organisms** that may infect humans includes not only microorganisms such as certain **bacteria** and **fungi**, but also **viruses**, some **protozoa** (single-celled animals) and certain non-vertebrate animals in the phyla of **flatworms** and of **roundworms** (pages 170–1).

9 State the differences in structure between a bacterial cell and a virus.

Not all bacteria or fungi are parasitic and pathogenic – only relatively few species are. On the other hand, no virus can function outside a host organism, so we can say that all viruses are parasitic. Remember, a virus consists of a nucleic acid core surrounded by a protein coat (page 19). Viruses, once introduced into a host cell, take over the machinery of protein and nucleic acid synthesis, and coerce their host cells to manufacture more virus components and assemble them.

Antibiotics against infection

Many bacterial diseases of humans and other animals can be successfully treated with antibiotics. **Antibiotics** are naturally occurring substances that slow down or kill microorganisms. They are obtained mainly from fungi or bacteria, and are substances which such organisms manufacture in their natural habitats. An antibiotic, when present in low concentrations, may inhibit the growth of other microorganisms.

Since their original discovery, over 4000 different antibiotics have been isolated, but only about 50 have proved to be safe to use as drugs. The antibiotics which are effective over a wide range of pathogenic organisms are called **broad spectrum antibiotics**. Others are effective with just a few pathogens. Many antibiotics in use today have been synthesised.

How do antibiotics work?

Most antibiotics are so extremely effective at disrupting bacterial metabolism that whole populations are quickly suppressed. Figure 7.15 shows an actively dividing bacterial cell. A key process here is the formation and laying down of the new dividing wall. Bacterial cells have a rigid wall containing giant, complex molecules of amino-sugars and peptide units (polymers) rather than the polysaccharides of plant cell walls. Some bacteria have additional wall layers.

Figure 7.15 How antibiotics work

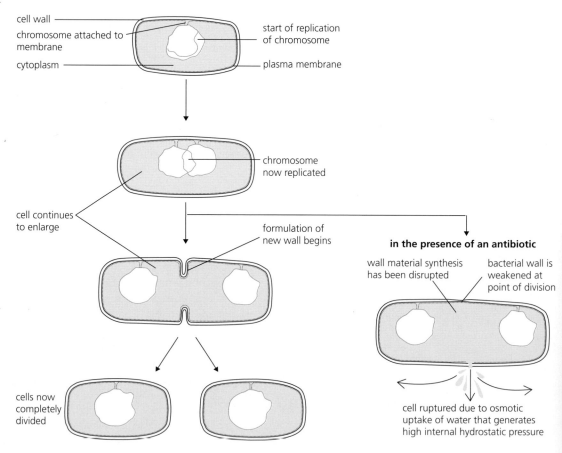

In division and growth, bacteria are vulnerable to antibiotic action because the antibiotic molecules enter the bacterial cells and disrupt the metabolic reactions of wall formation and growth.

Other bacteria have dormant spores whose growth is stopped by antibiotics, by similar mechanisms.

Viruses, on the other hand, are not living cells and have no metabolism of their own to be interfered with. Viruses reproduce using metabolic pathways in their host cell that are not affected by antibiotics. Antibiotics cannot be used to prevent viral diseases.

10 Explain why antibiotics are effective against bacteria but not viruses.

The body's defence against infectious disease

The **first line of defence** is the skin. Both our skin and the internal linings of lungs, trachea and gut are potential ports for entry to the body's tissues and organs by pathogens. Not surprisingly, protective measures have evolved at these surfaces.

The **external skin** is covered by keratinised protein of the dead cells of the epidermis (Figure 7.43, page 221). This is a tough and impervious layer, and an effective barrier to most organisms unless the surface is broken, cut or deeply scratched. However, folds or creases in the

Figure 7.16 The life cycle of *Schistosoma* and the spread of schistosomiasis

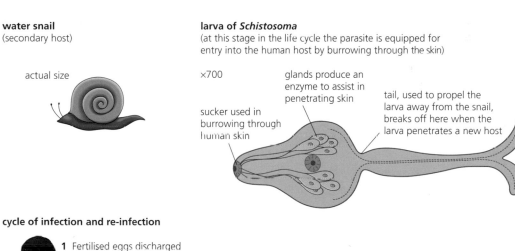

water snail
(secondary host)

actual size

larva of *Schistosoma*
(at this stage in the life cycle the parasite is equipped for entry into the human host by burrowing through the skin)

×700

glands produce an enzyme to assist in penetrating skin

sucker used in burrowing through human skin

tail, used to propel the larva away from the snail, breaks off here when the larva penetrates a new host

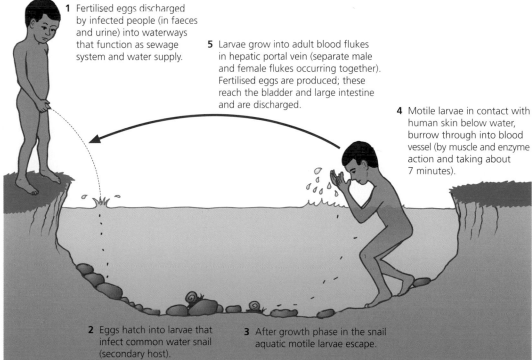

cycle of infection and re-infection

1 Fertilised eggs discharged by infected people (in faeces and urine) into waterways that function as sewage system and water supply.

5 Larvae grow into adult blood flukes in hepatic portal vein (separate male and female flukes occurring together). Fertilised eggs are produced; these reach the bladder and large intestine and are discharged.

4 Motile larvae in contact with human skin below water, burrow through into blood vessel (by muscle and enzyme action and taking about 7 minutes).

2 Eggs hatch into larvae that infect common water snail (secondary host).

3 After growth phase in the snail aquatic motile larvae escape.

skin that are permanently moist can harbour microorganisms that degrade the barrier and cause infection, as in athlete's foot. Also, the aquatic larvae of the pathogenic flatworm *Schistosoma*, known as a blood worm, may burrow through, when people bathe in infected water (Figure 7.16). Clearly, the body requires additional lines of defence.

> **11 Explain** how the skin acts as a barrier against many pathogens, yet is often traversed by *Schistosoma*.

The **internal surfaces** of our breathing apparatus (the trachea, bronchi and the bronchioles) and of the gut are all lined by moist epithelial cells. These vulnerable internal barriers are protected by the secretion of copious quantities of **mucus**, and by the actions of **cilia** removing the mucus.

Cilia are organelles that project from the surface of certain cells. Cilia occur in large numbers on the lining (epithelium) of the air tubes (bronchi) serving the lungs where they sweep the fluid mucus across the epithelial surface, away from the delicate air sacs of the lungs.

In the gut, digestive enzymes provide some protection, as does the strong **acid secreted in the stomach** on arrival of food (page 181).

> **12 Suggest** how mucus secreted by the lungs may protect lung tissue.

However, all these internal barriers may be crossed by certain pathogens – and often are. It is fortunate there are internal lines of defence too.

First, the body responds to localised damage by **inflammation**. Inflammation is the initial, rapid, localised response the tissues make to damage (cuts, scratches, bruising, or deep wounds). The site becomes swollen, warm and painful. The volume of blood is increased at the damaged site. **Leucocytes (white cells)** escape from the enlarged capillaries with plasma, and function in the tissue fluid, especially at the sites of inflammation. These cells originate in the bone marrow and are initially distributed by the blood circulation all over the body.

The leucocytes of the body and blood circulation play a complex part in the resistance to infection – their roles are detailed below.

Meanwhile, if a blood vessel is ruptured when the skin is damaged, then the **blood clotting mechanism** is activated, so that the vessel is quickly sealed off.

Phagocytic leucocytes

Some of the leucocytes have the role of engulfing foreign material including invading bacterial cells. Certain of these leucocytes are short-lived cells of the plasma. Others are the long-lived, rubbish-collecting cells found throughout the body tissues. Both types of cell take up material into their cytoplasm, much as the protozoan *Amoeba* is observed to feed, by a mechanism known as **phagocytosis** (Figure 7.17). Once inside the cell, the material taken up is destroyed in a controlled way by the activity of lysosomes.

Immunity: lymphocytes and the antigen–antibody reaction

Other leucocytes are responsible for the body's **antibody reaction** to infection or invasion of foreign matter – this is the basis of our immune system.

Immunity is based on the body's ability to recognise 'self' (body cells and specific proteins, for example) and to distinguish 'self' from 'non-self' substances (produced by an invading organism, for example). Any 'non-self' substance is called an **antigen**. This ability to recognise antigens and to take steps to overcome them is the property of special white cells called **lymphocytes**. Each type of lymphocyte recognises one specific antigen. In the presence of an antigen, these cells divide rapidly, producing many cells – known as a clone. These cloned lymphocytes then secrete the antibody specific to that antigen.

An **antibody** is a special kind of protein constructed in the shape of a Y, whose top contains an antigen-binding site (Figure 7.18). Millions of different types of antibodies are produced – as many as there are types of foreign matter (antigens) invading the body. The amino acid sequence of the antigen-binding site differs according to the chemistry of the antibody it binds with. It is the antigen-binding site that gives each antibody its specificity.

Figure 7.17 Phagocytosis of a bacterium

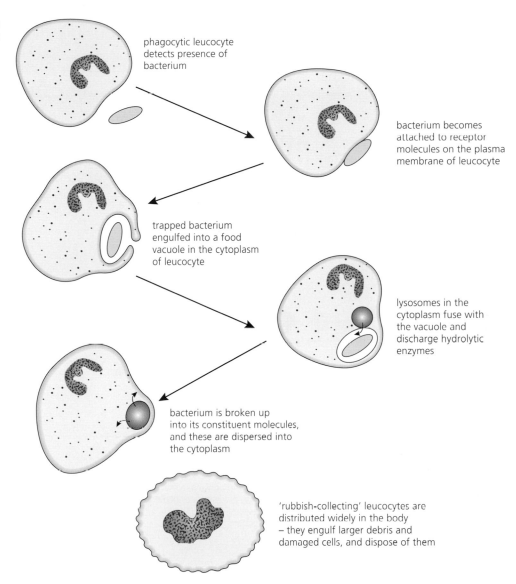

phagocytic leucocyte detects presence of bacterium

bacterium becomes attached to receptor molecules on the plasma membrane of leucocyte

trapped bacterium engulfed into a food vacuole in the cytoplasm of leucocyte

lysosomes in the cytoplasm fuse with the vacuole and discharge hydrolytic enzymes

bacterium is broken up into its constituent molecules, and these are dispersed into the cytoplasm

'rubbish-collecting' leucocytes are distributed widely in the body – they engulf larger debris and damaged cells, and dispose of them

So a huge range of **different antibody-secreting lymphocytes** exists, each type recognising one specific antigen. The more antigens we encounter, the more antibodies we are able to form, should they be required. In the presence of an invasion by an antigen, the immune system responds: the appropriate antibody-secreting lymphocytes rapidly divide, and sufficient antibodies necessary to overcome the antigen are secreted. However, this type of lymphocyte also has a short life span. Once the harmful effects of the invading antigen are neutralised, the respective lymphocytes disappear from the blood circulation. But 'knowledge' of the antigen is not lost, because lymphocytes we call **memory cells** remain behind, stored in the lymph nodes. With the aid of our memory cells, our body can respond rapidly, if the same antigen re-invades. We say we have **immunity** to that antigen.

Antibodies destroy antigens in different ways. Antigens that are toxins may be inactivated by reaction with the antibody, and bacterial cells may be clumped together so they 'precipitate' and can be engulfed by phagocytic cells. Antibodies may attach to foreign matter, ensuring its recognition by phagocytic cells. Antibodies may also act by destroying bacterial cell walls, causing lysis of the bacterium.

13 Deduce which synthetic machinery of the lymphocytes is active in the production of the components of their antibodies.

Figure 7.18 Formation and function of an antibody

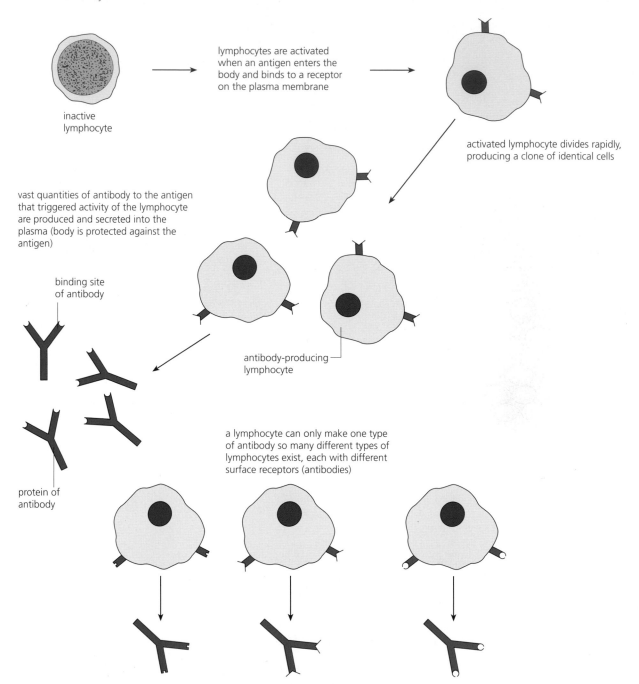

lymphocytes are activated when an antigen enters the body and binds to a receptor on the plasma membrane

inactive lymphocyte

activated lymphocyte divides rapidly, producing a clone of identical cells

vast quantities of antibody to the antigen that triggered activity of the lymphocyte are produced and secreted into the plasma (body is protected against the antigen)

binding site of antibody

antibody-producing lymphocyte

protein of antibody

a lymphocyte can only make one type of antibody so many different types of lymphocytes exist, each with different surface receptors (antibodies)

Human immunodeficiency virus (HIV) and AIDS

Human immunodeficiency virus (HIV) was first identified in 1983 as the cause of a disease of the human immune system known as **acquired immune deficiency syndrome (AIDS)**.

HIV is a tiny virus, less than 0.1 μm in diameter (Figure 7.19). It consists of two single strands of RNA which, together with enzymes, are enclosed by a protein coat. A membrane derived from the human host cell in which the virus was formed encapsulates each new virus particle leaving the host cell.

Figure 7.19 The human immunodeficiency virus (HIV)

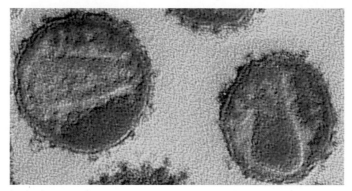

TEM of HIV (×300 000)

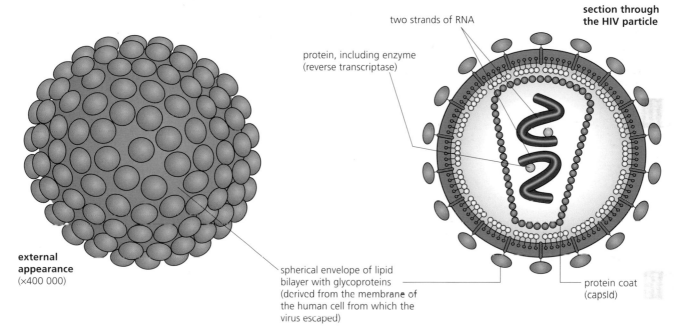

two strands of RNA

protein, including enzyme (reverse transcriptase)

section through the HIV particle

external appearance (×400 000)

spherical envelope of lipid bilayer with glycoproteins (derived from the membrane of the human cell from which the virus escaped)

protein coat (capsid)

HIV was first detected in central Africa in the 1950s, perhaps as a mutation of a similar virus present in African green monkeys (but other theories about the origin of HIV exist). From Africa, HIV was spread to the Caribbean and later to the USA and Europe. Now, HIV and AIDS occur worldwide. AIDS is probably already the greatest current threat to public health because it kills people in the most productive stage of their lives.

HIV is a retrovirus

The word 'retrovirus' is not self-explanatory; the term needs explaining. A **retrovirus** reverses the normal flow of genetic information, which is from the DNA of genes to messenger RNA in the cytoplasm (page 69). The idea that information always flows in this direction in cells is called the **central dogma of cell biology**. However, in retroviruses the information in RNA in the cytoplasm is translated into DNA within a host cell, and then becomes attached to the DNA of a chromosome in the host's nucleus.

How does a retrovirus work?

Taking HIV as an example, the virus binds to a host cell (lymphocyte) membrane (Figure 7.20), and the core of the virus passes inside. Inside the host cell, the RNA and virus enzymes are released. One enzyme from the virus is called **reverse transcriptase**. This enzyme catalyses the copying of the genetic code of each of the virus's RNA strands into a DNA double helix. This DNA then enters the host nucleus and is 'spliced' into the host's DNA of a chromosome (Figure 7.21). Here it may be replicated with the host's genes every time the host cell divides. The viral genes remain **latent**, giving no sign of their presence in the host cells at this stage.

Figure 7.20 HIV infection of a white cell

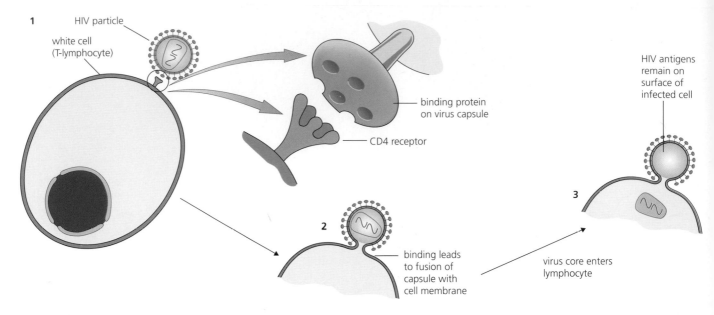

Figure 7.21 How HIV becomes part of the white cell's genome

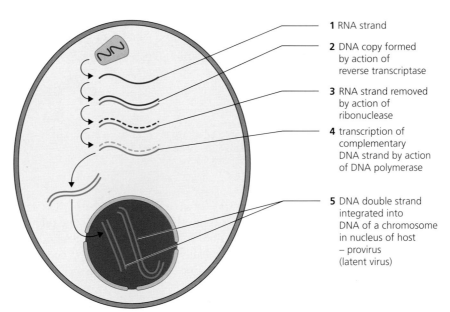

1 RNA strand

2 DNA copy formed by action of reverse transcriptase

3 RNA strand removed by action of ribonuclease

4 transcription of complementary DNA strand by action of DNA polymerase

5 DNA double strand integrated into DNA of a chromosome in nucleus of host – provirus (latent virus)

The onset of AIDS

At a later stage, some event in the patient's body activates the HIV genes and the outcome is AIDS. The average interval between HIV infection and the onset of AIDS is about 8–10 years. The result of activation is the synthesis of viral messenger RNA. This then passes out into the cytoplasm, and there codes for viral proteins (enzymes and protein coat) at the ribosomes. Viral RNA (single-stranded), enzymes and coat protein are formed into viral cores. These move against the cell membrane and 'bud-off' new viruses (Figure 7.22). These infect more lymphocytes and the cycle is rapidly repeated. Without treatment, this process causes the body's reserve of lymphocytes (T-cells) to decrease very quickly. Eventually, no infection, however trivial, can be resisted; death follows (Figure 7.23).

Figure 7.22 Activation of the HIV genome and production of new HIV

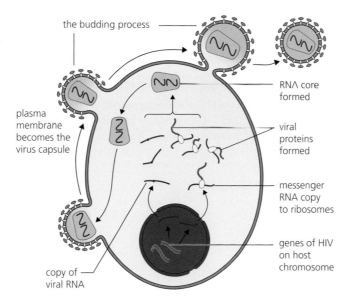

the budding process

viral proteins and RNA being synthesised and new HIV cores assembled, then budding off with part of the host plasma membrane as each capsule

plasma membrane becomes the virus capsule

RNA core formed

viral proteins formed

messenger RNA copy to ribosomes

genes of HIV on host chromosome

copy of viral RNA

Figure 7.23 Profile of an AIDS infection

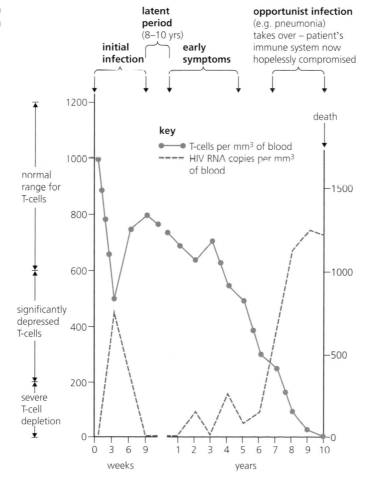

initial infection

latent period (8–10 yrs)

early symptoms

opportunist infection (e.g. pneumonia) takes over – patient's immune system now hopelessly compromised

death

normal range for T-cells

significantly depressed T-cells

severe T-cell depletion

key

T-cells per mm³ of blood

HIV RNA copies per mm³ of blood

weeks

years

Treatment, prevention and the social consequences of AIDS

Infection with HIV is possible through contact with blood or body fluids of infected people, such as may occur during sexual intercourse, sharing of hypodermic needles by intravenous drug users, and breast feeding of a newborn baby. Also, blood transfusions and organ transplants will transmit HIV, but donors are now screened for HIV infection in most countries. HIV is *not* transferred by contact with saliva on a drinking glass, or by sharing a towel, for example. Nor does the female mosquito transmit HIV when feeding on human blood (page 595).

Figure 7.24 Worldwide incidence of HIV infection (WHO, 2000)

The spread of HIV and the eventual onset of AIDS in patients are outpacing the current efforts of scientists and doctors to prevent them. The WHO charts the spread of this pandemic (Figure 7.24).

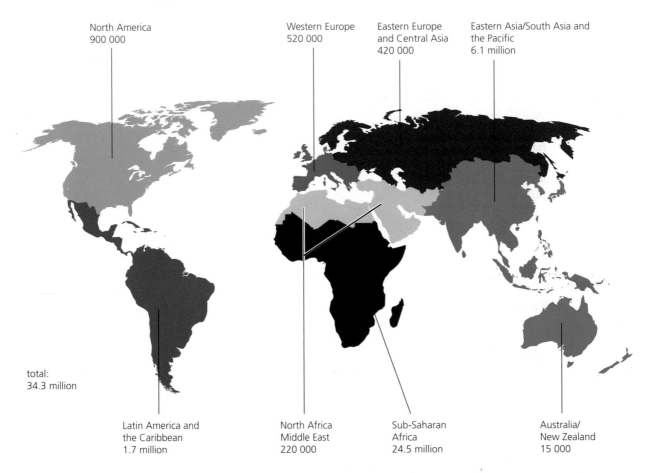

North America
900 000

Western Europe
520 000

Eastern Europe
and Central Asia
420 000

Eastern Asia/South Asia and
the Pacific
6.1 million

total:
34.3 million

Latin America and
the Caribbean
1.7 million

North Africa
Middle East
220 000

Sub-Saharan
Africa
24.5 million

Australia/
New Zealand
15 000

HIV infection and AIDS are difficult to treat. We have already noted that viruses are not controlled by antibiotics. Once the presence of HIV has been confirmed, patients may be offered drugs that slow down the progress of the infection – a combination of drugs that reduces the number of HIV-infected cells, at least temporarily. The three most popular drugs (AZT and two protease inhibitors) interrupt the steps of nucleic acid reverse transcription. A combination of drugs is used to prevent HIV from rapidly developing resistance to any one drug, and to avoid dangerous or unpleasant side-effects that some patients experience.

Ideally, a vaccine against HIV would be the best solution – one designed to wipe out infected lymphocytes and HIV particles in the patient's blood stream. The work of several laboratories is dedicated to this solution. The problem is that in the latent state of the infection, the infected (T4) lymphocyte cells frequently change their membrane marker proteins because of the presence of the HIV genome within the cell. Effectively, HIV can hide from the body's immune response by changing its identity.

Current strategies for preventing the spread of HIV are:

- practising 'safe sex' by using condoms to prevent transmission of the virus through infected blood or semen (condoms need to be freely available to the sexually active population);
- use of sterile needles by intravenous drug users (sterile needles need to be freely available);
- effective education programmes so that the vulnerable understand the cause and effects of HIV infection, and the best steps to remain healthy, whether or not they are literate.

TOK Link

Sexually transmitted diseases are rampant among teenagers in developed countries. Worldwide, there is a relentless rise in cases of AIDS. What are the ideal practical responses to the risk of infection by:

- vulnerable individual citizens?
- national governments?

Why may current responses be proving ineffective?

■ Extension

Recent studies have shown that the prevalence of AIDS is significantly higher in uncircumcised males. Circumcised males were seven times less likely to transmit HIV to, or receive HIV from, their partner. The reason for this is the mucous membrane of the inner surface of the foreskin has cells with receptors that HIV can exploit. Consequently, it is possible that HIV infection of future generations might be reduced if male circumcision were practised more widely. But health workers point out that if this were to encourage males to participate in unsafe sex with numerous partners, it would defeat the object.

In fact, AIDS is just one of several **sexually transmitted diseases (STDs)** currently on the increase in various parts of the world. But the **social implications of the AIDS pandemic** are devastating the economies and social life of communities in many less-developed countries and threatening to do the same in many others. The social consequences are summarised in Table 7.8.

Table 7.8 The social consequences of AIDS

	Social consequence
Psychological	Patient, family and friends suffer grief, loneliness and guilt.
Economic	Where the producer or wage-earner is incapacitated, poverty results or is increased. Infected people may be stigmatised, and deprived of housing or employment.
Child development and education	Children may become orphans at early age, older ones having to rear siblings with little support, and unable to proceed with education or training.
Child health	Offspring may be infected at birth or during breast feeding, leading to early ill-health and death.
Medical services provision	Meagre resources are diverted to treat long-term symptoms, without hope of cure. Other diseases not treated properly.
National factors	Reduction in numbers of the economically productive members of the community and incapacity of many of the more sexually active members cramp aspirations and achievements for a nation.

14 Describe why AIDS patients typically die from common infectious diseases that are not normally fatal.

15 Distinguish between the following pairs:

a antigens and antibodies;
b antibiotics and vaccines;
c vector and host.

Effects of HIV on the immune system

We have seen that HIV specifically attaches to antibody-secreting lymphocytes and takes over their nucleic acid and protein synthesis machinery. As the virus becomes active after a dormant period, the number of these lymphocytes drops profoundly, leaving the patient vulnerable to attack by opportunistic infections such as pneumonia and meningitis (Figure 7.23, page 201). This is because, with the reduction in the number of active lymphocytes, there is a dramatic loss in the ability to produce antibodies to a wide range of common infections.

■ Gaseous exchange

All living things respire.

> **Cellular respiration is the controlled release of energy in the form of ATP from organic compounds in cells. It is a continuous process in all cells.**

To support aerobic cellular respiration, cells take in oxygen from their environment and give out carbon dioxide, by a process called gaseous exchange (Figure 7.25).

> **Gaseous exchange is the exchange of gases between an organism and its surroundings, including the uptake of oxygen and the release of carbon dioxide in animals and plants.**

The exchange of gases between the individual cell and its environment takes place by **diffusion**. For example, in cells respiring aerobically there is a higher concentration of oxygen outside the cells than inside, and so there will be a continuous net inward diffusion of oxygen.

Figure 7.25 Gaseous exchange in an animal cell

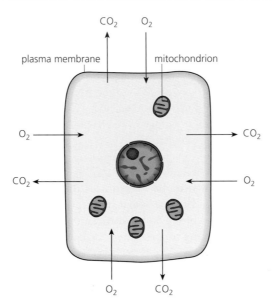

What speeds up diffusion? In living things there are three factors which effectively determine the rate of diffusion in practice.

- The size of the **surface area** available for gaseous exchange (the respiratory surface). The greater this surface area, the greater the rate of diffusion. Of course, in a single cell, the respiratory surface is the whole plasma membrane.
- The **difference in concentration**. A rapidly respiring organism will have a very much lower concentration of oxygen in the cells and a higher than normal concentration of carbon dioxide. The greater the gradient in concentration across the respiratory surface, the greater the rate of diffusion.
- The **length of the diffusion path**. The shorter the diffusion path, the greater the rate of diffusion, so the respiratory surface must be as thin as possible.

Gaseous exchange in animals

We can see that the surface area of singled-celled animal is large in relation to the amount of cytoplasm it contains – here the surface of the cell is sufficient for efficient gaseous exchange. On the other hand, large, multicellular animals have very many of their cells too far from the body surface to receive enough oxygen by diffusion alone.

In addition, animals often develop an external surface of tough or hardened skin that provides protection to the body, but which is not suitable for gaseous exchange. These organisms require an alternative respiratory surface.

Active organisms have an increased metabolic rate, and the demand for oxygen in their cells is higher than in sluggish and inactive organisms. So for many reasons, large active animals such as **mammals** have specialised organs for gaseous exchange. In mammals, the respiratory surface consists of **lungs**. Lungs provide a large, thin surface area, suitable for gaseous exchange. However, the lungs are in a protected position inside the thorax (chest), so air has to be brought to the respiratory surface there. The lungs must be ventilated.

A ventilation system is a pumping mechanism that moves air into and out of the lungs efficiently, thereby maintaining the concentration gradient for diffusion.

In addition, in mammals the conditions for diffusion at the respiratory surface are improved by:

16 List three characteristics of an efficient respiratory surface and explain how each influences diffusion.

- a blood circulation system, which rapidly moves oxygen to the body cells as soon as it has crossed the respiratory surface, thereby maintaining the concentration gradient;
- a respiratory pigment, which increases the oxygen-carrying ability of the blood. This is the haemoglobin of the red cells which are by far the most numerous of the cells in our blood circulation.

The working lungs of mammals

The structure of the human thorax is shown in Figure 7.26. Lungs are housed in the **thorax**, an airtight chamber formed by the **rib-cage** and its muscles (**intercostal muscles**), with a domed floor, the **diaphragm**. The diaphragm is a sheet of muscle attached to the body wall at the base of the rib-cage, separating thorax from abdomen. The internal surfaces of the thorax are lined by the **pleural membrane**, which secretes and maintains pleural fluid. Pleural fluid is a lubricating liquid derived from blood plasma that protects the lungs from friction during breathing movements.

Lungs connect with the pharynx at the rear of the mouth by the trachea. Air reaches the trachea from the mouth and nostrils, passing through the larynx (voice box). Entry into the larynx is via a slit-like opening, the glottis. Above is a cartilaginous flap, the **epiglottis**. Glottis and epiglottis work to prevent the entry of food into the trachea. The trachea initially runs beside the oesophagus. Incomplete rings of cartilage in the trachea wall prevent collapse under pressure from a large bolus of food passing down the oesophagus.

Figure 7.26 The structure of the human thorax

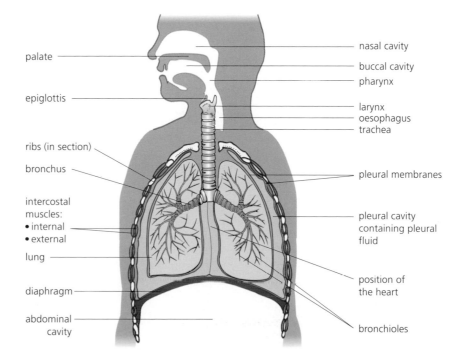

Figure 7.27 Water loss in gaseous exchange in humans

Exhaled air is saturated with water vapour, an invisible component except in freezing weather or when breathed on to a very cold surface.

The water balance of the body:

- about 3 dm^3 is taken in and lost daily
- about 10–15% of this total is lost from the lungs.

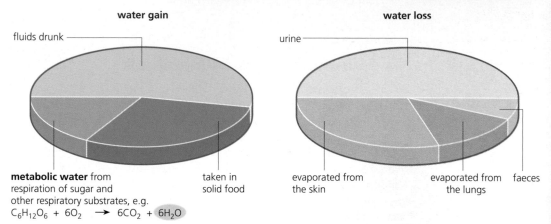

water gain

fluids drunk

metabolic water from respiration of sugar and other respiratory substrates, e.g.
$C_6H_{12}O_6 + 6O_2 \rightarrow 6CO_2 + 6H_2O$

taken in solid food

water loss

urine

evaporated from the skin

evaporated from the lungs

faeces

The trachea then divides into two **bronchi**, one to each lung. Within the lungs the bronchi divide into smaller bronchioles. The finest bronchioles end in air sacs (**alveoli**). The walls of bronchi and larger bronchioles contain smooth muscle, and are also supported by rings or tiny plates of cartilage, preventing collapse that might be triggered by a sudden reduction in pressure that occurs with powerful inspirations of air.

Lungs are extremely efficient, but of course they cannot prevent some water loss during breathing – an issue for most terrestrial organisms (Figure 7.27).

Ventilation of the lungs

Air is drawn into the alveoli when the air pressure in the lungs is lower than atmospheric pressure, and it is forced out when pressure is higher than atmospheric pressure. Since the thorax is an airtight chamber, pressure changes in the lungs occur when the volume of the thorax changes (Table 7.9 and Figure 7.28).

The volume of the thorax is increased when the ribs are moved upwards and outwards, and the diaphragm dome is lowered. These movements are brought about by contraction of the diaphragm and external intercostal muscles.

The volume of the thorax is decreased by the diaphragm muscles relaxing and the diaphragm becoming more dome-shaped by pressure from below (natural elasticity of the stomach and liver, displaced and stretched at inspiration). Also, the internal intercostal muscles contract. The ribs now move down and inwards.

17 Compare roles of the internal and external intercostal muscles during ventilation of the lungs (Figure 7.28 and Table 7.9).

Table 7.9 The mechanism of lung ventilation – a summary

Inspiration (inhalation)	Structure/outcome	Expiration (exhalation)
muscles contract, flattening the diaphragm and pushing down on contents of abdomen	**diaphragm**	muscles relax, pressure from abdominal contents pushes diaphragm into a dome shape
contract, moving rib-cage up and out	**external intercostal muscles**	relax
relax	**internal intercostal muscles**	contract, moving rib-cage down and in
increases	**volume of thorax cavity**	decreases
falls below atmospheric pressure	**air pressure of thorax**	rises above atmospheric pressure
in	**air flow**	out

Figure 7.28 The ventilation mechanism of the lungs

inspiration:
- external intercostal muscles contract
- internal intercostal muscles relax
- diaphragm muscles contract

} ribs moved upwards and outwards, and the diaphragm down

expiration:
- external intercostal muscles relax
- internal intercostal muscles contract
- diaphragm muscles relax

} ribs moved downwards and inwards, and the diaphragm up

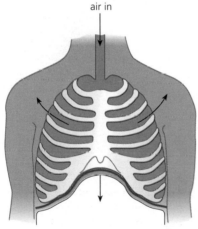

air in

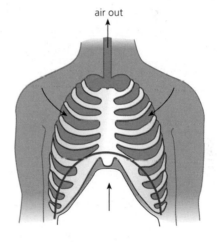

air out

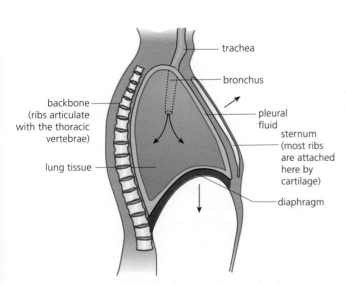

trachea

bronchus

backbone (ribs articulate with the thoracic vertebrae)

pleural fluid

sternum (most ribs are attached here by cartilage)

lung tissue

diaphragm

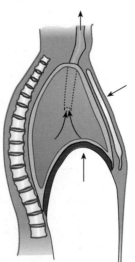

volume of the thorax (and therefore of the lungs) increases; pressure is reduced below atmospheric pressure and air flows in

volume of the thorax (and therefore of the lungs) decreases; pressure is increased above atmospheric pressure and air flows out

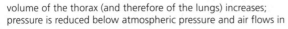

Alveolar structure and gaseous exchange

The lung tissue consists of the alveoli, arranged in clusters, each served by a tiny bronchiole. Alveoli have elastic connective tissue as an integral part of their walls. A capillary system wraps around the clusters of alveoli (Figure 7.29). Each capillary is connected to a branch of the pulmonary artery and is drained by a branch of the pulmonary vein. The pulmonary circulation is supplied with deoxygenated blood from the right side of the heart, and returns oxygenated blood to the left side of the heart to be pumped to the rest of the body.

Figure 7.29 Gaseous exchange in the alveoli

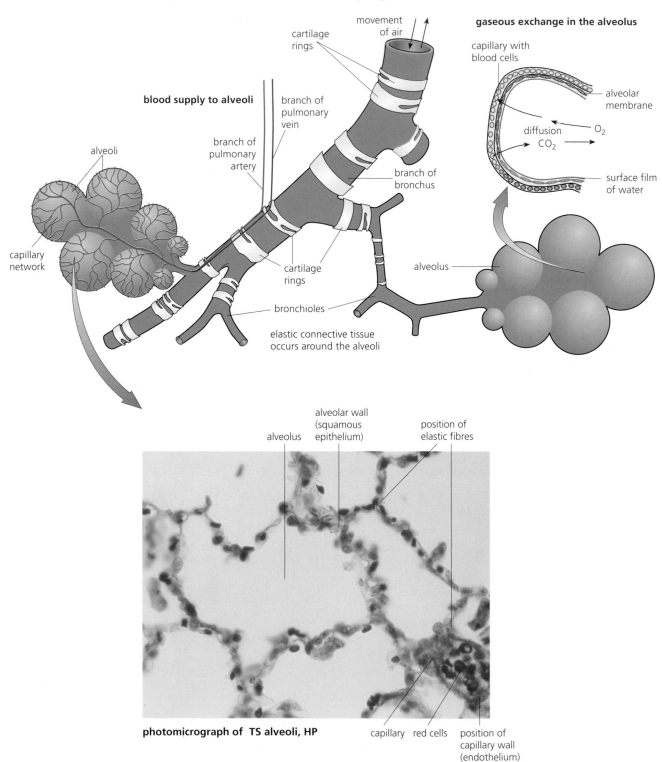

blood supply to alveoli

movement of air

cartilage rings

branch of pulmonary vein

branch of pulmonary artery

alveoli

capillary network

branch of bronchus

cartilage rings

bronchioles

elastic connective tissue occurs around the alveoli

gaseous exchange in the alveolus

capillary with blood cells

alveolar membrane

diffusion O_2
CO_2

surface film of water

alveolus

alveolar wall (squamous epithelium)

position of elastic fibres

alveolus

photomicrograph of TS alveoli, HP

capillary   red cells   position of capillary wall (endothelium)

There are some 700 million alveoli in our lungs, providing a surface area of about 70 m^2 in total. This is an area 30–40 times greater than that of the body's external skin. The wall of an alveolus is one cell thick, and is formed by pavement epithelium. Lying very close is a capillary, its wall also composed of a single layer of flattened (endothelium) cells. The combined thickness of walls separating air and blood is typically 5 μm. The capillaries are extremely narrow, just wide enough for red cells to squeeze through, so red cells are close to or in contact with the capillary walls.

Blood arriving in the lungs is low in oxygen but high in carbon dioxide. As blood flows past the alveoli, gaseous exchange occurs by diffusion. Oxygen dissolves in the surface film of water, diffuses across into the blood plasma and into the red cells where it combines with haemoglobin to form oxyhaemoglobin. At the same time, carbon dioxide diffuses from the blood into the alveoli (Table 7.10).

Component	Inspired air/%	Alveolar air/%	Expired air/%
oxygen	20	14	16
carbon dioxide	0.04	5.5	4.0
nitrogen	79	81	79
water vapour	variable	saturated	saturated

Table 7.10 The composition of air in the lungs

18 Explain why, if the concentration of carbon dioxide was to build up in the blood of a mammal, this would be harmful.

Efficiency of lungs as organs of gaseous exchange

The lungs of mammals are just one evolutionary response to the need for efficient organs of gaseous exchange in compact multicellular animals. Alternative arrangements include the system of tubes that pipe air directly to respiring cells of insects, the internal gills of fish, and the lungs of birds in which air travels completely through, to and from the air sacs beyond.

How effective are mammalian lungs?

Air flow in the lungs of mammals is tidal, in that air enters and leaves by the same route. Consequently there is a residual volume of air that cannot be expelled. Incoming air mixes with and dilutes the residual air, rather than replaces it. The effect of this is that air in the alveoli contains significantly less oxygen than the atmosphere outside (Table 7.10).

Nevertheless, the lungs are efficient organs. Their success is due to numerous features of the alveoli that adapt them to gaseous exchange. These are listed in Table 7.11.

Feature	Effects and consequences
surface area of alveoli	a huge surface area for gaseous exchange (50 m^2 = area of doubles tennis court)
wall of alveoli	very thin, flattened (squamous) epithelium (5 μm) – diffusion pathway is short
capillary supply to alveoli	network of capillaries around each alveolus supplied with deoxygenated blood from pulmonary artery and draining into pulmonary veins – maintains the concentration gradient of O_2 and CO_2
surface film of moisture	O_2 dissolves in water lining the alveoli; O_2 diffuses into the blood in solution

Table 7.11 Features of alveoli that adapt them to efficient gaseous exchange

19 Explain the difference between gaseous exchange and cellular respiration.

20 Explain why a significant amount of our total daily water loss occurs from the lungs (Figure 7.27).

■ Nerves, hormones and homeostasis 6.5.1–6.5.12

Control and communication within the body involves both the **nervous system** and **hormones from the endocrine glands**. We now look at these systems, in turn.

Introducing the nervous system

The nervous system is built from nerve cells called **neurones**. A neurone has a **cell body** containing the **nucleus** and the bulk of the cytoplasm. From the cell body run fine cytoplasmic **fibres**. Most fibres are very long indeed.

Neurones are specialised for the transmission of information in the form of impulses. An **impulse** is a momentary reversal in the electrical potential difference in the membrane of a neurone. The transmission of an impulse along a fibre occurs at speeds between 30 and 120 metres per second in mammals, so nervous coordination is extremely fast, and responses are virtually immediate. Impulses travel to particular points in the body, served by the fibres. Consequently, the effects of impulses are localised rather than diffuse.

Neurones are grouped together to form the **central nervous system**, which consists of the **brain** and **spinal cord**. To and from the central nervous system run nerves of the **peripheral nervous system**. Communication between the central nervous system and all parts of the body occurs via these nerves (Figure 7.30).

Figure 7.30 The organisation of the mammalian nervous system

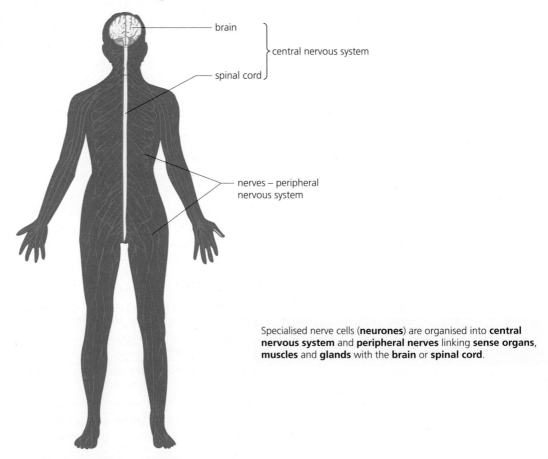

- brain
- central nervous system
- spinal cord
- nerves – peripheral nervous system

Specialised nerve cells (**neurones**) are organised into **central nervous system** and **peripheral nerves** linking **sense organs**, **muscles** and **glands** with the **brain** or **spinal cord**.

Looking at neurone structure

Three types of neurone make up the nervous system (sensory neurones, relay neurones and motor neurones). The structure of a motor neurone is shown in Figure 7.31.

The motor neurones have many fine **dendrites** which bring impulses towards the cell body, and a single long **axon** which carries impulses away from the cell body. The function of the motor neurone is to carry impulses from the central nervous system to a muscle or gland (known as an **effector**).

Figure 7.31 Motor neurone structure

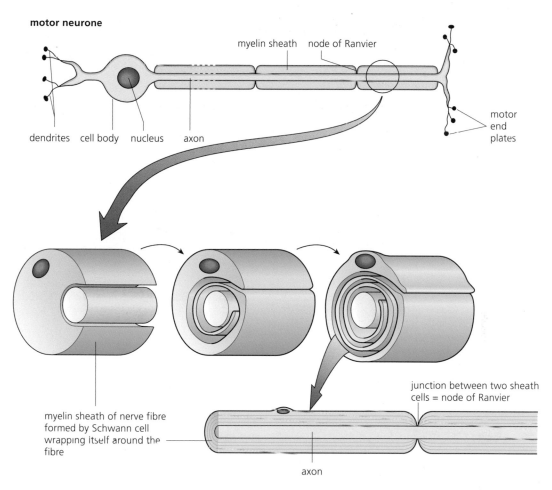

A neurone is surrounded by many supporting cells, one type of which, Schwann cells, become wrapped around the axons of motor neurones, forming a structure called a **myelin sheath**. Myelin consists largely of lipid, and has high electrical resistance. Frequent junctions occur along a myelin sheath, between the individual Schwann cells. The junctions are called nodes of Ranvier.

Neurones and the transmission of an impulse

Neurones transmit information in the form of impulses. An impulse is transmitted along nerve fibres, but it is not an electrical current that flows along the 'wires' of the nerves. As stated above, an impulse is a momentary reversal in electrical potential difference in the membrane – a change in the position of charged ions between the inside and outside of the membrane of the nerve fibres. This reversal flows from one end of the neurone to the other in a fraction of a second.

Between conduction of one impulse and the next the neurone is sometimes said to be resting, but this not the case. The 'resting' neurone membrane actively sets up and maintains the electrical potential difference between the inside and the outside of the fibre.

How is this done?

The resting potential

The resting potential is the potential difference across a nerve cell membrane when it is not being stimulated. It is normally about −70 millivolts (mV).

The resting potential difference is re-established across the neurone membrane after a nerve impulse has been transmitted. We say the nerve fibre has been **repolarised**.

The resting potential is the product of two processes:

1 **The active transport of potassium ions (K⁺) in across the membrane, and sodium ions (Na⁺) out across the membrane.** This occurs by a K⁺/Na⁺ pump, using energy from ATP (Figure 1.30, page 29). The concentration of potassium and sodium ions on opposite sides of the membrane is built up, but this in itself makes no change to the potential difference across the membrane.

2 **Facilitated diffusion of K⁺ ions out, and Na⁺ ions back in.** The important point here is that the membrane is far more permeable to K⁺ ions flowing out than to Na⁺ ions returning. This causes the tissue fluid outside the neurone to contain many more positive ions than are present in the tiny amount of cytoplasm inside. As a result, a **negative charge** is developed inside compared to outside and the resting neurone is said to be **polarised**. The difference in charge or potential difference (about −70 mV), is known as the **resting potential** (Figure 7.32).

Figure 7.32 The establishment of the resting potential

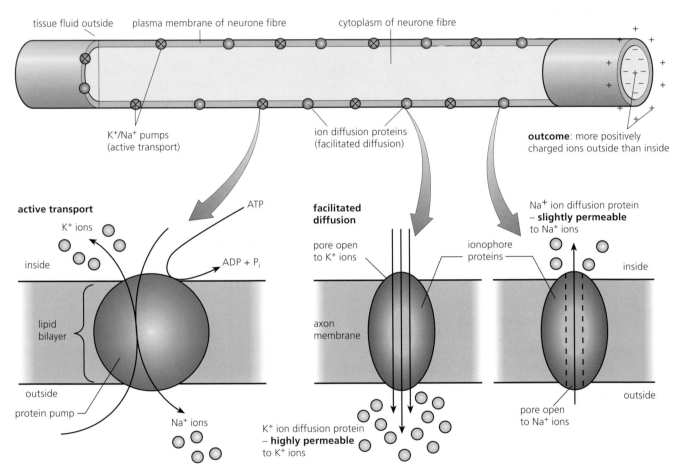

The next event, sooner or later, is the passage of an impulse, known as an **action potential**.

The action potential

The action potential is the potential difference produced across the plasma membrane of the nerve cell when stimulated, reversing the resting potential from about −70 mV to about +40 mV.

An action potential is triggered by a stimulus received at a receptor cell or sensitive nerve ending. The energy of the stimulus causes a temporary and local reversal of the resting potential. The result is that the membrane is briefly **depolarised**.

This change in potential across the membrane occurs because of pores in the membrane called **ion channels**. These special channels are globular proteins that span the membrane. They have a central pore with a **gate** that can open and close. One type of channel is permeable to sodium ions, and another to potassium ions. During a resting potential these channels are all closed.

The transfer of energy of the stimulus first opens the gates of the **sodium channels** in the plasma membrane and sodium ions diffuse in, down their **electrochemical gradient**.

What causes an electrochemical gradient?

The electrochemical gradient of an ion is due to its electrical and chemical properties.

- **Electrical properties** are due to the charge on the ion (an ion is attracted to an opposite charge).
- **Chemical properties** are due to concentration in solution (an ion tends to move from a high to a low concentration).

With sodium channels opened, the cytoplasm of the neurone fibre (the interior) quickly becomes progressively more positive with respect to the outside. When the charge has been **reversed** from −70 mV to +40 mV (due to the electrochemical gradient), an **action potential has been created** in the neurone fibre (Figure 7.33).

The action potential then runs the length of the neurone fibre. At any one point it exists for only two thousandths of a second (2 milliseconds), before the resting potential starts to be re-established. So action potential transmission is exceedingly quick.

Almost immediately an action potential has passed, the sodium channels close and the **potassium channels** open. Now, potassium ions can exit the cell, again down an electrochemical gradient, into the tissue fluid outside. The interior of the neurone fibre starts to become less positive again. Then the potassium channels also close. Finally, the resting potential is re-established by the action of the sodium/potassium pump and the process of facilitated diffusion.

21 Deduce the source of energy used to:

a establish the resting potential

b power an action potential.

Figure 7.33 The action potential

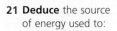

the gates are sometimes referred to as voltage-gated channels

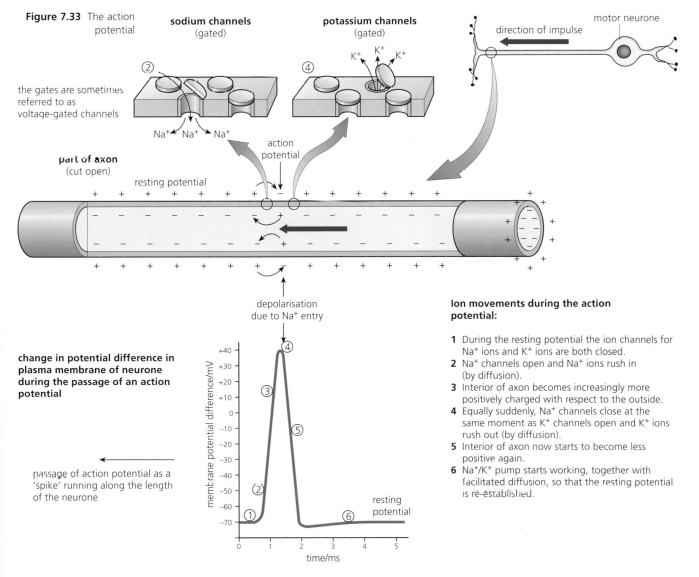

change in potential difference in plasma membrane of neurone during the passage of an action potential

passage of action potential as a 'spike' running along the length of the neurone

Ion movements during the action potential:

1 During the resting potential the ion channels for Na^+ ions and K^+ ions are both closed.
2 Na^+ channels open and Na^+ ions rush in (by diffusion).
3 Interior of axon becomes increasingly more positively charged with respect to the outside.
4 Equally suddenly, Na^+ channels close at the same moment as K^+ channels open and K^+ ions rush out (by diffusion).
5 Interior of axon now starts to become less positive again.
6 Na^+/K^+ pump starts working, together with facilitated diffusion, so that the resting potential is re-established.

The refractory period

For a brief period, following the passage of an action potential, the neurone fibre is no longer excitable. This is the **refractory period**, and it lasts only 5–10 milliseconds in total. The neurone fibre is not excitable during the refractory period because there is a large excess of sodium ions inside the fibre and further influx is impossible. Subsequently, as the resting potential is progressively restored, it becomes increasingly possible for an action potential to be generated again. Because of the refractory period, the maximum frequency of impulses is between 500 and 1000 per second.

The all-or-nothing principle

Obviously stimuli are of widely different strengths: for example, a light touch and the pain of a finger hit by a hammer. A stimulus must be at or above a minimum intensity, known as the **threshold of stimulation**, in order to initiate an action potential. Either the depolarisation is sufficient to fully reverse the potential difference in the cytoplasm (from −70 mV to +40 mV), or it is not. If not, no action potential arises. With all subthreshold stimuli, the influx of sodium ions is quickly reversed, and the full resting potential is re-established.

However, as the **intensity of the stimulus increases**, the **frequency** at which the **action potentials pass** along the fibre **increases** (the individual action potentials are all of standard strength). For example, with a very persistent stimulus, action potentials pass along a fibre at an accelerated rate, up to the maximum possible permitted by the refractory period. This means the effector (or the brain) is able to recognise the intensity of a stimulus from the frequency of action potentials (Figure 7.34).

Figure 7.34 Weak and strong stimuli and the threshold value

stimuli below the threshold value: not sufficient to reverse polarity of the membrane to +40 mV	**brief stimulus just above threshold value:** needed to cause depolarisation of the membrane of the sensory cell, and thus trigger an impulse	**stronger, more persistent stimulus**	**much stronger stimulus:** has stimulated almost the maximum frequency of impulses

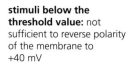

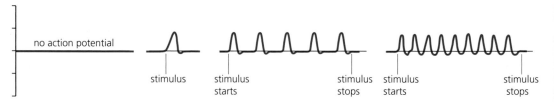

no action potential

stimulus | stimulus starts | stimulus stops | stimulus starts | stimulus stops

Junctions between neurones

The synapse is the link point between neurones. A synapse consists of the swollen tip (synaptic knob) of the axon of one neurone (**pre-synaptic neurone**) and the dendrite or cell body of another neurone (**post-synaptic neurone**). At the synapse, the neurones are extremely close but they have **no direct contact**. Instead there is a tiny gap, called a **synaptic cleft**, about 20 nm wide (Figure 7.35).

The practical effect of the synaptic cleft is that an action potential can only cross it via specific chemicals, known as **transmitter substances**. Transmitter substances are all relatively small, diffusible molecules. They are produced in the Golgi apparatus in the synaptic knob, and held in tiny vesicles before use.

Acetylcholine (ACh) is a commonly occurring transmitter substance (the neurones that release acetylcholine are known as cholinergic neurones). Another common transmitter substance is **noradrenalin** (from adrenergic neurones). In the brain, the commonly occurring transmitters are glutamic acid and dopamine.

Steps of synapse transmission

You may find it helpful to follow each step in Figure 7.36, the diagram of this event.

Figure 7.35 A synapse in section

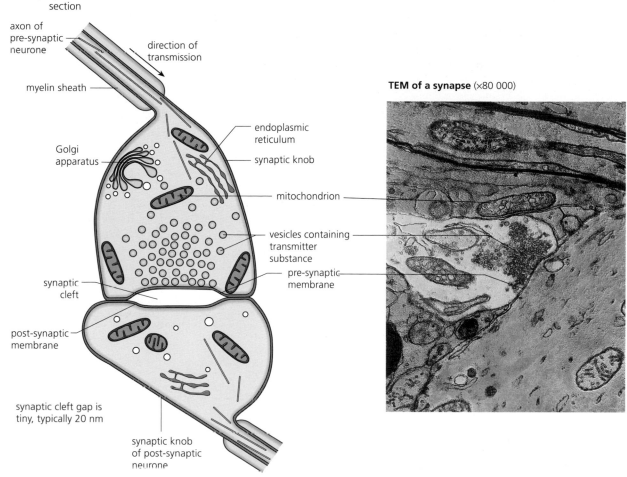

axon of pre-synaptic neurone

direction of transmission

myelin sheath

Golgi apparatus

endoplasmic reticulum

synaptic knob

mitochondrion

vesicles containing transmitter substance

pre-synaptic membrane

synaptic cleft

post-synaptic membrane

synaptic cleft gap is tiny, typically 20 nm

synaptic knob of post-synaptic neurone

TEM of a synapse (×80 000)

1 The arrival of an action potential at the synaptic knob opens **calcium ion channels in the pre-synaptic membrane**, and calcium ions flow in from the synaptic cleft.

2 The calcium ions cause **vesicles of transmitter substance** to fuse with the pre-synaptic membrane and release transmitter substance into the synaptic cleft.

3 The transmitter substance diffuses across the synaptic cleft and binds with a **receptor protein**.

In the **post-synaptic membrane** there are specific receptor sites for each transmitter substance. Each of these receptors also acts as a channel in the membrane which allows a specific ion (e.g. Na^+, or Cl^- or some other ion) to pass. The attachment of a transmitter molecule to its receptor instantly **opens the ion channel**.

When a molecule of ACh attaches to its receptor site, a Na^+ channel opens. As the sodium ions rush into the cytoplasm of the post-synaptic neurone, **depolarisation** of the post-synaptic membrane occurs. As more and more molecules of ACh bind, it becomes increasingly likely that depolarisation will reach the **threshold level**. When it does, an **action potential is generated** in the post-synaptic neurone. This process of build-up to an action potential in post-synaptic membranes is called **facilitation**.

4 The transmitter substance on the receptors is immediately **inactivated** by enzyme action. For example, the enzyme cholinesterase hydrolyses ACh to choline and ethanoic acid, which are inactive as transmitters. This causes the ion channel of the receptor protein to close, and so allows the resting potential in the post-synaptic neurone to be re-established.

5 The inactivated products from the transmitter re-enter the pre-synaptic knob, are **resynthesised** into transmitter substance, and packaged for re-use.

Figure 7.36 Chemical transmission at the synapse

how a synapse works

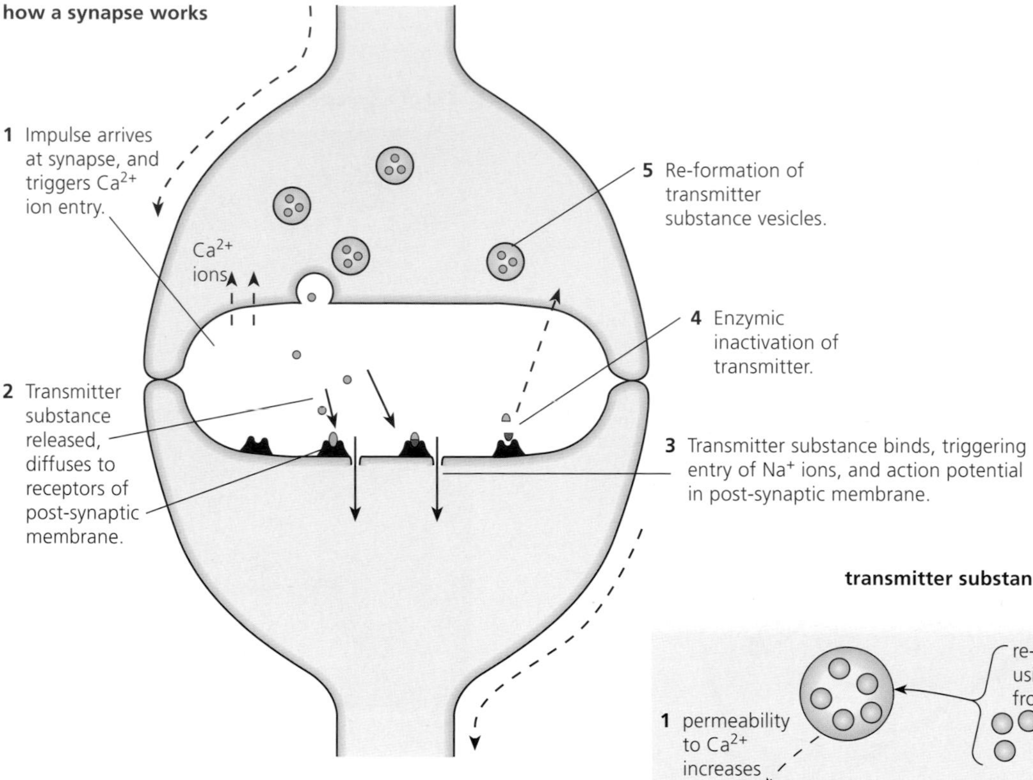

1 Impulse arrives at synapse, and triggers Ca²⁺ ion entry.

Ca^{2+} ions

5 Re-formation of transmitter substance vesicles.

4 Enzymic inactivation of transmitter.

2 Transmitter substance released, diffuses to receptors of post-synaptic membrane.

3 Transmitter substance binds, triggering entry of Na⁺ ions, and action potential in post-synaptic membrane.

transmitter substance cycle

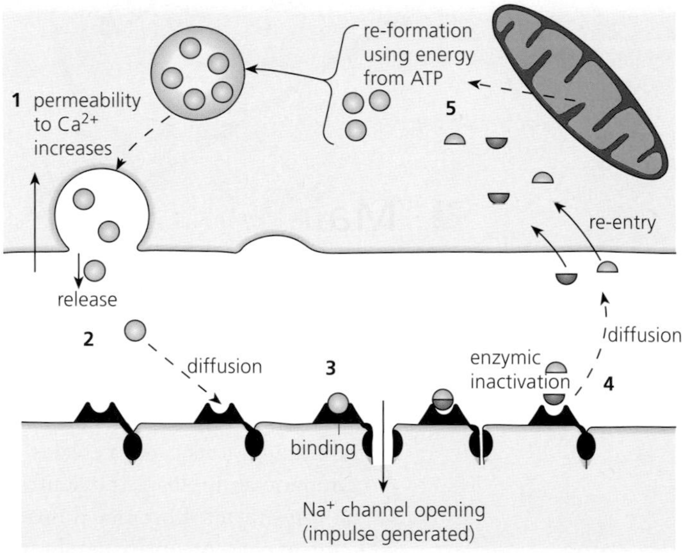

re-formation using energy from ATP

1 permeability to Ca^{2+} increases

5

release

re-entry

2

diffusion

3

enzymic inactivation

4

diffusion

binding

Na⁺ channel opening (impulse generated)

22 Identify the role of:

  a the Golgi apparatus
  b mitochondria in the synaptic knob.

Introducing the endocrine system

Hormones are chemical substances produced and secreted from the cells of the ductless or **endocrine glands**. In effect, hormones carry messages about the body – but in a totally different way from the nervous system.

Hormones are transported indiscriminately in the blood stream, but they act only at specific sites, called **target organs**. Although present in small quantities, hormones are extremely effective messengers, helping to control and co-ordinate body activities. Once released, hormones typically cause changes to specific metabolic reactions of their target organs, but a hormone circulates in the blood stream only briefly. In the liver, they are broken down and the breakdown products are excreted in the kidneys. So, long-acting hormones must be secreted continuously to be effective.

An example of a hormone to be discussed is insulin, released from endocrine cells in the pancreas. Insulin regulates blood glucose (page 222). The positions of endocrine glands of the body are shown in Figure 7.37.

Figure 7.37 The human endocrine system

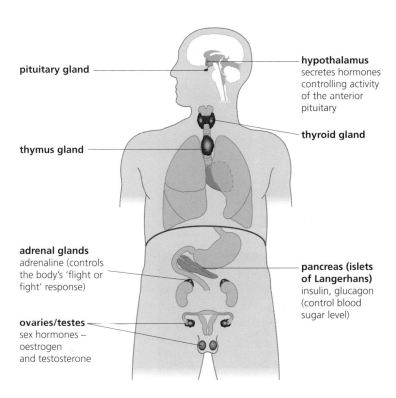

pituitary gland

hypothalamus
secretes hormones controlling activity of the anterior pituitary

thyroid gland

thymus gland

adrenal glands
adrenaline (controls the body's 'flight or fight' response)

pancreas (islets of Langerhans)
insulin, glucagon (control blood sugar level)

ovaries/testes
sex hormones – oestrogen and testosterone

Maintaining a constant internal environment – homeostasis

Living things face changing and sometimes hostile environments; some external conditions change slowly, others dramatically. For example, temperature changes quickly on land exposed to direct sunlight, but the temperature of water exposed to sunlight changes very slowly (page 39).

How do organisms respond to environmental changes?

An animal that is able to maintain a constant internal environment, enabling it to continue normal activities, more or less whatever the external conditions, is known as a **regulator**. For example, mammals and birds maintain a high and almost constant body temperature over a very wide range of external temperatures. Their bodies are at or about the optimum temperature for the majority of the enzymes that drive their metabolism. Their muscles contract efficiently, and the nervous system co-ordinates responses precisely, even when external conditions are unfavourable. They are often able to avoid danger, and perhaps they may also benefit from the vulnerability of prey organisms which happen to be **non-regulators**. So regulators may have greater freedom in choosing where to live. They can exploit more habitats with differing conditions than non-regulators.

Homeostasis is the name for this ability to maintain a constant internal environment. Homeostasis means 'staying the same'. The internal environment consists of the blood circulating in the body and the fluid circulating among cells (tissue fluid) that forms from it, delivering nutrients and removing waste products while bathing the cells. Mammals are excellent examples of animals that hold internal conditions remarkably constant. They successfully regulate and maintain their blood pH, oxygen and carbon dioxide concentrations, blood glucose, body temperature and water balance at constant levels or within narrow limits (Figure 7.38).

How is homeostasis achieved?

Figure 7.38 Homeostasis in mammals

Mammals are a comparatively recent group in terms of their evolutionary history, yet they have successfully settled in significant numbers in virtually every type of habitat on Earth. This success is directly linked to their ability to control their internal environment by homeostasis.

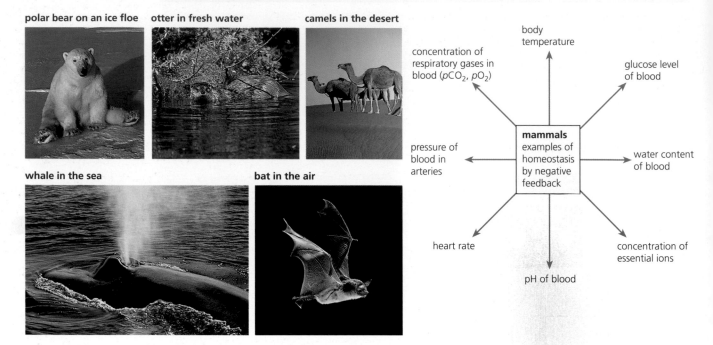

Negative feedback – the mechanism of homeostasis

Negative feedback is the type of control in which conditions being regulated are brought back to a set value as soon as it is detected that they have deviated from it. We see this type of mechanism at work in a system to maintain the temperature of a laboratory water bath. Analysis of this familiar example will show us the components of a negative feedback system (Figure 7.39).

A negative feedback system requires a **detector** device that measures the value of the variable (the water temperature in the water bath) and transmits this information to a **control unit**. The control unit compares data from the detector with a pre-set value (the desired water temperature of the water bath). When the value from the detector is below the required value, the control unit activates an **effector** device (a water heater in the water bath) so that the temperature starts to be raised. Once data from the detector register in the control box that the water has reached the set temperature, the control box switches off the response (the water heater). How precisely the variable is maintained depends on the sensitivity of the detector, but negative feedback control typically involves some degree of 'overshoot'.

In mammals, regulation of body temperature, blood sugar level, and the amounts of water and ions in blood and tissue fluid (**osmoregulation**) are regulated by negative feedback. The detectors are specialised cells in either the brain or other organs, such as the pancreas. The effectors are organs such as the skin, liver and kidneys. Information passes between them via the nerves of the nervous system or via hormones (the endocrine system), or both. The outcome is an incredibly precisely regulated internal environment.

Homeostasis in action

Control of body temperature

The regulation of body temperature, known as **thermoregulation**, involves controlling the amount of heat lost and heat gained across the body surface. Heat may be transferred between an animal and the environment by convection, radiation and conduction, and the body loses heat by evaporation (Figure 7.40).

Figure 7.39 Negative feedback, the mechanism

components of a negative feedback control system

input
– change to the *system*

detector
measures level of the *variable*

control unit
level of operation is set here, and information from detector *received* and *compared with set value*, and *commands to effector* despatched from here

effector
brings about a second change to system (in opposite direction to the input)

output
– condition restored to *set value*

feedback loop
establishes the change has been corrected, and causes the *effector to be switched off*

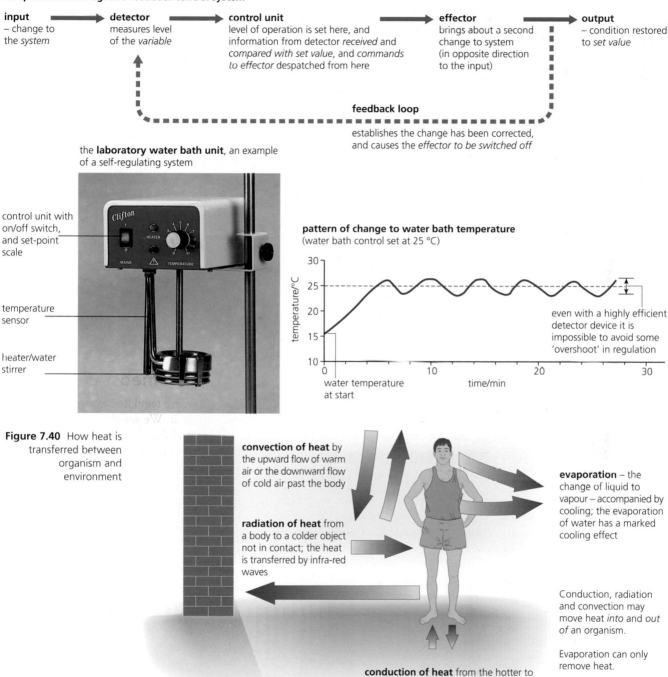

the **laboratory water bath unit**, an example of a self-regulating system

control unit with on/off switch, and set-point scale

temperature sensor

heater/water stirrer

pattern of change to water bath temperature
(water bath control set at 25 °C)

even with a highly efficient detector device it is impossible to avoid some 'overshoot' in regulation

water temperature at start

time/min

Figure 7.40 How heat is transferred between organism and environment

convection of heat by the upward flow of warm air or the downward flow of cold air past the body

radiation of heat from a body to a colder object not in contact; the heat is transferred by infra-red waves

evaporation – the change of liquid to vapour – accompanied by cooling; the evaporation of water has a marked cooling effect

Conduction, radiation and convection may move heat *into* and *out of* an organism.

Evaporation can only remove heat.

conduction of heat from the hotter to the colder of two surfaces in contact

Mammals maintain a high and relatively constant body temperature, using the heat energy generated by metabolism within their bodies (or by generating additional heat in the muscles when cold) and carefully controlling the loss of heat through the skin. An animal with this form of thermoregulation is called an **endotherm**, meaning 'inside heat'. Birds too have perfected this mechanism. Humans hold their inner body temperature (core temperature) just below 37 °C. In fact, human core temperature only varies between about 35.5 and 37.0 °C within a 24-hour period, when we are in good health. Under low external temperature, however, only the temperature of the trunk is held constant; there is a progressive fall in temperature along the limbs (Figure 7.41).

Figure 7.41 Body temperature of a human

body temperature over a 48-hour period

The body temperatures shown were taken with the thermometer under the tongue. Although this is a region close to the body 'core', temperatures here may be altered by eating/drinking, and by the breathing in through the mouth of cold air, for example. More accurate values are obtained by taking the rectal temperature.

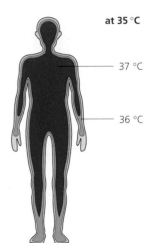

temperature distribution in environments at 20 °C and at 35 °C

The lines, **isotherms**, connect sites of equal temperature. The shaded area is the core, and around this the temperature varies according to the temperature of the surrounding air (**ambient temperature**).

23 Deduce the times and conditions under which body temperature typically varies from the normal in a 24-hour period (Figure 7.41).

Heat production in the human body

The major sources of heat are the biochemical reactions of metabolism that generate heat as a waste product. Heat is then distributed by the blood circulation – we might say that heat is transferred by the blood circulation. The organs of the body vary greatly in the amount of heat they yield. For example, the liver is extremely active metabolically, but most of its metabolic reactions require an input of energy (they are **endergonic reactions**) and little energy is lost as heat. Mostly, the liver is thermally neutral.

The bulk of our body heat (over 70%) comes from other organs, mainly from the heart and kidneys, but also from the lungs and brain (which, like a computer central processing unit, needs to be kept cool). While the body is at rest, the skeleton, muscles and skin, which make up over 90% of the body mass, produce less than 30% of the body heat (Figure 7.42). Of course, in times of intense physical activity, the skeletal muscles generate a great deal of heat as a waste product of respiration and contraction.

Figure 7.42 Heat production in the body at rest

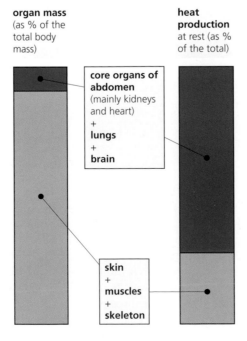

24 State what it means to say that most reactions in liver cells are endergonic.

The roles of the skin in thermoregulation

Heat exchanges occur at the skin. The structure of the skin is shown in Figure 7.43. Heat loss at the skin may be varied by:

- arterioles supplying **capillary networks** being dilated (**vasodilation**) when the body needs to lose heat, but constricted (**vasoconstriction**) when the body needs to retain heat;
- **hair erector muscles**, which contract when heat must be lost but relax when heat loss must be increased;
- **sweat glands**, which produce sweat when the body needs to lose heat, but do not when the body needs to retain heat.

Figure 7.43 The skin and temperature regulation

The operation of these mechanisms is shown in Figure 7.43.

structure of the skin

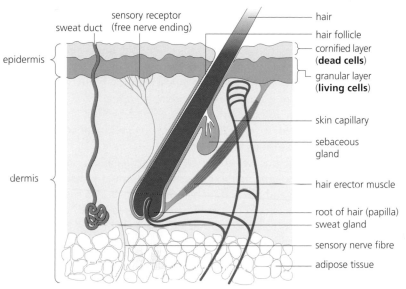

role of the sweat glands in regulating heat loss through the skin

warm conditions

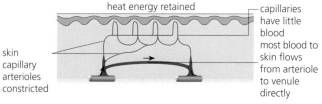

role of capillaries in regulating heat loss through the skin

In skin that is especially exposed (e.g. outer ear, nose, extremities of the limbs) the capillary network is extensive, and the arterioles supplying it can be dilated or constricted.

warm conditions

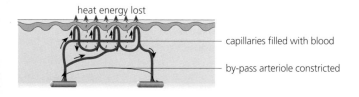

cold conditions

role of the hair in regulating heat loss through the skin

warm conditions

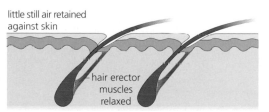

The hair erector muscles may be contracted or relaxed.

still air is a poor conductor of heat

cold conditions

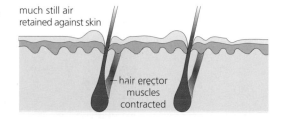

Other mechanisms in thermoregulation

If the body experiences persistent cold then heat production is increased. Under chilly conditions, heat output from the body muscles is raised by contraction of skeletal muscles that is not co-ordinated and is known as **shivering**. This raises muscle heat production about five times above basal rate.

Regulation of blood glucose

Transport of glucose to all cells is a key function of the blood circulation. In humans, the **normal level of blood glucose** is about 90 mg of glucose in every 100 cm^3 of blood, but it can vary. For example, during an extended period without food, or after prolonged and heavy physical activity, blood glucose may fall to as low as 70 mg. After a meal rich in carbohydrate has been digested, blood glucose may rise to 150 mg.

The maintenance of a constant level of this monosaccharide in the blood plasma is important for two reasons.

1 Respiration is a continuous process in all living cells. To maintain their metabolism, cells need a regular supply of glucose, which can be quickly absorbed across the cell membrane. Glucose is the principal respiratory substrate for many tissues. Most cells (including muscle cells) hold reserves in the form of glycogen which is quickly converted to glucose during prolonged physical activity. However, glycogen reserves may be used up quickly. In the brain, glucose is the only substrate the cells can use and there is no glycogen store held in reserve.

   If our blood glucose falls below 60 mg per 100 cm^3, we have a condition called **hypoglycaemia**. If this is not quickly reversed, we may faint. If the body and brain continue to be deprived of adequate glucose levels, convulsions and coma follow.

2 An abnormally high concentration of blood glucose, known as **hyperglycaemia**, is also a problem. Since high concentration of any soluble metabolite lowers the water potential of the blood plasma, water is drawn from the cells and tissue fluid by osmosis, back into the blood. As the volume of blood increases, water is excreted by the kidney to maintain the correct concentration of blood. As a result, the body tends to become dehydrated, and the circulatory system is deprived of fluid. Ultimately, blood pressure cannot be maintained.

For these reasons, it is critically important the blood glucose is held within set limits.

Mechanism for regulation of blood glucose

After the digestion of carbohydrates in the gut, glucose is absorbed across the epithelial cells of the villi (Figure 7.5, page 183) into the hepatic portal vein (Figure 7.11, page 189). The blood carrying the glucose reaches the liver first. If the glucose level is too high, glucose is withdrawn from the blood and stored as glycogen. But even so, blood circulating in the body immediately after a meal has a raised level of glucose. At the pancreas, the presence of an excess of blood glucose is detected in patches of cells known as the islets of Langerhans (Figure 7.44). These islets are hormone-secreting glands (endocrine glands); they have a rich capillary network, but no ducts that would carry secretions away. Instead, their hormones are transported all over the body by the blood. The islets of Langerhans contain two types of cell, α **cells** and β **cells**.

Figure 7.44 Islet of Langerhans in the pancreas

TS of pancreatic gland showing an islet of Langerhans

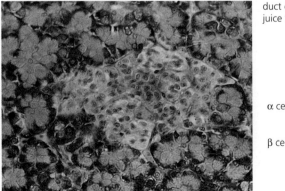

drawing of part of pancreatic gland

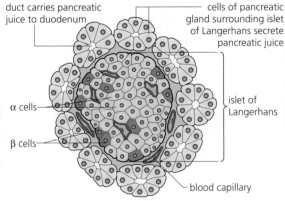

duct carries pancreatic juice to duodenum

cells of pancreatic gland surrounding islet of Langerhans secrete pancreatic juice

α cells

β cells

islet of Langerhans

blood capillary

25 Explain what liver cells receive from blood from the hepatic artery that is not present in blood from the hepatic portal vein.

26 Predict what type of organelle you would expect to see most frequently when a liver cell is examined by EM.

Figure 7.45 The sites of blood glucose regulation

In the presence of a **raised blood glucose** level, the β cells are stimulated. They secrete the hormone **insulin** into the capillary network. Insulin stimulates the uptake of glucose into cells all over the body, but especially by the liver and the skeletal muscle fibres. It also increases the rate at which glucose is used in respiration, in preference to alternative substrates (such as fat). Another effect of insulin is to trigger conversion of glucose to glycogen in cells (**glycogenesis**), and of glucose to fatty acids and fats, and finally the deposition of fat around the body.

As the blood glucose level reverts to normal this is detected in the islets of Langerhans, and the β cells respond by stopping insulin secretion. Meanwhile the hormone is excreted by the kidney tubules and the blood insulin level falls.

When the **blood glucose level falls below normal**, the α cells of the pancreas are stimulated. These secrete a hormone called **glucagon**. This hormone activates the enzymes that convert glycogen and amino acids to glucose (**gluconeogenesis**). Glucagon also reduces the rate of respiration (Figures 7.45 and 7.46)

As the blood glucose level reverts to normal, glucagon production ceases, and this hormone in turn is removed from the blood in the kidney tubules.

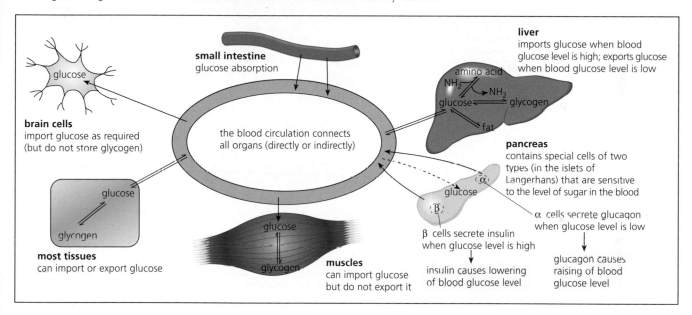

Figure 7.46 Glucose regulation by negative feedback

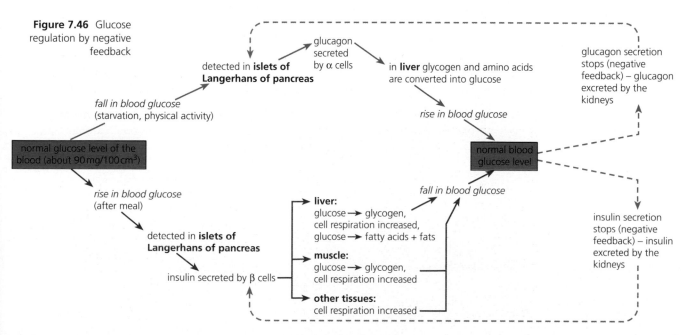

The disease diabetes

Diabetes is the name for a group of diseases in which the body fails to regulate blood glucose levels. **Type I diabetes** results from a failure of insulin production by the β cells. **Type II diabetes** (diabetes mellitus) is a failure of the insulin receptor proteins on the cell membranes of target cells (Figure 7.47). As a consequence, blood glucose is more erratic and generally, permanently raised. Glucose is also regularly excreted in the urine. If this condition is not diagnosed and treated, it carries an increased risk of circulatory disorders, renal failure, blindness, strokes or heart attacks.

Figure 7.47 Diabetes, cause and treatment

type I diabetes, 'early onset diabetes'

affects young people, below the age of 20 years

due to the destruction of the β cells of the islets of Langerhans by the body's own immune system

symptoms:
- constant thirst
- undiminished hunger
- excessive urination

treatment:
- injection of insulin into the blood stream daily
- regular measurement of blood glucose level

patient injecting with insulin, obtained by genetic engineering

type II diabetes, 'late onset diabetes'

the common form (90% of all cases of diabetes are of this type)

common in people over 40 years, especially if overweight, but this form of diabetes is having an increasing effect on human societies around the world, including young people and even children in developed countries, seemingly because of poor diet

symptoms:
mild – sufferers usually have sufficient blood insulin, but insulin receptors on cells have become defective

treatment:
largely by diet alone

■ Reproduction

6.6.1–6.6.6

Reproduction is the production of new individuals by an existing member or members of the same species. It is a fundamental characteristic of living things; the ability to self-replicate in this way sets the living world apart from the non-living. In reproduction, a parent generation effectively passes on a copy of itself in the form of the genetic material, to another generation, the offspring. The genetic material of an organism consists of its chromosomes, made of nucleic acid (page 63).

Organisms reproduce either asexually or sexually and many reproduce by both these methods. However, mammals reproduce by **sexual reproduction** only.

In sexual reproduction, two **gametes** (specialised sex cells) fuse to form a **zygote** which then grows into a new individual. Fusion of gametes is called **fertilisation**. In the process of gamete formation, a nuclear division by **meiosis** (page 94) halves the normal chromosome number. That is, gametes are **haploid**, and fertilisation restores the **diploid** number of chromosomes (Figure 7.48). Without the reductive nuclear division in the process of sexual reproduction, the chromosome number would double in each generation. Remember, the offspring produced by sexual reproduction are unique, in complete contrast with offspring formed by asexual reproduction.

Figure 7.48 Meiosis and the diploid life cycle

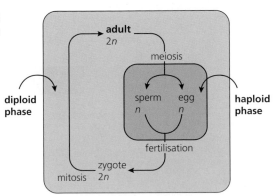

Sexual reproduction in mammals

In mammals, like most vertebrates, the sexes are separate (unisexual individuals). In the body, the reproductive and urinary (excretory) systems are closely bound together, especially in the male, so biologists refer to these as the urinogenital system. Here, just the reproductive systems are considered (Figures 7.49 and 7.50).

Male and female gametes are produced in paired glands called **gonads**, the testes and ovaries.

The male reproductive system

- Two **testes** (singular, **testis**) are situated in the scrotal sac, hanging outside the main body cavity; this allows the testes to be at the optimum temperature for sperm production, a temperature 2–3 °C lower than the normal body temperature. As well as producing the male gametes, **spermatozoa** (singular, **spermatozoon**) or sperms, the testes also produce the male sex hormone, **testosterone**; the testes are, therefore, also endocrine glands (page 216).
- Ducts which store the sperms and carry them in a fluid, called **seminal fluid**, to the outside of the body during a process called an **ejaculation**.
- Ducted or exocrine glands which secrete the nutritive seminal fluid in which the sperms are transported; these include the **seminal vesicles** and **prostate gland**.
- The **penis**, through which the urethra runs. This duct carries semen during an ejaculation (and urine during urination) to the outside. The penis also contains spongy erectile tissue that can fill with blood when the male is sexually stimulated. This causes the penis to enlarge, lengthen and become rigid, in a condition known as an **erection**. The erect penis penetrates the vagina in sexual intercourse.

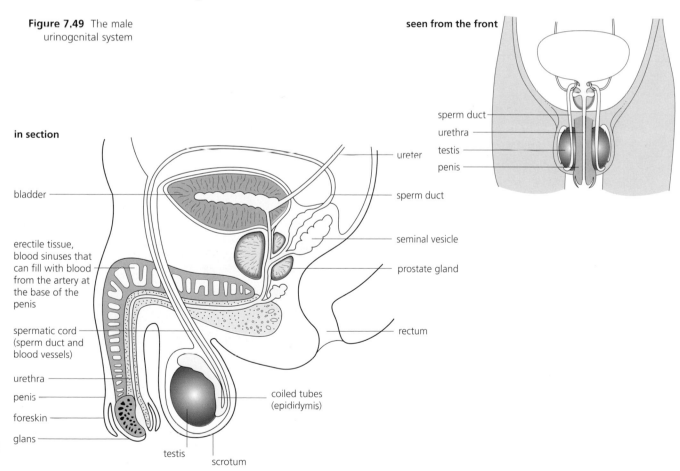

Figure 7.49 The male urinogenital system

The female reproductive system

- The **ovaries** are held near the base of the abdominal cavity. As well as producing the female gametes, ova or **egg cells**, the ovaries are also endocrine glands, secreting the female sex hormones **oestrogen** and **progesterone**.
- A pair of **oviducts** extend from the uterus and open as funnels close to the ovaries. The oviducts transport egg cells, and are the site of fertilisation.
- The **uterus**, which is about the size and shape of an inverted pear, has a thick muscular wall and an inner lining of mucous membrane richly supplied with arterioles. This lining, called the **endometrium**, undergoes regular change in a 28-day cycle. The lining is built up each month in preparation for implantation and early nutrition of a developing embryo, should fertilisation occur. If it does not occur, the endometrium disintegrates and menstruation starts.
- The **vagina**, a muscular tube that can enlarge to allow entry of the penis, and exit of a baby at birth. The vagina is connected to the uterus at the **cervix**, and it opens to the exterior at the **vulva**.

Figure 7.50 The female urinogenital system

seen from the front

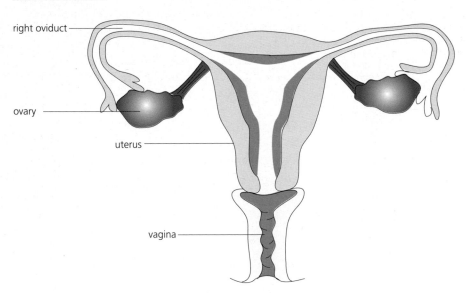

in section

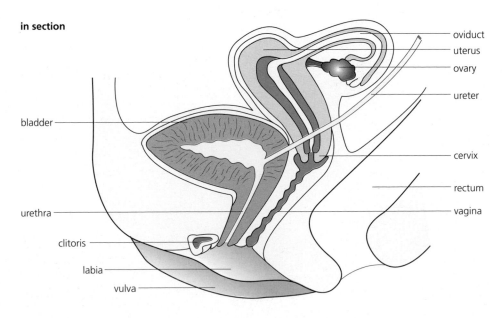

Primary and secondary sexual characteristics

The primary sexual characteristics of a male or a female are possession of their respective reproductive organs. We have seen that in humans, gender is primarily determined by the sex chromosomes, XX or XY (Figure 4.22, page 112).

The **secondary sexual characteristics** are those that develop in males and females at **puberty**, the time in growth and development at the beginning of sexual maturation. At this time there is a significant increase in the production of the **sex hormones** by the gonads, testosterone in cells of the testes, and oestrogen and progesterone in cells of the ovaries. These hormones are chemically very similar molecules; they are manufactured from the steroid **cholesterol** that has been synthesised in the liver and absorbed as part of the diet. (Steroids are a form of lipid.)

Perhaps the most noticeable effect of the increased secretion of the sex hormones is the stimulation they cause in muscle protein formation and bone growth. Because of this effect, testosterone, oestrogen and progesterone are known as **anabolic steroids** (anabolic means 'build up'). The effects of the female sex hormones are less marked, in this respect, than those of testosterone in the male, and the onset of puberty occurs, on average, about two years earlier in girls (Figure 7.51).

Figure 7.51 The onset of the secondary sexual characteristics

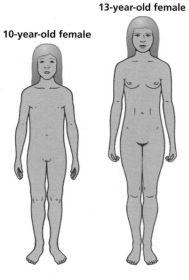

10-year-old female

13-year-old female

Secondary sexual characteristics of a human female:

- maturation of the ovaries, and enlargement of the vagina and uterus

- development of the breasts

- widening of the pelvis

- deposition of fat under the skin of the buttocks and thighs

- growth of pubic hair and hair under the arm pits

- monthly ovulation and menstruation

- changes in behaviour associated with a sex drive.

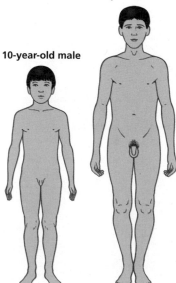

10-year-old male

16-year-old male

Secondary sexual characteristics of a human male:

- development and enlargement of the testes, scrotum, penis and glands of the reproductive tract

- increased skeletal muscle development

- enlargement of the larynx, deepening the voice

- growth of pubic hair, underarm hair, and body hair

- continuous production of sperms, and in the absence of sexual intercourse, occasional erections and the discharge of seminal fluid

- changes in behaviour associated with a sex drive.

Roles of hormones in the control of reproduction

The onset of puberty is triggered by a part of the brain called the hypothalamus. Here, production and secretion of a releasing hormone causes the nearby pituitary gland (the 'master' endocrine gland) to produce and release into the blood circulation two hormones, **follicle-stimulating hormone (FSH)** and **luteinising hormone (LH)**. They are so named because their roles in sexual development were discovered in the female, although they do operate in both sexes. Their first effects are to enhance secretions of the sex hormones. Then, in the presence of FSH, LH and the respective sex hormone, there follows the development of the secondary sexual characteristics, and the preparation of the body for its role in sexual reproduction.

In females

In the female reproductive system, the secretion of oestrogen and progesterone is cyclical, rather than at a steady rate. Together with FSH and LH, the **changing concentrations of all four hormones** bring about a repeating cycle of changes that we call the **menstrual cycle**.

The menstrual cycle consists of **two cycles**, one in the **ovaries** and one in the **uterus lining**. The ovarian cycle is concerned with the monthly preparation and shedding of an egg cell from an ovary, and the uterus cycle, with the build-up of the lining of the uterus. 'Menstrual' means 'monthly'; the combined cycles take 28 days (Figure 7.52).

Figure 7.52 Hormone regulation of the menstrual cycle

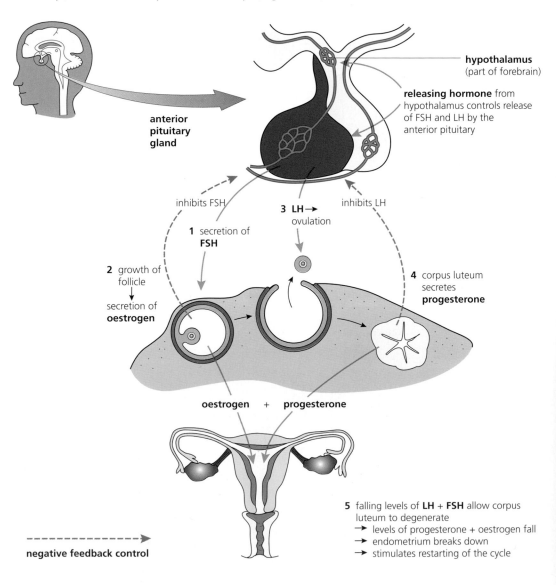

By convention the start of the cycle is taken as the first day of menstruation (bleeding), which is the shedding of the endometrium lining of the uterus. The steps, also summarised in Figure 7.53, are as follows.

1 **FSH** is secreted by the pituitary gland, and stimulates development of several immature egg cells (in primary follicles) in the ovary. Only one will complete development into a mature egg cell (now in the ovarian follicle).

Figure 7.53 Changing levels of hormones in the menstrual cycle

2 The developing follicle then secretes **oestrogen**. Oestrogen has two targets:
  a in the uterus, it stimulates the build-up of the endometrium, the lining for a possible implantation of an embryo, should fertilisation take place;

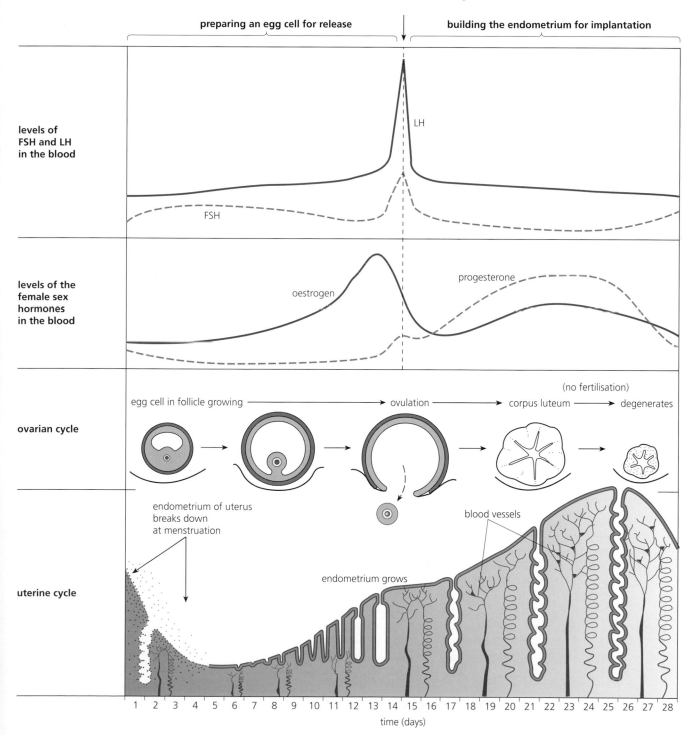

b in the pituitary gland, oestrogen inhibits the further secretion of FSH, which prevents the possibility of further follicles being stimulated to develop, and is an example of **negative feedback control** (Figure 7.53).

3 The concentration of oestrogen continues to increase to a peak value just before the mid-point of the cycle. This high and rising level of oestrogen suddenly stimulates the secretion of **LH** and, to a slightly lesser extent, FSH, by the pituitary gland. LH stimulates **ovulation** (the shedding of the mature egg cell from the ovarian follicle and its escape from the ovary).

As soon as the ovarian follicle has discharged its egg, LH also stimulates the conversion of the vacant follicle into an additional, temporary gland, called a **corpus luteum**.

4 The corpus luteum secretes **progesterone** and, to a lesser extent, oestrogen. Progesterone has two targets:

a in the uterus, it continues the build-up of the endometrium, further preparing for a possible implantation of an embryo, should fertilisation take place;

b in the pituitary gland, it inhibits further secretion of LH, and also of FSH; this is a second example of **negative feedback control**.

5 The levels of FSH and LH in the blood stream now rapidly decrease. Low levels of FSH and LH allow the corpus luteum to degenerate. As a consequence, the level of progesterone and oestrogen also fall. Soon the level of these hormones is so low that the extra lining of the uterus is no longer maintained. The **endometrium breaks down** and is lost through the vagina in the first five days or so of the new cycle. Falling levels of progesterone again cause the secretion of FSH by the pituitary.

A new cycle is under way.

6 **If the egg is fertilised** (the start of a pregnancy), then the developing embryo itself immediately becomes an endocrine gland, secreting a hormone that circulates in the blood and maintains the corpus luteum as an endocrine gland for at least 16 weeks of pregnancy. When eventually the corpus luteum does break down, the **placenta** takes over as an endocrine gland, secreting oestrogen and progesterone. These hormones continue to prevent ovulation, and maintain the endometrium.

27 Identify the critical hormone changes that respectively trigger ovulation, and cause degeneration of the corpus luteum.

In males

In the male, the secretion of sex hormone commences in pre-natal development, and is a continuous process, rather than cyclic. Testosterone secretion has the following roles:

- it initiates the pre-natal development of male genitalia;
- it triggers and regulates the development of secondary sexual characteristics;
- it maintains the sex drive (libido) in the adult.

Infertility, and *in vitro* fertilisation

In mammals, fertilisation – the fusion of male and female gametes to form a **zygote** – is internal. It occurs in the upper part of the oviduct. As the zygote is transported down the oviduct, mitosis and cell division commence. By the time the embryo has reached the uterus, it is a solid ball of tiny cells. Division continues and the cells organise themselves into a fluid-filled ball, the **blastocyst**, which becomes embedded in the endometrium of the uterus, a process known as **implantation**. In humans, implantation takes from day 7 to day 14 approximately (Figure 12.35, page 384).

Not all partners are fertile in this way. Either the male or female or both may be infertile, due to a number of different causes (Table 7.13).

In some cases, a couple's infertility may be overcome by the process of fertilisation of eggs outside the body (*in vitro* fertilisation, IVF). The key step in IVF is the successful removal of sufficient eggs from the ovaries. To achieve this, normal menstrual activity is temporarily suspended with hormone-based drugs.

Then the ovaries are induced to produce a large number of eggs simultaneously, at a time controlled by the doctors. In this way, the correct moment to collect the eggs can be known accurately.

■ Extension: Contraception

People who make a study of human population growth (demographers) have predicted that by 2050 the Earth may have 10 billion human inhabitants – that is, very many more than we currently have. The projections suggest that the world population will stabilise at this level. Can such a total human population be sustained by the Earth's resources?

If we think not, an immediate task would be to reduce the **birth rate**. The mechanisms for birth control exist. **Contraception** is any procedure which prevents conception. There are many different methods, some easier and more reliable than others. It is a convention to divide them into **mechanical**, **chemical** and **behavioural** (Table 7.12).

Mechanical	barrier between sperm and egg	■ condom – sheath fitted to erect penis ■ femidom** – sheath fitted to the vagina ■ diaphragm or cap** – 'cup' fitted over the cervix
	prevention of implantation	■ loop or coil** – fitted inside the uterus
Chemical – prevention of ovulation by use of hormones	combined pill	■ oestrogen and progesterone** – daily for 21 days
	mini-pill	■ progesterone** – daily at the same time each day
Behavioural	rhythm method – calculating a time when fertile eggs are not present and sperms cannot survive until ovulation	■ if ovulation occurs at days 13–15, egg may survive till day 18 and sperms introduced on or after day 8 may survive to ovulation; so intercourse not practised on days 8–18; ovulation detected by body temperature changes

Table 7.12 Alternative methods of contraception

** methods that can be used without involvement of the male partner, thereby giving the female partner control of contraception

■ Extension: Sexually transmitted diseases (STDs) and contraception

STDs cause enormous suffering worldwide. However, apart from AIDS, they are seldom mentioned or discussed.

Earlier in the last century, the common STDs were the bacterial infections **gonorrhoea** and **syphilis**, both becoming particularly prevalent in communities after both the First and Second World Wars.

Today, STDs due to *Chlamydia* (a bacterium), to herpes simplex virus, and to human papilloma viruses (genital warts) are adding to patient numbers. AIDS and the special factors in HIV transmission have already been discussed (page 198).

STDs are mostly transmitted between infected people who are sexually active. The more sexual partners a person has, the greater their risk of infection. In many cases, 'safe sex' using **barrier contraception** (such as the condom) **reduces the risks**, but now that oral contraception may be preferred, risks have increased enormously. Another source of infection comes at birth for newborn babies of infected mothers.

In males	In females
failure to achieve or maintain an erect penis	conditions in cervix cause death of sperms
structurally abnormal sperms sperms with poor mobility short-lived sperms too few sperms	conditions in uterus prevent implantation of blastocyst
blocked sperm duct preventing semen from containing sperms	oviducts blocked or damaged, preventing egg from reaching sperms
	eggs fail to mature or be released

Table 7.13 Causes of infertility

Figure 7.54 *In vitro* fertilisation – the process

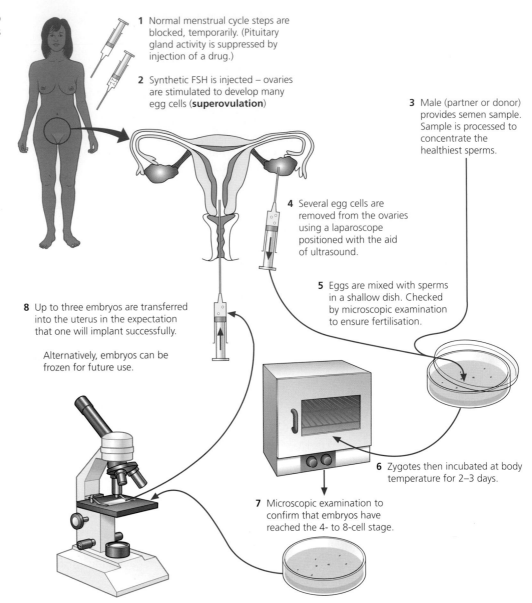

1 Normal menstrual cycle steps are blocked, temporarily. (Pituitary gland activity is suppressed by injection of a drug.)

2 Synthetic FSH is injected – ovaries are stimulated to develop many egg cells (**superovulation**)

3 Male (partner or donor) provides semen sample. Sample is processed to concentrate the healthiest sperms.

4 Several egg cells are removed from the ovaries using a laparoscope positioned with the aid of ultrasound.

5 Eggs are mixed with sperms in a shallow dish. Checked by microscopic examination to ensure fertilisation.

8 Up to three embryos are transferred into the uterus in the expectation that one will implant successfully.

Alternatively, embryos can be frozen for future use.

6 Zygotes then incubated at body temperature for 2–3 days.

7 Microscopic examination to confirm that embryos have reached the 4- to 8-cell stage.

Egg cells are then isolated from surrounding follicle cells, and mixed with sperms. If fertilisation occurs, the fertilised egg cells are incubated so that embryos at the eight-cell stage may be placed in the uterus. If one (or more) imbed there, then a normal pregnancy may follow.

The first 'test-tube baby' was born in 1978. The steps of IVF are illustrated in Figure 7.54. Today, the procedure is regarded as a routine one.

Ethical issues raised by IVF

IVF raises many issues for society. Infertility is a personal problem that generates stress and unhappiness in those affected. Many of these couples may seek assistance. Medical treatments involved are expensive, and their deployment inevitably deflects finite resources away from other needs. Success rates are very low.

In the face of the world's booming human population and the large numbers of parentless children seeking adoption, some argue against these sorts of development in reproduction technology.

Another controversial issue is that current fertility treatments tend to create several embryos, all with the potential to become new people. However, the embryos that are not selected for implantation ultimately must be destroyed – a stressful task in itself.

Ethical issues are listed in Table 7.14.

Favourable arguments	Critical arguments
For some otherwise childless couples, desired parenthood may be achieved.	Allows infertility due to inherited defects to be passed on (unwittingly) to the offspring who may then experience the same problem in adulthood.
Allows men and women surviving cancer treatments the possibility of having children later, using gametes harvested prior to radiation treatment or chemotherapy.	Excess embryos are produced to ensure success, and so an embryologist has to select some new embryo(s) to live, and to allow the later destruction of other potential human lives.
Permits screening and selection of embryos before implantation stage to avoid an inherited disease.	Multiple pregnancies have been a common outcome, sometimes producing triplets, quads or sextuplets. This can lead to increased risk to the mother's health, risks of premature birth, and put the babies at risk of conditions such as cerebral palsy.
If IVF treatment were to be banned, the state may be interfering in the lives of individuals with medical problems that otherwise could be cured.	Infertility is not always strictly a health problem; it may have arisen in older parents who chose to delay having a family (a life-style issue).
Offspring produced by IVF are much longed-for children who will more certainly be loved and cared for.	There is an excess of unwanted children, cared for in orphanages or in foster homes. These children may have benefited from adoption by couples, childless or otherwise, keen to be caring parents.

Table 7.14 Ethical issues raised by IVF

28 **Outline** key points that might be put by a genetic counsellor who felt that some alternative way to establish a family was more appropriate for a particular childless couple seeking IVF treatment.

■ *Examination questions – a selection*

Questions 1–8 are taken from past IB Diploma biology papers.

Q1 **a** Draw a diagram of the heart showing the chambers, valves and associated blood vessels. (4)
  b Outline the control of the heart beat. (6)
  c Discuss the structure and function of the blood vessels that are found in a human. (8)
    Standard Level Paper 2, May 06, QB5

Q2 Which of the following is correct for a pathogen?

	Can be a virus	Can cause antibody response	Is an antigen
A	✔	✘	✘
B	✔	✔	✘
C	✘	✔	✔
D	✔	✔	✔

Higher Level Paper 1, May 05, Q18

Q3 Which of the following correctly explains the functions of parts of the digestive system?

	Stomach	Small intestine	Large intestine
A	digests proteins	absorbs vitamin K	absorbs water
B	absorbs water	digests carbohydrates	digests proteins
C	digests lipids	digests proteins	absorbs water
D	digests proteins	absorbs glucose	absorbs water

Standard Level Paper 1, May 05, Q25

Q4 **a** Explain how the skin and mucous membranes prevent entry of pathogens into the body. (3)
  b Explain why antibiotics are used to treat bacterial but not viral diseases. (2)
    Standard Level Paper 2, May 03, Q5

Q5 Which hormone affects the heart beat?
   A glucagon
   B insulin
   C adrenaline
   D oxytocin

Higher Level Paper 1, May 04, Q19

Q6 **a** Draw a labelled diagram of an adult male reproductive system. (4)

   b Outline the process of *in vitro* fertilisation (IVF). (6)

   c Discuss the advantages and disadvantages of genetic engineering. (8)

Standard Level Paper 2, May 04, QB5

Q7 **a** Draw a diagram of the human digestive system. (4)

   b Describe the role of enzymes in the process of digestion of proteins, carbohydrates and lipids in humans. (6)

   c Explain how blood glucose concentration is controlled in humans. (8)

Standard Level Paper 2, May 03, QB8

Q8 Where are the chemoreceptors that detect the changes in blood pH and levels of glucose found?

	Changes in blood pH	Changes in blood glucose
A	brain stem	small intestine
B	carotid vein	liver
C	carotid artery	pancreas
D	venae cavae	liver

Higher Level Paper 1, May 02, Q17

Questions 9–12 cover other syllabus issues in this chapter.

Q9 **a** In the absorption of digested food molecules in the small intestine, explain where each of the following structures occurs and how each contributes to the absorption process:
    i villi (2)
    ii capillary networks (2)
    iii microvilli (2)
    iv protein pumps. (2)

   b Explain the term *assimilation*, and state where it occurs in the body. (3)

Q10 Blood has roles in transport and in the body's defences against disease. By means of a table, identify the specific roles of each component of the blood (plasma, red cells, white cells, platelets) in these functions. (8)

Q11 a The human immune deficiency virus (HIV) is a retrovirus that is responsible for the disease called AIDS. Explain what *retrovirus* means. (3)

   b With the onset of AIDS, the immune system is said to become 'hopelessly compromised'. Explain this, and outline how HIV brings this about. (3)

Q12 a In gaseous exchange, oxygen from the air reaches mitochondria in respiring cells of the body. Identify the precise pathway that oxygen takes and the processes by which it is moved at each step in this journey into the innermost human body cells. (6)

   b The regulation of the concentrations of oxygen and carbon dioxide in the blood is by negative feedback. Explain the principle and outline the mechanism of negative feedback in homeostasis. (4)

Nucleic acids and proteins

STARTING POINTS

- The **chromosomes** of eukaryotes are found in the nucleus and consist of **DNA** and **protein**.
- DNA exists as a **double helix**, the strands held by **complementary base pairing** and **hydrogen bonds**.
- **Replication of DNA** occurs during interphase of **mitosis** by unwinding of the double helix and formation of new complementary strands.
- In **protein synthesis**, the **genetic code** of the chromosome is **transcribed** into a single strand of **messenger RNA (mRNA)** which passes out to ribosomes in the cytoplasm.
- In a **ribosome** the sequence of triplets of bases in mRNA is **translated** into the sequence of amino acids that condense together to form **proteins**.
- This chapter extends the study of nucleic acids, proteins and enzymes begun in Chapter 2, pages 37–75.

We have seen that **nucleic acids** are very long, thread-like macromolecules of alternating sugar and phosphate molecules (forming a 'backbone') with a nitrogenous base – either cytosine (C), guanine (G), adenine (A), thymine (T), or uracil (U) – attached to each sugar molecule along the strand. Furthermore, nucleic acids are described as the information molecules of cells, and they fulfil this role throughout the living world – the genetic code is a universal one.

The structures of the two types of nucleic acid, **deoxyribonucleic acid (DNA)**, and **ribonucleic acid (RNA)**, are compared in Table 2.7, page 69. We have also noted that in eukaryotes, while DNA occurs only in the nucleus, RNA is found in both the cytoplasm and the nucleus.

1 Distinguish between an organic base, a nucleoside, a nucleotide, and a nucleic acid

In this chapter, the way **DNA is structured** and **packaged** in chromosomes is discussed, prior to looking again at the **replication of DNA**, the **transcription** of the genetic code, and its **translation** into the sequence of amino acids selected to build specific polypeptides. Finally, the structure and roles of **cell proteins**, particularly those that function as **enzymes**, are examined.

Chromosome structure and the packaging of DNA

7.7.1–7.7.5

DNA occurs in the chromosomes in the nucleus, along with protein. Actually, more than 50% of a chromosome is built of **protein**. While some of the proteins of the chromosome are enzymes involved in copying and repair reactions of DNA, the bulk of chromosome protein has a **support and packaging role** for DNA.

Why is packaging necessary?

Well, take the case of human DNA. In the nucleus, the total length of the DNA of the chromosomes is over 2 metres. We know this is shared out between 46 chromosomes, and that each chromosome contains one, very long DNA molecule. Chromosomes are different lengths (Figure 4.1, page 92), but we can estimate that within a typical chromosome of 5 μm length, there is a DNA molecule approximately 5 cm long. This means that about 50 000 μm of DNA is packed into 5 μm of chromosome.

This phenomenal packaging is achieved by the much-coiled DNA double helix being looped around protein beads called **nucleosomes**, as illustrated in Figure 8.1.

The packaging protein of the nucleosome, called **histone**, is a basic (positively charged) protein containing a high concentration of amino acid residues with additional base groups ($-NH_2$), such as lysine and arginine (Figure 8.17, page 254). In nucleosomes, eight histone molecules combine to make a single bead. Around each bead, the DNA double helix is wrapped in a double loop.

Figure 8.1 The structure of a nucleosome

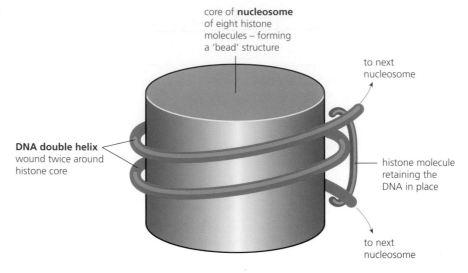

core of **nucleosome** of eight histone molecules – forming a 'bead' structure

to next nucleosome

DNA double helix wound twice around histone core

histone molecule retaining the DNA in place

to next nucleosome

Figure 8.2 The packaging of DNA in the chromosome

electron micrograph of metaphase chromosome (×40 000) – at this stage the chromosome is at maximum condensed state (supercoiled)

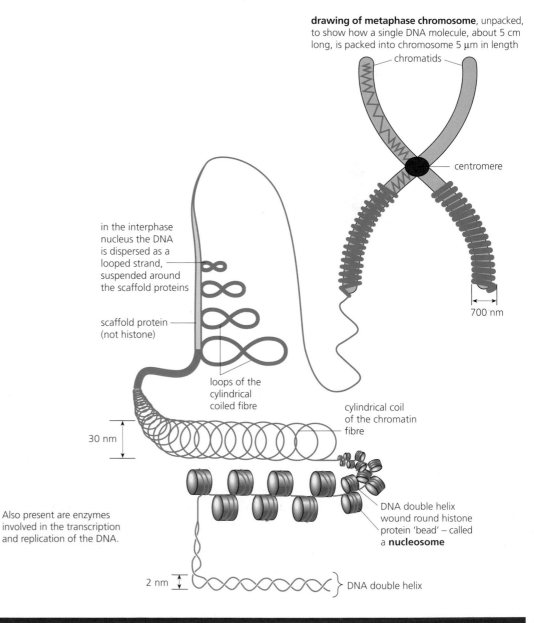

drawing of metaphase chromosome, unpacked, to show how a single DNA molecule, about 5 cm long, is packed into chromosome 5 μm in length

chromatids

centromere

700 nm

in the interphase nucleus the DNA is dispersed as a looped strand, suspended around the scaffold proteins

scaffold protein (not histone)

loops of the cylindrical coiled fibre

cylindrical coil of the chromatin fibre

30 nm

DNA double helix wound round histone protein 'bead' – called a **nucleosome**

Also present are enzymes involved in the transcription and replication of the DNA.

2 nm

DNA double helix

2 Suggest a main advantage of chromosomes being 'supercoiled' in metaphase of mitosis.

The whole beaded thread is itself coiled up, forming the chromatin fibre. The chromatin fibre is again coiled, and the coils are looped around a 'scaffold' protein fibre, made of a **non-histone protein**. This whole structure is folded (supercoiled) into the much-condensed metaphase chromosome, as shown in Figure 8.2. Clearly, the nucleosomes are the key structures that facilitate supercoiling of these phenomenal lengths of DNA that are packed in the nuclei. Furthermore, they facilitate access to selected lengths of the DNA (particular genes) during transcription – a process we will discuss shortly.

Discovery of the role of DNA as information molecule

Since about 50% of a chromosome consists of protein, it is no wonder that people once speculated that protein of the chromosomes might be the information substance of the cell. For example, there is more chemical 'variety' within protein's structure than in nucleic acid. However, this idea proved incorrect. We now know that the DNA of the chromosomes holds the information that codes for the sequence of amino acids from which the proteins of the cell cytoplasm are built.

How was this established?

The unique importance of DNA was shown by an experiment with a bacteriophage virus. A **bacteriophage** (or **phage**, as it is known) is a virus that parasitises a bacterium. We know that viruses consist of a protein coat surrounding a nucleic acid core (page 19). Once a virus has gained entry to a host cell it may take over the cell's metabolism, switching it to the production of new viruses. Eventually, the remains of the host cell break down (lysis) and the virus particle escapes, usually to repeat the infection with new host cells. The life cycle of a bacteriophage, a virus with a complex 'head' and 'tail' structure, is shown in Figure 8.3.

Figure 8.3 The life cycle of a bacteriophage

TEM of bacteriophage infecting a bacterium

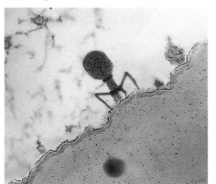

structure of the phage

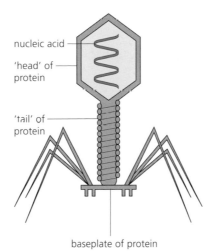

nucleic acid

'head' of protein

'tail' of protein

baseplate of protein

steps to replication of the phage

1 The phage attaches to the bacterial wall and then injects the virus DNA.

2 Virus DNA takes over the host's synthesis machinery.

3 New viruses are assembled and then escape to repeat the infection cycle.

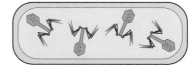

Two experimental scientists, Martha Chase and Alfred Hershey, used a bacteriophage that parasitises the bacterium *Escherichia coli* (page 16) to answer the question of whether genetic information lies in the protein (coat) or the DNA (core) (Figure 8.4).

Two batches of the bacteriophage were produced, one with radioactive phosphorus (^{32}P) built into the DNA core (hence the DNA was labelled) and one with radioactive sulphur (^{35}S) built into the protein coat (hence the protein was labelled). Sulphur occurs in protein, but there is no sulphur in DNA. Likewise, phosphorus occurs in DNA, but there is no phosphorus in protein. Thus the radioactive labels were specific.

Two identical cultures of *E. coli* were infected, one with the ^{32}P-labelled virus and one with the ^{35}S-labelled virus. Subsequently, radioactively labelled viruses were obtained only from the bacteria infected with virus labelled with ^{32}P. In fact, the ^{35}S label did not enter the host cell at all. Their experiment clearly demonstrated that it is the DNA part of the virus which enters the host cell and carries the genetic information for the production of new viruses.

Figure 8.4 The Hershey–Chase experiment

The question was answered using:

1 phage labelled with radioactive sulphur (^{35}S) – sulphur is a component of protein *but not of DNA*

2 phage labelled with radioactive phosphorus (^{32}P) – phosphorus is a component of DNA *but not of protein*

Is it the **protein coat** or the **DNA** of a bacteriophage that enters the host cell and takes over the cell's machinery, so causing new viruses to be produced?

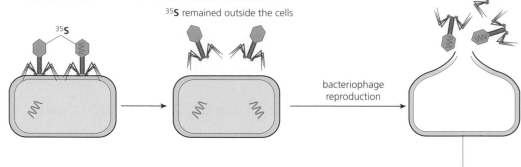

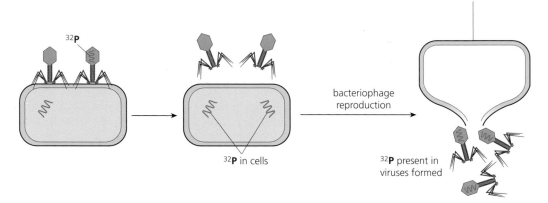

Only the DNA part of the virus got into the host cell (and radioactively labelled DNA was present in the new viruses formed). It was the virus DNA that controlled the formation of new viruses in the host, so Hershey and Chase concluded that **DNA carries the genetic message**.

3 Deduce what would have been the outcome of the Hershey–Chase experiment if protein had been the carrier of genetic information.

Base pairing and 'direction' in the DNA molecule

The structure of the DNA molecule as a double helix, proposed by Watson and Crick in 1953, is illustrated in Figure 2.27 (page 65). In terms of its function, the key feature of DNA is **base pairing**.

Discovery of the principle of base pairing by Watson and Crick was achieved by interpretation of the work of Edwin Chargaff. In 1935, Chargaff had analysed the composition of DNA from a range of organisms, and found rather remarkable patterns. The significance of these patterns was not immediately obvious, though. His discoveries were:

- the numbers of purine bases (adenine and guanine) always equalled the number of pyrimidine bases (cytosine and thymine);
- the number of adenine bases equalled the number of thymine bases, and the number of guanine bases equalled the number of cytosine bases.

What does this mean?

The organic bases found in DNA are of two distinct types with contrasting shapes:

- cytosine and thymine are pyrimidines or **single-ring** bases;
- adenine and guanine are purines or **double-ring** bases.

Only a **purine will fit with a pyrimidine** between the sugar–phosphate backbones, when base pairing occurs (Figure 8.5).

Figure 8.5 Direction, base pairing and hydrogen bonding in the DNA double helix

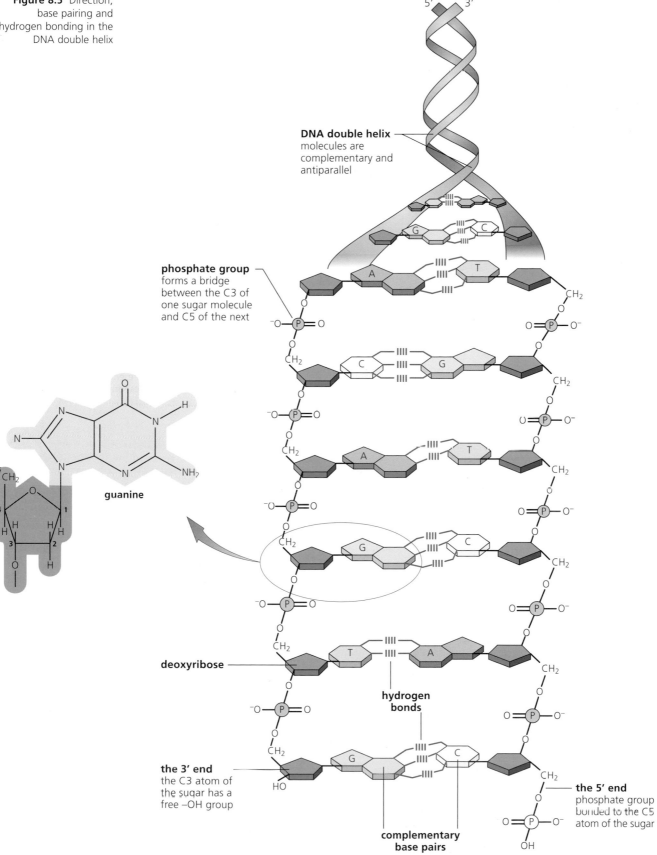

DNA double helix
molecules are complementary and antiparallel

phosphate group
forms a bridge between the C3 of one sugar molecule and C5 of the next

guanine

deoxyribose

the 3′ end
the C3 atom of the sugar has a free –OH group

hydrogen bonds

complementary base pairs

the 5′ end
phosphate group bonded to the C5 atom of the sugar

From the model of DNA in Figure 8.5 we can also see that when A pairs with T, they are held together by two hydrogen bonds; when C pairs with G, they are held by three hydrogen bonds. **Only these pairs can form hydrogen bonds.**

Because of base pairing and the formation of specific hydrogen bonds, the sequence of bases in one strand of the helix determines the sequence of bases in the other – a principle we know as complementary base pairing.

Note that we can identify **direction** in the DNA double helix. The phosphate groups along each strand are bridges between carbon-3 of one sugar molecule and carbon-5 of the next, and one chain runs from 5' to 3' while the other runs from 3' to 5'. That is, the two chains of DNA are **antiparallel**, as illustrated in Figure 8.5. The existence of direction in DNA strands becomes important in replication and when the genetic code is transcribed into mRNA.

4 In base pairing, organic bases are held together (A–T, C–G) by hydrogen bonds. **Describe** what a hydrogen bond is.

Chromosomes, genes and 'nonsense' DNA sequences

We know more about the structure of the human genome than about any other vertebrate genome. The **Human Genome Project**, the initiative to map the entire human genome, has established that the three million bases of our chromosomes represent far fewer genes than was expected (page 131). In fact, only a relatively small part of the total DNA in the nucleus occurs in genes. It is a fact that the bulk of our DNA does not code for proteins at all.

So, what are the different types of DNA present?

Well, about 30% of the human genome is made up of **genes** and base sequences relating to genes. The latter category includes the exons and introns of genes, of which more shortly (page 245). Also included are regions that contain promoters and regulatory sequences, of which there will again be further discussion shortly (page 244).

That leaves 70% of our DNA in the category of non-coding or **'nonsense' DNA**. Of this:

- about 80% of sequences are unique or low-copy-number sequences of bases;
- about 20% are moderately and highly repetitive DNA, and are divided as follows:
  - sequences in which base sequences are repeated from a few times up to 10^5 times per genome (moderately repetitive);
  - sequences in which between 5 and 300 base pairs per repeat occur, duplicated more than 10^5 times per genome (highly repetitive); it is these sequences that make up the **satellite DNA**, which is successfully exploited in **DNA profiling** (page 129).

We will return to the issue of nonsense DNA briefly, when we discuss the maturation of mRNA prior to it leaving the nucleus for the ribosomes.

Replication – DNA copying itself

7.2.1–7.2.3

The way that DNA of the chromosome is replicated was introduced in Chapter 2 (page 66). The key features are:

- replication must be an extremely accurate process since DNA carries the genetic message;
- replication is quite separate from cell division; replication of DNA takes place in the **interphase** nucleus, well before the events of nuclear division;
- strands of the DNA double helix are built up individually from free **nucleotides** (the structure of a nucleotide is shown in Figure 2.25, page 63);
- before nucleotides can be condensed together, the DNA double helix has to **unwind**, and the hydrogen bonds holding the strands together must be broken, allowing the two strands of the helix to separate;
- the enzyme **helicase** brings about the unwinding process and holds the strands apart for replication to occur;
- **both strands act as templates**; nucleotides with the appropriate complementary bases line up opposite the bases of the exposed strands (A with T, C with G);

- **hydrogen bonds form** between complementary bases, holding the nucleotides in place;
- finally, the sugar and phosphate groups of adjacent nucleotides of the new strand condense together, catalysed by the enzyme **DNA polymerase**;
- the two strands of each DNA molecule wind up into a double helix;
- one strand of each new double helix came from the parent chromosome and one is a newly synthesised strand, an arrangement known as **semi-conservative replication** because half the original molecule is conserved;
- DNA polymerase also has a role in '**proof-reading**' the new strands; any mistakes that start to happen (such as the wrong bases attempting to pair up) are immediately corrected and each new DNA double helix is exactly like the original.

5 Predict the experimental results you would expect to see if the Meselson–Stahl experiment (Figure 8.6) were carried on for three generations.

■ Extension: The evidence for DNA replication

Experimental evidence that DNA is replicated semi-conservatively, and not by some other mechanism, came from growing a culture of the bacterium *E. coli* (page 16) in a medium (food source) where the available nitrogen contained only the heavy nitrogen isotope, ^{15}N. Consequently, the DNA of the bacterium became entirely 'heavy'.

These bacteria were then transferred to a medium of the normal (light) isotope, ^{14}N. New DNA manufactured by the cells was now made of ^{14}N. The change in concentration of ^{15}N and ^{14}N in the DNA of succeeding generations was measured. Interestingly, the bacterial cell divisions in a culture of *E. coli* are naturally synchronised; every 60 minutes, they all divided again.

The DNA was extracted from samples of the bacteria from each succeeding generation and the DNA in each sample was separated. This was done by placing the sample on top of a salt solution of increasing density, in a centrifuge tube. On being centrifuged, the different DNA molecules were carried down to the level where the salt solution was of the same density. Thus, DNA with 'heavy' nitrogen ended up nearer the base of the tubes, whereas DNA with 'light' nitrogen stayed near the top of the tubes. Figure 8.6 shows the results that were obtained.

Figure 8.6 DNA replication is semi-conservative

1 **Meselson and Stahl** 'labelled' nucleic acid (i.e. DNA) of the bacterium *Escherichia coli* with 'heavy' nitrogen (^{15}N), by culturing in a medium where the only nitrogen available was as $^{15}NH_4^+$ ions, for several generations of bacteria.

2 When DNA from labelled cells was extracted and centrifuged in a density gradient (of different salt solutions) all the DNA was found to be 'heavy'.

3 In contrast, the DNA extracted from cells of the original culture (before treatment with ^{15}N) was 'light'.

4 Then a labelled culture of *E.coli* was switched back to a medium providing unlabelled nitrogen only, i.e. $^{14}NH_4^+$. Division in the cells was synchronised, and:
- after **one generation** all the DNA was of intermediate density (each of the daughter cells contained (i.e. *conserved*) one of the parental DNA strands containing ^{15}N alongside a newly synthesised strand containing DNA made from ^{14}N)
- after **two generations** 50% of the DNA was intermediate and 50% was 'light'. This too agreed with semi-conservative DNA replication, given that in only half the cells was labelled DNA present (one strand per cell).

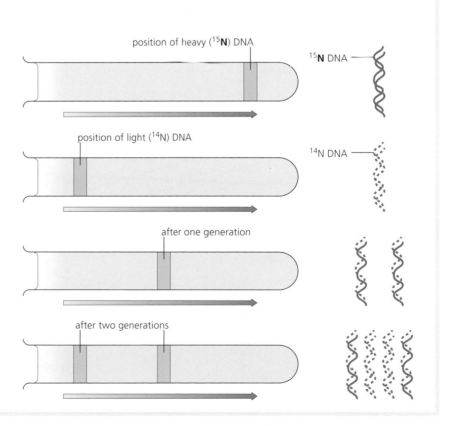

position of heavy (^{15}N) DNA
^{15}N DNA

position of light (^{14}N) DNA
^{14}N DNA

after one generation

after two generations

Events at the replication fork

In eukaryotic chromosomes, replication is initiated at many points along the DNA double helix. At each advancing replication fork, DNA replication always occurs in the 5' → 3' direction. This is because the DNA polymerase that catalyses the condensation reaction (known as **DNA polymerase III**) can only work in this direction. So, it is the 5' end of a free DNA nucleotide which is added to 3' end of a chain of nucleotides.

The consequence of 5' → 3' replication is that, since both strands of DNA are replicated simultaneously, the details of the mechanism must vary in the strand that runs 3' → 5' (Figure 8.7). Here, after helicase has catalysed the uncoiling of the DNA double helix, causing exposure of the base sequence of the two template strands, the enzyme **RNA primase** adds a short RNA primer to the exposed 3' → 5' strand. To this, **DNA polymerase III** then adds succeeding free nucleotides by complementary base pairing, working in the 5' → 3' direction, away from the direction of the advancing replication fork.

Relatively short lengths of replicated DNA are formed by this process, known as **Okazaki fragments** after the biochemist who discovered this phenomenon. Later, the RNA primer between fragments is removed and replaced with DNA by **DNA polymerase I**, and then fragments are annealed into one continuous strand by ligase.

Figure 8.7 The steps to DNA replication

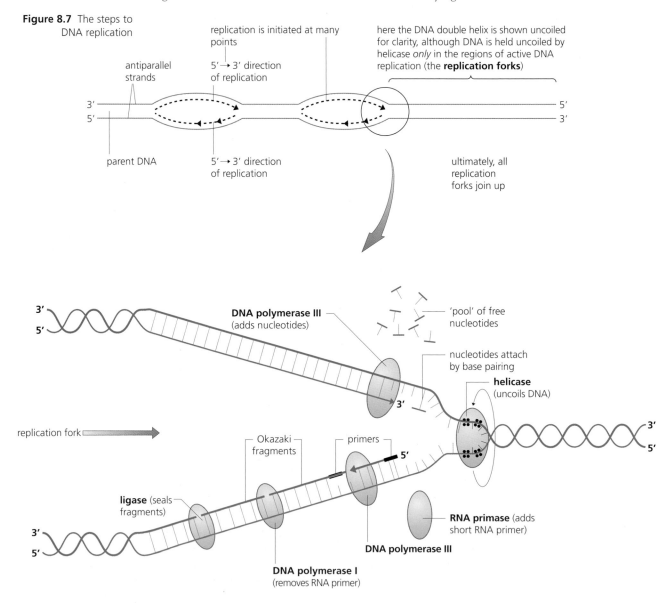

Meanwhile, on the exposed 5' → 3' strand, **DNA polymerase III** adds nucleotides by complementary base pairing to the free 3' end of the new strand, in the same direction as the replication fork. This process proceeds continuously, immediately behind the advancing helicase, as fresh template is exposed.

A note on 'nucleosides' and 'nucleotides'

The combination of a pentose sugar with a base forms a compound known as a **nucleoside**. Then, the combination of nucleoside with phosphate group forms a **nucleotide**. Table 8.1 lists the five nucleotides which are components of nucleic acids.

Base	+ pentose sugar	= Nucleoside	+ H$_3$PO$_4$	= Nucleotide
adenine		adenosine		adenosine phosphate
thymine		thymidine		thymidine phosphate
uracil		uridine		uridine phosphate
cytosine		cytidine		cytidine phosphate
guanine		guanosine		guanosine phosphate

Table 8.1 The common nucleosides and nucleotides found in cells

Nucleotides combined by the action of DNA polymerase are not in their monophosphate form, but are as **nucleoside triphosphates**: adenosine triphosphate (ATP), thymidine triphosphate, cytidine triphosphate, and guanosine triphosphate, as base pairing dictates. In each condensation reaction, two of the three phosphate groups are excluded.

So, it is chemically correct to refer to the nucleotides involved in DNA replication as nucleoside triphosphates.

■ DNA in protein synthesis – the genetic code

7.3.1–7.3.4, 74.1–7.4.7

The roles of nucleic acid in protein synthesis are introduced in Chapter 2, page 71. The key features are as follows.

- The DNA molecule in a single chromosome codes for a very large number of proteins. Within this extremely long molecule, the relatively short length of DNA that codes for a single protein is called a **gene**.
- Proteins are very variable in size and, therefore, so are genes. A few genes are as short as 75–100 nucleotides. Most are at least 1000 nucleotides long, and some are longer.
- Only 20 amino acids are used in protein synthesis; all cell proteins are built from them. The unique properties of each protein lie in:
  – which amino acids are involved in its construction;
  – the sequence in which these amino acids are joined.
- It is the sequence of the four bases (C, G, A and T) in a gene that dictates the order in which specific amino acids are assembled and combined.
- The code's sequence lies in one of the two strands of DNA – the coding strand. The other strand is complementary to it. As we shall shortly discover, the correct name of the coding strand is the **antisense strand** (see Table 8.2).
- The code is a three-letter or triplet code – a sequence of three of the four bases stands for one of the 20 amino acids, and is called a 'codon'. The genetic code has more codons than there are amino acids, and most amino acids have two or three similar codons that code for them (a degenerate code). Some codons represent 'punctuations' – that is, they are 'start' and 'stop' triplets.

There are three major steps in the process by which the information of the gene is used to determine how the protein molecule is constructed:

- Stage 1, **transcription** occurs in the nucleus.
  A copy of the code is made by building a molecule of **messenger RNA (mRNA)**. This is catalysed by RNA polymerase, and involves complementary base pairing, with the antisense strand used as the template. The mRNA strand then leaves the nucleus through pores in the nuclear membrane. It passes to ribosomes in the cytoplasm where the information can be 'read' and is used.
- Stage 2 occurs in the cytoplasm.
  Amino acids are activated for protein synthesis by combining with short lengths of a different sort of RNA, called **transfer RNA (tRNA)**. There is a different tRNA for each of the 20 amino acids involved in protein synthesis. One end of each tRNA molecule is a site where a particular amino acid can attach. At the other end, is a sequence of three bases called an **anticodon**. This anticodon is complementary to the codon of mRNA that codes for the specific amino acid.
- Stage 3, **translation** occurs in ribosomes in the cytoplasm.
  A protein is assembled, one amino acid residue at a time, as a ribosome moves along the messenger RNA 'reading' the codons. Complementary anticodons of the amino acid–tRNA slot into place and are temporarily held in position by hydrogen bonds. While held there, the amino acids of neighbour amino acid–tRNAs are joined by peptide linkages.

Regulation of gene expression

The cell nucleus contains many more genes than are required to be active at any one moment. For example, in a multicellular organism, every nucleus contains the coded information relating to the development and maintenance of all mature tissues and organs. Both during development and later, this genetic information is used selectively. Genes function (are **expressed**) only in cells they relate to, when they are needed. For example, a gene for the enzyme pepsin is present in all cells of our body but it is active only in cells of the gastric glands in the stomach. Similarly, the gene for insulin production is active only in cells of the islets of Langerhans in the pancreas.

How is gene expression regulated?

A mechanism for control of gene expression was first discovered in **prokaryotes**. However, it is now appreciated that this mechanism does not operate in eukaryotes, so the details do not concern us here.

In **eukaryotes**, genes are only transcribed if an RNA polymerase enzyme binds to a region of DNA situated close to the gene, known as a **promoter**. The special features of promoters in eukaryotic chromosomes are:

- some permit repeated, unrestricted binding of RNA polymerase, resulting in continuous expression of the gene;
- some require a **regulatory protein** to be present and bound, prior to binding of RNA polymerase and gene expression (regulatory proteins are the products of other genes, often on different chromosomes);
- some regulatory proteins must first be activated by reaction with a steroid hormone or some other metabolite, before binding of RNA polymerase and gene expression.

Other aspects of eukaryotic gene regulation concern:

- the change that may occur to the messenger RNA immediately after it has been formed by transcription and in which introns are removed (see 'Some eukaryotic genes are discontinuous', below);
- the changes that may occur to proteins formed by translation of the mRNA code, out in the cytoplasm (see 'Post-translational modification of protein', page 251).

Both of these processes are under the control of specific genes, although these are often found on other chromosomes; they too are part of the story of how gene action is brought about.

The sequence of events in transcription in eukaryote chromosomes

The steps to the expression of a gene begin when the genetic information in DNA is **transcribed** into a molecule of **mRNA** by complementary base pairing. mRNA is an intermediary molecule between the information in the gene and the formation of the protein it codes for, out in the cytoplasm. Remember, mRNA is single-stranded nucleic acid in which the base uracil pairs with adenine in place of thymine found in DNA. The events of transcription in eukaryote chromosomes are illustrated in Figure 8.8.

Look at the sequence of events described there, now.

The enzyme **RNA polymerase** binds to a **promoter region**, the 'start' signal for transcription, located immediately before the gene, and the new nucleic acid strand is formed in the 5' → 3' direction.

During transcription, only one strand of the DNA double helix serves as a **template** for synthesis of mRNA. This is called the **antisense strand**. The partner strand is called the sense strand. Sense and antisense strands are compared in Table 8.2 below.

Sense strand	Antisense strand
carries the promoter sequence of bases to which RNA polymerase binds and begins transcription	is the template sequence for transcription by complementary base pairing by RNA polymerase
has the same base sequence as the mRNA (the mRNA has U in place of T)	has the same base sequence as the tRNA (the tRNA has base U in place of T)
carries the terminator sequence of bases at the termination of each gene that cause RNA polymerase to stop transcription	is 'read' in the 3' → 5' direction, and mRNA synthesis occurs in the 5' → 3' direction (by addition of 5' end of a nucleotide to the 3' end of the RNA molecule already synthesised)

Table 8.2 Sense and antisense strands of DNA

RNA polymerase draws on the pool of **free nucleotides**. As with DNA replication, these nucleotides are present in the form of nucleoside triphosphates (although in RNA synthesis uridine triphosphate replaces thymidine triphosphate). As the RNA is formed, it falls away from the antisense strand that has acted as template, and hydrogen bonds re-form between the two DNA strands.

6 Explain what is meant by antiparallel strands.

The process continues until a base sequence known as the **terminator** is reached. At this signal, both RNA polymerase and the completed, new strand of mRNA are freed from the site of the gene.

Some eukaryotic genes are discontinuous

Where the exact sequence of bases in a particular gene has been determined, it is sometimes discovered that **non-coding sequences** are present. In other words, some eukaryotic genes have units of non-gene DNA *within their boundaries*.

The sections that carry meaningful information are called **exons**, whereas the intervening lengths of DNA (interruptions, in effect) are called **introns**. Genes split in this way are common in higher plants and animals, although others contain no introns at all.

When a split gene is transcribed into mRNA, the newly formed mRNA contains the sequence of introns and exons exactly as they occur in the DNA. The persistence of nonsense sequences would undoubtedly present problems in the subsequent protein-synthesis steps.

In fact, an enzyme-catalysed reaction known as **post-transcriptional modification**, removes the introns at this stage. The production of this enzyme is also under the control of a gene. The short lengths of nonsense transcribed into the RNA sequence of bases are disposed of. The resulting (shortened) length of mRNA is described as **mature**. It passes out into the cytoplasm, to ribosomes, where it is involved in protein synthesis (Figure 8.9).

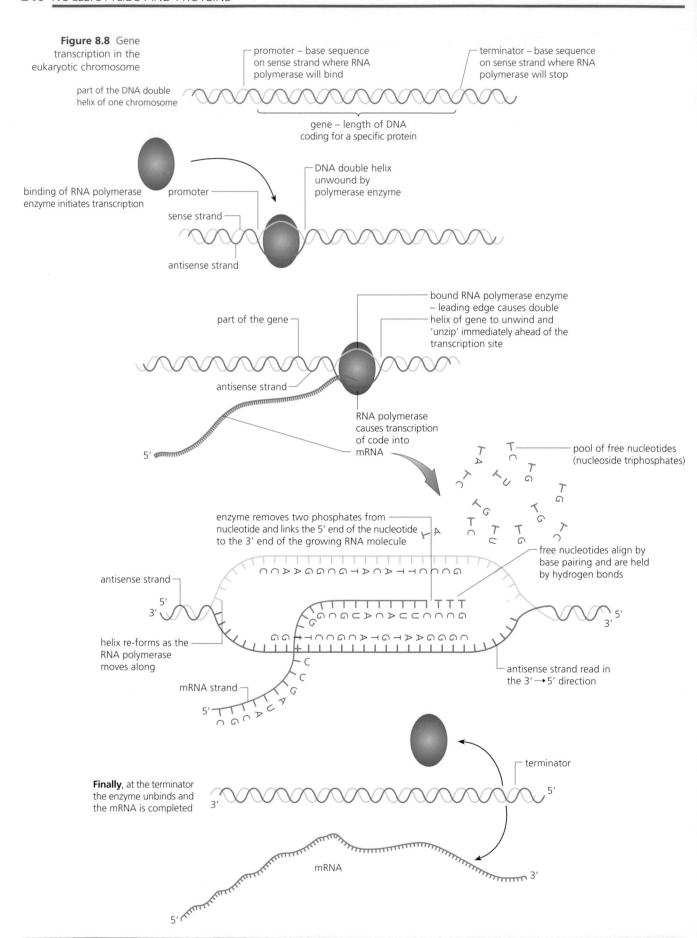

Figure 8.8 Gene transcription in the eukaryotic chromosome

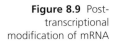

Figure 8.9 Post-transcriptional modification of mRNA

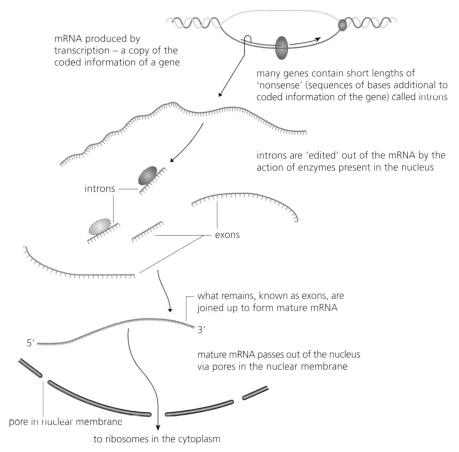

mRNA produced by transcription – a copy of the coded information of a gene

many genes contain short lengths of 'nonsense' (sequences of bases additional to coded information of the gene) called introns

introns are 'edited' out of the mRNA by the action of enzymes present in the nucleus

introns

exons

what remains, known as exons, are joined up to form mature mRNA

5'

3'

mature mRNA passes out of the nucleus via pores in the nuclear membrane

pore in nuclear membrane

to ribosomes in the cytoplasm

Translation – protein synthesis in ribosomes

The first step to protein synthesis in the **cytoplasm** involves the **activation of amino acids** by combining them with short lengths of a different sort of RNA, called **transfer RNA (tRNA)**. This activation process occurs in the cytoplasm and requires ATP. It is this tRNA, once attached to its amino acid, which facilitates the translation of the three-base sequences of each codon of mRNA into a sequence of amino acids in a protein.

All tRNAs have a cloverleaf shape, but there is a different tRNA for each of the 20 amino acids involved in protein synthesis (Figure 8.10). At one end of the tRNA molecule is a site where **one particular amino acid** can be joined (and no other type). At the other end, there is a sequence of three bases called an **anticodon**. This anticodon is complementary to the codon of mRNA that codes for that specific amino acid. Of course, the amino acid is attached to its tRNA by enzyme action and these enzymes are specific to the particular amino acids (and types of tRNA) to be used in protein synthesis. Thus, the structure of the tRNA allows recognition by a specific tRNA-activating enzyme which attaches a specific amino acid to the tRNA. The specificity of the enzymes is a way of ensuring the correct amino acids are used in the right sequence. Some amino acids have more than one type of tRNA specific to them.

The next step, the translation process, occurs in the **ribosomes**. These tiny organelles consist of a large and a small subunit, both composed of RNA (known as rRNA) and protein, as illustrated in Figure 8.11. During translation, the mRNAs bind with the small subunit. Here occur the three sites where the tRNAs interact:

- at the **first site**, codons of the incoming tRNA bind to specific tRNA–amino acids through their anticodons (**complementary base pairing**);
- the **second site** is where the amino acid attached to its tRNA is condensed with the growing polypeptide chain by **formation of a peptide linkage**;
- the **third site** is where the **tRNA leaves** the ribosome following transfer of its amino acid to the growing protein chain.

Figure 8.10 Transfer RNA (tRNA) and amino acid activation

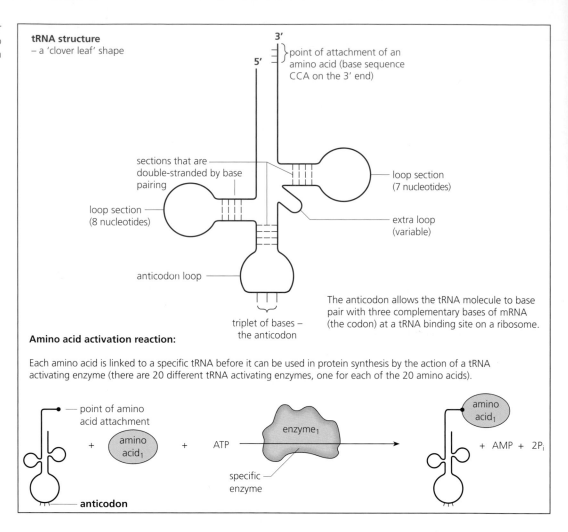

tRNA structure
– a 'clover leaf' shape

3'

}point of attachment of an amino acid (base sequence CCA on the 3' end)

5'

sections that are double-stranded by base pairing

loop section (7 nucleotides)

loop section (8 nucleotides)

extra loop (variable)

anticodon loop

triplet of bases – the anticodon

The anticodon allows the tRNA molecule to base pair with three complementary bases of mRNA (the codon) at a tRNA binding site on a ribosome.

Amino acid activation reaction:

Each amino acid is linked to a specific tRNA before it can be used in protein synthesis by the action of a tRNA activating enzyme (there are 20 different tRNA activating enzymes, one for each of the 20 amino acids).

point of amino acid attachment

+ amino acid$_1$ + ATP

enzyme$_1$

specific enzyme

amino acid$_1$

+ AMP + 2P$_i$

anticodon

Figure 8.11 Ribosome structure and function

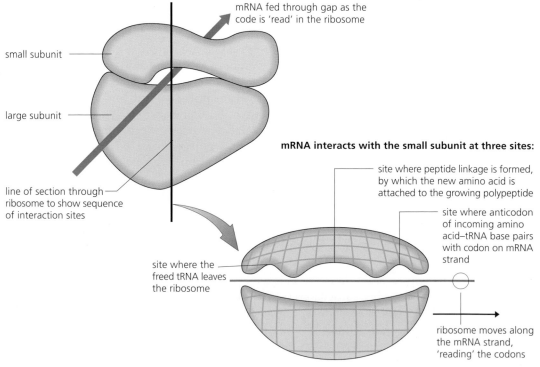

mRNA fed through gap as the code is 'read' in the ribosome

small subunit

large subunit

line of section through ribosome to show sequence of interaction sites

mRNA interacts with the small subunit at three sites:

site where peptide linkage is formed, by which the new amino acid is attached to the growing polypeptide

site where anticodon of incoming amino acid–tRNA base pairs with codon on mRNA strand

site where the freed tRNA leaves the ribosome

ribosome moves along the mRNA strand, 'reading' the codons

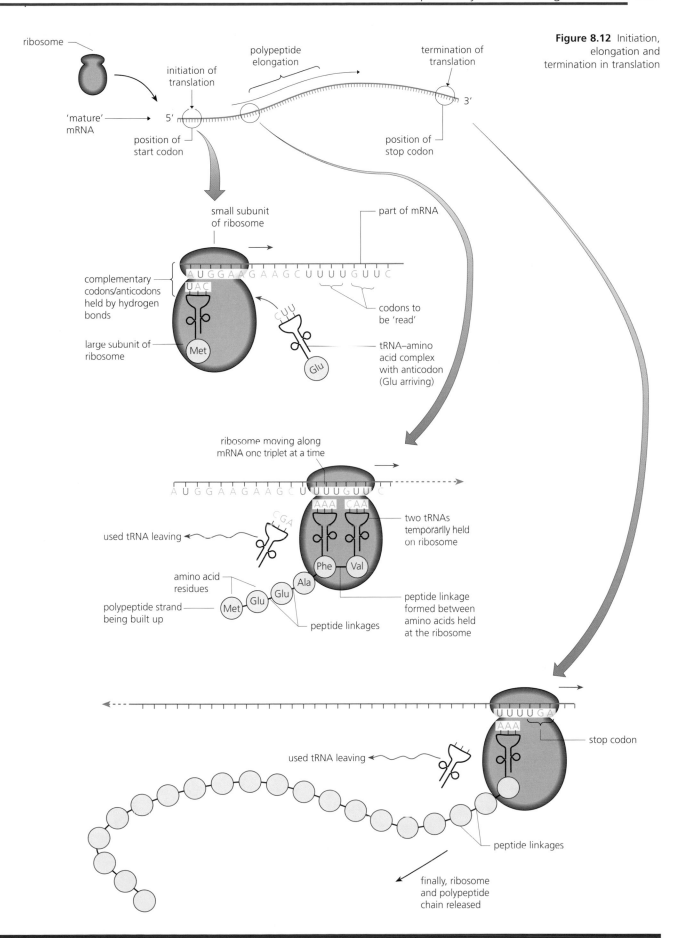

Figure 8.12 Initiation, elongation and termination in translation

In the ribosome a protein chain is assembled, one amino acid residue at a time. This occurs as the ribosome moves along the messenger RNA 'reading' the codons from the **'start'** codon.

Translation occurs in the 5' → 3' direction, the organelle moving along the mRNA from the 'start' codon towards the 3' end and the **'stop'** codon. As the ribosome moves along, complementary anticodons of the **specific amino acid–tRNA complex** slot into place. They are temporarily held in position by hydrogen bonds.

While held there, the amino acids of neighbour amino acid–tRNAs are joined by **peptide linkages** (Figure 2.15, page 52). This frees the first tRNA which moves back into the cytoplasm for re-use. Once this is done, the ribosome moves on to the next mRNA codon. The process continues until a 'stop' codon occurs (Figure 8.12).

Many ribosomes occur freely in the cytoplasm, and these are the site of synthesis of proteins that remain in the cell and fulfil particular roles there. It is common for several ribosomes to move along the mRNA at one time; the structure (mRNA, ribosomes and their growing protein chains) is called a **polysome** (Figure 8.13).

Other ribosomes are bound to the membranes of the rough endoplasmic reticulum (**rER**, page 15), and these are the site of synthesis of proteins that are subsequently secreted from cells or packaged in lysosomes there.

7 Draw and **label** the structure of a peptide linkage between two amino acids.

8 State the sequence of changes catalysed by RNA polymerase.

Figure 8.13 A polysome

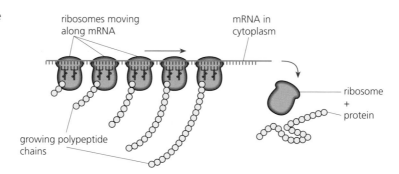

Deciphering of the genetic code

The sequence of bases (A, C, G, and T) in DNA carries the genetic code, specifying the 20 amino acids from which cell proteins are built. It was clear to Watson and Crick from the outset that combinations of three bases would be most likely to code for the amino acids. This was because:

- a doublet code (AA, AG, AC, AT, GA, etc.) could specify only 16 amino acids ($4^2 = 16$);
- a four-base code could specify 256 amino acids ($4^4 = 256$), far more possibilities than are needed.

In a triplet code, there are still more possibilities than are required, and it was later found that the spare capacity is used rather than left unused (this is why the genetic code is described as a **degenerate** code).

The code was first 'cracked' by the preparation of lengths of nucleic acid (synthetic mRNA, in effect) in which one 'word' was repeated (UUU–UUU–UUU, CCC–CCC–CCC etc).

Subsequently, synthetic mRNAs with known, variable sequences of nucleotides were produced. These mRNAs were added in turn to cell-free protein-synthesising systems containing all 20 amino acids. Each polypeptide formed was analysed. In this way, the complete code was deciphered.

Two amino acids were found to be coded for by a single triplet, and a few other amino acids were each coded for by two codons. However, most amino acids were coded for by several triplets, up to a maximum of six. The genetic code (for mRNA) is given in Figure 8.14. Note that certain 'words' code for a 'full stop', rather than an amino acid. The codon for methionine is the 'start' codon.

Figure 8.14 The genetic code – a universal code

The 20 amino acids used in protein synthesis

Amino acids	Abbreviations
alanine	Ala
arginine	Arg
asparagine	Asn
aspartic acid	Asp
cysteine	Cys
glutamine	Gln
glutamic acid	Glu
glycine	Gly
histidine	His
isoleucine	Ile
leucine	Leu
lysine	Lys
methionine	Met
phenylalanine	Phe
proline	Pro
serine	Ser
threonine	Thr
tryptophan	Trp
tyrosine	Tyr
valine	Val

The genetic code in circular form

The codons are those of messenger RNA (where uracil, U, replaces thymine, T).

Read the code from the centre of the circle outwards along a radius. For example, serine is coded by UCU, UCC, UCA or UCG, or by AGU or AGC.

In addition, some codons stand for 'stop', signalling the end of a peptide or protein chain.

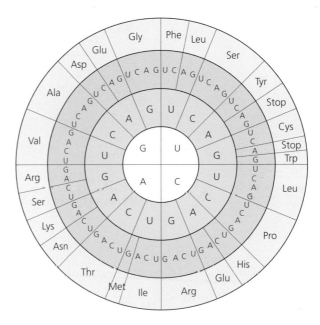

9 The sequence of bases in a sample of mRNA was found to be:

GGU–AAU–CCU–UUU–GUU–ACU–CAU–UGU.

Predict:
a the sequence of amino acids coded for by this sequence of bases
b the sequence of bases in the antisense strand of DNA from which this mRNA was transcribed.

Post-translational modification of protein

When a protein exits from translation at a ribosome, it may take up its active, three-dimensional shape and be functional immediately. For example, it may be active as an enzyme in the cytoplasm in some essential, continuous biochemical pathway. On the other hand, many proteins are in the form of inactive precursors requiring processing steps. These steps occur after translation and so are known as **post-translational modifications** (Figure 8.15). In fact, it is often important for proteins to become active only at particular sites. For example, the protein-digesting enzyme trypsin is produced in the pancreas but in an inactive form (trypsinogen, page 649) which will not digest the proteins of the pancreas cells in which it is formed.

Figure 8.15 Protein synthesis and post-translational modification

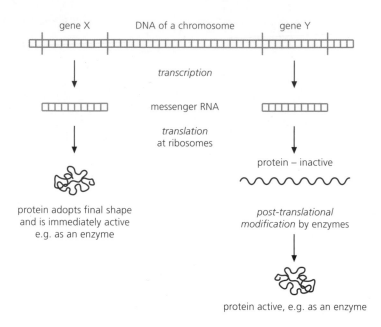

10 **Distinguish** between the different forms of protein in the nucleus.

The central dogma

We have seen that the information of genes is copied by transcription into mRNA, and that these single strands of nucleic acid pass to the ribosomes in the cytoplasm during protein synthesis. This is a **one-way flow** of coded information from nucleus to cytoplasm and has been named the **central dogma of molecular biology**.

The term 'one-way flow' draws attention to the direction in which information travels – from the nucleus to the cytoplasm, *and never the other way round* (Figure 8.16).

Figure 8.16 Steps to protein synthesis and the central dogma

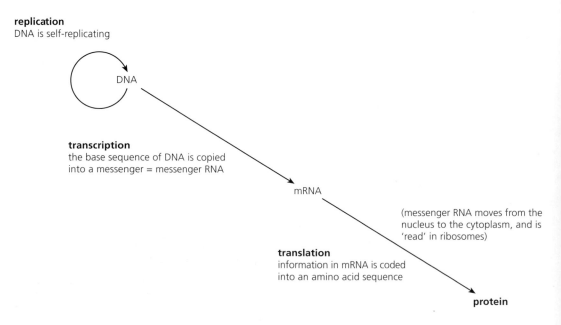

Incidentally, if this principle did not apply, events in cells due to environmental changes might lead to changes in the characteristics that particular genes code for.

Since this principle of molecular biology was asserted by Crick and Watson, it has been discovered that occasional reversing of the flow of information does occur.

You will remember that human immunodeficiency virus (HIV) is an RNA virus (page 198). Once HIV nucleic acid is inside a host cell, an enzyme called **reverse transcriptase** catalyses the copying of the RNA strand to form a DNA double helix. Reverse transcriptase is an enzyme the virus introduces into the host cell. The DNA this enzyme synthesises then enters the host nucleus and becomes attached to a host chromosome. There it functions as other genes do, eventually being transcribed, leading to HIV replication and the death of the host cell.

TOK Link

What limitations are placed on advancement of knowledge if we hold dogmas dogmatically?

The genetic engineer's tool-kit

The enzyme reverse transcriptase may be extracted from retroviruses (of which there are many besides HIV) and it is used in genetic modification. In fact, reverse transcriptase is an important enzyme in the genetic engineer's tool-kit (Table 8.3). The steps to the reverse transcription reaction are illustrated in Figure 7.21 (page 200). Genetic engineers make use of purified enzymes extracted mainly from microorganisms or viruses to manipulate nucleic acids in very precise ways.

Enzyme	Natural source	Application in genetic modification
restriction enzymes (restriction endonuclease)	cytoplasm of bacteria (combats viral infection by breaking up viral DNA)	breaks DNA molecules into shorter lengths, at specific nucleotide sequences
DNA ligase	with nucleic acid in the nucleus of all organisms	joins together DNA molecules during replication of DNA
polymerase	with nucleic acid in the nucleus of all organisms	synthesises nucleic acid strands, guided by template strand of nucleic acid
reverse transcriptase	in retroviruses only	synthesis of a DNA strand complementary to an existing RNA strand

Table 8.3 The genetic engineer's tool-kit of enzymes

The special value of reverse transcriptase to the genetic engineer lies in the fact that mRNA is often present in large quantities in cells, compared to the original DNA (the gene) from which it has been synthesised. Moreover, mRNA is easily extracted from cells.

For example, the gene for insulin is present in human pancreatic tissue, but it is difficult to extract and contains introns as well as exons (thus providing additional problems for the genetic engineer). But the mRNA complementary to the gene for insulin is relatively easy to extract and can be used to synthesise a version of the gene that contains only exons.

There are many cases of the successful application of reverse transcriptase in the production of modified microorganisms leading to the commercial production of important biochemicals. Continuing from the insulin example above, reverse transcription is exploited in the production of human insulin in strains of the genetically modified bacterium *E. coli*, for the treatment of type I diabetes. The steps of this process are illustrated in Figure 18.21 (page 573).

11 Explain the value of the discovery of reverse transcriptase to molecular biologists.

■ Proteins

We know that proteins are built up by condensation reactions between **amino acids**. We have seen that amino acids are molecules that have a basic amino group ($-NH_2$) and an acidic carboxyl group ($-COOH$), attached to the same carbon atom (page 51). These are the reactive or **functional groups** of the molecule; they are the groups that participate in the condensation reactions that form peptide linkages.

The remainder of the amino acid molecule, the side chain or **–R part** as it is known, may be very variable. Something of the variety of amino acids is shown in Figure 8.17. We can see that, while amino acids have the same basic structure, they are all rather different in character, because of the different R groups they carry. Categories into which many of the amino acids found in cell proteins fit are:

- **acidic amino acids**, having additional carboxyl groups (e.g. aspartic acid);
- **basic amino acids**, having additional amino groups (e.g. lysine);
- **amino acids with hydrophilic properties** (water soluble) have polar R groups (e.g. serine);
- **amino acids with hydrophobic properties** (insoluble) have non-polar R groups (e.g. alanine).

The bringing together of differing amino acids in contrasting combinations produces proteins with very different properties. The amino acid residues of proteins affect their shape, where they occur in cells, and the functions they carry out. We will see examples of this when the functions of cell membranes and enzymes are discussed.

Figure 8.17 The range of amino acids used in protein synthesis

acidic amino acids
(additional carboxyl group):
e.g. **aspartic acid**

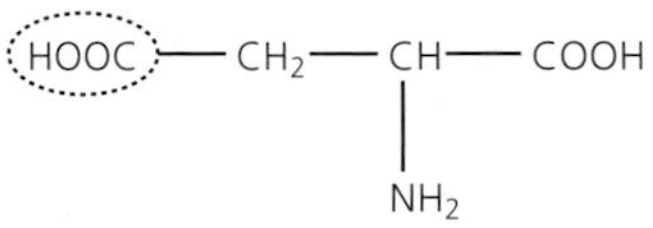

basic amino acids
(additional amino group):
e.g. **lysine**

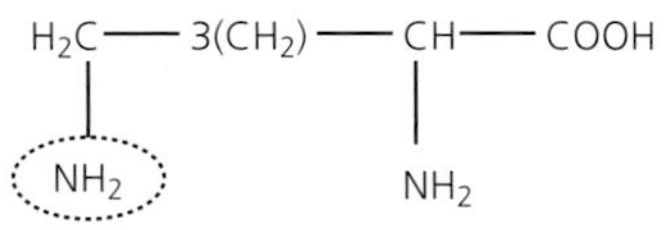

acidic amino acids with hydrophilic properties
(water soluble, polar R group):
e.g. **serine**

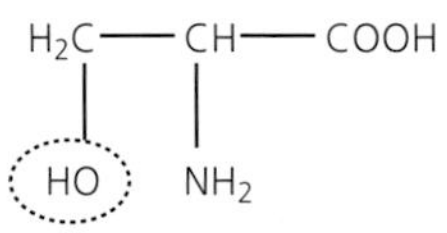

amino acids with hydrophobic properties
(insoluble, non-polar R group):
e.g. **alanine**

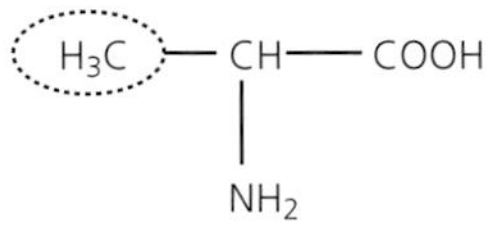

The structure of proteins

There are four levels of protein structure, each of significance in biology.

The **primary structure** of a protein is the sequence of amino acid residues attached by peptide linkages. Proteins differ in the variety, number and order of their constituent amino acids. We have seen how, in the living cell, the sequence of amino acids in the polypeptide chain is controlled by the coded instructions stored in the DNA of the chromosomes in the nucleus, mediated via mRNA. Changing just one amino acid in the sequence of a protein alters its properties, often quite drastically. This sort of mistake or mutation does happen (page 100).

The **secondary structure** of a protein develops when parts of the polypeptide chain take up a particular shape, immediately after formation at the ribosome. Parts of the chain become folded or twisted, or both, in various ways.

The most common shapes are formed either by coiling to produce an α **helix** or folding into β **sheets** (Figure 8.18). These shapes are permanent, held in place by hydrogen bonds (page 38).

Figure 8.18 The secondary structure of protein

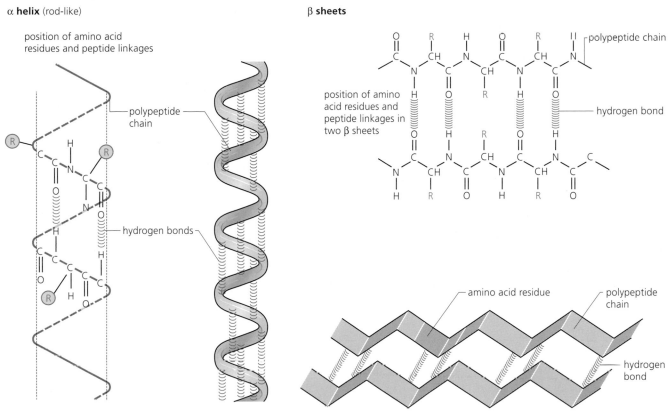

α **helix** (rod-like)

position of amino acid residues and peptide linkages

polypeptide chain

hydrogen bonds

β **sheets**

polypeptide chain

position of amino acid residues and peptide linkages in two β sheets

hydrogen bond

amino acid residue

polypeptide chain

hydrogen bond

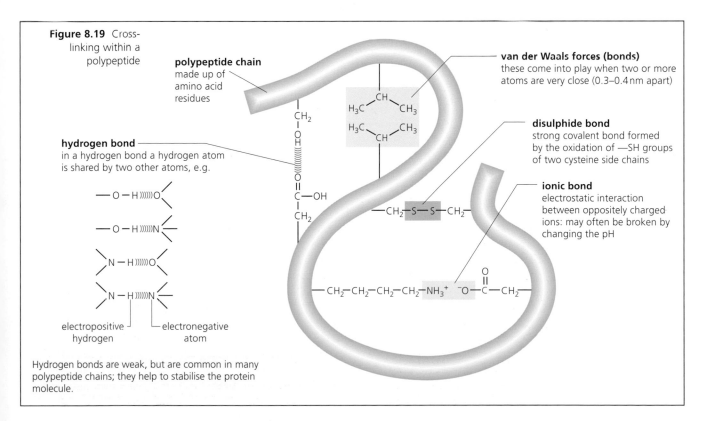

Figure 8.19 Cross-linking within a polypeptide

polypeptide chain
made up of amino acid residues

hydrogen bond
in a hydrogen bond a hydrogen atom is shared by two other atoms, e.g.

—O—H⟩⟩⟩⟩⟩O⟨

—O—H⟩⟩⟩⟩⟩N⟨

⟩N—H⟩⟩⟩⟩⟩O⟨

⟩N—H⟩⟩⟩⟩⟩N⟨

electropositive hydrogen

electronegative atom

Hydrogen bonds are weak, but are common in many polypeptide chains; they help to stabilise the protein molecule.

van der Waals forces (bonds)
these come into play when two or more atoms are very close (0.3–0.4 nm apart)

disulphide bond
strong covalent bond formed by the oxidation of —SH groups of two cysteine side chains

ionic bond
electrostatic interaction between oppositely charged ions: may often be broken by changing the pH

Figure 8.20 Lysozyme – primary, secondary and tertiary structure

primary structure
(the sequence of amino acids)

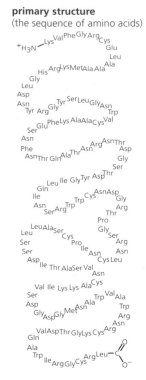

secondary structure
(the shape taken up by parts of the amino acid chain)

β sheets

α helix

tertiary structure
(the three-dimensional structure of the protein)

Figure 8.21 Haemoglobin – a quaternary protein of red cells

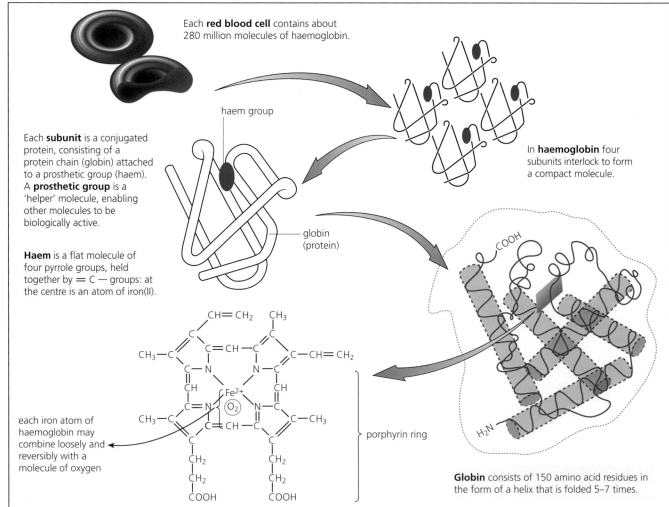

Each **red blood cell** contains about 280 million molecules of haemoglobin.

In **haemoglobin** four subunits interlock to form a compact molecule.

Each **subunit** is a conjugated protein, consisting of a protein chain (globin) attached to a prosthetic group (haem). A **prosthetic group** is a 'helper' molecule, enabling other molecules to be biologically active.

Haem is a flat molecule of four pyrrole groups, held together by ═ C ─ groups: at the centre is an atom of iron(II).

haem group

globin (protein)

each iron atom of haemoglobin may combine loosely and reversibly with a molecule of oxygen

porphyrin ring

COOH

H_2N

Globin consists of 150 amino acid residues in the form of a helix that is folded 5–7 times.

12 Describe three types of bond that contribute to a protein's secondary structure.

The **tertiary structure** of a protein is the precise, compact structure, unique to that protein, which arises when the molecule is further folded and held in a particular complex shape. This shape is made permanent by four different types of bonding, established between adjacent parts of the chain (Figure 8.19). The primary, secondary and tertiary structure of the protein lysozyme is shown in Figure 8.20.

The **quaternary structure** of protein arises when two or more proteins become held together, forming a complex, biologically active molecule. An example is haemoglobin, consisting of four polypeptide chains held around a non-protein haem group, in which an atom of iron occurs (Figure 8.21).

Fibrous and globular proteins – contrasting tertiary structures

Some proteins take up a tertiary structure that is a long, much-coiled chain, and are called fibrous proteins. They have long, narrow shapes. Examples of fibrous proteins are **collagen**, a component of bone and tendons (Figure 8.22), and **keratin**, found in hair, horn and nails. Fibrous proteins are often insoluble.

Figure 8.22 Collagen – example of a fibrous protein

Collagen:

- is the most abundant structural protein in animals –
  skin is largely composed of collagen, forming a mat in the deeper layers;
  it is also a major component of bones, teeth and tendons

- chemically consists of three polypeptide chains, each about 1000 amino acid residues long, wound together as a triple helix – a unique arrangement in proteins – with an appearance of a twisted rope

- has a primary structure of glycine (the smallest amino acid) at every third point in the chain in which the repeating sequence is glycine–proline–hydroxyproline. The R groups of these amino acids are ring structures that prevent collagen from folding or forming pleated sheeets; collagen is forced to take up the triple helix shape

- is an insoluble protein that is assembled by cells as procollagen, a soluble molecule built to make collagen outside the cell, with cross-links formed between the polypeptide chains as they are assembled

- when assembled, binds with other components such as calcium phosphate in bone.

three long polypeptide molecules, coiled together to form a triple helix

every third amino acid is glycine (the smallest amino acid) and the other two amino acids are mostly proline and hydroxyproline

covalent bonds form between the polypeptide chains – together with many hydrogen bonds

Patients with brittle bone disease (see below) may suffer multiple fractures of their bones.

The disease arises because the patient's collagen does not form links to the mineral component of bone.

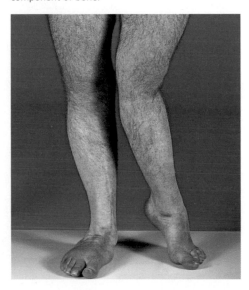

Other proteins take up a tertiary structure that is more spherical, and are called **globular proteins** (Figure 8.23). They are mostly highly soluble in water. Enzymes, such as **catalase**, are typical globular proteins. Some of our hormones are globular proteins, too, including **insulin** (page 222).

Figure 8.23 Insulin – example of a globular protein

Insulin is a hormone produced in the β cells of the islets of Langerhans in the pancreas by ribosomes of the rough endoplasmic reticulum (rER) as a polypeptide of 102 amino acid residues (preproinsulin).

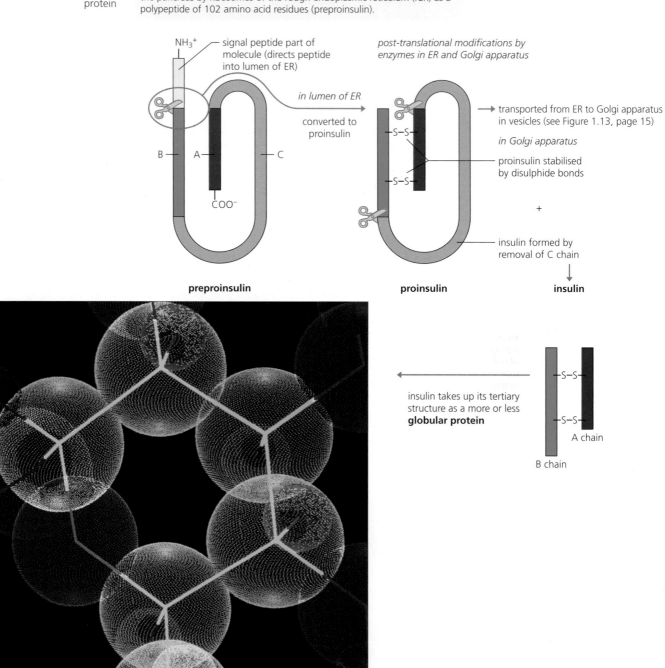

computer-generated image of 3D shape of insulin

Polar and non-polar amino acids in proteins

Amino acids with polar R groups have hydrophilic properties. When these amino acids are built into protein in prominent positions they may influence the properties and functioning of the proteins in cells. Similarly, amino acids with non-polar R groups have hydrophobic properties.

Examples of these outcomes are illustrated in Figures 8.24 (for cell membrane proteins) and 8.25 (for an enzyme that occurs in the cytoplasm).

Figure 8.24 Polar and non-polar amino acids in membrane proteins

plasma membrane (fluid mosaic model)
(diagrammatic cross-sectional view)

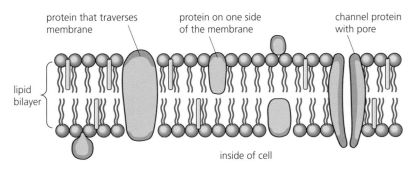

protein that traverses membrane

protein on one side of the membrane

channel protein with pore

lipid bilayer

inside of cell

position of **non-polar amino acid residues** (make bulk of protein hydrophobic – compatible with hydrocarbon tail of phospholipid molecules of bilayer)

position of **polar amino acid residues** (make surface of protein hydrophilic – this part of protein molecule protrudes or is exposed to cytosol)

Figure 8.25 Polar and non-polar amino acids in superoxide dismutase

Superoxide dismutase is an enzyme common to all cells – breaking down superoxide ions as soon as they form as by-products of the reactions of metabolism.

The molecule is approximately saucer-shaped, with active site centrally placed.

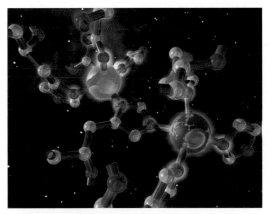

computer simulation of tertiary structure of superoxide dismutase

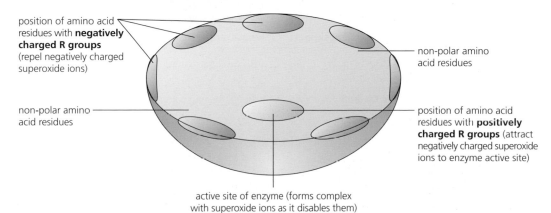

position of amino acid residues with **negatively charged R groups** (repel negatively charged superoxide ions)

non-polar amino acid residues

non-polar amino acid residues

position of amino acid residues with **positively charged R groups** (attract negatively charged superoxide ions to enzyme active site)

active site of enzyme (forms complex with superoxide ions as it disables them)

Roles of proteins

Some proteins have a structural role in cells and organisms, others have biochemical or physiological roles. The roles of proteins are reviewed in Table 8.4.

Whatever their roles are in metabolism, cell proteins are in a continuous state of flux. They are continuously built up, used, and broken down again into their constituent amino acids, to be rebuilt or replaced by fresh proteins, according to the needs of the cells. This dynamic state of cell proteins is shown in Figure 8.26.

Figure 8.26 The dynamic state of cell proteins

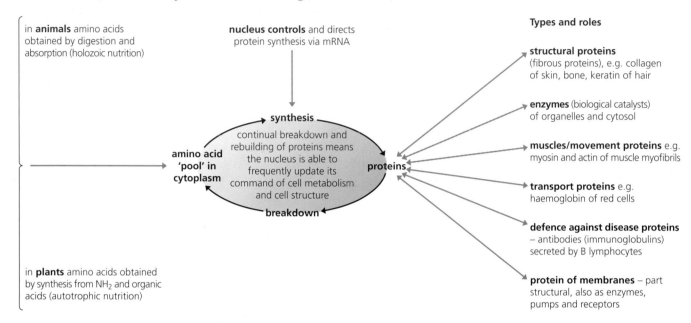

in **animals** amino acids obtained by digestion and absorption (holozoic nutrition)

nucleus controls and directs protein synthesis via mRNA

Types and roles

structural proteins (fibrous proteins), e.g. collagen of skin, bone, keratin of hair

enzymes (biological catalysts) of organelles and cytosol

synthesis

continual breakdown and rebuilding of proteins means the nucleus is able to frequently update its command of cell metabolism and cell structure

amino acid 'pool' in cytoplasm

proteins

breakdown

muscles/movement proteins e.g. myosin and actin of muscle myofibrils

transport proteins e.g. haemoglobin of red cells

defence against disease proteins – antibodies (immunoglobulins) secreted by B lymphocytes

protein of membranes – part structural, also as enzymes, pumps and receptors

in **plants** amino acids obtained by synthesis from NH_2 and organic acids (autotrophic nutrition)

Function	Role / examples
Biological catalysts – enzymes	Alter the speed of chemical reactions, making possible biochemical changes of organisms under the normal conditions of life (e.g. digestive enzyme pepsin and carbonic anhydrase of red cells).
Defence against disease	Antibodies secreted by B-lymphocytes (a type of white cell) in response to non-self substances (antigens) that may invade the body. Antibody proteins are known as immunoglobulins.
Transport of respiratory gases	Haemoglobin in red cells – a conjugated protein (non-protein haem part attached to globin protein) which combines with oxygen in the lungs and frees the oxygen (dissociates) in respiring tissues.
Muscle movement	Myosin and actin proteins of voluntary muscle myofibrils bring about muscle contraction by reaction with ATP, triggered by calcium ions (page 368).
Chemical messengers	Hormones are chemical messengers produced and secreted by cells of endocrine glands. Some are polypeptides or proteins (e.g. ADH, page 374, and insulin). Other hormones are steroids (lipids).
Structure and support	Fibrous proteins (e.g. collagen of bone, and keratin of hair).

Table 8.4 The functions of cellular proteins

Proteins also occur in membranes where they fulfil some of the above roles.

13 Outline three ways membrane proteins are important to the functioning of a cell.

Enzymes

Figure 8.27 Metabolism, an overview

synthesis of complex molecules used in growth and development and in metabolic processes, e.g. proteins, polysaccharides, lipids, hormones, growth factors, haemoglobin, chlorophyll

anabolism: energy-requiring reactions, i.e. **endergonic reactions**

nutrients → sugars, amino acids, fatty acids, i.e. smaller organic molecules

catabolism energy-releasing reactions, i.e. **exergonic reactions**

release of simple substances, e.g. small inorganic molecules, CO_2, H_2O, mineral ions

There are literally many thousands of chemical reactions taking place within cells and organisms. **Metabolism** is the name we give to the totality of these enzyme-catalysed chemical reactions of life, and the molecules involved are collectively called metabolites. Many metabolites are made in organisms, but others are imported from the environment – for example, nutrients from food substances taken in, water, and the gases carbon dioxide or oxygen.

Metabolism actually consists of chains (linear sequences) and cycles of enzyme-catalysed reactions, such as we see in respiration (page 270), photosynthesis (page 284), protein synthesis (page 247), and very many other pathways. All these reactions may be classified as one of just two types, according to whether they involve the build-up or breakdown of organic molecules.

- In **anabolic reactions**, larger molecules are built up from smaller molecules (Figure 8.27). Examples of anabolism are the synthesis of proteins from amino acids and the synthesis of polysaccharides from simple sugars.
- In **catabolic reactions**, larger molecules are broken down (Figure 8.27). Examples of catabolism are the digestion of complex foods and the breakdown of sugar in respiration.

Overall:

metabolism = anabolism + catabolism

Metabolism and energy

Chemical energy exists in the structure of molecules. Every molecule contains a quantity of stored energy equal to the quantity of energy needed to synthesise it originally. Chemical energy does not exist in the chemical bonds of molecules, but rather in the structural arrangement of the molecule.

When glucose is oxidised to carbon dioxide and water in aerobic cell respiration, energy is transferred. This energy is no longer in store but is on the move; it is **active energy**. Actually, only part of the stored energy in a molecule is available, known as free energy, and can be used to do work. Reactions that release free energy are known as **exergonic reactions** (Figure 8.28). The oxidation of glucose is an example of an exergonic reaction.

On the other hand, reactions that require energy are called **endergonic reactions** (Figure 8.28). The synthesis of a protein from amino acids is an example of an endergonic reaction.

Figure 8.28 Exergonic and endergonic reactions

In an **exergonic reaction** the products have less stored energy than the reactants.

A+B → AB
+ **free energy given out**, as work done, or heat, or both

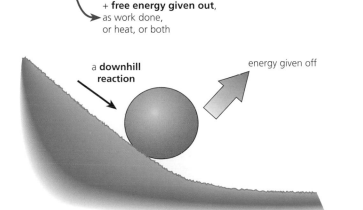
a **downhill reaction**
energy given off

In an **endergonic reaction** energy has to be put in, because the products have more stored energy than the reactants.

C+D → CD
+ **free energy input**

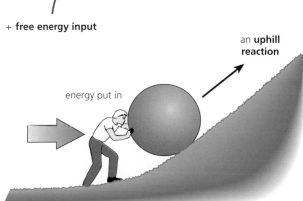
an **uphill reaction**
energy put in

The many endergonic reactions that occur in metabolism are made possible by being coupled to exergonic reactions. Coupling occurs through **ATP**, which is referred to as the **energy currency** molecule in biology (Figure 3.4, page 78). Molecules of ATP work in metabolism by acting as common intermediates, linking energy-requiring and energy-yielding reactions. Metabolic processes mostly involve ATP, directly or indirectly.

Enzymes work by lowering the energy of activation

As molecules react they become unstable, high-energy intermediates, but only momentarily. We say they are in a transition state because the products are formed immediately. The products have a lower energy level than the substrate molecules. The minimum amount of energy needed to raise substrate molecules to their transition state is a called the **activation energy**. This is the energy barrier that has to be overcome before the reaction can happen.

> **Enzymes work by lowering the amount of energy required to activate the reacting molecule.**

Another model of what is going on is the boulder (substrate) perched on a slope, prevented from rolling down by a small hump (activation energy) in front of it. The boulder can be pushed over the hump, or the hump can be dug away (= lowering the activation energy), allowing the boulder to roll, and shatter at a lower level (products) (Figure 8.29).

Figure 8.29 Activation energy

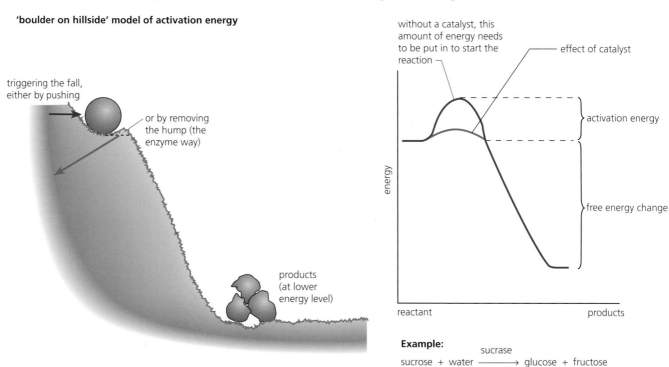

'boulder on hillside' model of activation energy

triggering the fall, either by pushing

or by removing the hump (the enzyme way)

products (at lower energy level)

without a catalyst, this amount of energy needs to be put in to start the reaction

effect of catalyst

activation energy

free energy change

energy

reactant   products

Example:

$$\text{sucrose} + \text{water} \xrightarrow{\text{sucrase}} \text{glucose} + \text{fructose}$$

Enzyme specificity and 'induced fit'

We have seen that enzymes are highly specific in their action, which makes them different from most inorganic catalysts. They are specific because of the way enzymes bind with their substrate at the active site, which is a pocket or crevice in the protein. To emphasise this, the binding of enzyme and substrate is sometimes referred to as the **lock and key hypothesis** of enzyme action (page 53). The necessity of binding the substrate at the active site of the enzyme before catalysis explained why changes in temperature and pH affected enzyme action since these changes often caused the shape of the enzyme molecules to change (Figures 2.18 and 2.19, pages 55–6).

However, the lock and key model does not fully account for the combined events of binding and simultaneous chemical change observed in most enzyme-catalysed reactions. At the active site, the arrangement of certain amino acid residues in the enzyme exactly matches certain groupings on the substrate molecule, enabling the enzyme–substrate complex to form. As the complex is formed, it seems an essential, critical **change of shape** is induced in the enzyme molecule. It is this shape change that is important in momentarily raising the substrate molecule to the transitional state in which it is able to react.

With a transitional state achieved, other amino acid residues of the active site bring about the breaking of particular bonds in the substrate molecule, at the point where it is temporarily held by the enzyme. Because different enzymes have different arrangements of amino acids in their active sites, each enzyme catalyses either a single chemical reaction or a group of closely related reactions (Figures 8.30 and 8.31). In other words, induced fit also accounts for the broad specificity of some enzymes (that is, the ability of some enzymes to bind to several substrates).

Figure 8.30 The induced fit model of enzyme action

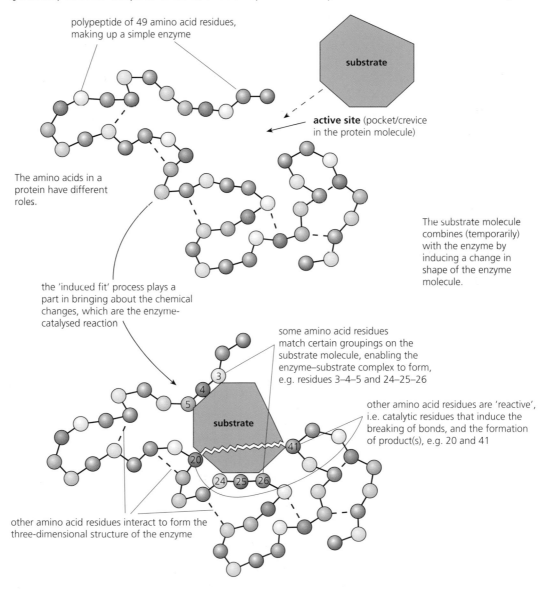

polypeptide of 49 amino acid residues, making up a simple enzyme

substrate

active site (pocket/crevice in the protein molecule)

The amino acids in a protein have different roles.

The substrate molecule combines (temporarily) with the enzyme by inducing a change in shape of the enzyme molecule.

the 'induced fit' process plays a part in bringing about the chemical changes, which are the enzyme-catalysed reaction

some amino acid residues match certain groupings on the substrate molecule, enabling the enzyme–substrate complex to form, e.g. residues 3–4–5 and 24–25–26

other amino acid residues are 'reactive', i.e. catalytic residues that induce the breaking of bonds, and the formation of product(s), e.g. 20 and 41

substrate

other amino acid residues interact to form the three-dimensional structure of the enzyme

Specificity:
- some amino acid residues allow a particular substrate molecule to 'fit'
- some amino acid residues bring about particular chemical changes.

Figure 8.31 Computer-generated image of induced fit in action

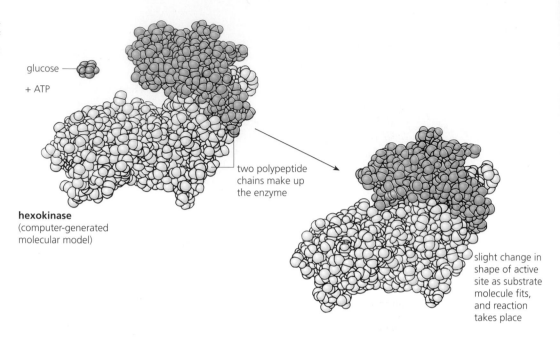

glucose

+ ATP

hexokinase
(computer-generated molecular model)

two polypeptide chains make up the enzyme

slight change in shape of active site as substrate molecule fits, and reaction takes place

14 Explain the differences between the 'lock and key' and 'induced fit' hypotheses of enzyme action.

Inhibitors of enzymes

Certain substances present in cells (and some which enter from the environment) may react with an enzyme, altering the rate of reaction. These substances are known as **inhibitors**, since their effects are generally to lower the rate of reaction. Studies of the effects of inhibitors have helped our understanding of:

- the chemistry of the active site of enzymes;
- the natural regulation of metabolism and which pathways operate;
- the ways certain commercial pesticides and some drugs work, namely by inhibiting specific enzymes and preventing particular reactions.

For example, molecules that sufficiently resemble the substrate in shape may compete to occupy the active site. They are known as **competitive inhibitors**. The enzyme that catalyses the reaction between carbon dioxide and the acceptor molecule in photosynthesis is known as ribulose bisphosphate carboxylase (Rubisco, page 285) and is competitively inhibited by oxygen in the chloroplasts.

Because these inhibitors are not acted on by the enzyme and turned into products, as normal substrate molecules are, they tend to remain attached. However, if the concentration of the substrate molecule is raised to a sufficiently high level, the inhibitor molecules are progressively displaced from the active sites.

Alternatively, an inhibitor may be unlike the substrate molecule, yet still combine with the enzyme. In these cases, the attachment occurs at some other part of the enzyme, probably quite close to the active site. Here the inhibitor either partly blocks access to the active site by substrate molecules, or it causes the active site to change shape and thus be unable to accept the substrate. These are called **non-competitive inhibitors**, since they do not compete for the active site. Adding excess substrate does not overcome their inhibiting effects (Figure 8.32). Cyanide ions combine with cytochrome oxidase but not at the active site. Cytochrome oxidase is a respiratory enzyme present in all cells, and is a component in a sequence of enzymes and carriers that oxidise the hydrogen removed from a respiratory substrate such as glucose, forming water.

Features and examples of competitive and non-competitive inhibition of enzymes are set out in Table 8.5.

Figure 8.32 Competitive and non-competitive inhibitors, the principles

When the initial rates of reaction of an enzyme are plotted against substrate concentration, the effects of competitive and non-competitive inhibitors are seen to be different.

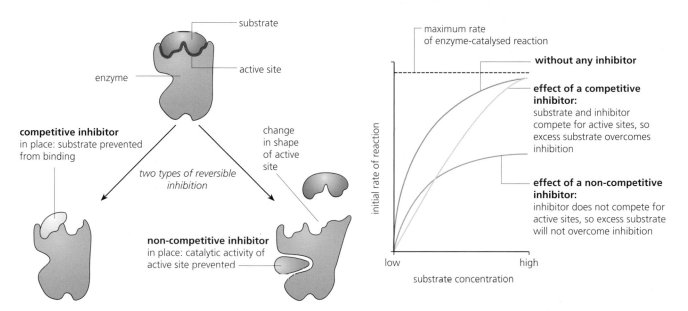

Competitive inhibition	Non-competitive inhibition
inhibitor chemically resembles the substrate molecule and occupies (blocks) the active site	inhibitor chemically unlike the substrate molecule, but reacts with bulk of enzyme, reducing accessibility of active site
with a low concentration of inhibitor, increasing concentration of substrate eventually overcomes inhibition as substrate molecules displace inhibitor	with low concentration of inhibitor, increasing concentration of substrate cannot prevent binding – some inhibition remains at high substrate concentration
Examples: ■ O_2 competing with CO_2 for active site of Rubisco ■ malonate competing with succinate for active site of succinate dehydrogenase	Examples: ■ cyanide ions blocking cytochrome oxidase in terminal oxidation in cell aerobic respiration ■ nerve gas Sarin blocking acetyl cholinesterase in synapse transmission

Table 8.5 Competitive and non-competitive inhibition of enzymes compared

The role of allostery in the control of metabolic pathways

Many metabolic pathways are switched off by a process known as **allosteric inhibition**. Allosteric enzymes have two sites. One is the active site of the enzyme and the other is an additional site on the molecule where another substance can lock in. Once such a substance is locked in, the whole enzyme is altered, resulting in inactivation of the active site.

Individual pathways in metabolism may be regulated and adjusted by means of allosteric inhibition. A case in point is end-product inhibition (Figure 8.34). Here, the **final product** inhibits the enzyme that catalyses the **first step** in the pathway.

So, in end-product inhibition, as the product molecules accumulate, the steps in their production are switched off. But these product molecules may now become the substrates in subsequent metabolic reactions. If so, the accumulated product molecules will be removed, and production of new product molecules will recommence.

■ Extension: Enzymes and the control of metabolism

The metabolic pathways of cells and tissues are numerous, and many interconnect. We have seen that the reactions of metabolism are made possible by the presence of specific enzymes. In addition, the enzyme machinery of cells plays a part in the **control** of the pathways of metabolism (Figure 8.33). How do enzymes achieve this?

- The **specificity** of enzymes means that a reaction occurs only in the presence of a specific enzyme. If the enzyme is not present, the reaction cannot occur.
- Because enzymes are **effective in very small amounts**, the production of a specific enzyme leads to immediate reactions and the formation of products.
- Where enzymes compete for the same substrate molecule, the amount of each enzyme present and **how readily each forms its enzyme–substrate complex** decides the extent to which pathways operate.
- Many enzymes are always present in cells, but some are **enzymes produced only in the presence of the substrate**. This is a case of the substrate molecule triggering the synthesis machinery by which the enzymes are produced.

Figure 8.33 Some metabolic pathways and the roles of enzymes

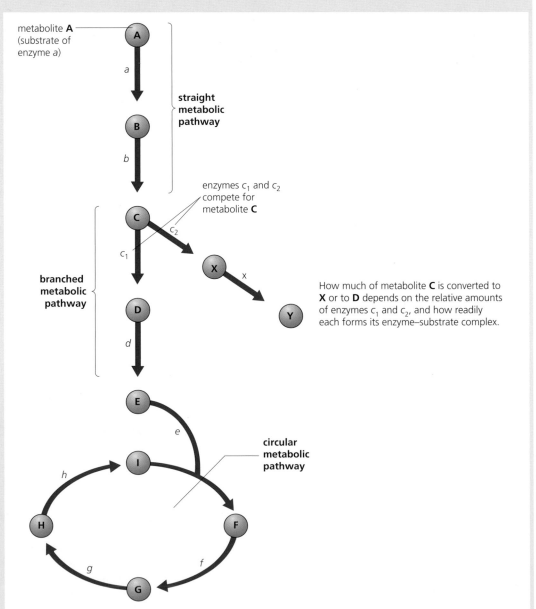

metabolite **A** (substrate of enzyme *a*)

straight metabolic pathway

enzymes c_1 and c_2 compete for metabolite **C**

branched metabolic pathway

How much of metabolite **C** is converted to **X** or to **D** depends on the relative amounts of enzymes c_1 and c_2, and how readily each forms its enzyme–substrate complex.

circular metabolic pathway

Figure 8.34 End-product
inhibition of metabolism

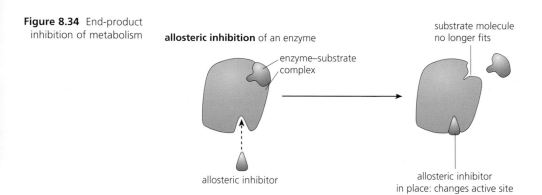

allosteric inhibition of an enzyme

enzyme–substrate
complex

substrate molecule
no longer fits

allosteric inhibitor

allosteric inhibitor
in place: changes active site

regulation of a metabolic pathway by end-product inhibition
(an example of allosteric inhibition)

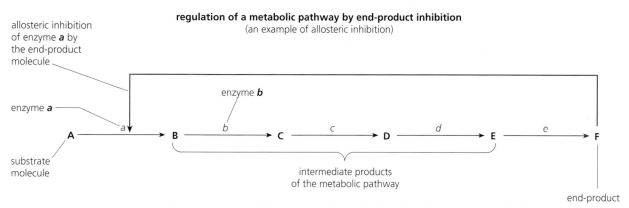

allosteric inhibition
of enzyme *a* by
the end-product
molecule

enzyme *a*

enzyme *b*

substrate
molecule

A   *a*   B   *b*   C   *c*   D   *d*   E   *e*   F

intermediate products
of the metabolic pathway

end-product

This is an example of the regulation of a metabolic pathway by **negative feedback**.

■ *Examination questions – a selection*

Questions 1–4 are taken from past IB Diploma biology papers.

Q1 How do enzymes speed up biochemical reactions?
   A By being used up in the reaction.
   B By increasing activation energy.
   C By changing the pH of the reaction.
   D By lowering activation energy.
         Higher Level Paper 1, May 05, Q24

Q2 Which molecule is involved in the process of transcription?
   A DNA polymerase
   B Helicase
   C DNA ligase
   D mRNA
         Higher Level Paper 1, May 03, Q12

Q3 Which process involves the removal of introns?
   A the reaction catalysed by RNA polymerase
   B the formation of mature eukaryotic mRNA
   C the activation of reverse transcriptase
   D the binding of ribosomes to mRNA
         Higher Level Paper 2, May 02, Q21

Q4 The diagram below illustrates a simple metabolic pathway.

metabolite   metabolite   metabolite   metabolite

P —*enzyme 1*→ Q —*enzyme 2*→ R —*enzyme 3*→ S

Which response shows allosteric feedback inhibition?

	Metabolite	Site of binding of metabolite
A	P	allosteric site of enzyme 1
B	S	allosteric site of enzyme 1
C	P	active site of enzyme 1
D	S	active site of enzyme 1

         Higher Level Paper 2, May 02, Q23

Questions 5–8 cover other syllabus issues in this chapter.

Q5 a State the **two** types of organic molecule that form the bulk of chromosomes of eukaryotes, and their approximate proportions. (3)
   b Suggest why the complex structural packaging of these molecules in chromosomes may be essential in the nucleus. (2)
   c By means of an annotated diagram, explain the composition and structure of a nucleosome. (4)

Q6 a DNA replication is semi-conservative and occurs in the 5' → 3' direction. Explain the meaning of this statement. (6)
   b By means of a fully annotated diagram, outline the steps to replication at a replication fork, making explicit the role of each of the essential enzymes. (6)

Q7 a Construct a concise flow diagram of the sequence of key events in transcription in the eukaryotic nucleus up to the point when mRNA is about to pass into the cytoplasm. (8)
   b Identify to what extent translation in prokaryotes differs from this. (3)
   c List the differences in composition between mRNA and the DNA of chromosomes. (3)

Q8 a Proteins are essential components of organisms. Describe the key property of the proteins specifically involved in:
    i biological catalysis
    ii movement driven by muscle fibres
    iii structural support
    iv the movement of molecules across membranes. (8)
   b Outline the differences between the primary and tertiary structures of proteins. (4)
   c Identify the types of bonds that maintain the secondary structure of protein. (5)
   d Membrane proteins typically arrange themselves with component amino acids that are non-polar and others that are polar in contrasting positions. With the aid of an annotated diagram, explain the property of the molecules of the lipid bilayer of membranes that causes this. (8)

9 Energy transfer in cells II

STARTING POINTS
- **Respiration** occurs in every living cell, making energy available to maintain cells and to carry out activities and functions.
- Cellular respiration requiring oxygen, **aerobic respiration**, involves the oxidation of sugar to carbon dioxide and water.
- Green plants manufacture glucose by **photosynthesis**, using the raw materials carbon dioxide and water and energy from sunlight. Oxygen is produced as a waste product.
- **Chloroplasts** are the photosynthetic organelles. Chloroplasts contain chlorophyll needed for the transfer of light energy into chemicals like glucose during photosynthesis.
- This chapter extends discussion of cell respiration and photosynthesis begun in Chapter 3, pages 76–90.

Respiration and photosynthesis have traditionally been summarised in single equations:

Cellular respiration

glucose + oxygen → carbon dioxide + water + ENERGY
$$C_6H_{12}O_6 + 6O_2 \rightarrow 6CO_2 + 6H_2O + ENERGY$$

Photosynthesis

carbon dioxide + water + ENERGY → glucose + oxygen
$$6CO_2 + 6H_2O + ENERGY \rightarrow C_6H_{12}O_6 + 6O_2$$

At first sight it seems that the one process is simply the reverse of the other. In fact these equations are merely 'balance sheets' of the inputs and outputs. Photosynthesis and respiration occur by different pathways with many enzymes unique to one or the other.

In this chapter, the **biochemical events in respiration** and **photosynthesis** are considered in detail, beginning with aerobic respiration.

The steps of aerobic cellular respiration 8.1.1–8.1.6

In cellular respiration, the chemical energy of organic molecules such as glucose is made available for use in the living cell. Much of the energy transferred is lost in the form of heat energy, but cells are able to retain significant amounts of chemical energy in **adenosine triphosphate** (ATP, page 78). ATP, found in all cells, is the universal energy currency in living systems. ATP is a relatively small, soluble molecule. It is able to move, by facilitated diffusion, from the mitochondria where it is synthesised to all the very many sites where energy is required, such as in muscles for contraction movements (page 368), in membranes for active transport (page 23) and in ribosomes for protein synthesis (page 248).

How is energy transferred from respiratory substrates like glucose?

In summary, glucose is a relatively large molecule containing six carbon atoms all in a reduced state. During aerobic cellular respiration, glucose undergoes a series of enzyme-catalysed oxidation reactions (Figure 9.1). These reactions are grouped into three major phases:

- **glycolysis**, in which glucose is converted to pyruvate;
- the **Krebs cycle**, in which pyruvate is converted to carbon dioxide;
- the **electron-transport system**, in which hydrogen removed in oxidation reactions of glycolysis and the Krebs cycle is converted to water, and the bulk of the ATP is synthesised.

Figure 9.1 The three phases of aerobic cellular respiration

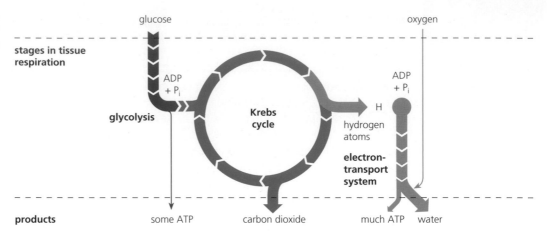

Respiration as a series of redox reactions

The terms '**reduction**' and '**oxidation**' recur frequently in respiration.

What do these terms mean?

In cellular respiration, glucose is oxidised to carbon dioxide, but at the same time, oxygen is reduced to water (Figure 9.2). In fact, tissue respiration is a series of oxidation–reduction reactions, so described because when one substance in a reaction is oxidised another is automatically reduced. The short-hand name for **red**uction–**ox**idation reactions is **redox reactions**.

In biological oxidation, oxygen atoms may be added to a compound, but alternatively, hydrogen atoms may be removed. In respiration, all the hydrogen atoms are gradually removed from glucose. They are added to hydrogen acceptors, which are themselves reduced.

Since a hydrogen atom consists of an electron and a proton, gaining hydrogen atom(s) (a case of reduction) involves gaining one or more electrons. In fact, the best definition of **oxidation is the loss of electrons**, and **reduction is the gain of electrons**. Remembering this definition has given countless people problems, so a mnemonic has been devised:

OIL RIG = **O**xidation **I**s **L**oss of electrons; **R**eduction **I**s **G**ain of electrons.

Redox reactions take place in biological systems because of the presence of a compound with a strong tendency to take electrons from another compound (an **oxidising agent**) or the presence of a compound with a strong tendency to donate electrons to another compound (a **reducing agent**).

Another feature of oxidation and reduction is **energy change**. When reduction occurs, energy is absorbed (an **endergonic reaction**, Figure 8.28, page 261). When oxidation occurs, energy is released (an **exergonic reaction**).

Figure 9.2 Respiration as a redox reaction

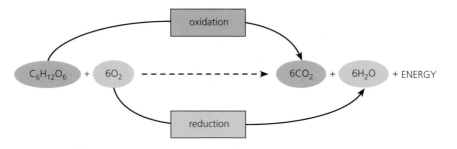

oxidation involves:
• addition of oxygen
• removal of hydrogen
• loss of electrons
• release of energy

reduction involves:
• removal of oxygen
• addition of hydrogen
• gain of electrons
• uptake of energy

An example of energy release in oxidation is the burning of a fuel in air. Here, energy is given out as heat. In fact, the amount of energy in a molecule depends on its degree of oxidation. An oxidised substance has less stored energy than a reduced substance, illustrated by the fuel molecule methane (CH_4) which has more stored chemical energy than carbon dioxide (CO_2).

Cellular respiration

Glycolysis

Glycolysis is a linear series of reactions in which a 6-carbon sugar molecule is broken down to two molecules of the 3-carbon pyruvate ion (Figure 9.3). The enzymes of glycolysis are located in the cytoplasm outside organelles (known as the cytosol), rather than in the mitochondria. Glycolysis occurs by four stages:

- **Phosphorylation** by reaction with ATP is the way glucose is first activated, forming glucose phosphate. Conversion to fructose phosphate follows, and a further phosphate group is then added at the expense of another molecule of ATP. So, two molecules of ATP are consumed per molecule of glucose respired, *at this stage of glycolysis*.
- **Lysis** (splitting) of the fructose bisphosphate now takes place, forming two molecules of 3-carbon sugar, called **triose phosphate**.
- **Oxidation** of the triose phosphate molecules occurs by removal of hydrogen. The enzyme for this reaction (a dehydrogenase) works with a coenzyme, **nicotinamide adenine dinucleotide (NAD)**. NAD is a molecule that can accept hydrogen ions (H^+) and electrons (e^-). In this reaction, the NAD is reduced to NADH and H^+ (reduced NAD):

$NAD^+ + 2H^+ + 2e^- \rightarrow NADH + H^+$ (sometimes represented as $NADH_2$)

(Reduced NAD can pass hydrogen ions and electrons on to other acceptor molecules (see below), and when it does, it becomes oxidised back to NAD.)

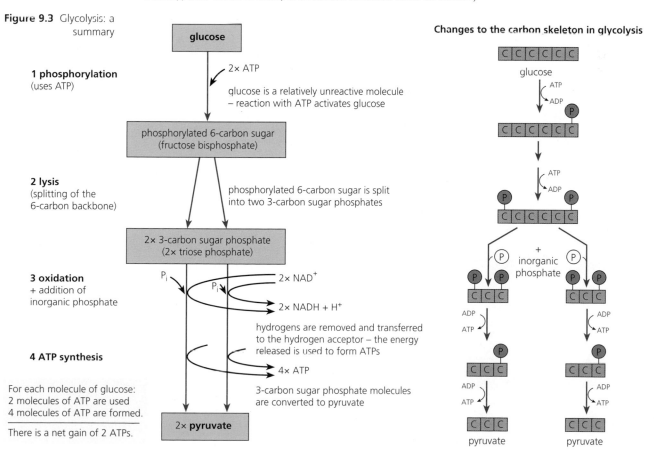

Figure 9.3 Glycolysis: a summary

1 phosphorylation
(uses ATP)

2 lysis
(splitting of the 6-carbon backbone)

3 oxidation
+ addition of inorganic phosphate

4 ATP synthesis

For each molecule of glucose:
2 molecules of ATP are used
4 molecules of ATP are formed.

There is a net gain of 2 ATPs.

glucose

2× ATP

glucose is a relatively unreactive molecule – reaction with ATP activates glucose

phosphorylated 6-carbon sugar (fructose bisphosphate)

phosphorylated 6-carbon sugar is split into two 3-carbon sugar phosphates

2× 3-carbon sugar phosphate (2× triose phosphate)

P_i P_i

2× NAD$^+$

2× NADH + H$^+$

hydrogens are removed and transferred to the hydrogen acceptor – the energy released is used to form ATPs

4× ATP

3-carbon sugar phosphate molecules are converted to pyruvate

2× **pyruvate**

Changes to the carbon skeleton in glycolysis

C C C C C C
glucose

ATP
ADP

C C C C C C

ATP
ADP

C C C C C C

+
inorganic phosphate

C C C   C C C

ADP   ADP
ATP   ATP

C C C   C C C

ADP   ADP
ATP   ATP

C C C   C C C
pyruvate   pyruvate

■ **ATP formation**, which occurs twice in the reactions by which each triose phosphate molecule is converted to pyruvate. This form of ATP synthesis is described as **at substrate level** in order to differentiate it from the bulk of ATP synthesis that occurs later in cell respiration, during operation of the electron-transport chain (see below). As two molecules of triose phosphate are converted to pyruvate, four molecules of ATP are synthesised *at this stage of glycolysis*. So in total, there is a **net gain of two ATPs in glycolysis**.

---

1 **State** which of the following are produced during glycolysis:

carbon dioxide	NADH	ATP	pyruvate
lactate	glycogen	NAD$^+$	glucose

---

2 Using the scale bar in Figure 9.4, **calculate** the length and width in microns of the mitochondrion shown in section in the TEM.

Figure 9.4 TEM of a mitochondrion, with an interpretive drawing

The mitochondria and the steps of the Krebs cycle

From this point on, the steps of aerobic cell respiration occur within organelles known as **mitochondria** (singular, **mitochondrion**). This is where the enzymes concerned with the Krebs cycle and electron transport are all located.

Mitochondria are found in the cytoplasm of all eukaryotic cells, usually in very large numbers. The structure of a mitochondrion is best investigated by transmission electron microscopy. The clarity of the resulting TEMs often makes possible a line drawing to show the mitochondrion's double membrane around the matrix, and the way the inner membrane intucks to form cristae (Figure 9.4). Of course, the mitochondrion is a three-dimensional structure.

TEM of a mitochondrion. Mitochondria are the site of the aerobic stage of respiration.

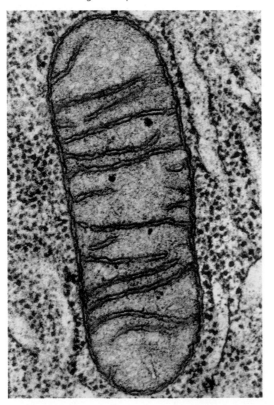

scale bar

1 μm

interpretive drawing

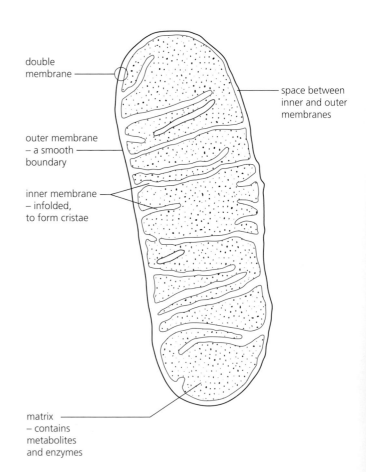

double membrane

outer membrane – a smooth boundary

inner membrane – infolded, to form cristae

space between inner and outer membranes

matrix – contains metabolites and enzymes

Link reaction

Pyruvate diffuses into the matrix of the mitochondrion as it forms, and is metabolised there.

First, the 3-carbon pyruvate is decarboxylated by removal of carbon dioxide and, at the same time, oxidised by removal of hydrogen. Reduced NAD is formed. The product of this **oxidative decarboxylation** reaction is an acetyl group – a 2-carbon fragment. This acetyl group is then combined with a coenzyme called coenzyme A (CoA), forming **acetyl coenzyme A (acetyl CoA)**. The production of acetyl coenzyme A from pyruvate is known as the link reaction because it connects glycolysis to reactions of the **Krebs cycle**, which now follow.

$$\text{pyruvate} \xrightarrow[\text{CoA}]{\text{NAD}^+ \quad\quad \text{NADH + H}^+ \quad\quad \text{CO}_2} \text{acetyl CoA}$$

Krebs cycle

The Krebs cycle is named after Hans Krebs who discovered it, but it is also sometimes referred to as the citric acid cycle, after the first intermediate acid formed.

The acetyl coenzyme A enters the Krebs cycle by reacting with a **4-carbon organic acid** (oxaloacetate, OAA). The products of this reaction are a **6-carbon acid** (citrate) and coenzyme A which is released and re-used in the link reaction.

The citrate is then converted back to the 4-carbon acid (an acceptor molecule, in effect) by **the reactions of the Krebs cycle**. These involve the following changes:

- **two molecules of carbon dioxide are given off**, in separate decarboxylation reactions;
- **a molecule of ATP is formed**, as part one of the reactions of the cycle; as in glycolysis, this ATP synthesis is at substrate level;
- **three molecules of reduced NAD are formed**;
- **one molecule of another hydrogen acceptor**, the coenzyme flavin adenine dinucleotide (FAD) is reduced (NAD is the chief hydrogen-carrying coenzyme of respiration but FAD has this role in the Krebs cycle).

Figure 9.5 The Krebs cycle: a summary

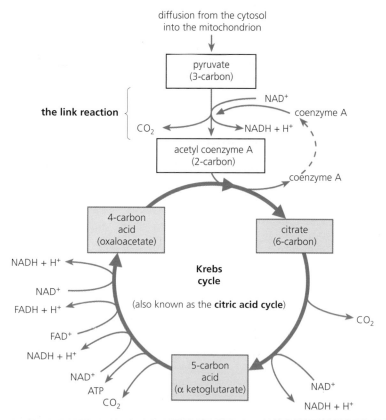

There are several other organic acid intermediates in the cycle not shown here.

Because glucose is converted to two molecules of pyruvate in glycolysis, the whole Krebs cycle sequence of reactions 'turns' twice for every molecule of glucose that is metabolised by aerobic cellular respiration (Figure 9.5).

Now we are in a position to summarise the changes to the molecule of glucose that occurred in the reactions of glycolysis and the Krebs cycle. A 'budget' of the products of glycolysis and two turns of the Krebs cycle is shown in Table 9.1.

Step	Product			
	CO_2	ATP	reduced NAD	reduced FAD
glycolysis	0	2	2	0
link reaction (pyruvate → acetyl CoA)	2	0	2	0
Krebs cycle	4	2	6	2
Totals	$6CO_2$	4 ATP	10 reduced NAD	2 reduced FAD

Table 9.1 Net products of aerobic respiration of glucose at the end of the Krebs cycle

3 **Outline** the types of reaction catalysed by:

  a dehydrogenases
  b decarboxylases.

■ **Extension:** ## Fats can be respired

In addition to glucose, **fats** (lipids) are also commonly used as respiratory substrates – they are first broken down to **fatty acids** (and glycerol). Fatty acid is 'cut up' into 2-carbon fragments and fed into the Krebs cycle via **coenzyme A**. Vertebrate muscle is well adapted to the respiration of fatty acids in this way (as is our heart muscle), and they are just as likely as glucose to be the respiratory substrate.

Terminal oxidation and oxidative phosphorylation

The removal of pairs of hydrogen atoms from various intermediates of the respiratory pathway is a feature of several of the steps in glycolysis and the Krebs cycle. On most occasions, oxidised NAD is converted to reduced NAD, but once in the Krebs cycle an alternative hydrogen-acceptor coenzyme, FAD, is reduced.

In the final stage of aerobic respiration, the hydrogen atoms (or their electrons) are transported along a **series of carriers**, from the reduced NAD (or FAD), to be combined with oxygen to form water.

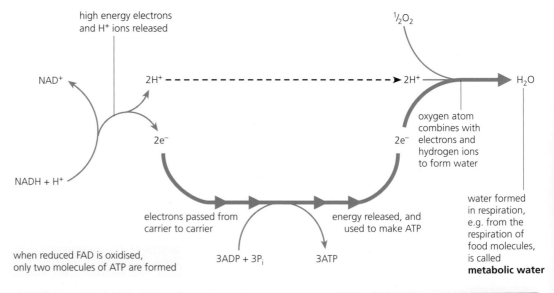

Figure 9.6 Terminal oxidation and the formation of ATPs

4 Suggest how the absence of oxygen in respiring tissue might 'switch off' both the Krebs cycle and terminal oxidation.

As electrons are passed between the carriers in the series, **energy is released**. Release of energy in this manner is controlled and can be used by the cell. The energy is transferred to ADP and P_i, to form ATP. Normally, for every molecule of reduced NAD which is oxidised (that is, for every pair of hydrogens) approximately three molecules of ATP are produced.

The process is summarised in Figure 9.6. The total yield from aerobic respiration is 38 ATPs per molecule of glucose respired.

Phosphorylation by chemiosmosis?

How could a mitochondrion use the energy made available in the flow of electrons between carrier molecules to drive the synthesis of ATP?

It was a biochemist, Peter Mitchell, who first suggested the chemiosmotic theory when he was at an independently funded research institute in Cornwall, UK. This was in 1961; at the time he was studying the metabolism of bacteria. His hypothesis was not generally accepted for many years, but about two decades later he was awarded a Nobel Prize for his discovery.

Chemiosmosis is a process by which the synthesis of ATP is coupled to electron transport via the movement of protons (Figure 9.7). The electron-carrier proteins are arranged in the inner mitochondrial wall in a highly ordered way. These carrier proteins oxidise the reduced coenzymes, and energy from the oxidation process is used to pump hydrogen ions (protons) from the matrix of the mitochondrion into the space between inner and outer mitochondrial membranes.

Here they accumulate – incidentally, causing the pH to drop. Because the inner membrane is largely impermeable to ions, a significant **gradient in hydrogen ion concentration** builds up across the inner membrane, generating a potential difference across the membrane. This represents a store of potential energy. Eventually, the protons do flow back into the matrix, but this occurs via the channels in **ATP synthetase** enzymes (ATPase), also found in the inner mitochondrial membrane. As the protons flow down their concentration gradient through the enzyme, the energy is transferred as ATP synthesis occurs.

5 When ATP is synthesised in mitochondria, **explain** where the electrochemical gradient is set up, and in which direction protons move.

Figure 9.7 Mitchell's chemiosmotic theory

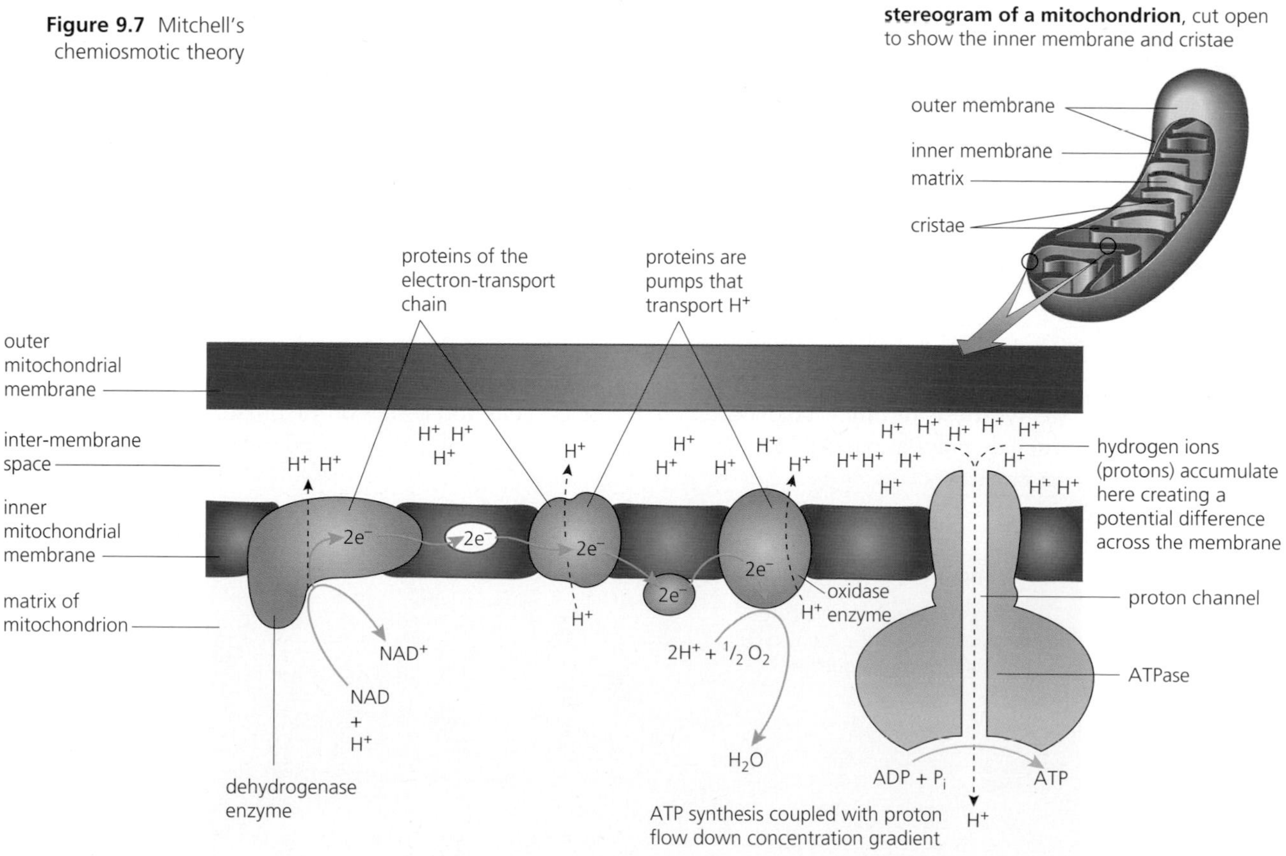

Site of cellular respiration – structure in relation to function

The location of the stages of cellular respiration are summarised in Figure 9.8. Once pyruvate has been formed from glucose in the cytosol, the remainder of the pathway of aerobic cell respiration is located in the mitochondria. The relationship between structure and function in this organelle is summarised in Table 9.2.

Table 9.2 Mitochondrial structure in relation to function

Structure	Function / role
external double membrane	permeable to pyruvate, CO_2, O_2 and NAD/NADH + H^+
matrix	site of enzymes of link reaction and Krebs cycle
inner membrane	surface area greatly increased by intucking to form cristae – since the electron-transport chain and ATP synthetase enzymes are housed here, opportunities for ATP synthesis are enhanced
	impermeable to hydrogen ions (protons) – permitting the establishment of a potential difference between the inter-membrane space and the matrix
inter-membrane space	relatively tiny space – allowing the accumulation of hydrogen ions (protons) to generate a large concentration difference with matrix, facilitating phosphorylation

Figure 9.8 The site of respiration in the eukaryotic cell

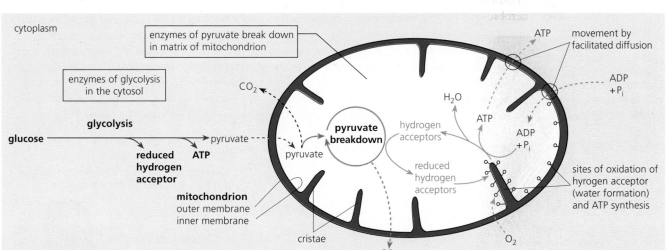

Extension: Respiration as a source of intermediates

We have seen that the main role of respiration is to provide a pool of ATP, and that this is used to drive the endergonic reactions of synthesis. But the compounds of the glycolysis pathway and the Krebs cycle (**respiratory intermediates**) may also serve as the **starting points of synthesis of other metabolites** needed in the cells and tissues of the organism. These include polysaccharides like starch and cellulose, glycerol and fatty acids, amino acids, and many others.

6 **Distinguish** between the following pairs:

a substrate and intermediate
b glycolysis and the Krebs cycle
c oxidation and reduction

The steps of photosynthesis

8.2.1–8.2.6

Just as the mitochondria are the site of reactions of the Krebs cycle and respiratory ATP formation, so the **chloroplasts** are the organelles where the reactions of photosynthesis occur.

Chloroplasts are found in green plants. They contain the photosynthetic pigments along with the enzymes and electron-transport proteins for the reduction of carbon dioxide to sugars and for ATP formation, using light energy. The detailed structure of chloroplasts is investigated with the transmission electron microscope. TEMs of thin sections of a chloroplast show the arrangement of the membranes within this large organelle (Figure 9.9).

You can see there is a double membrane around the chloroplast, and that the inner of these membranes intucks at various points to form a system of branching membranes. Here, these membranes are called **thylakoids**. Thylakoid membranes are organised into flat, compact, circular piles called **grana** (singular, **granum**), almost like stacks of coins. Between the grana are loosely arranged tubular membranes suspended in a watery matrix, called the **stroma**.

Chlorophyll, the photosynthetic pigment that absorbs light energy, occurs in the grana. Also suspended in the matrix are starch grains, lipid droplets and ribosomes. We shall see that the structure, composition and arrangements of membranes are central to the biochemistry of photosynthesis, just as the mitochondrial membranes are the sites of many of the reactions of aerobic cell respiration.

Figure 9.9 TEM of a chloroplast, with an interpretive drawing

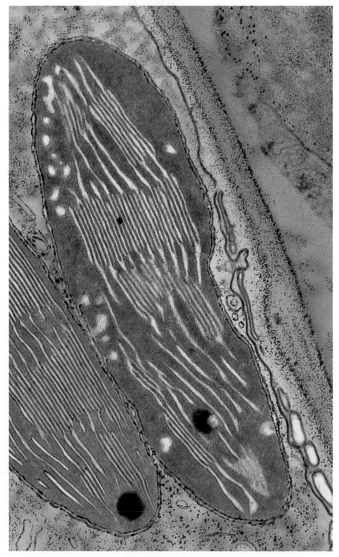

TEM of a thin section of a chloroplast (×15 000)

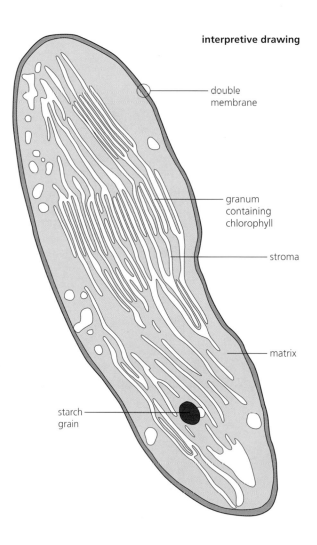

interpretive drawing

double membrane

granum containing chlorophyll

stroma

matrix

starch grain

The reactions of photosynthesis

Photosynthesis is a complex set of many reactions that take place in illuminated chloroplasts. However, biochemical studies of photosynthesis by several teams of scientists have established that the many reactions by which light energy brings about the production of sugars, using the raw materials water and carbon dioxide, fall naturally into two inter-connected stages (Figure 9.10).

- **The light-dependent reactions**, in which light energy is used directly to split water (known as **photolysis** for obvious reasons). Hydrogen is then removed and retained by the photosynthesis-specific hydrogen acceptor, known as $NADP^+$. ($NADP^+$ is very similar to the coenzyme NAD^+ of respiration, but it carries an additional phosphate group, hence NADP.) At the same time, ATP is generated from ADP and phosphate, also using energy from light. This is known as photophosphorylation. Oxygen is given off as a waste product of the light-dependent reactions. This stage occurs in the grana of the chloroplasts.

- **The light-independent reactions**, in which sugars are built up using carbon dioxide. Of course, the products of the light-dependent reactions (ATP and reduced hydrogen acceptor NADPH + H^+) are used in sugar production. This stage occurs in the stroma of the chloroplast. It requires a continuous supply of the products of the light-dependent reactions, but does not directly involve light energy (hence the name). Names can be misleading, however, because this stage is an integral part of photosynthesis, and photosynthesis is a process that is powered by light energy.

Figure 9.10 The two sets of reactions of photosynthesis, inputs and outputs

We shall now consider both sets of reactions, in order to understand more about how these complex changes are brought about.

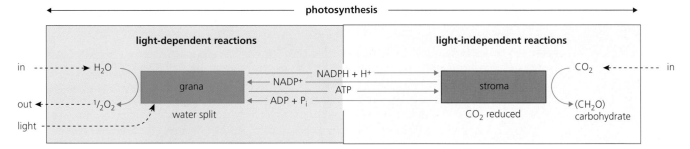

The light-dependent reactions

In the light-dependent stage, light energy is trapped by photosynthetic pigment, chlorophyll. Chlorophyll molecules do not occur haphazardly in the grana. Rather, they are grouped together in structures called **photosystems**, held in the thylakoid membranes of the **grana** (Figure 9.11).

Figure 9.11 The structure of photosystems

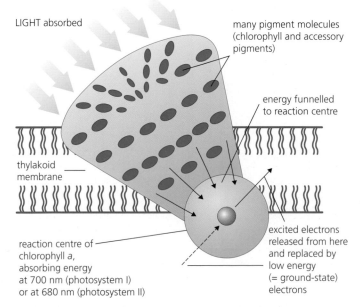

In each photosystem, several hundred chlorophyll molecules plus accessory pigments (carotene and xanthophylls) are arranged. All these pigment molecules harvest light energy, and they funnel the energy to a single chlorophyll molecule of the photosystem, known as the **reaction centre**. The different pigments around the reaction centres absorb light energy of slightly different wavelengths.

There are **two types of photosystem** present in the thylakoid membranes of the grana, identified by the wavelength of light that the chlorophyll of the reaction centre absorbs:

■ **photosystem I** has a reaction centre activated by light of wavelength 700 nm. This reaction centre is referred to as P700;
■ **photosystem II** has a reaction centre activated by light of wavelength 680 nm. This reaction centre is referred to as P680.

Photosystems I and II have specific and differing roles, as we shall see shortly. However, they occur grouped together in the thylakoid membranes of the grana, along with specific proteins that function quite specifically. These consist of:

■ **enzymes** catalysing
– splitting of water into hydrogen ions, electrons and oxygen atoms;
– formation of ATP from ADP and phosphate (P_i);
– conversion of oxidised H-carrier ($NADP^+$) to reduced carrier ($NADPH + H^+$);
■ **electron carrier molecules**.

7 **Construct** a table of the components of photosystems that identifies the role of each.

When light energy reaches the reaction centre, **ground-state electrons** of the key chlorophyll molecule are raised to an 'excited state' by the light energy received. As a result, **high-energy electrons** are released from this chlorophyll molecule, and these electrons bring about the biochemical changes of the light-dependent reactions. The spaces vacated by the high-energy (excited) electrons are continuously refilled by non-excited or ground-state electrons.

We will examine this sequence of reactions in the two photosystems next.

First, the excited electrons from photosystem II are picked up and passed along a chain of electron carriers. As these excited electrons pass, some of the energy causes the pumping of hydrogen ions (protons) from the chloroplast's matrix into the thylakoid spaces. Here they accumulate, causing the pH to drop. The result is a proton gradient that is created across the thylakoid membrane, and which sustains the synthesis of ATP. This is another example of chemiosmosis (see below).

As a result of these energy transfers, the excitation level of the electrons falls back to ground state and they come to fill the vacancies in the reaction centre of photosystem I. Thus, electrons have been transferred from photosystem II to photosystem I.

Meanwhile the 'holes' in the reaction centres of photosystem II are filled by electrons (in their ground state) from water molecules. In fact, the positively charged 'vacancies' in photosystem II are powerful enough to cause the splitting of water (photolysis), in the presence of a specific enzyme. The reaction this enzyme catalyses then triggers release of hydrogen ions and oxygen atoms, as well as ground-state electrons.

The oxygen atoms combine to form molecular oxygen, the waste product of photosynthesis. The hydrogen ions are used in the reduction of $NADP^+$ (see below).

Photophosphorylation

In the grana of the chloroplasts, the synthesis of ATP is coupled to electron transport via the movement of protons by chemiosmosis, as it was in mitochondria (Table 9.3). Here it is the hydrogen ions trapped within the thylakoid space which flow out via ATP synthetase enzymes, down their electrochemical gradient. At the same time, ATP is synthesised from ADP and P_i.

We have seen that the excited electrons which provided the energy for ATP synthesis originated from water, and move on to fill the vacancies in the reaction centre of photosystem II. They are subsequently moved on to the reaction centre in photosystem I, and finally are used to reduce $NADP^+$. Because the pathway of the electrons is linear, the photophosphorylation reaction in which they are involved is described as **non-cyclic photophosphorylation**.

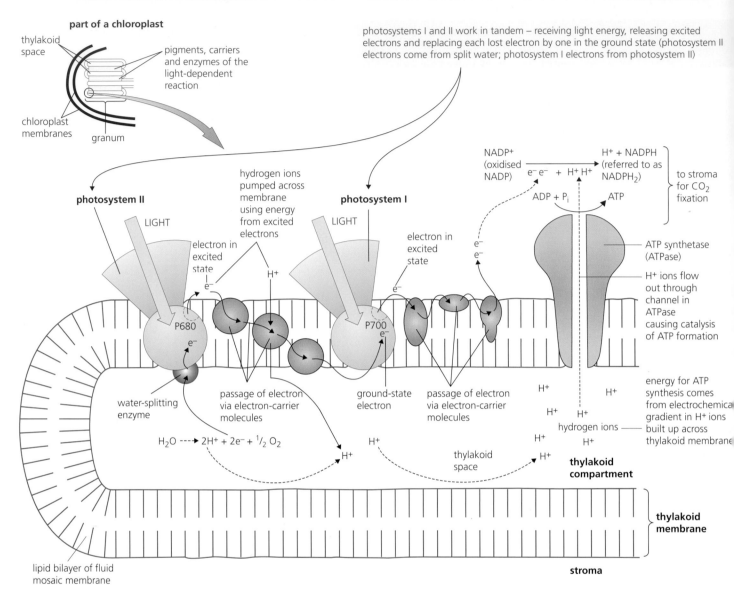

part of a chloroplast

thylakoid space

pigments, carriers and enzymes of the light-dependent reaction

chloroplast membranes

granum

photosystems I and II work in tandem – receiving light energy, releasing excited electrons and replacing each lost electron by one in the ground state (photosystem II electrons come from split water; photosystem I electrons from photosystem II)

photosystem II

LIGHT

electron in excited state

e^-

P680

e^-

water-splitting enzyme

hydrogen ions pumped across membrane using energy from excited electrons

H^+

passage of electron via electron-carrier molecules

$H_2O \dashrightarrow 2H^+ + 2e^- + \frac{1}{2} O_2$

photosystem I

LIGHT

electron in excited state

e^-

P700

e^-

ground-state electron

passage of electron via electron-carrier molecules

H^+

thylakoid space

e^-

e^-

NADP$^+$ (oxidised NADP)

$e^- \; e^- \; + \; H^+ H^+$

$H^+ + NADPH$ (referred to as NADPH$_2$)

ADP + P$_i$ ATP

to stroma for CO$_2$ fixation

ATP synthetase (ATPase)

H^+ ions flow out through channel in ATPase causing catalysis of ATP formation

H^+ H^+

H^+ H^+

H^+ H^+

hydrogen ions

H^+ H^+

thylakoid compartment

energy for ATP synthesis comes from electrochemical gradient in H$^+$ ions built up across thylakoid membrane

thylakoid membrane

lipid bilayer of fluid mosaic membrane

stroma

Figure 9.12 The light-dependent reaction

8 In non-cyclic photophosphorylation, **deduce** the ultimate fate of electrons displaced from the reaction centre of photosystem II.

The excited electrons from photosystem I are then picked up by a different electron acceptor. Two at a time, they are passed to NADP$^+$, which, with the addition of hydrogen ions from photolysis, is reduced to form NADPH + H$^+$.

By this sequence of reactions, repeated again and again at very great speed throughout every second of daylight, the products of the light-dependent reactions (**ATP + NADPH + H$^+$**) are formed (Figure 9.12).

ATP and reduced NADP do not normally accumulate, however, as they are immediately used in the fixation of carbon dioxide in the surrounding stroma (light-independent reactions, page 283). Then the ADP and NADP$^+$ diffuse back into the grana for re-use in the light-dependent reactions.

Photosynthesis in chloroplasts		Cell respiration in mitochondria
thylakoid space in grana	**site of proton (H$^+$) accumulation**	space between inner and outer membranes of mitochondria
from water molecules after photolysis has occurred	**origin of protons**	from reduced hydrogen acceptors (e.g. NADH + H$^+$)
sunlight	**energy source**	glucose and respiratory intermediates
diffuses to stroma and used to sustain reduction of carbon dioxide in light-independent reactions	**fate of ATP formed**	diffuses into matrix of mitochondria and to cytosol and mainly involved in anabolic reactions of metabolism

Table 9.3 Chemiosmosis in mitochondria and chloroplasts compared

Studying the light-dependent reactions with isolated chloroplasts

Chloroplasts can be isolated from green plant leaves, and suspended in buffer solution of the same concentration as the cytosol (using an isotonic buffer). Suspended in such a buffer, it has been found that the chloroplasts are undamaged, and function much as they do in the intact leaf. So, these isolated chloroplasts can be used to investigate the reactions of photosynthesis – for example, to show they evolve oxygen when illuminated. This occurs provided the natural electron acceptor enzymes and carrier molecules are present.

In the research laboratory, a sensitive piece of apparatus called an **oxygen electrode** is used to detect the oxygen given off by isolated chloroplasts.

Alternatively, a **hydrogen-acceptor dye** that changes colour when it is reduced can be used. The dye known as DCPIP is an example. DCPIP does no harm when added to chloroplasts in a suitable buffer solution, but changes from blue to colourless when reduced. The splitting of water by light energy (photolysis) is the source of hydrogen that turns DCPIP colourless. The photolysis of water and the reduction of the dye is represented by the equation:

$$2DCPIP + 2H_2O \rightarrow 2DCPIPH_2 + O_2$$

In Figure 9.13 the steps of isolation of chloroplasts and the investigation of their reducing activity are shown.

9 In the experiment shown in Figure 9.13, isolated chloroplasts are retained in isotonic buffer, standing in an ice bath. **Explain** the significance of this step.

Figure 9.13 The reducing activity of isolated chloroplasts

1 green leaves are ground up, and the slurry filtered to remove leaf debris

isotonic buffer
blender
muslin
filtered leaf extract
centrifuge tube
ice

2 the filtered extract is centrifuged at low speed to remove heavier debris (e.g. cell wall fragments) and the heaviest organelles (e.g. nuclei)

centrifuge tubes with filtered leaf extract
centrifuge head
motor (variable speed)
decanted
debris (discarded)
chloroplast suspension

3 the chloroplast suspension is centrifuged at high speed to precipitate the chloroplasts

liquid is now discarded
pellet of chloroplasts
chloroplasts resuspended in isotonic buffer and stored in ice (low temperature prevents autolysis)

4 isolated chloroplasts treated with DCPIP (blue dye)

DCPIP + chloroplasts in the light
DCPIP + chloroplasts in the dark
blue–green colour (green chloroplasts + blue dye)
LIGHT
lightproof wrapper
turns green (blue dye turned colourless)
remains blue–green

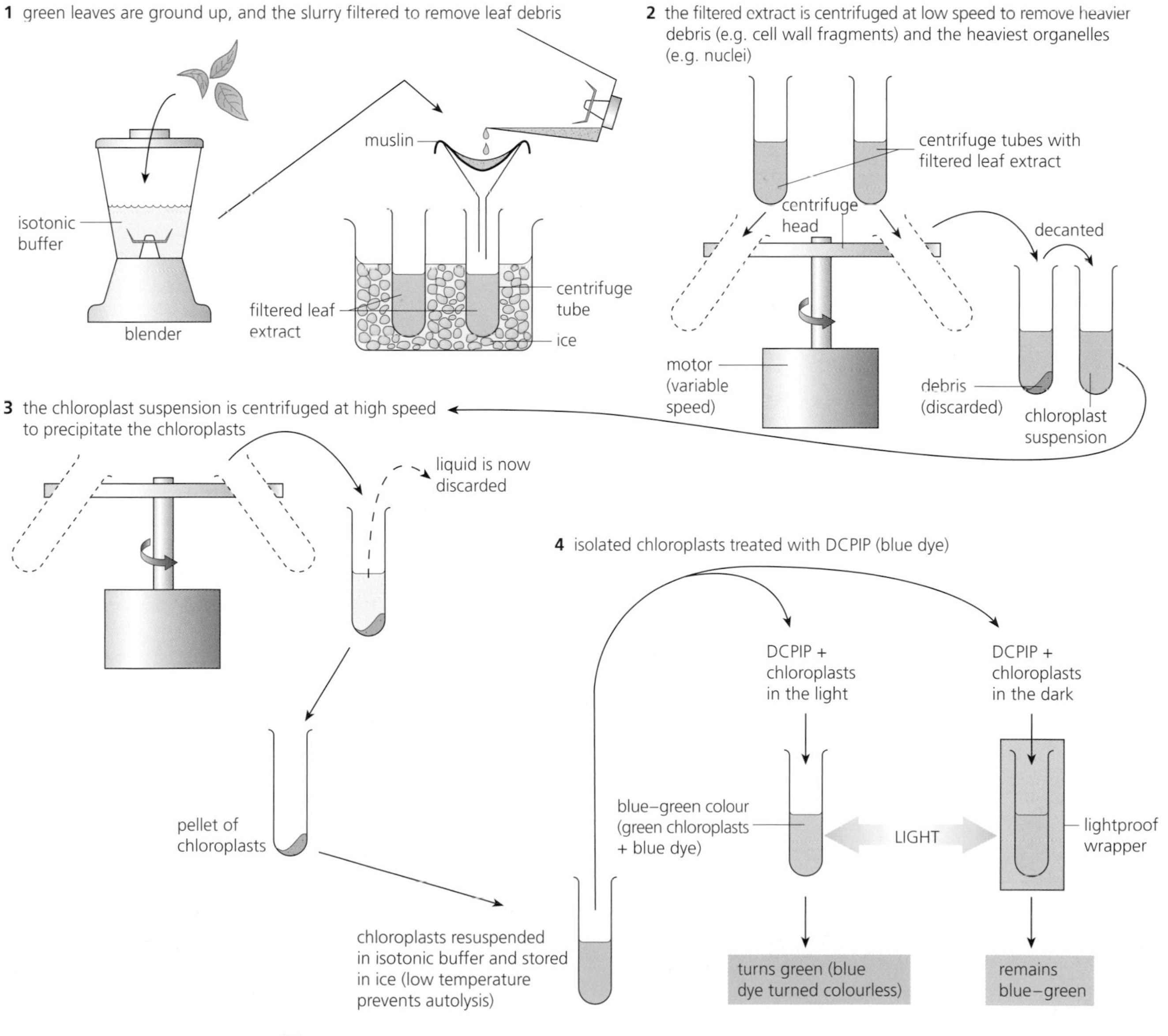

■ Extension: The light-dependent reactions and the source of oxygen

The explanation of the light-dependent reactions tells us that the oxygen given off in photosynthesis is derived exclusively from water (rather than carbon dioxide).

An experiment using water containing the isotope oxygen-18 confirmed this was correct. Illuminated suspensions of photosynthetic cells were provided with either carbon dioxide enriched with $C^{18}O_2$ or water enriched with $H_2^{18}O$. From both, the oxygen evolved was analysed to determine the oxygen-18 concentration, as shown in Figure 9.14.

Figure 9.14 Photolysis of water

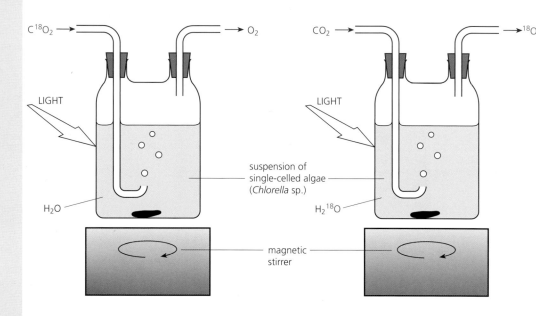

two identical cultures, one supplied with $C^{18}O_2$ and the other with $H_2^{18}O$

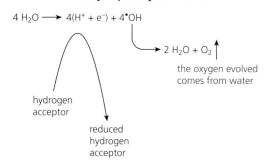

Pathway of photolysis of water

$$4\,H_2O \longrightarrow 4(H^+ + e^-) + 4\,{}^\bullet OH$$

hydrogen acceptor

reduced hydrogen acceptor

$2\,H_2O + O_2$

the oxygen evolved comes from water

Incidentally, this experiment established that the traditional balanced equation for photosynthesis

$$6CO_2 + 6H_2O + \text{LIGHT ENERGY} \rightarrow C_6H_{12}O_6 + 6O_2$$

is incorrect because it implies that some or all of the oxygen evolved comes from carbon dioxide. This is because it shows 12 oxygen atoms are produced, but the six water molecules on the left-hand side of the equation contain only six.

The summary equation for photosynthesis is **less misleading** when written as:

$$6CO_2 + 12H_2O + \text{LIGHT ENERGY} \rightarrow C_6H_{12}O_6 + 6O_2 + 6H_2O$$

The light-independent reactions

In the light-independent reactions, carbon dioxide is converted to carbohydrate. These reactions occur in the **stroma** of the chloroplasts, surrounding the grana.

How is this brought about?

The pathway by which carbon dioxide is reduced to glucose was investigated by a method we now call **feeding experiments**. In these particular experiments, radioactively labelled carbon dioxide was fed to cells. $^{14}CO_2$ is taken up by the cells in exactly the same way as non-labelled carbon dioxide is, and is then fixed into the same products of photosynthesis.

Figure 9.15 Investigation of the light-independent reactions of photosynthesis

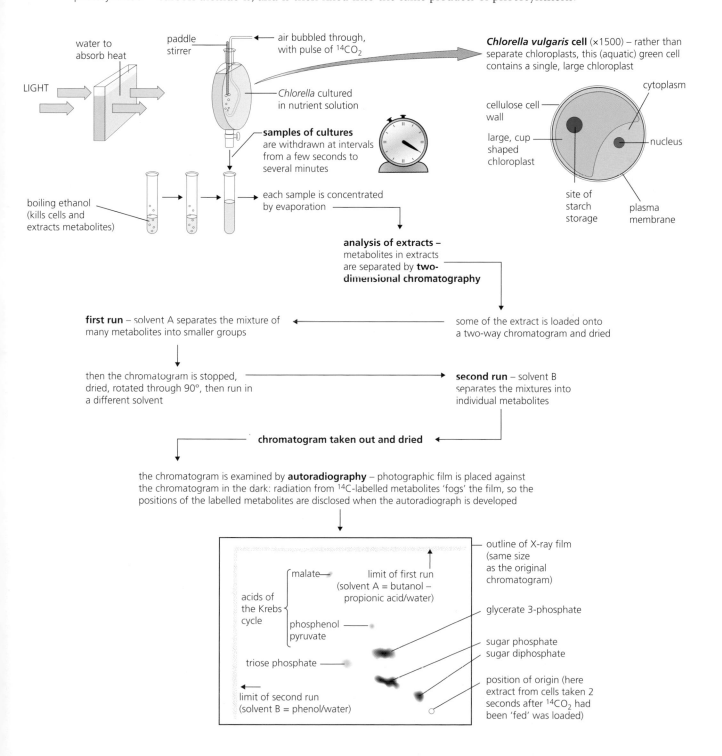

So, a brief pulse of labelled $^{14}CO_2$ was introduced into the otherwise continuous supply of $^{12}CO_2$ to photosynthesising cells in the light, and its progress monitored. Samples of the photosynthesising cells, taken at frequent intervals after the $^{14}CO_2$ had been fed, contained a sequence of radioactively labelled intermediates, and (later) products, of the photosynthetic pathway. These compounds were isolated by **chromatography** from the sampled cells and identified (Figure 9.15).

The experimenters chose for their photosynthesising cells a culture of *Chlorella*, a unicellular alga. They used these in place of mesophyll cells (page 296), since they have identical photosynthesis, but allowed much easier sampling.

The whole technique was pioneered by a team at the University of California, led by Melvin Calvin in the middle of the last century. He was awarded a Nobel Prize in 1961. The chromatography technique that the team exploited was then a relatively recent invention, and radioactive isotopes were only just becoming available for biochemical investigations.

10 Calvin used a suspension of aquatic, unicellular algal cells in his 'lollipop flask' (Figure 9.15) to investigate the fixation of carbon dioxide in photosynthesis. **Suggest** what advantages were obtained by this choice, compared to the use of cells of intact green leaves.

Figure 9.16 The path of carbon in photosynthesis

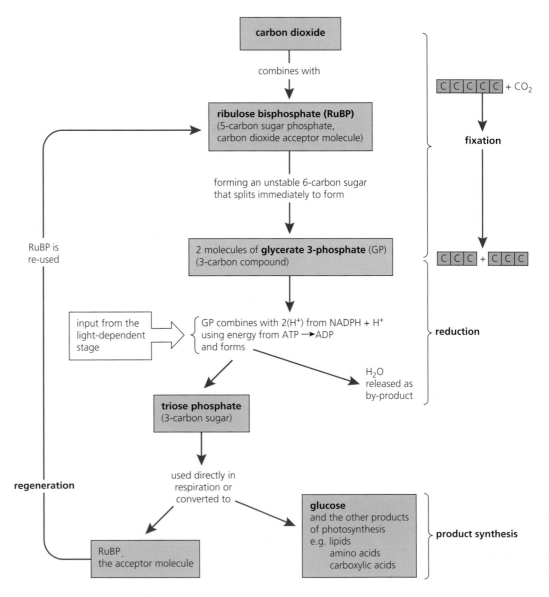

The steps of the light-independent reactions

The experiments of Calvin's team established the details of the path of **carbon from carbon dioxide to glucose** and other products (Figures 9.16 to 9.19). They showed that:

- The first product of the fixation of carbon dioxide is **glycerate 3-phosphate (GP)**. This is known as the **fixation step**.
- This initial product is immediately reduced to the 3-carbon sugar phosphate, **triose phosphate**, using **NADPH + H⁺** and **ATP**. This is the **reduction step**.
- Then the triose phosphate is further metabolised to produce **carbohydrates** such as **sugars**, **sugar phosphates** and **starch**, and later **lipids**, amino acids such as **alanine**, and organic acids such as **malate**. This is the **product synthesis step**.
- Some of the triose phosphate is metabolised to produce the molecule that first reacts with carbon dioxide (the acceptor molecule). This is the **regeneration of acceptor step**. The reactions of this regeneration process are today known as the **Calvin cycle** (Figure 9.18).

This done, a big problem remained.

Which intermediate is the actual acceptor molecule?

At first, a 2-carbon acceptor molecule for carbon dioxide was sought, simply because the first product of carbon dioxide fixation was known to be a 3-carbon compound. None was found.

Eventually the acceptor molecule proved to be a 5-carbon acceptor (**ribulose bisphosphate**). When carbon dioxide has combined, the 6-carbon product immediately split into two 3-carbon GP molecules – hence the initial confusion.

The enzyme involved is called **ribulose bisphosphate carboxylase** (commonly shortened to **Rubisco**). Rubisco is by far the most common protein of green plant leaves, as you would expect.

Figure 9.17 Summary of the light-independent reactions

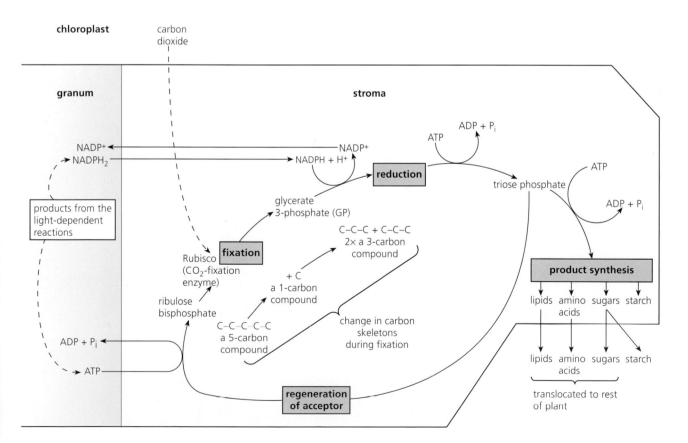

Figure 9.18
Regeneration of ribulose
bisphosphate – Calvin
cycle

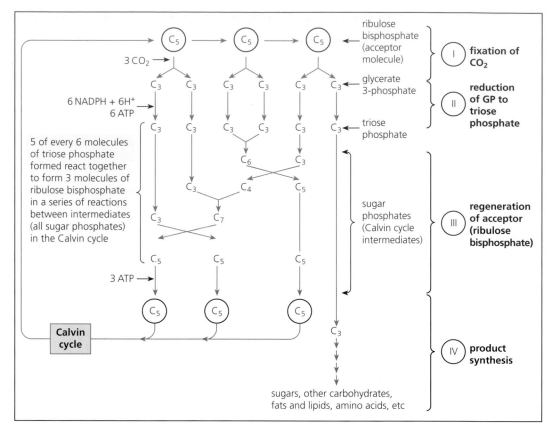

Figure 9.19 The product
synthesis steps of
photosynthesis

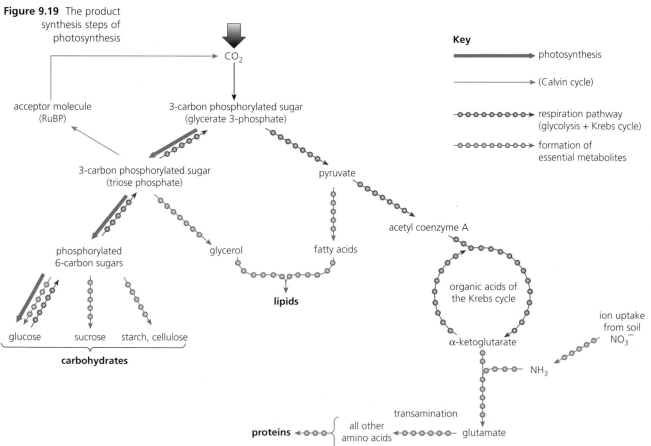

Chloroplast, grana and stroma – the venue for photosynthesis

We have seen that the grana are the site of the light-dependent reactions and the stroma the site of the light-independent reactions of photosynthesis. Table 9.4 identifies how the structure of the chloroplast facilitates function.

Structure of chloroplast	Function / role
double membrane bounding the chloroplast	contains the grana and stroma, and is permeable to CO_2, O_2, ATP, sugars and other products of photosynthesis
photosystems with chlorophyll pigments arranged on thylakoid membranes of grana	provide huge surface area for maximum light absorption
thylakoid spaces within grana	restricted regions for accumulation of protons and establishment of the gradient
fluid stroma with loosely arranged thylakoid membranes	site of all the enzymes of fixation, reduction and regeneration of acceptor steps of light-independent reactions, and many enzymes of the product synthesis steps

Table 9.4 Structure and function in chloroplasts

11 **Distinguish** between the following:

 a light-dependent reactions and light-independent reactions
 b photolysis and photophosphorylation.

12 **Deduce** the significant difference between the starting materials and the end-products of photosynthesis.

Light and photosynthesis

8.2.7–8.2.8

Visible light represents a small part of the spectrum of electromagnetic radiation reaching the Earth from the Sun (Figure 3.8, page 83). We have seen that the photosynthetic pigments that constitute chlorophyll absorb the various wavelengths of visible light to varying extents. The technique of chromatography has shown that chlorophyll present in green plants is a mixture of four pigments: chlorophyll α and β, and two carotenoids, carotene and xanthophylls. A **colorimeter** is the apparatus we use to find out the absorption spectrum of chlorophyll once this has been extracted from leaves (Figure 3.10, page 85).

The action spectrum for photosynthesis

Clearly, chlorophyll absorbs most strongly in the blue and red parts of the spectrum. But which wavelengths present in white light are most effective in bringing about the light-dependent reactions of photosynthesis?

The **action spectrum** for photosynthesis may be obtained most simply by using a photosynthometer, as illustrated in Figure 3.14, page 89. This apparatus allows estimation of the efficiency of photosynthesis in an aquatic plant such as *Elodea*. Here, the volume of oxygen produced in unit time is measured under particular conditions – for example, at different wavelengths. A light source that projects different wavelengths in turn is required. The amount of oxygen produced consistently at each wavelength is measured, and the table of results indicates the more effective wavelengths.

More accurate data may be obtained when oxygen evolution from a suspension of algal cells or from isolated chloroplasts is measured, using an **oxygen electrode**. The oxygen electrode is an especially accurate instrument for measuring the concentration (partial pressure) of oxygen present in solution. The suspension is constantly stirred, and so changes in oxygen production – for example, as light intensity or carbon dioxide concentration is varied – are detected.

13 **Discuss** the likely limitations of using a simple photosynthometer (Figure 3.14, page 89) to obtain an action spectrum of photosynthesis.

The **absorption spectrum** for chlorophyll pigments and the action spectrum for photosynthesis show that the wavelengths of light absorbed by chlorophyll pigments, namely the red and blue light, are very similar to the wavelengths that cause photosynthesis. The absorption and action spectra match quite well. So the wavelengths optimally absorbed are the ones that provide most energy for photosynthesis; both blue and red light are used by green plants as the energy source for photosynthesis (Figure 9.20).

Figure 9.20 Absorption and action spectra compared

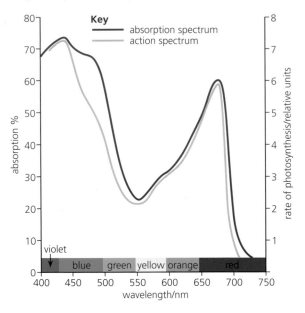

14 Distinguish between the following:

a chlorophyll and chloroplast
b stroma and grana
c absorption spectrum and action spectrum.

Incidentally there is one part of the two curves where they diverge somewhat – in the upper wavelengths of blue light. Light absorption at this point is largely by particular photosynthetic pigments (carotenes) and is not fully used in photosynthesis. Carotenes are ancillary pigments – meaning they are pigments that do not directly contribute light energy to a reaction centre, but rather pass the energy to the other photosynthetic pigments first. This energy transfer between pigments is clearly not 100% efficient.

Light as a limiting factor in photosynthesis

By definition, light is an essential for photosynthesis. Green plant cells in the dark are unable to photosynthesise at all; under this condition, cells of the plant take in oxygen from the atmosphere for aerobic cell respiration.

As light starts to reach green cells, at dawn for example, photosynthesis starts, and some oxygen is produced. Oxygen consumption in respiration continues, of course. Eventually the light intensity increases to the point where photosynthetic oxygen production is equal to oxygen consumption in respiration. Now the leaf is neither an oxygen importer nor exporter.

This point is known as the **compensation point** (Figure 9.21). Then, as the Sun rises higher in the sky and the light intensity increases further, the rate of photosynthesis also increases; the leaf becomes a net exporter of oxygen.

We have already noted the general effect of increasing light intensity on the rate of photosynthesis (Figure 3.16, page 90).

At low light intensities the rate of photosynthesis increases linearly with increasing light. Here the low light intensity (lack of sufficient light) is limiting the rate of photosynthesis. Light is a factor limiting the rate of photosynthesis under these conditions.

However, as light intensity is raised further, a point is reached where increasing light intensity produces no further effect on the rate of photosynthesis. Here, some factor other than light is limiting photosynthesis. What may now be rate-limiting?

The limiting factor at this point is disclosed when the investigation is repeated at higher carbon dioxide concentration (Figure 9.22). *Look at this graph now; follow the annotations.*

Figure 9.21 Light intensity and the compensation point

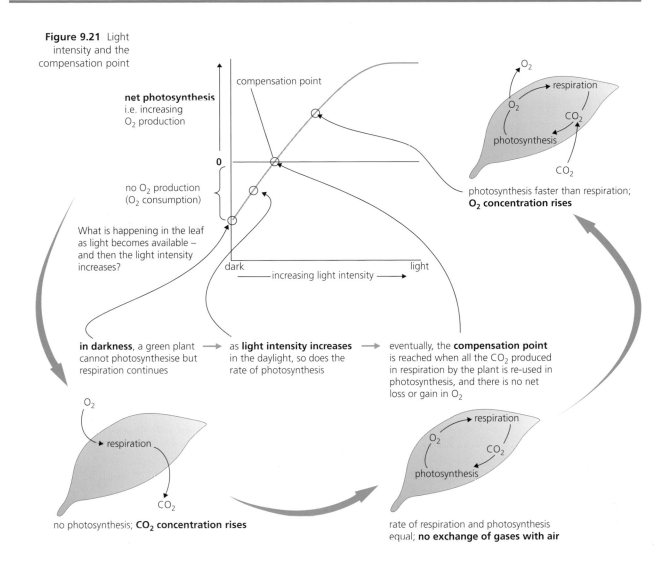

net photosynthesis
i.e. increasing
O_2 production

compensation point

0

no O_2 production
(O_2 consumption)

What is happening in the leaf as light becomes available – and then the light intensity increases?

dark ⟶ increasing light intensity ⟶ light

in darkness, a green plant cannot photosynthesise but respiration continues

as **light intensity increases** in the daylight, so does the rate of photosynthesis

eventually, the **compensation point** is reached when all the CO_2 produced in respiration by the plant is re-used in photosynthesis, and there is no net loss or gain in O_2

O_2
respiration
CO_2

no photosynthesis; **CO₂ concentration rises**

O_2
respiration
CO_2
photosynthesis

rate of respiration and photosynthesis equal; **no exchange of gases with air**

O_2
respiration
O_2
CO_2
photosynthesis
CO_2

photosynthesis faster than respiration; **O₂ concentration rises**

Figure 9.22 The effect of light intensity on the rate of photosynthesis

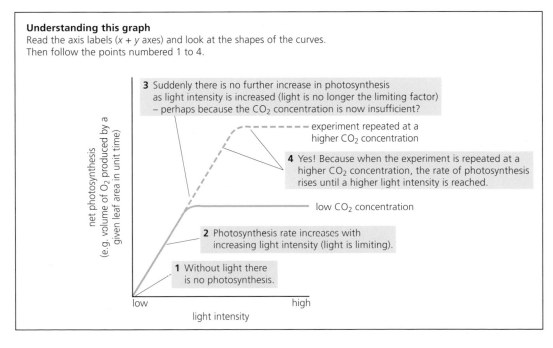

Understanding this graph
Read the axis labels (*x* + *y* axes) and look at the shapes of the curves.
Then follow the points numbered 1 to 4.

3 Suddenly there is no further increase in photosynthesis as light intensity is increased (light is no longer the limiting factor) – perhaps because the CO_2 concentration is now insufficient?

experiment repeated at a higher CO_2 concentration

4 Yes! Because when the experiment is repeated at a higher CO_2 concentration, the rate of photosynthesis rises until a higher light intensity is reached.

low CO_2 concentration

net photosynthesis
(e.g. volume of O_2 produced by a given leaf area in unit time)

2 Photosynthesis rate increases with increasing light intensity (light is limiting).

1 Without light there is no photosynthesis.

low   high
light intensity

The results of these earlier, physiological investigations fit well with our current understanding. Photosynthesis is a biochemical process involving a series of interconnected reactions. All these reactions contribute to the overall rate; photosynthesis depends on several essential conditions being favourable. At any one time, the rate of photosynthesis will be limited by the slowest of these reactions – the overall rate will be limited by the factor that is in shortest supply. This factor, which ever one it is, is known as the **limiting factor**. Clearly, a limited supply of either light (Figure 9.22) or carbon dioxide (Figure 9.23) could limit the rate of photosynthesis, since both of these are essential. Clearly, both light intensity and carbon dioxide concentration can be limiting factors in photosynthesis.

Figure 9.23 The effect of carbon dioxide concentration on photosynthesis

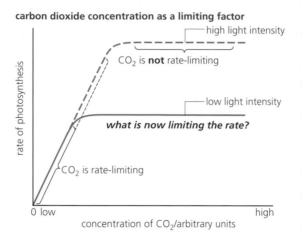

Carbon dioxide-limiting conditions and cyclic photophosphorylation

When the carbon dioxide concentration becomes the limiting factor, we know that the light-independent reactions may be slowed relative to the light-dependent reactions.

An outcome is that NADPH accumulates in the stroma and the concentration of $NADP^+$ reduces. Then, without an adequate supply of oxidised H-acceptor ($NADP^+$), photosystems II and I are unable to operate together, as they do in non-cyclic photophosphorylation (Figure 9.12, page 280). Now it has been found that another type of ATP formation occurs under these conditions, called **cyclic photophosphorylation** (Figure 9.24).

Figure 9.24 Cyclic photophosphorylation

Cyclic photophosphorylation occurs when the CO_2 concentration is the limiting factor (and with relatively high light intensity), so that the light-independent reactions are slowed relative to the light-dependent reactions. **NADPH accumulates in the stroma.**

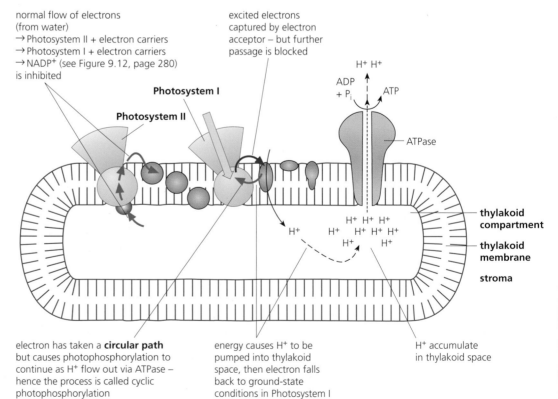

In cyclic photophosphorylation, excited electrons from the reaction centre in photosystem I fall back to their point of origin. They do this via electron carriers that transfer energy from those electrons and pump H⁺ into the thylakoid space. ATP synthesis by chemiosmosis follows. The Z-diagram illustrates this (Figure 9.25).

This type of photophosphorylation is called cyclic because the electrons have returned to the photosystem from which they originated (a cyclic path, rather than a linear one).

Figure 9.25 A comparison of cyclic- and non-cyclic photophosphorylation (the so-called Z diagram)

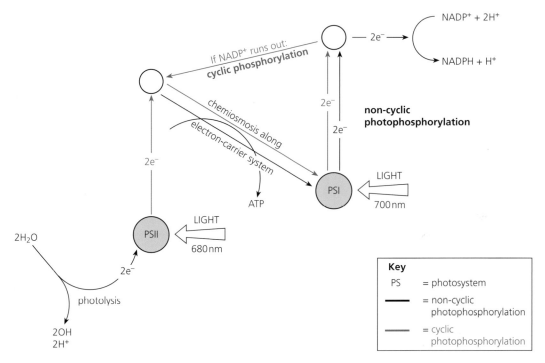

15 In cyclic photophosphorylation, **predict** which of the following occur:

photoactivation of photosystem I
reduction of NADP⁺
production of ATP.

The effect of changing temperature on the rate of photosynthesis

The effect of temperature on the rate of photosynthesis, under controlled laboratory conditions, is shown in Figure 9.26. It can be seen that the effect of increasing temperature, say from about 15 °C to 25 °C, actually depends on the light intensity.

Under low light intensities, a rise in temperature has less effect than it does under higher intensities. Of course, at very much higher temperatures, the rate of all metabolic reactions falls away since all cell enzymes are denatured by excess heat energy (page 55).

The graph in Figure 9.26 has been interpreted as showing that photosynthesis is made up of the two sequential sets of reactions we have been studying: light-dependent reactions (which, like all photochemical events, are largely temperature indifferent) and light-independent reactions (which, like all biochemical steps catalysed by enzymes, are temperature sensitive).

Can you see why?

The arguments are as follows:

- If photosynthesis includes **photochemical reactions** – temperature-insensitive changes brought about by light energy – then under conditions of low light intensity (when these photochemical reactions are rate limiting), a rise in temperature should have little effect. This is what happens (Figure 9.26, curve B).
- If photosynthesis also includes **enzymic reactions** – temperature-sensitive changes involving enzymes – then under conditions of high light intensity (when enzymic reactions are rate limiting), a rise in temperature should have a significant effect. It should increase the rate of photosynthesis. This, too, is what happens (Figure 9.26, curve A).

Figure 9.26 The effect of temperature on the rate of photosynthesis

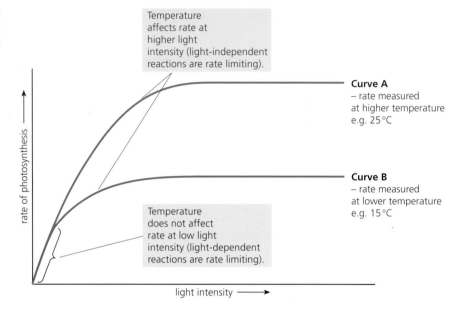

This reasoning provided the first evidence that photosynthesis is made up of two sequential sets of reactions:

- **light-dependent reactions** – photochemical steps largely unaffected by temperature;
- **light-independent reactions** – biochemical reactions catalysed by enzymes and therefore temperature sensitive. Here a 10 °C rise in temperature has the effect of doubling the rate of reaction.

In fact, this understanding of the nature of photosynthesis was deduced from the above experimental evidence before it was confirmed by biochemical techniques, using chloroplasts isolated from the leaf.

■ *Examination questions – a selection*

Questions 1–5 are taken from past IB Diploma biology papers.

Q1 What is acetyl (ethanoyl) CoA?

I   an intermediate in carbohydrate metabolism under aerobic conditions

II   a product of the oxidation of fatty acids in lipid metabolism

III   an intermediate in carbohydrate metabolism under anaerobic conditions

  A I and II only   **C** II and III only
  B I and III only   **D** I, II and III

              Higher Level Paper 1, May 03, Q15

Q2 Which of the following is produced during glycolysis?

  A NADH   **C** glucose
  B CO_2 **D** glycogen

              Higher Level Paper 1, May 05, Q26

Q3 Isocitrate dehydrogenase is an enzyme of the Krebs cycle. Its activity in the presence and absence of ADP is shown below.

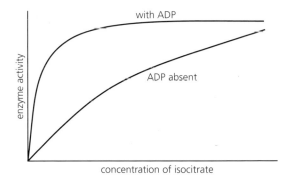

concentration of isocitrate

What effect will a high level of energy consumption have on the activity of this enzyme?

  A The activity will increase.
  B The activity will decrease.
  C The enzyme will maintain a constant activity.
  D The activity will fluctuate up and down.

              Higher Level Paper 1, May 04, Q27

Q4 At which stage of photosynthesis is light involved most directly?

  A reduction of $NADP^+$ to $NADPH_2$
  B chemiosmosis
  C the synthesis of chlorophyll
  D the photoactivation of chlorophyll

              Higher Level Paper 1, May 06, Q29

Q5 Which of the following statements about pyruvate is true?

  A It contains less energy than glucose per molecule.
  B Every molecule of glucose is converted to one molecule of pyruvate.
  C Pyruvate is produced in the mitochondria.
  D Under aerobic conditions, pyruvate is converted to lactate.

              Higher Level Paper 1, May 06, Q28

Questions 6–10 cover other syllabus issues in this chapter.

Q6 Although oxidation may be illustrated by reference to the addition of oxygen to a substance, oxidation is defined precisely as 'loss of electrons'. Explain this definition fully.   (4)

Q7 Chemiosmosis is a process by which the synthesis of ATP is coupled to electron transport via the movement of protons. Draw and annotate a diagram to show how the structure of the membranes of a mitochondrion (given the position of electron carriers and specific enzymes within it) allows a large proton gradient to be formed, and ATP synthesis to follow.   (8)

Q8 Draw a diagram of a chloroplast to show its structure as disclosed by electron micrography. Annotate this drawing to link function to structures where possible.   (6)

Q9 **a** Explain as concisely as you are able the distinctive nature of non-cyclic and cyclic photophosphorylation.   (6)

    b Describe the specific circumstances which cause cyclic photophosphorylation to occur.   (2)

Q10 **a** Explain the concept of limiting factors in photosynthesis, with reference to light intensity and the concentration of carbon dioxide.   (4)

    b Draw a fully annotated graph of net photosynthesis rate (*y* axis) against light intensity (*x* axis) at low and high concentrations of carbon dioxide.   (4)

10 Plant science

STARTING POINTS

- Green plants (**Plantae**) are **autotrophic** (self-feeding) organisms, manufacturing their own nutrients from simple, inorganic molecules.
- Green plants show wide diversity, including the mosses (**bryophytes**), the ferns (**filicinophytes**), the conifers (**coniferophytes**), and the flowering plants (**angiospermophytes**).
- **Photosynthesis** is the process by which green plants manufacture **carbohydrates** from carbon dioxide and water, using **energy from sunlight**; oxygen is the waste product. Photosynthesis occurs in specialised organelles called **chloroplasts**.
- Photosynthesis can be divided into two linked steps – the **light-dependent reactions** in the **grana** produce NADPH + H$^+$ and ATP, and the **light-independent reactions** in the **stroma** fix carbon dioxide to carbohydrate.
- Energy is transferred in cells by **aerobic cellular respiration**. ATP is the **universal energy currency** of cells. ATP is a reactant in energy-requiring reactions (e.g. protein synthesis) and processes (e.g. active transport mechanisms).
- Cells of organisms are surrounded by an aqueous solution, and **exchange of molecules** between cells and their environment occurs in solution across the plasma membrane (of **fluid mosaic** construction), either by **diffusion** (osmosis is a special case), or **active transport** (by protein pumps in the membrane), or by **bulk transport** (via the movements of vesicles, for example).
- In **sexual reproduction**, two sex cells (**gametes**) fuse (**fertilisation**) to form a **zygote**. The zygote develops into a new organism, similar but not identical to its parents. Gamete formation involves **meiosis** (a reduction nuclear division).

The green plants (**Plantae**) make up one of the five kingdoms of living things (Figure 6.43, page 176). The features that make the green plants distinctly different from other organisms are as follows.

- There is a wall around each cell, the chief component of which is **cellulose**. Cellulose is a polysaccharide, and is an extremely tough, protective material.
- Cell organelles called **chloroplasts** are the site of photosynthesis. By photosynthesis, the plant generates energy-rich nutrients from simple, inorganic substances (carbon dioxide, water and inorganic ions, such as nitrates and phosphates).

In the long history of life, green plants evolved about 500 million years ago, from aquatic, single-celled organisms called green algae (possibly very similar to *Chlorella*, Figure 9.15, page 283). The present-day diversity of green plants was introduced in Chapter 6, pages 137–77. Today, it is the angiospermophytes (flowering plants) that are the dominant terrestrial plants. The fossil record indicates they achieved this dominance early in their evolutionary history – about 100 million years ago.

In this chapter, **flowering plant structure** and **growth**, **internal transport mechanisms**, and **reproduction** are discussed.

Plant structure and growth

The flowering plants or angiospermophytes dominate plant life in almost every habitat across the world. Some are trees and shrubs with woody stems, but many are non-woody (herbaceous) plants. Whether woody or herbaceous, the plant consists of stem, leaves and root.

The **stem** supports the leaves in the sunlight, and transports organic materials (such as sugar and amino acids), ions and water between the roots and leaves. At the top of the stem is a **terminal bud** or terminal growing point, and in the axil of each leaf is an **axillary bud**. New cells are produced at these growing points.

A **leaf** consists of a leaf blade connected to the stem by a leaf stalk. The leaf is an organ specialised for photosynthesis.

The **root** anchors the plant and is the site of absorption of water and ions from the soil.

The structure of the sunflower, *Helianthus annus*, a herbaceous plant, illustrates these features (Figure 10.1).

Figure 10.1 The structure of the sunflower plant, *Helianthus annus*

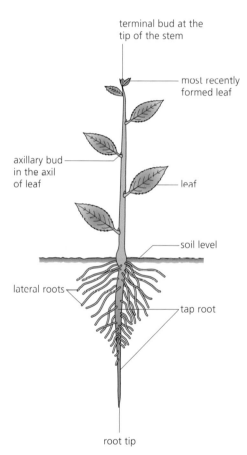

terminal bud at the tip of the stem

most recently formed leaf

axillary bud in the axil of leaf

leaf

soil level

lateral roots

tap root

root tip

The distribution of tissues in the stem of the sunflower

A **tissue map** (sometimes called a low-power diagram) is a drawing that records the relative positions of structures within an organ or organism, as seen in section; it does not show individual cells.

From the tissue map in Figure 10.2, it can be seen that the stem is an organ surrounded or contained by a layer called the **epidermis**, and that it contains **vascular** tissue (**xylem** for water transport and **phloem** for transport of organic solutes) in a discrete system of veins or **vascular bundles**. In the stem, the vascular bundles are arranged in a ring, positioned towards the outside of the stem, rather like the steel girders of a ferro-concrete building.

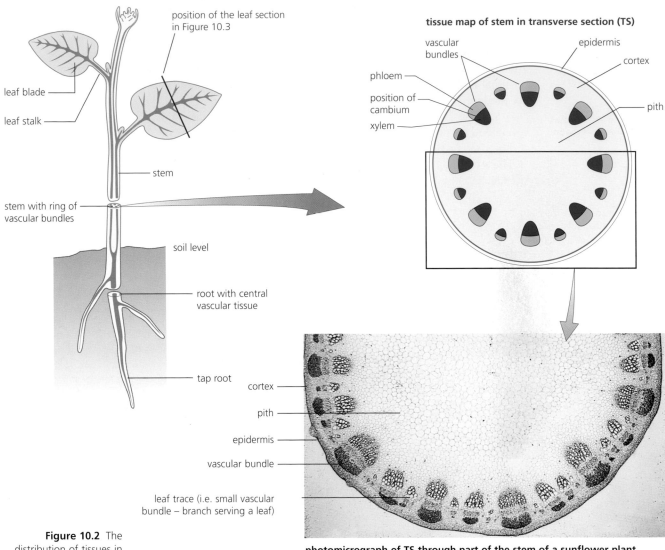

young sunflower plant showing positions of the sections shown below and in Figure 10.3

position of the leaf section in Figure 10.3

leaf blade

leaf stalk

stem

stem with ring of vascular bundles

soil level

root with central vascular tissue

tap root

tissue map of stem in transverse section (TS)

vascular bundles

epidermis

cortex

phloem

position of cambium

pith

xylem

cortex

pith

epidermis

vascular bundle

leaf trace (i.e. small vascular bundle – branch serving a leaf)

Figure 10.2 The distribution of tissues in the stem

photomicrograph of TS through part of the stem of a sunflower plant (*Helianthus*) (×20)

The distribution of tissues in the leaf

A tissue map showing the distribution of tissues in a leaf is shown in Figure 10.3. Like the stem, the leaf is contained by a single layer of cells, the **epidermis**, and also contains vascular tissue in a system of vascular bundles. The vascular bundles in leaves are often referred to as **veins**. The bulk of the leaf is taken up by a tissue called **mesophyll**, and the cells here are supported by veins arranged in a branching network.

Dicotyledonous and monocotyledonous plants

The flowering plants are divided into two groups with distinguishing structural features, and known as the **monocotyledons** and **dicotyledons**. The sunflower is a typical dicotyledonous plant (Figure 10.1) and the grasses are a major family of monocotyledonous plants (Figure 10.4). The defining difference between members of the two groups is the number of seed leaves (**cotyledons**) present in the embryo. (Cotyledons are structurally simpler leaves than the normal leaves of these plants that develop later.) The important common differences are identified in Table 10.1.

Figure 10.3 The distribution of tissues in a leaf

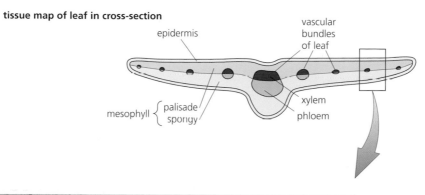

tissue map of leaf in cross-section

epidermis

vascular bundles of leaf

mesophyll { palisade / spongy }

xylem

phloem

photomicrograph of part of a leaf in cross-section (×180)

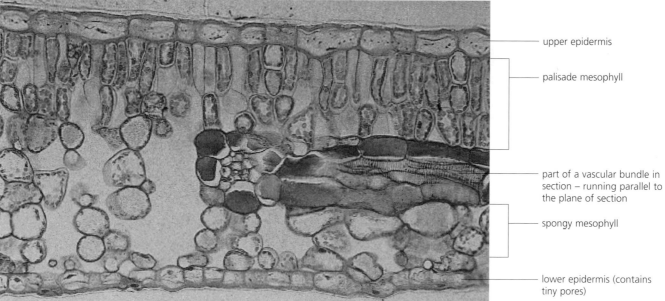

upper epidermis

palisade mesophyll

part of a vascular bundle in section – running parallel to the plane of section

spongy mesophyll

lower epidermis (contains tiny pores)

Figure 10.4 A plant of annual meadow grass (*Poa* sp.) showing monocotyledonous features

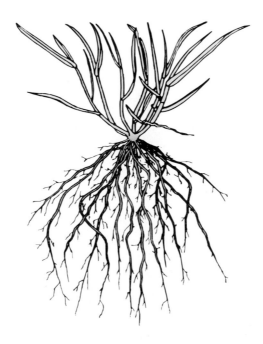

1 **Draw** and **label** a dicotyledonous plant and a monocotyledonous plant growing near your school or home, identifying their diagnostic features that can be observed with a simple microscope (hand lens).

Dicotyledons (e.g. sunflower)		Monocotyledons (e.g. meadow grass)
embryo in seed has two cotyledons	**cotyledons**	embryo in seed has one cotyledon
broad leaves with veins forming a network	**veins in leaves**	bayonet or strap-shaped leaves with parallel veins
vascular bundles of stem in a ring	**vascular bundles in stem**	vascular bundles of stem numerous and scattered
branched roots	**root growth**	unbranched roots
parts of the flowers (sepals, petals, etc.) in fours or fives	**flower parts (floral organs)**	parts of the flowers (sepals, petals, etc.) in threes.

Table 10.1
Monocotyledons and dicotyledons – the differences

Leaf structure and function

Leaves are the organs specialised for **photosynthesis**, in which light energy is used to build sugar from carbon dioxide obtained from the air, and water obtained from the soil.

The leaf is a thin structure with a large surface area in which **mesophyll cells** are spread out over a wide area, so maximising the amount of light absorbed. The mesophyll cells in the upper layer are called palisade cells. They are packed with **chloroplasts** – the organelles in which photosynthesis occurs.

The **epidermis** is a tough, transparent layer with an external waxy **cuticle**. The cuticle is impervious and effectively reduces water vapour loss from the leaf surface. (As a leaf warms in the light it is inevitably vulnerable to loss of water vapour by evaporation.) The epidermis has many **stomata** (singular, **stoma**), mainly in the lower surface. These are tiny pores that occur between specialised epidermal cells called **guard cells**. They are the sites of inward diffusion of carbon dioxide. Within the leaf's mesophyll tissue are continuous **air spaces** that enhance diffusion of carbon dioxide to the cells.

Between the mesophyll cells lies a complete **network of vascular bundles** which is so extensive that no mesophyll cell is more than a few cells away from a bundle. This is important because it is **xylem** in the vascular bundles that delivers water from the root system, and **phloem** that transports sugars, formed in the light, to sites of use and storage in the rest of the plant.

Another role of this network is mechanical **support**. Mesophyll tissue (rarely more than 10–15 cells thick) is supported by the turgidity of all its cells, contained within the non-elastic epidermis, and reinforced by the network of bundles. Leaves are relatively delicate structures, yet have to withstand destructive forces such as wind and rain, at times.

These features are illustrated in Figure 10.5, and summarised in Table 10.2.

2 **Outline** the properties of cellulose that make it an ideal material for plant cell walls.

Feature / structure	Role/function
thin structure of large surface area	maximises light absorption by chloroplasts in the (upper) palisade mesophyll cells
tough, transparent epidermis with waxy cuticle	contains and protects delicate mesophyll cells, particularly from excessive water loss
stomata	site of inward diffusion of carbon dioxide
continuous air spaces between mesophyll cells	pathway of diffusion between external air and surface of mesophyll cells
network of vascular bundles	supports leaf tissue and enables xylem and phloem to service mesophyll cells closely
xylem of vascular bundles	delivers water to leaf cells
phloem of vascular bundles	transports products of photosynthesis to rest of plant

Table 10.2 Functional adaptations of green leaves

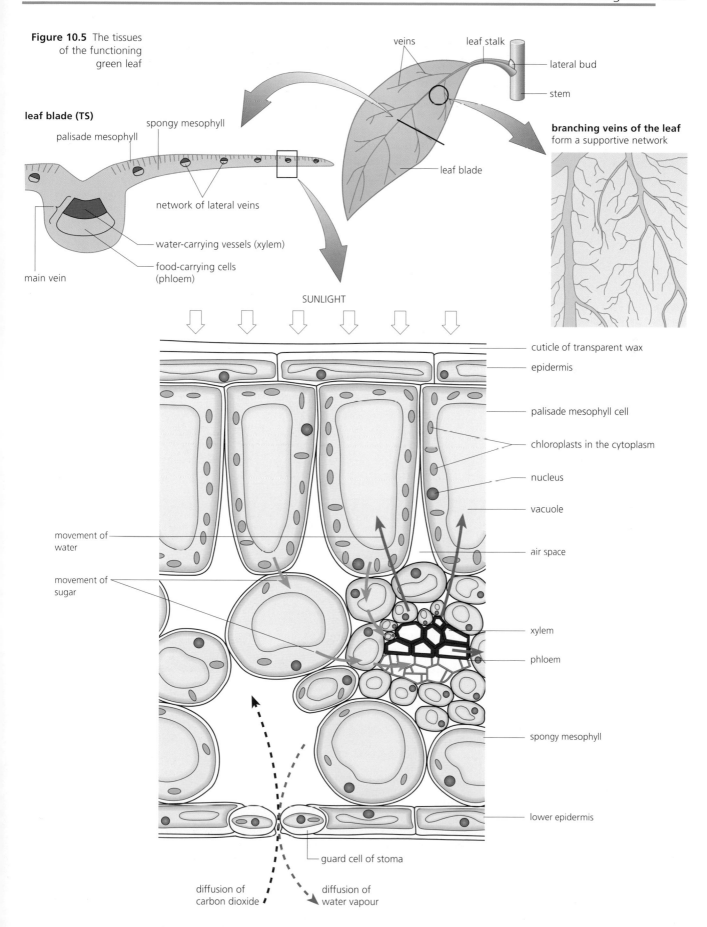

Figure 10.5 The tissues of the functioning green leaf

leaf blade (TS)

palisade mesophyll

spongy mesophyll

network of lateral veins

water-carrying vessels (xylem)

food-carrying cells (phloem)

main vein

veins

leaf stalk

lateral bud

stem

leaf blade

branching veins of the leaf form a supportive network

SUNLIGHT

cuticle of transparent wax

epidermis

palisade mesophyll cell

chloroplasts in the cytoplasm

nucleus

vacuole

air space

movement of water

movement of sugar

xylem

phloem

spongy mesophyll

lower epidermis

guard cell of stoma

diffusion of carbon dioxide

diffusion of water vapour

Plant structures can be modified for different functions

We have seen that flowering plant organs (stem, leaf and root) have clearly defined roles in the functioning of a plant such as the sunflower. These same organs have evolved other (or additional), specialised functions in some plants, in particular circumstances.

For example, leaves, stems and roots have become modified for **storage of food reserves** by plants surviving an unfavourable season for growth (Figure 10.6). In bulbs such as the onion plant, it is leaves (or **leaf bases**, actually) that are the site of food reserves on which subsequent growth is initially supported. Similarly, **underground stems** can be the site of storage of food reserves (e.g. the potato), as indeed may be the **main root** (e.g. the carrot).

Not all flowering plants support themselves upright, as free-standing organisms. The habit of creeping growth (on walls and fences), or climbing (particularly over other, taller plants), is often observed. With this growth habit, materials normally invested in supporting the plant body can be used alternatively – for example, in extensive leaf growth – to obvious advantage. Climbing plants frequently form **tendrils** by which they secure their positions. Tendrils are typically forms of modified stems or leaves (Figure 10.7).

Figure 10.6 Plant organs modified for food storage

Plant organ	Example
stem	e.g. stem tuber of potato 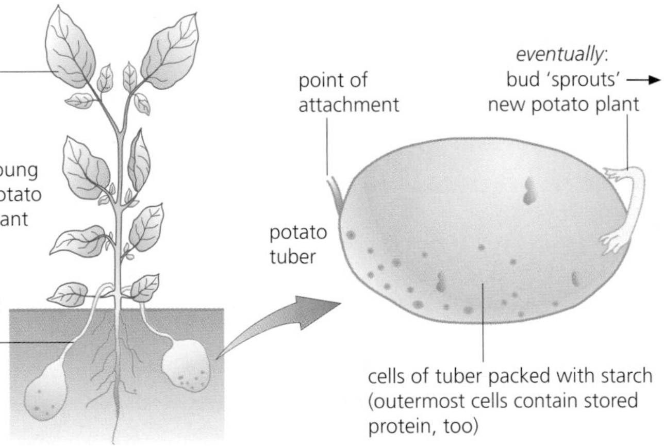
root	e.g. carrot, a modified main (tap) root 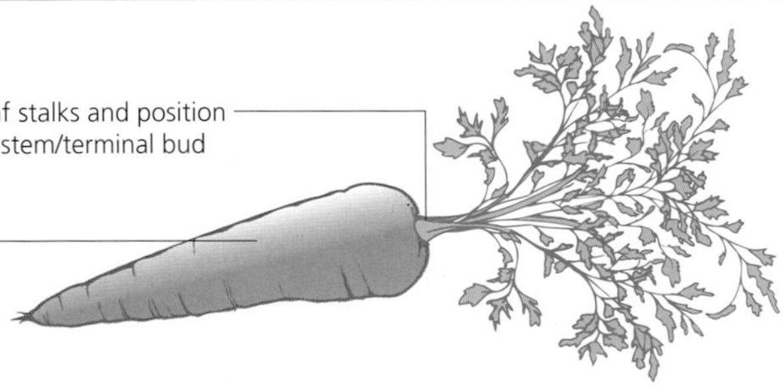
leaf	e.g. bulb of onion 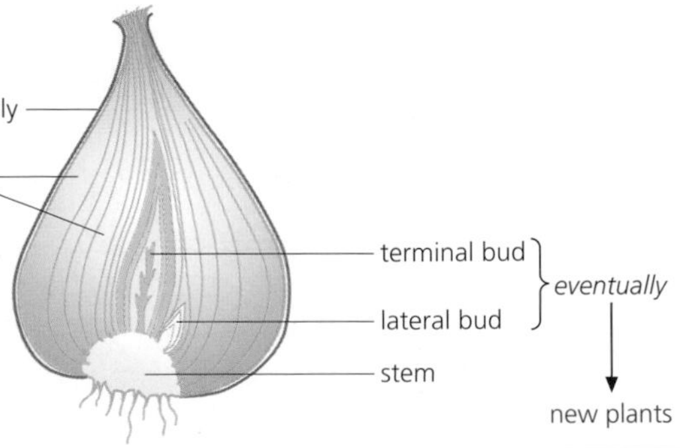

Figure 10.7 Tendrils of climbing plants

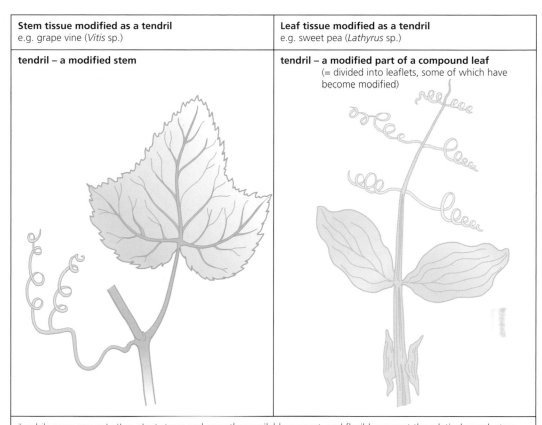

Stem tissue modified as a tendril e.g. grape vine (*Vitis* sp.)	Leaf tissue modified as a tendril e.g. sweet pea (*Lathyrus* sp.)
tendril – a modified stem	**tendril – a modified part of a compound leaf** (= divided into leaflets, some of which have become modified)

Tendrils grow around other plant stems and any other available support, and flexibly support the relatively weak stem and leaves of the climbing plant in a favourable position.

Plant growth – the role of meristems in dicotyledonous plants

Cells of a plant that are capable of dividing repeatedly are described as **meristematic** cells. A meristem is a group of cells that retain the ability to divide by mitosis. Once a plant has grown past the early embryo stage (an embryonic plant is present in the seed), subsequent growth of the plant occurs by cell division at the meristems (Table 10.3). In Figure 10.8, two types of meristem are identified, namely **apical meristems** and **lateral meristems**, and the growth they are responsible for is illustrated.

Apical meristems occur at the tips of the stem and root and are responsible for primary growth. This leads to an increase in the length of stem and root. First, the new cells formed by **division** rapidly increase in size. Then, this cell **enlargement** phase is followed by cell **differentiation** as the new, enlarging cells become specialised. For example, new cells of the ground tissue (Figure 10.16), contained within the external layer of cells known as the epidermis, form. So do cells of the vascular tissue. These contain water-carrying cells (xylem) and elaborated-food-carrying cells (phloem), and these are assembled as extensions to the existing vascular bundles. These are the primary tissues that make up stems (and roots), and so apical meristems are also called **primary meristems**. Between phloem and xylem of the bundles, a few meristematic cells remain after primary growth, and these form a meristematic tissue called **cambium**.

Lateral meristems form from the cambium cells in the centre of vascular bundles, between the outer phloem tissue and the inner xylem tissue. When the lateral meristem forms and grows, it causes the secondary growth of the plant. Secondary growth involves additions of vascular tissue (secondary phloem and secondary xylem), and results in an increase in the girth of the stem. The first stage in secondary growth occurs when the cambium in the vascular bundles grows into a complete cylinder around the stem. Growth of the lateral meristem increases the circumference of the stem, and also increases the strength of the stem.

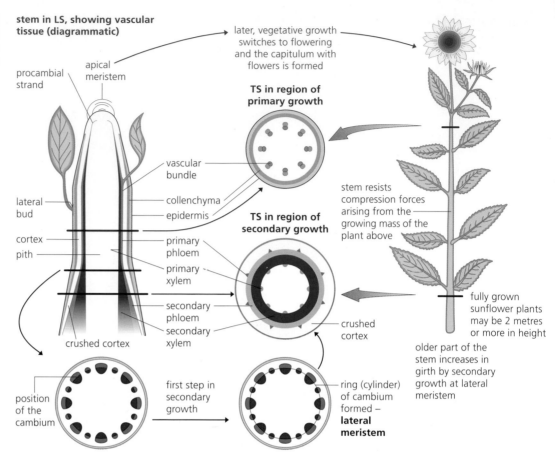

Figure 10.8 The roles of apical and lateral meristems in the growth of stems

Growth due to apical meristem		Growth due to lateral meristem
occurs at tip of stems and roots	**position of meristem**	occurs laterally, between primary phloem and primary xylem
product of embryonic cells	**origin**	cambium – meristematic cells left over from primary growth
produces initial tissues of actively growing plant from the outset	**timing of activity**	functions in older stems (and roots), and in woody plants from the outset
forms epidermis, ground tissues, and primary phloem and xylem	**cell products**	forms mainly secondary phloem and xylem (and often fibres)
produces growth in length and height of plant	**outcome for stem**	produces growth in girth of stem, plus strengthening of stem

Table 10.3 Growth due to apical and lateral meristems compared

The control of plant growth

Among the internal factors that play a part in control of plant growth and sensitivity are substances known as plant growth hormones or, better, as **plant growth substances**. In learning about these substances, bear the following points in mind:

- there are five major types of compound, naturally occurring in plants, that we classify as plant growth substances, one of which is known as **auxin**;
- these substances tend to interact with each other in the control of growth, rather than working in isolation;
- plant growth substances occur in low concentrations in plant tissues, making their extraction and investigation quite challenging.

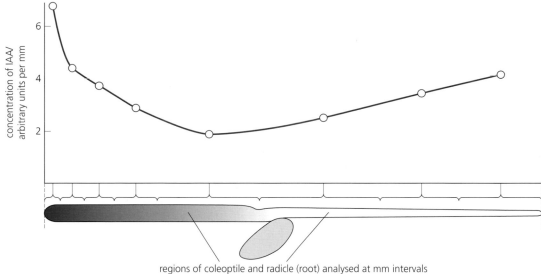

Figure 10.9 Distribution of auxin (IAA) in a young, growing plant

regions of coleoptile and radicle (root) analysed at mm intervals

Auxin is manufactured by cells undergoing repeated cell division, such as those found at the stem and root tips. Consequently, the concentration of auxin is highest there (Figure 10.9). Auxin is then transported to the region of growth behind the tip where it causes cells to elongate. In the process, the auxin is used up and inactivated.

Plant stems and light

The response of green plants to light is **complex** and very interesting.

In the **dark**, plant stems grow thin and weak, and they bear tiny, undeveloped leaves, yellow in colour. The shoots of plants in the dark are said to be etiolated. You can demonstrate this by covering growing plants to exclude the light from them completely for a while. By contrast, shoots grown in **full light** are short, with sturdy stems. The leaves are fully expanded and dark green in colour.

We already know that sunlight is essential for photosynthesis, to sustain plant nutrition. But we cannot also say that light is essential for plant growth in length. Quite the contrary in fact – light inhibits plant stem growth – but light *is* essential for chlorophyll formation and leaf expansion.

The shoots grown in unilateral light confirm this. (Unilateral light is a beam of light coming from one direction.) Here, the stems grow towards the light.

We explain this on the basis that growth on the illuminated side of the stem is inhibited by light, but stem growth is unchecked on the dark side, so a growth curvature results. This confirms that light does inhibit plant stem growth in length.

To investigate this response, we can mark a growing stem at regular intervals, using a felt-tip marker pen. Some of the marked stems are then exposed to unilateral light and others to normal illumination. This reveals that the region where elongation of the stem occurs is also the region of growth curvature in unilateral light. So we conclude that the response of the plant stem to unilateral light is a **growth response**.

Growth movements of plant organs in response to an external stimulus in which the direction of the stimulus determines the direction of the response are called **tropic movements** or tropisms. For example, when the stem tip responds by growing towards the light, it is said to be **positively phototropic**.

3 **Construct** a list of the various effects of light on plant growth and development.

Figure 10.10 The coleoptile as an experimental organ

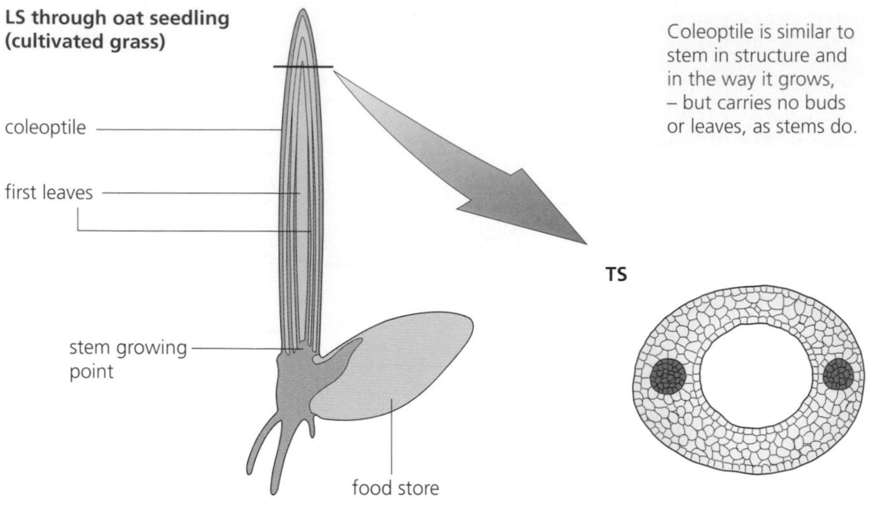

LS through oat seedling (cultivated grass)

Coleoptile is similar to stem in structure and in the way it grows, – but carries no buds or leaves, as stems do.

coleoptile

first leaves

stem growing point

food store

TS

Figure 10.11 Auxin and positive phototropism – establishing the connection

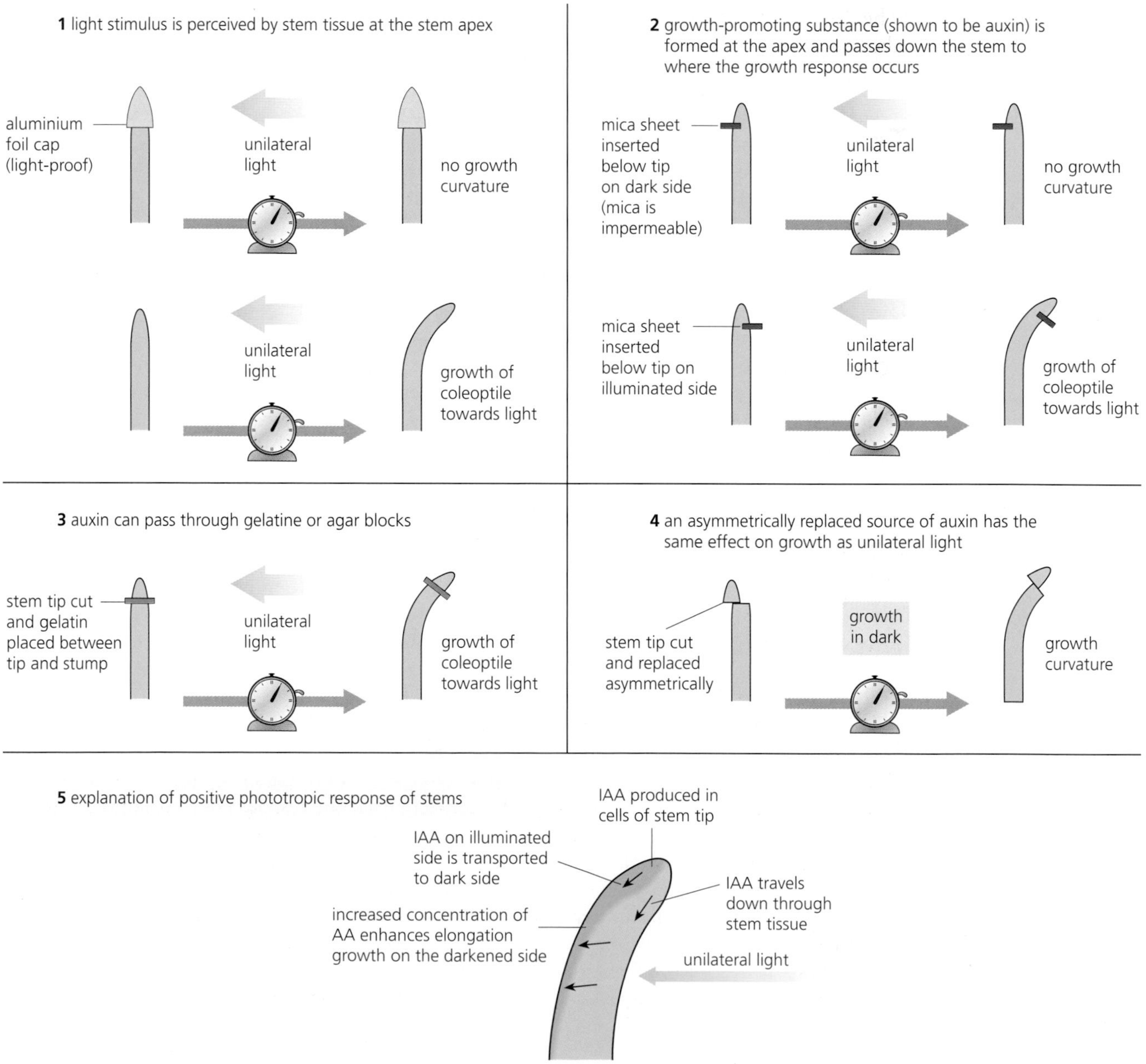

1 light stimulus is perceived by stem tissue at the stem apex

aluminium foil cap (light-proof)

unilateral light

no growth curvature

unilateral light

growth of coleoptile towards light

2 growth-promoting substance (shown to be auxin) is formed at the apex and passes down the stem to where the growth response occurs

mica sheet inserted below tip on dark side (mica is impermeable)

unilateral light

no growth curvature

mica sheet inserted below tip on illuminated side

unilateral light

growth of coleoptile towards light

3 auxin can pass through gelatine or agar blocks

stem tip cut and gelatin placed between tip and stump

unilateral light

growth of coleoptile towards light

4 an asymmetrically replaced source of auxin has the same effect on growth as unilateral light

stem tip cut and replaced asymmetrically

growth in dark

growth curvature

5 explanation of positive phototropic response of stems

IAA produced in cells of stem tip

IAA on illuminated side is transported to dark side

IAA travels down through stem tissue

increased concentration of AA enhances elongation growth on the darkened side

unilateral light

Using coleoptiles to investigate phototropism

The **coleoptile** is a sheath of tissue, unique to the grass family, which encloses the shoot of a germinating grass seedling, but only as long as it grows up through the soil (Figure 10.10). The coleoptile grows rather like a stem does, but it is uncluttered by leaves or buds, so its growth is easily observed.

Experiments to investigate phototropism by examining the responses of oat coleoptiles (oat is a cultivated grass species) to unilateral light led to the discovery of auxin. Much later, auxin was isolated, analysed, and identified as **indoleacetic acid (IAA)**.

If the tip of the stem or coleoptile is cut off, stood on a small gelatine (or agar) block for a short while, and the *block* then placed on a cut stump of stem or coleoptile, growth in length is continued. The explanation is that the plant growth substance auxin has passed from the coleoptile into the gelatine block, and when the gelatine took the place of a stem tip, the auxin then passed down into the tissue and stimulated elongation of the cells. This technique has been used to investigate auxin actions.

The effect of light on auxin distribution was discovered in experiments with coleoptiles exposed to unilateral light. Here it is the auxin passing down the coleoptile that is redistributed to the darkened side, causing differential growth and the curvature of the stem (Figure 10.11). (The degree of curvature is proportional to the amount of auxin, up to a certain concentration. Above this, additional auxin inhibits growth.)

Transport in angiosperms

9.2.1–9.2.11

Transport within flowering plants is of nutrients (carbon dioxide, water, and essential ions), oxygen for respiration, and elaborated foods (mainly sugar and amino acids). Plant growth substances are also transported, as illustrated by the movements of auxin, discussed above. Transport of water, ions and elaborated food substances involve the functioning vascular bundles, and it is this transport that is discussed now.

Root system, absorption and uptake

The root system provides a huge surface area in contact with soil, for plants have a system of branching roots that continually grow at each root tip, through the soil. This is important because it is the dilute solution that occurs around soil particles that the plant draws on for **essential ions** and the huge volume of **water** it requires.

Contact with the soil is vastly increased by the **region of root hairs** that occur just behind the growing tip of each root (Figure 10.12). Root hairs are extensions of individual epidermal cells, and are relatively short-lived. As root growth continues, fresh resources of soil solution are exploited.

4 List the features of root hairs that facilitate absorption from the soil.

Water uptake

Water uptake occurs from the soil solution in contact with the root hairs. Uptake is largely by mass-flow through the interconnecting 'free' spaces in the cellulose cell walls, but there are three possible routes of water movement through plant cells and tissues, in total, as illustrated in Figure 10.13.

- **Mass flow** through the interconnecting free spaces between the cellulose fibres of the plant cell walls. This free space in cellulose makes up about 50% of the wall volume. This route is a highly significant one in water movement about the plant. This pathway, entirely avoiding the living contents of cells, is called the apoplast. The **apoplast** also includes the water-filled spaces of dead cells (and the hollow xylem vessels – as we shall shortly see).
- **Diffusion** through the cytoplasm of cells, and via the cytoplasmic connections between cells (called plasmodesmata). This route is called the **symplast**. As the plant cells are packed with many organelles, these offer resistance to the flow of water and so this pathway is not the major one.

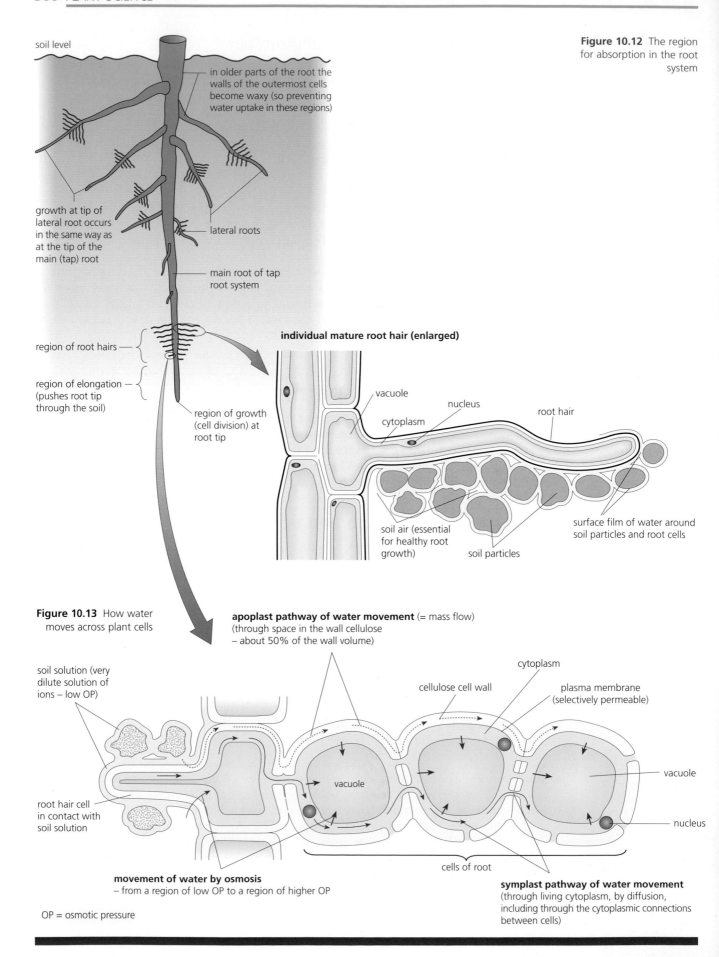

soil level

in older parts of the root the walls of the outermost cells become waxy (so preventing water uptake in these regions)

growth at tip of lateral root occurs in the same way as at the tip of the main (tap) root

lateral roots

main root of tap root system

region of root hairs —

region of elongation — (pushes root tip through the soil)

region of growth (cell division) at root tip

Figure 10.12 The region for absorption in the root system

individual mature root hair (enlarged)

vacuole

nucleus

root hair

cytoplasm

soil air (essential for healthy root growth)

soil particles

surface film of water around soil particles and root cells

Figure 10.13 How water moves across plant cells

apoplast pathway of water movement (= mass flow) (through space in the wall cellulose – about 50% of the wall volume)

cytoplasm

cellulose cell wall

plasma membrane (selectively permeable)

soil solution (very dilute solution of ions – low OP)

vacuole

vacuole

root hair cell in contact with soil solution

nucleus

cells of root

movement of water by osmosis – from a region of low OP to a region of higher OP

symplast pathway of water movement (through living cytoplasm, by diffusion, including through the cytoplasmic connections between cells)

OP = osmotic pressure

5 **Explain** the difference between the symplast and the apoplast.

■ **Osmosis** from vacuole to vacuole of the cells, driven by a gradient in osmotic pressure. This is not a significant pathway of water transport across the plant, but it is the means by which individual cells absorb water.

While all three routes are open, the bulk of water crosses the root tissue to the xylem via the apoplast (Figures 10.13 and 10.18).

Ion uptake

Ion uptake by the roots from the surrounding soil solution is by active transport.

In active transport, metabolic energy is used to drive the transport of molecules and ions across cell membranes. Active transport has characteristic features distinctly different from those of movement by diffusion, for example.

■ **Active transport may occur against a concentration gradient** – that is, from a region of low to a region of higher concentration. The cytosol of a cell normally holds some reserves of ions essential to metabolism, like nitrate ions in plant cells. These reserves of useful ions do not escape; the cell membranes retain them inside the cell. Indeed, when additional ions become available to root hair cells, they are actively absorbed into the cells, too. In fact, plant cells tend to hoard valuable ions like nitrates and calcium ions, even when they are already at higher concentration inside the cytoplasm than outside the cell.
■ **Active uptake is a highly selective process.** For example, in a situation where sodium nitrate (Na^+ and NO_3^- ions) is available to the root hairs, it is likely that more of the NO_3^- ions are absorbed than the Na^+, since this reflects the needs of the whole plants.
■ **Active transport involves special molecules of the membrane, called pumps.** The pump molecule picks up particular ions and transports them to the other side of the membrane, where they are then released. The pump molecules are globular proteins that traverse the lipid bilayer. Movements by these pump molecules require reaction with ATP; by this reaction, metabolic energy is supplied to the process. Most membrane pumps are specific to particular molecules or ions and this is the way selective transport is brought about. If the pump molecule for a particular substance is not present, the substance will not be transported.

It is the presence of numerous specific protein pumps in the plasma membranes of all the root hair cells that makes possible the efficient way that ions reaching the cell surface are absorbed (Figure 10.14). Roots are metabolically very active, and they require a supply of oxygen for aerobic cell respiration. By this process, the required supply of ATP for ion uptake is maintained.

Ions must reach the cell membranes

Soil solution contains ions at relatively low concentrations; so how are plasma membranes of the root hair cell supplied with them, in adequate quantities? Well, there are three mechanisms that maintain an adequate supply of ions.

1 The **mass flow of water through the free spaces in the cellulose walls** (the apoplast pathway of water movement – Figure 10.13) delivers fresh soil solution alongside the root hair plasma membranes, continuously.

6 **Explain** the significance of root hair cells being able to take up nitrate ions from the soil solution even though their concentration in the cell is already higher than in the soil.

7 **Suggest** why plants often fail in soil which is persistently waterlogged.

2 The active uptake of valuable ions from the soil solution of the apoplast maintains a **concentration gradient**, so ions diffuse from higher concentrations outside the apoplast to the solution of lower concentration immediately adjacent to the protein pumps.
3 Many species of **plants live in a mutualistic relationship with species of soil-inhabiting fungi**. In this relationship, the fungal hyphae receive a supply of sugar from the plant root cells. Plants generally have an excess of sugar. In return, the fungal hyphae release to the root cells ions that have previously been taken up as and when they became available in the soil. The spread of fungal hyphae through the surrounding soil is very extensive. The periodic death and decay of other organisms on or in the soil, releases a supply of ions – very often some distance from the plant roots. Nevertheless, plant roots obtain many of these ions later, from the fungal hyphae, thereby establishing that the plant–fungus relationship is one of mutual benefit.

Figure 10.14 The active uptake of ions by protein pumps in root hair cell membranes

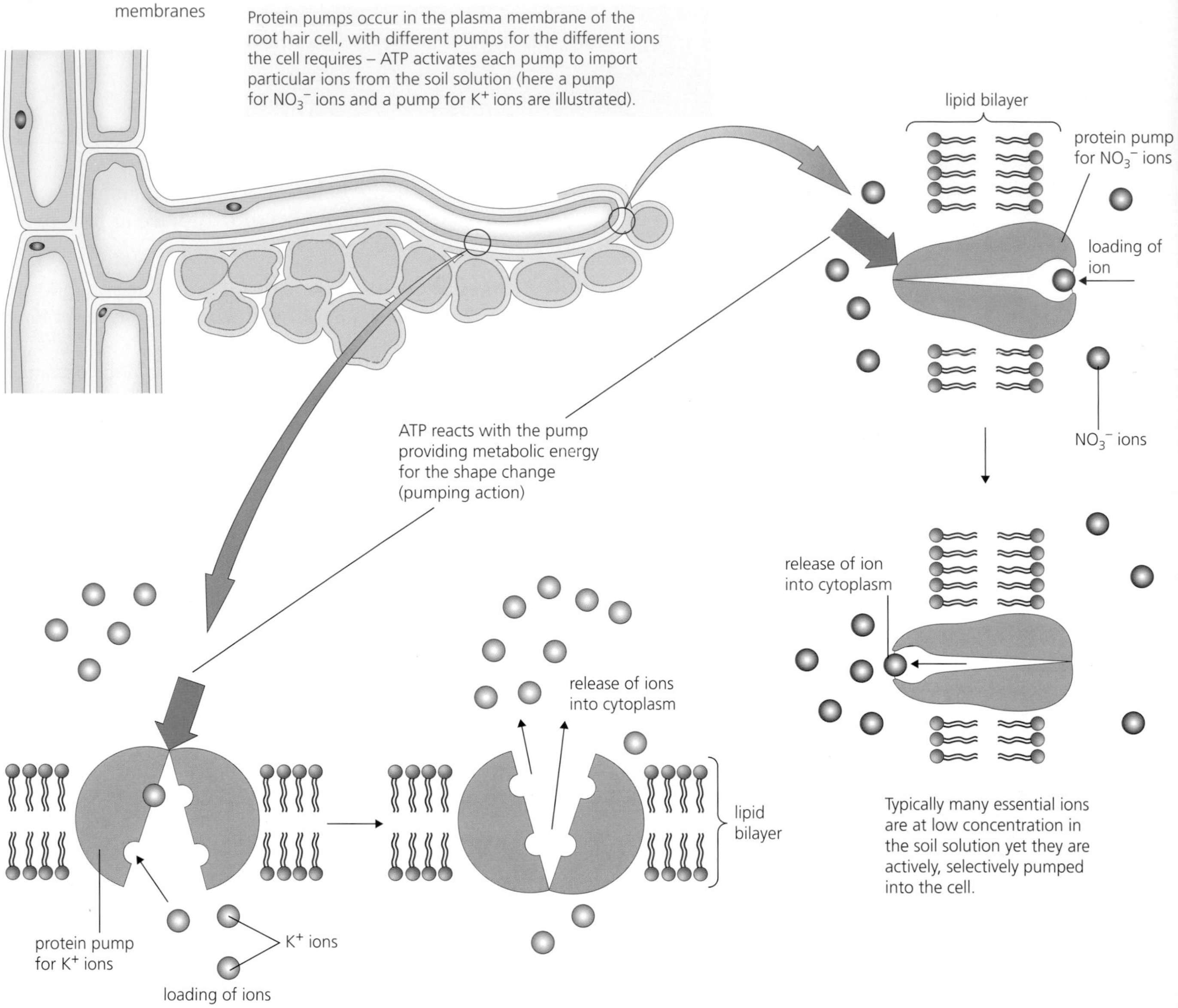

Protein pumps occur in the plasma membrane of the root hair cell, with different pumps for the different ions the cell requires – ATP activates each pump to import particular ions from the soil solution (here a pump for NO_3^- ions and a pump for K^+ ions are illustrated).

lipid bilayer

protein pump for NO_3^- ions

loading of ion

NO_3^- ions

ATP reacts with the pump providing metabolic energy for the shape change (pumping action)

release of ion into cytoplasm

release of ions into cytoplasm

lipid bilayer

Typically many essential ions are at low concentration in the soil solution yet they are actively, selectively pumped into the cell.

protein pump for K^+ ions

K^+ ions

loading of ions

The stem, support and water transport

The stem supports **leaves in the light**, and **transports water and ions** between the roots and the whole **aerial system** (leaves, flowers, and buds). It also transports **organic nutrients** (amino acids, sugars, etc.), as we shall see shortly.

The ground tissues consist of living cells that make up the bulk of the stem (and root) of herbaceous (non-woody) plants. These cells, known as parenchyma, show little structural adaptation. However, they have an important role in **support of the herbaceous stem**. This they achieve by means of turgidity, which exerts pressure on surrounding cells, and on the tough, continuous epidermis (as we saw in the leaf). How effective this is in maintaining the aerial system in an upright position is demonstrated when a herbaceous plant wilts (Figure 10.15). Incidentally, these ground tissue cells are also sites of starch storage in many plants.

The outermost layers of ground tissue cells of the stem often have additional layers of cellulose thickening laid down unevenly. These are known as collenchyma cells (Figure 10.16).

Figure 10.15 A herbaceous plant with and without adequate water

with turgid ground tissue cells

wilted

Figure 10.16 The structure of ground tissue

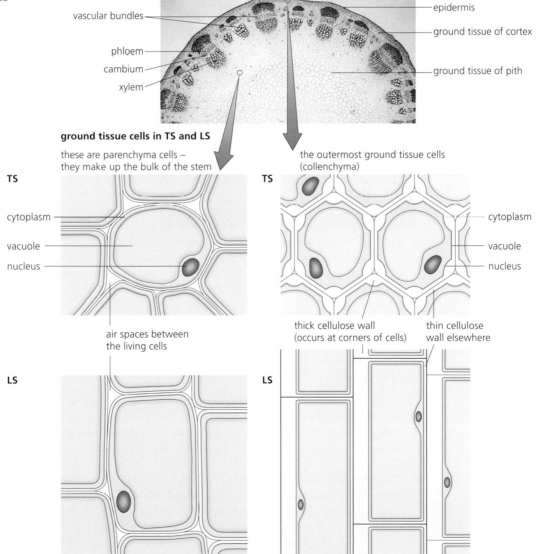

photomicrograph of TS of part of stem of sunflower (*Helianthus*)

vascular bundles

phloem

cambium

xylem

epidermis

ground tissue of cortex

ground tissue of pith

ground tissue cells in TS and LS

these are parenchyma cells – they make up the bulk of the stem

TS

cytoplasm

vacuole

nucleus

air spaces between the living cells

LS

the outermost ground tissue cells (collenchyma)

TS

cytoplasm

vacuole

nucleus

thick cellulose wall (occurs at corners of cells)

thin cellulose wall elsewhere

LS

Additional support to the stem comes from the walls of the **xylem tissue** (water-carrying) which are strengthened with cellulose thickenings that are hardened with a chemical substance, **lignin** (Figure 10.17). In **woody plants**, it is lignified cells like the xylem that supply virtually all the support to the stem. The great strength a piece of wood has is evidence of how strong lignin makes a block of plant tissue, otherwise composed only of cellulose cell walls.

Transport of water through the plant

Transport of water through the plant occurs in the xylem tissue. In a root, the xylem is centrally placed; in the stem, xylem occurs in the ring of vascular bundles, as we saw in Figure 10.2. Nevertheless, xylem of root and stem are connected.

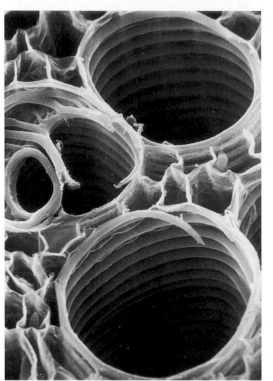

Figure 10.17 SEM of spiral xylem vessels

Xylem begins as elongated cells with cellulose walls and living contents, connected end to end. During development, the end walls are dissolved away so that mature xylem vessels are **long, hollow tubes**. The living contents of a developing xylem vessel are used up in the process of depositing cellulose thickening to the inside of the lateral walls of the vessel, and hardening this by the deposition of lignin. Consequently, xylem is extremely tough tissue and is strengthened internally; it is able to resist negative pressure (suction) without collapsing in on itself. Figure 10.17 is a scanning electron micrograph (SEM) of spirally thickened xylem vessels. Note that other vessels may have differently deposited thickening; many have rings of thickening, for example.

We have already seen that water uptake occurs from the soil solution, mainly at the root hairs (Figure 10.12). This occurs largely by mass flow through the interconnecting free spaces in the cellulose cell walls (apoplast – Figure 10.13).

A tissue map of a root tissue in transverse section shows that the centrally placed vascular tissue is contained by the **endodermis**. The endodermis is a layer of cells unique to the root. At the endodermis, a waxy strip in the radial walls blocks the passage of water by the apoplast route momentarily. This waxy strip is called the **Casparian strip**. Water passes through the endodermis by osmosis.

Meanwhile, in the leaves, evaporation of water occurs and water vapour diffuses out of the stomata, a process called **transpiration**.

> **Transpiration is the evaporation of water vapour through stomata of green plant leaves (and stems).**

Water lost by leaf cells inevitably raises the osmotic pressure in these cells, causing water uptake from surrounding cells, and so from the xylem vessels of the network of veins there. Consequently, a stream of water is drawn up the xylem of the stem by a force generated by transpiration in the leaves, sometimes called the transpiration stream, or the **transpiration pull**.

The properties of water in relation to the chemistry of cell walls ensure the water column coheres to the lateral walls of the xylem and the water column does not break under tension (i.e. negative pressure or suction). This is known as the **cohesive property of water** (page 40). So, a continuous column of water is maintained, moving from root cell walls to leaf cell walls. Much of this water ultimately evaporates – it is lost from the plant as vapour (Figure 10.18).

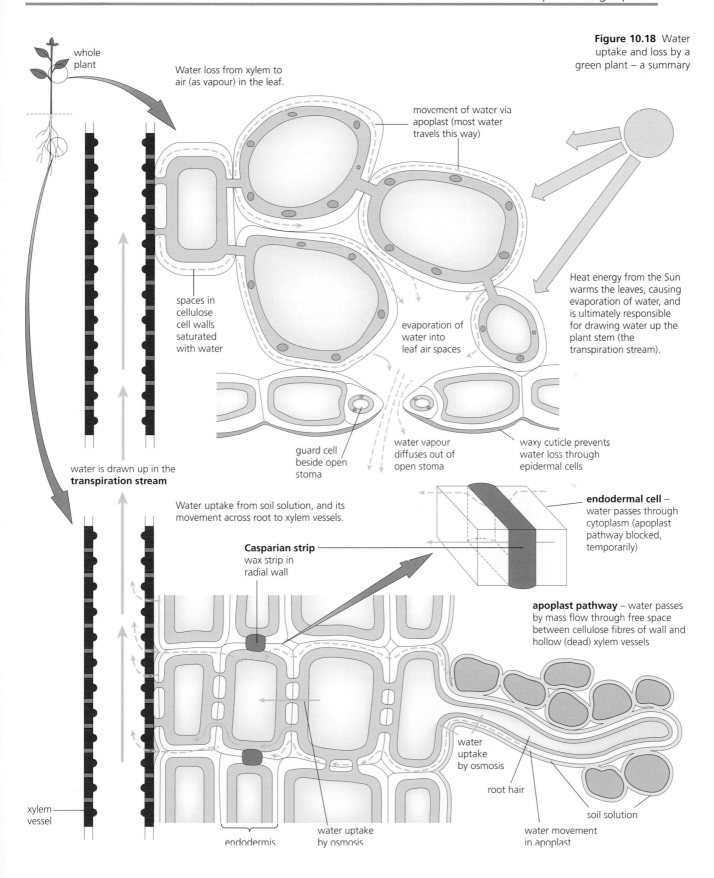

whole plant

Water loss from xylem to air (as vapour) in the leaf.

movement of water via apoplast (most water travels this way)

Figure 10.18 Water uptake and loss by a green plant – a summary

spaces in cellulose cell walls saturated with water

evaporation of water into leaf air spaces

Heat energy from the Sun warms the leaves, causing evaporation of water, and is ultimately responsible for drawing water up the plant stem (the transpiration stream).

guard cell beside open stoma

water vapour diffuses out of open stoma

waxy cuticle prevents water loss through epidermal cells

water is drawn up in the **transpiration stream**

Water uptake from soil solution, and its movement across root to xylem vessels.

endodermal cell – water passes through cytoplasm (apoplast pathway blocked, temporarily)

Casparian strip wax strip in radial wall

apoplast pathway – water passes by mass flow through free space between cellulose fibres of wall and hollow (dead) xylem vessels

water uptake by osmosis

root hair

soil solution

xylem vessel

endodermis

water uptake by osmosis

water movement in apoplast

8 Explain the consequence of the Casparian strip for the apoplast pathway of water movement.

Stomata and transpiration

The tiny pores of the epidermis of leaves through which gas exchange can occur are known as stomata (Figure 10.19). Most stomata occur in the epidermis of leaves, but some do occur in stems. In the broad, flattened leaves typical of many dicotyledonous plants, stomata are concentrated in the lower epidermis. Each stoma consists of two elongated guard cells. These cells are attached to ordinary epidermal cells that surround them and are securely joined together at each end. However, guard cells are detached and free to separate along the length of their abutting sides. When they separate, a pore appears between them.

Stomata open and close due to change in turgor pressure of the guard cells. They open when water is absorbed by the guard cells from the surrounding epidermal cells. The guard cells then become fully turgid, and they each push into the epidermal cell beside them (because of the way cellulose is laid down in the walls, Figure 10.19). A pore develops between the guard cells. When water is lost and the guard cells become flaccid, the pore closes again. This has been demonstrated experimentally (Figure 10.20).

Stomata tend to open in daylight and be closed in the dark (but there are exceptions to this). This diurnal pattern is overridden, however, if and when the plant becomes short of water and starts to wilt. For example, in very dry conditions when there is an inadequate water supply, stomata inevitably close relatively early in the day (turgor cannot be maintained). This curtails water vapour loss by transpiration and halts further wilting. Adequate water reserves from the soil may be taken up subsequently, thereby allowing the opening of stomata again – for example, on the following day. The effect of this mechanism is that stomata regulate transpiration in that they prevent excessive water loss when this is threatened (Figure 10.21).

9 Suggest why changes in the turgor of guard cells cause opening of stomata.

Figure 10.19 The distribution and structure of stomata

distribution of stomata in typical dicotyledonous leaf

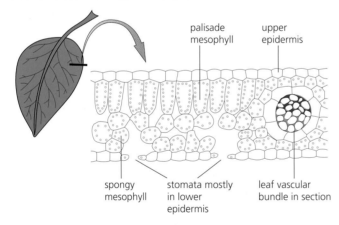

palisade mesophyll

upper epidermis

spongy mesophyll

stomata mostly in lower epidermis

leaf vascular bundle in section

lower surface of leaf – showing distribution of stomata among the epidermal cells (photomicrograph) (×100)

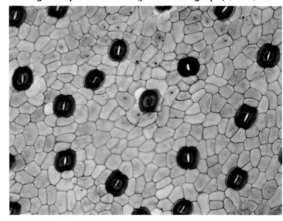

structure of individual stoma (photomicrograph) (×500)

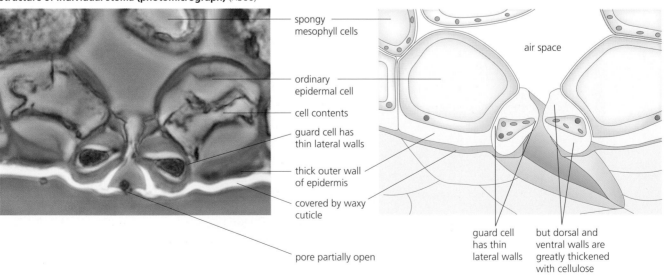

spongy mesophyll cells

air space

ordinary epidermal cell

cell contents

guard cell has thin lateral walls

thick outer wall of epidermis

covered by waxy cuticle

pore partially open

guard cell has thin lateral walls

but dorsal and ventral walls are greatly thickened with cellulose

Figure 10.20 It's turgor pressure that does it!

In an experimental demonstration that turgor pressure of the guard cells causes the opening of the stomatal pore, a microdissection needle was inserted into a guard cell.

A fully open pore
due to turgid guard cells

B microdissection needle (fine hollow tube) inserted into one guard cell vacuole

needle pushed in | cell sap (fluid) escapes

C half-open pore
due to collapse of turgor

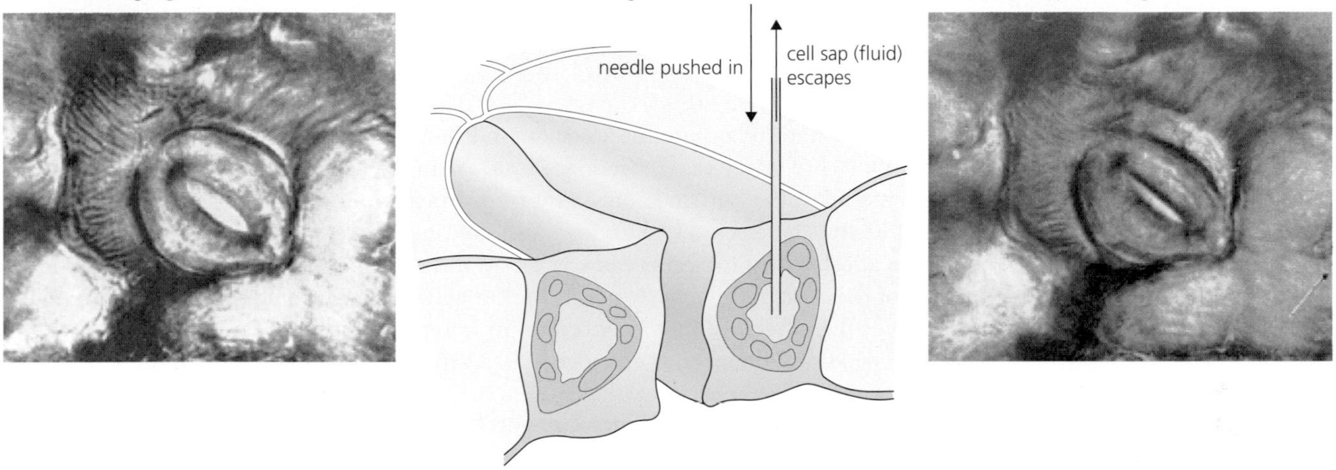

Observation: on release of the turgor pressure in one guard cell, the distinctive shape of the cell when the pore is open was lost. 'Half' of the pore disappeared.

Figure 10.21 Stomatal opening and environmental conditions

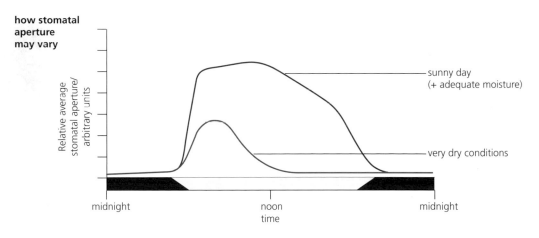

how stomatal aperture may vary

Relative average stomatal aperture/ arbitrary units

sunny day (+ adequate moisture)

very dry conditions

midnight — noon — midnight
time

10 Examine Figure 10.21. **Suggest** why the stomatal apertures of the plant in very dry conditions differed in both maximum size and duration of opening from those of the plant with adequate moisture.

Abscisic acid (ABA) and water stress conditions

Abscisic acid is another plant growth regulator found to occur in stems, leaves and fruits. Many of the effects of ABA result from its interaction with other growth regulator substances, including its effects on seed germination, *but these do not concern us here*. ABA is important in leaves because its presence assists plant survival at times of physiological stress, such as prolonged drought. In these conditions, the level of ABA present is raised, and it maintains stomatal closure, reducing water loss.

The rate of transpiration may be investigated using a potometer (Figure 10.22) and is found to be dramatically affected by **environmental conditions** around the plant.

Why is this so?

Transpiration occurs because water molecules continuously evaporate from the cellulose walls of cells in the leaf which are saturated with water. This makes the air in the air spaces between mesophyll cells more or less saturated with water vapour. If the air outside the plant is less saturated (less humid – as it very often is) *and the stomata are open*, water vapour will diffuse out into the drier air outside.

In effect, transpiration is an unfortunate consequence of plant structure and nutrition that can only be slowed or stopped by closure of the stomata. In the light, plants tend to dry out the soil they grow in! Thus we can see how changes in environmental conditions will affect transpiration, and why.

For example:

1 **Light** affects transpiration because the stomata tend to be open in the light, and open stomata are essential for loss of water vapour from the leaf. There is also an indirect effect of light because it comes from the Sun and contains infra-red rays which warm the leaf and raise its temperature. Light is an essential factor for transpiration.

2 **Temperature** affects transpiration because it causes the evaporation of water molecules from the surfaces of the cells of the leaf. A rise in the concentration of water vapour within the air spaces increases the difference in concentration in water vapour between the leaf's interior and the air outside, and diffusion is enhanced. So an increase in temperature of the leaf raises the transpiration rate.

3 **Wind** sweeps away the water vapour molecules accumulating outside the stomata of the epidermis of the leaf surface, so enhancing the difference in concentration of water vapour between the leaf interior and the outside. Movements of air around the plant enhance transpiration.

4 **Humid air**, if it collects around a leaf, decreases the difference in concentration of water vapour between the interior and exterior of the leaf, so slowing diffusion of water vapour from the leaf. High humidity slows transpiration.

Figure 10.22
Investigating transpiration and the factors that influence it

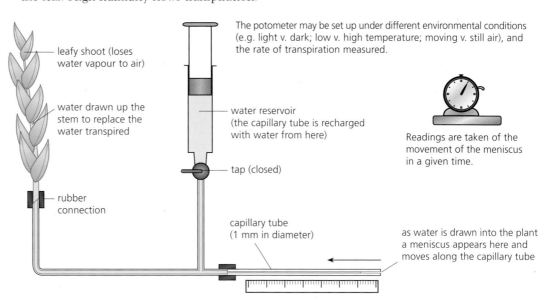

- leafy shoot (loses water vapour to air)
- water drawn up the stem to replace the water transpired
- rubber connection

The potometer may be set up under different environmental conditions (e.g. light v. dark; low v. high temperature; moving v. still air), and the rate of transpiration measured.

- water reservoir (the capillary tube is recharged with water from here)
- tap (closed)
- capillary tube (1 mm in diameter)

Readings are taken of the movement of the meniscus in a given time.

as water is drawn into the plant a meniscus appears here and moves along the capillary tube

Xerophytes – plants of permanently dry and arid conditions

Most native plants of temperate and tropical zones, and most of our crop plants, grow best in habitats with adequate rainfall, well-drained soils, and with their aerial system (stem and leaves) exposed to moderately dry air. Loss of water vapour from the leaves may be substantial in drier periods, particularly in the early part of the day, but excessive loss from the leaves is prevented by the responses of the stomata (Figure 10.21). Any deficit is normally made good by the water uptake that continues, day and night. It is the structure of these sorts of plants (known as mesophytes) that we have been considering in this chapter.

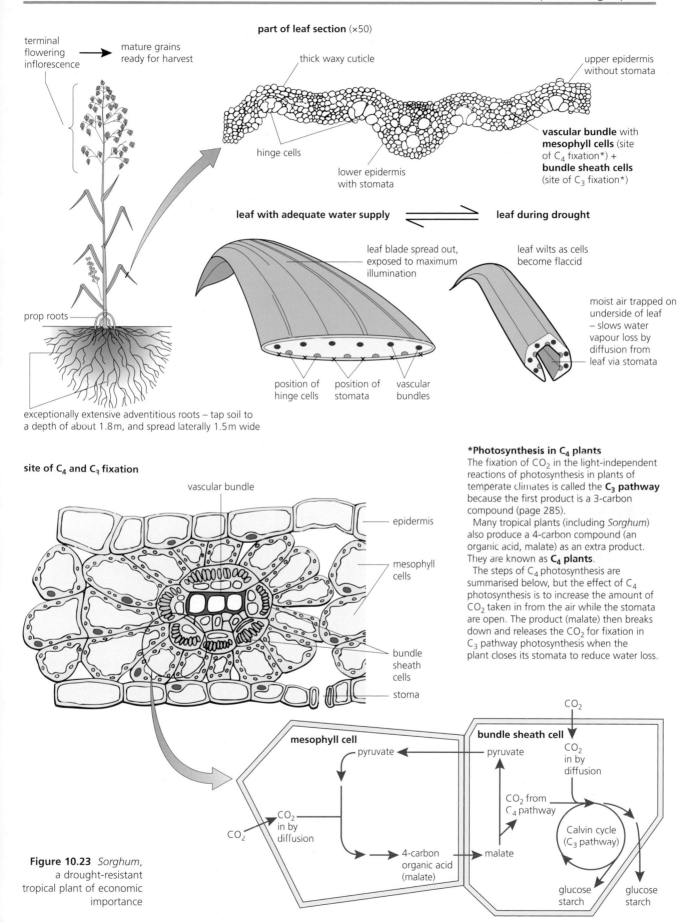

part of leaf section (×50)

terminal flowering inflorescence

mature grains ready for harvest

thick waxy cuticle

upper epidermis without stomata

hinge cells

lower epidermis with stomata

vascular bundle with **mesophyll cells** (site of C_4 fixation*) + **bundle sheath cells** (site of C_3 fixation*)

leaf with adequate water supply ⇌ **leaf during drought**

leaf blade spread out, exposed to maximum illumination

leaf wilts as cells become flaccid

prop roots

moist air trapped on underside of leaf – slows water vapour loss by diffusion from leaf via stomata

position of hinge cells

position of stomata

vascular bundles

exceptionally extensive adventitious roots – tap soil to a depth of about 1.8m, and spread laterally 1.5m wide

site of C_4 and C_3 fixation

vascular bundle

epidermis

mesophyll cells

bundle sheath cells

stoma

*Photosynthesis in C_4 plants
The fixation of CO_2 in the light-independent reactions of photosynthesis in plants of temperate climates is called the **C_3 pathway** because the first product is a 3-carbon compound (page 285).

Many tropical plants (including *Sorghum*) also produce a 4-carbon compound (an organic acid, malate) as an extra product. They are known as **C_4 plants**.

The steps of C_4 photosynthesis are summarised below, but the effect of C_4 photosynthesis is to increase the amount of CO_2 taken in from the air while the stomata are open. The product (malate) then breaks down and releases the CO_2 for fixation in C_3 pathway photosynthesis when the plant closes its stomata to reduce water loss.

Figure 10.23 *Sorghum*, a drought-resistant tropical plant of economic importance

CO_2

bundle sheath cell

CO_2 in by diffusion

mesophyll cell

pyruvate

pyruvate

CO_2 from C_4 pathway

CO_2 in by diffusion

Calvin cycle (C_3 pathway)

CO_2

4-carbon organic acid (malate)

malate

glucose starch

glucose starch

On the other hand, **xerophytes** are plants able to survive and often grow well in habitats where water is scarce. These plants show features that directly or indirectly help to minimise water loss, due to transpiration. Their adaptations are referred to as **xeromorphic features**, and these are summarised in Table 10.4.

Table 10.4 Xeromorphic features

Structural features	Effect
exceptionally thick cuticle to leaf (and stem) epidermis	prevents water loss through the external wall of the epidermal cells
layer of hairs on the epidermis	traps moist air over the leaf and reduces the diffusion
reduction in the number of stomata	reduces outlets through which moist air can diffuse
stomata in pits or groves	moist air trapped outside the stomata, reducing diffusion
leaf rolled or folded when short of water (cells flaccid)	reduces area from which transpiration can occur
superficial roots	exploit overnight condensation at soil surface
deep and extensive roots	exploit a deep water table in the soil
Biochemical features	**Effect**
C_4 photosynthesis pathway (Figure 10.23) operates in addition to normal photosynthesis (C_3)	enhances photosynthetic CO_2 fixation in daylight while stomata are open – allowing the stomata to be closed in dry conditions
CAM metabolism (Figure 10.25)	retains CO_2 from the air in organic acids in cells overnight (in the dark) while stomata are open, and then releases this CO_2 into leaf air space in the light (stomata now closed) for fixation in photosynthesis

Figure 10.24 Marram grass (*Ammophila*), a pioneer plant of sand dunes

marram grass has the ability to grow in the extremely arid environment of sand dunes, accelerating the build-up of sand

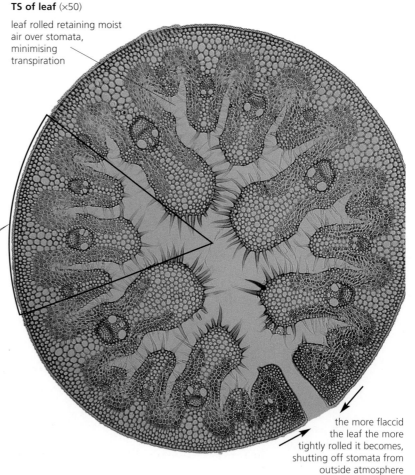

TS of leaf (×50)

leaf rolled retaining moist air over stomata, minimising transpiration

the more flaccid the leaf the more tightly rolled it becomes, shutting off stomata from outside atmosphere

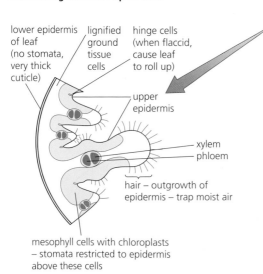

lower epidermis of leaf (no stomata, very thick cuticle)

lignified ground tissue cells

hinge cells (when flaccid, cause leaf to roll up)

upper epidermis

xylem
phloem

hair – outgrowth of epidermis – trap moist air

mesophyll cells with chloroplasts – stomata restricted to epidermis above these cells

Xerophytic plants typically show some of the adaptations listed below.

- **Sorghum** (*Sorghum*), a grain plant that thrives in extremely arid conditions, shows marked adaptations in its leaf structure and root system, and in its C_4 photosynthesis (Figure 10.23).
- **Marram grass** (*Ammophila*), a wild grass plant of sand dunes, has leaves that, at first glance, look more like stems (Figure 10.24).
- **Stonecrop** (*Sedum*), a plant of dry stone walls and rocky slopes, shows pronounced structural and biochemical adaptations (Figure 10.25).

Figure 10.25 Stonecrop (*Sedum*) – a plant of dry walls and rocky slopes

Sedum occurs in habitats where water is rarely available.

Sedum belongs to the angiospermophyte family Crassulaceae – succulent (fleshy) xerophytic plants. They show many xeromorphic features (Table 10.4), but their special feature is **crassulacean acid metabolism** (**CAM**).

In CAM plants, stomata are open in the night only (transpiration is at a minimum), and they fix CO_2 into the organic acid malate.

In the light, the stomata close, and the malate breaks down to release CO_2 into the air spaces of the plant. This CO_2 is fixed by C_3 photosynthesis (page 285), with minimal loss of water vapour from the plant.

Biochemical events in the photosynthetic cells of *Sedum*

Night
Stomata open: CO_2 assimilated into malic acid and stored as malate in the vacuoles.

Day
Stomata closed: malate from the vacuoles converted to CO_2 and pyruvate, and these products are used to make starch.

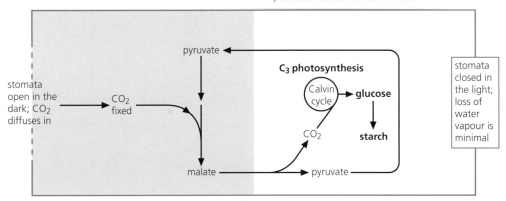

11 Suggest why it is that, of all the environmental factors which affect plant growth, the issue of water supply is so critical.

12 Explain why we can describe the external epidermis of the leaf of marram grass as botanically equivalent to the lower epidermis of a mesophyte leaf.

The stem and organic solute transport

Translocation is the movement of manufactured food (sugars and amino acids, mainly) which occurs in the phloem tissue of the vascular bundles. Sugars are made in the leaves (in the light) by photosynthesis and transported as sucrose. The first-formed leaves, once established, transport sugars to sites of new growth (new stem, new leaves and new roots). In older plants, sucrose is increasingly transported to sites of storage, such as the cortex of roots or stems, and in seeds and fruits (see below).

Amino acids are mostly made in the root tips. Here, absorption of nitrates occurs which the plant uses in the synthesis of amino acids. After their manufacture, amino acids are transported to sites where protein synthesis is occurring. These are mostly in the buds, young leaves and young roots, and in developing fruits.

Translocation is not restricted to organic compounds manufactured within the plant. Chemicals that are applied to plants, for example by spraying, and are then absorbed by the leaves, may be carried all over the organism. Consequently, pesticides of this type are called systemic.

Phloem tissue consists of **sieve tubes** and **companion cells**. Sieve tubes are narrow, elongated elements, connected end to end to form tubes. The end walls, known as **sieve plates**, are perforated by pores. The cytoplasm of a mature sieve tube has no nucleus, nor many of the other organelles of a cell. However, each sieve tube is connected to a companion cell by strands of cytoplasm passing through gaps (called pits) in the walls. The companion cells are believed to service and maintain the cytoplasm of the sieve tube, which has lost its nucleus.

Phloem is a living tissue, and has a relatively high rate of aerobic respiration during transport. In fact, transport of manufactured food in the phloem is an active process, using energy from metabolism.

Figure 10.26 The structure of phloem and the mass flow hypothesis of phloem transport

Phloem transport may occur in either direction in stem, leaves and roots, and is believed to occur by mass flow, as shown in Figure 10.26.

How does mass flow work?

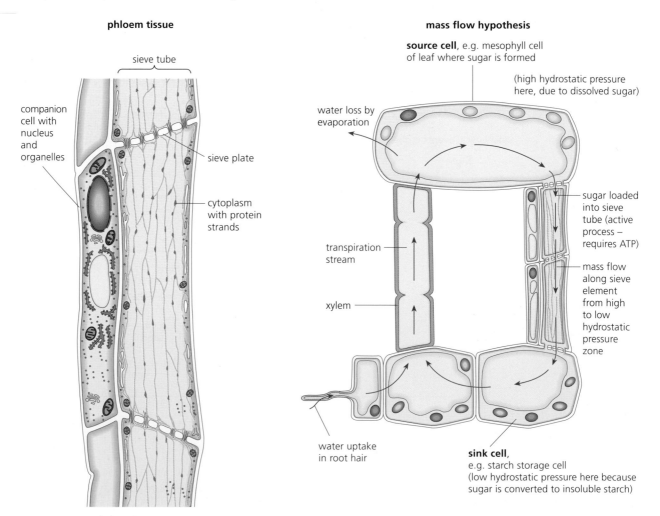

Solutes are loaded into the phloem sieve tubes (a process requiring ATP), and then solutes flow through the phloem from a region of high hydrostatic pressure to a region of low hydrostatic pressure. Hydrostatic pressure is high in and around photosynthesising cells in the light (mesophyll cells of the leaf), and in the phloem sieve tubes nearby, because of the presence of sugar, which generates a high osmotic pressure. Consequently water flows in, raising the hydrostatic pressure still further. This is called a source area.

Hydrostatic pressure is low in cells where sugar is converted to starch and stored (for example, ground tissue cells of the stem and root) and in the phloem sieve tubes nearby. Here the removal of sugar lowers the osmotic pressure, and water flows away. Starch storage cells like these are called sink areas.

13 Describe the differences between transpiration and translocation.

Reproduction in flowering plants

9.3.1–9.3.6

Flowering plants contain their reproductive organs in the flower. Flowers are often hermaphrodite structures, carrying both male and female parts.

The parts of flowers occur in rings or whorls, attached to the swollen tip of the flower stalk, called the receptacle. The **sepals** (collectively, the calyx) enclose the flower in the bud, and are usually small, green and leaf-like. The **petals** (collectively, the corolla) are often coloured and conspicuous, and may attract insects or other small animals. The stamens are the male parts of the flower, and consist of **anthers** (housing pollen grains) and the **filament** (stalk). The carpels are the female part of the flower. There may be one or many, free-standing or fused together. Each carpel consists of an **ovary** (containing ovules), a **stigma** (surface receiving pollen), and a connecting style.

Figure 10.27 The buttercup (*Ranunculus*) flower

The buttercup flower is shown in Figure 10.27, and other flowers common in different parts of the world are shown in Figure 10.28.

the inflorescence of buttercup (*Ranunculus acris*)

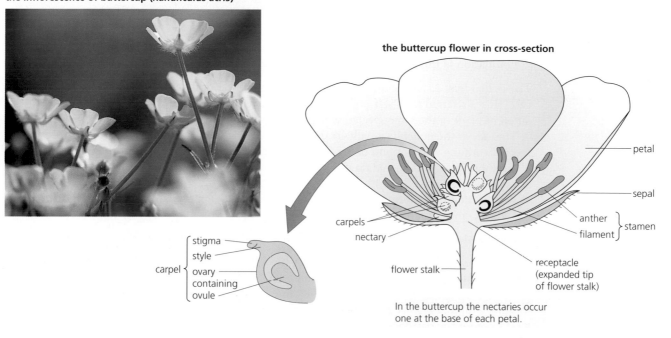

the buttercup flower in cross-section

In the buttercup the nectaries occur one at the base of each petal.

Figure 10.28 Other animal-pollinated flowers common in parts of the world

Bougainvillea rosenka Native of tropical and sub-tropical South America. The flowers are small but surrounded by brightly coloured leaves (bracts).

Hibiscus syriacus Native of warm temperate, tropical and sub-tropical regions throughout the world. The large, trumpet-shaped flowers have five petals.

Pollination and fertilisation

Pollination is the transfer of pollen from a mature anther to a receptive stigma.

The pollen may come from the anthers of the same flower or flowers of the same plant, in which case, this is referred to as **self-pollination**. Alternatively, pollen may come from flowers on a different plant of the same species, which is referred to as **cross-pollination**.

Transfer of the pollen is usually by **insects** or by the **wind**, although in the flowers of certain species, running water or bird or bat visitors to the flowers may be the agent that carries out pollination. Insect-pollinated flowers typically produce a sugar solution, called nectar, which attracts insects to the flower.

Fertilisation in flowering plants can occur only after an appropriate pollen grain has landed on the stigma, and germinated there.

Fertilisation is the fusion of male and female gametes to form a zygote.

The pollen grain produces a pollen tube which grows down between the cells of the style, and into the ovule through the micropyle (Figure 10.29). Incidentally, the pollen tube delivers two male nuclei. One of these male nuclei then fuses with the egg nucleus in the embryo sac, forming a diploid zygote. The other fuses with another nucleus which triggers formation of the food store for the developing embryo. This 'double fertilisation' is unique to flowering plants.

Figure 10.29 Fertilisation in a flowering plant

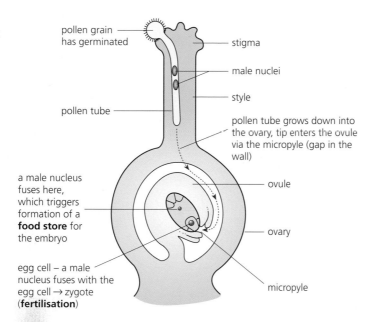

pollen grain has germinated

stigma

male nuclei

style

pollen tube

pollen tube grows down into the ovary, tip enters the ovule via the micropyle (gap in the wall)

a male nucleus fuses here, which triggers formation of a **food store** for the embryo

ovule

ovary

egg cell – a male nucleus fuses with the egg cell → zygote (**fertilisation**)

micropyle

14 **Explain** the differences between pollination and fertilisation in the flowering plant.

■ **Extension:** Because many flowers are hermaphrodite there is the potential for self-fertilisation that cannot arise in a unisexual organism. If self-fertilisation occurs, the offspring produced will show less variation from their parents than if fertilisation occurs between gametes from different individuals. So it is interesting to note that several mechanisms that prevent self-fertilisation are common in hermaphrodite flowers, such as the stamens and stigmas maturing at different times. This means that when the stigma is receptive the stamens are not releasing pollen grains, and vice versa.

Seed formation and dispersal

The seed develops from the fertilised ovule and contains an embryo plant and a food store. After fertilisation:

■ The zygote grows by repeated mitotic division to produce cells that form an **embryonic plant**, consisting of an embryo root, an embryo stem, and either a single cotyledon (seed leaf) or two cotyledons. (Remember, the phylum Angiospermophyta is divided into two classes, according to the number of cotyledons present. The monocotyledons have a single seed leaf, the dicotyledons have two.)
■ Formation of **stored food reserves** is triggered. In many seeds, the developing food store is absorbed into the cotyledons, rather than remaining as a separate store, packed round the embryonic plant. For example, this is the case in peas and beans (Figure 10.30). Note that formation of food reserves can only occur if fertilisation occurs – in the absence of fertilisation, food reserves are not moved into the unfertilised ovule.

As the seed matures, the outer layers of the ovule become the protective seed coat or **testa** and the whole ovary develops into the **fruit**. Next, the water content of the seed decreases, and the seed moves into a dormancy period. In a mature, fully dormant seed, water makes up only 10–15% of seed weight.

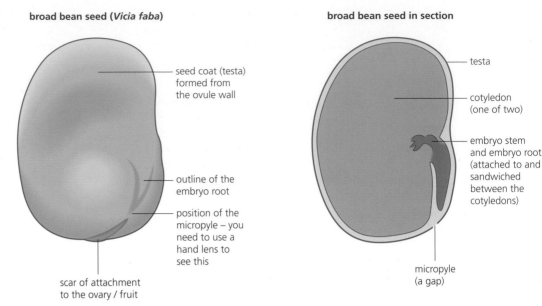

Figure 10.30 The structure of a dicotyledonous seed

broad bean seed (*Vicia faba*)

seed coat (testa) formed from the ovule wall

outline of the embryo root

position of the micropyle – you need to use a hand lens to see this

scar of attachment to the ovary / fruit

broad bean seed in section

testa

cotyledon (one of two)

embryo stem and embryo root (attached to and sandwiched between the cotyledons)

micropyle (a gap)

15 **State** a fruit or vegetable we eat that originates from:

a an ovary containing one seed

b an ovary containing many seeds

c several ovaries fused together, containing many seeds.

The **seed** is a form in which the flowering plant may be dispersed. If offspring seeds eventually germinate some distance apart, there is more likelihood they will not be competing for the same resources of space, water and light.

Seed dispersal is the carrying of the seed away from the vicinity of the parent plant.

The plant structures to aid dispersal that have evolved variously exploit air currents (wind), passing animals or flowing water to transport seeds. In a few plants, seeds are flung away from the ripening fruit by an explosive mechanism. All seeds are compact, nutritious, and relatively lightweight – in effect they are food packages to a hungry animal. In the process, many seeds taken in this way are dropped or lost in transit, and so these seeds, too, may have been successfully dispersed.

The physiology of seed germination

Many seeds do not germinate as soon as they are formed and dispersed. Such seeds are said to have a **dormant period** and germinate only when this has elapsed. Dormancy may be imposed within the seed, due to:

■ **incomplete seed development** that causes the embryo to be immature, and which is overcome in time;
■ the **presence of a plant growth regulator** – abscisic acid, for example – that inhibits development, and which only disappears from the seed tissues with time;
■ an **impervious seed coat** that is eventually made permeable – for example, by abrasion with coarse soil or by the action of microorganisms;
■ a **requirement for pre-chilling** under moist conditions, before the seed can germinate; some seeds need to be held at or below 5 °C for up to 50 days (possibly the equivalent of winter in temperate climates).

Once dormancy is overcome, germination occurs if the following essential external conditions are met (Table 10.5).

■ **Water** uptake has occurred so that the seed is fully hydrated and the embryo is enabled to be physiologically active.
■ **Oxygen** is present at a high enough partial pressure to sustain aerobic respiration. Growth demands a continuous supply of metabolic energy in the form of ATP that is best generated by aerobic cell respiration in all the cells.

■ **A suitable temperature** exists, one that is close to the optimum temperature for the enzymes involved in the mobilisation of stored food reserves, the translocation of organic solutes in the phloem, and the synthesis of intermediates for cell growth and development. For example, wheat seeds germinate in the range 1–35 °C, and maize in the range 5–45 °C.

The **steps of germination** are summarised in Figure 10.31. Note that a plant growth regulator, **gibberellic acid (GA)**, is produced by the cells of the embryo. GA passes to the food stored in the cotyledons. Here protein reserves are converted to **hydrolytic enzymes** which hydrolyse the stored food reserves. The main event is the production of the enzyme **amylase** which hydrolyses starch to maltose. This disaccharide is then hydrolysed to glucose. The resulting soluble sugar (and other compounds) sustain **respiration** and also provide the **building blocks for synthesis** of the intermediates essential for new cells.

Figure 10.31 Metabolic events of germination in a starchy seed

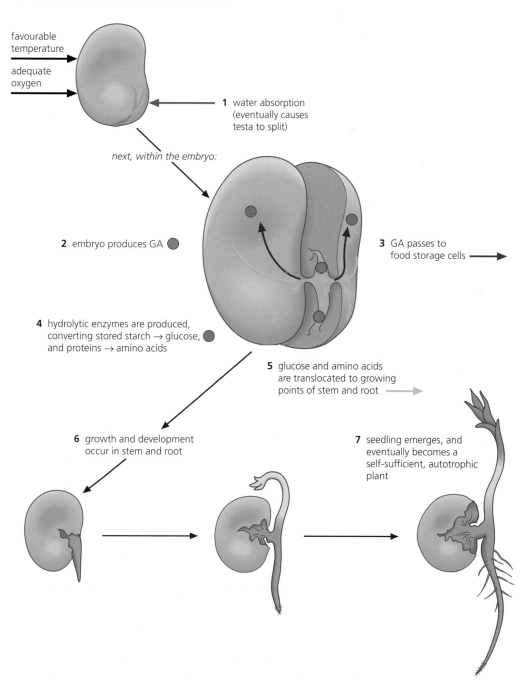

External	Internal
water uptake – hydration of the cytoplasm of cells of embryo	overcoming of dormancy
ambient **temperature** – within optimum range for enzyme action	production of GA by embryo cells to initiate biochemical changes of germination, leading to production of hydrolytic enzymes for mobilisation of stored food
oxygen – to sustain aerobic cell respiration	

Table 10.5 Conditions for germination

The control of flowering

You will be well aware that plants flower at different times of the year; very many species have a precise season when flowers are produced. At other times, no flowers are formed on these plants.

How is flowering switched on by environmental conditions?

The answer is that day length provides important signals, and that a different plant pigment molecule is involved in the process.

Plant development and phytochrome

A blue–green pigment called **phytochrome** is present in green plants in very low concentrations. The amount of phytochrome is not sufficient to mask chlorophyll, and it has been a substance difficult to isolate and purify from plant tissue, although this has been done.

Phytochrome is a very large conjugated protein (protein molecule + pigment molecule, combined), and it is a highly reactive molecule. It is not a plant growth substance, but it is a photoreceptor pigment, able to absorb light of particular wavelength, and change its structure as a consequence. It is likely to react with different molecules around it, according to its structure.

Two forms of phytochrome

We know that phytochrome exists in two interconvertible forms.

One form, referred to as P_R, is a blue pigment which absorbs mainly red light of wavelength 660 nm (this is what the $_R$ stands for).

The other form is P_{FR}, a blue–green pigment which mainly absorbs far-red light of wavelength 730 nm.

When P_R is exposed to light (or red light on its own) it is converted to P_{FR}. However, in the dark (or if exposed to far-red light alone) it is converted back to P_R.

$$P_R \underset{\substack{\text{darkness} \\ \text{(slow)} \quad \text{(or far-red light)} \\ \text{(fast)}}}{\overset{\substack{\text{light} \quad \text{(or red light)} \\ \text{(slow)} \quad \text{(fast)}}}{\rightleftharpoons}} P_{FR}$$

Where plant growth and development are influenced by light, this is known as **photomorphogenesis**. Phytochrome is the pigment system involved in photomorphogenesis. We know this because the red–far-red absorption spectrum of phytochrome corresponds to the action spectrum of some specific effects of light on development (see pages 287–8 if you have forgotten the terms 'absorption spectrum' and 'action spectrum').

It appears that it is P_{FR} that is the active form of phytochrome, stimulating some effects in plant development and inhibiting others. In particular, P_{FR} controls of the onset of flowering.

Photoperiodism is the response of an organism to changing length of day. Many plants flower only at a particular time of the year, and plants where flowering is controlled by day length fall into two categories (Figure 10.32).

- **Short-day plants** – these are plants which flower only if the period of darkness is longer than a certain critical length. If darkness is interrupted by a brief flash of red light the plant will not flower, but this is reversed by a flash of far-red light.

Interpretation

Phytochrome in P_{FR} form inhibits flowering in short-day plants. The very long nights required by short-day plants allow the concentration of P_{FR} to fall to a low level, removing the inhibition. A flash of light in the darkness reverses this, but a flash of far-red light reverses the reversal, and flowering still takes place.

■ **Long-day plants** – these are plants which flower only if the period of uninterrupted darkness is less than a certain critical length each day.

Interpretation

Phytochrome in P_{FR} form promotes flowering in long-day plants. The long period of daylight causes the accumulation of P_{FR}, because P_R is converted to P_{FR}.

Figure 10.32 Flowering related to day length

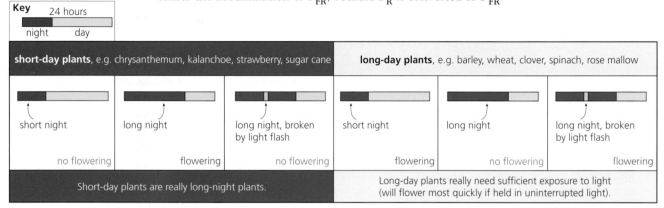

Extension: ## The conversion of vegetative buds to flower buds

It is the leaves of plants that are sensitive to day length, yet the structural switch to flowering occurs in a stem apex. It has been assumed that a growth regulator substance is formed in leaves under the correct regime of light and dark, and is then transported to the stem apex where it causes the switch in development. For example, a leaf that has been exposed to the correct photoperiod, if immediately grafted onto another plant of the same type, will cause flowering there.

A hormone is believed to exist, and has been named **florigen**, but it has not been isolated. Since it is P_{FR} that is enzymically active, this substance might cause the formation of an enzyme which promotes the formation of florigen in long-day plants but inhibits its formation in short-day plants. Much remains to be discovered about the control of flowering (Figure 10.33).

Figure 10.33 Phytochrome and flowering, a suggested hypothesis

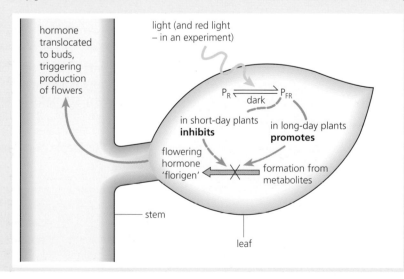

■ *Examination questions – a selection*

Questions 1–4 are taken from past IB Diploma biology papers.

Q1 Which of the following would be an adaptation made by a xerophyte plant?
   A reduced root surface area
   B increased air space
   C increased number of stomata
   D a thicker cuticle

Higher Level Paper 1, May 05, Q39

Q2 What are the differences between the transport of minerals in the apoplast and the symplast of the root?

	Apoplast	Symplast
A	they travel through the cytoplasm of the root cells	they travel through the intercellular spaces
B	their movement is blocked by the endodermis	their movement continues across the endodermis
C	they enter by active transport	they enter by passive transport
D	they cross between cells by the plasmodesmata	they cannot travel via the plasmodesmata

Higher Level Paper 1, May 04, Q40

Q3 The diagrams show the distribution of tissues in the root and in the leaf of a dicotyledonous plant.

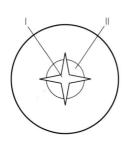 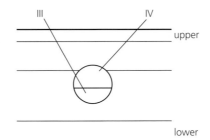

Which tissues are phloem?
   A I and III only
   B I and IV only
   C II and III only
   D II and IV only

Higher Level Paper 2, May 03, Q38

Q4 What conditions are needed for the germination of all seeds?
   I light   II sufficient water   III oxygen

   A I and II only
   B I and III only
   C II and III only
   D I, II and III

Higher Level Paper 1, May 02, Q40

Questions 5–10 cover other syllabus issues in this chapter.

Q5 The leaf is the site of the bulk of photosynthesis in the flowering plant. Outline, by means of concise notes, **five** structural features of leaves that specifically favour photosynthesis and the ways they may enhance this process.   (5 + 5)

Q6 *"Transpiration is an unfortunate consequence of plant structure and plant nutrition; it cannot be described as a purposeful process!"*
Suggest how you may support and justify this statement to a sceptical biologist.   (6)

Q7 a Explain what *meristems* are.   (1)
   b Identify the key features of meristematic plant cells.   (3)
   c Explain the difference between an apical and a lateral meristem by reference to the growth they make possible.   (4)

Q8 a Define *translocation* and *transpiration*.   (4)
   b Identify the sources of energy for movement of substances in:
      i translocation
      ii transpiration.   (4)
   c By means of a fully annotated drawing, describe the structure of phloem tissue.   (6)
   d List the structural features of phloem tissue that are not shown by xylem tissue.   (3)
   e Outline the essential features of the mass flow hypothesis of phloem transport.   (6)

Q9 a Draw a fully labelled half-flower diagram of an insect-pollinated flower you have studied.   (6)
   b State what insects may visit this flower.   (1)
   c Identify the features of this flower that may attract insects.   (3)
   d Explain how pollination is brought about in this flower.   (4)

Q10 a List the ways guard cells of stomata differ from the ordinary epidermal cells around them.   (3)
   b Explain why stomatal pores close as leaves wilt, irrespective of whether the leaf is in the light or dark.   (2)
   c Outline the ideal conditions for stomata to be fully open.   (4)

11 Genetics II

STARTING POINTS
- In **diploid organisms** chromosomes occur in pairs, called **homologous chromosomes**, one coming originally from each parent. A gene occupies a position on a chromosome, its **locus**. Genes at a locus exist in two or more forms, called **alleles**.
- **Meiosis**, the nuclear division in which the new cells formed have **half the chromosome number** of the parent cell, is associated with sexual reproduction and the production of gametes.
- Gregor Mendel's **monohybrid cross** established that characteristics may be controlled by a pair of alleles that **segregate** in equal numbers into different gametes. Segregation occurs in meiosis.
- Genes on the same chromosome are **linked** and may be inherited together. Characteristics controlled by genes on the **sex chromosomes** are sex-linked characteristics.
- **Mutations** (abrupt changes) may arise in genes or chromosomes.
- This chapter extends aspects of the study of genetics begun in Chapter 4, pages 91–116.

The painstaking experimental work on inheritance by **Gregor Mendel** (Figure 4.13, page 103), although overlooked in his life-time, supplied the foundations for **modern genetics**, once it was rediscovered, read and understood.

Heredity is responsible for many of the similarities and differences (**variations**) between parents and offspring. We know that many variations that are inherited may be discrete or **discontinuous variations**, such as we saw in tall or dwarf pea plants (page 104). Alternatively, other characteristics of organisms show continuous variation over a range (such as height in humans). These are known as **continuous variations**.

In this chapter, **chromosome behaviour in meiosis** and the causes of **genetic variation in gametes** are considered first. Mendel's investigation of the **dihybrid cross** and the **Law of Independent Assortment** are explained, and their relation to meiosis established. Then, gene linkage, **crossing over** and the formation of **recombinants** are discussed. Finally, how continuous variation may also be genetically controlled in **polygenic inheritance** is demonstrated.

Meiosis and genetic variety in gametes 10.1.1–10.1.3

Meiosis is an essential event in life cycles that include sexual reproduction, because at fertilisation the chromosome number is doubled.

The events in meiosis have already been established in Chapter 4. Meiosis is a nuclear division that is slower and more complex than mitosis, for it involves two successive divisions of the nucleus (**meiosis I** and **meiosis II**), but both of these divisions superficially resemble mitosis.

We have already seen that in meiosis I the **homologous chromosomes separate**, and that in meiosis II the **chromatids separate**.

Take a look at these points, shown in Figure 4.5 on page 95, now.

Equally important is the fact that there is no interphase between meiosis I and II, so no replication of the chromosomes occurs during meiosis. (Remember, chromosomes replicate to form chromatids during interphase, well before nuclear divisions occur.)

Meiosis consists of two nuclear divisions but only one replication of the chromosomes.

Figure 11.1 What happens in meiosis

MEIOSIS I

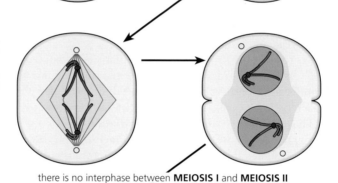

prophase I (early)
During interphase the chromosomes replicate into chromatids held together by a centromere (the chromatids are not visible). Now the chromosomes condense (shorten and thicken) and become visible.

prophase I (mid)
Homologous chromosomes pair up (becoming **bivalents**) as they continue to shorten and thicken. Centrioles duplicate.

prophase I (late)
Homologous chromosomes repel each other. Chromosomes can now be seen to consist of chromatids. Sites where chromatids have broken and rejoined, causing crossing over, are visible as chiasmata.

metaphase I
Nuclear membrane breaks down. Spindle forms. Bivalents line up at the equator, attached by centromeres.

anaphase I
Homologous chromosomes separate. Whole chromosomes are pulled towards opposite poles of the spindle, centromere first (dragging along the chromatids).

telophase I
Nuclear membrane re-forms around the daughter nuclei. The chromosome number has been halved. The chromosomes start to decondense.

there is no interphase between **MEIOSIS I** and **MEIOSIS II**

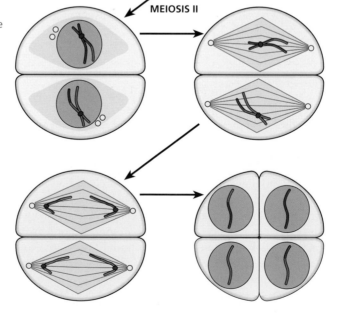

MEIOSIS II

prophase II
The chromosomes condense and the centrioles duplicate.

metaphase II
The nuclear membrane breaks down and the spindle forms. The chromosomes attach by their centromere to spindle fibres at the equator of the spindle.

anaphase II
The chromatids separate at their centromeres and are pulled to opposite poles of the spindle.

telophase II
The chromatids (now called chromosomes) decondense. The nuclear membrane re-forms. The cells divide.

The process of meiosis

Once started, meiosis proceeds steadily as a continuous process of nuclear division. The steps of meiosis are explained in four distinct phases (**prophase**, **metaphase**, **anaphase** and **telophase**), but this is just for convenience of analysis and description – there are no breaks between the phases in nuclear divisions.

The behaviour of the chromosomes in the phases of meiosis is shown in Figure 11.1. For clarity, the drawings show a cell with a single pair of homologous chromosomes.

Meiosis I – prophase I

What happens to chromosomes during prophase I is especially complex. They appear in the light microscope as single threads with many tiny bead-like thickenings along their lengths. These thickenings represent an early stage in the process of shortening and thickening by coiling that continues throughout prophase. This packaging of DNA in the chromosome is shown in Figure 8.2, page 236. Of course, each chromosome is already replicated as two chromatids but individual chromatids are not visible as yet.

Formation of bivalents

As the chromosomes continue to thicken, homologous chromosomes are seen to come together in specific pairs, point by point, all along their length. The product of pairing is called a **bivalent**. Remember, in a diploid cell each chromosome has a partner that is the same length and shape and with the same linear sequence of alleles.

The homologous chromosomes of the bivalents continue to shorten and thicken. Later in prophase, the individual chromosomes can be seen to be double-stranded, as the sister chromatids of which each consists become visible.

Crossing over

Within the bivalent, during the coiling and shortening process, breakages of the chromatids occur frequently. Breakages are common in non-sister chromatids at the same points along the length of each. Broken ends rejoin more or less immediately, but where the rejoins are between non-sister chromatids, swapping of pieces of the chromatids has occurred, hence the term 'crossing over'.

The point of join between different chromatids is called a **chiasma** (plural, **chiasmata**). Virtually every pair of homologous chromosomes forms at least one chiasma at this time, and to have two or more chiasmata in the same bivalent is very common (Figures 11.2 and 11.3).

In the later stage of prophase I, the attraction and tight pairing of the homologous chromosomes ends, but the attraction between sister chromatids remains for the moment. This attraction of sister chromatids keeps the bivalents together. The chromatids are now at their shortest and thickest.

Later still, the centrioles present in animal cells (page 7) duplicate, and start to move apart as a prelude to spindle formation. Plant cells are without a centriole.

Finally, the disappearance of the nucleoli and nuclear membrane marks the end of prophase I.

Metaphase I

Next, the spindle forms and the bivalents become attached to individual microtubules of the spindle by their centromeres. The bivalents are now arranged at the equatorial plate of the spindle framework – we say that they line up at the centre of the cell. By the end of metaphase I, the members of the bivalents start to repel each other and separate. However, at this point they are held together by one or more chiasmata, and this gives temporary but unusual shapes to the bivalents.

Anaphase I

The homologous chromosomes of each bivalent now move to opposite poles of the spindle, but with the individual chromatids remaining attached by their centromeres. The attraction of sister chromatids has lapsed, and they separate slightly – both are clearly visible. However, they do not separate yet, but go to the same pole. Consequently, meiosis I has separated homologous pairs of chromosomes but not the sister chromatids of which each is composed.

Figure 11.2 Formation of chiasmata

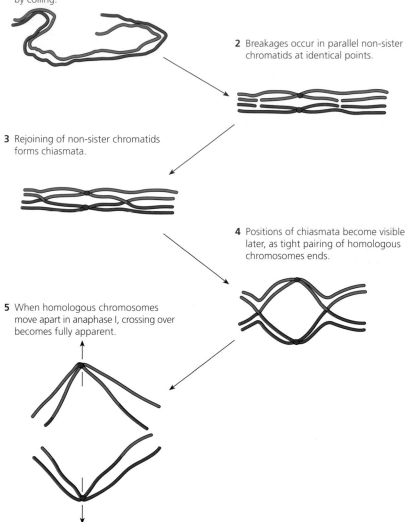

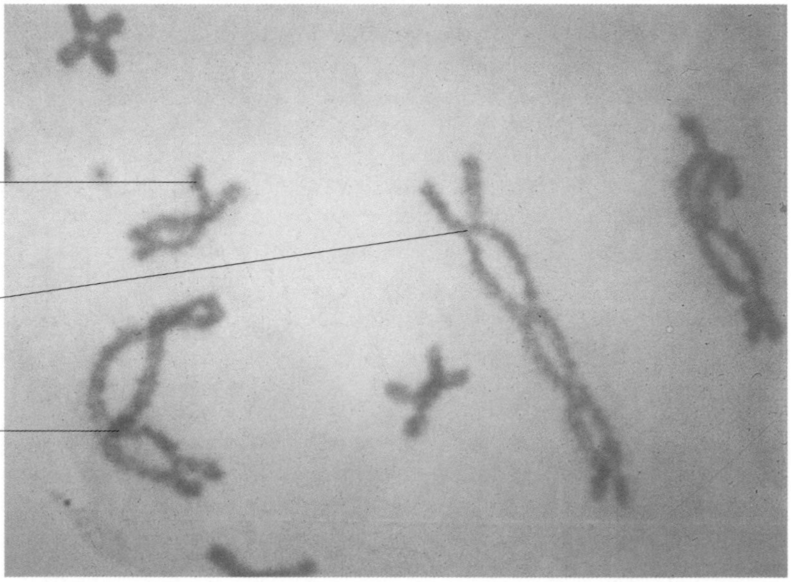

1 Homologous chromosomes commencing pairing to form a bivalent as they continue to shorten and thicken by coiling.

2 Breakages occur in parallel non-sister chromatids at identical points.

3 Rejoining of non-sister chromatids forms chiasmata.

4 Positions of chiasmata become visible later, as tight pairing of homologous chromosomes ends.

5 When homologous chromosomes move apart in anaphase I, crossing over becomes fully apparent.

Figure 11.3 Photomicrograph of bivalents held together by chiasmata

bivalent (paired homologous chromosomes)

chiasma

chiasma

Telophase I

The arrival of homologous chromosomes at opposite poles signals the end of meiosis I. The chromosomes tend to uncoil to some extent, and a nuclear membrane re-forms around both nuclei. The spindle breaks down. However, these two cells do not go into interphase, but rather continue into meiosis II, which takes place at right angles to meiosis I. Meiosis II is remarkably similar to mitosis.

Meiosis II – prophase II

The nuclear membranes break down again, and the chromosomes shorten and re-thicken by coiling. Centrioles, if present, move to opposite poles of the cell. By the end of prophase II the spindle apparatus has re-formed, but is present at right angles to the original spindle.

Metaphase II

The chromosomes line up at the equator of the spindle, attached by their centromeres.

Anaphase II

The centromeres divide and the chromatids are pulled to opposite poles of the spindle, centromeres first.

Telophase II

Nuclear membranes form around the four groups of chromatids, so that four nuclei are formed. Now there are four cells, each with half the chromosome number of the original parent cell. Finally, the chromatids – now recognised as chromosomes – uncoil and become apparently dispersed as chromatin. Nucleoli re-form.

The process of meiosis is now complete, and is followed by division of the cells (cytokinesis, page 33).

Meiosis and genetic variation

The variation in the genetic information carried by different gametes that arises in meiosis is highly significant for the organism, as we shall see. The four haploid cells produced by meiosis differ genetically from each other because of:

- **Independent assortment of maternal and paternal homologous chromosomes**
  The way the bivalents line up at the equator of the spindle in meiosis I is entirely random. Which chromosome of a given pair goes to which pole is unaffected by (independent of) the behaviour of the chromosomes in other pairs. This was introduced in Figure 4.7, but it is represented again here in terms of the critical steps in meiosis where it occurs (Figure 11.4). These illustrations show a parent cell with only four chromosomes, for clarity. Of course, the more bivalents there are in the nucleus, the more variation is possible. In humans, there are 23 pairs of chromosomes, so the number of possible combinations of chromosomes that can be formed as a result of independent assortment is 2^{23}. This is over 8 million.
- **Crossing over of segments of individual maternal and paternal homologous chromosomes**
  This results in new combinations of genes on the chromosomes of the haploid cells produced, as illustrated in Figure 11.5. Crossing over generates the possibility of an almost unimaginable degree of variation. For example, if we were to assume for sake of discussion that there are 30 000 individual genes on the human chromosome complement, all with at least two alternative alleles, and that crossing over was equally likely between all of these genes, then there would be $2^{30\,000}$ different combinations. Of course, all these assumptions would be inaccurate to varying extents, but the point that virtually unlimited recombinations are possible is established.

Figure 11.4 Genetic variation due to independent assortment

Independent assortment is illustrated in a cell with two pairs of chromosomes.

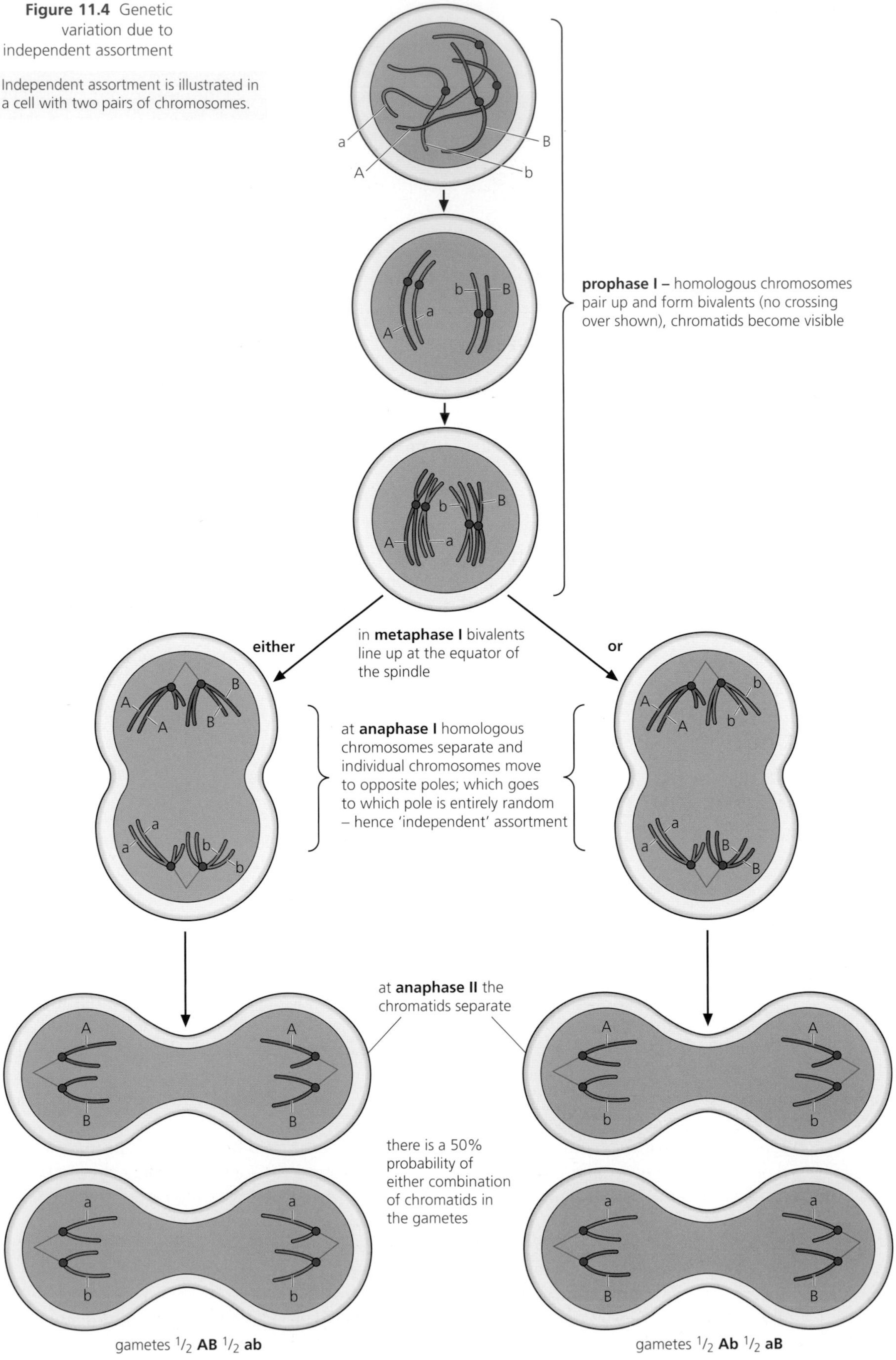
a
A
B
b
b
B
a
A
b
B
A
a
prophase I – homologous chromosomes pair up and form bivalents (no crossing over shown), chromatids become visible
either
or
in **metaphase I** bivalents line up at the equator of the spindle
at **anaphase I** homologous chromosomes separate and individual chromosomes move to opposite poles; which goes to which pole is entirely random – hence 'independent' assortment
A
A
B
B
a
a
b
b
A
A
b
b
a
a
B
B
at **anaphase II** the chromatids separate
A
B
A
B
A
b
A
b
there is a 50% probability of either combination of chromatids in the gametes
a
b
a
b
a
B
a
B
gametes $^1/_2$ **AB** $^1/_2$ **ab**
gametes $^1/_2$ **Ab** $^1/_2$ **aB**

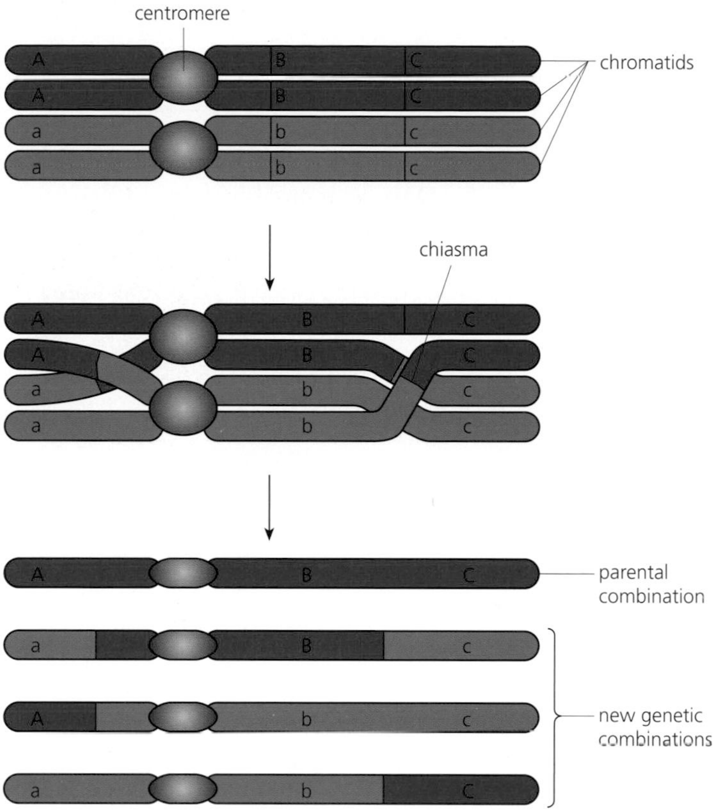

Figure 11.5 Genetic variation due to crossing over

The effects of chiasmata on genetic variation are illustrated in one pair of homologous chromosomes. Typically, two or three chiasmata form between the chromatids of a bivalent in prophase I.

Homologous chromosomes paired in a bivalent with alleles ABC and abc.

If the chromatids break at corresponding points along their length, their rejoining may cause crossing over.

The chromatids finally separate and move to haploid nuclei in meiosis II, producing new genetic combinations – chromatids carry alleles ABC, aBc, Abc and abC.

A note on recombinants

Offspring with new combinations of characteristics different from those of their parents are called **recombinants**.

Recombination in genetics is the re-assortment of alleles or characters into different combinations from those of the parents. We have seen that recombination occurs for genes located on separate chromosomes (unlinked genes) by chromosome assortment in meiosis (Figure 11.4), and for genes on the same chromosomes (linked genes) by crossing over during meiosis (Figure 11.5).

1 **Distinguish** the essential differences between mitosis and meiosis.

Dihybrid crosses and gene linkage · 10.1.4–10.1.5, 10.2.1–10.2.6

The contribution to our understanding of the mechanism of inheritance made by Gregor Mendel was introduced on page 103, by discussion of his investigation of the inheritance of a single pair of contrasting characteristics, namely of tall and dwarf pea plants. This was his so-called **monohybrid cross**.

Mendel also investigated the simultaneous inheritance of **two pairs of contrasting characters**, again using the garden pea plant. This he referred to as a **dihybrid cross**.

For example: Mendel crossed (P generation) pure-breeding pea plants from **round seeds** with **yellow cotyledons** (seed leaves) with pure-breeding plants from **wrinkled seeds** with **green cotyledons**. All the progeny (F$_1$ generation) were **round, yellow peas**.

When plants grown from these seeds were allowed to self-fertilise the following season, the resulting seeds (F$_2$ generation) – of which there were more than 500 to be classified and counted – were of the following four phenotypes, and were present in the ratio shown below:

Phenotypes	round seed with yellow cotyledons	round seed with green cotyledons	wrinkled seed with yellow cotyledons	wrinkled seed with green cotyledons
Ratio	**9**	**3**	**3**	**1**

Mendel noticed that two new combinations, not represented in the parents (i.e. **recombinations**) appeared in the progeny: both round and wrinkled seeds can turn up with either green or yellow cotyledons.

Thus, the two pairs of factors were inherited independently. He had noticed that either one of a pair of contrasting characters could be passed to the next generation. This meant that a heterozygous plant must produce four types of gametes in equal numbers (Figures 11.6 and 11.7).

Figure 11.6 Mendel's dihybrid cross

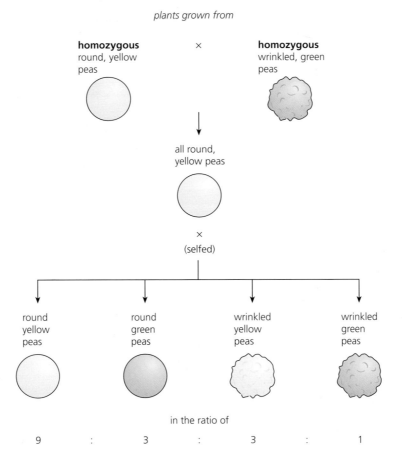

2 In Figure 11.6, **identify** the progeny that are:

a heterozygous
b recombinants.

3 **Deduce** the positions of the genes for round/wrinkled and for yellow/green cotyledons within the nucleus of the pea plant. Explain the significance of their location (which was unknown to Mendel).

Mendel confirmed the results of his first dihybrid cross by carrying out experiments with peas showing other pairs of contrasting characteristics (and also with other species of plant).

He published his results through his local natural history and agricultural research society, and by regular correspondence with certain influential scientists of the time. However, we cannot be confident that anyone apart from Mendel himself saw the significance of his discoveries in his life-time.

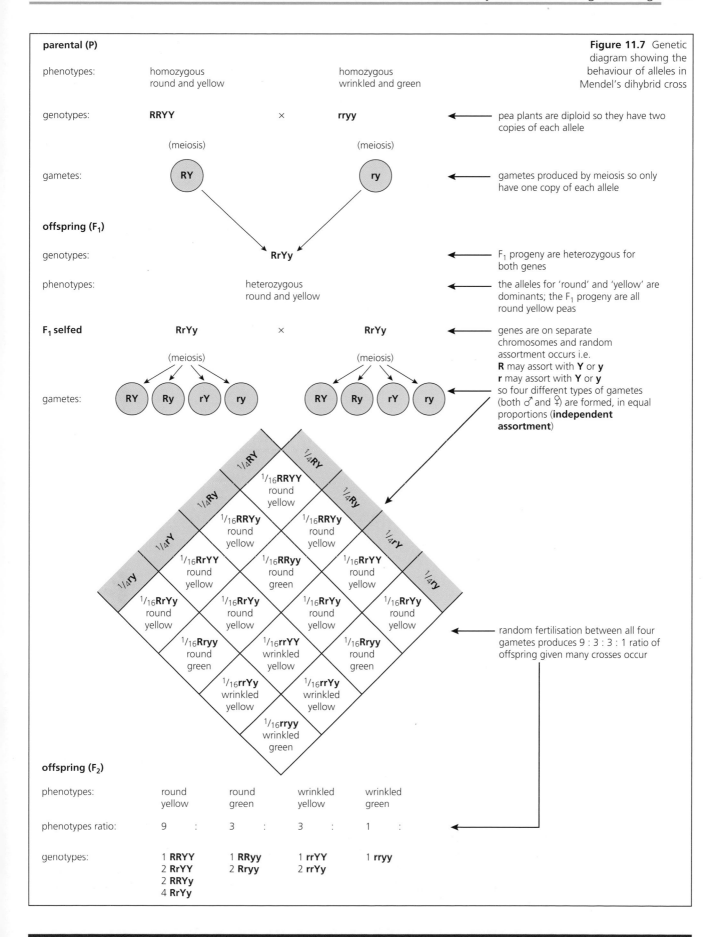

Figure 11.7 Genetic diagram showing the behaviour of alleles in Mendel's dihybrid cross

Mendel did not express the outcome of the dihybrid cross as a succinct Second Law. However, today we call Mendel's Second Law the **Law of Independent Assortment**. It is stated as:

Two or more pairs of alleles segregate independently of each other as a result of meiosis, provided the genes concerned are not linked by being on the same chromosome.

The relationship between Mendel's Law of Independent Assortment and meiosis is detailed in Table 11.1.

Mendel's dihybrid cross	Feature of meiosis
Within an organism there are breeding factors controlling characteristics like round or wrinkled seeds, and yellow or green cotyledons.	Each chromosome holds a linear sequence of genes.
These factors remain intact from generation to generation.	A particular gene always occurs on the same chromosome in the same position after each nuclear division.
There are two factors for each characteristic in each cell.	The chromosomes of a cell occur in pairs, called homologous pairs.
One factor comes from each parent. (A recessive factor is not expressed in the presence of a dominant factor.)	One of each pair came originally from one parent and the other from the other parent.
Factors separate in reproduction; either can be passed to an offspring. Only one of the factors can be in any gamete.	At the end of meiosis, each cell (gamete) contains a single member of each of the homologous pairs of chromosomes present in the parent cell.
The factors for seed shape and seed colour segregate independently of each other as a result of meiosis.	The genes for seed shape and seed colour are on separate chromosomes.
The 9:3:3:1 ratio shows that all four types of gamete are equally common. The inheritance of the two characteristics is separate.	The arrangement of bivalents at the equatorial plate of the spindle is random; maternal and paternal homologous chromosomes are independently assorted. In a large number of matings, all possible combinations of chromosomes will occur in equal numbers.

Table 11.1 How the Law of Independent Assortment relates to meiosis

The dihybrid test cross

Look back to Chapter 4, page 106, to remind yourself of the issue that the **monohybrid test cross** sorts out.

Why is a test cross sometimes necessary?

In the case of dihybrid inheritance, too, while homozygous recessive genotypes such as wrinkled green peas (**rryy**) can be recognised in the phenotype, homozygous round yellow peas (**RRYY**) and heterozygous round yellow peas (**RrYy**) look exactly the same (Figure 11.7). They can only be distinguished by the progeny they produce, as illustrated in a dihybrid test cross (Figure 11.8).

Unlike the monohybrid test cross, where the outcome is a ratio of 1:1, the dihybrid test cross outcome is a ratio of 1:1:1:1. We will return to this point later.

TOK Link

Given the absence of understanding of chromosomes, genes and meiosis at the time, is it appropriate to describe Mendel's scientific contributions as 'nothing but trained and organised common sense'?

Drosophila **and the dihybrid cross**

Mendel died in 1884 – in relative obscurity, at least as far as the scientific community was concerned. Few seemed to know of his scientific work and those who were aware of it did not appear to understand his results. But his papers were rediscovered in 1900, as a result of careful literature searches by people keen to advance our understanding of inheritance. Mendel's results came to be confirmed and then extended by many others, using a range of species.

Figure 11.8 Genetic diagram of the dihybrid test cross

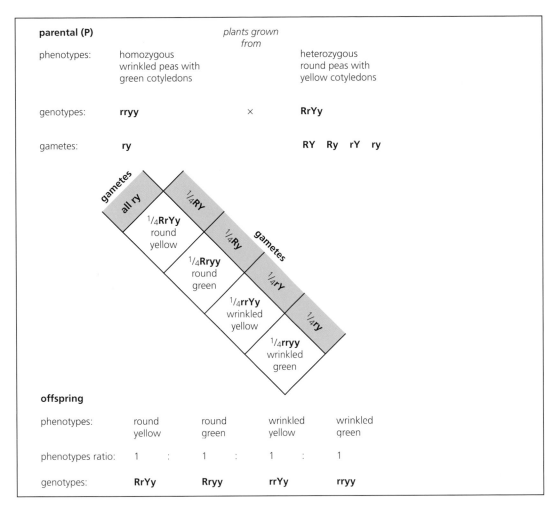

parental (P)   *plants grown from*

phenotypes: homozygous wrinkled peas with green cotyledons   heterozygous round peas with yellow cotyledons

genotypes: **rryy**   ×   **RrYy**

gametes: **ry**   **RY Ry rY ry**

offspring

phenotypes:	round yellow	round green	wrinkled yellow	wrinkled green
phenotypes ratio:	1 :	1 :	1 :	1
genotypes:	**RrYy**	**Rryy**	**rrYy**	**rryy**

Drosophila melanogaster (the fruit fly) was first selected by an American geneticist called **Thomas Morgan** in 1908 as an experimental organism for investigation of Mendelian genetics in an animal. Morgan was awarded a Nobel Prize in 1933 because by his experiments he had:

- shown that Mendel's 'factors' are linear sequences of genes on chromosomes (what is now called the **Chromosome Theory of Inheritance**);
- discovered sex chromosomes and sex linkage;
- demonstrated crossing over, and the exchange of alleles between chromosomes, resulting from chiasmata formed during meiosis.

Drosophila commonly occurs around rotting vegetable material. This form is often called the wild type, simply to differentiate it from the various naturally occurring mutant forms.

Why has this insect become such a useful experimental animal in the study of genetics?

Drosophila has four pairs of chromosomes (Figure 11.9). From mating to emergence of adult flies (generation time) takes about 10 days at 25°C. One female produces hundreds of offspring. These flies are relatively easily handled, cultured on sterilised artificial medium in glass bottles, and they can be temporarily anaesthetised for setting up cultures and sorting progeny.

A dihybrid cross can be shown in *Drosophila* – for example, by crossing normal flies (wild type) with flies homozygous for vestigial wing and ebony body (Figure 11.10). These characteristics are controlled by genes not on the sex chromosomes. All chromosomes other than the sex chromosomes are called **autosomal chromosomes** (see below).

The genes concerned in this *Drosophila* cross are on separate autosomal chromosomes, so they are unlinked genes. SAQ 5 on page 338 sets the task of determining the genotypes of offspring of the F$_2$ generation of this dihybrid cross in *Drosophila*, summarised in Figure 11.10.

4 **Define** what is meant by the term 'mutant'.

Figure 11.9 Wild-type *Drosophila* (photograph) and some common mutants (drawings)

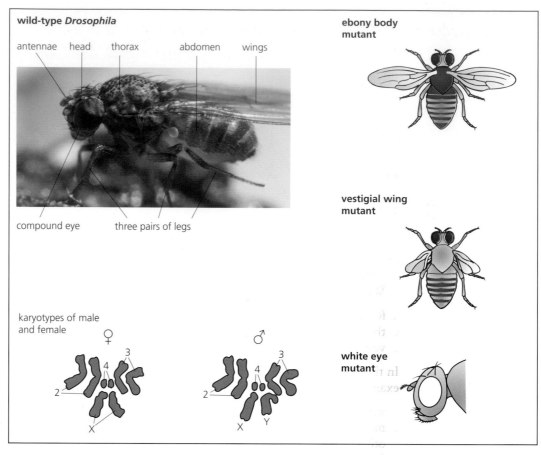

wild-type *Drosophila*

antennae   head   thorax   abdomen   wings

compound eye   three pairs of legs

karyotypes of male and female

ebony body mutant

vestigial wing mutant

white eye mutant

Figure 11.10 A dihybrid cross in *Drosophila* – a summary

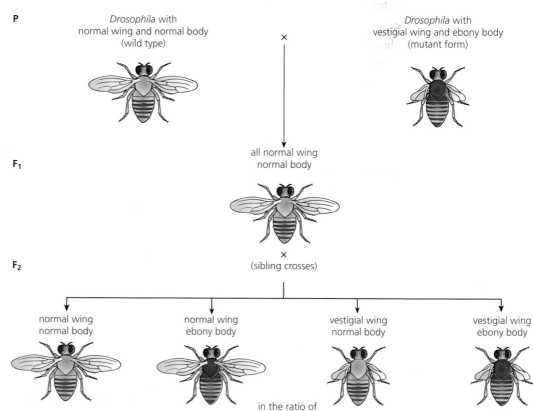

P

Drosophila with normal wing and normal body (wild type)

×

Drosophila with vestigial wing and ebony body (mutant form)

F₁

all normal wing normal body

F₂

×
(sibling crosses)

normal wing normal body

normal wing ebony body

vestigial wing normal body

vestigial wing ebony body

in the ratio of

9 : 3 : 3 : 1

5 **Construct** a genetic diagram for the dihybrid cross shown in Figure 11.10, using the layout as given in Figure 11.7.
Determine the genotypes of the offspring of the F₂ generation.

■ Extension: Probability and chance in genetic crosses

We can see that there is an expected ratio of offspring of 9:3:3:1 when the dihybrid cross is carried out. Actually, the offspring produced in many dihybrid cross experiments do not exactly agree with the expected ratio. This is illustrated by the results of an experiment with mutant forms of *Drosophila* in Table 11.2.

Offspring in F$_2$ generation	normal wing, grey body = 315	normal wing, ebony body = 108	vestigial wing, grey body = 101	vestigial wing, ebony body = 32	total = 556
Predicted ratio	9	3	3	1	
Expected numbers of offspring	313	104	104	35	

Table 11.2 Observed and expected offspring

Clearly, these results are fairly close to the ratio 9:3:3:1, but they are not the predicted ratio, precisely.

What, if anything, went wrong?

Well, we can expect this ratio among the progeny only if three conditions are met:

- fertilisation is entirely random;
- there are equal opportunities for survival among the offspring;
- very large numbers of offspring are produced.

In the above experiment with *Drosophila*, the exact ratio may not be obtained because, for example:

- more male flies of one type may have succeeded in fertilising females than of the other type;
- more females of one type may have died before reaching egg laying condition than of the other type;
- fewer eggs of one type may have completed their development than of the other type.

Similarly, in breeding experiments with plants such as the pea plant, exact ratios may not be obtained because of parasite damage or by the action of browsing predators on the anthers or ovaries in some flowers, or because some pollen types fail to be transported by pollinating insects as successfully as others, perhaps.

Gene linkage

In humans, the nucleus contains 46 chromosomes, although we have seen that these are only clearly visible as such during the nuclear divisions, mitosis or meiosis. In fact, it is particularly in metaphases of these divisions, when the chromosomes are at their shortest, and are arranged at the plate of the spindle, that it is particularly easy to see them. It is from photomicrographs of this stage that **karyotypes** are constructed (Figure 4.1, page 92).

A human karyotype shows us that one pair of our chromosomes are the **sex chromosomes**. These carry the critical gene that determines sex. The remainder of our set of chromosomes carry genes that determine characteristics of the growth, development and functioning of all other aspects of the body. These chromosomes are known as the autosomes (Figure 11.11).

Linkage groups

There are many thousands of genes per cell in an organism, whereas the number of chromosomes is often less than 50 and very rarely exceeds 100. Each chromosome, then, consists of many genes; it may be thought of as a linear series of genes that are all linked together.

The genes carried on a particular chromosome are called a linkage group.

Figure 11.11
Chromosomes as
autosomes and sex
chromosomes

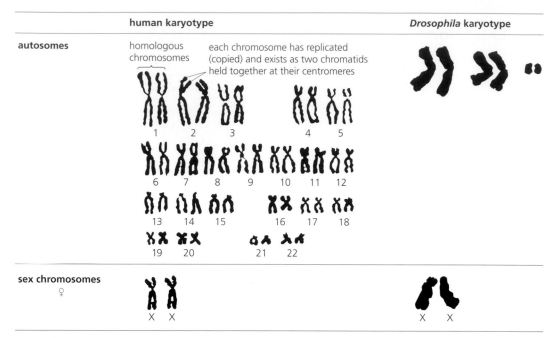

Obviously, genes of a linkage group will tend to be inherited together. And, in the case of a dihybrid cross involving linked genes, the Mendelian ratio we would expect from a cross with two pairs of contrasting characteristics in the F_2 generation (9:3:3:1) would not be obtained.

In fact, we might expect the ratio to be the same as that from crosses of one pair of contrasting characteristics in the F_2 generation, namely 3:1. This would certainly be the case if no chiasmata formed **between** the linked genes during prophase of meiosis, between non-sister chromatids.

The first example of this was discovered by experimental geneticists in 1906, very soon after Mendel's work was rediscovered. This experiment caused a mystery because linkage was not understood at that time. In studies of the inheritance in the **sweet pea plant**, plants homozygous for purple flowers and elongated pollen grains were crossed with plants homozygous for red flowers and rounded pollen grains. The offspring (the F_1 generation) had purple flowers and elongated pollen grains. Clearly, the alleles responsible for these characteristics were dominant.

When the F_1 generation plants were selfed, it was anticipated that the two pairs of alleles would segregate independently of each other, producing the four possible combinations (two parental types and two recombinant types) of a dihybrid cross in the expected ratio of 9:3:3:1.

This did not happen!

Instead, the progeny included a higher proportion of the parental characteristics (purple flowers and elongated pollen, and red flowers and round pollen) at the expense of the new combinations (purple flowers with round pollen, and red flowers with elongated pollen).

From Figure 11.12 it can be seen that this outcome is due to:

- gene linkage;
- where the chiasmata occur along the length of the chromosome.

6 The relative positions of linked genes have been extensively studied in organisms such as *Drosophila* by determining the proportions of recombinants in large samples of crosses. Recombination experiments have allowed the construction of gene maps of individual chromosomes, but this is not the case with humans. **Explain** why this is so, and **outline** how linkage is now investigated in human chromosomes.

parents homozygous purple flowers, elongated pollen × homozygous red flowers, round pollen

Figure 11.12 Crossing over in the sweet pea plant

genotypes:

$$\dfrac{F \quad E}{F \quad E} \qquad \dfrac{f \quad e}{f \quad e}$$

gametes:

$\left(\dfrac{F \; E}{}\right) \qquad \left(\dfrac{f \; e}{}\right)$

flowers of sweet pea (*Lathyrus odoratus*)

offspring (F₁) heterozygous purple flowers, elongated pollen

$$\dfrac{F \quad E}{f \quad e}$$

× self

When the F₁ offspring are selfed, the F₂ offspring that result depend on whether a chiasma forms *between* these alleles *or elsewhere* along the chromosome during meiosis, in gamete formation.

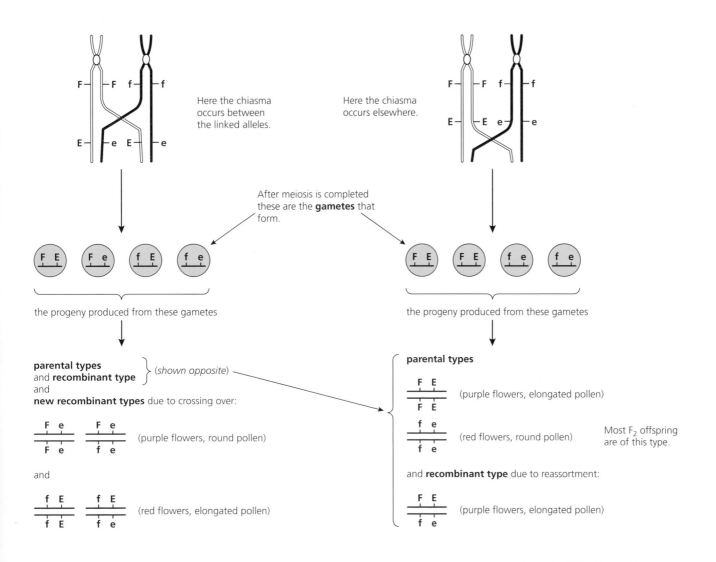

Here the chiasma occurs between the linked alleles.

Here the chiasma occurs elsewhere.

After meiosis is completed these are the **gametes** that form.

the progeny produced from these gametes

the progeny produced from these gametes

parental types and **recombinant type** } (*shown opposite*) and **new recombinant types** due to crossing over:

$$\dfrac{F \quad e}{F \quad e} \qquad \dfrac{F \quad e}{f \quad e}$$ (purple flowers, round pollen)

and

$$\dfrac{f \quad E}{f \quad E} \qquad \dfrac{f \quad E}{f \quad e}$$ (red flowers, elongated pollen)

parental types

$$\dfrac{F \quad E}{F \quad E}$$ (purple flowers, elongated pollen)

$$\dfrac{f \quad e}{f \quad e}$$ (red flowers, round pollen)   Most F₂ offspring are of this type.

and **recombinant type** due to reassortment:

$$\dfrac{F \quad E}{f \quad e}$$ (purple flowers, elongated pollen)

Figure 11.13 Linkages, crossing over and the test cross

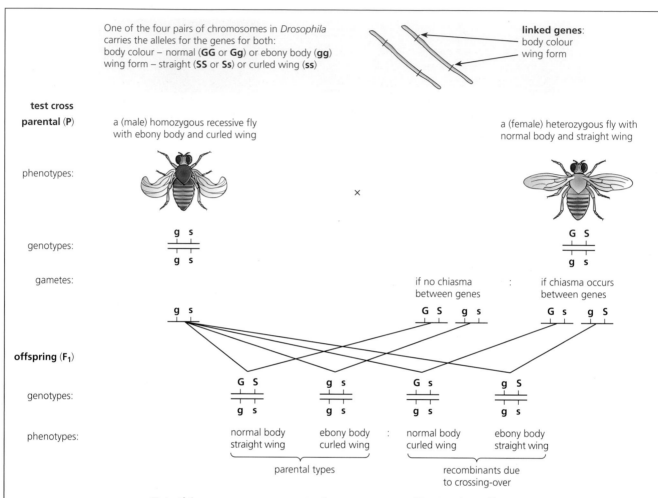

One of the four pairs of chromosomes in *Drosophila* carries the alleles for the genes for both:
body colour – normal (**GG** or **Gg**) or ebony body (**gg**)
wing form – straight (**SS** or **Ss**) or curled wing (**ss**)

linked genes:
body colour
wing form

test cross
parental (P)

a (male) homozygous recessive fly with ebony body and curled wing

a (female) heterozygous fly with normal body and straight wing

phenotypes:

×

genotypes:

$\dfrac{g \quad s}{g \quad s}$

$\dfrac{G \quad S}{g \quad s}$

gametes:

if no chiasma between genes : if chiasma occurs between genes

g s

G S   g s

G s   g S

offspring (F$_1$)

genotypes:

$\dfrac{G \quad S}{g \quad s}$ $\dfrac{g \quad s}{g \quad s}$ $\dfrac{G \quad s}{g \quad s}$ $\dfrac{g \quad S}{g \quad s}$

phenotypes:

normal body straight wing   ebony body curled wing   :   normal body curled wing   ebony body straight wing

parental types   recombinants due to crossing-over

Note: If these genes were on separate chromosomes we would expect these offspring in the ratio 1:1:1:1 (**dihybrid test cross**), but these genes are linked, and if no crossing over occurred we would expect parental types only, in the ratio 1:1 (**monohybrid test cross**).

The outcome of this experiment was:

Offspring	Phenotypes	Genotypes	Numbers obtained
parental types	normal body straight wing	$\dfrac{G \quad S}{g \quad s}$	536
	ebony body curled wing	$\dfrac{g \quad s}{g \quad s}$	481
recombinants	normal body curled wing	$\dfrac{G \quad s}{g \quad s}$	101
	ebony body straight wing	$\dfrac{g \quad S}{g \quad s}$	152

The majority of the offspring were parental types, so more chiasmata in this chromosome occur somewhere other than between these two genes.

Gene linkage and the test cross

The role of the test cross is to differentiate between the homozygous dominant and the heterozygous dominant since their appearance (their phenotype) is identical (pages 106 and 336).

The possibility of crossing over complicates the outcome of a test cross involving two genes that are linked, as Figure 11.13 shows.

This illustration comes from an investigation of inheritance in *Drosophila*, where a fly homozygous for ebony body and curled wing was crossed with a fly heterozygous for normal body and straight wing. Note that the characteristic 'curled wing' is different from the characteristic 'vestigial wing' shown in Figure 11.10 (a cross concerned with two contrasting characteristics controlled by genes on separate chromosomes – a straightforward dihybrid cross).

7 **Deduce** what recombinants may be formed in a test cross involving the linked genes:

$$\frac{tb}{tb} \times \frac{TB}{tb}$$

Polygenes and continuous variation 10.3.1–10.3.2

We began the story of genetics in Chapter 4 with an investigation of the inheritance of height in the garden pea (page 104), where one gene with two alleles gave tall or dwarf plants. This clear-cut difference in an inherited characteristic is an example of **discontinuous variation** – there is no intermediate form, and no overlap between the two phenotypes.

In fact, **very few characteristics of organisms are controlled by a single gene**. Mostly, characteristics of organisms are controlled by a number of genes. Groups of genes which together determine a characteristic are called **polygenes**.

> **Polygenic inheritance is the inheritance of phenotypes that are determined by the collective effect of several genes.**

The genes that make up a polygene are often (but not necessarily always) located on different chromosomes. Any one of these genes has a very small or insignificant effect on the phenotype, but the combined effect of all the genes of the polygene is to produce infinite variety among the offspring.

Many features of humans are controlled by polygenes, including body weight and height. The graph of the variation in the heights of a population of 400 people, in Figure 11.14, shows continuous variation in height between the shortest at 160 cm and the tallest at 186 cm and a mean height of 173 cm. Human height is controlled by several different genes.

Figure 11.14 Human height as a case of polygenic inheritance

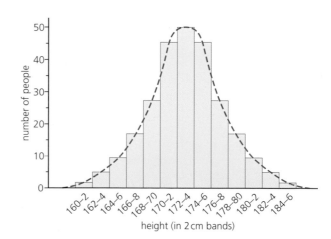

Human height is determined genetically by interactions of the alleles of several genes, probably located at loci on different chromosomes.

Variation in the height of adult humans
The results cluster around a mean value and show a normal distribution. For the purpose of the graph, the heights are collected into arbitrary groups, each of a height range of 2 cm.

Human skin colour

The colour of human skin is due to the amount of the pigment called **melanin** that is produced in the skin. Melanin synthesis is genetically controlled. It seems that three, four or more separately inherited genes control melanin production. The outcome is an almost continuous distribution of skin colour from very pale (no alleles coding for melanin production) to very dark brown (all alleles for skin colour code for melanin production).

In Figure 11.15, polygenic inheritance of human skin colour involving only two independent genes is illustrated. This is because dealing with all four genes is unwieldy (Figure 11.16), and the principle can be demonstrated clearly enough using just two genes.

It should be noted, too, that both human height and skin colour are characteristics that may also be influenced by environmental factors.

Figure 11.15 Human skin colour as a characteristic controlled by two independent genes – an illustration of polygenic inheritance

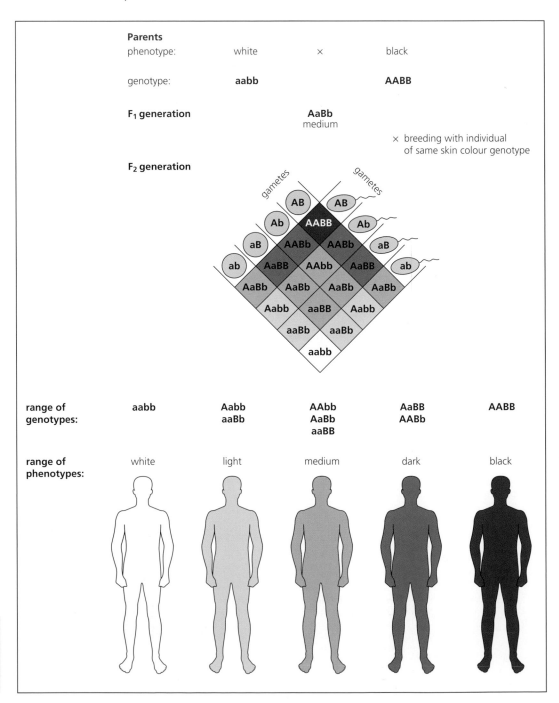

8 **Derive** the ratio of phenotypes produced in the F₂ generation shown in Figure 11.15.

Polygenic inheritance in a plant species

Many other examples of polygenic inheritance have been discovered. A good example, one in which only three genes interact together to control the phenotype, is the colour of the grain (a fruit) in certain varieties of wheat, *Triticum vulgare*.

In this case, for all three of these genes there are only two alleles. Despite this limitation, the full range of colours obtained varies from dark red (genotype $R^1R^1R^2R^2R^3R^3$) to white (genotype $r^1r^1r^2r^2r^3r^3$), with five intermediate shades of pink (Figure 11.16).

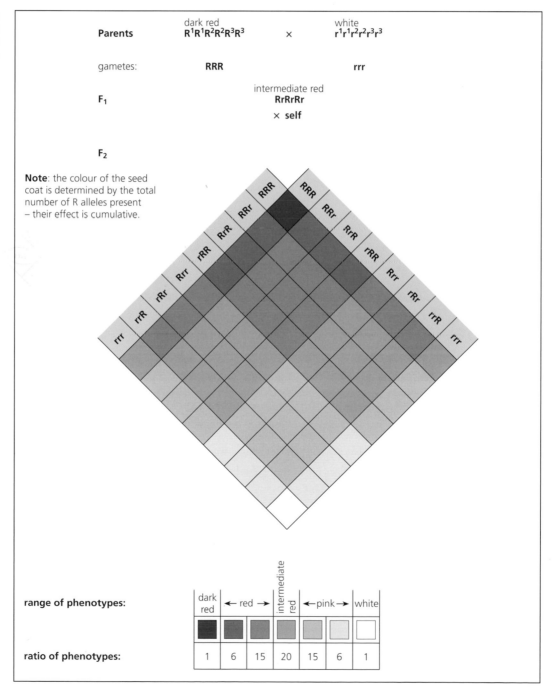

Figure 11.16 Inheritance of seed coat colour in *Triticum vulgare*, a case of polygenic inheritance

Continuous variation

We can see that the number of genes controlling a characteristic does not have to be large before the variation in a phenotype becomes more or less continuous, where a large group of offspring are produced. The outcome is that the characteristics controlled by polygenes tend to show **continuous variation**.

Nevertheless, the individual genes concerned are inherited in accordance with the principles established above. However, there are so many intermediate combinations of alleles that the discrete ratios are not observed. Even where only two genes constitute the polygene, significant variation results where the effect of the alleles is additive.

■ **Extension:** ## Other forms of gene interaction

We have seen that polygenic inheritance adds to the range of phenotypes that may exist. In fact, there are also other mechanisms by which genetic variety is controlled. It is helpful at this stage to be aware of the existence of some of these mechanisms, although knowing about how they operate is beyond the scope of this course.

Cases where characteristics are controlled by two or more genes, one or more of which **masks or modifies** the expression of the other(s) to various degrees, include:

■ plumage pigmentation and comb form in the domestic fowl;
■ agoutie coat colour in some mice;
■ shell banding in the snail *Cepaea nemoralis*.

These and several other examples have similarly been much studied and widely reported on.

Another important factor that may affect the appearance of the phenotype is the effect of **environmental conditions** (already mentioned above). For example, a tall plant may appear almost dwarf if it has been consistently deprived of adequate essential mineral ions.

Similarly, the physique of humans may be greatly affected by the levels of nourishment received, particularly as children.

We must remember then, that the phenotype of an organism is the product of both its genotype and the **influences of the environment**.

■ *Examination questions – a selection*

Questions 1–6 are taken from past IB Diploma biology papers.

Q1 Which response describes the behaviour of chromosomes in metaphase I and anaphase II of meiosis?

	Metaphase I	Anaphase II
A	chromosomes line up at the equator	separation of homologous chromosomes
B	tetrads (bivalents) line up at the equator	separation of homologous chromosomes
C	chromosomes line up at the equator	separation of sister chromatids
D	tetrads (bivalents) line up at the equator	separation of sister chromatids

Higher Level Paper 1, May 03, Q24

Q2 In garden peas, the pairs of alleles coding for seed shape and seed colour are unlinked. The allele for smooth seeds (S) is dominant over the allele for wrinkled seeds (s). The allele for yellow seeds (Y) is dominant over the allele for green seeds (y).

If a plant of genotype Ssyy is crossed with a plant of genotype ssYy, which offspring are recombinants?

A SsYy and Ssyy
B SsYy and ssYy
C SsYy and ssyy
D Ssyy and ssYy

Higher Level Paper 1, May 03, Q26

Q3 A polygenic character is controlled by two genes each with two alleles. How many different possible genotypes are there for this character?

  A 2
  B 4
  C 9
  D 16

  Higher Level Paper 2, May 04, Q30

Q4 If red (RR) is crossed with white (rr) and produces a pink flower (Rr), and tall (D) is dominant to dwarf (d), what is the phenotypic ratio from a cross of Rrdd and rrDd?

  A 9:3:3:1
  B 50% pink, 50% white and all tall
  C 1:1:1:1, in which 50% are tall, 50% are dwarf, 50% are pink and 50% are white
  D 3:1

  Higher Level Paper 1, May 05, Q30

Q5 If the haploid number of an organism is 8, how many gametes are possible, not considering the effects of crossing over?

  A 16
  B 64
  C 128
  D 256

  Higher Level Paper 1, May 06, Q40

Q6 **a** Define the term *gene linkage* and outline an example of a cross between two linked genes. (8)
  b Describe the inheritance of ABO blood groups, including an example of the possible outcomes of a homozygous blood group A mother having a child with a blood group O father. (5)
  c Outline sex linkage. (5)

  Higher Level Paper 2, November 05, QB8

Questions 7–10 cover other syllabus issues in this chapter.

Q7 **a** Explain the essential differences between prophase of mitosis and prophase I of meiosis. (4)
  b Identify the events in meiosis that result in gametes having different chromosome content. (4)
  c Describe the steps in meiosis by which a chiasma is formed. (4)

Q8 **a** Mendel conducted many experiments with garden pea plants, but some later workers used the fruit fly *Drosophila* in experimental genetics investigations. Suggest **three** reasons why this insect was found to be useful. (3)
  b When dihybrid crosses are carried out the progeny are rarely present in the exact proportions predicted. Explain why small deviations of this sort arise in dihybrid crosses with:
  i garden pea plants (3)
  ii *Drosophila*. (3)

Q9 In *Drosophila*, mutants with scarlet eyes and vestigial wings are recessive to flies with red eyes and normal wings. (These contrasting characters are controlled by single genes on different chromosomes, i.e. they are not linked on a single chromosome.) Explain the phenotypic ratio to be expected in the F_2 generation when normal flies are crossed with scarlet eyes/vestigial wing mutants and sibling crosses of the F_1 offspring are then conducted. Show your reasoning by means of a genetic cross diagram. (8)

Q10 Distinguish between the following pairs:
  a *discontinuous variable* and *continuous variable* (4)
  b *monohybrid cross* and *dihybrid cross* (4)
  c *linkage* and *crossing over* (4)
  d *autosomes* and *sex chromosomes* (4)
  e *X chromosomes* and *Y chromosomes* (4)
  f *multiple alleles* and *polygenes* (4)

12 Human physiology, health and reproduction II

STARTING POINTS

- The **blood circulation** has a role in the body's **defence against disease**.
- The **immune system** responds to the presence of foreign matter (**antigens**), including **pathogens**, by producing **antibodies** by special **leucocytes** (white cells).
- **Energy** is transferred in cells by cell respiration. **ATP**, the universal energy currency, is a reactant in **energy-requiring reactions** and **processes**.
- **Neurones** are the basic units of the **nervous system**, which consists of **receptors** (sense organs) linked to **effectors** (**muscles** or glands) by pathways of neurones called **reflex arcs**.
- **Excretion** is the removal of **waste products** of metabolism, including carbon dioxide, expelled at the lungs.
- **Homeostasis** involves maintaining the internal environment of the body between narrow limits. This includes **osmoregulation** in which the balance of **water** and **solutes** in body fluids is maintained at a constant level despite variations in intake.
- **Sex hormones** (testosterone, oestrogen and progesterone) have roles in the onset of **sexual maturity**, and the **production of sperm and egg cells**.
- Cell divisions by **mitosis** lead to the production of identical new cells. By **meiosis** the number of chromosomes per nucleus is halved – an essential step in **gamete production**.
- This chapter extends study of aspects of the structure and functioning (**physiology**) of the mammal begun in Chapter 7, pages 178–234.

We think of the **blood circulation** as the essential transport system for the body, but it also plays an intricate part in our resistance to harmful invasions. It is particularly the **white cells** that combat **infection**.

In the operation of the **nervous system**, changes that bring about responses, called **stimuli**, are detected by **receptors** (sense organs), but it is an **effector** (including our muscles) that brings about a response. Since in mammals, receptors and effectors are widely spaced, an efficient system of internal communication is essential.

Mammals are **regulators**, able to keep their internal environment in a steady state under a wide variety of external conditions. Negative feedback is the type of control mechanism that operates in **homeostasis**.

In mammals the **sexes are separate**. The **male reproductive system** includes the testes, in which sperms are produced. The **female reproductive system** includes the ovaries, in which oocytes are formed, and the uterus, where early development of the offspring occurs.

In this chapter, we extend study of the body's mechanisms of **defence against disease**. Then, the roles of the skeletal, muscular and nervous systems in bringing about **movement** are investigated, followed by discussion of the roles of the **kidneys** in excretion and osmoregulation – an aspect of homeostasis. **Human reproduction** is revisited in an investigation of the structure of the gonads and the process of gamete formation. Finally, the steps of fertilisation, the processes of pregnancy and birth, and the roles of certain hormones of the systems are considered.

Defence against infectious disease   11.1.1–11.1.7

Our intact skin is no easy barrier for pathogens to cross – mostly they are prevented from entry to the body. However, the defences of the skin are sometimes broken down, and so it is fortunate there are also internal lines of defence. The body responds to localised damage (cuts and abrasions, for example) by **inflammation**. Inflammation is the initial, rapid, localised response the tissue makes to damage. As a result, the volume of blood in the damaged area is increased. If a blood vessel has been ruptured, then the **blood clotting mechanism** is activated. In the blood and tissue fluid, the **immune system** operates. We will examine the blood clotting mechanism, first.

The blood clotting mechanism

In the event of a break in our closed blood circulation, the danger arises of a loss of blood and possibly a fall in blood pressure. It is by the clotting of blood that escapes are prevented, either at small haemorrhages, or at cuts and other wounds. In these circumstances, a clot both stops the outflow of blood and reduces invasion opportunities for pathogens. Subsequently, repair of the damaged tissues can get under way. Initial conditions at the wound trigger a **cascade of events** by which a blood clot is formed.

What is meant by 'a cascade of events'?

First, **platelets** collect at the site. These are components of the blood that are formed in the bone marrow along with the erythrocytes (red cells) and leucocytes (white cells), and are circulated throughout the body, suspended in the plasma, with the blood cells (Figure 7.7, page 186).

Platelets are actually cell fragments, disc-shaped and very small (only 2 µm in diameter) – too small to contain a nucleus. Each platelet consists of a sack of cytoplasm rich in vesicles containing enzymes, and is surrounded by a plasma membrane. Platelets stick to the damaged tissues and clump together there (at this point they change shape from sacks to flattened discs with tiny projections that interlock). This action alone seals off the smallest breaks.

The collecting platelets release a **clotting factor** (a protein called thromboplastin) which is also released by damaged tissues at the site. This clotting factor, along with vitamin K and calcium ions, always present in the plasma, causes a soluble plasma protein called **prothrombin** to be converted to the active, proteolytic enzyme **thrombin**. The action of this enzyme is to convert another soluble blood protein, **fibrinogen** to insoluble **fibrin** fibres at the site of the cut. Red cells are trapped within the mass of fibres, and the blood clot has formed (Figure 12.1).

Figure 12.1 The blood clotting mechanism

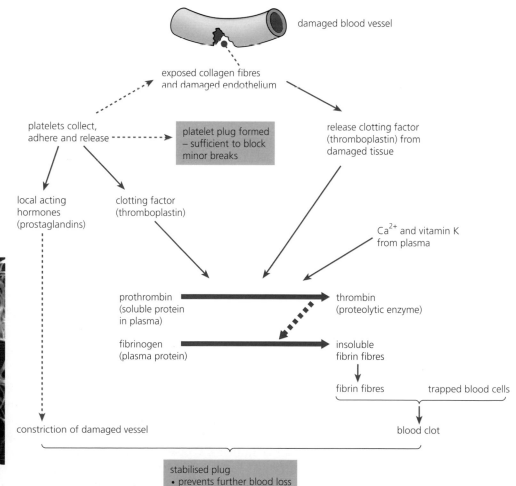

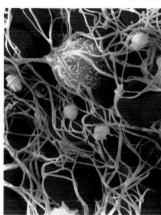

SEM of blood clot showing meshwork of fibrin fibres and trapped blood cells

It is most fortunate that clot formation is not normally activated in the intact circulation; clotting is triggered by the abnormal conditions at the break. These complex steps of clotting may be seen as an essential **fail-safe mechanism**. This is necessary because casual formation of a blood clot within the intact circulation system immediately generates the risk of a dangerous and possibly fatal blockage in the lungs, heart muscle or brain.

---

1 Identify the correct sequence of the following events during blood clotting:

fibrin formation; clotting factor release; thrombin formation.

The immune system and the response to invasion

It is the leucocytes in the blood that provide our main defences **once invasion of the body by harmful microorganisms has occurred**. Among the millions of erythrocytes (red cells) of our blood circulation are the relatively few leucocytes (white cells).

Leucocytes are not restricted to the blood circulation. Not only do they continually circulate in the arteries, capillaries and veins, they move through the walls of these vessels into tissues and organs. Very many occur in lymph of the lymph nodes and vessels, and many are found in organs like the lungs (page 196) and in the liver, and elsewhere in the body.

It is special leucocytes called **lymphocytes** that are responsible for the immune response. Lymphocytes make up 20% of the leucocytes circulating in the blood plasma. Lymphocytes detect matter entering from outside our bodies (including foreign macromolecules and microorganisms) as different from 'self' (body cells and our own proteins). 'Non-self' invading macromolecules and microorganisms are known as **antigens**.

What recognition of 'self' entails

Cells are identified by specific molecules – markers that are lodged in the outer surface of the plasma membrane. These molecules, which identify a cell, are highly variable **glycoproteins** on the cell surface.

You can see glycoproteins on the plasma membrane in Figure 1.19, page 21.

The glycoproteins that identify cells are known as the **major histocompatability complex** antigens – but we can refer to them as MHC. There are genes on one of our chromosomes (chromosome 6) that code for MHC, so each individual's MHC is genetically determined and is a feature we inherit. As with all inherited characteristics that are products of sexual reproduction, variation occurs. Each of us has distinctive MHC antigens present on the plasma membrane of most of our body cells. Unless you have an identical twin, your MHC antigens are unique.

So, lymphocytes of our immune system have **antigen receptors** that recognise our own MHC antigens, and differentiate these from foreign antigens detected in the body.

The principle of challenge and response

Our lymphocytes all appear the same, but we have two distinct types, based on the ways they function:

- B-lymphocytes (**B-cells**) secrete antibodies (**humoral immunity**);
- **T-cells** assist B-cells and may attack infected cells (**cell-mediated responses**).

As B- and T-cells are formed (in the red bone marrow) and then mature, they develop **immunocompetence**. This means they acquire an ability to recognise one specific antigen. An immunocompetent cell has a specific receptor protein on its cell surface. Each cell has lots of these receptor molecules that are capable of binding to only **one type of antigen**. The receptors on B-cells are actually attached copies of the antibody that will be secreted later, if the antigen is encountered.

Immunocompetent lymphocytes are stored in the lymph nodes. Here all the different lymphocytes, each with multiple copies of their antigen receptor, are found.

If antigens invade the body, they reach the tissue fluids and lymph, and encounter a lymphocyte with the corresponding receptor, typically in a lymph node. The lymphocytes challenged in this way immediately respond by growing and dividing repeatedly, leading to vast numbers of cells producing antibodies. The antibodies eventually overcome and dispose of the source of the foreign antigens.

Clonal selection and a polyclonal response

The product of vast numbers of identical plasma cells, as described above, is known as **clonal selection**, for obvious reasons.

Invading microorganisms have a complex chemical exterior – their wall or plasma membrane. Here are exposed very many different types of antigen. Consequently, a typical pathogen activates many different types of B-cell, triggering the secretion of many different antibodies, all of which attach and attack that pathogen. The activation of many different cloning events in this way is called **polyclonal selection**.

'Memory' in the immune system

After each immune response event has overcome the source of antigens, the plasma cells that secreted the antibodies are disposed of. Antibody-secreting cells are relatively short-lived. However, some of the cells produced in the cloning episode become memory cell lymphocytes. Memory cells survive in the body, mostly in the lymph nodes, typically for years after the event.

If the antigen returns, the body is able to respond quickly. We say that we have immunity.

Types of immunity

At the start of life, a mammal acquires **passive immunity** from the antibodies in its mother's blood circulation. Only later, after birth and direct stimulation by antigens, is **active immunity** acquired.

> **Passive immunity is immunity due to the acquisition of antibodies from the mother (in whom active immunity has arisen), via the placenta while in the uterus, and then via the first-formed milk, received immediately after birth. This milk is known as colostrum. Alternatively, antibodies can be received by injection, and so confer passive immunity.**

Note that passive immunity fades away eventually because the offspring cannot also receive the necessary memory cells, and so is unable to make the antibodies itself.

2 Outline in tabulated form the parts played by the blood in the protection of the body.

> **Active immunity is immunity due to the production of antibodies by the organism, after the body's defences have been exposed to antigens.**

Note that the exposure to antigens which generates active immunity may occur due to infection by a pathogen, as already described (**natural acquired immunity**), or following inoculation with a vaccine (**artificial acquired immunity**).

Steps of antibody production

We have seen that lymphocytes are involved in repelling an invasion by the production of antibodies, and that lymphocytes consist of two types, T-lymphocytes and B-lymphocytes. Both types are formed by divisions of the **stem cells** in the bone marrow, and undergo a development process in preparation for their distinctive roles (Figure 12.2).

T-lymphocytes (T-cells) leave the bone marrow during development, and differentiate in the **thymus gland** before circulating and storage in lymph nodes. It is while they are present in the thymus gland that the body apparently selects out the lymphocytes that would otherwise react to the body's own cells.

The role of T-cells is **cell-mediated immunity** – an immune response not directly involving antibodies, although some have a role in the activation of B-cells, as we shall see shortly. Some T-cells are effective against pathogens located within host cells.

B-lymphocytes (B-cells) complete their maturation in the bone marrow, prior to circulating in the body and being stored in lymph nodes. The role of the majority of B-cells, after recognition and binding to a specific antigen, is to proliferate into cells (called **plasma cells**) that **secrete antibodies** into the blood system. This is known as **humoral immunity**.

Both T-cells and B-cells have molecules on the outer surface of their plasma membrane that enable them to recognise antigens, but each lymphocyte has only one type of surface receptor. Consequently, each lymphocyte can recognise only one type of antigen.

Figure 12.2
T-lymphocytes and
B-lymphocytes

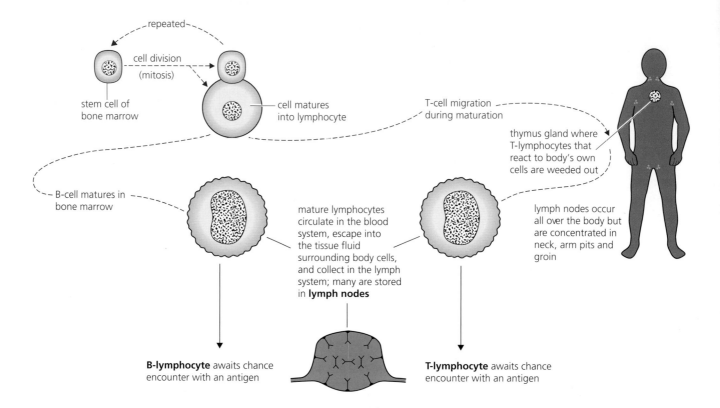

3 Explain the significance of the role of the thymus gland in destroying T-cells that would otherwise react to body proteins.

When an infection occurs the leucocyte population responds. Their numbers increase enormously, and many collect at the site of the invasion. A complex response to infection is begun. The special roles of T-cells and B-cells in this response are as follows, and are illustrated in Figure 12.4 (page 354).

1 On the arrival of a specific antigen in the body, B-cells with surface receptors (antibodies) that recognise that particular antigen, bind to it.

   What exactly is an antibody?

   An antibody is a special protein called an **immunoglobulin**, made of four polypeptide chains held together by disulphide bridges (—S—S—), forming a molecule in the shape of a Y. The arrangement of amino acid residues in the polypeptides that form the fork region in this molecule is totally unique to that antibody. It is this region that forms the highly specific binding site for the antigen (Figure 12.3). Antibodies initially occur attached to the plasma membrane of B-cells, but later are also mass-produced and secreted by cells derived from the B-cell by exocytosis, but only after that B-cell has undergone an **activation step** (step 5, below).

2 On binding to the B-cell, the antigen is taken into the cytoplasm by phagocytosis, before being expressed on the plasma membrane of the B-cell.

Figure 12.3 The structure of an antibody

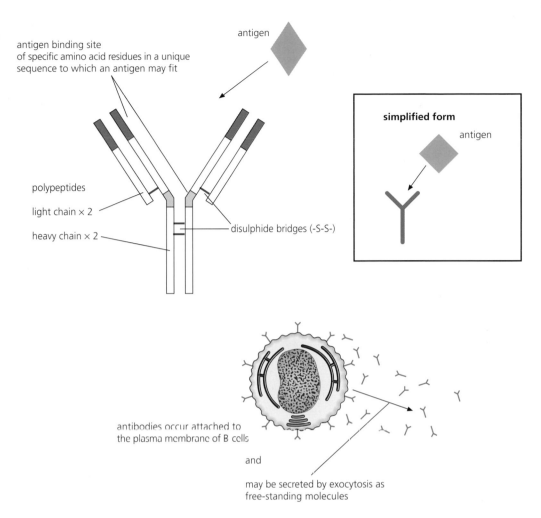

antigen binding site of specific amino acid residues in a unique sequence to which an antigen may fit

antigen

polypeptides

light chain × 2

heavy chain × 2

disulphide bridges (-S-S-)

simplified form

antigen

antibodies occur attached to the plasma membrane of B cells

and

may be secreted by exocytosis as free-standing molecules

3 Meanwhile, T-cells can only respond to antigens when presented on the surface of other cells. Phagocytic cells of the body, including **macrophages**, engulf antigens they encounter. This occurs in the plasma and lymph. Once these antigens are taken up, the macrophage presents them externally by attaching the antigen to their surface membrane protein, MHC antigens. This is called **antigen presentation** by a macrophage.

4 T-cells come in contact with these macrophages and briefly bind to them. The T-cell is immediately activated. They are armed or **activated helper T-cells**.

5 Activated helper T-cells now bind to B-cells with the same antigen expressed on their plasma membrane (step 2 above), and the activated T-cell sends a message to the B-cell, activating it. This is the activation step mentioned in step 1 above. It is now an armed or **activated B-cell**.

6 Activated B-cells immediately divide very rapidly by mitosis, forming a clone of cells called plasma cells. A TEM of plasma cells shows them to be packed with rough endoplasmic reticulum (rER). It is in these organelles that the antibody is mass-produced and exported from the B-cell by exocytosis. The antibodies are normally produced in such numbers that the antigen is overcome (Figure 12.4).

   As noted above, the production of an activated B-cell, its rapid cell division to produce a clone of plasma cells, and the resulting production of antibodies that react with the antigen is called clonal selection. Sometimes several different antibodies react with the one antigen – polyclonal selection.

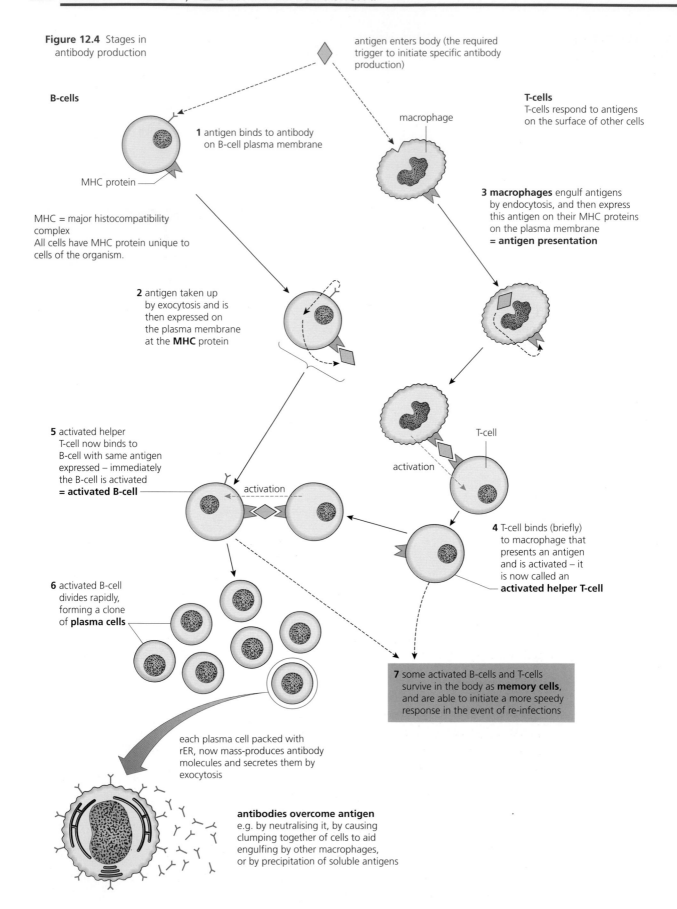

Figure 12.4 Stages in antibody production

antigen enters body (the required trigger to initiate specific antibody production)

B-cells

1 antigen binds to antibody on B-cell plasma membrane

MHC protein

MHC = major histocompatibility complex
All cells have MHC protein unique to cells of the organism.

2 antigen taken up by exocytosis and is then expressed on the plasma membrane at the **MHC** protein

T-cells
T-cells respond to antigens on the surface of other cells

macrophage

3 macrophages engulf antigens by endocytosis, and then express this antigen on their MHC proteins on the plasma membrane
= antigen presentation

5 activated helper T-cell now binds to B-cell with same antigen expressed – immediately the B-cell is activated
= activated B-cell

activation

T-cell

activation

4 T-cell binds (briefly) to macrophage that presents an antigen and is activated – it is now called an **activated helper T-cell**

6 activated B-cell divides rapidly, forming a clone of **plasma cells**

7 some activated B-cells and T-cells survive in the body as **memory cells**, and are able to initiate a more speedy response in the event of re-infections

each plasma cell packed with rER, now mass-produces antibody molecules and secretes them by exocytosis

antibodies overcome antigen
e.g. by neutralising it, by causing clumping together of cells to aid engulfing by other macrophages, or by precipitation of soluble antigens

Figure 12.5 Profile of antibody production in infection and re-infection

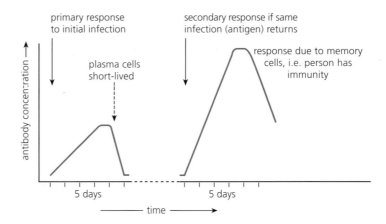

Memory cells are retained in lymph nodes. They allow a quick and specific response if the same antigen reappears.

primary response to initial infection

plasma cells short-lived

secondary response if same infection (antigen) returns

response due to memory cells, i.e. person has immunity

antibody concentration →

5 days

5 days

—— time ——→

7 After these antibodies have tackled the foreign matter and the disease threat it introduced, they disappear from the blood and tissue fluid, along with the bulk of the specific B-cells and T-cells responsible for their formation. However, certain of these specifically activated B-cells and T-cells are retained in the body as memory cells. These are long-lived cells, in contrast to plasma cells and activated B-cells. Memory cells make possible an early and effective response in the event of a re-infection of the body by the same antigen (Figure 12.5). This is the basis of natural immunity (see below).

4 Identify where antigens and antibodies may be found in the body.

■ Extension: Additional roles for T-cells

We have noted that T-cells of the immune system identify antigens **when presented on the surface of cells** (as opposed to responding to free antigens in the plasma of the blood or in tissue fluid, as B-cells do).

A **virus** causes a disease only when it has entered a host cell and then has converted the host metabolic machinery to the mass-production of more viruses (page 237). However, a virus-infected cell also automatically 'advertises' the presence of the virus within, early in the invasion, by attaching antigens from the virus's protein coat onto the exterior of the plasma membrane.

The immune system, in the form of special T-cells, recognises these antigens. The killer T-cell attaches to the infected cell and then destroys it; the infection is overcome. Killer T-cells are known as **cytotoxic T-cells**.

T-cells and cancer

A similar response occurs with body cells that have become cancerous. This is because cancer cells develop **tumour-associated antigens (TAA)** on their surface. Chance encounters between T-cells and cancer cells with exposed TAA sensitise the T-cells (we say the T-cells have become armed). They then become active as **cytotoxic cells**. In this condition, the cancer cells may be destroyed.

Unfortunately, the immune system is generally less efficient at dealing with cancerous tumours than it is with infections. This may be because cancer cells are almost identical to healthy body cells from which they formed. Consequently, they also carry MHC proteins on their plasma membranes, marking them out as the body's own cells. We saw that T-cells pass through the thymus gland during formation, where T-cells that attack the body's own cells are removed. It is likely that the dual messages on cancer cells (TAA alongside MHC proteins) may disable cytotoxic T-cells to some extent.

It is now helpful to summarise the complex roles of B-cells and T-cells in the immune system (Figure 12.6).

Figure 12.6 The roles of B-cells and T-cells in the immune system – a summary

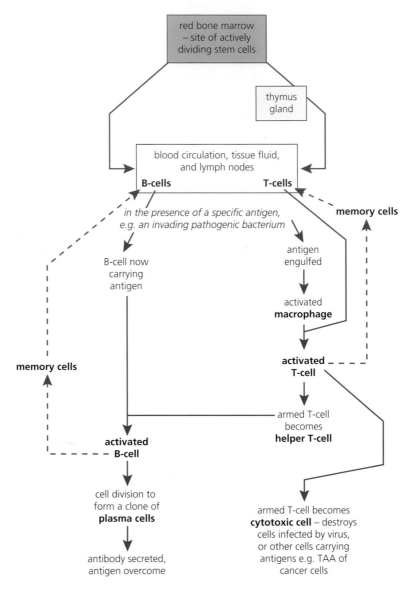

5 **Distinguish** between a plasma cell and memory cells of the immune system.

Monoclonal antibody production and their uses

We have seen that antibodies are secreted by plasma B-cells and are effective in the destruction of antigens within the body.

Antibodies also have great potential in modern medicine, where they can be made available. The trouble has been that the plasma cells from which they are derived are short-lived. **Monoclonal antibodies** are a recent invention by which antibodies are made available in the long term, for applications in new circumstances. They are already used widely in medicine and research.

A monoclonal antibody is a single antibody that is stable and that can be used over a period of time. Each specific antibody is made by one particular type of B-cell. The problem of the normally brief existence of a plasma cell is overcome by fusing the specific lymphocyte with a cancer cell which, unlike other body cells, goes on dividing indefinitely. The resulting cell divides to form a clone of cells which persists, and which conveniently goes on secreting the antibody in significant quantities (Figure 12.7).

Figure 12.7 Formation of monoclonal antibodies

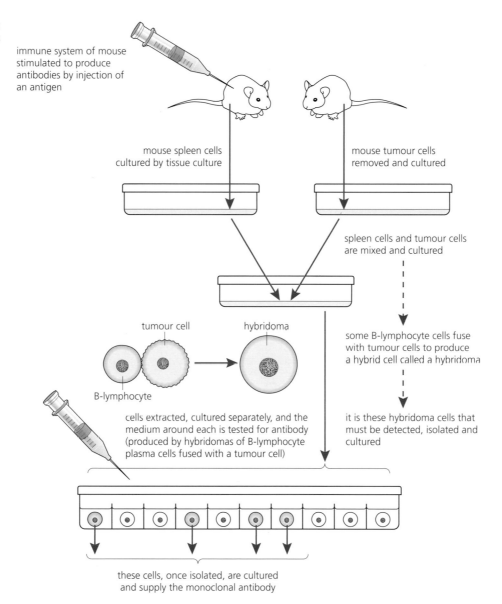

The use of monoclonal antibodies in medicine is already established, and is under further development in these and other areas. For example, in **diagnosis**, monoclonal antibodies are used in pregnancy testing.

A pregnant woman has a significant concentration of the hormone human chorionic gonadotrophin (HCG) (page 387) in her urine, whereas a non-pregnant woman has a negligible amount. Monoclonal antibodies to HCG have been engineered to also carry (become attached to) coloured granules, so that in a simple test kit the appearance of a coloured strip in one compartment provides immediate, visual confirmation of pregnancy. How this works is illustrated in Figure 12.8.

Figure 12.8 Detecting pregnancy using monoclonal antibodies

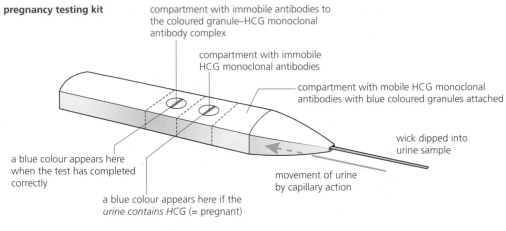

pregnancy testing kit

compartment with immobile antibodies to the coloured granule–HCG monoclonal antibody complex

compartment with immobile HCG monoclonal antibodies

compartment with mobile HCG monoclonal antibodies with blue coloured granules attached

wick dipped into urine sample

a blue colour appears here when the test has completed correctly

movement of urine by capillary action

a blue colour appears here if the *urine contains HCG* (= pregnant)

how the positive test result is brought about

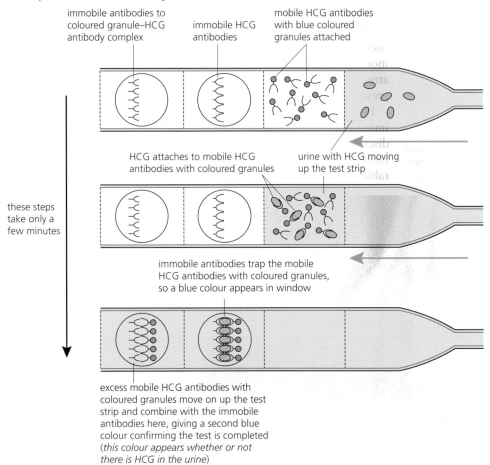

immobile antibodies to coloured granule–HCG antibody complex

immobile HCG antibodies

mobile HCG antibodies with blue coloured granules attached

these steps take only a few minutes

HCG attaches to mobile HCG antibodies with coloured granules

urine with HCG moving up the test strip

immobile antibodies trap the mobile HCG antibodies with coloured granules, so a blue colour appears in window

excess mobile HCG antibodies with coloured granules move on up the test strip and combine with the immobile antibodies here, giving a second blue colour confirming the test is completed (*this colour appears whether or not there is HCG in the urine*)

Monoclonal antibodies also have applications in the **treatment** of disease. For example, cancer cells carry specific tumour-associated antigens (TAA) on their plasma membrane. Monoclonal antibodies to TAA have been produced. Then, drugs to kill cells or inhibitors to block key tumour proteins have been attached, so cancer cells can be specifically targeted and killed. The advantage here is that many drugs and treatments effective against cancer are harmful to other, healthy cells. The specificity of antibodies avoids this problem.

The original monoclonal antibodies were developed from mouse cells (Figure 12.7), but patients have developed an adverse reaction to antibodies made this way, since they are foreign proteins to the patient's immune system. Genetically engineered antibodies that will be compatible with the patient's immune system are sought, to avoid triggering the immune response.

Vaccination – the process of immunisation

It has long been known that people who recovered from plague or smallpox rarely contracted those diseases again. The possibility of a patient acquiring immunity from smallpox was apparently appreciated in the East in the seventeenth century, if not earlier. An English ambassador's wife tried to introduce the practice of vaccination in Britain at the start of the eighteenth century. Vaccination was practised in Turkey at the time, and she had observed how successful it was there. Sadly, she had little success.

The first attempt in the West at immunisation was made by **Edward Jenner (1749–1823)**, a country doctor from Gloucestershire, UK. At the time, many people who got smallpox died of it, but *not* those who had earlier contracted cowpox (workers who handled cows typically did so at some stage). Jenner saw the significance of this protection the patients had acquired. He extracted fluid from a cowpox pustule on an infected milkmaid, and injected it into the arm of an eight-year-old boy (Figure 12.9). The child got a mild infection, but when exposed to smallpox, remained healthy. Jenner named this technique **vaccination**, after the cowpox *vaccinia* (a virus). Of course, he did not understand the cause of smallpox; the chemical nature of viruses was not reported until 1935.

The French scientist **Louis Pasteur (1822–95)** discovered that cultures of chicken cholera bacterium, allowed to age for 2–3 months, produced only a mild infection of cholera when inoculated into chickens. The old cultures had become less pathogenic – today we say they had **attenuated**. Fresh, virulent strains of the chicken cholera bacterium failed to infect chickens previously exposed to the mild form of the disease.

Pasteur, one of the greatest experimentalists in microbiology, had notable successes in immunisation (Figure 12.9). However, he recognised the original contribution of Jenner to the discovery of immunity by using the name vaccine for injections of the attenuated organisms that he developed to prevent chicken cholera disease, and (later) anthrax (due to a bacterium) and rabies (due to a virus).

Figure 12.9 Edward Jenner and Louis Pasteur at work

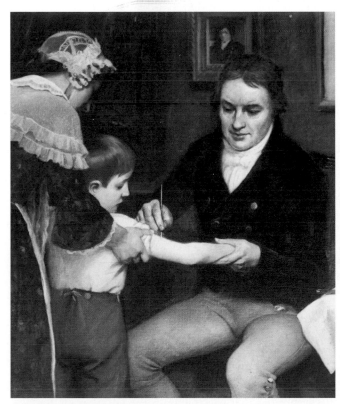

Jenner inoculating James Phipps, from a drawing by William Thompson, c. 1880 (*by courtesy of the Wellcome Trustees*)

Pasteur made a major contribution to our understanding of diseases of humans and other animals; working with dogs, he showed that an injection of the attenuated rabies microorganism can produce immunity to the disease

Vaccines today

The deliberate administration of antigens that have been made harmless, after they are obtained from disease-causing organisms, in order to confer immunity in future, is a very important contribution to public health today.

Vaccines are administered either by injection or by mouth. They cause the body's immune system to briefly make antibodies against the disease (*without becoming infected*), and then to retain the appropriate memory cells. Active artificial immunity is established in this way. The profile of response in terms of antibody production caused by any later exposure to the antigen is exactly the same as if the immunity was acquired after the body overcame an earlier infection (Figure 12.5).

Vaccines are manufactured from dead or attenuated bacteria, or from inactivated viruses, purified polysaccharides from bacterial walls, toxoids, and even recombinant DNA produced by genetic engineering.

So successful has vaccination been *where vaccines are widely available and the take up is by about 85–90% of the relevant population* that, in many human communities, some formerly common and dangerous diseases have become very uncommon occurrences. As a result, the public in such communities have sometimes become casual about the threat such diseases still pose (see below). The recommended schedule of vaccinations for children brought up in one developed country can be accessed via the website www.doh.gov.uk

6 Identify the steps of plasma cell formation that the existence of memory cells avoids.

Controversy about vaccination

The issues that vaccination can raise with the general public are shown by cases such as the controversy that raged over the **combined measles, mumps and rubella (MMR) vaccine**.

MMR vaccine was first licensed for use in 1975. For MMR vaccine, attenuated viruses are extracted from separate cell cultures and freeze-dried. The dried measles, mumps and rubella strains are then mixed together. In this condition, they remain stable until added to distilled water, for injection. The preparation must then be used within 6 hours. Children under a year old are rarely vaccinated because they are protected by antibodies from their mother (passive immunity). Infants in the UK, for example, receive their first MMR injection aged 15–24 months, and they receive a booster injection between three and five years of age.

Dr Andrew Wakefield, a gastroenterologist employed at the Royal Free Hospital in London at the time (1998), studied 12 children who had all apparently developed autism within 14 days of being given MMR. He published his suggestion (in the medical journal *Lancet*) that for some children, inoculation with the MMR vaccine triggered an inflammatory bowel condition. In this state, the gut might become leaky, allowing 'rogue peptides' into the blood circulation, quickly leading to brain damage – in particular, to autism.

Autism is a life-long disorder in which children withdraw into themselves, reject human contact, and may become impossible to handle. To the families in which it occurs, autism can be most distressing. The film *Rain Man*, in which Dustin Hoffman starred, raised the profile of this disease, so it is more widely recognised now.

Dr Wakefield noted 'We did not prove an association', meaning this was a suggestion that needed following up (and it was). However, his ideas immediately received widespread publicity, and have lead to public anxiety sufficient to cause a marked fall in the take-up of MMR vaccine.

Why do some parents confidently blame MMR for their child's condition?

Autism, when it arises, does so at about 18 months. We have noted the MMR vaccine is first given when children are around 15 months old. When autism does develop soon after inoculation, it is inevitable that there will *appear* to be a connection, whether there is or not (page 683).

To date, no study has produced any evidence that MMR causes autism. Major investigations and follow-up studies have been undertaken with large samples of children in Australia, in Finland, and in Japan. In communities where the opinion is that cases of autism are on the increase, it is noted that the increase began before MMR was introduced, and the incidence of autism continued to rise even when the numbers of children receiving MMR reached a plateau. There is no doubt in the minds of health authorities that vaccination is the safest option for children and their parents. However, after the BSE (bovine spongiform encephalitis, page 596) episode in the UK, governments in the developed world have a major problem in convincing doubters.

Benefits and dangers arising from the general practice of vaccination are listed in Table 12.1.

TOK Link

The coincidence of autism onset and MMR administration may be described as circumstantial evidence. What part, if any, can it play in scientific discovery?

Benefits	Dangers
With the assistance of an effective vaccine, dangerous disease may be eradicated, as was smallpox in 1977. Poliomyelitis may also soon be eradicated; the Salk vaccine was developed in 1955, and the (oral) Sabin vaccine in 1962.	In the worst cases, vaccines can actually cause the disease they are designed to prevent. This is extremely rare.
Vaccines prevent diseases that otherwise may result in very unpleasant and sometimes life-threatening conditions; for example, measles is a major cause of infant death in many less-developed countries.	Vaccines can cause occasional adverse reactions; for example, MMR may trigger tenderness, slight fever and rashes in mild cases, and seizures, allergic reactions, and anaphylactic shock in serious cases (but none has been fatal). These reactions are rare. Whooping cough vaccine may cause brain damage.
Long-term disability from disease can be prevented. Disability for unborn children can be prevented since rubella infections in pregnant women can infect the unborn child, leading to deafness, blindness, brain damage and heart disease.	As the incidence of a disease begins to fall dramatically due to an immunisation programme, rare side-effects of the vaccine, appearing in very a small proportion of those vaccinated, can become unacceptable to the public, leading to serious loss of confidence in what are, in fact, favourable treatments.

Table 12.1 Benefits and dangers of vaccination, today

7 State what we mean by immunity.

Muscles and movement

11.2.1–11.2.8

Movement is a characteristic of all living things. It occurs within cells (e.g. cytoplasmic streaming), within organisms (e.g. pumping action of the heart), and as movements of whole organisms, known as **locomotion**. It is the issue of **muscular locomotion** in humans that is examined here.

Roles of the components of our locomotory system

Locomotion is the result of the interactions of nervous, muscular and skeletal systems. The component parts and their roles in locomotion are as follows:

- **Bones** support and partially protect the body parts. Also, they articulate with other bones at **joints**, and they provide anchorage for the muscles. In mammals, the skeleton consists of the axial skeleton (skull and vertebral column) and the appendicular skeleton (limb girdles and limbs). In our study of exercise physiology, we shall be more concerned with the latter.
- **Ligaments** hold bones together, and form protective capsules around the moveable joints. Ligaments are made of fibres of strong but very slightly elastic connective tissue.
- **Muscles** cause movements by contraction. Skeletal muscle is one of three types of muscle in the mammal's body. Skeletal muscles occur in pairs, anchored to bones across joints. They are arranged so that when one of the pair contracts the other is stretched, a system known as antagonistic pairs (Figure 12.10). Contractions of skeletal muscle may either maintain the posture and position of the body, or go on to bring about movement at joints.
- **Tendons** attach muscles to bones at their points of anchorage. They are cords of dense connective tissue.

Figure 12.10 Muscles operate in antagonistic pairs

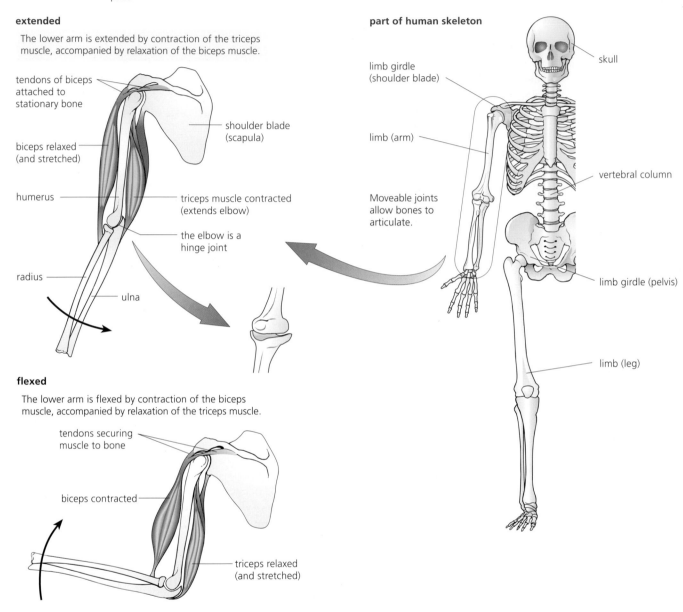

extended

The lower arm is extended by contraction of the triceps muscle, accompanied by relaxation of the biceps muscle.

tendons of biceps attached to stationary bone

shoulder blade (scapula)

biceps relaxed (and stretched)

humerus

triceps muscle contracted (extends elbow)

the elbow is a hinge joint

radius

ulna

flexed

The lower arm is flexed by contraction of the biceps muscle, accompanied by relaxation of the triceps muscle.

tendons securing muscle to bone

biceps contracted

triceps relaxed (and stretched)

part of human skeleton

skull

limb girdle (shoulder blade)

limb (arm)

vertebral column

Moveable joints allow bones to articulate.

limb girdle (pelvis)

limb (leg)

- **Nerves** are bundles of many nerve fibres of individual nerve cells (called neurones). They connect the central nervous system (brain and spinal cord) with other parts of the body, including the skeletal muscle. Nerve impulses are transmitted in a few milliseconds, travelling along individual nerve fibres to particular points in the body. Nervous control is therefore precise and specific as well as quick. Nerve impulses stimulate muscles to contract, and the nervous system as a whole co-ordinates movement.

How do these components work together to bring about movements at joints?

Moveable joints in the body are of different types, but they all permit controlled movements, and are all examples of **synovial joints** because a thick viscous fluid, the synovial fluid, is secreted and retained in the joint, to help lubricate it. We will consider first a hinge joint, as found in the human elbow.

The human elbow joint

Moveable joints are contained in fibrous **capsules** attached to the immediately surrounding bone. The capsule consists of tough connective tissue but is flexible enough to permit movement. Also present at the joint, but outside the capsule, are ligaments that hold the bones together, preventing dislocations.

At the elbow, the humerus of the upper arm articulates with the radius and ulna of the lower arm at a hinge joint (Figure 12.11 and Table 12.2). At the joint a fluid-filled space separates the articulating surfaces. This fluid, the **synovial fluid**, is secreted by the **synovial membrane**. The fluid nourishes the living cartilage layers that cover the articulating surfaces of the bones as well as serving as a lubricant.

Components	Functions
humerus, radius and ulna	the bones of the skeleton, together with the muscles attached across joints, function as a system of levers to maintain body posture and bring about actions, typically movements
biceps muscle	anchored to shoulder blade and attached to radius so contraction flexes the lower arm (and stretches triceps)
triceps muscle	anchored to shoulder blade and attached to ulna so contraction extends the lower arm (and stretches biceps)
ligaments	hold bones (humerus, radius and ulna) in correct positions at the joint (combats dislocation)
capsule	contains and protects the joint without restricting movement
synovial membrane	secretes synovial fluid
synovial fluid	lubricates the joint, nourishes the cartilage, and removes any (harmful) detritus from worn bone and cartilage surfaces
cartilage	firm, flexible material – a slippery covering that reduces friction

Table 12.2 Components of the elbow joint (a synovial joint) and their functions

Figure 12.11 The hinge joint of the elbow

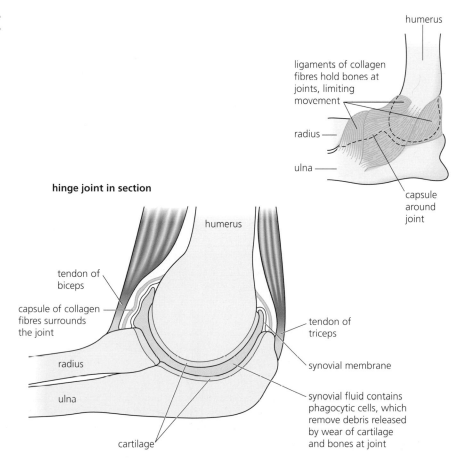

Comparative movements at joints

You will have noticed that we have contrasting degrees of movement at our knees and hips (and at shoulder and elbow). This is because of a fundamental difference in the types of joints involved (Figure 12.12 and Table 12.3).

At the hip is a **ball and socket joint**, which is also a synovial joint. In this type of joint, the ball-like surface of one bone (here, the femur of the upper leg) fits into a cup-like depression on another bone (here, the pelvic girdle or hip bone). In the hip joint, the socket is called the acetabulum. This type of joint permits movements in all three planes, a type of movement described as circumduction.

At the knee is a **hinge joint**, which like that of the elbow, restricts movement to one plane. This is because of the shape of the articulating surfaces, and also the ligaments that hold the bones together. Movements at the knee are described as flexions and extensions.

Figure 12.12 Movement at hip and knee joints

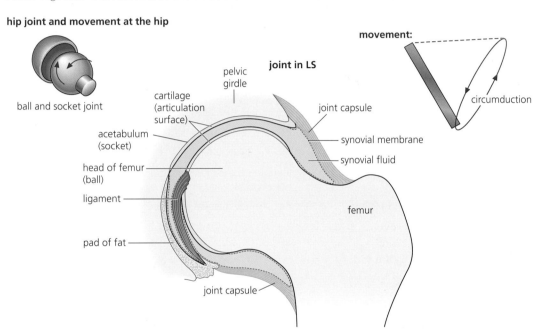

hip joint and movement at the hip

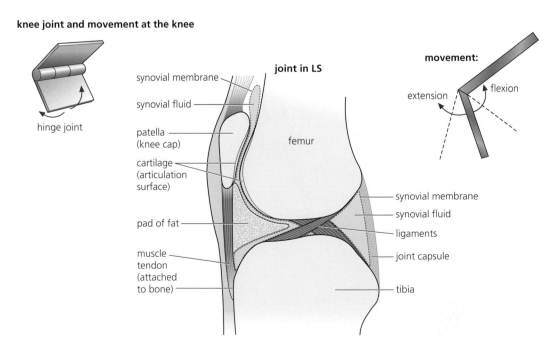

knee joint and movement at the knee

	hip joint		knee joint
type	synovial – ball and socket		synovial – hinge
articulating bones	acetabulum of pelvic girdle and femur (head)		femur and tibia
additional bones	none		knee cap (patella)
articulating surface(s)	between acetabulum and head of femur		between femur and tibia and between femur and patella
permitted movement	circumduction		flexion and extension

Table 12.3 Movement of hip and knee joints compared

8 When the tendon that secures the patella is tapped, a knee jerk is observed. Sketch a diagram and **annotate** it to show the structures and the events involved in the knee jerk response.

Muscle structure

We have seen that muscles that cause locomotion are attached to the moveable parts of skeletons and are known as **skeletal muscles**. Skeletal muscles are attached by **tendons** and work in antagonistic pairs, as illustrated in Figure 12.10.

Skeletal muscle consists of bundles of muscle fibres (Figure 12.13). A muscle **fibre** is a long, multinucleate cell. The remarkable feature of a muscle fibre is the ability to shorten to half or even a third of the relaxed or resting length. Fibres appear striped under the light microscope, so skeletal muscle is also known as striated muscle. Actually, each fibre is itself composed of a mass of myofibrils, but we need the electron microscope to see this.

Figure 12.13 The structure of skeletal muscle

skeletal muscle cut to show bundles of fibres

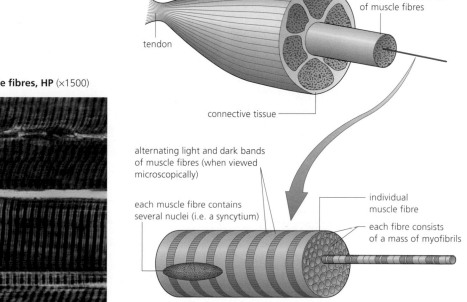

photomicrograph of LS voluntary muscle fibres, HP (×1500)

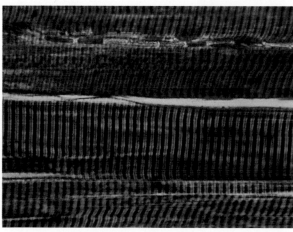

The ultrastructure of skeletal muscle

By use of the electron microscope we can see that each muscle fibre consists of very many parallel **myofibrils** within a plasma membrane known as the **sarcolemma**, together with cytoplasm. The cytoplasm contains **mitochondria** packed between the myofibrils. The sarcolemma infolds to form a system of transverse tubular endoplasmic reticulum, known as **sarcoplasmic reticulum**. This is arranged as a network around individual myofibrils. The arrangements of myofibrils, sarcolemma and mitochondria, surrounded by the sarcoplasmic membrane, are shown in Figure 12.14.

Figure 12.14 The ultrastructure of a muscle fibre

electron micrograph of TS through part of a muscle fibre, HP (×36 000)

stereogram of part of a single muscle fibre

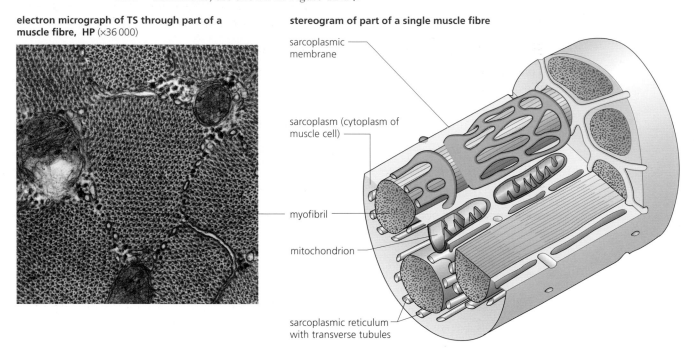

sarcoplasmic membrane

sarcoplasm (cytoplasm of muscle cell)

myofibril

mitochondrion

sarcoplasmic reticulum with transverse tubules

Figure 12.15 The ultrastructure of a myofibril

electron micrograph of LS through part of voluntary muscle fibre, HP (×36 000)

sarcomere

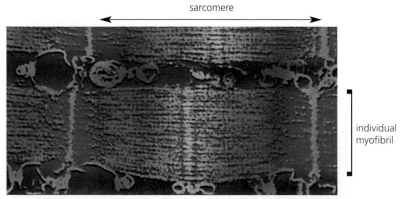

individual myofibril

interpretive drawing of the thick filaments (myosin) and thin filaments (actin)

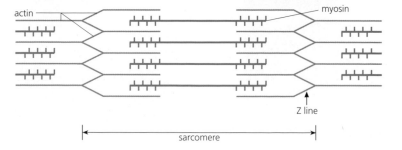

actin

myosin

Z line

sarcomere

The striped appearance of skeletal muscle is due to an interlocking arrangement of two types of protein filaments, known respectively as **thick** and **thin filaments**, that make up the myofibrils. These protein filaments are aligned, giving the appearance of stripes (alternating **light and dark bands**). This is shown in the more highly magnified electron micrograph and interpretive drawing in Figure 12.15.

The **thick filaments** are made of a protein called **myosin**. They are about 15 nm in diameter. The longer, **thin filaments** are made of another protein, **actin**. Thin filaments are about 7 nm in diameter, and are held together by transverse bands, known as **Z lines**. Each repeating unit of the myofibril is, for convenience of description, referred to as a **sarcomere**. So we can think of a myofibril as consisting of **a series of sarcomeres attached end to end**.

Skeletal muscle contracts by sliding of the filaments

Thick filaments lie in the central part of each sarcomere, sandwiched between thin filaments. When skeletal muscle contracts, the **actin** and **myosin filaments slide past each other**, in response to nervous stimulation, causing shortening of the sarcomeres (Figure 12.16). This occurs in a series of steps, sometimes described as a ratchet mechanism. A great deal of **ATP** is used in the contraction process.

Shortening is possible because the thick filaments are composed of many myosin molecules, each with a **bulbous head** which protrudes from the length of the myosin filament. Along the actin filament are a complementary series of binding sites to which the bulbous heads fit. However, in muscle fibres at rest, the binding sites carry **blocking molecules** (a protein called **tropomyosin**), so binding and contraction are not possible. The contraction of a sarcomere is best described in the following four steps.

1 The myofibril is stimulated to contract by the arrival of an **action potential**. This triggers release of calcium ions from the sarcoplasmic reticulum, to surround the actin molecules. Calcium ions now react with an additional protein present (**troponin**) which, when so activated, triggers the removal of the blocking molecule, tropomyosin. The **binding sites are now exposed**.

9 Explain the relationship to a muscle of:

a a muscle fibre
b a myofibril
c a myosin filament.

Figure 12.16 Muscle contraction of a single sarcomere

change in a single sarcomere in relaxed and contracted myofibril

Muscles contract as the actin and myosin filaments slide between each other, shortening each sarcomere.

relaxed **contracted**

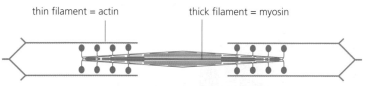
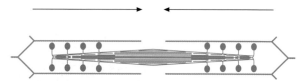

electron micrographs of muscle fibres, relaxed (left) and contracted (right)

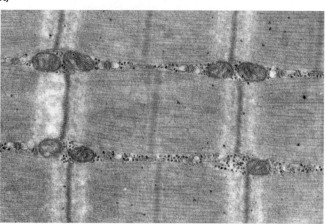

Figure 12.17 The sliding-filament hypothesis of muscle contraction

Arrival of action potential at myofibril releases Ca^{2+} ions from sarcoplasmic reticulum.

Ca^{2+} ions react with a protein (troponin), activating it. Activated troponin reacts with tropomyosin at the binding sites on the actin molecules, thereby exposing the binding sites.

Each myosin molecule has a 'head' that reacts with ATP → ADP + P_i which remain bound.

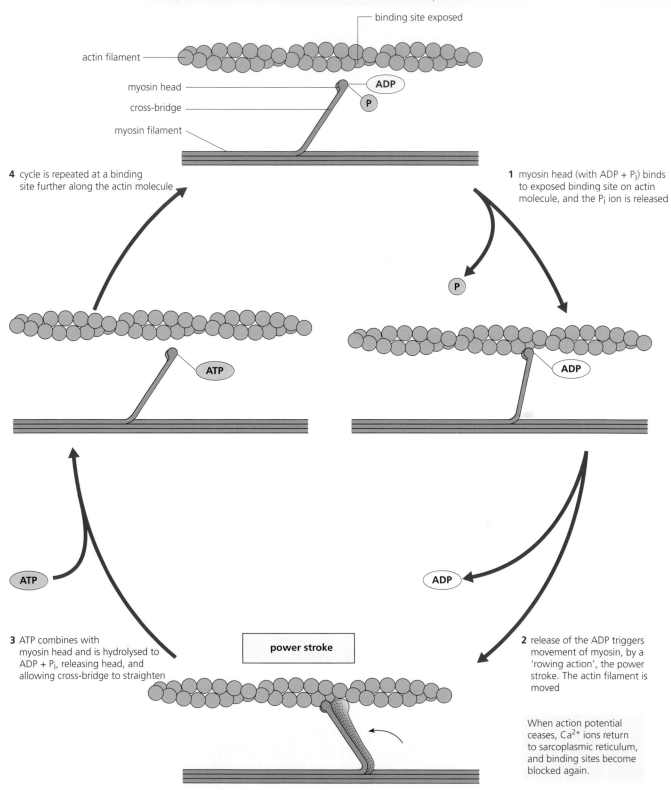

binding site exposed

actin filament

myosin head

ADP

P

cross-bridge

myosin filament

4 cycle is repeated at a binding site further along the actin molecule

ATP

1 myosin head (with ADP + P_i) binds to exposed binding site on actin molecule, and the P_i ion is released

P

ADP

ATP

ADP

3 ATP combines with myosin head and is hydrolysed to ADP + P_i, releasing head, and allowing cross-bridge to straighten

power stroke

2 release of the ADP triggers movement of myosin, by a 'rowing action', the power stroke. The actin filament is moved

When action potential ceases, Ca^{2+} ions return to sarcoplasmic reticulum, and binding sites become blocked again.

2 Each bulbous head to which ADP and P_i are attached (called a **charged bulbous head**) reacts with a binding site on the actin molecule beside it. The phosphate group (P_i) is shed at this moment.

3 The ADP molecule is then released from the bulbous head, and this is the trigger for the **rowing movement** of the head, which tilts by an angle of about 45°, pushing the actin filament along. At this step, the **power stroke**, the myofibril has been shortened (**contraction**).

4 Finally, a fresh molecule of **ATP binds** to the bulbous head. The protein of the bulbous heads includes the enzyme ATPase, which catalyses the hydrolysis of ATP. When this reaction occurs, the ADP and inorganic phosphate (P_i) formed remain attached, and the **bulbous head is now 'charged'** again. The charged head detaches from the binding site and straightens.

This cycle of movements is shown is Figure 12.17. The cycle is repeated many times per second, with thousands of bulbous heads working along each myofibril. ATP is rapidly used up, and the muscle may shorten by about 50% of its relaxed length.

Muscles, controlled movements, and posture

Muscles are involved in maintaining body posture and in subtle, delicate movements, as well as in vigorous or even violent actions. Consequently, nervous control of muscle contraction may cause relaxed muscle to contract slightly, moderately or fully, depending on the occasion. In these differing states of contraction, the overall lengths of the sarcomeres are changed accordingly. These relative changes are illustrated diagrammatically in a single sarcomere in Figure 12.18. Below them is a representation of part of a myofibril, seen at a particular stage of contraction. This representation is not diagrammatic, but is based on an interpretation of a TEM. (See the TEMs in Figure 12.16, for example.) SAQ 10 is concerned with analysing the state of contraction of myofibrils.

10 a Identify the approximate state of contraction illustrated in the sketch of a TEM of a myofibril shown in Figure 12.18.
b Sketch a similar myofibril, fully contracted. Label your drawing (sarcomere, Z lines, light band and dark band).

Figure 12.18 Analysing states of contraction in striated muscle fibres

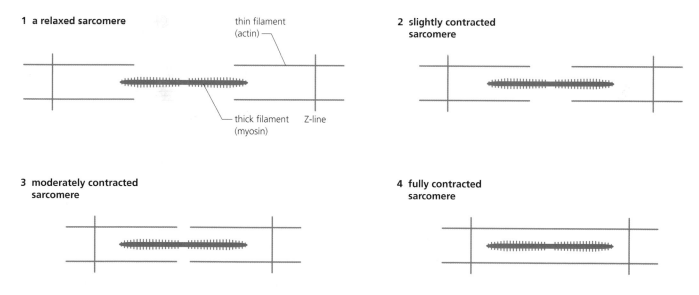

1 **a relaxed sarcomere**

thin filament (actin)

thick filament (myosin) Z-line

2 **slightly contracted sarcomere**

3 **moderately contracted sarcomere**

4 **fully contracted sarcomere**

sketch representing a myofibril at a particular stage in contraction, based on interpretation of a TEM of a sample of striated muscle

■ The kidney – excretion and osmoregulation

11.3.1–11.3.9

The chemical reactions of metabolism produce by-products, some of which would be toxic if allowed to accumulate in the organism.

> **Excretion is the removal from the body of the waste products of metabolism. It is a characteristic activity of all living things. Metabolites present in excessive concentrations are also excreted.**

In mammals, excretion plays an important part in the process by which the internal environment is regulated to maintain more or less constant conditions (homeostasis). Associated with excretion, and very much part of homeostasis, is the process of osmoregulation.

> **Osmoregulation is the maintenance of a proper balance of water and dissolved substances in the organism.**

Why is the issue of nitrogenous excretion so important in animals?
The reason is that animals break down excess proteins and amino acids by a process called **deamination** – the first step is the removal of the amino groups. Once removed, a likely initial product is **ammonia**, which is extremely toxic to cells if it is allowed to accumulate. So, the amino group is converted into some other nitrogenous excretory product for safe disposal in most animals. **Urea** is a chemical compound synthesised from carbon dioxide and ammonia. In dilute solution, urea is safely excreted from the body in mammals.

The human kidney – an organ of excretion and osmoregulation

The kidneys regulate the internal environment by constantly adjusting the blood composition. The waste products of metabolism are transported from the metabolising cells by the blood circulation, removed from the blood in the kidneys, and excreted in a solution called urine. The concentrations of inorganic ions, such as Na^+ and Cl^-, and of water in the body are also regulated in the kidneys, which are, therefore, also organs of osmoregulation.

This function of the kidneys is another example of **homeostasis by negative feedback** (page 218), a characteristic of the body of mammals. For a summary of osmoregulation by the kidney see Table 12.4, page 376.

The position of the kidneys in humans is shown in Figure 12.19. Each kidney is served by a renal artery and drained by a renal vein. Urine from the kidney is carried to the bladder by the **ureter**, and (occasionally) from the bladder to the exterior by the **urethra**, when the bladder

Figure 12.19 The human urinary system

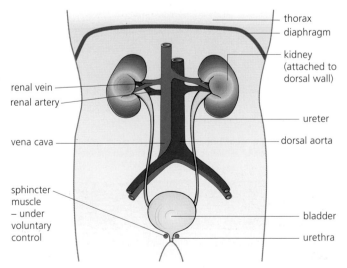

sphincter muscle is relaxed. Together these structures are known as the urinary system. In section, a kidney can be seen to consist of an outer **cortex** and inner **medulla**. These are made up of a million or more tiny tubules, called **nephrons**, together with their blood supply. Part of a nephron is in the cortex and part in the medulla. A nephron is a thin-walled tubule about 3 cm long. **Capillary networks** are crucial to the functioning nephron (Figure 12.20).

Figure 12.20 The kidney and its nephrons – structure and roles

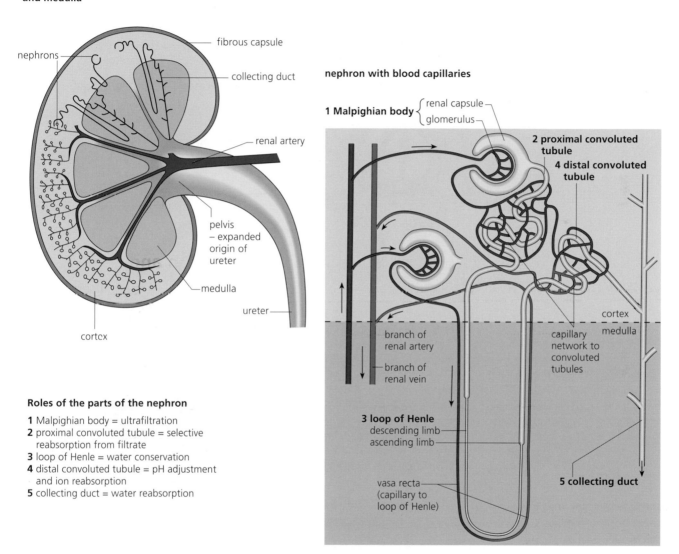

LS through kidney showing positions of nephrons in cortex and medulla

Roles of the parts of the nephron

1 Malpighian body = ultrafiltration
2 proximal convoluted tubule = selective reabsorption from filtrate
3 loop of Henle = water conservation
4 distal convoluted tubule = pH adjustment and ion reabsorption
5 collecting duct = water reabsorption

11 Distinguish between excretion, egestion, osmoregulation and secretion by means of both definitions and examples.

The formation of urine

In humans, about 1.0–1.5 litres of urine are formed each day, typically containing about 40–50 g of solutes of which **urea** (about 30 g) and **sodium chloride** (up to 15 g) make up the bulk. The nephron produces urine in a continuous process which we can conveniently divide into five steps, to show how the blood composition is so precisely regulated. These steps are discussed in turn below.

Step 1: Ultrafiltration in the renal capsule

In the glomerulus, water and relatively small molecules of the blood plasma, including useful ions, glucose and amino acids, are forced out of the capillaries, along with urea, into the lumen of the capsule. This is described as **ultrafiltration** because it is powered by the pressure of the blood, which drives substances through an extremely fine sieve-like structure.

The **blood pressure** here is high enough for ultrafiltration because the input capillary (afferent arteriole) is wider than the output capillary (efferent arteriole). The 'sieve' is made of two layers of cells (the endothelium of the capillaries of the glomerulus and the epithelium of the capsule), between which is a basement membrane.

You can see this arrangement in Figure 12.21.

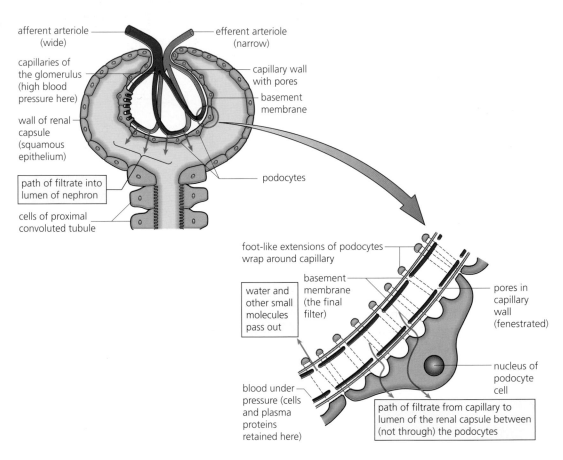

Figure 12.21 The site of ultrafiltration

afferent arteriole (wide)
efferent arteriole (narrow)
capillaries of the glomerulus (high blood pressure here)
capillary wall with pores
basement membrane
wall of renal capsule (squamous epithelium)
podocytes
path of filtrate into lumen of nephron
cells of proximal convoluted tubule

foot-like extensions of podocytes wrap around capillary
basement membrane (the final filter)
water and other small molecules pass out
pores in capillary wall (fenestrated)
nucleus of podocyte cell
blood under pressure (cells and plasma proteins retained here)
path of filtrate from capillary to lumen of the renal capsule between (not through) the podocytes

Notice that the cells of the capsule wall are called **podocytes** because they have foot-like extensions that form a network with tiny slits between them (a situation we call **fenestrated**). Similarly, the endothelium of the capillaries has **pores**, too. This detail has only become apparent from studies using the electron microscope – these filtration gaps are very small indeed.

The entire contents of blood are *not* forced out. Not only are blood cells retained, but the majority of blood proteins and polypeptides dissolved in the plasma are also retained in the circulating blood. This is because of the presence of the **basement membrane**.

12 State the source of energy for ultrafiltration in the glomerulus.

Step 2: Selective reabsorption in the proximal convoluted tubule

The proximal convoluted tubule is the longest section of the nephron. The walls are one cell thick and are packed with mitochondria (ATP is required for the active transport). The cell membrane in contact with the filtrate has a brush border of microvilli which enormously increase the surface area for reabsorption. A large part of the filtrate is reabsorbed into the capillary network here (Figure 12.22).

The individual mechanisms of transport are:

- movement of water by **osmosis**;
- **active transport** of glucose and amino acids across membranes;
- movement of mineral ions by a combination of **active transport, facilitated diffusion,** and some **exchange of ions**;
- **diffusion** of urea;
- movement of proteins by **pinocytosis**.

Figure 12.22
Reabsorption in the proximal convoluted tubule

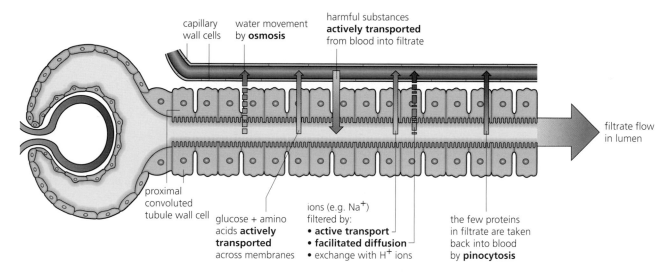

13 Cells of the walls of the proximal convoluted tubule have a brush border. **Describe** what this means, and **explain** how it helps in tubule function.

Step 3: Water conservation in the loop of Henle

Urea is expelled from the body in solution, so water loss in excretion is inevitable. However, mammals are able to form urine that is more concentrated than the blood (when necessary), thereby reducing the water loss to a minimum. The role of the loop of Henle with its **descending** and **ascending limbs**, together with a parallel blood supply, the **vasa recta**, is to create and maintain a high concentration of salts in the tissue fluid in the **medulla of the kidney**. This is brought about by a **countercurrent multiplier mechanism**. It is the building up of a high concentration of salts in the tissue of the medulla that causes water to be reabsorbed from the filtrate in the collecting ducts. The collecting ducts run through the medulla.

The roles of the vasa recta are to:

- absorb water that has been absorbed into the medulla at the collecting ducts;
- remove carbon dioxide and deliver oxygen to the metabolically active cells of the loop of Henle without removing the accumulated salts from the medulla.

Figure 12.23 explains how the countercurrent mechanism works. Notice that the descending and ascending limbs lie close together.

Look first at the second half of the loop, the ascending limb.

Here, sodium and chloride ions are pumped out into the medulla but water is retained inside the ascending limb. Opposite, the descending limb is permeable here, so sodium and chloride ions diffuse in. Water passes out into the medulla tissue, due to the salt concentration in the medulla. As the filtrate flows down the descending limb, this water loss increases the salt concentration in the loop, making the filtrate more concentrated.

Consequently, sodium ions and chloride ions diffuse out down their concentration gradient, around the 'hairpin' zone at the base of the descending limb, adding to the concentration of ions in the medulla. How this concentration helps in the formation of concentrated urine is explained in step 5 below.

Figure 12.23 The functioning loop of Henle

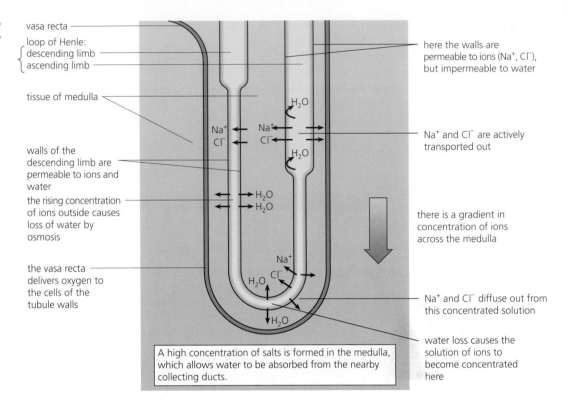

vasa recta

loop of Henle:
descending limb
ascending limb

tissue of medulla

walls of the descending limb are permeable to ions and water

the rising concentration of ions outside causes loss of water by osmosis

the vasa recta delivers oxygen to the cells of the tubule walls

here the walls are permeable to ions (Na^+, Cl^-), but impermeable to water

Na^+ and Cl^- are actively transported out

there is a gradient in concentration of ions across the medulla

Na^+ and Cl^- diffuse out from this concentrated solution

water loss causes the solution of ions to become concentrated here

H_2O
Na^+
Cl^-
H_2O
H_2O
H_2O
Na^+
Cl^-
H_2O
H_2O

A high concentration of salts is formed in the medulla, which allows water to be absorbed from the nearby collecting ducts.

Step 4: Blood pH and ion concentration regulation in the distal convoluted tubule

Here the cells are of the same structure as those of the proximal convoluted tubule, but their role is to adjust the composition of the blood, and in particular the **pH**. An initial tendency for the pH of the blood to change is buffered by the blood proteins, but if the blood does begin to deviate from pH 7.4, then the concentration of hydrogen ions and hydroxyl ions in the blood is adjusted, along with the concentration of hydrogencarbonate ions. Consequently, blood pH does not vary outside the range pH 7.35–7.45, but the pH of urine varies from pH 4.5 to pH 8.2.

Also in the distal convoluted tubule, the selective reabsorption of ions useful in metabolism occurs from the filtrate.

Step 5: Water reabsorption in the collecting ducts

The collecting ducts are where the **water content of the blood** (and therefore of the whole body) is regulated (Figures 12.24 and 12.25). When the water content of the blood is low, **antidiuretic hormone (ADH)** is secreted from the posterior pituitary gland. When the water content of the blood is high, little or no ADH is secreted.

The permeability of the walls of the collecting ducts to water is variable (a case of facilitated diffusion) – the presence of ADH causes the walls of the collecting ducts to be fully permeable. This allows water to be withdrawn from the filtrate of the tubule into the medulla, due to the high concentration of sodium and chloride ions there (see step 3 above). This water is taken up and redistributed in the body by the blood circulation, and only small amounts of concentrated urine are formed. Meanwhile, the ADH circulating in the blood is slowly removed at the kidneys.

When no ADH is secreted, the walls of the collecting ducts become less permeable. The result is that large quantities of very dilute urine are formed.

14 Predict in what circumstances in the body ADH is released.

Figure 12.24 Water reabsorption in the collecting ducts

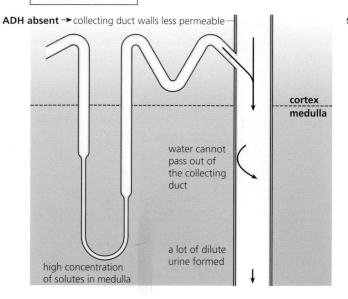

When we have:
• drunk a lot of water.

ADH absent → collecting duct walls less permeable

cortex
medulla

water cannot pass out of the collecting duct

high concentration of solutes in medulla

a lot of dilute urine formed

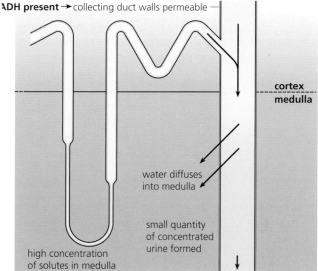

When we have:
• taken in little water
• sweated excessively
• eaten salty food.

ADH present → collecting duct walls permeable

cortex
medulla

water diffuses into medulla

high concentration of solutes in medulla

small quantity of concentrated urine formed

Figure 12.25 Homeostasis by osmoregulation in the kidneys – a summary

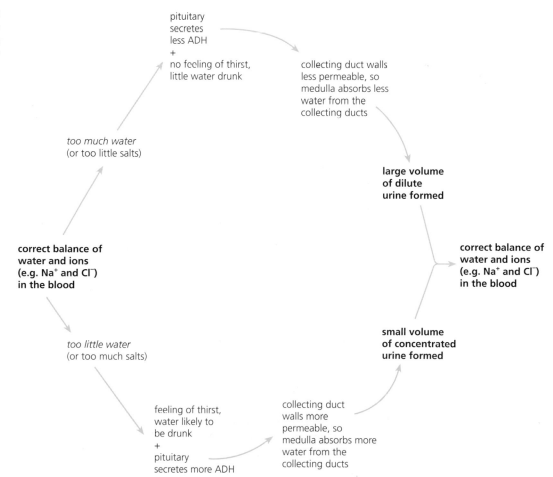

pituitary secretes less ADH
+
no feeling of thirst, little water drunk

collecting duct walls less permeable, so medulla absorbs less water from the collecting ducts

too much water (or too little salts)

large volume of dilute urine formed

correct balance of water and ions (e.g. Na⁺ and Cl⁻) in the blood

correct balance of water and ions (e.g. Na⁺ and Cl⁻) in the blood

too little water (or too much salts)

small volume of concentrated urine formed

feeling of thirst, water likely to be drunk
+
pituitary secretes more ADH

collecting duct walls more permeable, so medulla absorbs more water from the collecting ducts

Differences in composition of blood plasma, glomerular filtrate and urine

The composition of urine excreted from the body is inevitably very variable. It is greatly influenced by our diet (including salt intake and amount of protein consumed), water intake, degree of physical activity, environmental conditions, water loss by other routes (particularly in sweat), and of course by our state of health, as the urine of diabetics illustrates (see below).

On the other hand, the composition of the blood is held more or less constant. This is due to the efficiency of the homeostatic mechanisms of the body, particular those operating at the kidney tubules.

Similarly, the composition of the filtrate passing into the renal capsule is remarkably constant. This is a result of ultrafiltration in the glomerulus, the pressure of the blood, and the sizes of blood proteins and polypeptides dissolved in the plasma – they are mostly too large to be filtered.

In Table 12.4, we have evidence of the power of the ultrafiltration mechanism and the scale of selective reabsorption. And we see the largest divergence in concentration when the composition of the filtrate is compared with composition of urine, formed in one day.

Substance	Total amount in the plasma	Filtered (per day)	Reabsorbed (per day)	Urine (excreted per day)
water	3 litres	180 litres	178–179 litres	1–2 litres
glucose	2.7 g	162.0 g	162.0 g	0.0 g
urea	0.9 g	54.0 g	27.0 g	27.0 g**
proteins + polypeptides	200.0 g	2.0 g	1.9 g	0.1 g
Na⁺ ions	9.7 g	579.0 g	575.0 g	4.0 g
Cl⁻ ions	10.7 g	640.0 g	633.7 g	6.3 g

Table 12.4 Composition of blood, glomerular filtrate and urine

**some is also secreted by the cells of the tubule into the urine

The composition of urine of diabetic patients

The diseases known as diabetes were introduced in Chapter 7, page 224. In either form – early-onset diabetes (type I diabetes) and diabetes mellitus (type II diabetes) – blood glucose levels are erratic and generally frequently well above the normal blood glucose level of about 90 mg glucose per 100 cm³ of blood. This is especially the case after a meal has been digested and the products of digestion absorbed in the small intestine.

An outcome of this condition is the failure of the kidney tubules to reabsorb all the glucose that is forced out of the blood plasma during ultrafiltration. Consequently, the urine of diabetic patients typically has raised and erratic concentrations of glucose. This is one symptom that indicates the likelihood of a patient being a diabetic.

■ Reproduction

11.4.1–11.4.15

In sexual reproduction, sex cells (**gametes**) fuse to form a zygote which then grows into a new individual. The gametes are produced in paired glands called gonads – male gametes or **sperms**, are formed in **testes** (Figure 7.49, page 225); female gametes, ova or **oocytes** (singular, ovum or **oocyte**) are formed in **ovaries** (Figure 7.50, page 226).

The process of gamete formation, known as **gametogenesis**, involves not only mitosis but also meiotic division, thereby halving the normal chromosome number. That is, gametes are haploid. **Fertilisation** restores the diploid number of chromosomes.

The structure of the gonads and the steps of gamete formation are what we consider first.

15 Suggest what evidence there is that, in nature, only some individuals of any species succeed in reproducing themselves.

Gametogenesis

In gametogenesis, many gametes are produced, although relatively few of them are ever used in reproduction. The processes of gamete formation in testes and ovaries have a common sequence of phases.

First, there is a **multiplication phase** in which the gamete mother cells divide by mitotic cell division (Figure 1.33, page 32). This division is then repeated to produce many cells with the potential to become gametes.

Secondly, each developing sex cell undergoes a **growth phase**.

Third and finally, comes the **maturation phase**. This involves meiosis and results in the formation of the haploid gametes. The products of meiosis I are secondary **spermatocytes** and secondary **oocytes**, and the products of meiosis II are **spermatids** and **ova**. The steps of meiosis are described on page 328, Figure 11.1.

These phases in sperm and ova production are summarised in Figure 12.26; the differences between gametogenesis in testis and ovary are listed in Table 12.5 (page 382).

Figure 12.26 The phases and changes during gametogenesis

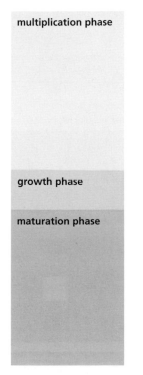

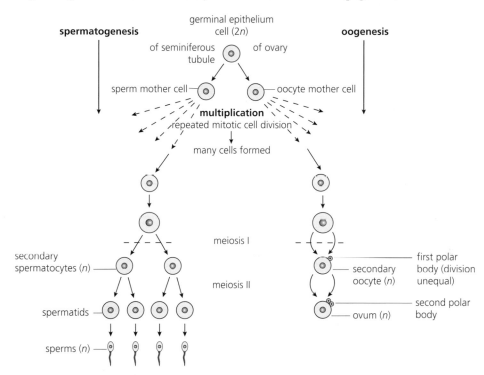

The structure and functioning of the testis

In the human fetus, testes develop high on the posterior abdominal wall and migrate to the scrotum in about the seventh month of pregnancy. In the scrotum, the paired testes are held at a temperature 2–3 °C below body temperature after birth. This lower temperature is eventually necessary for sperm production – testes that fail to migrate do not later produce sperms.

Spermatogenesis begins in the testes at puberty and continues throughout life. Each testis consists of many **seminiferous tubules**. These are lined by germinal epithelial cells which divide repeatedly. Tubules drain into a system of channels leading to the epididymis, a much coiled tube which leads to the **sperm duct**. Between the individual seminiferous tubules is connective tissue containing blood capillaries, together with groups of **interstitial cells**. These latter cells are hormone-secreting (the testis is also an endocrine gland). Testes are suspended by a spermatic cord containing the sperm duct and blood vessels (Figure 12.27).

In the seminiferous tubules, the **germinal epithelium cells** are attached to the basement membrane, along with the **nutritive cells**. Cells from the subsequent steps of sperm production (spermatogonia, primary spermatocytes, secondary spermatocytes and spermatids) occur lodged in the surface of Sertoli cells (nutritive cells) on which they are dependent until they mature into spermatozoa (sperms) (Figures 12.28 and 12.29).

Figure 12.27
Photomicrograph of testis
tissue in section, and
interpretive drawing

**photomicrograph of TS of seminiferous
tubule, LP** (×500)

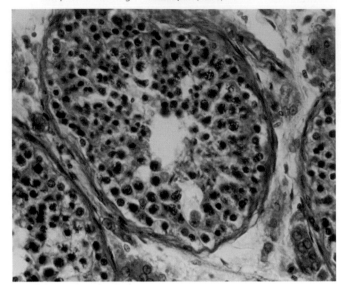

position of nutritive cells
with sperm mother cells

position of
basement membrane

secondary spermatocytes

position of germinal
epithelium

position of
spermatids

position of interstitial cells
(secrete testosterone)

Figure 12.28 Structure
of a seminiferous tubule –
site of sperm production

photomicrograph of TS of seminiferous tubule, HP (×1000)

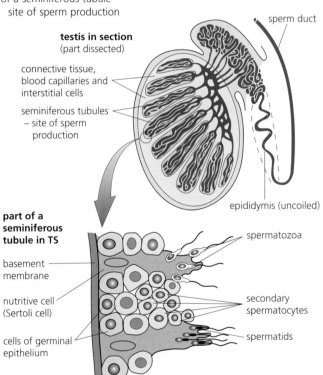

testis in section
(part dissected)

connective tissue,
blood capillaries and
interstitial cells

seminiferous tubules
– site of sperm
production

sperm duct

epididymis (uncoiled)

**part of a
seminiferous
tubule in TS**

basement
membrane

nutritive cell
(Sertoli cell)

cells of germinal
epithelium

spermatozoa

secondary
spermatocytes

spermatids

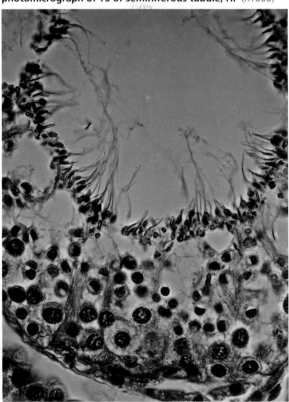

The mature sperms, and the production of semen

The sperms are immobile when first formed. From the seminiferous tubules they pass into the much-coiled epididymis where maturation is completed and storage occurs. During an ejaculation, the sperms are moved by waves of contraction in the muscular walls of the sperm ducts. Sperms are transported in a nutritive fluid secreted by glands, mainly the seminal vesicles and prostate gland. These glands add their secretions just at the point where the sperm ducts join with the urethra, below the base of the penis (Figure 7.49, page 225). As well as providing nutrients for the sperms, semen is a slightly alkaline fluid, the significance of which we will return to later. During an ejaculation, the sphincter muscle at the base of the bladder is closed.

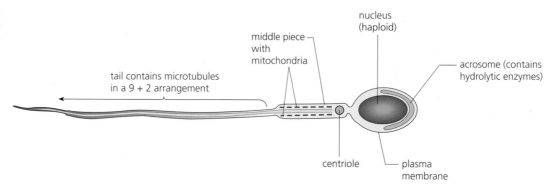

Figure 12.29 The structure of a mature spermatozoon

The roles of hormones in spermatogenesis

The onset of puberty is triggered by a part of the brain called the hypothalamus. Here, production and secretion of a releasing hormone causes the nearby **pituitary gland** (the master endocrine gland) to produce and release into the blood circulation two hormones, known as **follicle-stimulating hormone (FSH)** and **luteinising hormone (LH)**. These hormones are so named because their roles in sexual development in humans were first discovered in the female reproductive system. However, FSH and LH operate in males also (Figure 12.30).

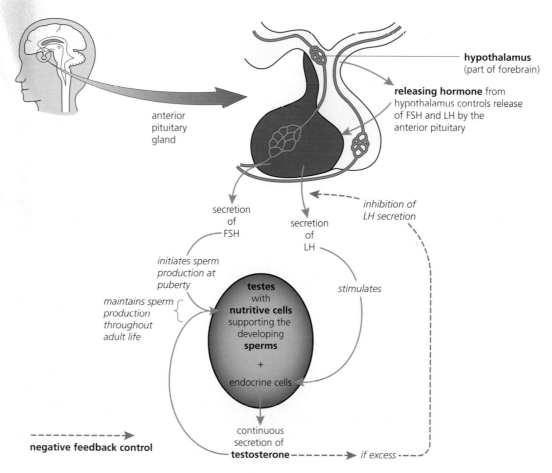

Figure 12.30 Hormone regulation of sperm production

So, at puberty, hormone from the hypothalamus triggers the secretion of FSH and LH by the anterior lobe of the pituitary. In the male, the first effect of FSH is to initiate sperm production in the testes. LH stimulates the endocrine cells of the testes to secrete testosterone. Subsequently, testosterone and FSH together maintain continued sperm production and the growth of the essential Sertoli cells that support sperms with nutrients as they grow and develop in the testes.

Subsequently, secretion of testosterone continues throughout life. Over-activity of testosterone is regulated by **negative feedback control**, as an excessively high level of testosterone in the blood inhibits secretion of LH. Only when the concentration of LH in the blood has fallen significantly will testosterone production recommence. (Similarly, over-activity of the nutritive cells inhibits secretion of FSH for a while.)

The structure and functioning of the ovaries

In the female, the ovaries are about 3 cm long and 1.5 cm thick. These paired structures are suspended by ligaments near the base of the abdominal cavity. As well as producing egg cells, the ovaries are also endocrine glands. They secrete the female sex hormones **oestrogen** and **progesterone**. A pair of oviducts extend from the uterus and open as funnels close to the ovaries. The oviducts transport oocytes, and are the site of fertilisation. In the event of fertilisation, development of the fetus will occur in the uterus.

The steps of oogenesis occur in the ovary. Ovulation, the process by which an egg is released to the oviduct, occurs at the secondary oocyte stage. Development of a secondary oocyte into an ovum is triggered in the oviduct if fertilisation occurs. Consequently, a thin section through a mature ovary examined by light microscopy shows developing oocytes at differing stages (Figure 12.31).

Figure 12.31
Photomicrograph of an ovary in section, and interpretive drawing

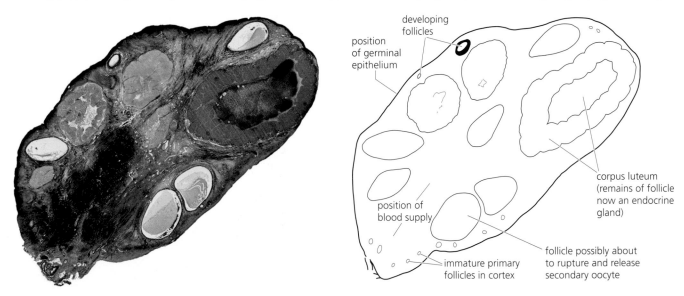

developing follicles

position of germinal epithelium

corpus luteum (remains of follicle now an endocrine gland)

position of blood supply

follicle possibly about to rupture and release secondary oocyte

immature primary follicles in cortex

The structure of the ovary and the steps of oogenesis

Oogenesis begins in the ovaries of the fetus before birth, but the final development of oocytes is only completed in adult life (Figure 12.32). The germinal epithelium, which lines the outer surface of the ovary, divides by mitotic cell division (page 32) to form numerous oogonia. These cells migrate into the connective tissue of the ovary, where they grow and enlarge to form oocytes. Each oocyte becomes surrounded by layers of follicle cells, and the whole structure is called a **primary follicle**.

By mid-pregnancy, production of oogonia in the fetus ceases – by this stage there are several million in each ovary. Very many degenerate, a process that continues throughout life. At the onset of puberty, the number of primary oocytes remaining is about 250 000. Less than 1% of these follicles will complete their development; the remainder never become secondary oocytes or ova.

Between puberty at about 11 years and the cessation of ovulation at menopause, typically about 55 years of age, primary follicles begin to develop further. Several start growth each month, but usually only one matures. Development involves progressive enlargement, and at the same time, the follicles move to the outer part of the ovary. The primary follicle then undergoes **meiosis I** (page 328), but the cytoplasmic division that follows is unequal, forming a tiny polar body and a **secondary oocyte**. The second meiotic division, **meiosis II**, then begins, but it does not go to completion. In this condition the **egg cell** (it is still a secondary oocyte) is released from the ovary (ovulation), by rupture of the follicle wall (Figure 12.32).

Figure 12.32 The ovary, and stages in oogenesis

summary of changes from oogonium to ovum – steps in the growth and maturation phases of gametogenesis in the ovary

diagrammatic representation of the sequence of events in the formation of a secondary oocyte for release and the subsequent changes in the ovary

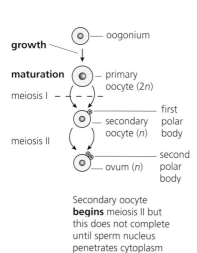

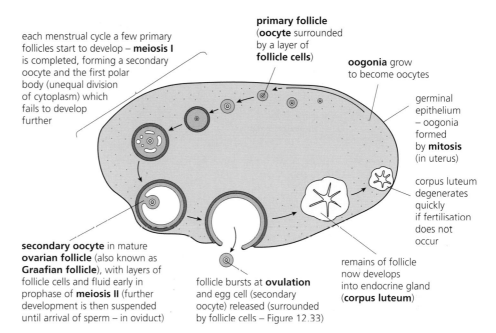

Figure 12.33 The structure of a mature secondary oocyte

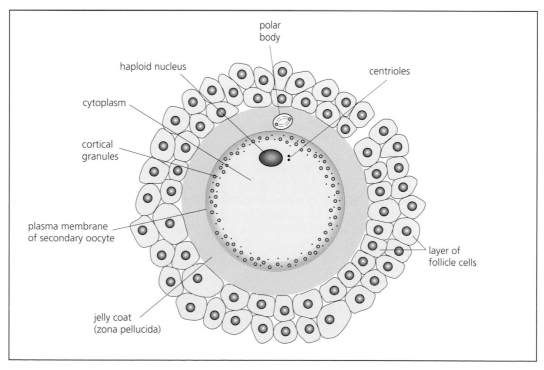

16 Distinguish
between the roles of
FSH in sperm and
ovum production.

Ovulation occurs from one of the two ovaries about once every 28 days. Meanwhile, the remains of the primary follicle immediately develop into the yellow body, the **corpus luteum**. This is an additional but temporary endocrine gland with a role to play if fertilisation occurs (see below).

Gametogenesis in testis and ovary are compared in Table 12.5.

Spermatogenesis	Oogenesis
Spermatogonia formed from the time of puberty, throughout adult life.	Oogonia formed in the embryonic ovaries, long before birth.
All spermatogonia develop into sperms, nurtured by the nutritive cells of the seminiferous tubules of the testes.	Oogonia become surrounded by follicle cells, forming tiny primary follicles, and remain dormant within ovary cortex. Most fail to develop further – they degenerate.
Millions of sperms are formed *daily*.	From puberty, a few primary oocytes undergo meiosis I to become secondary oocytes *each month*. Only one of these secondary oocytes, surrounded by a much enlarged follicle, forms a Graffian follicle – the others degenerate.
Four sperms are formed from each spermatogonium.	One ovum is formed from each oogonium (the polar bodies degenerate, too).
Sperms released from the body by ejaculation.	Graffian follicle releases secondary oocyte into oviduct at ovulation.
Meiosis I and II go to completion during sperm production.	Meiosis II reaches prophase and then stops until a male nucleus enters the secondary oocyte, triggering completion of meiosis II.
Sperms are small, mobile gametes.	Fertilised ovum is non-motile and becomes lodged in the endometrium of the uterus where cell divisions lead to embryo formation.

Table 12.5
Spermatogenesis and
oogenesis compared

Fertilisation

In mammals, fertilisation is internal and occurs in the upper part of the oviduct. The sperms are introduced into the female during sexual intercourse. The erect penis is placed in the vagina, and semen may be ejaculated (3–5 cm^3, in humans) close to the cervix. Typically, more than one hundred million sperms are deposited. The pH of the vagina is quite acid, but the alkaline secretion of the prostate gland, a component of the semen, helps to neutralise the acidity and provides an environment in which sperms can survive.

Waves of contractions in the muscular walls of the uterus and the oviducts assist in drawing semen from the cervix to the site of fertilisation. In this way, a few thousand of the sperms reach the upper uterus and swim up the oviducts. One or more of the few sperms that reach a secondary oocyte pass between the follicle cells surrounding the oocyte. Next, the coat that surrounds the oocyte, which is made of glycoprotein and called the zona pellucida, has to be crossed (Figure 12.34). This is made possible by hydrolytic enzymes which are packaged in the tip of the head of the sperm, called the **acrosome**. In contact with the zona pellucida, these enzymes are released and digest a pathway for the sperm to the oocyte membrane. This process is part of the activation processes, called **capacitation**, in which sperms are prepared for fertilisation.

The head of the sperm, containing the male nucleus, is then able to fuse with the oocyte membrane. The male nucleus enters the oocyte. As this happens, granules in the outer cytoplasm of the oocyte release their contents outside the oocyte by exocytosis. The result is that the oocyte plasma membrane cannot be crossed by another sperm.

As the sperm nucleus enters the oocyte, completion of meiosis II is triggered, and the second polar body is released. The male and female haploid nuclei come together to form the diploid nucleus of the zygote. Fertilisation is completed.

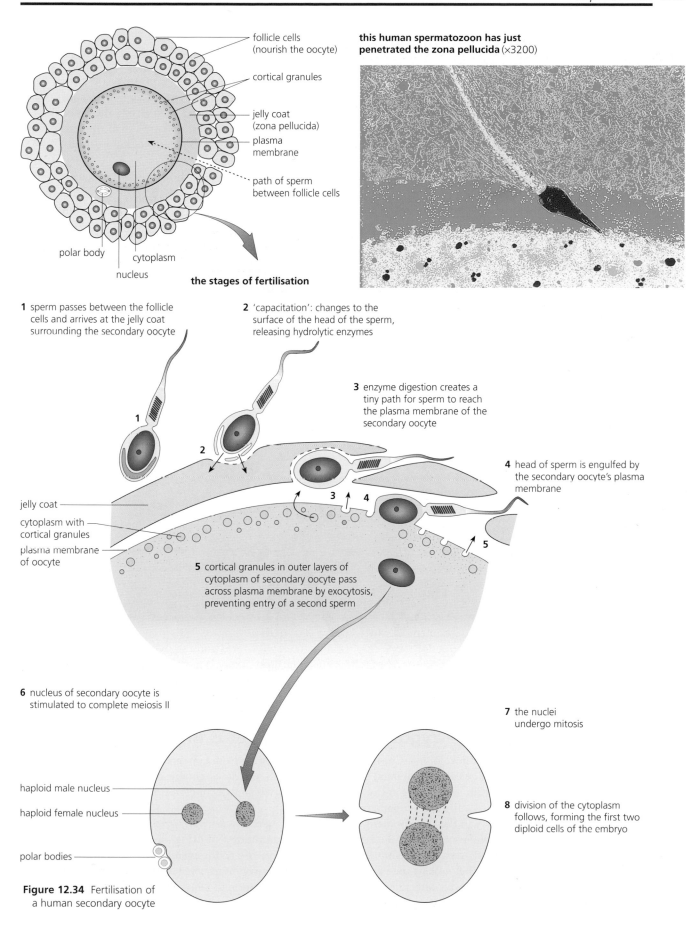

follicle cells
(nourish the oocyte)

cortical granules

jelly coat
(zona pellucida)

plasma
membrane

path of sperm
between follicle cells

polar body

cytoplasm

nucleus

the stages of fertilisation

**this human spermatozoon has just
penetrated the zona pellucida** (×3200)

1 sperm passes between the follicle
cells and arrives at the jelly coat
surrounding the secondary oocyte

2 'capacitation': changes to the
surface of the head of the sperm,
releasing hydrolytic enzymes

3 enzyme digestion creates a
tiny path for sperm to reach
the plasma membrane of the
secondary oocyte

4 head of sperm is engulfed by
the secondary oocyte's plasma
membrane

jelly coat

cytoplasm with
cortical granules

plasma membrane
of oocyte

5 cortical granules in outer layers of
cytoplasm of secondary oocyte pass
across plasma membrane by exocytosis,
preventing entry of a second sperm

6 nucleus of secondary oocyte is
stimulated to complete meiosis II

7 the nuclei
undergo mitosis

haploid male nucleus

haploid female nucleus

polar bodies

8 division of the cytoplasm
follows, forming the first two
diploid cells of the embryo

Figure 12.34 Fertilisation of
a human secondary oocyte

Early development and implantation

Fertilisation occurs in the upper oviduct. As the zygote is transported down the oviduct by ciliary action, mitosis and cell division commence. The process of the division of the zygote into a mass of daughter cells is known as **cleavage**. This is the first stage in the growth and development of a new individual. The embryo does not increase in mass at this stage. By the time the embryo has reached the uterus it is a solid ball of tiny cells called **blastomeres**, no larger than the fertilised egg cell from which it has been formed. Division continues and the blastomeres organise themselves into a fluid-filled ball, the blastocyst (Figure 12.35).

In humans, by day 7 the blastocyst consists of about 100 cells. It now starts to become embedded in the endometrium, a process known as **implantation**. Implantation takes from day 7 to day 14 approximately. At this stage, some of the blastomeres appear grouped as the **inner cell mass**, and these cells will eventually become the fetus. Once implanted, the embryo starts to receive nutrients directly from the endometrium of the uterus wall (Figure 12.36).

Figure 12.35 The site of fertilisation and early stages of development

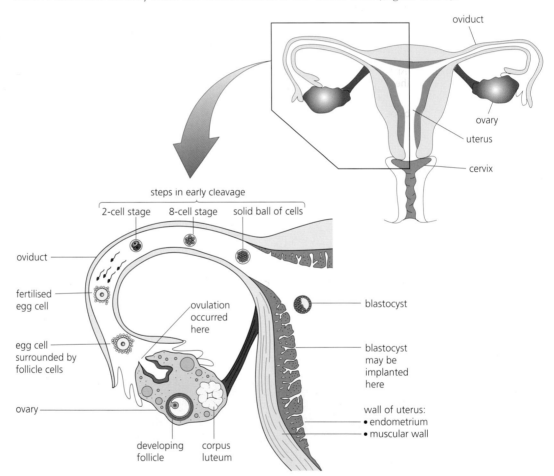

Gestation – zygote to embryo to fetus in humans

The period of development in the mother's body, lasting from conception to birth, is known as **gestation** (40 weeks in humans). The rate of growth and development during gestation is much greater than in any other stage of life. In the first two months of gestation, the developing offspring is described as an **embryo**.

From early in the development of the embryo, this tiny, delicate structure is contained, supported and protected by the **amniotic sac** and **amniotic fluid** (Figure 12.37). It is the outer layers of the tissues of the embryo that grow and give rise to the **membranes**, and also the **placenta** (see below). By the end of two months' development, the beginning of the principal adult organs can be detected, and the placenta is operational. During the rest of gestation, the developing offspring is called a **fetus**.

Figure 12.36 The embryo at implantation

blastocyst at about day 7

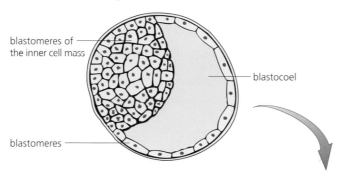

blastomeres of the inner cell mass

blastomeres

blastocoel

implanted (14 days after fertilisation)

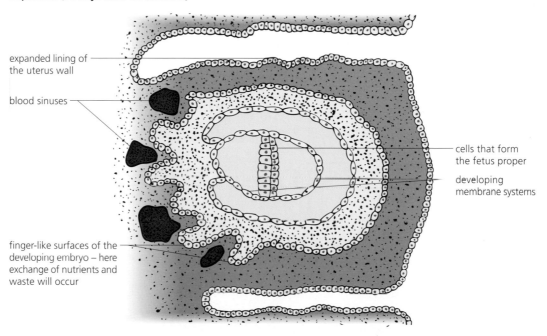

expanded lining of the uterus wall

blood sinuses

cells that form the fetus proper

developing membrane systems

finger-like surfaces of the developing embryo – here exchange of nutrients and waste will occur

Figure 12.37 Human embryo at the six-week stage

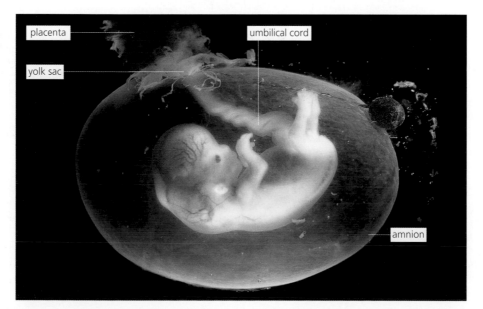

placenta

yolk sac

umbilical cord

amnion

The placenta – structure and function

The **placenta** is a disc-shaped structure composed of maternal (endometrial) and fetal membrane tissues. Here the maternal and fetal blood circulations are brought very close together over a huge surface area, but they do not mix. Placenta and fetus are connected by arteries and a vein in the umbilical cord (Figure 12.38).

Exchange in the placenta is by diffusion and active transport. Movements across the placenta involve:

- **respiratory gases**, which are exchanged; oxygen diffuses across the placenta from the maternal haemoglobin to the fetal haemoglobin (page 669), and carbon dioxide diffuses in the opposite direction;
- **water**, which crosses the placenta by osmosis; **glucose**, which crosses by facilitated diffusion; and **ions** and **amino acids**, which are transported actively;
- **excretory products**, including urea, leaving the fetus;
- **antibodies** present in the mother's blood, which freely cross the placenta so the fetus is initially protected from the same diseases that the mother has protection from (**passive immunity**, page 351).

The placenta is a barrier to bacteria, although some viruses can cross it.

Figure 12.38 The placenta – site of exchange between maternal and fetal circulations

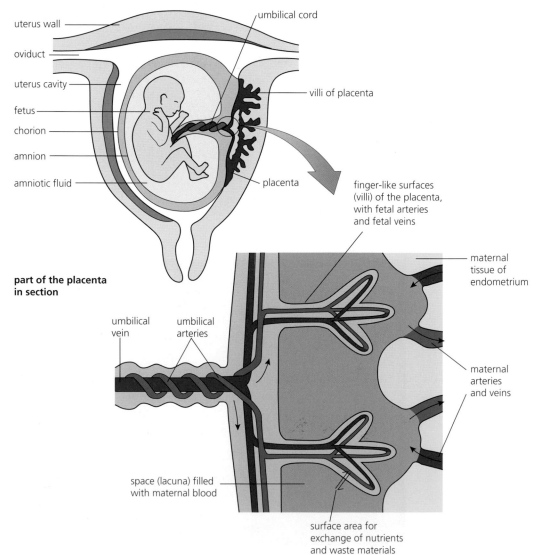

17 Explain why it is so important that the blood of mother and offspring do not mix together in the placenta.

18 List the features of structure of the placenta which contribute to efficient exchange and **explain** why each is important.

The placenta as endocrine gland

The placenta is also an endocrine gland, initially producing an additional sex hormone known as **human chorionic gonadotrophin (HCG)**. HCG appears in the urine from about seven days after conception. We have already noted that it is the presence of HCG in a sample of urine that is detected using monoclonal antibodies in a pregnancy-testing kit (Figure 12.8, page 358).

HCG is initially secreted by the cells of the blastocyst, but later it comes entirely from the placenta. The role of HCG is to maintain the corpus luteum as an endocrine gland (secreting oestrogen and progesterone) for the first 16 weeks of pregnancy. When the corpus luteum eventually does break down, the placenta itself secretes oestrogen and progesterone (Figure 12.39). Without maintenance of these hormone levels, conditions favourable to a fetus are not maintained in the uterus, and a spontaneous abortion results.

Figure 12.39 Blood levels of sex hormones during gestation

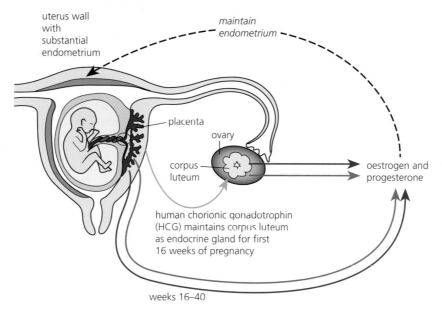

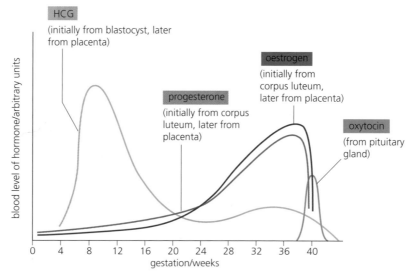

19 Suggest why the immediate production of HCG by the embryo while it still consists of relatively few cells is significant in a successful outcome to gestation.

The process of birth and its hormonal control

Figure 12.40 The positive feedback loop in the control of labour

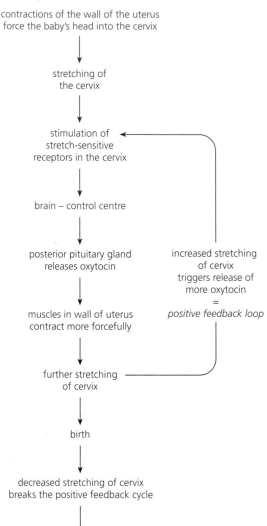

contractions of the wall of the uterus force the baby's head into the cervix

↓

stretching of the cervix

↓

stimulation of stretch-sensitive receptors in the cervix

↓

brain – control centre

↓

posterior pituitary gland releases oxytocin

↓

muscles in wall of uterus contract more forcefully

↓

further stretching of cervix

increased stretching of cervix triggers release of more oxytocin
=
positive feedback loop

↓

birth

↓

decreased stretching of cervix breaks the positive feedback cycle

↓

oxytocin release by posterior pituitary terminated

20 Distinguish between negative and positive feedback processes.

Immediately before birth, the level of **progesterone** declines sharply. As a result, progesterone-driven inhibition of contraction of the muscle of the uterus wall is removed.

At the same time, the posterior pituitary begins to release a hormone, **oxytocin** (Figure 12.39). This relaxes the elastic fibres that join the bones of the pelvic girdle, especially at the front, and thus aids dilation of the cervix for the head (the widest part of the offspring) to pass through. Oxytocin also stimulates rhythmic contractions of the muscles of the uterus wall. Subsequently, control of contractions during birth occurs via a **positive feedback loop** (Figure 12.40). The resulting powerful, intermittent waves of contraction of the muscles of the uterus wall start at the top of the uterus and move towards the cervix. Progressively during this process (known as labour), the rate and strength of the contractions increase, until they expel the offspring.

Finally, less powerful uterine contractions separate the placenta from the endometrium, and cause the discharge of the placenta and remains of the umbilicus as the afterbirth.

■ **Extension:** Lactation

During pregnancy, the mammary glands are prepared for milk production by the action of hormones. Just before birth, lactation commences. Lactation is the production, secretion and ejection of milk.

In the first 2–3 days the milk, at this stage called **colostrum**, provides sugar and protein, but no fat. Also present are **antibodies** that aid survival during first exposures to potentially dangerous microorganisms.

Milk formed later is an almost complete diet, providing 1.5–2.0% protein, 3.5% fat, 6.5% milk sugar (lactose), and 0.3% minerals such as Ca^{2+} ions, vitamins A, B, C and D, and water. Milk is deficient in iron, and offspring have to rely on iron stored in their liver until their diet changes and develops.

■ *Examination questions – a selection*

Questions 1–6 are taken from past IB Diploma biology papers.

Q1 The diagram shows the immune system identifying an infected cell in the body. What is the structure labelled X?

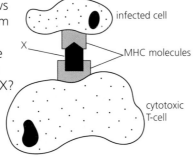

- **A** antigen
- **B** antibody
- **C** IgA
- **D** IgM

Higher Level Paper 1, May 02, Q31

Q2 Which structure of the kidney responds to ADH by reabsorbing water?
- **A** proximal convoluted tubule
- **B** loop of Henle
- **C** glomerulus
- **D** collecting duct

Higher Level Paper 1, May 02, Q37

Q3 The diagram shows the structure of testis tissue as seen using a light microscope. Which is the primary spermatocyte?

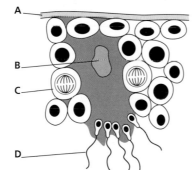

Higher Level Paper 2, May 03, Q35

Q4 The diagram below shows a human elbow joint.

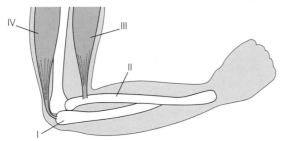

Which response correctly identifies the ulna and the extensor muscle?

	Ulna	Extensor muscle
A	I	III
B	I	IV
C	II	IV
D	II	III

Higher Level Paper 1, May 03, Q36

Q5 Which of the following parts of the male reproductive system contribute to the production of semen?
- I epididymis
- II seminal vesicle
- III bladder
- IV prostate

- **A** II only
- **B** II and IV only
- **C** I, II and IV only
- **D** I, II, III and IV

Higher Level Paper 1, May 04, Q32

Q6 Which of the following occur(s) at birth in the mother's body?
- I increase in oxytocin
- II increase in uterine contractions
- III increase in levels of progesterone

- **A** I only
- **B** I and II only
- **C** II and III only
- **D** I, II and III

Higher Level Paper 1, May 06, Q24

Questions 7–10 cover other syllabus issues in this chapter.

Q7 **a** Distinguish between passive and natural immunity. (4)
b Outline the sequence of steps by which the human body may acquire naturally active immunity to a viral infection. (6)

Q8 Muscles contract when the fibres shorten. This shortening is brought about when myosin and actin filaments of the sarcomeres slide past each other. Explain by means of annotated drawings how ATP and calcium ions (Ca^{2+}) enable the myosin and actin filaments to interact to shorten a muscle. (10)

Q9 **a** Outline the principle of a countercurrent mechanism. (4)
b Describe the roles of:
  i the vasa recta
  ii the descending and ascending limbs of the loop in water conservation by the loop of Henle. (8)

Q10 **a** Identify the stage in gestation at which the placenta forms, and the tissues involved. (4)
b Explain why is it essential that maternal and fetal blood circulations do not mix in the placenta. (4)
c Describe what substances are required by the fetus and how each is transferred to the fetal blood at the placenta. (6)
d Outline the additional role of the placenta as an endocrine gland. (3)

Answers to self-assessment questions (SAQs) in Chapters 1–12

1 Cells – the building blocks

page 1

1 The processes characteristic of living things are:
- transfer of energy (respiration)
- metabolism
- movement and locomotion
- reproduction
- feeding or nutrition
- excretion
- responsiveness or sensitivity
- growth and development

page 2

2 a $1\,mm = 1000\,\mu m$.
   Since $^{1000}/_{100} = 10$, 10 cells of $100\,\mu m$ will fit along a 1 mm line.
   b The drawing of *E. coli* is 64 mm in length (actual length $2.0\,\mu m$). Therefore, magnification $= 64 \times 1000/2 = \times 32\,000$.

page 5

3 a

Dimensions/ mm	Surface area/ mm²	Volume/ mm³	SA:V ratio
$1 \times 1 \times 1$	6	1	6:1 = 6.0
$2 \times 2 \times 2$	24	8	24:8 = 3.0
$4 \times 4 \times 4$	96	64	96:64 = 1.5
$6 \times 6 \times 6$	216	216	216:216 = 1.0

   b Small cells and organisms have a large surface area to volume ratio (that is, the surface area available for diffusion). As the cell increases in size, the surface area to volume ratio decreases very rapidly (i.e. less of the cytoplasm has access to the cell exterior).
   c As cell size increases, the efficiency of diffusion for the removal of waste products decreases.

page 8

4 **Emergent properties** of humans may include behavioural traits such as playfulness (a quality typical of many mammals) and anticipation of danger, and affective (emotional) traits such as loyalty and sadness, perhaps.
What have you listed?

page 12

5 The maximum length of the image of the *Amoeba* in the photomicrograph is 129 mm. From the scale bar shown here, 28 mm = 0.1 mm = $100\,\mu m$. So the actual length of the *Amoeba* is $129/28 \times 100\,\mu m$, which is approximately $460\,\mu m$.

page 13

6 The magnification is $\times 60$ (6×10).

page 14

7 See **Magnification and resolution of an image**, page 13.

page 15

8 The electron microscope has powers of magnification and resolution that are greater than those of an optical microscope. The wavelength of visible light is about 500 nm, whereas that of the beam of electrons used is 0.005 nm. At best the light microscope can distinguish two points which are 200 nm ($0.2\,\mu m$) apart, whereas the transmission electron microscope can resolve points 1 nm apart when used on biological specimens. Given the sizes of cells and of the organelles they contain, it requires the magnification and resolution achieved in transmission electron microscopy to observe cell ultrastructure – in suitably prepared specimens.

page 17

9 The length of the image is approximately 60 mm. From the scale bar, $1\,\mu m = 23\,mm$. Therefore, the actual length of *E. coli* $= 60/23\,\mu m = 2.6\,\mu m$. The magnification of the image = $60 \times 1000/26 = $ approximately $\times 23\,000$.

page 19

10 The characteristics *not* shown by viruses are:
- transfer of energy (respiration)
- movement and locomotion
- responsiveness or sensitivity
- feeding or nutrition
- excretion
- metabolism

11 a A **cell wall** is characteristic of plant cells. It is entirely external to the cell, surrounding the plasma membrane. The wall is not an organelle. Plant cell walls are primarily constructed from cellulose, an extremely strong material. When a growing plant cell divides, a cell wall is laid down across the old cell, dividing the contents. This primary cell wall has more layers of cellulose added, forming the secondary cell wall. In some plant cells the secondary layers of cellulose become very thick indeed. Cell walls are absent from animal cells. Prokaryotes have cell walls, too, but chemically different from those of plants.
   The **plasma membrane** is the cell membrane that surrounds and contains the cytoplasm of all cells. It is constructed almost entirely of protein and lipid. The lipid of membranes is phospholipid, arranged as a bilayer. The proteins of cell membranes are globular proteins which are buried in and across the lipid bilayer, with most protruding above the surfaces. The whole structure is described as a fluid mosaic. See **Figure 1.19**, page 21.
   b The **nucleus** is the largest organelle in the eukaryotic cell, typically $10-20\,\mu m$ in diameter, and contains the chromosomes. These thread-like structures are visible at the time the nucleus divides; at other times they are dispersed as a diffuse network, called chromatin. The nucleus is surrounded by a double membrane, which contains many tiny pores, each only 100 nm in diameter. Pores are so numerous that they make up about one-third of the nuclear membrane's surface area. This suggests that communication between nucleus and cytoplasm is important. The appearance of the nucleus in electron micrographs is shown in Figure 1.13, page 15.
   The **nucleoid** is the genetic material of a prokaryote, and consists of a single, circular chromosome of DNA (helix), located in the cytoplasm, but attached at one point to the inner surface of the plasma membrane. Here the DNA is not supported by histone protein, as is the case with eukaryotic chromosomes. See Figure 1.15, page 16.
   c **Flagella** and **pili**, see **Figure 1.15**, page 16.

page 21

12

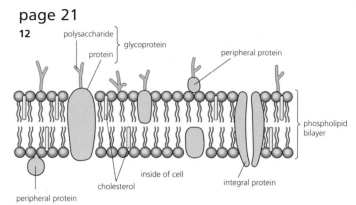

Diagrammatic cross-section of the fluid mosaic membrane

page 22

13 A **lipid bilayer** is demonstrated in **Figure 1.20**, page 22, in which, in the presence of sufficient water, molecules of lipid arrange themselves as a bilayer, with the hydrocarbon tails facing together. This latter is the situation in the plasma membrane.

Several organelles of eukaryotic cells have a **double membrane**, including chloroplasts and mitochondria, in which there are present an outer and an inner membrane, both of which consist of lipid bilayers.

So the difference between a lipid bilayer and a double membrane lies in the number of lipid bilayers present.

page 26

14 a

Dimensions/mm	SA:V ratio
10 × 10 × 10	600/1000 = 0.6
5 × 5 × 5	150/125 = 1.2
4 × 4 × 4	96/64 = 1.5
2.5 × 2.5 × 2.5	37.5/15.6 = 2.4

b

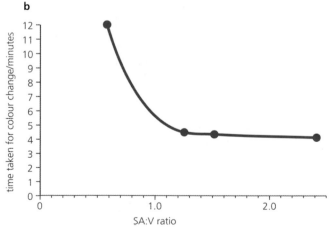

Graph of time taken for colour change against SA:V ratio

c Hydrogen ions enter the gelatine blocks by diffusion and there cause the observed colour change. Relatively large blocks (10 mm cubes) have a low SA:V ratio – meaning that little of the interior matter is close to the external environment, and the diffusion path is a long one. Here, colour change is slowest. The reverse is true of the smallest gelatine blocks (2.5 mm cubes).

page 26

15 Compare **Figure 1.26**, page 25, and **Figure 1.27**, page 25. The difference is the permeability of the membrane traversed; in facilitated diffusion this is due to the properties of the substance that passes – it triggers the opening of pores through which diffusion occurs.

page 27

16 The concentrated solution of glucose (where the concentration of free water molecules is low) will show a net gain of water molecules at the expense of the dilute glucose solution.

page 29

17 Uptake of ions is by active transport involving metabolic energy (ATP) and protein pump molecules located in the plasma membranes of cells. As with all aspects of metabolism, this is a temperature-sensitive process and occurs more speedily at 25 °C than at 5 °C.

Individual ions are pumped across by specific, dedicated protein molecules. Because there are many more sodium ion pumps than chloride ions pumps, more of the former ion is absorbed.

page 30

18 a See pages 28–30 for the differences between proteins and lipids.
  b See pages 47 and 51 for the differences between active transport and bulk transport.
  c See page 30 for the difference between endocytosis and exocytosis.

page 34

19

Stage of mitosis	a % of dividing cells at each stage of mitosis*	b Time taken by each step of mitosis (given an overall length of 60 minutes)
prophase	70	70/100 × 60 = 42 min
metaphase	10	10/100 × 60 = 6 min
anaphase	5	5/100 × 60 = 3 min
telophase	15	15/100 × 60 = 9 min

*Your pie chart should comprise sectors with the following angles at the centre: prophase 252°, metaphase 36°, anaphase 18° and telophase 54°.

page 35

20 Cancer cells divide uncontrollably, forming a tumour. The cells of a malignant tumour invade and damage surrounding organs. Cancer cells may detach and be transported by the blood circulation (metastasise) to distant sites in the body. Normal cells do not behave in this way.

The switch to uncontrolled growth of cancer cells is caused by the accumulation of harmful genetic changes (mutations) in a range of genetically controlled mechanisms that regulate the cell cycle.

The cell cycle is a regulatory loop. It ensures that DNA is faithfully copied and that the replicated chromosomes move to the new (daughter) cells. Further, cell division is restricted – only a selected range of cells can divide again. Normally, if any cell is severely damaged, or grows abnormally, or becomes redundant in the further development of an organ, it undergoes programmed cell death. Thus, many controls prevent cancerous cell behaviour in normal cells.

So cancer cells arise as a result of the coincidence of mutations in several normal growth and behaviour genes. Once some cancers are established, malignant tumour cells typically release a specific protein that dictates the formation of a network of blood vessels supplying the tumour. This occurs at the expense of the supply of nutrients to surrounding healthy cells, which enhances abnormal cell division and growth, and leads to further metastasis.

2 Chemistry of life

page 38

1 An **atom** is the smallest part of an element that can take part in a chemical change. The atoms of different elements are of different sizes, but all atoms are incredibly **small**. Because of the small size of atoms we cannot refer to their mass by a standard unit, like the gram, for example. Instead, we compare the mass of an atom relative to an agreed standard. For this purpose the reference atom is that of carbon (see diagram below). The carbon atom is given a **relative atomic mass** of 12 (A_r = 12). By comparison, atoms of hydrogen (A_r = 1) are much lighter than carbon, but atoms of nitrogen (A_r = 14) are slightly heavier, and atoms of potassium (A_r = 39) substantially heavier.

Atoms themselves are made of three kinds of smaller particle. They consist of a nucleus of **protons** (positively charged particles) and, usually, **neutrons**, which are uncharged particles. (The exception is the nucleus of the hydrogen atom which contains no neutron, only a single proton.) Around the nucleus occur incredibly tiny particles called **electrons** (negatively charged particles), moving in shells.

Protons and neutrons have virtually the same mass, and together make up the mass of the nucleus. Electrons have almost no mass at all. Actually, the neutron is made of two particles, a proton (+) and an electron (−), which explains why the charge on a neutron is neutral. **The atom is electrically neutral** because the number of protons in the nucleus is equal to the number of electrons in the orbits around. (Note that nucleus of an atom must not be compared or confused with the cell nucleus.)

Ions, on the other hand, are the **charged particles** formed when atoms combine together in **ionic bonding**.

Atoms combine in ways that produce a **stable arrangement of electrons in the outer shell** of each atom – atoms are most stable when their outer shell of electrons is complete. The first electron shell can hold up to 2 electrons and then it is full. The second shell can hold up to a maximum of 8 electrons, the third shell can hold up to 18 electrons, and the fourth shell can hold up to 32 electrons. (There are further shells in the largest atoms, but they do not concern us here because the elements that make up living things have atoms that are among the smallest and lightest in the Earth's crust.)

So, ions are very **stable** because their outermost electron shell is complete. Note that when sodium and chlorine ionically bond, the sodium ion is formed by losing an electron (and so is no longer neutral – it is positively charged), and the chlorine atom has gained an electron to become the chloride ion (and so is negatively charged), as shown in the diagram below.

The structure of a carbon atom

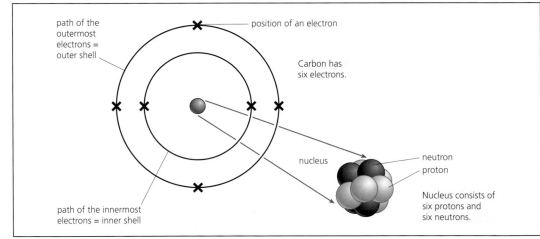

The formation of ions by ionic bonding

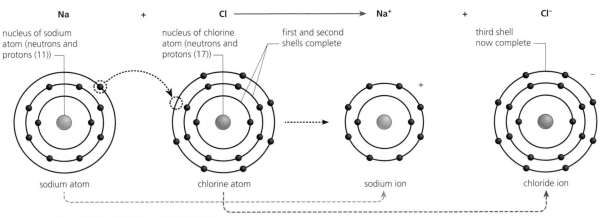

A sodium atom donates an electron to a chlorine atom.

Positively charged ions are called **cations**, and negatively charged ions are called **anions**. The table below shows some important ions that occur widely in living cells, and which have some specialised roles in functioning cells.

Positively charged ions (cations)

Na⁺ = sodium ion	Involved in the setting up of the action potential of a nerve fibre, and the flow of the action potential (impulse) (page 212).
K⁺ = potassium ion	Involved in the setting up of the action potential of a nerve fibre, and the flow of the action potential.
Ca²⁺ = calcium ion	Involved in the contraction of the muscle myofibrils by combining with blocking molecules, so that the myosin head of the cross bridge can attach to the actin (page 368).

Negatively charged ions (anions)

NO³⁻ = nitrate ion	Plants reduce nitrate to ammonia and combine it with an organic acid, forming an amino acid from which all 20 amino acids used to manufacture proteins are derived.
PO₄³⁻ = phosphate ion	The phosphate ion is combined with ADP to form ATP. ATP is the energy currency of cells, involved in energy-requiring reactions and processes, like protein synthesis, and muscle contraction.
HCO³⁻ = hydrogencarbonate ion	The form in which carbon dioxide is transported in the blood (plasma and red cells). It is formed when CO_2 reacts with water, catalysed by carbonic anhydrase enzyme.

2 Atoms bond in ways that produce a stable arrangement of electrons in the outer shell of each atom. The outer electron shells are completed either by **sharing electrons** to form **covalent bonds**, or by **giving and taking electrons** to form **ionic bonds**.

Ionic bonding to form sodium chloride (sodium ions and chloride ions) is illustrated above (page B392). Ionic bonding is the electrostatic attraction between oppositely charged particles. In solid sodium chloride (crystals of the salt), ionic bonds hold the ions together in a regular arrangement (known as a crystal lattice). In solution, however, water molecules surround the sodium and chloride ions, causing them to be separated and dispersed.

In **covalent bonding**, electrons are shared between atoms. Covalent bonds are the strongest bonds occurring in biological molecules. This means they need the greatest input of energy to break them. So, covalent bonds provide great stability to biological molecules, many of which are very large and elongated. Bonding of this kind is common in non-metal elements such as hydrogen, nitrogen, carbon and oxygen.

page 42

3 In a solution of glucose, water is the solvent and sucrose is the solute.

page 43

4 The causes and reasons for the **properties of water** – due to **H-bonds** – are explained in **Water** and **Figure 2.1** (pages 38–39). The mechanisms of the **cooling and solvent properties of water** are explained subsequently (page 39 and page 42).

1 In the **hydrogen molecule** a covalent bond is formed.

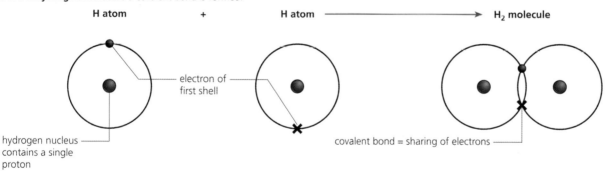

2 In **methane**, four single bonds are formed with hydrogen atoms to make the outer shell of carbon up to eight electrons.

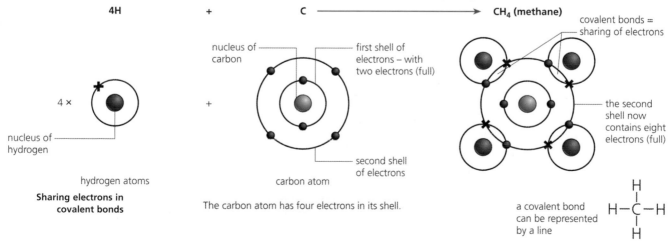

page 44

5

Non-organic C	Found in the biosphere
carbon dioxide	in the atmosphere and dissolved in fresh water and in sea water as hydrogencarbonate ions
carbonates (e.g. calcium and magnesium carbonate)	in the shells of species of non-vertebrate animals, mostly marine, but also of some fresh water and terrestrial habitats, and chalk and limestone rocks, principally formed from fossilised shells

6 The presence of sugar in the cytoplasm or vacuoles of cells has a powerful osmotic effect (see **Osmosis – a special case of diffusion**, page 26), whereas if glucose molecules are condensed to starch (or glycogen, in animal cells), these insoluble carbohydrate reserves have no effect on cell water relations. Meanwhile, starch and glycogen may be speedily hydrolysed to sugar if and when the need arises.

page 46

7 A **polymer** is a large organic molecule made of repeating subunits known as **monomers**, chemically combined together. Among the carbohydrates, starch, glycogen and cellulose are polymers built from a huge number of molecules of glucose (the monomer). The glucose monomers are combined together in different ways in the three, distinctive polymers.

page 48

8 See **Disaccharides** and **Condensation and hydrolysis reactions**, **Figure 2.8**, pages 45–46, and **Figure 2.11**, page 49.

page 50

9 The **hydrophobic properties** of a lipid are combined with the **hydrophilic properties** of an ionised phosphate group, resulting in a 'head and tail' molecule.

page 52

10 In a polypeptide of only five amino acids there can be 20^5 different types, or 3 200 000.

So in a polypeptide of 25 amino acids, 20^{25} different types, and in one of 50, 20^{50} different types of polypeptide can be formed. A polypeptide of more than 50 amino acid residues is by convention called a protein. So, there is virtually unlimited structural variation possible in proteins of cells. Remember, as the sequence of amino acids changes, so do their structure and properties.

page 54

11 Enzymes work by binding to their substrate molecule at a specially formed pocket on the enzyme – the active site. Most enzymes are large molecules, and the active site takes up a relatively small part of the total volume of the enzyme molecule. Nevertheless, the active site is a function of the overall shape of the globular protein, and if the shape of an enzyme changes for whatever reason, the catalytic properties may be lost.

page 56

12 Pre-incubation is required to ensure that when the reactants are mixed, the reaction occurs at the known, pre-selected temperature.

page 57

13 **pH** is a measure of acidity or alkalinity of a solution. Strictly, pH is a measure of the hydrogen ion concentration. The pH scale runs from 0 to 14, where pH 7 is neutral. This is the pH of pure water, where the concentrations of hydrogen ions (H^+) and hydroxide ions (OH^-) are low and equal in number. A solution of pH of less than 7 is an acidic solution, and strong acids have a pH of 0–2. Solutions of pH of more than 7 are alkaline.

A **buffer solution** acts to resist pH change when diluted or a little acid or alkali is added. Many buffers used in laboratory experiments contain a weak acid (such as ethanoic acid – vinegar) and its soluble salt (e.g. sodium ethanoate). In this case, if acid is added, the excess hydrogen ions are immediately removed by combination with ethanoate ions to form undissociated ethanoic acid. Alternatively, if alkali is added, the excess hydroxide ions immediately combine with hydrogen ions to form water. At the same time, more of the ethanoic acid dissociates, adding more hydrogen ions to the solution. The pH does not change in either case.

In the body of the mammal, the blood is very powerfully buffered by the presence of a mixture of phosphate ions, hydrogencarbonate ions and blood proteins. The blood is held between pH 7.35 and 7.45. pH is very important in living organism, largely because pH affects the shape of enzymes, almost all of which are proteins.

page 59

14 Approximately $0.23 \ cm^3 \, s^{-1}$

page 60

15 a see **Figure 2.22**, page 60.
   b Working with an excess of substrate molecules (a relatively high concentration of substrate), the effect of increase in the concentration of enzyme is to increase the rate of reaction. This is because, at any moment, proportionally more substrate molecules are in contact with an enzyme molecule.

page 61

16 *in vitro* = biological processes occurring in cell extracts (literally 'in glass')
   in vivo = biological processes occurring in living organisms (literally 'in life')

page 62

17 A catalyst is a substance that alters the rate of a chemical reaction, but remains unchanged at the end.

Inorganic catalysts	Enzymes
typically a metal like platinum in a finely-divided state (e.g. as platinised mineral wool)	typically made of protein (but occasionally RNA acts as an enzyme), so easily denatured (e.g. by high temperature)
able to withstand high temperatures, high pressures and extremes of pH, if necessary	extremely specific – most are specific to one type of substrate molecule, for example

page 64

18 **Nitrogenous base**
   Nitrogenous bases are organic compounds. The carbon backbones of nitrogenous bases are ring molecules containing two or more nitrogen atoms, covalently bonded together. They are derived from one of two parent compounds: purine (a double-ring compound) or pyrimidine (a single-ring compound).

Inorganic base

An inorganic base is a substance that can accept a hydrogen ion and so neutralise an acid. Strong bases are substances like sodium hydroxide. They are ionised compounds.

page 71

19

RNA involved in transcription	
messenger RNA (mRNA)	See **Transcription – the first step in protein synthesis**, page 69.

RNA involved in translation	
messenger RNA (mRNA)	mRNA is a linear molecule in the cytoplasm along which ribosomes move, 'reading' the genetic code and transcribing the information into a linear sequence of amino acid residues (i.e. primary structure of the protein)
transfer RNA (tRNA)	See **Amino acid activation** and **Figure 2.32**, pages 70–71.
ribosomal RNA	RNA is a major component of the ribosomes – organelles found in the cytoplasm and attached in rough endoplasmic reticulum (rER); here, the mRNA is 'read' and the protein molecules are formed (**Figure 2.33**, page 72). The structure of a ribosome is shown in **Figure 8.11**, page 248.

page 74

20

Proteins other than enzymes	Roles
'active' proteins in cell membranes	■ active uptake pumps (e.g. for ions) ■ hormone receptor sites ■ antigens of immune system
'active' proteins in body fluids (e.g. blood)	■ blood proteins (pH buffers) ■ blood clotting proteins ■ antibodies
structural proteins	■ hair of mammals ■ collagen fibres of tendons and ligaments
storage proteins (plants only)	■ grains of proteins deposited in the cells of some seeds and plant storage organs – available for re-use on germination and growth

3 Energy transfer in cells

page 78

1 See **ATP, the universal energy currency**, page 77.

page 80

2 Glycolysis (the conversion of glucose to pyruvate) which occurs in the cytosol (the aqueous part of the cytoplasm that surrounds organelles such as the mitochondria) does not require oxygen for completion.

page 81

3 Lactate and a limited amount of ATP are the final products of anaerobic respiration in muscle fibres.

page 82

4 In the respirometer, the far side of the U-tube manometer is the control tube (A). Here, conditions are identical to those in the respirometer tube, but in the former, no living material is present. However, any change in external temperature or pressure is equally experienced by both tubes, and their effects on the level of manometric fluid are equal and opposite, and they cancel out.

5

Mammals	source of glucose	Flowering plants
product of digestion of food items, particularly from carbohydrates hydrolysis of glycogen reserves in muscle cells	**source of glucose**	product of photosynthesis in the chloroplasts, mainly situated in the green leaves hydrolysis of stored starch

page 84

6 If a naked flame (Bunsen burner) is used to heat the water (Step 1), then the flame must be switched off before the propanone (acetone) is poured out – to avoid fire.

Care is needed when fresh leaves are immersed in boiling water using blunt forceps – to avoid a scalding accident.

The contents of centrifuge tubes to be placed in the centrifuge (Step 4) must be balanced in contents, so that they are of equal mass – to prevent damage to the centrifuge or to the tubes during centrifugation.

Pigment solution should be labelled with the contents and particularly the solvent, and stored in cool dark conditions –– so that they are not confused with any other materials, and so that solvent vapour is not accidentally exposed to a naked flame.

page 87

7 a Carbon: from carbon dioxide by reducing it to carbohydrate
b Hydrogen: from water by photolysis to form hydrogen and oxygen gas (waste product)

page 88

8 Starch in the green leaves held in the dark is converted to glucose and then to sucrose and the latter is carried (translocated) in the phloem sieve tubes to storage sites, typically in the stem and root cells – where it is converted back to starch and stored.

page 89

9 A thermometer is required in the glass tube with the *Elodea* (in a position that does not interfere with the supply of light to the plant), so that the temperature at which photosynthesis is measured is known. Also, it is advisable to check that the *Elodea* sample is not subjected to an unplanned rise in temperature as the intensity of light is increased, for example.

page 90

10 The biochemical steps of photosynthesis are dependent on the action and activity of numerous (protein) enzymes. These are progressively denatured and rendered inactive as the temperature is raised.

4 Genetics

page 92

1 See **Chromosomes occur in pairs**, page 91.

page 94

2 See **The significance of mitosis**, page 35, and **Abrupt change in hereditary information – mutations**, particularly **Chromosome mutations**, page 98.

page 100

3 **Figure 4.10** shows the karyotype of a male patient showing non-disjunction at chromosome 21.

page 102

4 See **Gene mutations**, page 98.

page 105

5 The presentation of a breeding experiment, such as that shown in **Figure 4.15**, is a prediction of the likely outcome. It represents the probable results, provided that:
- fertilisation is random
- there are equal opportunities for survival among the offspring
- large numbers of offspring are produced.

What is actually observed in a breeding experiment may not necessarily agree with the prediction. For example, there is a chance in this particular cross that:
- more pollen grains of one genetic constitution may fuse with egg cells than another
- more developing seeds of one type are predated and destroyed by insect larvae of species attacking the plant (so fewer zygotes of one type complete development)
- the cross produced too few progeny in total.

page 106

6 Below is a table showing how the Law of segregation relates to meiosis.

Mendel's monohybrid cross	Feature of meiosis
Within an organism there are breeding factors controlling characteristics like 'tall' and 'dwarf'. These factors remain intact from generation to generation.	Each chromosome holds a linear sequence of genes. A particular gene always occurs on the same chromosome in the same position after each nuclear division.
There are two factors for each characteristic in each cell.	The chromosomes of a cell occur in pairs, called homologous pairs.
One factor comes from each parent. (A recessive factor is not expressed in the presence of a dominant factor.)	One of each pair came originally from one parent and the other from the other parent.
Factors separate in reproduction; either can be passed to an offspring. Only one of the factors can be in any gamete.	At the end of meiosis each cell contains only one of the homologous pair of chromosomes present in the parent cell.
Mendel recognised the 3:1 ratio is the product of randomly combining two pairs of unlike factors (e.g. **T** and **t**) – the product of the binomial expression (where a recessive factor is not expressed in the heterozygote): $(T + t)(T + t) = 1TT + 2Tt + 1tt$	The arrangement of bivalents at the equatorial plate of the spindle is random; maternal and paternal homologous chromosomes are independently assorted. In a large number of matings all possible combinations of chromosomes will occur in equal numbers.

page 107

7 The layout of your monohybrid cross will be as in **Figure 4.17** (page 107), but the **parental generation** (**P**) will have the genotypes (if you have chosen C = allele for coat colour):
$C^R C^R \times C^W C^W$
where C^R represents the allele for red coat, and C^W represents the allele for white coat. The gametes the parental generation produces will be:
C^R and C^W
The **offspring (F₁)** will have genotype $C^R C^W$
and the phenotype will be roan.
In a **sibling cross of the F₁ generation** the gametes of both siblings will be:
$\frac{1}{2}C^R + \frac{1}{2}C^W$
From an appropriate Punnett grid, the offspring (**F₂**) to be expected and the proportions are as follows.

genotypes:	$C^R C^R$	$C^R C^W$	$C^W C^W$
ratio:	1	2	1
phenotypes:	red	roan	white

page 109

8 The **Jones** were A × B which might produce any one of:

AA × BB	= AB group
AO × BO	= AB or O groups
AA × BO	= AB or A groups
AO × BB	= AB or B groups

So the Jones could be the parents of *any* of the four children.
The **Lees** were B × O which might produce either of:

BB × OO	= B group
BO × OO	= B or O groups

So the Lees might be the parents of *either* the B group or the O group child.
The **Gerbers** were O × O which can produce only:

OO × OO	= O group

So the **Gerbers were parents of the O group child**
(and therefore the **Lees were the parents of the B group child**).
The **Santiagos** were AB × O which might produce:

AB × OO	= A or B groups

So the **Santiagos were the parents of the A group child** (since the Lees were the parents of the B group child).
So by elimination, the **Jones were the parents of the AB group child**.

9 a Liz and Diana
b (**i**) David and Anne   (**ii**) James
c Eight: Richard and Judith, Anne, Charles, Sophie, Chris, Sarah, and Gail
d James and William, Arthur and Diana, etc.

page 111

10 Given a homozygous normal-handed parent (**nn** – producing **n** gametes only) crossed with a heterozygous brachydactylous parent (**Nn** – producing 50% **N** and 50% **n** gametes), the probability of an offspring with brachydactylous hands is 50% or 0.5, as your genetic diagram and Punnett grid will show.

page 114

11 See **Sex linkage** and **Figure 4.24**, pages 113–114.

page 115

12 See **Sex linkage**, **Haemophilia** and **Figure 4.25**, pages 113–115.

5 Genetic engineering and biotechnology

page 117

1 The **genome** is the complement (genes) of an organism or of an individual cell. (See also **Table 4.2**, page 109, for other genetics terms.)

page 119

2 Protease enzymes hydrolyse proteins to shorter chain polypeptides, and finally to the individual amino acids which made up the primary structure of the protein.

3 See **The DNA double helix**, pages 64–66.

page 123

4 Complementary base pairing is explained on page 64 and illustrated in **Figure 2.27**, page 65.

5 The minimum length (in terms of nucleotides) of the artificial gene is:

$14 \times 3 = 42$ to code for the constituent amino acids
$2 \times 3 = 6$ to code for the 'stop' and 'start' codons
plus 6 for recognition by the sticky end restriction enzyme.
Total = 54

page 124

6 See **Figure 5.8**, page 125.

7 When the bacterium invades a host cell, the Ti plasmid becomes inserted into a chromosome, introducing genes for the synthesis of a plant growth substance (causing proliferation of host cells = tumour) and other genes present (or previously inserted) on the plasmid. In effect, the bacterium carries out genetic engineering on its own behalf.

page 128

8 The fruits of the cultivated grasses (which include wheat and rice) are the staples of human diets all over the world – providing the bulk of essential energy-rich foods. The ability of leguminous plants to fix atmospheric nitrogen for amino acid and protein production enables these plants to grow well without the addition of (expensive) nitrogen-based fertilisers. Food products from leguminous plants are also relatively rich in proteins. GM cultivated grasses that could also fix nitrogen (should they come about) would grow well without nitrogen-based fertilisers – and might add even more to human nutrition, contributing to the overcoming of protein deficiency as well as meeting energy needs.

page 131

9 a Genotype and genome: see answer to SAQ1, Chapter 5, above.
  b Restriction endonuclease and ligase: see **Figure 5.2** (page 119) and **Figure 5.6** (page 122).
  c Blunt ends and sticky ends: see **Figure 5.2** (page 119).
  d Bacterial chromosome and a plasmid: see **Vectors for cloning**, page 000. (Note that the bacterial chromosome is known as a nucleoid – see **Figure 1.15**, page 16.)

page 132

10 Alleles coding for proteins that cause genetic disease typically arise by mutation. Mutations occur at a steady rate in human populations. Consequently, genetic diseases are maintained at low levels in populations.

6 Ecology, evolution and biodiversity

page 138

1 The dominant plants set the way of life for many other inhabitants, largely by:
  - providing the principal source of nutrients
  - determining the living spaces (habitats/microhabitats)
  - influencing the environmental conditions.

page 139

2 b all the frogs of the lake – population
  a the whole lake – ecosystem
  f the mud of the lake – habitat
  c the flow of water through the lake – abiotic factor
  g the temperature variations in the lake – abiotic factor
  d all the plants and animals present – community
  e the total mass of vegetation growing in the lake – biomass

page 140

3

	Producer	Primary Consumer	Secondary consumer	Tertiary consumer
Food chain 1	phyto-plankton	zooplankton	common mussel	herring gull
Food chain 2	sea lettuce	grey mullet	pollack	seal

page 142

4 See **Feeding relationships – producers, consumers and decomposers**, page 138.

5 Primary consumers – humans who eat food of plant origin, only. All consumer trophic levels – humans who eat a diverse range of foods (e.g. hunter-gatherers).

page 144

6 See **Energy flow**, pages 142–144.

page 147

7 See **Figure 6.6 B**, and follow the 'cycling of materials' arrow.

page 148

8 a In the atmosphere: carbon dioxide gas
  b In the hydrosphere: hydrogencarbonate ions
  c In the lithosphere: carbonates (e.g. Ca_2CO_3)

page 150

9 a The % change in mean atmospheric carbon dioxide 1960–2000: in 1960, 315 ppm of CO_2; in 2000, 370 ppm of CO_2.
Increase in these 40 years was 55 ppm.
% gain was $\frac{55}{315} \times 100 = 17.5\%$
  b The atmospheric carbon dioxide varies between high and low values within each 12-month period of the graph due to photosynthesis on lands in the northern hemisphere – the peaks are winter levels, and troughs are summer levels of atmospheric CO_2.

page 155

10 a Favourable abiotic factors such as a continuing good food supply. Favourable biotic factors such as the absence of predators, and freedom from parasite attack.

b Intraspecific competition for resources and space as the population grows.

page 156

11 a Two soluble nutrients essential to phytoplankton growth are nitrate and phosphate ions.

b The numbers of phytoplankton decrease significantly by May and June due to a shortage of essential nutrients.

c The increasing quantity of nutrients in October came from the decay of the dead phytoplankton and zooplankton.

page 157

12 Sedimentary rocks are formed by deposition of the products of erosion of other rocks, most frequently when this material is swept down rivers to the sea, or enters large fresh water lakes, and settles in layers on the bottom.

See **Figure 6.19**, page 157.

page 159

13 The breeding of domesticated plants and animals has created varieties with little external resemblance to their wild ancestors. Darwin bred pigeons, and noted there were more than a dozen distinctive varieties of pigeon, all of which were descended from the rock dove (**Figure 6.20**). Darwin argued that if so much change can be induced in so few generations, then species must be able to evolve into other species by the gradual accumulation of minute changes, as environmental conditions alter and natural selection operates.

14 All these differing varieties of domesticated dog are capable of interbreeding to produce fertile offspring.

page 161

15 See **Neo-Darwinism**, page 160.

page 162

16 a Exposure of pathogenic bacteria to sub-lethal doses of antibiotic may increase the chances of resistance developing in that population of pathogens.

b By varying the antibiotics used, there is increased likelihood of killing all the pathogens in a population, including any now resistant to the previous antibiotics used. This approach works until multiple-resistance strains have evolved, such as in strains of *Clostridium difficile* and *Staphylococcus aureus*.

page 164

17 By 'evolution' we mean 'the gradual development of life in geological time'. For example, we know that life appeared on Earth about 3500 million years ago, and that most of the great diversity of living forms have appeared subsequently. Before early geologists realised that the Earth is extremely old, biblical calculations suggested that life had been created in 4004 BC, or 6000 years ago. If this were still believed, then there would be insufficient time for evolution by natural selection.

18 The impact of a meteorite or asteroid from space or the violent eruption of a volcano are examples of events that might have caused violent and speedy habitat change over a substantial part of the surface of the Earth.

page 165

19 Such names are precisely defined and internationally agreed; they facilitate cooperation between observers by ensuring the exact species that is being investigated and reported on.

page 166

20 Your answer depends largely on the types of plant growing in gardens where you are, and perhaps on the main uses they are put to; for example:
- vegetables (of root, leaf, fruit or seed origin)
- flowers (of particular seasons or perhaps soil types).

7 Human physiology, health and reproduction

page 178

1 **Saprotrophic nutrition:** in the decomposer organisms, mainly bacteria and fungi.

Parasitic nutrition: by organisms living on or in a host organism for much or all of their life cycle, and feeding on the host's tissues.

page 181

2 a See **Digestion, where and why**, page 178.

b Water, vitamins, minerals.

c Cellulose.

page 182

3 Protease enzymes of digestion are secreted in inactive forms to prevent autolysis of the cells of the gastric glands and pancreas in which they are formed.

page 184

4 **Absorption:** uptake into the body (blood circulation or lacteals) of the useful products of digestion, from the gut lumen.

Assimilation: uptake of nutrients into cells and tissues.

page 185

5 For example, it means that blood cannot be directed to a respiratory surface immediately before or after servicing tissues that are metabolically active (and so have a high rate of respiration). Rather, the blood circulates randomly around the blood spaces and blood vessels.

page 187

6 Phagocytic leucocytes function anywhere in the body that an infection occurs, but in addition to their presence in the blood plasma, lymph and lymph glands, they are always present in the airways and alveoli of the lungs, and in the liver, lining the rows of liver cells (hepatocytes) past which the blood flows.

page 192

7 These non-elastic strands keep the heart valve flaps pointing in the direction of the blood flow. They stop the valves turning inside out when the pressure rises abruptly within the ventricles.

page 193

8 Adrenaline is secreted in 'flight or fight' situations, when the individual is suddenly startled or attacked, or otherwise believes itself to be in danger. It prepares the body for exertion and high physical and mental performance.

page 194

9

Bacterial cell (see Figure 1.15, page 16)	Virus particle (see Figure 1.17, page 19)
small cells typically 5–10 µm	crystal structure when outside host cells (i.e. not cellular) all extremely small, 20–400 nm.
cell wall of complex biochemical composition (not cellulose)	no cell wall
plasma membrane surrounding cytoplasm	no cytoplasm or plasma membrane
nucleoid (circular length of DNA) in the cytoplasm, attached to the plasma membrane	no nucleoid; has a core of nucleic acid (DNA or RNA) surrounded by a protein coat called the capsid
no envelope present	some viruses have an additional envelope of protein and lipid – acquired as they leave the previous host cell

page 195

10 Antibiotics work by interfering with specific metabolic processes, typically the synthesis and laying down of new wall materials (see **Figure 7.15**, page 194). Bacteria have cell walls that are serviced metabolically (and a general metabolism within their cytoplasm), but viruses have neither.

page 196

11 This parasite has evolved a sucker (**Figure 7.16**, page 195) that is capable of burrowing through human skin submerged in infected water, if contact is maintained for a sufficiently long period.

12 A ciliated epithelium with numerous goblet cells lines the trachea and bronchi. The mucus secreted by the goblet cells traps any dust particles in the incoming air, thus protecting the alveoli in the lungs.

page 197

13 Antibodies are proteins secreted by the lymphocytes. Consequently, we know they are produced by ribosomes attached to endoplasmic reticulum (**rER**, page 250).

page 203

14 See **The onset of AIDS**, page 200.

15

Antigen	a substance capable of binding specifically to an antibody	Antibody	a protein produced by blood plasma cells derived from the B-lymphocytes when in the presence of a specific antigen; it binds, aiding destruction of the antigen

Antibiotic	an organic compound produced by microorganisms which selectively inhibits or kills other microorganisms	Vaccine	a preparation of microorganisms (or/ their antigens) which can induce protective immunity against the microorganism (pathogenic bacterium or virus), but which does not itself cause disease
Vector	an organism that transmits a disease-causing organism *or* a device for transferring genes during genetic engineering	Host	organism in or on which a parasite spends all or part of its life cycle

page 205

16

Characteristic	How it influences diffusion
a large, thin surface area	the greater the surface area and the shorter the distance that gases (O_2 and CO_2) have to diffuse, the quicker gas exchange occurs
a ventilation mechanism that moves air (or water) over the respiratory surface	the higher the concentration of oxygen on the 'supply side' of the respiratory membrane, the quicker gas can diffuse across the surface
a blood circulation that speeds up the removal of dissolved oxygen, with a respiratory pigment that increases the gas-carrying capacity of the blood	the quicker that oxygen is picked up and transported away from the gas exchange surface, the greater the rate of diffusion

The relationship of these factors is summarised by **Fick's Law of Diffusion**:

$$\text{rate of diffusion} \propto \frac{\text{surface area} \times \text{difference in concentration}}{\text{length of diffusion pathway}}$$

page 206

17

Inspiration		Expiration
relax	**internal intercostal muscles**	contract
contract	**external intercostal muscles**	relax
move upwards and outwards	**effects on rib cage**	move downwards and inwards

page 209

18 Carbon dioxide is an acidic gas which, if it were to accumulate in the blood, would alter the pH of the plasma solution. The normal pH of the blood is 7.4, and for life to be maintained it cannot be allowed to vary more than within the range pH 7.0–7.8. This is largely because blood pH affects the balance of essential ions which are transported in the plasma solution. Efficient removal of respiratory CO_2 at the lungs is as important to life as efficient uptake of O_2.

19 See **Gaseous exchange**, page 204.

20 The surfaces of the alveoli are moist, and oxygen gas dissolves in the surface film of water. It is oxygen in solution that diffuses into the red cells and combines with the haemoglobin there. Consequently the outgoing air contains water vapour that has evaporated during gaseous exchange.

page 213

21 a See **The resting potential**, page 211.
   b See **The action potential**, page 212.

page 216

22 a See **Junctions between neurones**, page 214.
   b See **Figures 7.35** and **7.36**, pages 215 and 216.

page 220

23 Body temperature falls significantly during sleep, but rises above normal during periods of physical activity.

24 **Endergonic reactions** require energy input, because the products have more potential energy than the reactants – see also **Figure 8.28**, page 261. **Note:** the alternative type of reaction is one in which the products have less potential energy than the reactants, and these reactions transfer energy as heat and work. They are called exergonic reactions.

page 223

25 The liver cells receive oxygen from the blood delivered by the hepatic artery.

26 Mitochondria are the type of organelle would you most expect to see when a liver cell is examined by EM.

page 230

27 See **Roles of hormones in the control of reproduction**, page 228.

page 233

28 *This is a personal issue which needs handling with great sensitivity. When you discuss a response to this question with your peers it is best if each individual explains their own approach and is listened to carefully. It may be that a consensus concerning a suitable response can be arrived at – but there are circumstances over issues of this sort where individuals cannot agree. In this situation, it is highly desirable to understand the approach of those you do not agree with rather than to have conflict.*

8 Nucleic acids and proteins

page 235

1 In summary:
   organic base + pentose sugar ──────────→ **nucleoside**
   nucleoside + phosphoric acid ──────────→ **nucleotide**
   many nucleotides condensed together ──────────→ **polynucleotide (nucleic acid)**
   See **Nucleotides** and **Figure 2.25**, page 63; **Nucleotides become nucleic acid** and **Figure 2.26**, page 64; **Table 8.1**, page 243.

page 237

2 Given the length of the DNA in each chromosome (of which there are 46 in human nuclei), together with the movements required of the chromosomes for a successful outcome of nuclear division (particularly mitosis, but also meiosis), compact packaging is essential. See **Chromosome structure and the packaging of DNA**, page 235; **Mitosis** and **Figure 1.33**, page 32.

page 238

3 Hershey and Chase would have expected that only the bacteria infected with virus labelled with ^{35}S (an element in proteins but not in nucleic acids) would have produced radioactive virus. Remember, they were not aware that the protein coat of the virus remained outside of the host cell at the time of infection.

page 240

4 A hydrogen bond is an electrostatic attraction between the positively charged region of one molecule and the negatively charged region of a neighbouring one; the attraction gives rise to a relatively weak bond (compared to a covalent bond). Collectively, the H-bonds of DNA hold the polynucleotide strands together. See **Hydrogen bonds** and **Figure 2.1**, page 38.

page 241

5 After three generations, 75% of the DNA would be 'light'.

The experimental results that would be expected if the Meselson–Stahl experiment were carried on for three generations

page 245

6 See **Base pairing and 'direction' in the DNA molecule** and **Figure 8.5**, page 238–239.

page 250

7 See **Figure 2.15**, page 52.

8 These are illustrated in sequence in **Figure 8.8**, page 246.

page 251

9 a The sequence of amino acids coded for by the sequence of bases is found using the genetic code (**Figure 8.14**):
   GGU AAU CCU UUU GUU ACU CAU UGU
   Gly Asn Pro Phe Val Thr His Cys
   b The sequence of bases in the antisense strand of DNA from which this mRNA was transcribed would have been:
   CCA TTA GGA AAA CAA TGA GTA ACA

page 252

10

Structural proteins supporting DNA	Enzymes
■ histones of nucleosomes ■ non-histone protein of 'scaffold'	■ helicase – unwinds DNA helix; holds strands apart for replication ■ DNA polymerase III, RNA primase, and polymerase I; involved in DNA replication ■ RNA polymerase; involved in transcription

See **Chromosome structure and the packaging of DNA**, page 235

See **Replication – DNA copying itself**, page 240, and **The sequence of events at transcription**, page 245

page 253

11 See **The central dogma** and **Table 8.3**, pages 252–253.

page 257

12 See **Figure 8.19**, page 255.

page 260

13 Membrane proteins are important structurally (see **Figure 1.19**, page 21) and as receptors, enzymes and molecular pumps (see **Figure 1.22**, page 23).

page 264

14

Lock and key hypothesis	Induced fit hypothesis
Refers to the pocket or crevice on the enzyme surface (at the active site) where the substrate molecule binds to the enzyme.	Binding occurs at the active site where the arrangement of certain amino acid residues matches certain groupings on the substrate molecule.
Binding is a prelude to catalysis, but this hypothesis does not explain the simultaneous chemical change as binding occurs.	As the complex forms, an essential, critical change of shape is induced in the enzyme molecule which raises the substrate molecule to the transitional state from which the catalysed reaction follows.

9 Energy transfer in cells II

page 272

1 The following are produced during glycolysis:
NADH
ATP
pyruvate.

2 Length = 6.25 µm, width = 2.1 µm.

page 274

3 a **Dehydrogenases**
In respiration, all the hydrogen atoms are gradually removed from glucose, catalysed by dehydrogenase enzymes. They are added to hydrogen acceptors, usually NAD (nicotinamide adenine dinucleotide, page 271), which itself is reduced. We can write this addition of hydrogen to its carrier as:
NAD + 2H $\longrightarrow$ NADH$_2$
but what actually happens is
NAD$^+$ + 2H $\longrightarrow$ NADH + H$^+$
So NAD is a coenzyme that works with specific dehydrogenase enzymes in the oxidation of substrate molecules by the removal of hydrogen.

b **Decarboxylases**
Decarboxylation is the removal of carbon from organic compounds by the formation of carbon dioxide. For example, glucose consists of six carbon atoms. All six carbon atoms are removed at different stages of respiration, one at a time, and given off as carbon dioxide. A specific decarboxylase enzyme is involved in each case. The first decarboxylation in aerobic respiration occurs in the reaction linking glycolysis with the Krebs cycle, when pyruvate is converted to a 2-carbon molecule. The other decarboxylation reactions of aerobic respiration occur in steps in the Krebs cycle.

page 275

4 In the absence of oxygen, reduced NAD (NADH$_2$) accumulates and oxidised NAD reserves are used up. In the absence of NAD$^+$, pyruvate production by glycolysis slows and stops, so subsequent steps in respiration stop too.

5 See **Figure 9.7**, page 275. Protons move from the inter-membrane space to the matrix (the interior) of the mitochondrion.

page 276

6 a Substrate and intermediate:
   Substrate = molecule that is the starting point for a biochemical reaction; it forms a complex with a specific enzyme.
   Intermediate = metabolite formed as a component of a metabolic pathway.
b Glycolysis and the Krebs cycle:
   See **Cellular respiration: Glycolysis** page 271, and **The mitochondria and the steps to the Krebs cycle**, page 272.
c Oxidation and reduction:
   See **Respiration as a series of redox reactions**, page 270.

page 279

7

Photosystem I	Role
many accessory pigment molecules	harvest light energy and funnel the energy to a single chlorophyll molecule of the reaction centre
reaction centre of chlorophyll a molecule absorbing light of 700 nm wavelength	has ground-state electrons that are raised to an excited state when light energy is received from accessory pigments – excited electrons passed to oxidised NADP
electron-carrier molecules	receive excited electrons and pass these on

Photosystem II	Role
many accessory pigment molecules	harvest light energy and funnel the energy to a single chlorophyll molecule of reaction centre
reaction centre of chlorophyll a molecule absorbing light of 680 nm wavelength	has ground-state electrons that are raised to an excited state when light energy is received from accessory pigments – excited electrons passed to reaction centre of photosystem I
water-splitting enzyme	catalyses splitting of water into hydrogen ions, electrons and oxygen atoms
electron-carrier molecules	receive excited electrons and pass these on; simultaneous pumping of protons from stroma to thylakoid compartment

See **Figure 9.12**, page 280.

page 280

8 Electrons displaced from the reaction centre of photosystem II in an excited state are first passed to the reaction centre of photosystem I. Here they are again raised to an excited state and this time they are passed to oxidised NADP (NADP$^+$) to form reduced NADP (NADPH + H$^+$).

page 281

9 An **isotonic** solution is of the same osmotic concentration as the chloroplasts which therefore are not disrupted by excess movement of water into or out of their delicate structure. As a **buffer** solution, this medium maintains the pH at that of the cell contents, thereby ensuring enzyme action is not interfered with.

The presence of **ice** keeps the solution and organelles at or just above 0 °C, thereby preventing unwanted biochemical reactions while the extracted organelles are held before investigation.

page 284

10 *Chlorella* cells in suspension function biochemically like mesophyll cells but they can be cultured in suspension, sampled without interference of the biochemistry of the other cells, and supplied directly and quickly with light, intermediates and inhibitors (if required) in such a way that all the cells are treated identically. Gaseous exchange and diffusion occurs without the complexity (and delays) of the intact leaf with its air spaces and stomata.

page 287

11 a Light-dependent reactions and light-independent reactions:
See **The reactions of photosynthesis**, and **Figure 9.10**, page 278.
b Photolysis and photophosphorylation:
See **The reactions of photosynthesis**, page 278.

12 The starting materials (carbon dioxide and water) are in an oxidised (low energy) state. The end product of photosynthesis – glucose – is in a reduced (higher energy) state.

13 The experimental material is a (more or less) intact plant, rather than isolated chloroplasts where the light is absorbed and exploited in the light reaction.
Difficult to precisely control the wavelength of light received by the chloroplasts, in the mesophyll cells, deep inside the leaves.
Difficult to ensure that the plant behaves identically at each wavelength over the extended period of time needed to collect a measurable sample of oxygen gas (evidence of the rate of respiration).

page 288

14 a Chlorophyll and chloroplast:
See **Investigating chlorophyll**, page 83, and **Chloroplast, grana and stroma – the venue for photosynthesis**, page 287.
b Stroma and grana:
See **The steps of photosynthesis** and Figure 9.9, page 277.
c Absorption spectrum and action spectrum:
See **Light and photosynthesis**, page 287.

page 291

15 In cyclic photophosphorylation, photoactivation of photosystem I and production of ATP occur. Reduction of NADP$^+$ does not occur (cyclic photophosphorylation occurs when NADPH has accumulated in the illuminated green leaf because the fixation of carbon dioxide is prevented), see **Figure 9.24**, page 290.

10 Plant science

page 297

1 The features you are likely to emphasise include:
Leaves – whether they are simple or the leaf blade is divided into leaflets; the arrangement of the 'veins' of the blade, whether they are parallel or in a network.
Stem – its length, and whether it branches or not, and how the leaves are attached.
Root – whether a tap root or a fibrous system.
Flowers – whether solitary or grouped together (an inflorescence), numbers of parts (typically in 3s, 4s, or 5s or multiples), and whether they are hermaphrodite flowers (they typically are).

page 298

2 The shape of the cellulose polymer allows close packing into long chains (**Figure 1.14**, page 16) held together by hydrogen bonds. These are laid down in porous sheets, and have great tensile strength. The monomer from which cellulose is assembled by condensation reaction is glucose, of which green plants typically have an excellent supply.

page 303

3 Light has diverse effects on plants, including:
- being required for the manufacture of sugar in photosynthesis
- inhibiting extension growth in length of stems (so plants growing in the dark 'bolt', whereas plants in full light are short and sturdy)
- causing positive phototropic growth and sun-tracking
- promoting expansion of leaf blades
- being required for the formation of chlorophyll (so plants in the dark are yellow)
- triggering the switch from vegetative growth to flowering in many species, in response to some particular regime of light and dark (day and night) cycles
- triggering germination in a few species.

page 305

4 The features of root hairs that facilitate absorption from the soil are:
- they greatly increase the surface area of the root
- they grow in close contact with the film of soil water that occurs around mineral particles where the essential resources (water and soluble ions) occur
- their walls are of cellulose and are in intimate contact with cells of the cortex in a region that is permeable to water.

page 307

5 See **Figure 10.13**, page 306.

6 Plant growth is dependent on a supply of chemically combined nitrogen (for amino acid and protein synthesis) of which nitrates are typically the most readily available. However, nitrates are also taken up by microorganisms, and may be released in the soil at times other than when plant demand is at its peak. They are also very soluble and are easily leached away into ground water in heavy rain. By taking up nitrate whenever it becomes available (and hording it in cells), plants can maintain growth at peak times.

7 Plant roots are metabolically very active and require oxygen for aerobic cell respiration and ATP formation (for ion uptake, for example). Waterlogged soil lacks soil air and the essential oxygen gas.

page 311

8 See **Transport of water through the plant**, and **Figure 10.18**, pages 310–311.

page 312

9 See **Stomata and transpiration**, and **Figures 10.19** and **10.20**, pages 312–313.

page 313

10 See **Stomata and transpiration**, and **Figures 10.19** and **10.20**, pages 312–313.

page 317

11 Transpiration is a direct consequence of plant structure, plant nutrition, and the mechanism of gaseous exchange in leaves. In effect, the living green plant is like a wick that steadily dries the soil around it. Put like this, transpiration is an unfortunate consequence of plant structure and metabolism, rather than a valuable process. It means that a constant, adequate supply of water is critical to plant growth; if the water supply fails, plants cannot move away.

12 In the veins and vascular bundles of the leaf, the water-conducting tissue (xylem) is on the upper side (with phloem below – because of their relative positions in stem vascular bundles with which they connect directly). So, looking at this feature of Marram grass leaf, we see the outer epidermis is strictly the lower epidermis.

page 319

13 See **Transport of water through the plant**, page 310 and **The stem and organic solute transport**, page 000.

page 321

14 See **Pollination and fertilisation**, page 320.

page 322

15

Ovary structure	Fruit or vegetable
a an ovary containing one seed	plum, peach, avocado
b an ovary containing many seeds	pea pod, runner bean
c several ovaries fused together, containing many seeds	gooseberry, cucumber, tomato

11 Genetics II

page 333

1

The process	Mitosis	Meiosis First division	Second division
Prophase	▪ chromosomes become visible, finally as 2 chromatids joined at the centromere ▪ nuclear membrane breaks down ▪ spindle forms	▪ chromosomes become visible ▪ homologous chromosomes pair to form bivalents ▪ nuclear membrane breaks down ▪ spindle forms	▪ chromosomes reappear as 2 chromatids joined at the centromere ▪ spindle forms

table continues

The process	Mitosis	Meiosis First division	Second division
Metaphase	▪ chromosomes at equator of spindle, attached by centromeres to fibre	▪ bivalents at equator of spindle, centromeres attached to a fibre	▪ chromosomes at equator of spindle, attached by centromeres to fibre
Anaphase	▪ centromeres divide ▪ chromatids move to opposite poles	▪ chromosomes (each two sister chromatids joined at the centromeres) move to opposite poles	▪ centromeres divide ▪ chromatids move to opposite poles
Telophase	▪ spindle breaks down ▪ nuclear membrane reforms ▪ cytoplasm divides	▪ spindle breaks down ▪ nuclear membrane may reform ▪ cytoplasm may divide or may be delayed	▪ spindle breaks down ▪ nuclear membrane reforms around both nuclei ▪ cytoplasm divides
The products			
	▪ 2 identical cells, each with the diploid chromosome number	▪ 2 non-identical nuclei each with the haploid chromosome number (1 of each homologous pair per nucleus)	▪ 4 non-identical cells, each with the haploid chromosome number
The consequences and significance			
	▪ produces identical diploid cells ▪ permits growth within multicellular organisms, and asexual reproduction	▪ produces haploid cells ▪ contributes to genetic variability by: – reducing chromosome number by half, permitting fertilisation, and the combination of genes from two parents – permitting random assortment of paternal and maternal homologous chromosomes – recombination of segments of individual maternal and paternal homologous chromosomes during crossing over	

page 334

2 From the information available in **Figure 11.6**:
  a the heterozygotes were the F_1 progeny – round and yellow;
  b the recombinants (due to reassortment) among the F_2 progeny were 'round and green' and 'wrinkled and yellow'.

3 These genes are on separate chromosomes (so there is no chance of recombinants due to crossing over, incidentally). Because the alleles of these genes are on separate chromosomes, the dihybrid ratio was obtained by Mendel. He would have surely been confused if (by chance) he had chosen two pairs of contrasting characters controlled by genes on the same chromosome.

page 337

4 See **Abrupt change in hereditary information – mutations**, page 98.

page 338

5 Using the lay-out given in **Figure 11.7**:

P	normal wing ×	vestigial wing
	normal body	ebony body
	homozygous	homozygous
	WWGG	**wwgg**
gametes	**WG** ×	**wg**

offspring (F₁) → offspring (F_1)

WwGg
genotype heterozygous
phenotype normal wing
      normal body

sibling cross   **WwGg** × **WwGg**

gametes   **WG Wg wG wg** × **WG Wg wG wg**

(Punnett grid)

offspring (F_2)

genotypes $\frac{1}{16}$ **WWGG** $\frac{1}{16}$ **WWgg** $\frac{1}{16}$ **wwGG** $\frac{1}{16}$ **wwgg**
$\frac{1}{8}$ **WWGg** $\frac{1}{8}$ **Wwgg** $\frac{1}{8}$ **wwGg**
$\frac{1}{8}$ **WwGG**
$\frac{1}{4}$ **WwGg**

| phenotypes | normal wing normal body | normal wing ebony body | vestigial wing normal body | vestigial wing ebony body |
| phenotype ratio | 9 :: | 3 : | 3 : | 1 |

page 340

6 In order to create gene maps of linkage groups, it is necessary to carry out crosses between known genotypes that yield large samples of offspring. From the outcomes it is possible to calculate statistically significant recombination frequencies. Obviously, it is quite impossible to conduct such breeding experiments with humans. Rather, it is the exercise to map the human genome (**Human Genome Project**, page 131) that has produced maps of the positions of the genes on each of our chromosomes.

page 343

7 The recombinants would be:
   Tb   **tB**
   tB   **tB**

page 344

8

Phenotypes	white	light	medium	dark	black
Range of genotypes	$\frac{1}{16}$ **aabb**	$\frac{2}{16}$ **Aabb** $\frac{2}{16}$ **aaBb**	$\frac{1}{16}$ **AAbb** $\frac{4}{16}$ **AaBb** $\frac{1}{16}$ **aaBB**	$\frac{2}{16}$ **AaBB** $\frac{2}{16}$ **AABb**	$\frac{1}{16}$ **AABB**
Phenotype ratio	1	4	6	4	1

12 Human physiology, health and reproduction II

page 350

1 See **Figure 12.1**, page 349.

page 351

2

Inflammation response	rapid, localised response to cuts, blows or bites – involves vasodilation of capillaries and increased permeability of blood vessels, bringing phagocytic white cells to site, for example
Clotting of blood	sealing of gaps due to local haemorrhage, cuts or breaks in vessels, see **The blood clotting mechanism**, page 349
Immune response	production of specific antibodies, see **The immune system and the response to invasion**, page 350

page 352

3 See **What recognition of 'self' entails**, page 350, and **Steps of antibody production**, page 351.

page 355

4 Antigens may be present more or less anywhere in the body that becomes contaminated from outside. Antibodies exist in the blood and lymph, and may be carried in the plasma solution anywhere that blood 'leaks out' to – including sites of invasions.

page 356

5 See pages 353–355, points 6 and 7.

page 360

6 The existence of memory cells avoids the steps in the production of activated T-cells.
   The particular memory cell, once re-activated by the re-invading antigen, switches into production of an excess of appropriate plasma cells and helper T-cells (**Figure 12.4**, page 354).

page 361

7 Immunity is resistance to the onset of disease after infection by harmful microorganisms or internal parasites. Long-lived specific immunity is a result of the action of the immune system; it may be acquired naturally by previous infection, or can be induced by vaccination. See **Types of immunity**, page 351.

page 365

8 See diagram at the top of page B405.

page 367

9 See **The ultrastructure of skeletal muscle**, and **Figures 12.13** and **12.15**, page 000.

The knee jerk reflex

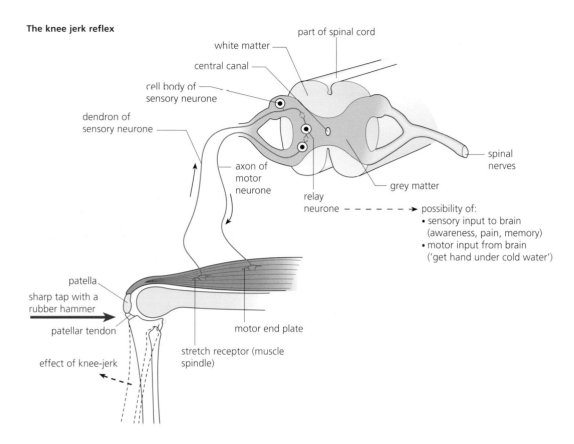

10 **a** The myofibril shown in the sketch has the same proportions of 'light' and 'dark' bands as the slightly contracted sarcomere shown above.

b Sketch of a fully contracted myofibril

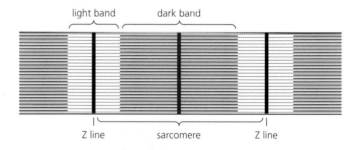

page 371

11

Excretion	elimination of the waste products of metabolism from the body (e.g. removal of urea from the blood and the formation of urine in the kidney tubules)
Egestion	disposal of waste from the body (e.g. defecation)
Osmoregulation	regulation of water potential – osmotic concentration – of body fluids by the control of water and salt content (e.g. actions of distal convoluted tubule and collecting duct of kidney)
Secretion	material produced and released from glandular cells (e.g. saliva by salivary glands)

page 372

12 The source of energy for ultrafiltration in the glomerulus is respiration of heart muscle that 'fuels' contractions of the ventricles and thus creates blood pressure in the glomerulus. This pressure is heightened by the efferent arteriole of the glomerulus being of smaller diameter than the afferent arteriole (see **Figure 12.21**).

page 373

13 See **Selective reabsorption in the proximal convoluted tubule**, and **Figure 12.22**, pages 372–373.

page 374

14 See **Figure 12.25**, page 375.

page 376

15 An excess of offspring are typically produced by breeding pairs, yet the numbers in most species remain fairly constant over time. When an excess of offspring do survive, there is generally strong competition for resources resulting in a speedy return to normal population numbers.

page 382

16 The role of FSH in sperm production, see **Figure 12.30**, page 379. The role of FSH in ovum production, see **Role of hormones in the control of reproduction**, and **Figure 7.52**, page 228.

page 386

17 The fetus is 'foreign' tissue to the mother (for example, they may not be of the same blood group) and carries antigens foreign to her (see **What recognition of 'self' entails**, page 350).

18

Structural feature	Importance
large, disc-shaped structure, composed of tissue of two two different organisms (fetal membranes and part of uterus wall)	large area for exchange of essential metabolites between different organisms
maternal and fetal blood circulations brought close together	conditions favour diffusion without meeting of the two blood circulations
finger-like projections of fetal membranes grow into the endometrium and become bathed by maternal blood	surface area enormously increased

page 387

19 The chief effect of HCG is to maintain the corpus luteum as an endocrine gland, at least for the first 16 weeks of the pregnancy. The maintenance of the corpus luteum means that the endometrium persists, to the benefit of the implanted embryo, and menstruation is prevented. (The premature demise of the corpus luteum, leading to degeneration of the endometrium during early pregnancy, is a possible cause of a miscarriage.)

page 388

20 In **negative feedback** the effect of a deviation from the normal or set condition is to create a tendency to eliminate the deviation. Negative feedback is a part of almost all control systems in living things. The effect of negative feedback is to reduce further corrective action of the control system once the set-point value is reached.

In **positive feedback** the effect of a deviation from the normal or set condition is to create a tendency to reinforce the deviation. Positive feedback intensifies the corrective action taken by a control system, so leading to a vicious-circle situation. Imagine a car in which the driver's seat was set on rollers (not secured to the floor), being driven at speed. The slightest application of the foot brake causes the driver to slide and to press harder on the brake as the car starts to slow, with an extreme outcome.

Biological examples of positive feedback are rare, but one can be identified at the synapse. When a wave of depolarisation (a nerve impulse) takes effect in the post-synaptic membrane, the entry of sodium ions triggers the entry of further sodium ions at a greater rate. This is a case of positive feedback. The depolarised state is established, and the impulse moves along the post-synaptic membrane.

Glossary

- Entries that are IB action verbs and entries that are IB syllabus-required definitions are coloured red and blue respectively.
- Entries are *aides-mémoire*, rather than formal definitions.

A

abiotic factor a non-biological factor (e.g. temperature) that is part of the environment of an organism

abscisic acid a plant growth substance tending to inhibit growth

absorption spectrum range of a pigment's ability to absorb various wavelengths of light

acetylcholine a neurotransmitter, liberated at synapses in the CNS

acid rain the cocktail of chemical pollutants that may occur in the atmosphere

action potential rapid change (depolarisation) in membrane potential of an excitable cell (e.g. a neurone)

action spectrum range of wavelengths of light within which a process like photosynthesis takes place

activation energy energy a substrate molecule must have before it can undergo a chemical change

active site region of enzyme molecule where substrate molecule binds

active transport movement of substances across a membrane involving a carrier protein and energy from respiration

adenine a purine organic base, found in the coenzymes ATP and NADP, and in nucleic acids (DNA and RNA) in which it pairs with thymine

adenosine diphosphate (ADP) a nucleotide, present in every living cell, made of adenosine and two phosphate groups linked in series, and important in energy transfer reactions of metabolism

adenosine triphosphate (ATP) a nucleotide, present in every living cell, formed in photosynthesis and respiration from ADP and P_i, and functioning in metabolism as a common intermediate between energy-requiring and energy-yielding reactions

adrenaline a hormone secreted by the adrenal medulla (and a neurotransmitter secreted by nerve endings of the sympathetic nervous system), having many effects, including speeding of heart beat, and the breakdown of glycogen to glucose in muscle and liver

aerobic respiration respiration requiring oxygen, involving oxidation of glucose to carbon dioxide and water

alimentary canal the gut; a tube running from mouth to anus in vertebrates, where complex food substances are digested and the products of digestion selectively absorbed into the body

allele an alternative form of a gene, occupying a specific locus on a chromosome

allele frequency the commonness of the occurrence of any particular allele in a population

alpha cell (pancreas) glucagon-secreting cell of the islets of Langerhans in the pancreas

alveolus air sac in the lung

amino acid building block of proteins, of general formula $R.CH(NH_2).COOH$

anabolism the building up of complex molecules from smaller ones

anaerobic respiration respiration in the absence of oxygen, involving breakdown of glucose to lactic acid or ethanol

analogous structure similar in structure but of different evolutionary origin

analyse interpret data to reach a conclusion

anion negatively charged ion

annotate add brief notes to a diagram, drawing or graph

anther part of the stamen in flowers, consisting of pollen sacs enclosed in walls that eventually split open, releasing pollen

antibody a protein produced by blood plasma cells derived from B lymphocytes when in the presence of a specific antigen, which then binds with the antigen, aiding its destruction

antibiotics organic compounds produced by some microorganisms which selectively inhibit or kill other microorganisms

anticodon three consecutive bases in tRNA, complementary to a codon on RNA

antidiuretic hormone (ADH) hormone secreted by the pituitary gland that controls the permeability of the walls of the collecting ducts of the kidney

antigen a substance capable of binding specifically to an antibody

apoplast collective name for the cell walls of a tissue or plant

apply use an idea, equation, principle, theory, or law in a new situation

aqueous humour fluid between lens and cornea of the eye

arteriole a very small artery

artificial classification classifying organisms on the basis of few, self-evident features

artificial selection selection in breeding exercises, carried out deliberately, by humans

asexual reproduction reproduction not involving gametes and fertilisation

assimilation uptake of nutrients into cells and tissues

atherosclerosis deposition of plaque (cholesterol derivative) on inner wall of blood vessels

atrio-ventricular node mass of tissue in the wall of the right atrium, functionally part of the pacemaker mechanism

atrio-ventricular valve tricuspid or bicuspid valve

atrium (plural, **atria**) one of the two upper chambers of the mammalian four-chambered heart

autolysis self-digestion

autotrophic (organism) self-feeding – able to make its own elaborated foods from simpler substances

autonomic the involuntary nervous system

auxin plant growth substance, indoleacetic acid

axon fibre carrying impulses away from the cell body of a neurone

B

bacillus a rod-shaped bacterium

bacteriophage a virus that parasitises bacteria (also known as a phage)

baroreceptor a sensory receptor responding to stretch, in the walls of blood vessels

basement membrane the thin fibrous layer separating an epithelium from underlying tissues

beta cell (pancreas) insulin-secreting cells of the islets of Langerhans in the pancreas

bicuspid valve valve between atrium and ventricle on the left side of the mammalian heart

bile an alkaline secretion of liver cells which collects in the gall bladder in humans, and which is discharged into the duodenum periodically

binary fission when a cell divides into two daughter cells, typically in reproduction of prokaryotes

binomial system double names for organisms, in Latin, the generic preceding the specific name

biological pest control control of pests and weeds by other organisms

biomagnification the process by which chemical substances become more concentrated at each trophic level

biomass total mass of living organisms in a given area (e.g. a quadrat)

biome a major life-zone over an area of the Earth, characterised by the dominant plant life present

biosphere the inhabited part of the Earth

biotechnology the industrial and commercial applications of biology, particularly of microorganisms, enzymology and genetic engineering

biotic factor the influence of living things on the environment of other living things

bivalent a pair of duplicated chromosomes, held together by chiasmata during meiosis

blastocyst embryo as hollow ball of cells, at the stage of implantation

blind spot region of the retina where the optic nerve leaves

body mass index (BMI) body mass in $kg/(\text{height in } m)^2$

bone marrow tissue special connective tissue filling the cavity of certain bones

boreal forest northern coniferous forests (example of a biome)

bovine somatotrophine (BST) hormone produced by the pituitary, controlling milk production

brain the coordinating centre of the nervous system

breed (animal) the animal equivalent of a plant variety

bronchiole small terminal branch of a bronchus

bronchus a tube connecting the trachea with the lungs

brush border tiny, finger-like projections (microvilli) on the surface of epithelial cells of the small intestine

buffer a solution which minimises change in pH when acid or alkali are added

bundle of His bundles of long muscle fibres that transmit myogenic excitation throughout the ventricle walls

C

C_3 **pathway** the light-independent reaction in photosynthesis, producing as its first product, a 3-carbon compound, glycerate 3-phosphate

C_4 **plants** plants with an additional carbon dioxide-fixation pathway that augments the supply of this raw material of photosynthesis at the chloroplast

calculate find an answer using mathematical methods

Calvin cycle a cycle of reactions in the stroma of the chloroplast by which some of the product of the dark reaction is re-formed as the acceptor molecule for carbon dioxide (ribulose biphosphate)

carrier an individual that has one copy of a recessive allele that causes a genetic disease in individuals that are homozygous for this allele

carrier protein one of the types of protein in plasma membranes, responsible for active transport across the membranes

cardiac cycle the stages of the heart beat, by which the atrial and then the ventricle walls alternately contract (systole) and relax (diastole)

carnivore flesh-eating animal

cartilage firm but plastic skeletal material (e.g. cartilage over bones at joints)

Casparian strip band of cells with impervious walls, found in plant roots

catabolism the breaking down of complex molecules in the biochemistry of cells

catalyst a substance that alters the rate of a chemical reaction, but remains unchanged at the end

cellular respiration controlled release (transfer) of energy from organic compounds in cells to form ATP

cellulase enzyme capable of hydrolysing cellulose

cellulose an unbranched polymer of 2000–3000 glucose residues, the major ingredient of most plant walls

central dogma the idea that transfer of genetic information from DNA of the chromosome to mRNA to protein (amino acid sequence) is irreversible

centromere constriction of the chromosome, the region that becomes attached to the spindle fibres in division

centrosome organelle situated near the nucleus in animal cells, involved in the formation of the spindle prior to nuclear division

cephalisation development of a head at the anterior of an animal

cerebellum part of hindbrain, concerned with muscle tone, posture and movement

cerebral cortex superficial layer of grey matter on extension of forebrain, much enlarged in humans and apes

cerebral hemispheres (cerebrum) the bulk of the human brain, formed during development by the outgrowth of part of the forebrain, consisting of densely packed neurones and myelinated nerve fibres

chemoautotroph an organism that uses energy from chemical reactions to generate ATP and produce organic compounds from inorganic substances

chemoheterotroph an organism that uses energy from chemical reactions to generate ATP and obtains organic compounds from other organisms

chemoreceptor a sense organ receiving chemical stimuli

chemosynthesis use of chemical energy from oxidation of inorganic compounds to synthesise organic compounds, typically from carbon dioxide and water

chiasma (plural, **chiasmata**) site of crossing over (exchange) of segments of DNA between homologous chromosomes

chloroplast organelle that is site of photosynthesis and contains chlorophyll

chlorophyll the main photosynthetic pigment of green plants, occurs in the grana membranes (thylakoid membranes) of the chloroplasts

cholesterol a lipid of animal plasma membranes; a precursor of the steroid hormones, in humans, formed in the liver and transported in the blood as lipoprotein

chromatid one of two copies of a chromosome after it has replicated

chromatin a nuclear protein material in the nucleus of eukaryotic cells at interphase; forms into chromosomes during mitosis and meiosis

choroid layer of blood vessels lying below the retina

chromosome visible in appropriately stained cells at nuclear division, each chromosome consists of a long thread of DNA packaged with protein; chromosomes replicate prior to division, into chromatids. Contents of nucleus appears as granular chromatin between divisions

chyme partly digested food as it leaves the stomach

cilium (plural, **cilia**) motile, hair-like outgrowth from surface of certain eukaryotic cells

citric acid cycle see *Krebs cycle*

clade the branch of a phylogenetic tree containing the set of all organisms descended from a particular common ancestor which is not an ancestor of any non-member of the group

cladistics method of classifying living organisms that makes use of lines of descent only (rather than phenotypic similarities)

climax community the mature (stable) stage of a succession of communities

clone a group of genetically identical individuals (or cells)

coccus spherical bacterial cell

CNS see nervous system

codominant alleles pairs of alleles that both affect the phenotype when present in a heterozygous state

codon three consecutive bases in DNA (or RNA) which specify an amino acid

coleoptile protective sheath around emerging leaves of germinating grass seeds

colon part of the gut, preceding the rectum

colostrum first milk secreted by the mother, after birth of young

commensalism a mutually beneficial association between two organism of different species

comment give a judgement based on a given statement or result of a calculation

community a group of populations of organisms living and interacting with each other in a habitat

compare give an account of similarities and differences between two or more items (e.g. by using a table)

compensation point the point where respiration and photosynthesis are balanced

condensation reaction formation of larger molecules involving the removal of water from smaller component molecules

cone (retinal cell) a light-sensitive cell in the retina, responsible for colour vision

conjugate protein protein combined with a non-protein part

connective tissue tissues that support and bind tissues together

conservation applying the principles of ecology to manage the environment

contractile vacuole a small vesicle in the cytoplasm of many fresh water protozoa that expels excess water

construct represent or develop in graphic form

cornea transparent covering at the front of the eye

corpus luteum glandular mass that develops from an ovarian follicle in mammals, after the ovum is discharged

cotyledon the first leaf (leaves) of a seed plant, found in the embryo

covalent bond bond between atoms in which electrons are shared

cristae folds in the inner membrane of mitochondria

crossing over exchange of genetic material between homologous chromosomes during meiosis

crypt of Lieberkuhn endocrine cells within the pancreas

cuticle layer of waxy material on outer wall of epidermis

cyanobacteria photosynthetic prokaryotes

cytokinesis division of cytoplasm after nucleus has divided into two

cytology study of cell structure

cytoplasm living part of the cell bound by the plasma membrane, excluding the nucleus

cytosol what remains of cytoplasm when the organelles have been removed

D

data recorded products of observations and measurements
qualitative data observations not involving measurements
quantitative data precise observations involving measurements

deamination the removal of NH_2 from an amino acid

deciduous loss at the end of the growing season (e.g. of leaves from broadleaved trees)

decomposer organisms (typically microorganisms) that feed on dead plant and animal material, causing matter to be recycled by other living things

degenerate code the triplet code contains more codons than there are amino acids to be coded, so most amino acids are coded for by more than one codon

deduce reach a conclusion from the information given

define give the precise meaning of a word or phrase as concisely as possible

denaturation a structural change in a protein that results in a loss (usually permanent) of its biological properties

dendrite a fine fibrous process on a neurone that receives impulses from other neurones

depolarisation (of axon) a temporary and local reversal of the resting potential difference of the membrane that occurs when an impulse is transmitted along the axon

derive manipulate a mathematical equation to give a new equation or result

describe give a detailed account including all relevant information

desertification the conversion of marginal cultivated land into desert, caused by climate change or by over-grazing or inferior cultivation

design produce a plan, object, simulation or model

determine find the only possible answer

detrital chain a food chain based on dead plant matter

detritivore an organism that feeds on detritus (dead organic matter)

dialysis separation of large and small molecules in solution by the inability of the former to pass through a selectively permeable membrane

diaphragm a sheet of tissues, largely muscle, separating thorax from abdomen in mammals

diastole relaxation phase in the cardiac cycle

dichotomous key one in which a group of organisms is progressively divided into two groups of smaller size

dicotyledon class of Angiospermophyta having an embryo with two seed leaves (cotyledons)

diffusion passive movement of particles from a region of high concentration to a region of low concentration

dihybrid cross one in which the inheritance of two pairs of contrasting characters (controlled by genes on separate chromosomes) is observed

diploid condition organisms whose cells have nuclei containing two sets of chromosomes

disaccharide a sugar that is a condensation product of two monosaccharides (e.g. maltose)

discuss give an account including, where possible, a range of arguments, assessments of the relative importance of various factors or comparisons of alternative hypotheses

distinguish give a difference between two or more different items

disulphide bond S—S bond between two S-containing amino acid residues in a polypeptide or protein chain

diuresis increased secretion of urine

division of labour the carrying out of specialised functions by different types of cell in a multicellular organism

DNA a form of nucleic acid found in the nucleus, consisting of two complementary chains of deoxyribonucleotide subunits, and containing the bases adenine, thymine, guanine and cytosine

dominant allele an allele that has the same effect on the phenotype whether it is present in the homozygous or heterozygous state

double bond a covalent bond involving the sharing of two pairs of electrons (rather than one)

double circulation in which the blood passes twice through the heart (pulmonary circulation, then systemic circulation) in any one complete circuit of the body

double fertilisation a feature of flowering plants in which two male nuclei enter the embryo sac, and one fuses with the egg cell and one with the endosperm nucleus

draw represent by means of pencil lines (with labels added)

duodenum the first part of the intestine after the stomach

E

ecology the study of relationships between living organisms and between organisms and their environment – a community and its abiotic environment

ecosystem a natural unit of living (biotic) components and non-living (abiotic) components (e.g. temperate deciduous forest)

edaphic factor factor influenced by the soil

effector an organ or cell that responds to a stimulus by doing something (e.g. a muscle contracting, a gland secreting)

egestion disposal of waste from the body (e.g. defecation)

egg cell an alternative name for an ovum

electron microscope (EM) microscope in which a beam of electrons replaces light, and the powers of magnification and resolution are correspondingly much greater

electron-transport system carriers that transfer electrons along a redox chain, permitting ATP to be synthesised in the process

embolism a blood clot blocking a blood vessel

embryo the earliest stages in development of a new animal or plant, from a fertilised ovum, entirely dependent on nutrients supplied by the parent

embryo sac occurs in the ovule of flowering plants, and contains the egg cell and endosperm nucleus

emulsify to break fats and oils into very tiny droplets

endemic species restricted to a particular region

endergonic reaction metabolic reaction requiring energy input

endocrine glands the hormone-producing glands that release secretions directly into the body fluids

endocytosis uptake of fluid or tiny particles into vacuoles in the cytoplasm, carried out at the plasma membrane

endoplasmic reticulum system of branching membranes in the cytoplasm of eukaryotic cells, existing as rough ER (with ribosomes) or as smooth ER (without ribosomes)

endosperm the stored food reserves within the seeds of flowering plants

endoskeleton an internal skeleton system

endothermic generation of body heat metabolically

endothelium a single layer of cells lining blood vessels and other fluid-filled cavities

enzyme mainly proteins (a very few are RNA) that function as biological catalysts

epidemiology the study of the occurrence, distribution and control of disease

epidermis outer layer(s) of cells

epiglottis flap of cartilage that closes of the trachea when food is swallowed

epiphyte plant living on the surface of other plants

epithelium sheet of cells bound strongly together, covering internal or external surfaces of multicellular organisms

erythrocyte red blood cell

estimate find an approximate value for an unknown quantity, based on the information provided and scientific knowledge

etiolation the condition of plants when grown in the dark

eukaryotic (cells) cells with a 'good' nucleus (e.g. animal, plant, fungi and protoctista cells)

evaluate assess the implications and limitations

evolution cumulative change in the heritable characteristics of a population

ex situ not in its original or natural position or habitat

excretion removal from the body of the waste products of metabolic pathways

exergonic reaction metabolic reaction releasing energy

exocytosis secretion of liquids and suspensions of very fine particles across the membrane of eukaryotic cells

exocrine gland gland whose secretion is released via a duct

exoskeleton skeleton secreted external to the epidermis of the body

exothermic chemical reaction that releases energy as heat (an endothermic reaction requires heat energy)

explain give a clear account including causes, reasons or mechanisms

expiratory emitting air during breathing

extensor muscle a muscle that extends or straightens a limb

F

F_1 generation first filial generation – arise by crossing parents (P), and when selfed or crossed via sibling crosses, produce the F_2 generation

facilitated diffusion diffusion across a membrane facilitated by molecules in the membrane (without the expenditure of metabolic energy)

fermentation anaerobic breakdown of glucose, with end-products ethanol and carbon dioxide or lactic acid

fetus a mammalian embryo when it becomes recognisable (e.g. the human embryo from 7 weeks after fertilisation)

fertilisation the fusion of male and female gametes to form a zygote

field layer the layer of herbaceous plants in a forest or wood

filter-feeding feeding on tiny organisms which are strained from the surrounding medium

fimbria (singular, **fimbrium**) thin,

short filaments protruding from some bacteria, involved in attachment

flaccid state of a tissue with insufficient water, as in wilting leaves

flagellum (plural, **flagella**) a long thin structure, occurring singly or in groups on some cells and tissues, and used to propel unicellular organisms, and to move liquids past anchored cells (flagella of prokaryotes and eukaryotes are of different internal structure)

flexor muscle a muscle that on contraction bends a limb (or part of a limb)

flower develops from the tip of a shoot, with outer parts (e.g. sepals, petals) surrounding the male and female reproductive organs

fluid mosaic model the accepted view of the structure of the plasma membrane, comprising a phospholipid bilayer with proteins embedded but free to move about

food chain a sequence of organisms within a habitat in which each is the food of the next, starting with a producer, which is photosynthetic

food web interconnected food chains

founder effect genetic differences that develop between an original breeding population and a small isolated interbreeding group of these organisms

fovea point on a retina of greatest acuity of vision

free energy part of the potential chemical energy in molecules that is available to do useful work when the molecules are broken

frequency commonness of an occurrence

fruit forms from the ovary after fertilisation, as the ovules develop into seeds

functional group the chemically active part of a member of a series of organic molecules

fungus heterotrophic, non-motile, multicellular (usually) eukaryotic organism with 'plant' body – a mycelium of hyphae with cell walls of chitin; the fungi constitute a separate kingdom

G

gall bladder sac beside the liver that stores bile, present in some mammals (e.g. humans)

gamete sex cell (e.g. ovum, sperm)

ganglion part of a nervous system, consisting of nerve cell bodies

gaseous exchange exchange of respiratory gases (oxygen, carbon dioxide) between cells/organism and the environment

gastric relating to the stomach

gene a heritable factor that controls a specific characteristic

gene mutation change in the chemical structure (base sequence) of a gene resulting in change in the characteristics of an organism or individual cell

gene pool all the genes (and their alleles) present in a breeding population

gene probe an artificially prepared sequence of DNA made radioactive with ^{14}C, coding for a particular amino acid residue sequence

gene therapy various mechanisms by which corrected copies of genes are introduced into a patient with a genetic disease

generator potential localised depolarisation of a membrane of a sensory cell

genetic code the order of bases in DNA (of a chromosome) that determines the sequence of amino acids in a protein

genetic counselling genetic advice to potential parents on the risks of having children with an inherited disease

genetic engineering change to the genetic constitution of individuals or populations by artificial selection

genome the genetic complement (genes) of an organism or of an individual cell – the whole of the genetic information of an organism

genotype the genetic constitution of an organism – the alleles of an organism

genus a group of similar and closely related species

germination the resumption of growth by an embryonic plant in seed or fruit, at the expense of stored food

gland cells or tissues adapted for secretion

global warming the hypothesis that the world climate is warming due to rising levels of atmospheric carbon dioxide, a greenhouse gas

glomerulus network of capillaries which are surrounded by the renal capsule

glycocalyx long carbohydrate molecules attached to membrane proteins and membrane lipids

glycogen a much-branched polymer of glucose, the storage carbohydrate of many animals

glycogenesis the synthesis of glycogen from glucose (the reverse is glycogenolysis)

glycolysis the first stage of tissue respiration in which glucose is broken down to pyruvic acid, without use of oxygen

glycoprotein membrane protein with a glycocalyx attached

glycosidic bond a type of chemical linkage between monosaccharide residues in polysaccharides

goblet cell mucus-secreting cell of an epithelium

Golgi apparatus a stack of flattened membranes in the cytoplasm, the site of synthesis of biochemicals

gonad an organ in which gametes are formed

gonadotrophic hormone follicle-stimulating hormone (FSH) and luteinising hormone (LH), secreted by the anterior pituitary, which stimulate gonad function

granum (plural, grana) stacked disks of membranes found within the chloroplast, containing the photosynthetic pigments, and the site of the light-dependent reaction of photosynthesis

grey matter regions of the brain and spinal cord consisting largely of nerve cell bodies

growth more or less irreversible increase in size and amount of dry matter

gut the alimentary canal

H

habitat the locality or surroundings in which an organism normally lives or the location of a living organism

haemoglobin a conjugated protein, found in red cells, effective at carrying oxygen from regions of high partial pressure (e.g. lungs) to regions of low partial pressure of oxygen (e.g. respiring tissues)

half-life the time taken for the ionising radiation emitted by a radioactive isotope to fall to half maximum

hallucinogen a drug capable of causing hallucinations

halophyte a plant adapted to survive at abnormally high salt levels (e.g. seashore or salt marsh plant)

haploid (cells) cells having one set of chromosomes, the basic set

heart rate number of contractions of the heart per minute

hepatic associated with the liver

herb layer layer of herbaceous plants (mainly perennials) growing in woodland

herbaceous non-woody

herbicide pesticide toxic to plants

herbivore an animal that feeds (holozoically) exclusively on plants

hermaphrodite organism with both male and female reproductive systems

heterotroph an organism incapable of synthesising its own elaborated nutrients

heterozygous having two different alleles of a gene

hexose a monosaccharide containing six carbon atoms (e.g. glucose, fructose)

hibernation passing the unfavourable season in a resting state of sleep

histology the study of the structure of tissues

histone basic proteins (rich in the amino acids arginine and lysine) that form the scaffolding of chromosomes

holozoic ingesting complex food material and digesting it

homeostasis maintenance of a constant internal environment

homeotherm organism that maintains a constant body temperature

homologous chromosomes chromosomes in a diploid cell which contain the same sequence of genes, but are derived from different parents

homologous structures similar due to common ancestry

homozygous having two identical alleles of a gene

hormone a substance, formed by an endocrine gland and transported in the blood all over the body, but triggering a specific physiological response in one type of organ or tissue

host an organism in or on which a parasite spends all or part of its life cycle

humus complex organic matter, the end-product of the breakdown of the remains of plants and animals, which covers the mineral particles of soil

hybrid an individual produced from a cross between two genetically unlike parents

hybridoma an artificially produced hybrid cell culture, used to produce monoclonal antibodies

hydrocarbon chain a linear arrangement of carbon atoms combined together and with hydrogen atoms, forming a hydrophobic tail to many large organic molecules

hydrogen bond a weak bond caused by electrostatic attraction between a positively charged part of one molecule and a negatively charged part of another

hydrolysis a reaction in which hydrogen and hydroxide ions from water are added to a large molecule causing it to split into smaller molecules

hydrophilic water loving

hydrophobic water hating

hydrophyte an aquatic plant

hydrosere a plant succession that originated from open water

hydrostatic pressure mechanical pressure exerted on or by liquid (e.g. water) also known as pressure potential

hyperglycaemia excess glucose in the blood

hypertonic solution a more concentrated solution (one with a less negative water potential) than the cell solution

hypha the tubular filament 'plant' body of a fungus, which in certain species is divided by cross walls into either multicellular or unicellular compartments

hypoglycaemia very low levels of blood glucose

hypothalamus part of floor of the rear of the forebrain, a control centre for the autonomic nervous system, and source of releasing factors for pituitary hormones

hypothesis a tentative (and testable) explanation of an observed phenomenon or event

hypotonic solution a less concentrated solution (one with a more negative water potential) than the cell solution

I

identify find an answer from a number of possibilities

immunisation (e.g. inoculation/ vaccination) the injection of a specific antigen, derived from a pathogen, to confer immunity against a disease

immunity resistance to the onset of a disease after infection by the causative agent

  active immunity immunity due to the production of antibodies by the organism itself after the body's defence mechanisms have been stimulated by antigens

  passive immunity immunity due to the acquisition of antibodies from another organism in which active immunity has been stimulated, including via the placenta, colostrum, or by injection of antibodies

immunoglobin proteins synthesised by the B lymphocytes of the immune system

immunology study of the immune system

immunosuppressant a substance causing temporary suppression of the immune response

implantation embedding of the blastocyst (developed from the fertilised ovum) in the uterus wall

impulse see *action potential*

imprinting process occurring soon after birth, causing young birds follow their mother

in situ in the original place (in the body or organism)

in vitro biological processes occurring in cell extracts (literally 'in glass')

in vivo biological process occurring in a living organism (literally 'in life')

inbreeding when gametes of closely related individuals fuse leading to progeny that is homozygous for some or many alleles

incubation period period between infection by a causative agent and the appearance of the symptoms of a disease

incus tiny, anvil-shaped bone, the middle ossicle of the middle ear in mammals

industrial melanism increasing proportion of a darkened (melanic) form of an organism, in place of the light-coloured form, associated with industrial pollution by soot

infectious disease disease capable of being transmitted from one organism to another

inhibitor (enzyme) a substance which slows or blocks enzyme action (a competitive inhibitor binds to the active site; a non-competitive inhibitor binds to another part of the enzyme)

inhibitory synapse synapse at which arrival of an impulse blocks forward transmissions of impulses in the post-synaptic membrane

innate behaviour behaviour that does not need to be learned

innervation nerve supply

inspiratory capacity amount of air that can be drawn into the lungs

intelligence the ability to learn by reasoning and to solve problems not yet experienced

interferon proteins formed by vertebrate cells in response to virus infections

intermediates metabolites formed as components of a metabolic pathway

interphase the period between nuclear divisions when the nucleus controls and directs the activity of the cell

interspecific competition competition between organisms of different species

intestine the gut

intracellular enzymes enzymes operating inside the cell

intraspecific competition competition between organisms of the same species

intron a non-coding nucleotide sequence of the DNA of chromosomes, present in eukaryotic chromosomes

invagination the intucking of a surface or wall

ion charged particle formed by the transfer of electron(s) from one atom to another

ionic bonding strong electrostatic attraction between oppositely charged ions

iris circular disc of tissue, in front of the lens of the eye, containing circular and radial muscles

irreversible inhibition inhibition by inhibitors that bind tightly and permanently to an enzyme, destroying its catalytic properties

islets of Langerhans groups of endocrine cells scattered through the pancreas

isomers chemical compounds of the same chemical formula but different structural formulae

isotonic being of the same osmotic concentration and therefore of the same water potential

isotopes different forms of an element, chemically identical but with slightly different physical properties, based on differences in atomic mass (due to different numbers of neutrons in the nucleus)

J

joule the SI unit of energy

K

keratin a fibrous protein found in horn, hair, nails, and in the upper layer of skin

kinesis random movements maintained by motile organisms until more favourable conditions are reached

kinetic energy energy in movement

kingdom the largest and most inclusive group in taxonomy

Krebs cycle part of tissue respiration

L

label add labels to a diagram

lactation secretion of milk in mammary glands

leaching washing out of soluble ions and nutrients by water drainage through soil

learned behaviour in animals, behaviour that is consistently modified as a result of experiences

leucocyte white blood cell

lichens permanent, mutualistic associations between certain fungi and algae, forming organisms found encrusting walls, tree trunks and rocks

ligament strong fibrous cord or capsule of slightly elastic fibres, connecting movable bones

light-independent step part of photosynthesis occurring in the stroma of the chloroplasts and using the products of the light-dependent step to reduce carbon dioxide to carbohydrate

light-dependent step part of photosynthesis occurring in grana of the chloroplasts, in which water is split and ATP and $NADPH_2$ are regenerated

lignin complex chemical impregnating the cellulose of the walls of xylem vessels, fibres and tracheids, imparting great strength and rigidity

lipid diverse group of organic chemicals essential to living things, insoluble in water but soluble in organic solvents such as ether and alcohol (e.g. lipid of the plasma membrane)

linkage group the genes carried on any one chromosome

lipoprotein a complex of lipid and protein of various types which are classified according to density (e.g. LDL, HDL)

list give a sequence of names or other brief answers with no elaboration

liver lobule polygonal block of liver cells, a functional unit within the liver structure

locus the particular position on homologous chromosomes of a gene

loop of Henle loop of mammalian kidney tubule, passing from cortex to medulla and back, important in the process of concentration of urine

lumen internal space of a tube (e.g. gut, artery, etc.) or sac-shaped structure

lymph fluid derived from plasma of blood, bathing all tissue spaces and draining back into the lymphatic system

lymph node tiny glands in the lymphatic system, part of the body's defences against disease

lymphatic system network of fine capillaries throughout the body of vertebrates, which drain lymph and return it to the blood circulation

lymphocyte type of white blood cell

lysis breakdown, typically of cells

lysosome membrane-bound vesicles, common in the cytoplasm, containing digestive enzymes

M

macromolecule very large organic molecule – rmm 10 000+ (e.g. protein, nucleic acid or polysaccharide)

macronutrients ions required in relatively large amounts by organisms

Malpighian body glomerulus and renal capsule of mammalian nephron

mandibles the lower jaw of vertebrates; in arthropods paired, biting mouthparts

matrix ground substance of connective tissue, and the innermost part of a mitochondrion

measure find a value for a quantity

mechanoreceptors a sensory receptor sensitive to mechanical stimulus

meiosis nuclear division with daughter cells containing half the number of chromosomes of the parent cell

melanic pigmented

menstrual cycle monthly cycle of ovulation and menstruation in human females

meristem plant tissue capable of giving rise to new cells and tissues

mesentery connective tissue holding body organs (e.g. gut) in position

mesophyll parenchyma cells containing chloroplasts

mesosome an invagination of the plasma membrane of a bacterium

metabolic pathway sequence of enzyme-catalysed biochemical reactions in cells and tissues

metabolic water water released within the body by oxidation, typically of dietary lipids

metabolism integrated network of all the biochemical reactions of life

metabolite a chemical substance involved in metabolism

metaphase stage in nuclear division (mitosis and meiosis) in which chromosomes become arranged at the equator of the spindle

microhabitat the environment immediately surrounding an organism, particularly applied to tiny organisms

micronutrient ions required in relatively small (trace) amounts by organisms

microtubule tiny, hollow protein tube in cytoplasm (e.g. a component of the spindle)

microvillus one of many tiny infoldings of the plasma membrane, making up a brush border

middle lamella a layer of pectins between the walls of adjacent cells

mitochondrion (plural, **mitochondria**) organelle in eukaryotic cells, site of Krebs cycle and the electron-transport pathway

mitosis nuclear division in which the daughter nuclei have the same number of chromosomes as the parent cell

mitral valve left atrio-ventricular valve

mode the most frequently occurring value in a distribution

monoclonal antibody antibody produced by a single clone of B lymphocytes; it consists of a population of identical antibody molecules

monocotyledon class of angiosperms having an embryo with a single cotyledon

monocyte large phagocytic white blood cell

monohybrid cross a cross (breeding experiment) involving one pair of contrasting characters exhibited by homozygous parents

monosaccharide simple carbohydrate (all are reducing sugars)

morphology form and structure of an organism

motile capable of moving about

motor area area of the brain where muscular activity is coordinated

motor end plate the point of termination of an axon in a voluntary muscle fibre

motor neurone nerve cell that carries impulses away from the central nervous system to an effector (e.g. muscle, gland)

mRNA single-stranded ribonucleic acid formed by the process of transcription of the genetic code in the nucleus, that then moves to ribosomes in the cytoplasm

mucilage mixture of various polysaccharides that become slippery when wet

mucosa the inner lining of the gut

mucus a watery solution of glycoprotein with protective and lubrication functions

muscle spindle sensory receptor in muscle, responding to stretch stimuli

mutagen an agent that causes mutation

mutant organism with altered genetic material (abruptly altered by a mutation)

mutation a change in the amount or the chemical structure (i.e. base sequence) of DNA of a chromosome

mutualism a case of symbiosis in which both organisms benefit from the association

mycelium a mass or network of hyphae

mycology the study of fungi

mycorrhiza a mutualistic association between plant roots and fungi, with the mycelium restricted to the exterior of the root and its cells (ectotrophic), or involving a closer

association between hyphae and root cell contents (endotrophic)

myelin sheath an insulating sheath of axons of nerve fibres, formed by the wrapping around of Schwann cells

myelinated nerve fibre nerve fibre insulated by a lipid sheath formed from membranes of Schwann cells

myofibril contractile protein filament from which muscle is composed

myogenic originating in heart muscle cells themselves, as in generation of the basic heart beat

N

natural classification organisms grouped by as many common features as possible, and therefore likely to reflect evolutionary relationships

nectary group of cells secreting nectar (dilute sugar solution) in a flower

nematocyst stinging cell of cnidarians (coelenterates) (e.g. *Hydra*)

Neolithic revolution the period of human development involving the first establishment of settled agriculture practices, and including the breeding and cultivation of crop plants and herd animals

nephron the functional unit of a vertebrate kidney

nerve bundle of many nerve fibres (axons), connecting the central nervous system with parts of the body

nerve cord in non-vertebrates, a bundle of nerve fibres and/or nerve ganglia running along the length of the body

nervous system organised system of neurones which generate and conduct impulses

autonomic nervous system (ANS) the involuntary nervous system

central nervous system (CNS) in vertebrates, the brain and spinal cord

parasympathetic nervous system part of the involuntary nervous system, antagonistic in effect to the sympathetic nervous system

peripheral nervous system (PNS) in vertebrates, neurones that convey sensory information to the CNS, and neurones that convey impulses to muscles and glands (effector organs)

sympathetic nervous system part of the involuntary nervous system, antagonistic in effect to the parasympathetic nervous system

neurone nerve cell

neurotransmitter substance chemical released at the pre-synaptic membrane of an axon, on arrival of an action potential, which transmits the action potential across the synapse

neutrophil a type of white blood cell

niche both the habitat an organism occupies and the mode of nutrition employed

node of Ranvier junction in the myelin sheaths around a myelinated nerve fibre

noradrenaline neurotransmitter substance in the sympathetic nervous system

nuclear division first step in the division of a cell, when the contents of the nucleus are subdivided by mitosis or meiosis

nuclear membrane double membrane surrounding the eukaryotic nucleus

nuclear pores organised gaps in the nuclear membrane, exit points for mRNA

nucleic acid polynucleotide chain of one of two types, deoxyribonucleic acid (DNA) or ribonucleic acid (RNA)

nucleus largest organelle of eukaryotic cells; controls and directs the activity of the cell

nucleolus compact region of nucleus where RNA is synthesised

nucleoside organic base (adenine, guanine, cytosine, thymine) combined with a pentose sugar (ribose or deoxyribose)

nucleotide phosphate ester of a nucleoside – an organic base combined with pentose sugar and phosphate (P_i)

nutrient a chemical substance found in foods that is used in the human body – any substance used or required by an organism as food

nutrition the process by which an organism acquires the matter and energy it requires from its environment

O

obesity condition of being seriously over-weight (BMI of 30+)

oestrous cycle reproductive cycle in female mammal in the absence of pregnancy

oestrous period of fertility (immediately after ovulation) during the oestrous cycle

olfactory relating to the sense of smell

omnivore an animal that eats both plant and animal food

oncogene a cancer-initiating gene

oocyte a female sex cell in the process of a meiotic division to become an ovum

oogamy union of unlike gametes (e.g. large ovum and tiny sperm)

opsonin type of antibody that attacks bacteria and viruses, facilitating their ingestion by phagocytic cells

order a group of related families

organ a part of an organism, consisting of a collection of tissues, having a definite form and structure, and performing one or more specialised functions

organelle a unit of cell substructure

organic compounds of carbon (except carbon dioxide and carbonates)

organism a living thing

osmoreceptor sense cells or organ stimulated by changes in water potential

osmoregulation control of the water balance of the blood, tissue or cytoplasm of a living organism

osmosis diffusion of free water molecules from a region where they are more concentrated (low solute concentration) to a region where they are less concentrated (high solute concentration) across a partially permeable membrane

outline give a brief account or summary

ovarian cycle the monthly changes that occur to ovarian follicles leading to ovulation and the formation of a corpus luteum

ovary female reproductive organ in which the female gametes are formed

ovarian follicle spherical structures found in the mammalian ovary, containing a developing ovum with liquid surrounded by numerous follicle cells, and from which a secondary oocyte is released at ovulation

ovum (plural, **ova**) a female gamete

ovulation shedding of ova from the ovary

ovule in the flowering plant flower, the structure in an ovary which, after fertilisation, grows into the seed

oxygen dissociation curve a graph of % saturation (with oxygen) of haemoglobin against concentration of available oxygen

oxyntic cells cells in the gastric glands secreting hydrochloric acid

P

pacemaker structure that is the origin of the myogenic heart beat, known as the sino-atrial node

Pacinian corpuscles sensory receptors in joints

pancreas an exocrine gland discharging pancreatic juice into the duodenum, combined with endocrine glands (islets of Langerhans)

parasite an organism that lives on or in another organism (its host) for most of its life cycle, deriving nutrients from its host

parenchyma living cells, forming the greater part of cortex and pith in primary plant growth

pathogen an organism or virus that causes a disease

partial pressure the pressure exerted by each component of a gas mixture, proportional to how much of the gas is present in the mixture; the partial pressure of oxygen in air is represented by the symbol pO_2 and is expressed in kilopascals (kPa)

pentadactyl having all four limbs (typically) terminating in five digits

pentose a 5-carbon monosaccharide sugar

peptide a chain of up to 20 amino acid residues, linked by peptide linkages

peptide linkage a covalent bonding of the α amino group of one amino acid to the carboxyl group of another (with the loss of a molecule of water)

perception the mental interpretation of sense data (i.e. occurring in the brain)

pericardium a tough membrane surrounding and containing the heart

peristalsis wave of muscular contractions passing down the gut wall

pesticide a chemical that is used to kill pests

petal modified leaf, often brightly coloured, found in flowers

phagocytic cells cells that ingest bacteria etc. (e.g. certain leucocytes, *Amoeba*)

phenotype the characteristics or appearance (structural, biochemical, etc.) of an organism

pheromone volatile chemical signal released into the air

phloem tissue that conducts elaborated food in plant stems

phosphate (P_i) phosphate ions, as involved in metabolism

phospholipid formed from a triacylglycerol in which one of the fatty acid groups is replaced by an ionised phosphate group

photoautotroph an organism that uses light energy to generate ATP and to produce organic compounds from inorganic substances

photoheterotroph an organism that uses light energy to generate ATP and obtains organic compounds from other organisms

photomorphogenesis effects on plant growth of light

photoperiodism day-length control of flowering in plants

photosynthesis the production of sugar from carbon dioxide and water, occurring in chloroplasts and using light energy, and producing oxygen as a waste product

photophosphorylation the formation of ATP, using light energy (in the light-dependent step of photosynthesis in the grana)

phototropism a tropic response of plants to light

phylogenetic classification a classification based on evolutionary relationships (rather than on appearances)

phylum a group of organisms constructed on a similar general plan, usually thought to be evolutionarily related

physiology the study of the functioning of organisms

phytoplankton photosynthetic plankton, including unicellular algae and cyanobacteria

pinocytosis uptake of a droplet of liquid into a cell involving invagination of the plasma membrane

pituitary gland the master endocrine gland, attached to the underside of the brain

placenta maternal and fetal tissue in the wall of the uterus, site of all exchanges of metabolites and waste products between fetal and maternal blood systems

plant growth substance substances produced by plants in relatively small amounts, that interact to control growth and development

plasma the liquid part of blood

plasma membrane the membrane of lipid and protein that forms the surface of cells (constructed as a fluid mosaic membrane)

plasmid small circular DNA that is independent of the chromosome in bacteria (R plasmids contain genes for resistance to antibiotics)

plasmolysis withdrawal of water from a plant cell by osmosis (incipient plasmolysis is established when about 50% of cells show some shrinkage of cytoplasm away from the walls)

plankton very small, aquatic (marine or fresh water) plants and animals, many of them unicellular, that live at or near the water's surface

plastid an organelle containing pigments (e.g. chloroplast)

platelets tiny cell fragments that lack a nucleus, found in the blood and involved in the blood clotting mechanism

pleural membrane lines lungs and thorax cavity and contains the pleural fluid

polarise the setting up of an electrical potential difference across a membrane

polarised light light in which rays vibrate in one plane only

pollen microspore produced in anthers (and male cones), containing male gamete(s)

pollen tube grows out of a pollen grain attached to a stigma, and down through the style tissue to the embryo sac

polygenic inheritance inheritance of phenotypic characters (such as height, eye colour in humans) that are determined by the collective effects of several different genes

polynucleotide a long, unbranched chain of nucleotides, as found in DNA and RNA

polymer large organic molecules made up of repeating subunits (monomers)

polypeptide a chain of amino acid residues linked by peptide linkages

polyploidy having more than two sets of chromosomes per cell

polysaccharides very high molecular mass carbohydrates, formed by condensation of vast numbers of monosaccharide units, with the removal of water

polysome an aggregation of ribosomes along a molecule of mRNA strand

population a group of organisms of the same species which live in the same area (habitat) at the same time

portal vein vein beginning and ending in a capillary network (rather than at the heart)

post-synaptic neurone neurone 'downstream' of a synapse

potential difference separation of electrical charge within or across a structure (e.g. a membrane)

potential energy stored energy

predator an organism that catches and kills other animals to eat

predict give an expected result

pre-synaptic membrane membrane of the tip of an axon at the point of the synapse

pre-synaptic neurone neurone 'upstream' of a synapse

prey–predator relationship the inter-relationship of population sizes due to predation of one species (the predator) on another (the prey)

proboscis a projection from the head, used for feeding

producer an autotrophic organism

productivity the amount of biomass fixed by producers (photosynthetically)

gross productivity total amount of organic matter produced

net productivity the organic matter of organisms less the amount needed to fuel respiration

prokaryote tiny unicellular organism without a true nucleus; they have a ring of RNA or DNA as a chromosome (e.g. bacteria and cyanobacteria)

prophase first stage in nuclear division, mitotic or meiotic

proprioceptor an internal sensory receptor

prosthetic group a non-protein substance, bound to a protein as part of an enzyme, often forming part of the active site, and able to bind to other proteins

protein a long sequence of amino acid residues combined together (primary structure), and taking up a particular shape (secondary and tertiary structure)

Protoctista kingdom of the eukaryotes consisting of single-celled organisms and multicellular organisms related to them (e.g. protozoa and algae)

protoplast the living contents of a plant cell, contained by the cell wall

protozoan a single-celled animal-like organism, belonging to a sub-kingdom, the Protozoa, of the kingdom Protoctista

pseudopodium a temporary extension of the body of an amoeboid cell, by which movement or feeding may occur

pulmonary circulation the circulation to the lungs in vertebrates having a double circulation

pulmonary ventilation rate breathing rate

pulse a wave of increased pressure in the arterial circulation, generated by the heart beat

pumps proteins in plasma membranes that use energy directly to carry substances across (primary pump) or work indirectly from metabolic energy (secondary pump)

pupil central aperture in the eye through which light enters

pure breeding homozygous, at least for the gene(s) specified

Purkinje fibres fibres of the bundle of His that conduct impulses between the atria and ventricles of the heart

pyloric sphincter circular muscle at the opening of the stomach to the duodenum

pyruvic acid a 3-carbon organic acid, $CH_3.CO.COOH$; product of glycolysis

Q

quadrat a sampling area enclosed within a frame

R

radical a short-lived, intermediate product of a reaction, formed when a covalent bond breaks, with one of the two bonding electrons going to each atom

radioactive dating using the proportions of different isotopes in fossilised biological material to estimate when the original organism was alive

reaction centres protein–pigment complexes in the grana of chloroplasts, sites of the photochemical reactions of photosynthesis

receptor a sense organ

recessive allele an allele that has an effect on the phenotype only when present in the homozygous state

reciprocal cross a cross between the same pair of genotypes in which the sources of the gametes (male and female) are reversed

recombinant a chromosome (or cell or organism) in which the genetic information has been rearranged

recombinant DNA DNA which has been artificial changed, involving joining together genes from different sources, typically from different species

recycling of nutrients the process by which materials from dead organisms are broken down and made available for re-use in the biosphere

Red Data Book an internationally produced record of actions for endangered species

redox reaction reaction in which reduction and oxidation happen simultaneously

reductive division meiosis, in which the chromosome number of a diploid cell is halved

reflex a rapid unconscious response

reflex action a response automatically elicited by a stimulus

reflex arc a functional unit in the nervous system, consisting of sensory receptor, sensory neurone, (possibly relay neurones), motor neurone and effector (e.g. muscle or gland)

refractory period the period after excitation of a neurone, when a repetition of the stimulus fails to induce the same response, divided into periods known as absolute and relative

relative atomic mass the ratio of the mass of an atom of an element to the mass of a carbon atom

renal capsule the cup-shaped closed end of a nephron which, with the glomerulus, constitutes a Malpighian body

renewable energy energy that comes from exploiting wave power, wind power, tidal power, solar energy, hydroelectric power or biological sources such as biomass

replication duplication of DNA by making a copy of an existing molecule

semi-conservative replication each strand of an existing DNA double helix acts as the template for the synthesis of a new strand

reproduction formation of new individual by sexual or asexual means

residual volume volume of air remaining in the lungs after maximum expiration

respiration the cellular process by which sugars and other substances are broken down to release chemical energy for other cellular processes

respiratory centre region of the medulla of the brain concerned with the involuntary control of breathing

respiratory pigment substance such as haemoglobin, which associates with oxygen

respiratory quotient ratio of the volume of carbon dioxide produced to the oxygen used in respiration

respiratory surface a surface adapted for gaseous exchange

respirometer apparatus for the measurement of respiratory gaseous exchange

response the outcome when a stimulus is detected by a receptor

resting potential the potential difference across the membrane of a neurone when it is not being stimulated (repolarised)

restriction enzymes enzymes, also known as endonucleases, that cut lengths of nucleic acid at specific sequences of bases

retina the light-sensitive layer at the back of the eye

retroviruses viruses which, on arrival in a host cell, have their own RNA copied into DNA which then attaches to the host DNA for a period

ribosome non-membranous organelle, site of protein synthesis

ribonucleic acid (RNA) a form of nucleic acid containing the pentose sugar ribose, found in nucleus and cytoplasm of eukaryotic cells (and commonly the only nucleic acid of prokaryotes), and containing the organic bases adenine, guanine, uracil and cytosine

rod cell one of two types of light-sensitive cell in the retina, responsible for non-colour vision

roughage indigestible matter (such as cellulose fibres) in our diet

ribulose bisphosphate the 5-carbon acceptor molecule for carbon dioxide, in the light-independent step of photosynthesis

S

saliva secretion produced by salivary glands

saltatory conduction impulse conduction 'in jumps', between nodes of Ranvier

saprotroph organism that feeds on dead organic matter (saprotrophic nutrition)

sarcolemma membranous sheath around a muscle fibre

sarcomere a unit of a skeletal (voluntary) muscle fibre, between two Z-discs

sarcoplasm cytoplasm around the myofibril of a muscle fibre

sarcoplasmic reticulum network of membranes around the myofibrils of a muscle fibre

saturated fat fat with a fully hydrogenated carbon backbone (i.e. no double bonds present)

Schwann cell cell which forms the sheath around nerve fibres

sclera the opaque, fibrous coat of the eyeball

secondary sexual characteristic sexual characteristic that develops under the influence of sex hormones (androgens and oestrogens)

secondary succession a plant succession on soil already formed, from which the community had been abruptly removed

secretion material produced and released from glandular cells

sedentary organism living attached to the substratum (e.g. rock or other surface)

seed formed from a fertilised ovule, containing an embryonic plant and food store

segmentation body plan built on a repeating series of similar segments (e.g. as in annelids)

selection differential survivability or reproductive potential of different organisms of a breeding population

self-pollination transfer of pollen from the anther to the stigma of the same plant (normally the same flower)

selfing self-pollination or self-fertilisation

semilunar valve half-moon shaped valves, preventing backflow in a tube (e.g. a vein)

seminiferous tubule elongated tubes in the testes, the site of sperm production

sense organ an organ of cells sensitive to external stimuli

sensory area an area of the cerebral cortex of the brain receiving impulses from the sense organs of the body

sensory neurone nerve cell carrying impulses from a sense organ or receptor to the central nervous system

sensory receptor a cell specialised to respond to stimulation by the production of an action potential (impulse)

sepal the protective outermost parts of a flower, usually green

seral stage / sere stages in a seral succession, the whole succession being known as a sere

sex chromosome a chromosome which determines sex rather than other body (soma) characteristics

sex linkage genes carried on only one of the sex chromosomes and which therefore show a different pattern of inheritance in crosses where the male carries the gene from those where the female carries the gene

sexual reproduction involves the production and fusion of gametes

show give the steps in a calculation or derivation

shrub layer the low-level (below trees) woody perennials growing in a forest or wood, normally most numerous in clearings (e.g. where a full-grown tree has died)

sibling offspring of the same parent

sieve tube a phloem element, accompanied by a companion cell, and having perforated end walls known as sieve plates

simple sugar monosaccharide sugar such as a triose sugar (3C), pentose sugar (5C), or hexose sugar (6C)

single access key contrasting or mutually exclusive characteristics are used to divide the group of organisms into progressively smaller groupings until individual organisms (species) can be identified

sino-atrial node cells in the wall of the right atrium in which the heart beat is initiated, also known as the pacemaker

sinus a cavity or space

sketch represent by means of a graph showing a line plus labelled but unscaled axes and with important features (e.g. intercepts) clearly indicated

solar energy electromagnetic radiation derived from the fusion of hydrogen atoms of the Sun, reaching Earth from space

solve obtain an answer using algebraic and/or numerical methods

somatic cell (soma) body cell – not a cell producing gametes (sex cell)

specialisation adaptation for a particular mode of life or function

speciation the evolution of new species

species a group of individuals of common ancestry that closely resemble each other and that are normally capable of interbreeding to produce fertile offspring

sperms motile male gametes of animals

spermatogonia male germ cells (stem cells) which make up the inner layer of the lining of the seminiferous tubules, and give rise to spermatocytes

spermocyte cell formed in seminiferous tubules of testes; develops into sperm

spindle structure formed from microtubules, associated with the movements of chromosomes in mitosis and meiosis

spiracle hole in the side of an insect (thorax and abdomen) by which the tracheal respiratory system connects with the atmosphere

spiral vessel protoxylem vessel with spirally arranged lignin thickening in lateral walls

spirometer apparatus for measurements of lung capacity and breathing rates

spore a small, usually unicellular reproductive structure from which a new organism arises

standing crop the biomass of a particular area under study

stamen male reproductive organ of the flower, consisting of filament and anther, containing pollen sacs where pollen is formed and released

state give a specific name, value or other brief answer (no supporting argument or calculation is necessary)

steroid organic molecule formed from a complex ring of carbon atoms, of which cholesterol is a typical example

stigma part of the carpel receptive to pollen

stimulus a change in the environment (internal or external) that is detected by a receptor and leads to a response

stoma (plural, **stomata**) pore in the epidermis of a leaf, surrounded by two guard cells

stretch receptor sensory receptor in muscles

stroke volume volume of blood pumped out by the heart per minute

stroma the membranous matrix of the chloroplast, site of the light-independent reaction in photosynthesis

style found in the female part of the flower (carpel), linking stigma to ovary

subthreshold stimulus a stimulus not strong enough to trigger an action potential

substrate a molecule that is the starting point for a biochemical reaction and that forms a complex with a specific enzyme

succession the sequences of different communities developing in a given habitat over a period of time

sugars compounds of a general formula $C_x(H_2O)y$, where x is approximately equal to y, and containing an aldehyde or a ketone group

suggest propose a hypothesis or other possible answer

summation combined effect of many nerve impulses

spatial many impulses arriving from different axons

temporal many impulses arriving via a single axon

suspensory ligament attaches lens to ciliary body in the vertebrate eye

symbiosis literally 'living together'; covering parasitism, commensalism and mutualism

symplast the pathway (e.g. of water) through the living contents of cells

synapse the connection between two nerve cells; functionally a tiny gap, the synaptic cleft, traversed by transmitter substances

synaptic knob the terminal swelling of a pre-synaptic neurone

synergism acting together and producing a larger effect than when acting separately

synovial fluid secreted by the synovial membrane at joints, having lubricating role

systematics the study of the diversity of living things

systemic circulation the blood circulation to the body (not the pulmonary circulation)

systemic pesticide pesticide that is absorbed and carried throughout the body

systole contraction phases in the cardiac cycle

T

target organ organ on which a hormone acts (although broadcast to all organs)

taste bud sense organ found chiefly on the upper surface of the tongue

taxis response by a motile organism (or gamete) where the direction of the response is determined by the direction of the stimulus

taxon a classificatory grouping

taxonomy the science of classification

telophase a phase in nuclear division, when the daughter nuclei form

template (DNA) the DNA of the chromosome, copied to make mRNA

tendon fibrous connective tissue connecting a muscle to bone

terminal bud bud at the apex of the stem

test cross testing a suspected heterozygote by crossing it with a known homozygous recessive

testa seed coat

testis male reproductive gland, producing sperms

thermogenesis generation of heat by metabolism

testosterone a steroid hormone, the main sex hormone of male mammals

thorax in mammals, the upper part of the body separated from the abdomen; in insects, the region between head and abdomen

threshold of simulation the level of stimulation required to trigger an action potential (impulse)

thrombosis blood clot formation, leading to blockage of a blood vessel

thylakoid membrane system of chloroplast

thyroid gland an endocrine gland found in the neck of vertebrates, site of production of thyroxine and other hormones influencing the rate of metabolism

tidal volume volume of air normally exchanged in breathing

tight junction point where plasma membranes of adjacent cells are sealed together

tissue collection of cells of similar structure and function

tissue fluid the liquid bathing cells, formed from blood minus cells and plasma proteins

tissue respiration biochemical steps by which energy is released from sugars

tonoplast membrane around the plant cell vacuole

total lung capacity volume of air in the lungs after maximum inhalation

toxic poisonous

toxin poison

toxoid inactivated poison

trachea windpipe

tracheal system system of tubes by which air is passed to tissues in insects

tracheole branch of the trachea

trait a tendency or characteristic

transcription when the DNA sequence of bases is converted into mRNA

transect arbitrary line through a habitat, selected to sample the community

transfer RNA (tRNA) short lengths of specific RNA that combine with specific amino acids prior to protein synthesis

translation the information of mRNA is decoded into protein (amino acid sequence)

translocation transport of elaborated food via the phloem

transmitter substances substances released into the synaptic cleft on arrival of an impulse at the pre-synaptic membrane to conduct the signal across the synapse

transpiration loss of water vapour from the aerial parts of plants (leaves and stem)

tricarboxylic acid (TCA) cycle the stage in tissue respiration in which pyruvate is broken down to carbon dioxide, and hydrogen is removed for subsequent oxidation

tricuspid valve right atrio-ventricular valve

triglyceride fatty acid ester of the 3-carbon alcohol, glycerol – forms into globules because of its hydrophobic properties

triose a 3-carbon monosaccharide

tripeptide a peptide of three amino acid residues

trophic level a level in a food chain defined by the method of obtaining food and in which all organisms are the same number of energy transfers away from the original source of the energy (photosynthesis)

tropism a growth response of plants in which the direction of growth is determined by the direction of the stimulus

tumour abnormal proliferation of cells, either benign (if self-limiting) or malignant (if invasive)

turgid having high internal pressure

U

ultrafiltration occurs through the tiny pores in the capillaries of the glomerulus

ultrastructure fine structure of cells, determined by electron microscopy

unisexual of one or other sex

unsaturated fat lipid with double bond(s) in the hydrocarbon chain

urea NH_2CONH_2, formed from amino groups deaminated from excess amino acid

ureter tube from kidney to bladder

urethra tube from bladder to exterior

uterine cycle cycle of changes to the wall of the uterus (approximately 28 days)

uric acid an insoluble purine, formed from the breakdown of nucleic acids and proteins

urine an excretory fluid produced by the kidneys, consisting largely of a dilute solution of urea

uterus the organ in which the embryo develops in female mammals

V

VO$_2$ the amount of oxygen being used in the body ($cm^3 kg^{-1} min^{-1}$); with increasingly vigorous exercise, VO_2 will increase, initially

VO$_2$max the maximal oxygen uptake by the body ($cm^3 kg^{-1} min^{-1}$) – even if the maximum physical effort is maintained, a situation is reached where further increase is impossible

vaccination conferring immunity from a disease by injecting an antigen (of attenuated microorganisms or inactivated component) so that the body acquires antibodies prior to potential infection

vascular bundle strands of xylem and phloem (often with fibres) separated by cambium; the site of water and elaborated food movements up and down the stem

vacuole fluid-filled space in the cytoplasm, especially large and permanent in plant cells

vagus nerve 10th cranial nerve; supplies many internal organs, including the heart

variety a taxonomic group below the species level

vasa recta capillary loop supplying the loop of Henle

vascular tissue xylem and phloem of plants

vasoconstriction constriction of blood supply to capillaries (of skin)

vasodilation dilation of blood supply to capillaries (of skin)

vector an organism that transmits a disease-causing organism, or a device for transferring genes during genetic engineering

venous return volume of blood returning to the heart via the veins per minute

vein vessel that returns blood to the heart

ventilation rate number of inhalations or exhalations per minute

ventral the underside

ventricle chamber, either of the centre of the brain, or of the heart

venule branch of a vein

vertebrate animal with a vertebral column

vesicle membrane-bound sac

vestibular apparatus the semicircular canals of the inner ear, concerned with balance

vestibular canal upper compartment of the cochlea

vestigial small, imperfectly developed structure

virus minute, intracellular parasite, formed of protein and nucleic acid

vital capacity the total possible change in lung volume – the maximum volume of air that can be exhaled after a maximum inhalation

vitalism theory early idea that organic compounds could only be produced in living cells

vitreous humour clear jelly of inner eye

W

water potential the tendency of water molecules to move

water table level of ground water in the Earth

wax complex form of lipid

weathering breakdown of rock

white matter nerve fibres wrapped in their myelin sheaths

X

xeromorphic modified to withstand drought

xerophyte plant showing modifications to withstand drought

xerosere succession of plants starting from dry terrain

xylem water-conducting vessels of plants

Y

yolk food stores of egg cells, rich in proteins and lipids

yolk sac membranous sac with numerous blood vessels, developed by vertebrate embryos around the yolk (e.g. in birds and reptiles) or as a component of the placenta (in mammals)

Z

zonation naturally occurring distribution of organisms in zones

zygote product of the fusion of gametes

zymogenic cells cells of gastric glands, secreting pepsinogen

Acknowledgements

The publishers have made every effort to contact copyright holders. If any have been inadvertently overlooked, they will be pleased to make the necessary arrangements at the earliest opportunity.

Photo credits
Thanks are due to the following for permission to reproduce copyright photographs.

Cover © David Aubrey/Science Photo Library; **p.6** Fig. 1.4 *l* Science Photo Library/J.C.Revy; **p.6** Fig. 1.4 *r* Gene Cox; **p.11** Fig. 1.8 Gene Cox; **p.12** Fig. 1.10 Science Photo Library/Andrew Syred; **p.13** Fig. 1.11 *l* Biophoto Associates; **p.13** Fig. 1.11 *r* from S.W. Hurry *The Microstructure of Cells*, John Murray, 1965, courtesy of Mr A.D. Greenwood; **p.14** Fig. 1.12 Science Photo Library/J.C.Revy; **p.15** Fig. 1.13 Dr Kevin S. Mackenzie, School of Medical Science, Aberdeen University; **p.16** Fig. 1.14 *t* Science Photo Library/Biophoto Associates; **p.16** Fig. 1.15 *b* Science Photo Library/ Kwangshin Kim; **p.19** Fig. 1.17 Science Photo Library/Barry Dowsett; **p.22** Fig. 1.21 *l* Science Photo Library/NIBSC; **p.22** Fig. 1.21 *r* Science Photo Library/Dr D. Fawcett; **p.32** Fig. 1.33 all Biophoto Associates; **p.34** Fig. 1.35 Gene Cox; **p.41** Fig. 2.3 Biophoto Associates; **p.41** Fig. 2.4 Science Photo Library/C.Nuridsany & M.Perennou; **p.43** Fig. 2.6 NHPA/B Jones & M Shimlock; **p.47** Fig. 2.9 Biophoto Associates; **p.50** Fig. 2.12 Gene Cox; **p.66** Fig. 2.28 *t* Science Photo Library/A. Barrington Brown; *bl* Science Photo Library; *br* Science Photo Library; **p.77** Fig. 3.2 *l* Andrew Lambert; *r* Getty Images/Mike Hewitt; **p.92** Fig. 4.1 *l* Biophoto Associates; *r* Biophoto Associates; **p.99** Fig. 4.8 *l* Biophoto Associates; *r* Science Photo Library/Hattie Young; **p.100** Fig. 4.10 Photolibrary/Scott Camazine; **p.103** Fig. 4.13 Science Photo Library; **p.110** Fig. 4.20 Science Photo Library/Dr P. Marazzi; **p.111** Fig. 4.21 Science Photo Library/Chris Bjornberg; **p.114** Fig. 4.24 Science Photo Library/Adam Hart-Davis; **p.123** Fig. 5.7 Science Photo Library/Will & Dent McIntyre; **p.125** Fig. 5.8 Science Photo Library/C.C.Studio; **p.126** Fig. 5.9 Frank Lane Picture Agency/N.Cattlin; **p.130** Fig. 5.11 Science Photo Library/David Parker; **p.134** Fig. 5.13 Roslin Institute, Edinburgh; **p.152** Fig. 6.15 *l* Still Pictures/N.Dickinson; **p.153** Fig. 6.16 *t* NHPA/Kevin Schafer; *b* NHPA/B&C Alexander; **p.157** Fig. 6.19 Visuals Unlimited/Ken Lucas; **p.158** Fig. 6.21 *tl* NHPA/Andy Rouse; *tr* NHPA/Henry Ausloos; *bl* Getty Images/Martin Ruegner; *br* Alamy/Kathy Wright; **p.183** Fig. 7.5 Gene Cox; **p.186** Fig. 7.8 Gene Cox; **p.188** Fig. 7.9 Gene Cox; **p.199** Fig. 7.19 Science Photo Library/Eye of Science; **p.206** Fig. 7.27 Alamy/David R. Frazier Photolibrary, Inc; **p.208** Fig. 7.29 Gene Cox; **p.215** Fig. 7.35 Science Photo Library/Prof S. Cinti; **p.218** Fig. 7.38 *tl* Natural Visions/Heather Angel; *tc* NHPA/Laurie Campbell; *tr* Science Photo Library/Tomas Friedman; *bl* Natural Visions/Heather Angel; *br* NHPA/Stephen Dalton; **p.219** Fig. 7.39 Nickel-Electro Ltd.; **p.222** Fig. 7.44 Gene Cox; **p.224** Fig. 7.47 Science Photo Library/Saturn Stills; **p.236** Fig. 8.2 Biophoto Associates; **p.237** Fig. 8.3 Science Photo Library/Biozentrum, University of Basel; **p.257** Fig. 8.22 Wellcome Photo Library; **p.258** Fig. 8.23 Science Photo Library/Alfred Pasieka; **p.259** Fig. 8.25 Science Photo Library/Phantatomix; **p.272** Fig. 9.4 Science Photo Library/CNRI; **p.277** Fig. 9.9 Science Photo Library/Dr Kari Lounatmaa; **p.296** Fig. 10.2 Gene Cox; **p.297** Fig. 10.3 Gene Cox; **p.309** Fig. 10.16 Gene Cox; **p.310** Fig. 10.17 Dr R.P.C. Johnson, Aberdeen University (retired); **p.312** Fig. 10.19 *r* Gene Cox; *l* Gene Cox; **p.313** Fig. 10.20 both from C.P. Whittingham (1964) *The Chemistry of Plant Processes*, Methuen, London; **p.316** Fig. 10.24 *l* Dr

C.J. Clegg; *r* Gene Cox; **p.317** Fig. 10.25 Alamy/Keith Pritchard/fstop2; **p.319** Fig. 10.27 NHPA/Gerry Cambridge; **p.320** Fig. 10.28 *t* Corbis/Bill Ross; *b* Science Photo Library/Jane Sugarman; **p.330** Fig. 11.3 Biophoto Associates; **p.338** Fig. 11.9 NHPA/Stephen Dalton; **p.341** Fig. 11.12 Photolibrary/Rowan Isaac; **p.349** Fig. 12.1 Science Photo Library/CNRI; **p.359** Fig. 12.9 *l* Corbis/Bettmann; *r* Science Photo Library/Jean-Loup Charmet; **p.365** Fig. 12.13 Gene Cox; **p.366** Fig. 12.14 *t* Mediscan/University of Aberdeen; **p.366** Fig. 12.15 *b* Science Photo Library/Biology Media; **p.367** Fig. 12.16 *l* Biophoto Associates; *r* Biophoto Associates; **p.378** Fig. 12.27 *l* Science Photo Library/Astrid & Hans-Frieder Michler; **p.378** Fig. 12.28 *r* Gene Cox; **p.380** Fig. 12.31 Science Photo Library/Jean-Claude Revy-A. Goujeon, ISM; **p.383** Fig. 12.34 Science Photo Library/Petit Format; **p.385** Fig. 12.37 Science Photo Library/Moscoso; **p.400** Fig. 13.8 FLPA/Angela Hampton; **p.401** Fig. 13.9 *r* Science Photo Library; *l* Science Photo Library/Dr P. Marazzi; **p.403** Fig. 13.10 reproduced by permission of Sainsbury's Supermarkets Ltd; **p.407** Fig. 13.13 *bl* Getty Images/Raymond K. Gehman/National Geographic; *tr* FLPA/Nigel Cattlin; *tl* Corbis/Dung Vo Trung/Sygma; *br* Corbis/Owen Franken; **p.408** Fig. 13.14 *b* Corbis/Wolfgang Kaehler; *t* Alamy/Robert Fried; **p.410** Fig. 13.16 Science Photo Library/Prof S. Cinti; **p.414** Fig. 13.19 *l* Corbis; *r* Rex Features/Sabah Arar; **p.418** Fig. 13.21 *tr* Dr C.J. Clegg; *br* NHPA/E.A.Janes; *l* PA Photos/DPA; **p.420** Fig. 13.22 Science Photo Library/BSIP VEM; **p.427** Fig. 14.4 Getty Images/Toru Yamanaka/AFP; **p.434** Fig. 14.7 PA Photos/Steve Mitchell; **p.437** Fig. 14.12 Getty Images/Dr Gladden Willis; **p.439** Fig. 14.14 *tl* Corbis/Gary Hershorn/Reuters; *tr* Getty Images/Farjana K. Godhuly/AFP; **p.439** Fig. 14.15 PA Photos/DPA; **p.458** Fig. 16.3 *b* Corbis/Theo Allofs/zefa; **p.463** Fig. 16.6 Dr C.J. Clegg; **p.464** Fig. 16.7 *r* Corbis/Owen Franken; *l* NHPA/Nick Garbutt; **p.465** Fig. 16.8 *l* Science Photo Library/Tony Wood; *r* GardenWorld Images/D.Gould; **p.466** Fig. 16.9 Getty Images/Nina Leen/Time Life Pictures; **p.467** Fig. 16.10 Prof A. Gray; **p.481** Fig. 16.22 *t* Getty Images/Chris McGrath; *b* Getty Images/Arthur Tilley; **p.485** Fig. 16.27 Science Photo Library/John Reader; **p.492** Fig. 16.33 la Grotte de Niaux, Niaux, Tarascon-sur-Ariège, Pyrenees, France; **p.507** Fig. 17.3 Gene Cox; **p.509** Fig. 17.4 NHPA/Nick Garbutt; **p.512** Fig. 17.6 Gene Cox; **p.513** Fig. 17.7 Gene Cox; **p.521** Fig. 17.12 Dr C.J. Clegg; **p.523** Fig. 17.13 Gene Cox; **p.529** Fig. 17.20 Science Photo Library/Omikron; **p.537** Fig. 17.24 all Prof Robert Turner, Wellcome Department of Imaging Neuroscience, Institute of Neurology, University College London; **p.542** Fig. 17.27 *l* FLPA/Fritz Polking; *r* FLPA/Silvestris Fotoservice; **p.543** Fig. 17.28 *l* FLPA/Jurgen & Christine Sohns; *r* Getty Images/Adrian Bailey/Aurora; **p.545** Fig. 17.29 Alamy/Penny Boyd; **p.547** Fig. 17.31 *t* FLPA/Nigel Cattlin; *b* FLPA/Foto Natura Stock; **p.548** Fig. 17.33 *l* FLPA/Frans Lanting/Minden Pictures; *tr* Nature Picture Library/Peter Oxford; *br* FLPA/Peggy Heard; **p.557** Fig. 18.3 *l* Science Photo Library/Dr Kari Lounatmaa; *r* Corbis/Ralph White; **p.559** Fig. 18.6 Gene Cox; **p.565** Fig. 18.15 Gene Cox; **p.578** Fig. 18.24 Corbis/Macduff Everton; **p.579** Fig. 18.25 *t* Anthony Blake Photo Library; *b* Anthony Blake Photo Library/ Gerrit Buntrock; **p.584** Fig. 18.32 Gene Cox; **p.592** Fig. 18.36 Science Photo Library/Matt Meadows/Peter Arnold Inc; **p.595** Fig. 18.39 Rex Features; **p.603** Fig. 19.3 *t* Educationphotos.co.uk/Walmsley; **p.603** Fig. 19.4 *b* Nature Picture Library/Chris Gomersall; **p.608** Fig. 19.9 *b* Alamy/Daniel L. Geiger/SNAP; *t* Alamy/WildPictures; **p.610** Fig. 19.10 *tl* NHPA/Rod Planck; *tr* NHPA/Martin Harvey; *bl* Premaphotos; *br* Dr C.J. Clegg;

B424 Acknowledgements

p.616 Fig. 19.16 *l* Corbis/Steven G. Smith; *r* Corbis/Eric and David Hosking; p.621 Fig. 19.20 Dr C.J. Clegg; p.625 Fig. 19.25 *l* Science Photo Library/John Devries; *r* NHPA/Stephen Dalton; p.628 Fig. 19.28 Alamy/CuboImages; p.630 Fig. 19.30 Science Photo Library/Dr G. Feldman/NASA/GSFC; p.631 Fig. 19.31 Alamy/Natural History Museum, London; p.647 Fig. 20.7 *t* Gene Cox; *b* Science Photo Library/Innerspace Imaging; p.648 Fig. 20.8 Dr Kevin S. Mackenzie, School of Medical Science, Aberdeen University; p.652 Fig. 20.10 Gene Cox; p.652 Fig. 20.11 Dr Kevin S. Mackenzie, School of Medical Science, Aberdeen University; p.662 Fig. 20.19 Corbis/Michael Keller; p.672 Fig. 20.27 Science Photo Library/Dr Jeremy Burgess; p.673 Fig. 20.28 Getty Images/Tim Graham; p.686 Fig. 22.1 Gary Seston; p.687 Fig. 22.2 Gary Seston; p.689 Fig. 22.3 Gary Seston.

Artwork credits

The publishers would like to thank the following for permission to reproduce copyright material:

p.118 Fig. 5.1 Modified, with permission, from Dr P. Moore (1994) *Recombinant DNA Technology* © The Biological Society; p.149 Fig. 6.13 *Climate Change 2001: The Scientific Basis* © The Intergovernmental Panel on Climate Change, quoted in F.Press, R.Siever, J.Grotzinger, T.H.Jordan (2004) *Understanding Earth* (4th edition); p.152 Fig. 6.15 cartoon © Scott Willis, San Jose Mercury News; p.163 Fig. 6.24 Adapted from A.D.Bradshaw and T.McNeilly (1981) *Evolution and Pollution*, Institute of Biology, *Studies in Biology* No. 130, by permission of Cambridge University Press; p.220 Fig. 7.41 Graph of human body temperature from J.H.Green (1963) *An Introduction to Human Physiology*, by permission of Oxford University Press; Isotherm diagrams from K.Schmidt-Nielson (1983) *Animal Physiology: Adaptation and Environment* (3rd edition) by permission of Cambridge University Press; p.251 Fig. 8.5 Adapted from E.J.Wood, C.A.Smith and W.R.Pickering (1997) *Life Chemistry and Molecular Biology* © Portland Press Ltd; p.393 Fig. 13.2 Images of children adapted from A.F.Walker (1990) *Cambridge Social Biology Topics: Human Nutrition*, by permission of Cambridge University Press; p.413 Fig. 13.18 Adapted from an article by Helen Carter (1998) copyright Guardian News and Media Limited; p.426 Fig. 14.3 David Graham, adapted from K.Weston, N.Wiggins-James, G.Thompson and S.Hartigan (2005) *Sport and PE* (3rd edition) Hodder Arnold; p.430 Table 14.2 Adapted from Colin Clegg (revised Stephen Ingham) (1995) *Exercise Physiology* © Feltham Press; p.434 Fig. 14.8 David Graham, adapted from K.Weston, N.Wiggins-James, G.Thompson and S.Hartigan (2005) *Sport and PE* (3rd edition) Hodder Arnold; p.449 Fig. 15.4 Adapted from Figure 12.13 in C.J.Clegg, with D.G.Mackean (2000) *Advanced Biology: Principles and Applications* (2nd edition) John Murray; p.451 Fig. 15.6 Adapted with permission from a method published on the Science and Plants for Schools (SAPS) website (see www.saps.org.uk); p.457 Fig. 16.2 Adapted from John Maynard Smith and E.Szathmáry (1999) *The Origins of Life*, by permission of Oxford University Press; p.488 Fig. 16.30 Map adapted from R.Lewin (1989) *Human Evolution: An Illustrated Introduction* © Blackwell Publishing Ltd.; Skull images reproduced from R.Leakey (1994) *The Origin of Humankind* © Weidenfeld & Nicolson, a division of The Orion Publishing Group, and John Brockman Associates; p.489 Fig. 16.31 Stuart Bailey, adapted from Paul Arnold 'Human Evolution', *Biological Sciences Review*, Volume 8, Number 4 (1996) © S.E.R.Bailey; p.497 Table 16.7 M.Ridley (1993) *Evolution* © Blackwell Publishing Ltd; p.523 Fig. 17.13 and p.524 Fig. 17.14 and Fig. 17.15 Adapted from J.Cheverton (1994) 'Animals in Action', *Biological Sciences Review*, Volume 7, Number 2, Philip Allan Updates, Philip Allan Publishers; p.526 Fig.17.17 Adapted from G.G.Simpson, C.S.Pittendrigh, L.H.Tiffany (1957) *Life, An Introduction to Biology*, Routledge; p.545 Fig.17.29 Adapted from *The Animal Mind* by James L. Gould and Carol Grant Gould. Copyright 1994 by Scientific American Library. Reprinted by permission of Henry Holt and Company, LLC.; p.546 Fig. 17.30 Adapted from G.G.Simpson, C.S.Pittendrigh, L.H.Tiffany (1957) *Life, An Introduction to Biology*, Routledge & Kegan Paul Ltd, © William S. Beck, Elizabeth Simpson Wurr, Helen S. Vishniac, Joan S. Burns; p.549 Fig. 17.34 Adapted from J.D.McCarthy (1966), *The Study of Behaviour*, Institute of Biology, *Studies in Biology* No. 3 (Edward Arnold), by permission of Cambridge University Press; p.599 Fig. 19.1 T.J.King (1989) *Selected Topics in Biology – Ecology* (2nd edition) Thomas Nelson & Sons Ltd; p.619 Fig. 19.19 Alastair Gray (Ed.) (1985), *World Health and Disease*, reproduced with kind permission of the Open University Press; p.621 Fig. 19.20 Data supplied by Dr John Cheverton, Head of Biology Department, Oakham School, Rutland, UK and the Upper Sixth Form Biologists; p.624 Fig. 19.23 Michael Madigan, John Martinko (2006) *Brock Biology of Micro-organisms* (11th edition) © Reprinted by permission of Pearson Education Inc., Upper Saddle River, NJ; p.625 Fig. 19.24 Adapted from M.Wade, L.Child and N.Adachi (1996) 'Japanese Knotweed – a cultivated coloniser', *Biological Sciences Review*, Volume 8, Number 3, © Biological Records Centre, ITE, Monks Woods; p.626 Fig. 19.27 Graph from the paper by Dr I. Newton of the Institute of Terrestrial Ecology, *Britain Since Silent Spring*, Institute of Biology Symposium; p.629 Fig.19.29 David L. Hawksworth and Francis Rose (1976) 'Lichens as Pollution Monitors', *Studies in Biology* No. 66, by permission of Cambridge University Press; p.676 Fig. 21.1 From C.J.Clegg (1967), 'Studies in tissue metabolism in stored potato tissue', MSc Thesis, University of London.

Thanks are due to the following sources of inspiration and data for illustrative figures:

p.141 Fig. 6.3b Adapted from *Introducing Ecology: Nature at Work*, British Museum (Natural History) London, and Cambridge University Press, 1978; p.195 Fig. 7.16 Alastair Gray (Ed.) (1985), *World Health and Disease*, Open University Press; p.239 Fig. 8.5 Adapted from E.J.Wood, C.A.Smith and W.R.Pickering (1997) *Life Chemistry and Molecular Biology*, Portland Press, London; p.286 Fig. 9.18 Adapted from D.O.Hall and K.K.Rao (1992) *Photosynthesis* (4th edition) Cambridge University Press; p.313 Fig. 10.20 C.P.Whittingham (1964) *The Chemistry of Plant Processes*, Methuen; p.483 Fig. 16.25 Matrix adapted from R.Lewin (1984) *Human Evolution*, Blackwell Scientific Publications, Boston; map adapted from R.Leakey (1994) *The Origin of Humankind*, Weidenfeld & Nicolson, a division of The Orion Publishing Group, and John Brockman Associates; p.501 Fig. 16.39 and p.502 Fig. 16.40 Adapted from *Man's Place in Evolution*, British Museum (Natural History), 1980, Cambridge University Press; p.527 Fig. 17.19 Adapted from D.McFarland (1981) *The Oxford Companion to Animal Behaviour*, Oxford University Press; p.612 Fig. 19.11 Julian Cremona (1988) *A Field Atlas of the Sea Shore*, Cambridge University Press; p.618 Fig. 19.18 T.King (1980) *Ecology*, Nelson; p.622 Fig. 19.21 Adapted from Stuart L. Pimm and Clinton Jenkins (2005) 'Sustaining the Variety of Life' © *Scientific American* Inc. 293:3. All rights reserved.

Text credits

p.623 Fig. 19.22 Adapted from an article in *The Times*, 2 February 2006, © Nick Meo.

Examination questions credits

The publishers would like to thank the International Baccalaureate Organization for permission to reproduce its intellectual property.

Index